W9-DGN-166

Principles and Practices of
TEACHING
READING

Principles and Practices of
TEACHING
READING
Third Edition

ARTHUR W. HEILMAN
Pennsylvania State University

CHARLES E. MERRILL PUBLISHING COMPANY
A Bell & Howell Company
Columbus, Ohio

International Standard Book Number: 0-675-09149-7

Library of Congress Catalog Card Number: 70-139777

3 4 5 6 7 8 9 10 / 76 75 74 73 72

Printed in the United States of America

To Bruce
and all other children
learning to read

Preface

The third edition of *Principles and Practices of Teaching Reading* reflects new developments and instructional concerns in the field of teaching reading. Two chapters deal with "The Culturally Different Child as a Learner" and "Developing and Expanding Concepts." The chapter on reading readiness has been completely revised, and material on teaching reading beyond the beginning stage has been reorganized and expanded. The fact that reading is a language process is constantly stressed throughout the book. One of the new chapters demonstrates ways to teach children about their language while teaching reading skills. Special emphasis is placed on teaching the relationship between intonation and meaningful reading.

Certain important premises found in previous editions continue to be stressed. These include:

1. Reading is part of the child's total growth process, and learning to read cannot be separated from social-emotional needs.
2. The purpose of the school is to develop and expand concepts along with the *tools* that will permit the child to assume responsibility for his own growth.
3. Beginning reading instruction should not consist of *either* code cracking *or* reading for meaning. Mastery of letter-sound relationships and sight word vocabulary and profiting from context clues must be taught concommitantly, not in sequence.
4. Following sound principles of instruction is a prerequisite for a successful instructional program.

The writer is indebted to a great number of students and teachers who through their research, writing, discussion, and comments have contributed much to this book. Particular thanks is due Dr. Hulda Groesbeck, Dr. Carl Callenbach, and Dr. Elizabeth Ann

Holmes who contributed to the preparation of particular chapters, and to Miss Ruby Thompson, the senior author of Chapter 3.

I wish to acknowledge the contribution of members of the Editorial Production and Art Staff of Charles E. Merrill Publishing, particularly Miss Julia Estadt, editor, and Mrs. Jocelyn Ritter, proofreader, who worked with me on this third edition.

Arthur W. Heilman

March, 1972

Contents

I

Principles: For All Instructional Levels

The principles found in this chapter can be thought of as guidelines that should govern teaching behavior. Principles do not spell out instructional practices that are to be followed, but they can provide the criteria for evaluating practices. It is possible that one could hold to certain principles which would preclude the use of a particular set of materials or methodology. More likely, however, one would adjust or adapt practices in order to make principles and practices compatible.

Sound principles of instruction tend to be learner-oriented, therefore they do not vary from grade level to grade level. They can be applied quite consistently to children who are noticeably different in regard to capacity, interest and experience.

1

1

Principles of
Teaching Reading

The decade of the 1970s has a good chance of being a memorable one with regard to teaching children to read. Even if it is *not* memorable, it will seem so simply because it followed the 1960s. This was the decade of the "ad-man." The virtues of a different panacea were extolled with every issue of one's favorite reading journal. New "breakthroughs" were announced frequently. Allegedly-new methods and materials were described superficially but enthusiastically in the popular press. Each new approach, the public was assured, was destined to revolutionize reading instruction in our schools. Much of our energy was expended in a relatively fruitless search for new miracle-materials:

> If one sought for a capsule description of American reading instruction during the past decade, the plausible one could well be "the frenzied search." The search was based on the false hope that there just might be a panacea for the ills which beset reading instruction. This false hope leads to many unproductive responses such as excessive concern with trivia, unwarranted loyalty—or hostility—to labels without concern for substance, or childlike faith in "breakthroughs" which later proved to be more of a triumph for Madison Avenue than for children in the classroom. The frenzied search was an era in which no significant changes occurred.(6) *

*Numbers in parentheses refer to numbered references at the end of the chapter.

3

We know now that it was naïve to think that materials and methodology determine the effectiveness of instruction. Today there is general agreement that reading programs never rise above the quality of instruction found in them. On the other hand, unless teachers and educators can evaluate teaching materials and their impact on learning, reading instruction will likely be dominated by efficient advertising and public relations programs. Teachers must learn to ask pertinent questions which are relevant to sound educational goals, and evaluation of particular materials should determine how they propose to achieve these goals. To be meaningful, evaluation must be based on understanding of children as learners, reading as a learning process, and learning to read as a long-term developmental process. These concepts lead to a discussion of *principles* of reading instruction.

As the term is used here, "principles" of teaching reading are those basic rules which constitute the theoretical framework out of which all practices are evolved. The principles do not spell out the best procedures or practices for particular situations. However, when one accepts a set of principles, he will be inconsistent if he uses practices which violate those principles.

Principles are necessarily stated in broad and general terms, but if we are to understand their meaning, they should never be vague or nebulous. The principles of teaching reading evolve from the best knowledge available in the fields of psychology, educational psychology, and curriculum planning, from studies in child growth and development, and from child-guidance and psychological clinics. In formulating these principles, it is necessary to consider all facets of human growth and development, including the intellectual, physiological, and emotional.

Most teachers are familiar with the principles discussed in the following pages. Like scientific laws, the principles of teaching reading are subject to modification or repeal as new data are discovered and new theories erected on the basis of this data. Some readers will undoubtedly feel that one (or more) of the following principles is not absolutely valid. Such questioning is healthy, especially if it stimulates the formulation of rational alternatives. If the following principles are a sound basis for teaching reading at all levels of instruction, there are many practices in our schools which need to be re-examined.

Principles

1. *Learning to read is a complicated process, one sensitive to a variety of pressures. Too much pressure or the wrong kind of pres-*

sure may result in non-learning. A fact that attests to the complexity of the reading process is that authorities have never agreed on one definition of reading. There are, however, many statements about the complexity of reading on which experts would agree. One such statement is that reading involves more than the mechanical process of correctly pronouncing words—it involves the recognition of meaning.

Reading is a language function. It is the manipulation of symbolic materials. Psychologists and other observers of human behavior tell us that the symbolic process is sensitive to pressures of any kind. Language is the most sensitive indicator of personal or emotional maladjustment. Yet in no area of learning in our schools is greater pressure brought to bear on the pupil than in the area of reading. This is partly due to the high value which our society places on education and to the recognition that education is based on reading skill.

Often the school and the home present a united front in exerting overt and subtle pressures on the child. (7) Reading is the first school task in which the child is deliberately or inadvertently compared with others in his peer group. It is the first task in which he must compete. How he fares in this competition has a tremendous impact on his ego, his concept of himself, and the attitudes of his peers toward him. But, most important, this is the first school activity in which his performance has a direct impact on his parents' egos. Parents may sense that their anxiety is not an intelligent or mature response. Insofar as the average parents can be coldly analytical of their motivation and involvement in their child's non-success in reading, they know their feelings are never far below the surface. These feelings of disappointment are perceived by the child as a judgment that he does not measure up to parents' expectations.

2. *Reading is a language process. The child being taught to read must understand the relationship between reading and his language.* Much has been written about "what the child brings to school" and that the school must *build on the skills children have acquired.* In the final analysis, the only thing the child brings to school that can transfer to learning to read is the language he uses.

Unfortunately, many of the child's early experiences in beginning reading tend to mask the fact that he is engaged in a language process. He is asked to focus on single words and letters within words. While such analysis is essential, instruction should prevent the new reader from *equating* these skills with reading. One more step is essential: Reading must incorporate the melody of oral language. This leads to the next principle.

3. *Instruction should lead children to understand that reading must result in meaning.* This principle applies to all stages of reading instruction. It means that reading is more than a mechanical process, even though mechanics are an essential part of the process. It rejects the thesis that beginning reading deals only with mechanics and that *meaning* is an additive to be inserted at some later point on the learning continuum.

If this principle is followed from the start, it mitigates the possibility that children will develop a *set* that reading is saying or sounding out words. For some reason, this particular set resists extinction, and unless children are reading for meaning they cannot translate print into the language patterns that it represents.

This principle does not imply that some instructional periods cannot focus on isolated skills such as letter-sound relationships. Obviously all facile readers master such skills, not in lieu of critical reading but as part of the process.

4. *Early in the learning process the child must acquire ways of gaining independence in identifying words whose meanings are known to him but which are unknown to him as sight words.* Pronouncing words is not reading, but sounding out words not known as sight words is essential in independent reading. The more widely a child reads, the less likely it is that he will know as a sight word every word he meets. Hence, developing independence in reading depends on acquiring methods of unlocking the pronunciation of words. The clues used in identifying words, discussed in later chapters, include unique configuration of words, structural analysis (prefixes, suffixes), context clues, and phonic analysis. Phonics is undoubtedly the most important of the word analysis skills.

The cooperative Reading Studies (2, 5) reported data on a number of methodological issues. In many instances the data failed to reveal any clear cut superiority for particular instructional procedures and materials. However, in regard to the efficacy of teaching letter-sound relationships, the findings were remarkably uniform. Programs of instruction which featured systematic phonics instruction resulted in consistently superior pupil reading achievement when compared with programs which did not.

The principle just discussed is not in conflict with number three above which states that the child must see reading as a meaning-making process. To read for meaning, one must be able to recognize printed word forms. Those words which are not instantly recognized must be analyzed by associating printed letters with speech sounds.

5. *Learning to read is an individual process*. Although group activities associated with reading enhance the learning process, and even though it is true that learning is partly a social process, each child in a group who learns how to read learns as an individual. The complicated stimuli confronting the child are mastered by an individual nervous system. Dividing a class into three or more smaller groups on the basis of reading ability may be a wise procedure, but this in itself will not teach the children how to read. Even though all children in the slowest group have the common characteristic that they are poor readers, grouping them physically in the classroom and psychologically in the teacher's mind is of negligible value unless the teacher adjusts learning situations to each child's need for instruction.

6. *Pupil differences must be a primary consideration in reading instruction*. This implies that instruction cannot be dominated by the grade-level system, promotion practices, or graded instructional materials. It is hypothesized that any classroom will house pupils whose present achievement and instructional needs vary greatly. Identical educational experiences, particularly reading the same material, cannot be equally effective for all. Differentiation of both instruction and free-choice reading will inevitably result in larger pupil differences, which in turn will call for more differentiation.

The culturally different child is now recognized by the school as providing a major challenge in regard to meeting his individual needs. We have known for years that extreme cultural-economic differences exist in our society. Further, we have known that these differences in culture and deficits in standard of living affected school learning. Until recently, however, this knowledge resulted in no significant changes in the curriculum on teaching methods. A school attended exclusively by culturally different black children would confront these children with a curriculum that was no different from the one found in a school 20 miles away in the suburbs.

The educational philosophies we verbalized were always adequate to take care of this problem, i.e., "fit the teaching to the child," "meet him where he is," "teach to his needs and interests," "build readiness for learning." Unfortunately, we never implemented this philosophy; however, some of the educational practices which resulted from the new awareness of poverty and the ghetto are discussed in Chapter 3.

7. *Reading instruction should be thought of as an organized, systematic, growth-producing activity*. If any combination of strictly

environmental factors will, in the absence of systematic instruction, produce optimum growth in reading, then instruction per se is superfluous. Sound instruction will start from the premise that the classroom environment is an integral part of instruction. The presence of adequate reading materials and the evolvement of a desirable classroom organization are prerequisites for good instruction. The absence of these precludes effective instruction, but their presence does not assure it.

8. *Proper reading instruction depends on the diagnosis of each child's weaknesses and needs.* This principle is applicable to ordinary classroom teaching, as well as to remedial reading. Individual diagnosis in reading has somehow become associated more with "retarded" readers and pupils with a clinical history of non-learning than with ordinary classroom procedure. Diagnosis has become associated too often with cure or remedy rather than with preventing the development of poor reading. In many cases, proper diagnosis will warn a teacher before bad habits or unhealthy emotional reactions cripple a potentially capable reader.

A survey test used as the basis for grouping children into poorest, average, and best categories is not in itself a diagnosis. To know that children A, B, and C are among the poorest in the class and that they are reading at least a year below their grade level tells us nothing about what it is that inhibits their reading progress. Nor does such a test tell us what aspect of reading should be attacked first in order to improve the child's reading. To determine that a child is reading below what might be expected is not diagnosis. It is an invitation to diagnosis.

9. *The best diagnosis is useless unless it is used as a blueprint for instruction.* Diagnosis itself has no salutary effect on the performance of the child tested. If diagnosis alone had salutary effects, it would be possible to raise a child's level of performance indefinitely by more and more diagnosis. It may be noted that extensive testing and metal filing cabinets full of individual folders do not necessarily make a better school. Testing in many American schools has become an end in itself. When test results are not used for instructional purposes, the educational objectives of the testing program are defeated.

There is no area of the curriculum in American schools more ideally suited to constant diagnosis than reading in the elementary and intermediate grades. The good teacher knows this and proceeds with continuous diagnosis of the children in her room. She knows that numerous factors inhibit progress in reading during this period. Any skill not mastered or only partially mastered may be instrumental in producing other reading problems. A teacher's manual or curriculum guide can point out a logical sequence for introducing skills and tasks, but it offers no help in determining what in the sequence has been learned. The manual or guide is like an artist's conception of the total edifice before it is constructed. Intelligent instruction must be based on accurate information regarding children's present accomplishments and weaknesses. In this sense, a thorough diagnosis is a blueprint for instruction.

10. *No child should be expected or forced to attempt to read material which at the moment he is incapable of reading.* Although applied here specifically to reading, this principle has a much wider application in our schools. All curriculum study and the placing of learning tasks at different points on the educational continuum are related to this principle. The principle should be followed in all areas of child growth and development—physical, social, emotional, intellectual. The principle amounts to a rejection of the myth that "the child is a miniature adult." We know that he is not. Today, informed teachers and parents expect the average child of six years to have developed social and emotional responses only to a level of maturity commensurate with his experience.

This principle is also related to the fact that different children develop at different rates and that the growth pattern of an individual child is not uniform. The data from which we derive norms or averages of physical, emotional, social, and intellectual growth warn us that there are differences in rates of development. The principle does not imply that children should avoid difficult tasks or that a child should be able to read a passage perfectly before he attempts to read it. It does imply that we cannot expect a child to perform up to a given standard when at the moment he is incapable of such performance. To do this is to expect the impossible.

The following episode, although it illustrates the point under discussion, is not advanced as being representative of teacher practice. Arrangements were made in an elementary school for thorough testing of a number of pupils who were not making expected academic progress. One fourth grade boy could read successfully no higher than primer level. The counselor inquired of the boy's teacher what reading program the boy was following. The teacher explained that for a while she had the boy attempt to read third grade materials. Failing in these, he was given second grade materials with no better success. Since the boy read these materials no better than he read the fourth grade texts, the teacher concluded that he might as well read the fourth grade books. Even teachers who would not endorse this solution may occasionally expect a child to do what he cannot do at the moment. Untold numbers of pupils face such a situation, and probably more instances occur because of lack of reading ability than for all other reasons combined.

A given child may have average or superior overall ability but currently may be below grade norm in his reading. With proper guidance, he may later master the reading process commensurate with his expected ability. Each child is entitled to the best guidance available. It is not conducive to social, emotional, or educational growth to subject a child to failure experiences because he is physically present in a classroom where arbitrary achievement goals have been set.

11. *A child capable of advancing to a higher level of reading should not be prevented from doing so.* This principle warns against instruction becoming a prisoner of graded materials. In the upper primary and intermediate levels, a child may be able to move through graded materials at a much faster pace than does the average reader. He may also have less need for and less interest in these materials. This child should be encouraged to move at his own pace and select materials of his own choosing.

12. *Any given technique, practice, or procedure is likely to work better with some children than with others. Hence, the teacher of reading must have a variety of approaches.* Virtually every method and procedure described in the vast literature on reading is reported to have been successful with some children and unsuccessful with others. Therefore, creativity and versatility are basic requirements for successful teaching. If a teacher begins to take sides in methodological squabbles, or if she begins to crystalize her ideas on an either/or basis, she is likely to be less receptive to other points of view and approaches which may be helpful to her teaching.

Authorities in the field of reading are in general agreement that "There is no one best method of teaching." The evidence indicates that one method is not necessarily superior to another. Regardless of the efficiency of a given method of teaching reading, it will produce its share of problem cases and impaired readers if used exclusively. If there are significant individual differences in the way children learn to read, it follows that different approaches are advisable. Unfortunately, children do not have identifiable characteristics which make it possible to know at a glance which approach will yield the highest return in learning. For this reason, flexibility, ingenuity, and creativity are essential to successful teaching, particularly for teaching reading.

When a teacher becomes enamored of one method to the exclusion of others, she shuts out the possibility of adjusting this method to individual pupil needs. Although such a teacher may be highly successful in teaching some of her pupils, she will inevitably produce a number of frustrated, unhappy misfits in the educational arena. If she is authoritarian and presses hard, some of her pupils will develop behaviors which result in such labels as "bad," "dull," "dreamers," "lazy," and "anti-social." These behaviors, instead of being interpreted as the logical psychological outcome of failure, frustration, and tension evolving from the reading situation, become in turn the explanations of why the child failed in reading.

13. *Learning to read is a long-term developmental process extending over a period of years.* This principle rests on two premises. First, every aspect of the instructional program is related to the ultimate goal of producing efficient readers. This is particularly important in light of the many recent "newer approaches" to beginning reading instruction. What is done during this period influences the child's concept as to what constitutes reading. In other words, beginning reading instruction can inculcate any one of a number of pupil "sets."

The second premise is that the child's early attitude toward reading is important from the educational standpoint. It can influence a student's reading habits for life. Nothing should be permitted to happen in beginning instruction which impairs later development of efficient reading.

There are several approaches to beginning reading which may result in a "fast start" or relatively high achievement at the end of a year of intensive instruction. The materials used stress analysis of letter sounds and, in the opinion of some observers, fail to achieve a balanced program. The overemphasis on analysis permits rapid initial growth, but carries with it the potential of producing readers who over-learn only this specific technique. Some pupils will tend to overrely on analysis to the detriment of smooth facile reading.

The question which teachers must answer is, "Do higher reading achievement scores at the end of grade one establish the procedures and materials used as the best approach to *beginning reading instruction?*" If principle 13 is accepted as valid, the question cannot be answered on the basis of the short-term achievement.

14. *The concept of readiness should be extended upward to all grades.* Few teachers maintain that readiness applies more to one level of education than to another. Nevertheless, in the area of reading, there seems to be a predilection for associating readiness with beginning or first grade reading. This is the level at which we have "readiness tests," and much of the literature on readiness is concerned with the beginning reader. Even though readiness has been achieved at one level of experience, it does not necessarily follow that readiness is retained at a higher level of experience. There should be as much concern with readiness at the third-, fourth-, or sixth-grade levels as there is at the first-grade level.

A good start is an important factor in the learning process. But a good start is not always half the race because reading is a continuous developmental process. What is learned today is the foundation for what is learned tomorrow. A smooth, unfaltering first step is not a guarantee that succeeding steps will be equally smooth. For example, some children display no complications in learning until they are asked to sound out a number of words not known at sight. At this point they encounter difficulties, the degree of which could not have been predicted on the basis of readiness tests administered in the first grade. Even so, some of these failures stem from non-readiness for the experience.

15. *Children should not be in the classroom if they have emotional problems sufficiently serious to make them uneducable at the moment or if they interfere with or disrupt the learning process.* Physical disturbances such as a slight temperature, an inflamed throat, an abscessed tooth, or a skin blemish are cause for removing a child from the classroom. Many schools require that children not come to school until inoculated against certain diseases; other schools strongly urge these precautions. These measures seem natural and logical today. The suggestion that serious emotional problems be corrected before a child can attend school will probably be scoffed at—today. Tomorrow the concept of emotional health will be as readily accepted as the concept of physical health. Just as the practice of "beating the devil" out of the "obsessed" came to an end, so we will stop trying to beat learning into a child who is at the moment uneducable.

The reason for emphasizing emotional health in a book on reading is that our entire educational structure is based on the ability to read. One of the principles stated earlier was that a child should not be expected to do something he cannot do. When a child is uneducable because of serious emotional involvements and we persist in drilling him on sight words which he cannot learn, we are violating this earlier principle. Unless the classroom teacher can overcome the barrier to learning, the uneducable child should leave the classroom while being treated and return when he is educable. The vast majority of youngsters with emotional problems can be helped with personal and environmental therapy. If the emotional problem is not severe, it is possible for some children to continue in school while receiving outside treatment; in some cases the treatment can take place concurrently with regular learning in the classroom. In the latter situation, the teacher is a key factor.

16. *Emphasis should be on prevention rather than cure. Reading problems should be detected early and corrected before they deteriorate into failure-frustration-reaction cases.* However excellent the instruction in our schools, some children will not profit as much as others. The early detection of impairments and immediate attention to them are cornerstones of effective reading instruction. Although this may be obvious, the emphasis in our schools is still on cure, not prevention. The following discussion of school practices explains in part how this came about.

Reading instruction in American schools has been under heavy criticism. Parallel with the criticism emerged many new materials, suggested modifications in practice, and suggested shifts in philosophy. A few of the methodological emphases include i/t/a, language-experience materials, individualized reading, words in color, and integration of writing with beginning reading instruction. Questions raised include: "Is readiness training essential? Should the content of instructional materials parallel children's language usage? Should initial reading instruction consist primarily of teaching letter-sound relationships?"

Reading instruction seems particularly susceptible to over-enthusiasm for whatever bears the "new" label. Too often, highly publicized "new approaches" capture the attention of the general public and of a number of educators. Based on the publicity the method-materials receive, one might surmise they would soon be in universal use. Generally, interest wanes, and approaches heralded as breakthroughs are deserted for some other new approach in which interest builds to a peak and then recedes. (14)

During periods of ferment, such as the present, it is easy to lose sight of fundamental principles of instruction. Much time and energy can be spent in climbing on and off so-called "instructional bandwagons." Occasionally a "new emphasis" in instruction emerges which has some excellent features but which may neglect certain essentials while overemphasizing others. To illustrate, assume we agree with the principles discussed above. It is still possible to overemphasize one or more to such a degree that others are either ignored or actually violated.

Sound principles of reading instruction should apply with equal validity to any instructional approach, and, by definition, they cannot reflect what might be called an either/or bias as to particular methodologies. If a set of principles are valid criteria for instructional practices, a sound reading program cannot be built by paying lip service to several valid assumptions while making only one the cornerstone of instruction.

Principles and practices should be compatible

It is logical that a book on teaching reading should open with a statement of the principles upon which good teaching is based. Principles should evolve ahead of practices so that teacher and school practices can be evaluated in light of these principles. The view accepted here is that the principles formulated above are sound and that teachers who find them so should follow them in teaching reading. Some of the techniques used by teachers in their daily practice may inadvertently or unconsciously inhibit them from applying the principles which they have accepted as sound and desirable.

Administrative practices affecting instruction

Most defections from sound principles of teaching reading probably stem from institutionalized practices that have become part of American education. The practices have often evolved from economic pressures or community pressures, sometimes advocated as emergency measures. It is doubtful if any of these practices have been accepted because someone thought that they would enhance the quality of American education.

Schools do not deliberately produce non-readers or impaired readers, but educators often sacrifice sound principles in the face of pressure. Emergencies produce compromises which tend to become permanent. These compromises often become standard procedure to such an extent that after a while they are defended on the basis that "we've been doing this for years." Some of the more obvious school practices which prevent teachers from doing as well as they know how are listed below.

Class size

Classes containing thirty-five to forty students are, unfortunately, numerous.* Teachers of reading in these classrooms complain that they cannot do the job. They mean that they cannot find time for thorough, ongoing diagnosis and individual programs for the children who need individual help. If this is true, large classes prevent teachers from following some of the principles we have discussed.

When conditions force one sound principle to be ignored, it is likely that other principles will also be violated. Some children will be expected to read materials which are too difficult. When a teacher lacks an accurate picture of a child's ability and specific reading weaknesses, she will have a tendency to expect him to read at grade level. When this happens, another danger is that pressures both overt and subtle will be brought on the child experiencing failure. These pressures are not conducive to reading facility, at least not for all children.

Promotion versus concept of mastery of skills

The problems arising from large classes are compounded by the widespread school practice of universal or almost universal promotion. We are not concerned here with the merits of promotion versus retention, but rather with pointing up the inevitable results of our present-day practices.

Our schools are set up on a grade-level basis in which the curricula of the various grades are progressively more difficult. Everyone agrees that the learning tasks in the second grade are more difficult than those in the first. This is inherent in the grade-level system. This arrangement is obviously logical, but the logic implies that children in the second grade have mastered the skills taught in the first grade, because the second grade curriculum is based on the assumption of mastery of first grade skills. In similar manner, the third grade curriculum is based on skills presumably mastered in the second grade.

As school systems adopted the practice of social promotion, one might expect that the grade-level concept would be abandoned or

*Some data relative to class size are misleading. Some school systems may report class size or pupil-teacher ratio as somewhat smaller than is actually the case. This can occur when supervising personnel, school counselors, nurses, psychologists, speech therapists, etc., are included as instructional staff. Class size, as used in this discussion, refers to the actual mean number of children present in one teacher's classroom during the school year.

drastically revised. In the majority of our schools neither of these things happened. The result is that today we find children moving from grade to grade mainly because they have been physically present in a particular grade for an academic year. True, many children master the skills required for the next year's curriculum, but many do not. And when many do not, the grade-level concept is unsound because it was not designed to function under these conditions. The higher the grade level under consideration, the more apparent becomes the inadequacy of our efforts to impose automatic promotion on a graded system. When we attempt to justify automatic promotion on the grounds that it is psychologically sound because promotion prevents failure, we are being unrealistic in our concept of failure. Children who progress through the grades without adequate skills to deal with the tasks expected of them experience failure every day they attend school.

The foregoing is not intended to imply that non-promotion is desirable. Such data as we have on retaining students in the same grade for another year indicate that this is also an ineffective practice. A truly ungraded primary school will accept various levels of competency. As students master certain skills, they move on to the next level of tasks. The emphasis on promotion abates and each child moves at his own pace.

School entrance based on chronological age

Another school practice that tends to produce problems in the teaching of reading is the use of chronological age as the criterion for admitting children to school. Educators generally agree that instruction should be based on readiness for attempting the tasks to be performed. Once the school and community accept the chronological-age criterion for entering school, however, it is a simple step for parents and communities to reason: "Johnny is six years old. Therefore, he is ready for school. If he is *in* school, he is ready for reading."

Systematic reading instruction not found in upper grades

Reading is taught systematically in the elementary grades. Reading instruction is part of the curriculum. As we go upward in the grades, more reading is required, but instruction in reading is not as systematic as in the lower grades. In practice, reading seems to be regarded as a skill to be acquired in the elementary and intermediate grades and used in all areas of the curriculum from that point on. Although most school administrators and teachers realize that many children need thorough, planned, deliberate instruction above the sixth grade, they are also aware that systematic instruction at these levels is lacking.

At the junior high and high school levels we tend to rely more on slogans than planned instruction. "Every teacher is a teacher of reading" is such a slogan. The slogan does not fit the facts because some teachers are not qualified to teach reading. The job calls for specific training, knowledge, and skills, just as it does at lower grade levels. It is wrong to assume that poor readers will outgrow poor reading habits when they reach these grades, and it is wrong to assume that poor readers will read widely and better because they have more reading assigned in these grades. If children entering seventh and eighth grades had mastered the fundamental reading skills required for the reading tasks in these grades, present practices in our schools would be justified. Research data for these upper grades tell a different story. It has been found that in these grades about one in four students functions at a level one grade below actual placement; more than 10 per cent function at a level two grades below, and 5 per cent at three grades below placement. (16)

We hear more and more criticism that students are not proficient readers and they they cannot meet the demands of the curriculum. There is a growing consensus that one of the major ills of our educational system is that the systematic teaching of reading is terminated too early.

Non-teaching activities

If teachers are trained professionals they should not expend time and energy in non-professional activities. Any encroachments on a teacher's time leaves less time for teaching, and non-teaching activities are closely related to children's failure to learn. A tired, harassed teacher can hardly be expected to be an effective teacher. A teacher responsible for a host of administrative duties will have less time and energy for creative teaching activities. It is unfortunate when teachers accept these encroachments which reduce their effectiveness and contribute to the failure and maladjustment of students.

Teacher morale and effectiveness of instruction would be greatly increased if teachers could have short periods of time, morning and afternoon, when they are completely free of all school activities and pressures—free from children, grading workbooks, preparing records, and filling out forms. Teachers now enjoying such free periods may be surprised to learn that many teachers do not.

These are a few of the school practices which have led observant teachers to the conclusion that we do not live in the best of all educational worlds. Too often teachers are not aware that they work under conditions which prevent them from applying sound reading principles. But if teaching is a profession, the violation of sound principles of teaching is unprofessional. There is a tendency to absolve teachers of responsibility for teaching practices resulting from over-crowded classrooms with the statement that the community desires large classes or that teachers have no recourse since class size is an administrative decision. Teachers who feel responsible for making professional decisions will perceive that these arguments are rationalizations. (9)

Evaluating classroom practices

While individual teachers may have little control over certain institutional practices in the school, they do have considerable freedom in the classroom. They also have great responsibility to children. Teacher behavior is a most powerful determiner of the child's ego development and self concept. The teacher not only dispenses or withholds rewards but she is also the most important factor in the child's learning to read.

Teaching involves awesome responsibility. Teachers have the power to choose or *adopt* methodology, determine *how* materials are used, and control classroom-learning climate. These are powerful influences on students' development and use of reading ability. How well or poorly a child progresses in reading will determine what options are open to him in later life. The following suggestions focus on instructional behaviors over which teachers have major control:

1. Initial instruction should be structured so as not to confuse the child as to what is involved in the reading process. Reading is *not* code cracking, *or* learning sight words, *or* using context clues. Instruction must involve all of these in the right combination.
2. Be suspicious of practices which may be effective in achieving a short term goal but which can inhibit later growth in reading!
3. Provide children with good models of oral reading.

4. A prerequisite for producing avid readers is to be one.
5. Avoid practices that would lead children to view reading as being exclusively a "school activity" or a joyless mechanical fact gathering process.
6. Resist being dominated by any one set of materials or methodology.
7. Remember that differentiation of instruction is the key to effective teaching.
8. Capitalize on children's interests. Provide options outside the textbook and permit children to harness their own egos to reading tasks.
9. Do not let potentially sound practices deteriorate into educational rituals. This applies to such things as grouping, diagnosis, grading, writing experience stories, completing IPI prescriptions, writing book reports, and answering questions at the end of chapters.

YOUR POINT OF VIEW?

The problems following each chapter are not intended primarily to test recall of material presented. The problems may serve as a basis for class discussion or, in some instances, library research papers.

Respond to the following problems:

1. In your opinion, which one of the principles discussed in this chapter is the most important for improving reading instruction? Provide a rationale for your choice.

2. Assume that you are assigned the task of improving the teaching of reading in your state and that you can eliminate or modify *one* school practice which is now prevalent. What would be your recommendation? Why?

3. "Individual differences in achievement increase as we move upward through the grades." Which one of the following factors would you prefer to defend as being most important in effecting these differences in achievement? Why?

   a. Pupil ability
   b. School promotion policies

    c. Competency of instruction
    d. Factors outside the school

Defend or attack the following statements:

1. Chronological age is the most practical and most justifiable criterion determining when children should enter school.

2. Parents' ego-involvement in their child's learning to read is a causal factor in many reading failures and is a major problem for the schools and first grade teachers.

3. Teachers have erred in accepting non-teaching activities as part of their occupational obligation.

4. There is little basis for assuming that the school can prevent a substantial number of reading failures among pupils.

BIBLIOGRAPHY

1. Allen, James E., Jr. "The Right To Read —Target for the 70's," *Elementary English* (April 1970), 487–92.

2. Bond, Guy. and Robert Dykstra, "The Cooperative Research Program in First-Grade Reading Instruction," *Reading Research Quarterly* (Summer 1967), 5–142.

3. Cutts, Warren G. (ed.), *Teaching Young Children to Read*, Washington: U.S. Office of Education, Bulletin No. 19, 1964.

4. Dale, R. R. "Anxiety About School Among First-Year Grammar School Pupils, and Its Relation to Occupational Class and Co-Education," *British Journal of Educational Psychology* (February 1969), 18–26.

5. Dykstra, Robert, "Summary of Second-Grade Phase of the Cooperative Research Program in Primary Reading Instruction," *Reading Research Quarterly* (Fall 1968), 49–70.

6. Heilman, Arthur W. "Moving Faster Toward Outstanding Instructional Programs," *Vistas in Reading*, Proceedings, International Reading Association, 11, 1966, 273–76.

7. Ilg, Frances L., and Louise Bates Ames, *School Readiness*. New York: Harper and Row Publishers, 1965.

8. Kingston, Albert J. "The Psychology of Reading," in *Forging Ahead In Reading*, Vol. 12, Part 1, J. Allen Figural (Ed.), Proceedings, International Reading Association, 425–32.

9. Lieberman, Myron, *Teaching as a Profession*. Englewood Cliffs, N.J.: Prentice-Hall, Inc., 1956.

10. Morrison, Coleman (ed.), *Children Can Learn to Read ... But How?* Rhode Island College Reading Conference Proceedings. Providence, Rhode Island: Oxford Press, 1964.

11. Rogers, Carl R., *Freedom To Learn*. Columbus, O.: Charles E. Merrill Publishing Co., 1969.

12. Rutherford, William L. "Five Steps To Effective Reading Instruction," *The Reading Teacher* (February 1971), 416–21.

13. Singer, Harry, "Research That Should Have Made a Difference," *Elementary English* (January 1970), 27–34.

14. Smith, Nila Banton, *American Reading Instruction*, Newark, Del.: International Reading Association, 1965.

15. Smith, Richard, Wayne Otto and Kathleen Harty, "Elementary Teacher's Preferences for Pre-Service and In-Service Training in the Teaching of Reading," *Journal of Educational Research* (July–August 1970), 445–49.

16. Stroud, J. B., *Psychology in Education* (rev. ed.), New York: Longmans, Green and Co., 1956, 375–77.

17. U. S. Office of Education, *Do Teachers Make A Difference?*, Washington, D.C., 1970.

II

Beginning Reading: The School's Clients

Our society places a very high value on learning to read. So high, in fact, that once children begin their formal education the school provides no curricular options that are not premised on reading ability. Despite the fact that educators know that there are tremendous individual differences among children, the system seems to function as if it were expected that all children will make approximately the same *amount* of progress in a *given time* under *any* instructional format. Since this expectation is not fulfilled, more and more educational problems are created.

Chapter 2 focuses on a number of learner characteristics found among children from the mainstream of our society. Chapter 3 describes the schools' attempts to teach reading to the culturally different (or linguistically different) child.

2

Children
as Readers

One of the reasons why we produce a large number of reading failures in our schools is that we have not really been able to adapt the "system" to meet individual differences. We have evolved instructional principles which recognize prospective learners as being unique, but all begin school on the basis of chronological age and pursue their educational growth within the framework of a grade-level system.

As evidence piles up that something has gone amiss — that our educational dreams are not being realized — we tend to tinker with the system; in reality, however, we make few significant changes. We reaffirm our belief that "readiness" is crucial, resort to in-class grouping practices, work out elaborate schemes for Individually Prescribed Instruction, inaugurate ungraded schools, search for new materials, and hire corporations to use their own products in teaching children.

Each of these and other proposals can be easily superimposed on the existing structure. If they do not achieve our goals, at least they stand as evidence that the schools are trying to do something to cope with individual differences. A review of classroom practices used over the years emphasizes a never ceasing search for ways to cope with this problem. Examples of some of these include:

The Dalton Plan	The several "tracks" approach
Winnetka Plan	Programmed materials
Various other "contract"	I.P.I. (Individually
plans	Prescribed Instruction)
The Unit Approach	P.L.A.N. (Programmed
Individualized Reading	Learning According
The Ungraded School	to Need)
The Joplin Plan	Team teaching
All types of Homogeneous	C.A.I. (Computer
grouping	Assisted Instruction)

There is no question that teaching individual learners is a most difficult task. It is easier to pledge support for the proposition that every child has the "right to read" than it is to deliver on that promise. What follows focuses on children as readers and attempts to point out some of the factors that need to be considered in instruction. There is a relationship between a child's cultural environment and the educational environment he enters called the school. Also, the environment in which beginning reading takes place has a vital influence on potential learners. Since children are different, they should not be treated as interchangeable parts within a classroom.

The Importance of
Cultural Differences

The American educational experiment of providing free compulsory education for all children embraced many commendable virtues and goals. It was fashionable to view the United States as a "melting pot" for the many cultures and ethnic groups that comprised the larger society. The school, as an institution established by the society, inherited the chief responsibility for the assimilating process. This process took a bit longer than might ideally have been hoped for, but in the final analyses the school functioned with some degree of success.

The school recently has been faced with a much more serious challenge — that of providing relevant education for large groups whose assimilation into the main stream of our society has been systematically resisted by that society. Many black, Chicano, American Indian, and impoverished white children have grown up in ghettos. The educational significance of this is that their contact with the main cultural stream was systematically curtailed. These children attended schools, but the curiculum and instructional procedures they found there were not compatible with their backgrounds. What went on in the school was really designed for a clientele who were already admitted to the main stream.

Under these circumstances, the achievement level of many culturally different children was minimized. As these children fell farther behind in what the school was teaching, they tended to be more and more abandoned by the school. The problems posed by the recent attempts to make the educational process relevant to these culturally different children are staggering. Problems of dialect, values, attitudes toward the school, and hostility to the past must be understood and accepted as teachers deal with these "children-as-readers." Discussion of these problems is found in Chapter 3.

Attitudes Toward Self and Adjustment

The reaction of the school and the home to reading skill has a very pronounced effect on the beginning reader. Children quickly see the importance which is attached to learning to read. Many beginning readers must fail because success is measured by an arbitrary criterion, grade level achievement. We will look briefly at the way in which attitudes and later behavior are influenced during the beginning reading period.

Among educators, parents, or psychologists, there would be few dissenters to the proposition that "getting the right start" in learning to read is of the greatest importance. For some children who experience difficulty, a poor start is often the key to later reading difficulty as well as a factor in maladjustment. The fact that some children can fail in the beginning stages of reading and still develop into adequate readers and well-adjusted individuals does not in the least militate against the fact that the beginning stage in reading is extremely important. It is during this period that the child develops attitudes toward himself, toward reading, and toward competition. These attitudes, in turn, are related to the motivations which may arouse anti-social behavior.

The child's attitude toward self is influenced by the attitudes of others toward him. There are parental reactions toward him as their child and as a learner, possibly complicated by an unconscious comparison of him with siblings. The teacher, in turn, reacts to the child as a learner, to his home and parents, and to the child as a problem if he develops behavior not condoned by the school. The child senses that his parents and his teacher feel that learning to read is extremely urgent. Pressures from home, school, and self do not always result in learning. There are many activities which may call for intense competition, but in most cases it is optional with the individual whether he elects to compete. In the elementary school, there is no choice of curricula, one including reading and the other not. The curriculum is *based* on reading. The non-reader has no place to hide except behind whatever defenses he can devise. Unfortunately, these are not honored as substitutes for reading by the society in which he lives. Examples of these defenses are:

> I'm too dumb to read.
> Don't-care attitude.
> Aggression.
> Withdrawal, daydreaming.
> Compensation.

Self-confidence is very important for the beginning reader. The child who lacks confidence in his own ability is likely to over-react when he encounters difficulty in learning to read. The type of home the child comes from and the relationships he has had with parents or adults will have already affected his confidence before he gets to school. It is the teacher's task to structure school experiences in such a way that the classroom will be an area of safety rather than a threat. This is one of the most difficult tasks confronting the teacher; it is also one of the most important. The task is difficult because the school is only one of several institutions which parcel out failure and success, ego-satisfaction, and frustration. It has no control over the home, neighborhood, or community. Children entering school have patterns of behavior which reflect experiences of rejection, overprotection, success, personal inadequacy, and the like. (48)

Today there are few educators who question that these experiences relate to learning. It is true that the school cannot undo the past experiences of each child, nor can it control the present in the community and home. A child may come to school with feelings of inadequacy so strong and so reinforced by his home that the school cannot satisfy his need for attention and acceptance. But the school can, in many cases, compensate to some degree for the unfulfilled needs of children. Chapter 1 dealt with practices found in many schools which tend to limit effective education. Even if teachers take the position that their only job is to teach an agreed upon curriculum, they must still understand that they teach the subject matter to potential learners. Factors which diminish this potential among learners are teaching problems.

An alert and observant teacher can see many clues which suggest how a particular child fits in with, or is accepted by, his peer group. Four children are playing in the sand box. Eddie approaches with the intention of joining the group, but is met with: "Get away from here!" "You can't play with us." "There's no more room — let us alone." These responses in themselves are not atypical of six-year-olds. What the teacher has to discover is whether this is just a group of "haves" protecting their domain, the sandbox, from a "have not," or whether this is an illustration of the group's rejection of Eddie.

There are two types of behavior, over-shyness and aggression, which pose special problems for the teacher and special threats to the learning situation. These behaviors are vastly different, yet it is safe to conclude that the same drives are often behind these apparent opposites in behavior. The shy child and the aggressive child both desire responses from others. Each has learned the behavior patterns which he uses in an attempt to cope with his environment. Each will also need some help in learning to use behavior that will be likely to lead to group acceptance rather than group rejection.

Attitudes
Toward Reading

Most first grade teachers would agree that one of the most important aims of the beginning reading period is to help the child develop a positive attitude toward reading. Failure in reading is likely to produce the opposite attitude. When the school sets an arbitrary goal or level of achievement, namely the reading of first grade material, the child feels that non-success in achieving this arbitrary standard is failure regardless of promotion policies.

A number of experienced teachers were given a conventional checklist of reading difficulties. This was a one-page list of difficulties which appear frequently among retarded readers. The teachers were asked to select the two problems which they thought would:

> Be present in most remedial reading cases
> Be the most serious problems noted

The majority of teachers gave as their first choice "aversion to reading." If one thought only in terms of the actual mechanics of reading, he might not include aversion as a reading problem. However, it *is* a problem in working with most reading failures. Once a child has developed a dislike for reading, stemming from failure, he is not likely to give up his aversion as a result of persuasion based on the authoritarian statements that reading is fun, pleasant, and important. The child's dislike of reading is a most logical reaction. The fact that the child will be told it is an unfortunate response will have little influence on its removal.

**Later Development
in Reading**

Attitudes and habits acquired by children during the beginning reading period influence later reading behavior. According to the experience of persons working with impaired readers in the upper elementary and intermediate grades, it is unsafe to assume that children will outgrow ineffective reading habits. Poor reading habits seem to feed on themselves and multiply. Common but serious pitfalls which threaten the beginning reader include:

1. Word-calling without comprehension; the mere mechanics of reading is equated with reading.
2. Failure to use punctuation properly. Unless the weakness is overcome, the child can never enjoy reading because he will continually distort or destroy meaning.
3. Failure to develop and use methods of attacking unknown words, i.e., structural analysis, phonic analysis, and context clues.
4. Development of crutches which become substitutes for actual sight recognition of words when the sight-word method is used. An inadequate stock of sight words accompanied by pressure to read beyond one's present ability can lead to numerous bad reading habits such as:

   (a) Guessing at unknown words
   (b) Miscalling words
   (c) Substituting words
   (d) Inserting or omitting words
   (e) Slow reading

These habits tend to be reinforced with practice rather than to disappear with time.

Parental Reactions
to Reading Problems

Parents' reaction to poor reading is a special problem. A parent who has worked with a child daily and weekends, who has drilled him on sight words, such as *them–then; when–where; these–those; but–buy;* etc., only to have the child miss these same words day after day, usually displays some hostility, either overt or unconscious, toward the child. Parental reactions can take many forms, but some variation of one of the following is very common. Shifting all blame to the child, the parents come to believe that he is lazy, obstinate, and deliberately trying to exasperate adults, or that he is just dull. Even when parents entertain the latter hypothesis, they usually continue to drill, pressure, or shame the child, evidently supposing that he can somehow be sharpened by this procedure.

Another reaction is to posit that the reading failure stems from some special defect other than lack of intelligence, such as poor vision. This assumption is a form of rationalization; the physical factor in question is not the real cause. The disability hypothesis is not destroyed by hearing or visual examinations which result in negative findings, because it can be reasoned that the diagnosis may be in error.

A third solution is to shift the blame outside the child-home orbit, with the most obvious recipient being the school. In a case where the reading problem has existed for several years, the present teacher is often excused, but some previous teacher, usually the first, is seen as the source of the trouble. This analysis, of course, can be correct. However, in many cases it is not. Many parents vacillate between the three positions, emphasizing different ones at different times.

Rarely are parents able to see how the home and patterns of overprotection, psychological rejection, excessively high standards, perfectionism, or unfilled psychological needs stemming from the family configuration, are related to reading failures. There is no doubt among clinicians who work with remedial cases that an emotionally unstable home environment is a factor in many such cases. Self-confidence, or the lack of it, is conditioned by home as well as school experiences. Initiative, self-direction, and social adequacy are determined by attitudes found in the home. Some parents have little insight into how their own expectations and responses to children's failures are related to reading difficulties.

If the reading problem is to a large degree a symptom of maladjustment in the home, working with reading alone is not going to the root of the problem. In cases where a child is referred to an outside agency, such as a child-guidance clinic or reading laboratory, parents are often counselled and worked with prior to, or concurrently with, reading instruction for the child. This, of course, is one of the most difficult problems facing the schools. At the present time, schools lack the authority and the facilities for dealing with home conditions which are closely related to school learning situations. Thus, the school is often handicapped in that it is forced to deal only with a symptom — poor reading — rather than with the basic cause of the poor reading. Parents are not likely to be aware of the fact that their attitudes and behavior are related to their child's poor reading, and attempts on the part of the school to probe this very sensitive area are likely to arouse strong resentment and hostility.

Sex Differences
in Learning to Read

One unexplained phenomenon associated with children as readers is the differential achievement between boys and girls during the initial stages of reading instruction. Research data compiled over the past few decades have reported conclusive evidence that girls as a group achieve significantly higher in *beginning reading* than do boys as a group.*

As one reviews the literature on early achievement in reading it becomes apparent that sex difference has significance for teachers who are interested in children as readers. The material that follows is advanced as representative of the data available on the topic.

Ayres (7) was one of the first to call attention to sex differences in school achievement. His book *Laggards in Our Schools* does not deal with differences in reading per se. However, he pointed out that 12.8 per cent more boys than girls repeated grades; that 17.2 per cent more girls than boys completed "common school" (eighth

---

*Previous editions of this text have devoted a full chapter to this topic. Since the school operated from the premise of no sex differences in learning to read, it was felt that a rather thorough review of the literature was somewhat mandatory. During the past decade, much has been written on the topic which, when coupled with the published results of the cooperative First and Second Grade Studies (USOE), has diminished the need for "making a case" that sex differences in early reading have existed in our schools.

grade); and that there was 13 per cent more retardation among boys.

St. John (39) reported no significant difference in the measured intelligence of approximately one thousand pupils in grades one through four, but stated that girls very distinctly excel boys in reading at grade levels one through four. The study covered a four-year period and reported that boys showed 7 per cent more repeating of grades or non-promotions than did girls.

Wilson, et al., (45) report a study covering three years at Horace Mann School. Boys and girls in first grade showed no differences on mental tests, but the authors state ". . . the difference between girls and boys in paragraph reading in this grade was statistically reliable." In reading at second grade level, "the average of chances was 88 in 100 that the girls would be superior." At third grade level, girls surpassed the boys but not significantly. It should be pointed out that the intelligence level of the pupils in this study was considerably above the mean for all children their age.

Alden, et al., (1) report data from children in grades two through six who were tested with the Durrell Sullivan Reading Capacity Test.* Over six thousand children were tested, and the number of boys who were one or more years retarded in reading was double that of girls in each of the first five grades. Table 1 gives the data on these sex differences.

One of the most significant studies on sex differences was reported by Stroud and Lindquist (42) in 1942. Over three hundred schools with 50,000 pupils were the source of data. The data compiled covered a number of years of testing in the Iowa schools, using the Iowa Every-Pupil Basic Skills Test. In this program, grades

TABLE 1

Sex Differences Between Boys and Girls in Reading Retardation Measuring One Year or More Retardation

Grade	Per cent Boys Retarded	Per cent Girls Retarded
2	9.7	4.2
3	14.7	7.1
4	23.6	12.0
5	25.5	11.6
6	13.7	9.9

*Harcourt, Brace and World, Inc., New York.

three through eight are tested on reading comprehension, vocabulary, word study skills, basic language skills, and arithmetic skills. The authors state, "Girls have maintained a consistent, and on the whole, significant superiority over boys in the subjects tested, save in arithmetic, where small insignificant differences favor boys." Table 2 shows the mean difference in reading comprehension scores between boys and girls for grades three through eight. It should be noted that the largest differences occur at grades three and four and decline significantly at grade six.

TABLE 2

Sex Differences in Reading Comprehension as Measured by the Iowa Every-Pupil Test of Basic Skills

Grade	Mean Differences (all favoring girls)	Significance Ratios
3	2.12	2.57
4	2.75	3.38
5	1.29	1.77
6	.30	.39
7	.10	.14
8	.47	.50

Hughes, (24) using the total comprehension scores from the Chicago Reading Tests, measured reading achievement of boys and girls in grades three through eight. She found that the greatest difference was at grade three where the girls achieved more than a half school-year above the boys. This difference favoring girls was significant at the 1 percent level. At grade four the difference favoring girls was significant at only the 5 percent level, while in grades five through eight girls made higher reading scores than did boys, but the differences were not statistically significant.

Nila, (34) during the first weeks of school, tested three hundred first graders on a number of individual and group readiness tests. She reports that on the basis of these test scores, the boys as a group and the girls as a group were equally ready to read. These pupils were tested at the end of the school year for reading achievement. Seventy-two were designated as reading failures; 45 of the failures, or 63 percent, were boys, and 37 percent were girls.

Gates (18) tested over thirteen thousand children in grades two through eight and compared girls' and boys' mean scores on three reading subtests at each grade level. He states, "In each of the twenty-one comparisons the mean raw score for girls is higher than the mean raw scores for boys, and most of the differences are significant."

Prescott (35) tested over 7,000 boys and 7,000 girls beginning first grade on the Metropolitan Readiness Test to determine whether or not this test showed sex differences. He reports that when chronological age is equated the performance of girls is superior to that of boys (difference favoring girls significant at the 5 percent level). Carroll (11) also found sex differences in reading readiness at first grade level. These differences were in favor of girls and were large enough to be satistically significant.

Cooperative USOE studies

During the school year 1964–65, 27 first grade reading studies were supported by grants from the U.S. Office of Education. Analyzing the data from these studies, Bond and Dykstra (10) reported that girls rated higher than boys on both readiness measures and reading achievement at the end of grade one. During the following year, 15 of these studies were continued into grade two. Dykstra (15) reported that girls maintained their superiority in reading achievement at the end of grade two.

Clinical data

Further data on sex differences in reading are found in reports from clinical sources, such as child-guidance clinics and remedial reading clinics. Rarely do the data from these sources deal primarily with sex differences. As a rule, the titles of reported research do not indicate that sex differences are discussed, but, almost without exception, these studies reveal a disproportionate number of referrals of boys as compared with girls and, also, an even more disproportionate percentage of seriously retarded readers among boys. The range of percentages is from approximately 65 percent boys and 35 percent girls to 90 percent boys and 10 percent girls. Monroe (31) reported an exhaustive study of over 400 children who had been referred to the Chicago Institute for Juvenile Research for various problems, including impaired reading. One group of 155 children was referred specifically for reading problems; in this group 86 percent were boys and 14 percent were girls.

Blanchard, (9) in discussing seventy-three consecutive cases seen at the Philadelphia Child Guidance Clinic, in which reading was given as one reason for referral or where a reading problem was found to exist, reports that sixty-three of these cases were boys, and ten cases were girls.

Young (46), investigating forty-one cases diagnosed as retarded in reading and referred to the Psycho-Educational Clinic, Harvard University, reports that thirty-seven of the cases were boys and four cases were girls. He further reports that over a period of years this same ratio held for all children referred who were retarded in reading but had at least average intelligence.

Preston (36) studied the effects of security-insecurity in the home, the school, and the social situation of retarded readers. In a sample of 100 reading failures possessing normal intelligence and no physical defects, there were seventy-two boys and twenty-eight girls.

Missildine (30), studying the emotional adjustment of thirty retarded readers picked at random from clinic files, reported twenty-five of the thirty were boys. All but two of the children in this study were below ten years of age.

McCollum (25), discussing forty severe reading disability cases referred to a reading clinic during one year, reports that 78 percent were boys. Axline (6) reported a study of thirty-seven second graders selected on the basis of reading retardation or non-reading. Twenty-eight, or 76 percent of the retarded readers, were boys. Vorhaus (44) described 225 reading disability cases seen at the New York University Reading Institute. One hundred seventy-eight, or 80 percent of these cases, were boys. All cases were reported as having average or better intelligence.

Fabian (17) reports on a group of 279 children given diagnostic tests at the Brooklyn Juvenile Guidance Center. Ninety-nine of these children were at least eight years of age, had I.Q.'s of eighty or above, and showed reading achievement at least 25 percent below expectation based on mental age. Of these ninety-nine children, sixty-seven were boys, and thirty-two were girls.

Many other clinical and remedial studies, particularly those of a "case study" nature, also report a preponderance of boys as remedial reading cases. However, these reports are not cited here because the number of cases they discuss is too small for evaluation.

Hypotheses as to causes of sex differences in reading

The data on sex differences in learning to read should not be dismissed as just another educational statistic. If we are interested in children as readers (and learners), then the school must evaluate all practices which might be related to this differential in beginning reading achievement. Today there is growing support for the hypothesis that these differences are probably not entirely traceable to the nervous systems of the learners. The methodological practices and educational climate found in classrooms are also a factor.

Several recent studies have contributed data which suggest that the cultural mileau of the school, *including instruction*, may play a significant role in producing sex differences in early reading performance. The important implication here is that there are variables within the learning environment which, when taken into consideration in instruction, tend to enhance the performance of boys. Two such variables are the teacher (her attitude and behavior patterns) and teaching materials.

McNeil and Keislar (26) found kindergarten boys' achievement superior to that of girls when beginning instruction relied exclusively on the use of programmed materials. When this instruction was followed by four months of teacher instruction (all women teachers), girls' achievement was superior to that of boys. The authors state, "The fact that the superiority in reading of boys was not maintained under teacher direction indicates that there are variables within the classroom which militate against the maximum performance of young male learners."

Heilman (20) conducted an intensive in-service program in which participating teachers studied and discussed research data relevant to sex differences in learning to read. These teachers did make a number of classroom and teaching adjustments. Boys taught by these teachers had higher mean scores on each of the subtests of the Stanford Achievement Test at the end of grade one than did boys taught by control-teachers in the same community. "In-service training which resulted in teacher awareness of sex differences in learning to read appears to have evoked classroom practices which tended to enhance the performance of boys."

Preston's (37) study of reading achievement of German children reports sex differences favoring boys. In addition, he reports more variability among scores made by girls, which is at variance with most findings of American studies. These data strongly suggest cultural influence as being important factors in learning the reading process.

A number of the hypotheses which have been advanced in an effort to explain why girls have consistently shown superiority over boys in early reading achievement are cited here.

1. *Boys and girls mature at different rates and some phases of growth are closely related to reading.* Since the data are conclusive that girls develop more rapidly than boys, this hypothesis is sometimes seen as the key to the problem under discussion. In skeletal development, girls as a group are superior to boys throughout the pre-school period, and by the age of six years they are at least a full year ahead of boys. Since boys are less physiologically mature, eye muscles and visual acuity may not be equal to the task of beginning reading, and their attention span may not be developed enough to allow for lengthy concentration on teacher guidance.

A long-term study carried out at the University of Michigan compares the chronological age at which boys and girls begin to read and the "rate of progress" made after each has mastered a certain level of reading ability. The authors report a significant difference favoring girls in the age of learning to read. However, once children achieved a reading age of eighty-four months on the Gates Primary Reading Test, no difference between boys' and girls' rate of advancement was found. (4)

2. *The school environment and curriculum at the primary level are more frustrating to boys than to girls.* This hypothesis is very closely related to the preceding one. For instance, if boys and girls mature at different rates it is logical to suppose that participating in the same classroom activity is not the same experience for each group. One group is more mature than the other, but each group is equally expected to do close work, make fine discriminations, sit quietly for extended periods of time, pay attention, cooperate, finish tasks, and inhibit aggression. Many educators think that these are the factors which frustrate boys as a group more than girls.

Robinson (38) is convinced that research supports a hypothesis of sex difference in reading achievement during the first few years of formal schooling, but she states: "At present it is not clear whether just being a girl gives a young child a better chance for early reading success or whether something inherent in the school situation or the social setting militates against the progress of boys." After pointing out that boys as a group produce more remedial reading problems, get lower school marks, have a higher incidence of non-promotion, and produce more "behavior problems" than do girls as a group, Smith and Jenson (40) conclude, "all these findings emphasize the fact that the school functions less effectively for boys than for girls."

3. *Basal reader materials are less motivating and satisfying to boys than to girls.* This idea is an extension of hypothesis two, since

the reading materials are naturally part of the curriculum. The rationale behind this hypothesis is that the rather sterile, repetitious "look, oh, look; see baby play" vocabulary and the rigid conformist mood, tone, and atmosphere contained in and conveyed by the pre-primers, primers, and early readers are considerably less challenging to boys than to girls. It is often alleged that the "content" is a far cry from what the culture has taught to and expects from boys. Therefore, beginning reading, which should be an exciting, challenging new adventure, is actually a dull, regressive sort of experience unless the teacher can project more excitement into the material.

4. *Most primary teachers are women.* Allen (2) states: "Social environments for males and females are not and never have been the same or equal," and points out that from this fact may stem differences in interests, values, and achievement. Bell (8) holds that the difference in reading success between boys and girls is related to their emotional relationships with their teachers. It is his opinion that it is easier for girls to identify with women teachers and that boys are not provided with enough opportunities for the expression of aggression. The various studies all agree that boys show more aggressive tendencies than do girls. The school frowns on aggressive behavior and this no doubt influences some teachers to react toward boys in a manner different from that manifested toward girls who, as a group, may have a reputation for being docile, quiet, and cooperative. Terman (43) states that there is ample indication that some sort of "halo" effect operates in the classroom to give girls higher teacher ratings or grades than would be merited on the basis of objective achievement test results. St. John (39) does not question the fact that in grades one through four girls "distinctly" excel boys in reading and general school achievement, but he states: "They (girls) excel *less* when achievement is measured by standard tests than when it is measured by *teacher marks*." [Emphasis added.]

5. *Boys are less motivated to learn to read.* This hypothesis is closely related to certain others that have previously been mentioned, but it is advanced often enough in the literature on reading to be considered independently. Nila (34) is of the opinion that girls are more likely to work up to the capacity of their abilities than are boys. She states: "The writer believes that the reason boys and girls who are equally ready to read do not make the same progress lies in the factor of motivation." Wilson, et al., (45) state: "It

would seem probable that the reasons for more rapid progress by girls are related to learning interests and dispositions, rather than to more subtle sex differences such as mental qualities or characteristics of femininity."

**Examples of
Children as Readers**

The previous discussion touched on some of the social-cultural and other environmental influences which shape and mold children as learners. The school cannot undo or revise the experiences a child has had prior to his arriving at school. The fact that children are so different when they come to school makes it imperative that the teacher discover those differences which are important factors in learning to read. Then she must develop a program of teaching which, at its maximum effectiveness, will help each child to grow at a rate commensurate with his ability. The teacher must guard against practices and classroom experiences which may damage the child psychologically and inhibit learning in the future. The discussion which follows attempts to show how differences among pupils are related to instruction.

Scott was a boy of average intelligence who gave the appearance of being shy. He was reluctant to respond in class or to join in the playground activities for fear that he would fail. He would give up easily, make no effort to get help from the teacher when it was needed, and was showing no progress in reading. He was socially immature and inadequate in the group. Within three or four months, he had been generally rejected by the group. While he seemed to accept this on the surface, he nevertheless harbored intense hostility.

He did not manifest this hostility through overt attacks on other children, but through such immature behavior as scribbling on another pupil's drawing, breaking another child's pencil, and putting his own coat on a hallway hook in place of another, which he would then drop on the floor. He displayed a tendency to tattle and call the teacher's attention to other pupils' shortcomings. Whatever form his aggression took, he always seemed to get caught.

Jerry was a boy of above average intelligence and, according to the teacher, just the opposite of Scott. She characterized him as being "pushy" in class, attempting to be the center of everything that went on. He was able to achieve leadership status among the class but still had an insatiable need to be the center of attention and to dominate others. Physically he was more mature than the other boys and extremely well-coordinated. Because his superiority in things physical was never questioned, he was never a problem as a bully.

Despite high ability, he made a poor adjustment in class. He was unable to work alone or carry any project through to its conclusion. Instead of doing assigned seat work, he would wander around the room in an attempt to get an audience. Jerry and Scott both got off to a very poor start in reading.

Doris, a girl of high average intelligence, was one of the most mature children in the class. Her language facility was above average and, while not the brightest child in the class, she was as well-informed as any. She was accepted by both boys and girls as a leader and yet did not insist on the leadership role. Her social adjustment was excellent both in and out of class. She enjoyed reading from the start. Making better than expected progress in beginning reading, she continued this same level of performance in the following years.

What were the real differences between these pupils? On the basis of C.A., I.Q., and M.A., they were fairly equal. All came from higher than average socio-economic homes. Each child had been read to a great deal prior to school and since early infancy. Each had many books at home and each had rich and varied experiences prior to entering school, which included family picnics, rides on trains, long trips by car, eating out with their families, and visits to large cities, farms, zoos, and parks. How did they differ?

Scott was the older of two boys. Both parents set very high standards for him. His parents were perfectionists, and he could never quite measure up to their expectations. He became very aware of this. It was impossible to do anything exactly right. His parents always nagged when he attempted anything, and his withdrawal was a most logical response. This response he soon learned and eventually over-learned. His ego was threatened by this inability to please his parents. When he really did wrong he was not rejected or severely punished. In fact, he was treated as an individual, for his parents tried to discover "Why did Scott do this?" The closest his psychological needs ever came to being fulfilled was when he was caught in some misbehavior which was a threat to his parents. School simply became a new and different arena, and he used the same weapons and approach, even though, from an adult standpoint, his responses were not the most logical ones available.

Reading became a threat to him very early in school. Like most parents, his were concerned about reading. They wanted him to get a good start. His confidence in himself and in his ability was already undermined, and he started from the premise that he would fail in reading. It is not surprising that with this emotional conflict he was unable to bring his energies to bear on the reading task. As tension from failure mounted, he used responses which further alienated him from people — his parents, peer group, and teacher. Needing acceptance more than anything else, and being denied it, he withdrew from any situation which in his mind might further jeopardize his status.

Jerry was the only child of parents who had both finished college, done graduate work, and acquired professional standing. They were quite concerned with status, but unconsciously so. They never verbalized comparisons between Jerry and members of his peer group. In their own minds such invidious comparisons were a sign of immaturity. Yet their need for Jerry to succeed, to be the best in all types of endeavor, while not perceived by them, was so close to the surface that it was clearly sensed by him. His security became tied up with excelling, with dominating others. Success was the safety region for him. Through it, he could dominate the home; it was the price paid for love, affection, and acceptance. As he grew to school age, most of his endeavors were rewarded by success. He was "superior."

Reading was a different story. He did not start school with a superiority in this skill. He found himself in a group where, in one particular skill, he was only average. He seemed never to be interested in reading. As other pupils' superiority in reading became marked, reading became a threat to him. A frontal attack on the problem was not the solution he chose. He elected to compensate. He withdrew from reading, disrupted class activities, interfered with others' learning, and tried to capture attention and maintain his status in numerous ways.

The needs and motives of the two boys were strikingly similar, as were their attitudes toward reading. Yet their overt reactions to a frustrating situation were quite different, so much so that the teacher identified the boys as being "just the opposite." Would knowing the background of each boy, as related here, help the teacher in dealing with their reading problems?

Our third case, Doris, was not a reading problem. This girl was a well-adjusted, thoroughly accepted child. She was the youngest of several siblings, adored by her family, but not spoiled. She did not have to compete for affection. An outward appearance of the home lives of all three children appeared to be similar. Yet only one of the three had found security at home. Could this factor have had an important relationship to reading?

The three children just described were members of the same first grade class. This class contained over twenty other children, some of whom would merit an equally extensive individual analysis if they were to be understood as beginning readers. Here, only an important fact or two concerning these twenty children will be mentioned; teachers' knowledge or experience will show why these facts are important in beginning reading.

Some of the children were barely old enough to enter school. Others were eight or nine months older. Some had attended kindergarten the previous year, others had not. Three children had attended nursery school since they were three years old. Two of the mothers worked outside the home during those years.

The I.Q.'s of children in this group ranged from 76 to 130. Three children measured 85 or below. Mental age varied as much as 24 months within the group. Education of parents ranged from one year in high school to graduate work in college. Occupation of the parents ranged from manual laborer to physician. Two children had medical records showing excessive illness during childhood. One child wore glasses. Children other than Scott and Jerry had emotional problems.

These and many other factors are definitely related to learning to read and to the differences in reading ability which will inevitably emerge in any first grade class. Being able to detect differences and understand their significance is an invaluable aid to the teacher as she plans experiences and sets goals for individuals in her group. From the potential learner's position, having a teacher with this ability to detect subtle but important differences is a form of insurance against being pushed too fast, losing self-confidence, and forming an aversion to school and to reading.

**Ego-Involved Behavior
in the Classroom**

Understanding the term ego-involvement, as used here, does not call for an extensive background in psychology. Teachers, like pupils and parents, have egos and know what it is like to have one's ego crushed. They also know the satisfaction felt when one's abilities and accomplishments are recognized by others.

Pupils like to do those things which are ego-satisfying and tend to dislike and resist doing those things which threaten the ego. Previous discussion has centered around the interaction between the learner and instruction. To posit that this interaction is important is to recognize the importance of the learner's ego. The first-grade teacher starts with one advantage that should be exploited to the fullest: *The child is potentially ego-involved in learning to read.* At this stage of his career the child has usually been conditioned to enjoy books and stories. The sense of accomplishment felt when he reads a pre-primer for the first time is probably as great as for any subsequent academic accomplishment. When the child becomes engrossed in the process of learning to read, the effect is to minimize many of the interferences to learning found in the average classroom.

Ego-involvement, if it is not centered on the learning task, can work against the teacher. The following examples of behavior observed in classroom situations will call to mind parallel incidents which teachers have observed. Each incident occurred in a classroom where the teaching was excellent, preparation of pupils for class discussion was thorough, and motivation of the group was above average.

In a first grade class the children had been divided into several groups, each of which practiced reading a story in a supplementary primer not being used by the class. Each group was to read its story to the class. In order that every pupil could make a contribution, one of the poorer readers was to show the pictures accompanying the story. In one group, a pupil other than the duly appointed one usurped this privilege and was slyly showing the picture from *his* book. The victim of this duplicity promptly and loudly called attention to the infringement. The disruption of learning resulted from the importance the child attached to the ego-satisfying activity of showing the pictures.

A similar situation occurred in another class where five pupils had practiced reading a story in which they each read a predetermined number of lines. When they read this story to the class, one child paused a moment in his reading and the next pupil started to read his remaining lines. The injured party interrupted and loudly asserted, "No, it isn't your turn yet." This behavior interfered with the learning process for the entire class and shows that no child likes to be deprived of his "performance time" with its attendant ego-satisfaction.

In another first grade class a film strip was being shown. The teacher selected children, one at a time, to walk up to the screen and indicate certain words by using a pointer. A motivational peak was reached each time a pupil was to be selected, followed by a lapse in interest until a new selection was to be made. Achieving the role of "demonstrator" had such strong status-building connotations that it worked against the intended mastering of the content of the film.

In a second grade discussion of pioneers and how they cleared the land to plant crops, one pupil seemed extremely eager to make a contribution and pumped his hand up and down vigorously. When called on, his contribution to the topic was nil, but he produced a lengthy story which cast him in the central role: "I looked at some seed yesterday at home, and I remember I said to myself: 'This looks just like the cotton seed we had yesterday in school.' I said it looks just like it and I wondered if it was cotton seed. I was going to bring it to school today. . . ."

One third grade class had studied a particular unit and was now ready to discuss it in class. Prior to the actual discussion, the teacher and pupils had worked out an outline of major points to be discussed, and the teacher had listed these points on the board. The outline was to serve both as a stimulus and as a means of keeping the discussion from wandering. One boy near the rear of the room held up his hand to make a contribution on item one, but since the entire class was prepared and responsive, all could not be called on. The discussion moved on through item two and was well into item three when this boy was finally called on. He gave an immediate answer which was in no way related to the question under discussion, but his response was logical and correct for item one.

The response was too spontaneous to support the hypothesis that he was caught without an answer for the question and simply talked to cover up. It was quite apparent that he had a contribution to make during the discussion of item one, and became so emotionally involved in this situation that he failed to make the shift to items two and three. His ego-involvement became a barrier to his own learning and interfered with group learning.

No teacher, regardless of her skill and experience, can prevent such incidents from occurring. From such incidents, however, the wise teacher will learn much about the needs of various pupils in her class. She will attempt to harness the children's egos to the reading tasks so that they will work for her instead of against her. She will realize that the more closely the beginning reading materials are related to the child and his interests, the easier it will be for him to become ego-involved in the reading situation. Illustrations of this point were observed in the same classrooms which provided the examples cited above.

John, a bright boy but a poor reader, could not read from the basal readers being used by the class. The teacher had John tell her a story involving one of his recent experiences. The teacher typed this story, using the easiest vocabulary possible. After reading it several times for him, she had John practice reading it. A flash card was made of each word he had difficulty in learning. John's progress in mastering the sight words was slow, but he did make progress. The last step was to fold a page of construction paper and fasten the typed story inside. On the front of this booklet John printed the words *John's Book.* He clutched his book tightly as he rushed out at the close of school. He would now earn praise and acceptance and restore some measure of self-esteem. Reading was less of a threat at that moment than it had been for many weeks.

Another teacher, whose practice it was to secure many different books for her second-grade class, was able to help a very poor reader by finding for him a large colorful book with exciting, full-page pictures and very little reading text. Many pupils in the class showed interest in this book and asked if they might have it when Fred finished reading it. Fred was credited with reading a book and this experience attracted him, at least for the moment, to books and reading. Every teacher knows how important these experiences are to a child. In the pre-reading stage, the child's name is probably the first word he learns. In addition, *his* birthday is announced on the board, and he learns the word used to designate *his* school, *his* street, *his* town. These relatively difficult words are learned after fewer exposures than are most words he learns during this period and illustrate the importance of ego-involvement in learning.

**Early
Readers**

Some children begin mastering the reading process at an early age without the benefit of formal instruction. In our society these early readers are often viewed with fascination and even awe. In his early studies of genius (upper one percent of population based on intelligence scores), Lewis M. Terman reported a high incidence of early readers. There are many case studies which report on individual children as early readers. The biographies of a number of famous individuals noted for high achievement in science, art, or literature also report early reading. This data, coupled with certain other case studies of early readers, has tended to associate early reading with genius or very high intellectual ability.

Data from recent studies by Durkin (14) has suggested that genius is not an absolute prerequisite for early reading. One group of 49 early readers had a median IQ of 121; and a second group of 156 children attained a median IQ of 133. While the data indicates most early readers in these groups measured relatively high in regard to intelligence, there were others in the group who fell within the average range.

Study of one group of subjects covered a five year span and provided interesting data on reading achievement for the 49 subjects. (14) The median grade-level achievement for the group at the beginning of grade one was 1.9. A median gain of 18 months was reported at the end of grade one and a three month gain was noted over the summer months. Thus the median reading achievement score for the group at the beginning of grade two was 4.0. The successive median grade level achievements reported were:

End of grade two	4.9	gain of nine months
End of grade three	5.3	gain of four months
End of grade four	6.7	gain of fourteen months
End of grade five	7.6	gain of nine months

The most rapid growth in reading achievement was recorded in grade one. At the end of fifth grade, the group of early readers had a median reading grade achievement of 7.6 which exceeded the normal expectancy (6.9) by seven months. This was approximately the degree of superiority noted at the beginning of grade one. The data on gains in achievement could likely be interpreted in different ways. Undoubtedly a study of individual children and an analysis of their progress would provide important clues that are masked by the group median scores presented here.

The debate on early instruction

Paralleling the recent emphasis on moving the teaching of subject matter downward in the grade level structure, there has been considerable discussion relative to providing formal reading instruction in kindergarten. Each highly publicized account of a child, or small group of children, who acquire some reading ability before entering school is interpreted in some quarters as evidence supporting earlier formal reading instruction.

Questions relative to the teaching of reading in the kindergarten are often posed in such a way as to lead protagonists into defending an either/or position. Polar positions preclude the possibility of arriving at a meaningful consensus. The question "Should reading be taught in the kindergarten?" is not the same as "Should some children be taught reading in the kindergarten?" The former can lead to logical analyses under such diverse titles as *Let's Not Teach Reading In Kindergarten* (28) and *Kindergartners Are Ready! Are We?* (22)

The early reading controversy is rooted in an important educational principle, to which lip service is paid by practically all educators. This principle is that "the school is to educate each child up to his maximum ability, taking each child where he is and moving him at his own pace." Speaking of learning the reading process, Newman (33) states, ". . . no child should be denied entré to probably the most important of our school-learned forms of expression if he is at the point in his development when it is opportune for him to take part in this expression himself. . . ."

When relatively few children attended kindergarten, the issue of reading could be safely ignored. With the rapid increase in kindergarten (and even earlier pre-school experiences) the problem of "What is the proper curriculum for kindergarten?" becomes a significant educational issue. To attempt to resolve this question by recourse to personal predilections results in a meaningless debate.

It is probable that one's concept of the role of the kindergarten will influence his attitude toward early reading instruction. If the kindergarten is seen as a *pre-school* experience, the principle referred to above may be waived. On the other hand, if kindergarten is seen as an integral part of the planned educational sequence, rather than as play time or an educational holding action, growth in significant educational processes would be expected.

In much of the discussion of reading instruction in the kindergarten there is either a tacit or openly expressed fear that if reading is taught, the situation can, and likely will, somehow get out of hand. Past practices in our schools would seem to indicate that such fears are well-founded. Newman (33) presents a rationale which favors reading instruction in the kindergarten, adding the reservation, ". . . but only if the reading activities are taught in such a way as to build enthusiasm for books and reading and the foundation for a lifelong interest in reading for pleasure and inquiry. This is a big 'if'. . . ."

In addition to the problem of what type of reading instruction might be appropriate for kindergarten, there is the question of "instruction for whom?" There is no experimentally established chronological or mental age at which children should begin receiving reading instruction. It is well-established that large numbers of children admitted to first grade on the basis of chronological age, rather than readiness for reading, do experience difficulty in learning. Many of these non-reading pupils react adversely to the pressures which accompany instruction under such conditions. The fear of many educators is expressed in the question "What is to prevent more of this type of pressure, administered even earlier in the child's educational career, if formal reading instruction is moved into the kindergarten?"

By a process of careful selection of research data, one can build a fairly strong case for earlier reading instruction for *some* children. No manipulation of data will result in a mandate for extending earlier instruction to *all* children.

There is good reason for raising the question of how well the school is equipped for making the proper differentiation of instruction. If we have failed to achieve a workable differentiation at the level at which we now introduce reading instruction, by what educational alchemy can we expect to achieve this goal by making the task much more complicated?

There is a related problem which should be considered. It is unrealistic to devise a new role for the kindergarten without revamping the curriculum and teaching practices of later grades. One of the saddest things that could happen to a community would be to develop an outstanding kindergarten program in which reading is taught to those children who are ready to read and in which the primary grades continued their present traditional grade-level-dominated teaching. Any gains made in reading would be lost if succeeding grades did not provide a flexible program built on on-going diagnosis of children's present achievement. A breakthrough achieved at any particular level must be accompanied by breakthroughs all along the educational continuum.

It might be argued that the above rationale is extraneous to the question of whether or not reading should be taught in the kindergarten. It should be kept in mind that the points raised are not advanced as arguments *against* the proposition, but rather as an effort to view it in a larger educational context.

"Should reading be taught in the kindergarten?" is the type of question heard too often in education. In essence, this is an abstraction, or even an isolated fragment of a much more complex question. The larger question should focus on "What are the experiences one would find in an ideal kindergarten?" As a first step in answering this question, one would have to determine the *purpose* of kindergarten.

It would take years of evaluation and re-evaluation to cut through the shibboleths developed in the past. Purpose could hardly be divorced from learning and learners. Is kindergarten to be characterized by an informal relaxed approach to growth? Growth in what areas? Is its purpose to take advantage of one of the "golden years" of great potential growth in formal learning? Or is it to "school break" the child and prepare him for the institutionalized environment of the school? Is kindergarten a last fling before institutionalism? Is it to be child-centered? If so, what does this mean? Does the kindergarten have a curriculum? Should much of the present first grade curriculum be moved down into kindergarten? Should kindergarten be renamed first grade?

Conclusion

There are large and significant differences among children as they begin learning to read. Teachers are generally aware of this fact, but classroom practices and habits of thought prevailing in the school and community sometimes tend to slight the significance of these pupil differences. Our society places a high value on reading ability, and as a result all children in the group are expected to progress at a somewhat uniform rate. Failure to do so is a very noticeable failure. When some children in the group do not meet fixed arbitrary standards of achievement, pressures from both school and home increase. Reading is particularly sensitive to pressure because it involves learning a complicated symbol system.

Children as beginning readers are quite pliable, yet there are many who cannot adjust to, or profit from, a lock-step educational philosophy which treats pupils as interchangeable parts in the classroom. These children may have an initial desire to learn to read, but the type of experience they have can affect their goals and behavior. Reading and other learning tasks prescribed by the school can be interpreted as threatening rather than as rewarding.

Ego-involvement is extremely important in learning. A child who fails to meet arbitrary group standards will not experience satisfaction from reading. Even when failure is not present, ego-involvement in learning tasks may lead the child away from the structured activity and thus disrupt learning for himself or others. Too much uniformity of instructional method used with a group that includes a wide range of interests and abilities will not be equally motivating or equally appropriate for each member of the group. This is the sole reason why instruction must be concerned with individual differences.

YOUR POINT OF VIEW?

Would you defend or attack the following statements?

1. The teacher, the school environment, and the curriculum inescapably function as barriers to, or means of, fulfilling the psychological needs of children.

2. A thoroughly differentiated instructional program in grade one which is based on sound ongoing diagnosis would materially reduce the difference between the reading achievement scores of boys when compared with girls.

3. The "halo effect" favoring girls is less likely to be found among experienced teachers than among beginning teachers.

4. Since research data tend to indicate that sex difference in reading are not significant at the end of the elementary school period, sex differences in learning to read are of little educational importance.

5. Inadequate reading ability, or failure to learn to read well enough to meet the demands of the school curriculum, is a factor in producing anti-social behavior.

6. If every child in the class were ego-involved in the learning tasks, there would be practically no discipline problems in the classroom.

7. Early experiences in learning to read have a considerable influence on pupils' later work habits and attitudes toward the school.

8. The teacher is not a causal factor in the disproportionate number of reading failures among boys as compared with girls.

9. Assume a forced choice item on a test required you to select one of the following broad categories as being the most influential causal factor in the production of sex differences in beginning reading. Which would you choose? Why?
   a. Physiological — maturational factors.
   b. Social — cultural — environmental factors.

10. Assume you have worked closely with a group of six-year olds who learned to read before entering school. Describe these children, touching on the behavioral characteristics you think they would display.

BIBLIOGRAPHY

1. Alden, Clara, Helen B. Sullivan, and Donald Durrell, "The Frequency of Special Reading Disabilities," *Education*, LXII (1942), 32–36.

2. Allen, C. N. "Recent Research on Sex Differences," *Psychological Bulletin*, XXXII (1935), 343–54.

3. Ames, Louise B. and Frances L. Ilg, "Sex Differences In Test Performance of Matched Girl-Boy Pairs In the 5 to 9 Year-old Age Range," *Genetic Psychology*, 104 (1964), 25–34.

4. Anderson, Irving H., Byron O. Hughes, and Robert W. Dixon, "Age of Learning to Read and Its Relation to Sex, Intelligence, and Reading Achievement in Sixth Grade," *Journal of Educational Research* (February 1956), 447–53.

5. _____, "The Rate of Reading Development and Its Relation to Age of Learning to Read, Sex, and Intelligence," *Journal of Educational Research* (March 1957), 481–94.

6. Axline, Virginia, "Nondirective Therapy for Poor Readers," *Journal of Consulting Psychology*, XI (1947), 61–69.

7. Ayres, Leonard, *Laggards in Our Schools*. New York, Russell Sage Foundation, 1909.

8. Bell, John E. "Emotional Factors in the Treatment of Reading Difficulties," *Journal of Consulting Psychology*, IX (1945), 125–31.

9. Blanchard, Phyllis, "Reading Difficulties in Relation to Difficulties of Personality and Emotional Development," *Mental Hygiene*, XX (1936), 384–413.

10. Bond, Guy and Robert Dykstra, "The Cooperative Research Program in First-Grade Reading Instruction," *Reading Research Quarterly* (Summer 1967), 5–142.

11. Carroll, Marjorie W. "Sex Differences in Reading Readiness at the First Grade Level," *Elementary English* (October 1948), 370–75.

12. Concannon, Sister Josephina, C.S.J. "Concept Development in Kindergarten." *The Catholic Educational Review* (November 1968), 516–22.

13. Criscuolo, Nicholas, "Sex Influences on Reading," *The Reading Teacher* (May 1968), 762–64.

14. Durkin, Dolores, "The achievement of pre-school readers: Two longitudinal studies," *Reading Research Quarterly* (Summer 1966), 5–36.

15. Dykstra, Robert, "Summary of Second-Grade Phase of the Cooperative Research Program in Primary Reading Instruction," *Reading Research Quarterly* (Fall 1968), 49–70.

16. Dykstra, Robert and Ronald Tinney, "Sex Differences in Reading Readiness—First-Grade Achievement and Second-Grade Achievement," *Reading and Realism*, J. Allen Figural (Ed.), Proceedings, International Reading Association, 13, Part 1, 1969, 623–28.

17. Fabian, A. A. "Reading Disability: An Index of Pathology," *American Journal of Orthopsychiatry* (April 1955), 319–29.

18. Gates, Arthur I. "Sex Differences in Reading Ability," *Elementary School Journal* (May 1961), 431–34.

19. Glass, Gerald G. "Students Misconceptions Concerning Their Reading," *The Reading Teacher* (May 1968), 765–68.

20. Heilman, Arthur W. *Effects of an Intensive In-Service Program on Teacher's Classroom Behavior and Pupil's Reading Achievement.* Cooperative Research Project No. 2709, USOE, 1965, 53.

21. Hillerich, Robert L. "Pre-Reading Skills in Kindergarten: A Second Report," *Elementary School Journal* (March 1965), 312–18.

22. ————, "Kindergartners Are Ready! Are We?" *Elementary English* (May 1965), 569–73.

23. ————, "An Interpretation of Research In Reading Readiness," *Elementary English* (April 1966), 359–64.

24. Hughes, Mildred C. "Sex Differences in Reading Achievement in the Elementary Grades," *Clinical Studies in Reading II*, Supplementary Educational Monographs no. 77. Chicago: University of Chicago Press, 102–6.

25. McCollum, Mary E. and Mary J. Shapiro, "An Approach to the Remediation of Severe Reading Disabilities," *Education* (March 1947), 488–93.

26. McNeil, John D. and Evan R. Keislar, *Oral and Non-oral Methods of Teaching Reading By an Auto-Instructional Device.* Cooperative Research Project No. 1413, USOE, 1963.

27. Means, Chalmers, "Sex Differences in Reading Achievement," *Improving Reading Through Classroom Practices.* Joint Proceedings of the Twenty-seventh Reading Conference and the Third Intensive Summer Workshop, Pennsylvania State University, 1966.

28. Micucci, Pat, "Let's *Not* Teach Reading in Kindergarten!" *Elementary English* (March 1964), 246–51.

29. Miller, Wilma H. "Home Prereading Experiences and First-Grade Reading Achievement," *Reading Teacher* (April 1969), 641–45.

30. Missildine, W. H. "The Emotional Background of Thirty Children with Reading Disabilities with Emphasis on Its Coercive Elements," *Nervous Child* (July 1946), 263–72.

31. Monroe, Marion, *Children Who Cannot Read*. Chicago: University of Chicago Press, 1932.

32. Mortensen, W. Paul, "Selected Pre-Reading Tasks, Socio-Economic Status and Sex," *Reading Teacher* (October 1968), 45–49.

33. Newman, Robert E. "The Kindergarten Reading Controversy," *Elementary English* (March 1966), 235–9.

34. Nila, Sister Mary, "Foundations of a Successful Reading Program," *Education* (May 1953), 543–55.

35. Prescott, George A. "Sex Differences in Metropolitan Readiness Test Results," *Journal of Educational Research* (April 1955), 605–10.

36. Preston, Mary J. "Reading Failure and the Child's Security," *American Journal of Orthopsychiatry*, X (1940), 239–52.

37. Preston, Ralph, "Reading Achievement of German and American Children," *School and Society*, XC (1962), 350–54.

38. Robinson, Helen M. "Factors which Affect Success in Reading," *Elementary School Journal* (January 1955), 266.

39. St. John, Charles W. "The Maladjustment of Boys in Certain Elementary Grades," *Educational Administration and Supervision*, XVIII (1932), 659–72.

40. Smith, C. A. and M. R. Jenson, "Educational, Psychological and Physiological Factors in Reading Readiness," *Elementary School Journal* (April 1936), 689.

41. Stanchfield, Jo M. "Differences in Learning Patterns of Boys and Girls," *Reading Difficulties: Diagnosis, Correction and Remediation*, International Reading Association, Newark, Del.: 1970, 202–213.

42. Stroud, J. B. and E. F. Lindquist, "Sex Differences in Achievement in the Elementary and Secondary School," *Journal of Educational Psychology* (1942), 657–67.

43. Terman, Lewis M. and Leona E. Tyler, "Psychological Sex Differences," *Manual of Child Psychology* (2nd ed.), L. Carmichael (ed.). New York: John Wiley & Sons, Inc., 1954, Chapter 17.

44. Vorhaus, Pauline G. "Rorschach Configurations Associated with Reading Disability," *Projective Techniques*, XVI (1952), 3–19.

45. Wilson, Frank T., Agnes Burke, and C. W. Flemming, "Sex Differences in Beginning Reading in a Progressive School," *Journal of Educational Research* (April 1939), 570–82.

46. Young, Robert A. "Case Studies in Reading Disability," *American Journal of Orthopsychiatry*, VIII (1938), 230–54.

47. Wright, Benjamin, "Postscript on Permissiveness," *Elementary School Journal* (April 1965), 393–4.

48. —————, and Shirley Tuska, "The Price of Permissiveness," *Elementary School Journal* (January 1965), 179–83.

3

The Culturally
Different Child
as a Learner*

The learners discussed in this chapter have been identified by several different labels: socially handicapped, economically deprived, culturally disadvantaged, linguistically different, dialect speakers, children without, the leftouts, the newcomers, the educationally handicapped, the socially deprived, the alienated ones, the underachievers, children from depressed areas, and the children of the poor. The list is exhaustive and yet no one term fully and adequately describes these children. The term "culturally different" will be used throughout this discussion.

The term culturally different refers to the economically deprived child who is not profiting from the *established curriculum* and who is not learning to read. The term includes speakers of dialects from all racial groups — black, white, Indian-American, Mexican-American, and Puerto Rican, etc.

Failure in reading has been the major educational problem of the children from these groups. Although these learners may differ in race, ethnic background, geographic placement, and cultural heritage, they share the common problem of reading failure. Since part of the problem is that the school is alien to these children, it is felt that if teachers know and understand them, the first objective of a good reading program has been met.

*This chapter contributed by Ruby Thompson, instructor at Pennsylvania State University.

The culturally different child has a life style that reflects these conditions:

1. Housing is usually substandard, crowded, and in unattractive surroundings. (The ghetto, dusty rural areas, tenement shacks, pitched tents, dilapidated trailers.)
2. Food and clothing are often inadequate according to nutritional and health standards.
3. Family ties are often unstable because of the restrictions imposed by the environment, poor economic conditions, and the psychological factors that these conditions manifest.
4. Groups are socially alienated from white middle-class society and therefore are not exposed to the social life that determines the criteria by which they are ultimately judged.
5. Jobs are usually those on the lower end of the continuum in terms of pay, prestige, and security.
6. Educational levels of parents seldom exceed junior high school.
7. Exposure to the crime, violence, and prevalence of immorality that are bred and nutured in their environments is early and continuous.

Although teachers can do little as individuals to change these conditions, they must be more sensitive to the deficits that such an environment may have imposed on the children. These include: the tendency to have a poor self-concept, low aspirational levels, to be tardy and absent frequently, to be poorly oriented to school and school tasks, to display hostility toward school and school authorities, to resist or reject values which are foreign to them and which are forced on them by teachers whom they tend to distrust.

As a potential reader, the culturally different learner will come to school speaking his natural language which is not the language upon which the curriculum was constructed. He may not have auditory discrimination for some "standard" English speech phonemes, and he will be much more limited than most middle-class children in his development of readiness-for-reading skills.

Several other characteristics that have been associated with the culturally different learner are either erroneous or misleading. Examples include the ideas that the parents do not care about their children's academic achievement, that the children do not want to learn, that the children are naturally prone to violence inside and outside the classroom, and that they are genetically inferior in regard to school learning tasks. Sociological studies and surveys have refuted the first three. Respect for individuals, coupled with understanding of the limitations of testing situations and lack of validity of testing instruments, have hopefully stemmed a rush to judgment on the latter issue.

Misconceptions about language, however, consistently pervade discussions of the culturally different child. Some of these are based on false premises about language. Others stem from inadequate research, unwarranted generalizations, and lack of understanding of the language facility of these children. These and other language factors are examined in the following discussion.

Myths and Facts
about Language

One myth that has enjoyed widespread dissemination is that culturally different children have very little language facility. The truth is that these children use language quite extensively with their peers on the playground and in their private huddles. They talk incessantly, and they do so in a style that is sophisticated for their ages. In these peer situations, children encounter no judgments about the quality of language. However, in the school, their use of language is often stifled because they fear teacher ridicule or criticism because their language *is different.*

The case of Gloria is an example of how schools and teachers can inhibit language expression. Gloria was a third grader who grew up in the South and hence had an accent that was quite noticeable in the northeastern school in which she was enrolled. She spoke what is commonly called "black dialect." Gloria was not a discipline problem but after the first few days in the classroom she simply would not talk. A prospective teacher, as part of her training, worked as a reading tutor to Gloria. The regular teacher's perception of the problem was that Gloria refused to talk or join in the reading activities. She would make only "yes" or "no" responses. The tutor, however, found that in their private sessions Gloria talked quite freely. When asked why she wouldn't talk in class, Gloria replied "'Cause they be laughing at me." The tutor found out later that the teacher had constantly tried to make Gloria change her pronunciation and syntax which, in effect, were interpreted as social judgments and to some degree as punishment.

The other children followed the teacher's example and soon Gloria became that "funny talking" girl. The tutor was sensitive to Gloria's problem and changed her focus from teaching word attack skills (which the teacher had suggested as Gloria's need) to a total class project in "language respect." A special program on dialects was developed and Gloria's reading of the black dialect was the turning point in the attitudes of the teacher and the class. Gloria talks now and her teacher listens to *what* she says instead of to *how* she says it.

Another myth is that of *linguistic deprivation*, which implies that these children have no true language system and that they know only a limited number of words which they put together in a haphazard fashion. However, a logical systematic structure is evident in their language usage. Also, the non-standard syntax is known to convey specific meaning. For example, it has been found that the absence or presence of the verb form *to be* in some dialects connotes a certain meaning. In the sentence "He working," the absence of the verb *is* indicates that "He is working just now [possibly for the day or for a little while]." In the sentence "He *be* working," (although the verb form is non-standard usage), the presence of the "be" indicates that "He is working [steadily]."

The use of the subject pronouns *he* and *she* are used consistently in some dialects as possessives. "Susie and *she* love," means Susie and *her* love; "That be *he* ball," means that that is *his* ball. If a child comes up to the teacher's desk and says "He laughing," she means that he is laughing at the moment. A cause for greater alarm might arise if she were to say: "He be laughing at me." This means that she is the constant center of ridicule.

These are just a few examples of the consistent and rigid structure of a non-standard dialect. Labov (44) notes that most linguists agree that non-standard dialects are highly structured systems, and John (39) sees the dialects termed non-standard as presenting operational linguistic wealths.

A third myth is that the culturally different child is unable to understand spoken standard English. Experience demonstrates that these children *do* understand standard English. Robert and Barry are black children in a Bedford-Stuyvesant ghetto. They communicate in their dialect with its slang expressions and linguistic system. Yet they can paraphrase, interpret, and explain record albums by the late Malcolm X, the late Dr. Martin Luther King, Jr., and other materials which are in standard English. They, as do other children like them, understand most of what they hear on radio and television and in the classroom if the *concepts are familiar* to their experiences. This is equally true of other English speaking minorities, even though they use a non-standard dialect in communicating.

An unanswered question that faces the reading teacher is whether or not the child who speaks a dialect should learn to speak standard English *before* he can learn to read it. Experimental data relative to this issue are, at the moment, inconclusive. However, in regard to an entirely separate issue, there is general agreement that the dialect speaker must learn to speak standard English, not because it is better, but because there are many situations in which his economic or social mobility will be hindered if he cannot use standard English. Whether an individual elects to use standard English is his decision, but it seems mandatory that the schools provide him with the tools so that he can exercise this option if he so elects. The following brief case history illustrates how reliance on a nonstandard dialect and lack of facility in the use of standard English created problems for a college student.

Pearl, having just received the Baccalaureate degree in Georgia, was a first-term graduate student at a northern state university. Her first school term outside of her native state was tragic. She failed two seminar courses, not because of the difficulty of the material, but because her speech was termed as "incomprehensible" by the professor.

She was thwarted in her attempts to receive financial aid because her file indicated that she was "unsatisfactory" for graduate school. One professor told her point blank that the way she talked was not representative of an educated person.

She spoke a black dialect which had been reinforced during the 22 years she lived and attended school in the rural south. One job application for a teaching position was turned down because the interviewer said she had a "speech" problem. Another faculty advisor suggested that she lacked the ability to function at this particular institution and that perhaps she should return to the south and attend one of the small black schools there. Frustrated, and in tears, the student sought the aid of the black ombudsman on campus.

After much red tape, calls to deans, and pleas for conditional readmission, Pearl was given another chance. Her second term consisted of a course in speech correction, a course in English composition, and private tutoring in "English as a second language." In essence, the student was given a crash program in learning standard English.

Many of her classmates, aware of her plight, helped her with her pronunciations and syntax and spent sessions listening to her talk. It was evident that it was her dialect, not lack of ability, that had very nearly terminated her college career.

The third term was better. Pearl was careful to try to speak distinctly and in standard English. It was not easy. Not only did she have to cope with changing her speech patterns, but also with her self-concept. She was angry with the school system she had left behind for "letting her get by." At many times during her retraining she felt inferior and inadequate.

While it was a fact that this student spoke a dialect, certain generalizations drawn from this fact worked against her. If teachers do not allow the myths to influence their teaching and the child's learning to read, a first step will have been made in working with the culturally different child. Because of the fact that for many of these children the school language is not their language, and because of the crucial relationship that exists between the language development and reading achievement of a learner, we shall take a closer look at the question of dialect.

Dialect
Divergencies

A young black college student was working with a large corporation during the summer break. At an orientation meeting, in which some simple technological processes were being discussed, the student was taking notes:

> The *floor* chart is basic to . . .
> A good *floor* chart must be constructed . . .
> *Floor* charts are keys to . . .

The notes were accurate except for one word; what the speaker was actually saying was:

> The *flow* chart is basic to . . .
> A good *flow* chart must be constructed . . .
> *Flow* charts are keys to . . .

There are highly qualitative differences in the meanings of "floor charts" and "flow charts" and this student heard and recorded a slightly different auditory signal than the speaker had intended. She transcribed what she heard and, in the process, misinterpreted much of the lecture. But she had written this key word the way she perceived it in her dialect.

This incident points up two of the major problems in teaching the culturally different learner to read — lack of experience with words and concepts and the masking of critical phonemes which cause semantic differences (the latter being a dialect factor).

Dialect, broadly conceived, is the way people speak in different parts of the country or in their specific social classes. The components of dialect are pronunciation, grammar, and vocabulary. McDavid (50) adds that a dialect is a variety of a given language that is mutually intelligible with other dialects of that language. Since many culturally different children speak a dialect, the question that has been raised by linguists and pondered by reading teachers is: Do dialect divergencies cause difficulties in learning to read standard English?

Most hypotheses relative to the question of dialect interference in learning to read have been stated in general terms. Martin and Castaneda (51) hold to the position that children who come to school speaking a dialect other than standard American English encounter noticeable difficulty in learning to read; they experience a higher failure rate than do children who speak standard American English. This is true. But do the children fail in reading because of their dialect or because of factors such as lack of experiences that relate to reading, the quality of instruction they receive, and teacher expectations of failure? These and other factors could work together to produce a high failure rate.

Skinner (64) implies that the dialect of Appalachia is the cause of children's reading problems in that geographical area, and that the critical need for Appalachian schools, or any group in an analogous position, is a preschool oral language program which teaches standard English. This, he feels, will give the Appalachian child a better chance of success when he encounters the printed word in the first grade.

York and Ebert (79) believe that a reasonable degree of speaking and understanding standard American English are necessary if children are to read the academic texts. Moore (54) sees the "language of the book" as tantamount to a foreign language in the case of the child who speaks a non-standard dialect. The problem is compounded when the child has a limited school vocabulary used in school books. Johnson (40) hypothesized that non-standard dialects may give rise to difficulties in the many communicative efforts of other subject areas as well as in reading. The following discussion focuses on some specific dialect differences that various authorities have mentioned as possible interferences with learning to read standard English.

Sound or phonological divergencies

Generally speaking, phonological divergencies refer to differences in speech sounds within words. A grapheme (written letter symbol) may represent different phonemes (speech sounds) in different dialects. For example, the standard English "poor" may be heard as "po' 'in some black dialects, while the standard English "head" may be pronounced as "haid" in non-standard dialect used by some white speakers. The standard English "something" may be heard as "sumpin" in non-standard English, and the word "oil" pronounced as "aul" in non-standard.

Standard English	*Non-Standard*	*Standard English*	*Non-Standard*
that	dat	nothing	nutin
get	git	going	gon
gore	go	thirst	tirs
other	udder	heard	hud
touch	taut, tech	girl	gul
poem	purm	iron	ion, arn
right	rat	I'm	ohm, ahm
help	hop, hep	earned	earnt

The phonological differences between the speech patterns of dialect speakers and standard English usage have been rather thoroughly researched. (7, 8, 30, 44) However, research has not established the degree to which these phonological variations influence learning to read standard English. Thus, a number of hypotheses have been advanced which focus on the issues of dialect interference and how beginning reading should be taught to dialect speakers.

Some possible interference effects of sound divergencies in reading achievement and reading instruction and instructional materials have been noted by Goodman (30) and Saville (61). They believe that phonics programs which attempt to teach the relationship between letters and sounds cannot be universally applicable to all non-standard dialects. The question is raised as to whether the use of materials such as i/t/a and others that are based on invariant pronunciation are appropriate for many of these learners. Furthermore, they point out that because a child learns at home to ignore certain speech sounds, meaning may be distorted for him when these phonemes are the critical distinguishable elements in a word.

Another foreseeable problem is the teacher's misinterpretation of the significance of "errors" they detect in children's oral reading. Some errors which are unrelated to the child's dialect can, and possibly should, be corrected on the spot. In other instances it may be unproductive at the moment to overemphasize errors which are perfectly logical in the child's dialect. When a child is compelled to insert phonemes that are ignored in his phonological system, he may end up with pronunciations that are unfamiliar and meaningless to him. These pronunciations may prove to be barriers to his progress in getting meaning from the printed page. (30) Other phonological differences may involve variations in intonation (pitch, stress, and rhythm of the dialect). If the teacher insists on intonation patterns in oral reading or speaking which are unfamiliar to the reader, frustration and loss of meaning may be the result.

In studies of black English dialect, it has been noted that a number of non-standard phonological patterns occur with considerable frequency. A few examples are dropping of certain final consonant sounds, omitting the sounds represented by *r* and *l*, substituting sounds (*th=d*), omitting some inflectional endings, and the like. These and other phonological variations result in generating hundreds of homonyms for the black dialect speaker which do not exist in standard English (told – toe – toll; road – row; past – pass; find – fine; seed – seat – see; hold – whole; call – called; etc.).

Melmed conducted a study using children in third grade as subjects. One of the experimental groups consisted of children whose oral language usage qualified them as black dialect speakers. The purpose of the study was to discover what effect the existence of these phonological pairs of words had on both auditory comprehension of standard English sentences and the effect on reading comprehension when the printed material included one of a pair of black dialect homonyms. Data revealed that "the black youngster did significantly poorer in auditory discriminating of word pairs which are homonyms in black English but different words in standard English." However, the black group ". . . showed no inability to comprehend these words while reading orally or silently."* One conclusion advanced was that confusion of the word pairs in the reading

---

*Paul Jay Melmed, *Black English Phonology: The Question of Reading Interference.* Monographs of the Language-Behavior Research Laboratory, University of California, Berkeley, February, 1971.

situation was minimal because the subjects utilized syntactical and contextual clues.

Grammatical and syntactical differences

Grammatical and syntactical divergencies refer to those differences in inflectional changes, verb forms, and verb auxiliaries, and to the ways in which words are put together in phrases and sentences. The following is an example that cuts across phonological, grammatical-syntactical differences and lack of a necessary concept. Assume a teacher read the sentence: "Edgar Allen Poe was a rich man." The students, drawing from the phonology, grammar, and syntax of their dialect may interpret the sentence to mean: "Edgar Allen (is) poor, was a rich man." The students have no concept of Edgar Allen Poe, writer; they assume that he is poor because of the phonological differences (poor=po) and because of the assumed syntactical link (Allen [is] poor).

The following are illustrative of grammatical divergencies found between standard English and a non-standard dialect:

Standard	*Non-Standard*
	Omission of "s" in plurals and possessives
He gets to work early.	He get to work early.
I saw four cows.	I saw four cow.
John's dog runs home.	John dog run home.
	Omission of "ed" ending
He walked home.	He walk home.
I knocked three times.	I knock three times.
	Changes and omissions of verb forms
They were here.	They *was* here.
He is here.	He *be* here.
I am here.	I *be* here.
He is going.	He going.
We are always happy.	We *be* happy. (always)
Now we are happy.	We happy. (now)

Saville (61) suggests that because the children have perfected the syntax of their dialect, which is not the syntax of the classroom

English, they will have difficulty reading the conventional basal reading materials. Goodman (30) points out that these grammatical divergencies will be reflected in the child's reading of standard texts and in his conversation. That is, he will substitute his dialect for what is written. This substitution process must be understood by the teacher if frustration is to be kept at a minimum. The intended meaning in listening activities may be misconstrued by both teacher and the pupil. This is especially true if the teacher does not realize the difference between school talk and the children's dialect, or if she is unable to accept the child's speech patterns.

Vocabulary Divergencies refer to word meanings and connotations of words that are peculiar to a dialect. Some examples are:

Standard	*Non-Standard*
Carry that ball.	*Tote* that ball.
We're going to a *party*.	We're going to a *gig*.
I heard a loud *rap* (knock) last night.	I heard a loud *rap* (discussion) last night.
He is *bad*. (naughty)	He is *bad*. (superlative for good)
I want to *dig* it. (lift dirt)	I want to *dig* it. (understand)
He is *bright*. (smart)	He is *bright*. (light complexioned)
The *spook* scared me. (ghost)	The *spook* scared me. (slang for black)
That is my *mother*.	That is my *mama*.
The *man* is here. (any male)	The *man* is here. (person in authority, usually a "white")
I saw a *pig*. (farm animal)	I saw a *pig*. (negative term for a policeman)
This stove is *hot*. (burning)	This stove is *hot*. (stolen)
The class is *on fire*. (particularly responsive)	This class is "on fire." (poor in performance achievement)

These and numerous other variations in meaning are thought to cause difficulty in reading from texts that use words that have peculiar meanings in a learners' dialect. If the word has a negative meaning in non-standard English, the teacher may find that she is guilty of unintentional insults and she may be placed in an embarrassing situation.

The preceding discussion identified a number of differences between standard English and certain non-standard dialects. Some authorities hold that these dialectical differences are barriers to learning to read standard English. However, among the group sharing this opinion there is no consensus as to the procedures the school should follow in dealing with the problem. The following are some points of view relative to when and how dialect differences should be dealt with.

1. *Teach standard English prior to reading instruction.* The proponents of this position recommend that language training in standard English be given to the dialect speaker so that he will be familiar with the grammatical and syntactical patterns he will find in his textbook and hear in his teacher's speech. Formal reading instruction is delayed until the language training program is completed. Training in language is achieved mainly by drill in which standard English is treated as a second language. Children repeat sentence patterns until they can generalize the grammar and syntax to other similar situations.

2. *Teach standard English in conjunction with the reading of dialect materials in planned units.* This alternative is based on the use of stories written in both the learner's dialect and standard English. The child is taught to see the differences between these dialect patterns, and he learns that the latter pattern is "school talk." Instruction centers chiefly on differences in grammar and syntax.

3. *Teach standard English through the "exemplar" method before and concommitant with formal reading instruction.* This approach seeks to teach the child patterns of standard English at opportune times. Conscious efforts are made to equip the child with skill in using standard English, but they are made with little regimentation. The teacher speaks using standard English patterns and exposes her learners to such patterns whenever possible.

4. *Teach children to read ignoring dialect differences in beginning reading stages. Then teach standard English as a tool of mobility in the upper grades and high school.* This position is posited on the idea that getting the child to talk and teaching him to read are the important emphases in beginning reading. Once the child has developed in word analysis skills and comprehension abilities, make him aware of variations in language usage and teach him alternate forms.

It seems unlikely that programs will be developed which utilize only one of these alternatives exclusively. It must be kept in mind that a child cannot instantly suspend the use of a dialect that he has used for years. Nor can he adapt completely to a different speech pattern. The learning of a new pattern must take place in a meaningful setting. If children do not understand why they are to speak in another way, they may resist language training in the classroom.

If language training in dialect differences is delayed until the upper grades, the self-concept of the learner must be reckoned with. Care must be taken to make him aware at this stage of the realistic values of "talking like the man."

The following principles for working with dialect speakers should be useful to teachers regardless of the methodology used.

1. Learning must be gradual and constantly reinforced for stability of gains.
2. Children must understand why they are being introduced to a different language pattern.
3. Care must be taken to remove "value" labels from the dialect of the learner and the dialect to be learned.
4. The learner's dialect must be respected by himself and by the teacher as a complete and usable linguistic system — not a "stepchild" of standard English.
5. Different learners will learn more readily from different techniques.

The teacher of beginning reading must know the different features of the learners' dialect and must be skilled in approaches for language training. With her also lies the task of determining which learners will benefit from language training for reading purposes and which will not. Some language training programs that have been used in working with the culturally different child are discussed in the reading approaches below.

Alternative Approaches for Working with the Culturally Different Learner

Most of the programs that have been suggested for dealing with the culturally different child appear to be modifications of existing programs. These may be new in the sense that they are deliberately planned for the economically deprived or culturally different child.

But there are few innovations other than suggestions that attempts at developing "readiness" and language facility be intensified. However, this emphasis on preparing the child to become a good risk for the learning environment found in the school may hopefully provide teachers with important insights relative to these learners.

Current approaches which focus on preparing and teaching the culturally different child to read fall under two broad headings. One can be labeled *pre-school intervention*, the other, *beginning reading strategies*.

Limitations of space preclude an intensive discussion of all the theory and teaching strategies suggested or used with the culturally different learner. Therefore, certain studies and points of view which illustrate major trends and philosophies will be examined.

Preschool approaches for the culturally different learner

When the culturally different learner enters first grade, his major school problem will be lack of preparatory experiences. The school is structured to provide learning experiences which, to a large degree, are foreign to these children. There are two obvious potential solutions: We may provide the child with the experiences he needs in order to cope with the tasks he must do in school, or we may alter the curriculum to fit the learner. The practice of providing readiness activities cuts across both of these alternatives. As readiness activities are varied to fit the learners' needs, the curriculum itself is altered.

In theory, readiness has for a long time been a part of most school programs. In one sense, these readiness programs represent a concession to children's nonreadiness for the schools' curricula. However, in actual practice the implementation of programs for readiness has always been more apparent than real. Shortly after children entered school, they received the formal reading instruction that had been planned for them. This occurred whether or not they were ready for these particular activities. Fortunately, many children had the background which enabled them to fit into the planned program. Many did not. For members of the latter group, had readiness training been realistically incorporated in their programs, many reading failures and frustrations might have been avoided.

While the culturally different child is on the same readiness continuum as other children, he has experience-deficits that are significant to the school. He may be so different in terms of school preparation that readiness programs, as traditionally carried out, are simply not adequate for making him a good risk for beginning reading instruction. Sometimes, even a well-structured program of readiness activities may fail with this child. This failure may be attributed to the culturally different child's need for more of, or for a different type of, activities than those offered by the schools. For this type of learner, there must be a rethinking of readiness that will use his strengths and concentrate on eliminating his weaknesses.

The preschool approaches discussed in this section have attempted to redefine readiness in terms of the needs of the culturally different learner. They differ somewhat in philosophy and technique but share the common goal of making the culturally different child ready for first-grade reading instruction. The approaches included here are: intensified readiness, academic-preschool intervention, enrichment programs, and the Montessori approach.

Intensification of the traditional readiness program

This approach to preschool training is based on the philosophy that the traditional readiness program has the major components needed to prepare the culturally different child for reading instruction, but that there will be a need for reinforcement that extends for a greater duration of time.

The intensified approach is advocated by Cohen (19) who selected seven areas for emphasis with the culturally different learner: letter knowledge, visual discrimination of letters and words, auditory discrimination of sounds in words, developing a love of books, and interest in printed symbols, story sense, and memory for sequence. These areas were stressed by Cohen because they were found to have high correlations with reading success in grade one, they are the kinds of specific activities that can be handled by the school, and finally because they are most directly related to beginning reading instruction.

The enrichment activities of the traditional preschool programs in the form of field trips, drama, and other creative activities are also included in this program. Together, these activities comprise a cluster that has been advocated for many years in the literature on readiness. This program eliminates those activities that have been alleged to have little bearing on reading success, such as identifying the sounds of animals, types of transportation, and musical instruments; matching geometric shapes; and drill in eye-hand-motor coordination.

The techniques for developing the seven readiness skills cited above are similar to readiness activities found in the regular school environment. Examples are listed without discussion.

Letter Knowledge and Recognition

1. Using letter form boards.
2. Using alphabet cards and commercial alphabet games.
3. Working with alphabet jingles and songs.

Visual Kinesthetic Discrimination of Letters and Words

1. Matching word cards with large envelopes which show a particular stimulus word.
2. Labeling items in the room until words are learned, and then switching the labels and challenging the children to make the correct match.
3. Copying words from charts or signs.

Auditory Discrimination

1. Reciting verses that emphasize repetitive sounds.
2. Singing along with children's records that emphasize specific sounds.
3. Designating a letter of the week and collecting words that begin with the sound of that letter.

Love of Books

1. Exposing children to a wide variety of colorful storybooks.
2. Stressing personal ownership of books.
3. Reading to children.

Story Sense and Memory for Sequence

1. Daily storytelling experiences.
2. Read-along activities with children anticipating events, retelling events in correct sequences, discussing personal experiences related to the story, dramatizing events.

Vocabulary for Reading

1. Acting out multimeaning variations of basal-words. (like, run, jump, look)
2. Testing children to see what oral labels they do not have for beginning reading material and teaching these.
3. Introducing trips, stories, and multimedia.

Attention to the Reading Task

1. Use of colorful picture books at the reading readiness level.
2. Providing a variety of activities that have to do with the printed page (marking pages, cutting pieces, drawing lines).
3. Directed reading activities (have children look at pictures

to find a specific item, or a specific color, or the number of items).

4. Training in left to right orientation. (19)

Children not Ready for Reading Readiness Activities. If, after a period of time, the learner does not respond, Cohen suggests that intensification alone may not be the answer. Many children from depressed areas have not had the experiences that prepare them for a reading readiness program. The problem that must then be dealt with is "readiness for learning." Cohen lists four major goals for a "readiness for learning" program:

One: Self Control. Teach the child self control in working with others in the formal classroom. This goal many be mainly achieved by the teacher ignoring misbehavior and rewarding good behavior.

Two: Class Decorum. School-break the child by teaching him the daily routines of the classroom, such as housekeeping, completing activities, conforming to rules, handling of books and other school materials, and developing attention span. The direct teaching approach is seen as perhaps the most effective procedure for teaching the daily routine. That is, the teacher openly modifies the child's behaviors with directions and stipulations. In some instances, the teacher must physically direct the pupils.

Three: Perceptual Training. Visual-motor-auditory skill development is, in essence, preparing the child in certain physiological areas and specifically includes:

1. eye-hand coordination
2. general coordination
3. eye movements
4. visual memory
5. form perception
6. visual imagery

Selected parts of such programs as Frostig's Program for the Development of Visual Perception, the Getman-Kane Program for Accelerated School Success, the Balance Board, the Walking Rail, and the Montessori Program (discussed later in this chapter) offer possible techniques for aiding the teacher. The teacher may wish to review such programs prior to developing her own activities.

Four: Language and Concepts. Teaching language and concepts necessary for beginning reading is thought by Cohen to be best met through the delineation of specific skills. For concept learning Cohen recommends the programming technique outlined by Fowler.* Using this technique, the teacher provides stimuli that are

---

*Paper presented at meeting of the American Educational Research Association, Chicago, February 12, 1965, p. 18.

designed and ordered sequentially to move the child from gross perceptions of objects to classifying objects according to their functions. The movement from simple discrimination to classifying is illustrated:

> Have the children *identify* an object from a large group of pictures.
>
> Have the children *match* related pictures (pictures of different houses, etc.).
>
> Have children *group* objects according to functions (bicycle, car, etc.).
>
> Have children *construct wholes from parts* (2–4 piece jig-saw puzzle).
>
> Have children *group* then *classify* objects according to functions (e.g., those useful to man: foods, clothing, tools).

For language development, Cohen suggests the sequence of stages developed by Pasamanick (19) as a guide for teaching the culturally different child to cope with the language of the school.

> STAGE I is based upon experiences familiar to the children and attempts to make the known more concrete. The naming of simple nouns and a few basic verbs are the focal points.
>
> EXAMPLE: Children would name objects such as *chair, table, hat, dress;* and verbs such as *running, walking, peeping, laughing.*

> STAGE II attempts to expand the child's noun and verb storehouse by having him combine two known words into a compound.
>
> EXAMPLE: hat + box = hatbox
> shoe + shine = shoeshine
> sing + along = singalong

> STAGE III concentrates on expanding the use of language as an expressive and descriptive tool through such activities as storytelling, show and tell, role playing, and relating experiences. These activities foster the development and use of sequencing skills, descriptive language, and word connectors.

> STAGE IV encourages the child to use past language learning to categorize, catalogue, and perform other reasoning tasks. To develop these abilities children may:

Group pictures under general headings:

	Animals	Clothing

Match pictures that relate.

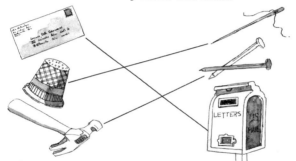

And classify objects and activities based on some common clue:

Things we clean with

Things we travel in; things that go fast

The high-intensity language sessions similar to the drill approach described in the academic preschool below is recommended for maximum development of selected language content.

Mills (52) summarizes the eclectic approach advocated by most writers who are proponents of the intensified readiness approach for culturally different learners.

> Since there is no one-best educational model for all disadvantaged preschoolers, compensatory educational experiences should be integrated with the best of traditional preschool practices . . . . [And that for some children] teachers should emphasize the "learning to learn" rather than the "learning to read" skills. (52:349)

The academic preschool

Perhaps the most radical procedures for making culturally different children ready for formal reading instruction are found in academic preschool programs. These programs concentrate on the direct teaching of specific language and reading skills. This is a teaching strategy in which the teacher presents stimuli designed to elicit specific language responses from the learner.

The Bereiter-Engelmann program (1, 12) is representative of the academic preschool approach and also serves as a model for the direct-instruction technique. Examples of this method and some of the specific language goals are provided below:

GOAL 1: To move from one word responses to complete affirmative and negative statements in reply to questions.

Teacher	*Pupils*
"What is this?"	"Dog."
"Say it all."	"This is a dog."
"Is this a dog?"	"Yes."
"Say it all."	"Yes, this is a dog."
"Is this a dog?"	"No."
"Say it all."	"No, this is not a dog."

GOAL 2: To respond with both affirmative and negative statements when told to "tell about something."

Teacher	*Pupil*
"Tell me about this ball."	"It is round." "It is black." "It is not big." "It is not square."

GOAL 3: To develop the ability to handle polar opposites for at least four concept pairs.

Teacher	*Pupil*
"If this is not up, what is it?"	"Down."
"Say it all."	"It is down."
"If this is not big, what is it?"	"It is little."

GOAL 4: To use the prepositions *on*, *in*, *under*, *over*, and *between* in statements describing arrangements.

Teacher	*Pupil*
"Where is the turkey?"	"The turkey is *on* the table."

"Where is the long line?"

"The long line is *under* the short line."

"Where is the number 2?"

1 2 3

"The number 2 is *between* the numbers 1 and 3."

GOAL 5: To name positives and negatives for at least four classes.

Teacher	Pupil
"Tell me something that is clothing."	"A hat is clothing." "A chair is not clothing."
"Tell me something that is food."	"An apple is food." "A pencil is not food."

GOAL 6: To perform simple "if-then" deductions.

Teacher	Pupil
"If the circle is big, what else do you know about it?"	"It is white."

Teacher	Pupil
"If the circle is little, what else do you know about it?"	"It is black."

GOAL 7: To use *not* in deductions.

Teacher	Pupil
"If the circle is white what else do you know about it?"	"It is not little."
"If the circle is black what else do you know about it?"	"It is not big."

The beginning reading program

The reading program is the extension of the language development program and is designed to familiarize children with letter names, to associate pictures visually with their naming words, to recognize and produce rhyming words, and to learn and use a limited number of sight words.

In the alphabet learning phase of the program, children familiarize themselves with the letter names of the alphabet through identity and position statements:

This is the letter A.

This is a big A.

This is a little A.

This A is standing up.

This A is lying down.

The child is taught first to spell words by letter sounds (CAT = kuh–ah–tuh) and is then presented clusters of words that follow the same spelling pattern (cat, fat, hat, bat). Word meanings are reinforced by yes-no questions of lexical terms.

Word recognition begins with the production of isolated words. A word is printed on the chalkboard and the rule "This is a word" is taught and followed by the identity statement, "This is the word MAN." The children then are encouraged to produce complete identity statements in answering questions such as, "Is this the word DOG?". "No that is not the word *dog*." "That is the word MAN." Action words are illustrated with gestures. Children are invited to suggest other words which they wish to learn. If there are no volunteers the teacher supplies another word.

Word placement exercises are used to teach visual discrimination of word forms and word meanings. Objects are labeled with 5″ x 8″ cards and identified by the teacher. "This card has a word on it. This is the word $\boxed{\text{TOY}}$." Five or more words are identified in this way and one word is placed on the proper object by the teacher. The children are asked: "This is the word what?" (Desk.) "So where does it belong?" (On the desk.) Each child has a turn at naming and placing a word. These words are then identified on the chalkboard. The rule "If all the letters are the same, the words are the same." is taught. The converse rule is also presented.

Word identity exercises help the children develop a small sight vocabulary which is used in developing simple sentences. First, the children are taught to recognize their own names and then receive drill on recognition of other children's names. Names of the parts of the body are also taught in this way. New sets of words (*is not, big*) are added for sentence making: "Joe is not big." Meaning is stressed in sentence reading by having children answer questions about their reading. "Is Joe big?" "No, Joe is not big." "Is Joe little?" "Yes, Joe is little." After children master the basic tasks, they are taught to read from teacher-prepared booklets.

This academic preschool program has been criticized on the basis that is a mechanistic conditioned-response approach and that it deals only with beginning reading. This latter criticism could also be leveled against other beginning programs (i/t/a, Words in Color, Programmed Reading, Computer Assisted Instruction). Jongsma (41) raises the "question of stability of gains" but feels that the specific and detailed objectives of the program will be helpful to teachers.

Results of the use of this type program are impressive. Bereiter and Engelmann (11) indicated that children from the first group using this approach scored from one-half to one and one-half years below average on pretests of language. By the end of the second year, their scores were approximately average for their age group. Mental age rose from about six months below average to about four months above average. Terminal achievement averaged at the 1.5 grade level in reading.

A second experimental group (1) with whom the same techniques were used over a two year period, showed a mean reading achievement of 2.6. Although experimental data are still somewhat limited, these studies have reported statistical data to support claims of the program's effectiveness.

Enrichment programs

The view that enrichment experiences are fundamental to offsetting the effects of economic deprivation is held by many educators. Several programs which place major emphasis on the development of readiness skills through enrichment activities have been proposed for use with the culturally different learner. The programs under Project Head Start may be looked at as prototypes of the enrichment-intervention model. The assumptions underlying these programs are:

> That from birth through six years of age are important years in human development; that children of the poor generally have not had the experiences and opportunities that support maximum development during this period; that effective programs for these children must be comprehensive, including health, nutrition, social services, and education; that for their own and their children's benefit, parents should be deeply involved in the design and implementation of local programs; and that a national child development program can focus attention on the needs of preschool and elementary school children from low-income families, and, through continued review of program

effectiveness, stimulate local institutions to do a better job of meeting these needs. (21:16)

Because of the diversity found in the numerous Head Start programs that were conducted, it is impossible to present a valid sketch of *the* program. Surveys of the curriculum emphasis found in the various programs indicated that a common feature was an attempt to influence sensory-motor development and language development. Only 50 percent of the directors responding indicated the development of pre-academic or academic skills as an important goal (21).

More specifically, it was found that few classes spent more than 5 percent of the time on auditory-discrimination training and that visual-perception training varied from 5 to 40 percent of class activities. Amounts of language training in the formal sense varied from 5 to 30 percent. Activities which occurred with the highest frequency were motor training, informal language stimulation, and social interaction.

Although the Head Start programs have enjoyed a fairly high degree of support, there is little data to indicate that they had a significant influence on later school achievement. In some instances it has been suggested that this influence was minimal because of the lack of emphasis on developing specific cognitive skills. Another factor that might also account for lack of success on some counts is the brief duration of training. It could hardly be expected that intervention programs that consisted of a few hours per day for a few weeks could be expected to compensate for several years of living in the ghetto or in depressed rural environments.

Enrichment through cognitive emphasis

Deutsch (24) developed a program for working with culturally different children which he describes as "enrichment intervention." Children are provided specific readiness training in auditory and visual discrimination, language and concept formation development, learning letter names and forms, sounding and blending of letters into words, and left-right orientation. Although labeled "enrichment," the program is based on systematic instruction aimed at cognitive development. Several other less extensive programs involving enrichment as the key to cognitive development had reported significant gains in reading readiness.

The Montessori method

The Montessori Method and philosophy cut across many of the preschool programs previously discussed. Since it does not fit under any of the labels used thus far, and since it represents a long-established program for the culturally different child, some of the major features of this program will be reviewed.

Kohlberg (43) cites data from his pilot research studies to support the view that there is much promise in the Montessori Method for stimulating the cognitive functioning that culturally different learners need for success in school.

One rationale given by Stevens (69) for using the Montessori Method with culturally different children is that this approach concentrates on the development of those skills and abilities in which these children are most lacking: language facility, vocabulary expansion, an environment conducive to learning, and structured experiences for developing attention and concentration. "It has demonstrated in many cultures that it can introduce language and related reading-readiness skills to children from disadvantaged backgrounds" and "can be greatly expanded and elaborated within our current understanding of learning theory." (69:48)

The Montessori Language Program (53) is somewhat analogous to a word recognition program and includes: (1) exercises of silence (i.e. paying attention); (2) stress on pronunciation of words; (3) recognition of printed symbols by shape; and (4) speech production through adequate manipulation of the vocal mechanisms. The language program does not deal with the language training that is felt necessary for the expression of concepts or for oral language usage.

The Montessori Reading Program (53) utilizes the "trace and say" task sequences which were designed to teach the child to recognize and pronounce letter sounds and to use these in word recognition. This writing-reading program stresses the sounds of the letters which is, in essence, a phonics approach. It is suggested that the time for beginning reading instruction will vary with different children, as will the pace at which they proceed. The child does not compete with the calendar or with other children. He competes only with himself.

Materials for the reading exercises consist of slips of paper or cards upon which familiar words and phrases are written. Both materials and tasks are simple: (1) the child reads (sounds out) the word and places it under the object it names; (2) phrase reading follows once the idea that "words represent thoughts" is grasped by the child. The phrase reading exercises are usually in the form of simple commands or directions which must be comprehended by the reader if they are to be carried out. The true reading in this program is thought of as "mental" rather than vocal. Oral reading is utilized for pronunciation, silent reading for meaning.

The total program encompasses not only major reading readiness skills, but also provides for "learning readiness" (a recommendation made also by Mills and Cohen). It lacks completeness in the area of language training. And this is the area where modifications may need to be made if it is to fully meet the needs of culturally different dialect speaking children.

Summary statement about preschools

These programs for the culturally different child demonstrate various approaches to compensatory education. Some programs, such as Head Start, stress enrichment experiences with incidental training in cognitive areas. Others, such as the academic preschools, stress cognitive development with less emphasis on enrichment experiences. Possibly an aim of future programs will be to establish experimentally the proper balance between these two.

In varying degrees, these programs have attempted to incorporate experiences and activities for developing:

positive self-concepts	visual discrimination of letter
visual and auditory perception	shapes
knowledge of letter names	sight vocabulary
and sounds	left-to-right-orientation
auditory discrimination of	language facility
letter sounds	concept formation

In many instances, the content of the traditional readiness program has been altered only slightly. In other programs, the actual teaching techniques appear to have been modified to fit the learner. Reports on the success of these programs suggest that, in many instances, gains may be short lived. This might be traceable to the fact that the program is terminated too soon or that the schools' follow-up program does not reinforce or build on the child's previous learnings. The descriptions of some programs have been too vague to invite replication. Exceptions to this criticism might be the academic preschool and the intensified traditional readiness programs. One of the major needs in this area is specific suggestions for the transition from the preschool program to a beginning reading program.

Beginning reading programs for the culturally different learner

Some of the suggestions relative to beginning reading instruction for the culturally different child are approaches that have been used for years in the regular classroom. Examples are the "language experience approach" and "individualized reading." Other theorists hold that these traditional approaches are inadequate unless they take into account the dialect differences which culturally different children bring to school. Still others propose that the materials for beginning reading be written in the child's dialect. This suggestion, which calls for development of vernacular texts, breaks new ground and is the center of some controversy.

The language experience approach

The major premise of the language experience approach is that the child should learn to read materials based on his personal experiences and written in his natural language patterns. Usually the pupil dictates a story which the teacher writes down. When a child provides a story from his own experiences, it is hypothesized that he will have little trouble expressing himself for he will use concepts he understands.

School-structured experiences that are to be the basis for later dictations must be something the child can relate to and understand or he will not talk about them. To take a group of Puerto Rican or black children from a ghetto environment to visit a museum or a group of Mexican-American children to a printing company may result in meager verbal concepts for use in an experience story. Appalachian youngsters may not be able to talk fluently about a visit to a large industrial development.

These kinds of experiences may be vivid but they may not be the kind about which the children can express ideas. Experiences of this type might well be delayed until children have had many chances at dictating experiences from familiar surroundings that will stimulate them to learn and use new words and concepts.

Arnold (4) and Stemmler (67) report success in using a modified language experience approach with culturally different learners. The modifications consisted of pretraining in standard English and the use of science materials as the experience sources. Children were coached to respond in standard English to questions about the science material. These answers were then read by the children. Other teacher-prepared charts written in standard English were also used.

Such modification represents a popular trend; however, the use of subject matter and standard English for experience stories should not cause teachers to minimize the use of children's personal experiences, nor should the stress on using standard English patterns be so rigorous as to stifle children's expression.

Transcribing Children's Stories. In transcribing the experience stories of culturally different learners, certain problems are likely to be encountered by the teacher. The following are prerequisites for teachers who would use this approach:

1. Urge the children to express themselves in oral language.
2. Refrain from placing value judgements on the content of the stories, or on the child's nonstandard English.
3. Be able to discriminate the phonology of the child's speech and translate this to standard spellings.
4. Understand the syntactical system used by the child and be able to transcribe it.

The following example is provided to illustrate these points. The child dictates:

> "Dos bums who lib up ober us, dey fight all de time. And when de lady boyfrien, he be comin in late, dey has a big ro. Yestuhday, dey fight cause when dey ma she come in, dey don't be no green left. Only thing lef be de pot likker. But den later on dey buys some wine and dey grub for days."

According to rules 1 and 2, the teacher must let the child speak, uninterrupted, without "corrections" that she might feel would make his speech sound "better." She must refrain from showing distaste at a child's experiences and the vocabulary used to express them. The conflicts that the child described may be as common-place in some life styles as is the angry middle-class parents who will not speak to each other for a week. According to rules 3 and 4 the teacher must understand the child's dialect and transcribe his syntactical patterns as follows:

> "Those bums who live up over us, they fight all the time. And when the boyfriend, he be coming in late, they have a big row. Yesterday, they fight cause when their mama she come in, there don't be no green left. Only thing left be the pot liquor. But then later on, they buy some wine and they groove for days."

In the example above, it will be noted that the teacher does not use spellings which fit the child's pronunciations. In all cases, she uses the standard English spellings for the materials the child dictates.

A review of the literature revealed no authority suggesting that nonstandard spellings be used. It is quite obvious that were they used, confusion in learning sight words and word attack skills would result. Stewart (70) points out that dialect spellings would have to be replaced by standard spelling patterns before the child was taught letter-sound relationships. Also, teachers would have to be trained in the transcription of nonstandard pronunciations.

When common sense principles are carefully observed, the language experience approach offers the culturally different learner the same benefits that accrue to other groups of learners.

The vernacular text approach

In some respects the vernacular texts closely parallel the beginning materials found in traditional basal readers. The chief difference is that the vernacular texts are written in the grammatical and syntactical patterns of the reader's dialect. Another basic difference is that the content of the vernacular texts is more typical of the minority-group child's life style than is the content of the traditional basal reader.

There are numerous proponents of vernacular texts. Baratz, writing in their support, states:

> The overwhelming evidence of the role that language interference can play in reading failure indicates that perhaps one of the most effective ways to deal with the literacy problems of Negro ghetto youth is to teach them using vernacular texts that systematically move from the syntatic structure of the ghetto community to those of the standard English speaking community. (7:114)

This position is based in part on an experiment which used third and fifth grade black children from the inner-city and white children from a low-middle-income community. The subjects were administered a sentence repetition test comprised of thirty sentences — fifteen in standard and fifteen in black dialect. White subjects were significantly better than black subjects in repeating standard English sentences; black subjects were significantly better than white subjects in repeating sentences in nonstandard dialect. Both groups exhibited "translation" problems when presented sentences that were outside of their primary code.

Baratz concluded that the most effective way to teach the inner-city Negro child to read is through an approach that uses his own language as the basis for initial readers. In other words, first teach the child to read in the vernacular, and then teach him to read in standard English. Such a reading program, she cautions, would not only require accurate vernacular texts for the dialect speaker, but also necessitates the creation of a series of "transition readers" that

On The Playground (A Vernacular Story)

On the playground in my neighborhood, there be a big merry-go-round. It be in the middle of the playground. In the evening after school, my mama, she take us there. We ride a long time. My baby brother, he cry when it be time to go. I don't cry 'cause I can stay late. My daddy, he come and get me when it be time for me to go. My grandmama say she know I like the playground. She be right. If I tell 'bout the time I try to jump on and fall off, mama won't let me stay by myself. I got me a secret. You got a secret too?

would move the child from vernacular texts to standard English texts. The ultimate success of such a reading program would be determined by the child's eventual ability to read standard English.

Stewart (70) advocates the use of dialect-based texts because such materials cut the double learning load otherwise faced by this child. He reasons that standard English must be acquired by these children but that while they are trying to develop effective word-recognition skills, they should not be burdened with deciphering unfamiliar syntactic structures. Having the child begin reading in sentence patterns from his dialect will facilitate his mastery of the necessary word-reading skills. Then, he may move to what is, for him, the unfamiliar patterns from standard English.

One hypothesis is given by Goodman (30) who contends that since it *is* true that learning to read a foreign language is a more difficult task than learning to read a native language, it must follow that it is harder for a child to read a dialect which is not his own than to learn to read his own dialect.

Tatham (72) reported that second and fourth graders of middle socio-economic status attained higher comprehension scores on material which included high frequency oral language patterns than on materials which included infrequent patterns. The results of the study led to this conclusion: A significant number of second and fourth graders comprehend material written with frequent oral language patterns better than materials written with infrequent oral language patterns. While this conclusion is specifically applicable to the population represented by the subjects tested, it seems reasonable that the same could be generalized to the culturally different learner.

The vernacular texts have been labeled by some as demeaning to the language of the ethnic group that it represents. It has also been alleged that these materials reinforce the language patterns that are thought to interfere with beginning reading success. These criticisms may be rooted in the feeling that the dialect speech is inferior to standard English. Or they may have been made when the idea of vernacular texts centered around materials written solely in the dialect with no provision for transition to standard English. These criticisms have been dealt with to some degree in the vernacular texts developed by a team of researchers and teachers. Leaverton, et al. (28, 46, 47) combined an oral language program with dialect readers. These texts, termed a bi-dialectal approach to beginning reading, have been used with black pupils in low-income areas of Chicago.

Taped conversations of the children's speech were obtained and analyzed for speech patterns. The speech samples revealed these differences in verb usage from standard English:

1. Absence of forms of the verb *be*. (Pat cute. Joe a boy. John running. We going to school in the morning.)
2. Absence of "were." (We tired yesterday.)
3. Absence of "s," third person singular. (Susie say to hurry.)
4. Failure to differentiate between present and past in both regular and irregular verb forms. (Last night he open the gate.) (Last year we lose the championship.)
5. Substitution of the verb *be* for other forms. (I be so happy. They be playing. We be going.)

Both the oral language program and the texts were designed with these aspects of verb usage as focal points. The instructional sequence for oral language training for either of the verb areas follows this form:*

The introduction of the use of IS with SHE

The teacher presents stimulus to elicit in a sentence the pattern of the child in the verb area being studied:

Teacher	*Possible Child Responses*
"Yesterday, one of the kindergarten girls said to me, "I got a nice teacher. She pretty too." But a boy said "My teacher is mean." Now boys and girls, let's pretend that you are in kindergarten. Tell me about your teacher. (46)	She nice. She not pretty. She is pretty. She wear pretty clothes. She got long hair. (46)

The teacher labels each response as either SCHOOL TALK OR EVERYDAY TALK and explains the differences:

Teacher: "Here are some things we said about our teacher — 'She pretty,' 'She nice.' Sometimes we said 'She is pretty.' and sometimes we said 'She pretty.' We are using different ways of saying almost the same thing. When we said "She pretty," we

---

*The following is paraphrased from Leaverton, et al., 1968.

were using EVERYDAY TALK. When we said, "She is pretty" we were using SCHOOL TALK. (46)

EVERYDAY TALK is what we use when we're just talking about anything and to anyone. We're usually not thinking about school or school work either. SCHOOL TALK is the way of talking that we're going to learn to use especially in school and outside of school, too. Our school books are written in SCHOOL TALK. Most of the time our teachers use SCHOOL TALK.

The teacher reads each sentence in turn to the children and tells them whether it is SCHOOL TALK or EVERYDAY TALK. These activities are followed by pattern practice drills and dialogues in SCHOOL TALK.

Reinforcing Drill

Teacher	Pupil
he	is (big).
she	is (little).
it	is (red). (46)

Dialogues for Reinforcement

The dialogues are memorized by the children who are all given turns to participate:

Girl	Boy
Today is a nice day.	Yes, it is.
You are pretty tall.	Yes, I am.
John is nice isn't he?	Yes, he is.
Is your sister nice?	Yes, she is.

The children are also given written exercises for practice in using SCHOOL TALK.

1. Five to ten sentences duplicated on sheets with a line below each sentence so that the child can rewrite the EVERYDAY TALK sentences in SCHOOL TALK.

   He big.

   _____ (He is big)

2. Sentences written in EVERYDAY TALK with a blank in the verb position. Children fill in from choices written below each sentence.

He _____ big. (46)

        is   am   are

Finally, at the close of each unit each child is asked to give an informal oral presentation using SCHOOL TALK.

Reading Program

The reading program (47) is built around a series of eight units or books. Each unit contains two versions of the same story, the EVERYDAY TALK version and the corresponding SCHOOL TALK story. Each book places emphasis on only one verb pattern. The progression from Book 1 through Book 7 is seen in the following examples:

Contrasting Verb Usage	EVERYDAY TALK	SCHOOL TALK
Book 1. *got* vs *have*	I got a mama.	I have a mama.
Book 2. omitting *is*, are use of is *are*	My mama she pretty.	My mama she is pretty.
Book 3. Omitting "s" use of "s" (3rd person singular)	My mama work.	My mama works.
Book 4. omitting *ed* ending use of *ed* ending	Yesterday my daddy work hard.	Yesterday my daddy worked hard.
Book 5. *do* vs *does*	My baby sister do her ABC's at home.	My baby sister does her ABC's at home.
Book 6. use of *be* vs and 7. use of *am, is, are*	When we be good, he be happy.	When we are good, he is happy.

Book 8 has only one set of stories. These stories serve as a review of standard verb forms introduced in the series. Space is provided in several of the books for children to write their own stories. The stories are about the child's life style with illustrations that feature the child's drawings and photographs of children in home and class-room settings. The book becomes the property of the child as he completes each unit.

After the child has completed the vernacular readers, he can move into basal readers or programs using individualized reading or the language experience approach. The use of picture dictionaries, phrase reading exercises, and silent reading for meaning are suggested to reinforce what has been taught. Phonics is introduced by using the names of the children to associate initial sounds with letters and then having children apply this learning to other words. (47)

Stewart, et al. (70) in their work at the Education Study Center have developed a three book series (*Ollie, Friends,* and *Old Tales*). These materials are available in both black-dialect and standard English versions. The standard English materials were developed primarily for use with control groups in studies designed to test the efficacy of the vernacular texts.

The Stewart materials do not deal with developing readiness skills or providing drill on translating black dialect into standard English. As a result, the language and sentence structure is more sophisticated than that found in early basals or in some vernacular materials. One potential advantage of this is story material that arouses and sustains reader interest. To cope with the difficulty level of the vocabulary, the authors suggest that the words found in the texts be pre-taught before children attempt to read the books. Thus, while these stories are viewed as part of the early reading program, they are not designed for the initial stage of beginning reading.

Both these materials and the Chicago Readers use standard spellings in the vernacular texts. However, in a few instances in the Stewart materials a grapheme-phoneme omission (*'cause* for *because*) is indicated by use of the apostrophe. The following is a verbatim copy of pages 22-30 of the story *Icarus**. In the texts, each page contains a picture plus two to four lines of print.

Icarus

It's a boy name Icarus.
Icarus a Greek name.
And he a Greek boy.

---

*William A. Stewart, *Old Tales,* Education Study Center, Washington, D.C., 1970. Used with permission of the author.

Icarus father made him some
wings out of wax and feathers.

Then Icarus father teach him
how to fly.
But Icarus he not suppose to fly
too far away.

His father tell him,
"Don't go near the sun, boy,
'cause your wings going to melt."

But Icarus he bad.
He don't do what his father say.
He fly right up to that old sun.

He get real close and he get hot.
His wings, they get hot, too,
and they start to melt.

Soon Icarus he ain't got no wings left
and he fall right out of the sky.

Icarus he feel real bad 'cause
he don't got no more wings.

His father going to be mad with him.
When he go home his father going
to hit him upside the head.

In discussing the use of vernacular texts several factors should be kept in mind.

1. Not all culturally different children will need such materials. Many of these children already speak standard English with enough proficiency that the use of vernacular texts may be confusing to them.
2. It is likely that different materials will have to be prepared for different groups of culturally different learners. Differences among the groups are just as significant as differences between any given dialect and standard English.
3. Teachers who expect to develop or use these materials must be familiar with the dialects involved.

Wolfram (74) suggests that until more experimental data are available on the efficacy of vernacular texts, teachers might simply accept the child's "dialect version" of standard English text material. In other words, beginning reading instruction should not focus on changing the child's pronunciation of words or his use of non-standard syntax.

Individualized Reading and the Culturally Different Child

Although individualized reading is widely discussed and practiced, there is so much variation in programs that no specific instructional guide is available. There are two major assets of this approach: one is flexibility and the other is openendedness. These same factors are also limitations in that they have inhibited meaningful research which could be replicated.

The discussion of individualized reading in Chapter 11 presents the philosophy and major practices associated with this approach.

There is some difficulty in fitting the individualized approach to beginning reading instruction, however, because there is no systematic methodology for using it at this level. The special advantages traceable to its use are more noticeable in the case of the independent reader than with the child who still needs to learn mechanics. Once the culturally different learner has gained independence in reading, he may profit from self-selection, self-pacing, ego-centered conferences, and the like to the same degree as do other groups. Since this approach has been strongly recommended as a follow-up to any beginning approach with culturally different children, the following suggestions may help teachers maximize its potential benefits.

Self Selection of reading materials can be an important asset in harnessing the culturally different child's ego to the reading task. To achieve this goal one needs not only a wide variety of books on topics of universal appeal but also materials that are of specific interest to these children. Books which portray their ethnic background and ethnic heroes must be available in the classroom collection. Teachers must remember to place on the reading shelves not only the "acceptable" stories, but also stories that focus on all aspects of the children's lives. The following lists contain titles that have been found by teachers to be popular with different ethnic groups:

Mexican Americans	*Black Americans*
Benito	Let My People Go
Citizen Pablo	The Riot Report
Manuela's Birthday	The Negro in America

A Mexican Boy's Adventure
Two Pesos for Catalina
Juanita
Popo's Miracle
And Now Miguel
Out from Under
First Book of Mexico
Blue Willow
No, No, Rosina
Awk!
Garbage Can Cat

Afro-Americans: Then and Now
Worth Fighting For
The Autobiography of Malcolm X
City Rhythms
What Harry Found When He Lost Archie
Tom B. and the Joyful Noise
Mary Jane
Roosevelt Grady
Martin Luther King, Jr.: Peaceful Warrior

Puerto Rican Americans

Getting to Know Puerto Rico
Young Puerto Rico
The Three Wishes
Juan Bobo and the Queen's Necklace
Perez and Martina
Barto Takes the Subway
Rosa-Too-Little
City High Five
Moncho and the Dukes
Sleep in Thunder
That Bad Carlos
Feast on Sullivan Street

American Indians

Walk in My Moccasins
Tall as Great Standing Rock
In My Mother's House
Nika Illahee
The American Indian
From Ungskah 1 to Oyaylee 10
Benny's Flag
Indian Two Feet and His Horse
Apache Boy
Snowbound in Hidden Valley
Indian Hill
Chief Seattle: Great Statesman

It is not suggested that books of this type constitute the entire reading fare for culturally different children. All good literature for children is appropriate, but the disadvantaged child, particularly, needs books and stories that deal with his culture and heroes from his ethnic group.

Criteria for selection of books and materials for the culturally different are similar to those which apply in any classroom.

1. The teacher must observe very closely the sociocultural principles. Not only must the title be appealing but the content of the books must not be beyond the child's experiences or conflict heavily with his cultural values.
2. The teacher must be aware of the linguistic principles of book selection. The child's language and the language of the book must not be far apart. (32)

Teacher-pupil conferences must be highly stimulating if the culturally different learner is to respond. The use of questions by the teacher must again reflect an understanding of the child's culture, his attitudes, and the mores and values peculiar to that culture. A teacher's unfamiliarity with or insensitivity to these factors may impose a communications barrier and defeat the total purpose of the conference. A question that might conflict with the experiences of the economically deprived child might be the one asked in relation to the following story during a conference.

The story is about a little boy whose life is in danger after he has shot himself in the brain. The boy is in another city visiting relatives and the hospital there has no surgeon. The only recourse is to call the surgeon in the boy's hometown. The hometown surgeon agrees to come right away, even after finding out that the boy's family is too poor to pay for his services. The call reaches the doctor at around nine o'clock and he promises to try to be at the hospital before midnight.

On his way out of town, the surgeon stops his car for a red light and a man in an old black coat with a gun gets in. The doctor is ordered to drive on. The doctor tries to explain where he is going but is not given the chance by the man in the old black coat. Soon, the doctor is ordered out of his car and is left standing on the road in the snow. The doctor calls a cab and arrives at the railway station only to find that the next train to his destination would not leave until midnight.

The doctor finally arrives at the hospital, but it is after two o'clock. He finds that he is too late; the boy died just an hour earlier. As the two doctors walk by the door of the hospital waiting room, the surgeon is introduced to the boy's father — the same man in the old black coat who took his car.*

Insensitive questioning: "Why do you think the boy's father would do such a bad thing as steal another man's car?"

Attaching the labels "steal" and "bad" to the man's actions might be insulting to the economically deprived child's values. For so long, the only way for him and for many whom he knew to survive was by taking. From this question he may be made to feel that all his deeds for survival have been "bad."

---

*Story retold from Billy Rose, "Why the Doctor Was Late". Courtesy of the Bell-McClure Syndicate as condensed in *Reader's Digest Readings* — English as a second language, copyright, 1964.

Perhaps a better question would be: "Why do you think the man in the black coat took the doctor's car instead of asking him for a ride?"

This question implies no judgments and allows the child to label the action and tell why he did so. From answers to questions such as this one, insights may be gained into the learner and his culture.

Diagnostic conferences with the culturally different child call for the teacher to be aware of the learner's syntactical and phonological system. Without this knowledge, the teacher will likely suggest corrections which are meaningless to the reader. For example:

Text	*Child's Reading*
We three boys were running.	We three boy be runnin'.
We passed a store.	We pass a sto.
Sam asked if we wanted to go in.	Sam, he ask do we wanna go in.
Joe did.	Joe, he do.
I did too.	I do too.
Sam went first.	Sam, he go firs.
Joe and I followed.	Joe and me follow.
The candy was good.	De candy good.

The teacher will be overevaluating if she lists the absence of final phonemes (boy*s*, runnin*g*, pass*ed*, ask*ed*, firs*t*) or the word (was) as "errors of omission." The adding of the italicized words (Sam *he*, Joe *he*) is not making "insertions" in the usual sense of the term, and using *do* for is and *be* for were do not meet the criteria for substitutions. The omission of certain phonemes, addition of certain pronouns, patterns of intonation, all reflect the characteristics of his dialect.

If the teacher is familiar with the language, vocabulary, and experiences of her children, she can, with minimum difficulty, plan for skills teaching. Chances are that the majority of the children will have similar pronunciations and attach similar meanings to most words. Informal diagnosis during the conferences can be the key to skills teaching for these groups.

Not only must individualized reading for the culturally different learner be built on the premise that "each child is a reader," it must also recognize the culturally different learner as a member of a specific group whose members have characteristics in common.

There will be skills teaching that this group membership may make necessary, but the child's interests and needs as an individual must be considered.

Summary

Beginning reading programs for the culturally different learner fall into two categories: They are either modifications of already existing approaches, or they are specifically centered around the learner's dialect.

The language experience approach is widely recommended for these children because the child reads and speaks in his natural language. Two innovations for this approach that are geared to the culturally different learner are the use of subject area content for dictation materials and stimulation of language usage before and during the reading.

Although the individualized approach is not feasible until independence in reading is gained, it has been cited in this chapter because it offers possibilities for use of dialect materials and ethnic content materials which create a reading environment which does not contradict, conflict with, or demean the reader's background.

The phonological differences between various dialects and standard English poses a real problem in regard to teaching letter-sound relationships. Neither linguists nor reading authorities have evolved programs for teaching these skills. However, the Bereiter-Engelmann approach resolves the problem to some degree since children are drilled on standard English before they move into reading.

The use of dialect or vernacular text materials for teaching reading to dialect speakers has been recommended by some authorities. While a number of the materials developed thus far are based on black dialect, the rationale for use of such materials has been generalized to other major dialects. Several factors have limited the use of dialect materials. These include the negative attitudes of parents and teachers; the absence of unequivocal experimental data as to the efficacy of these materials; and the fact that a great number of different materials would be needed in order to accommodate all dialect speakers.

In dealing with the culturally different child one important educational link is missing. In essence, this is the school's failure to provide continuity from the various pre-school programs into the primary grades. As Orem (55) has pointed out, any researcher who attempts to evaluate the values of a preschool approach designed for culturally different learners is faced at the outset with a major problem, for the schools do not offer the continuity needed to maximize the benefits of the preschool and hence may cancel out the benefits which might accrue from the earlier experiences.

YOUR POINT OF VIEW?

Defend or attack the following statements:

1. Of all the factors that influence academic achievement in the school, the dialect or language habits of the culturally different child is the most important.

2. Systematic instruction in standard English should precede reading instruction for children using a non-standard dialect.

3. a. In regard to the culturally different child, the major educational issue is that the school has ignored the needs and experiential backgrounds of these children.

   b. Agreement with statement a. is tantamount to charging the school with racism.

4. The potential efficacy of vernacular texts has been overrated by most proponents of this approach.

5. a. The school (and society) has tended to operate from the premise that non-standard dialects are inferior to standard English.

   b. The attitude expressed in a. relative to non-standard dialects is still prevalent.

6. *Premise:* "Language facility is the best single indicator of a child's mental ability."

   Statement: In the past, the school has made little effort to measure or evaluate the "language" of the culturally different, dialect speaking child.

7. *Discuss:* What change(s) in society (i.e. outside the school) would tend to minimize the "non-standard dialect problem" of blacks, chicanos, and other minority groups.

BIBLIOGRAPHY

1. *Academic Preschool, Champaign, Illinois.* Washington, D. C.: U. S. Government Printing Office, 1970.

2. Ahlfeld, Kathy, "The Montessori Revival," *The Education Digest,* (April 1970), 18–21.

3. Allen, Virginia F. "Teaching Standard English As A Second Dialect," *Teachers College Record* (February 1967), 355–370.

4. Arnold, Richard D. "English as a Second Language," *The Reading Teacher* (April 1968), 634–639.

5. Association for Supervision and Curriculum Development, NEA, *Educating The Children of the Poor,* Alexander Frazier (ed.), Washington, D. C., 1968.

6. Bailey, B. L. "A Crucial Problem in Language Intervention As It Relates to the Disadvantaged," *Supplement to the IRCD Bulletin* (Summer 1966), 1–2.

7. Baratz, Joan C. "Teaching Reading in an Urban Negro School System," in *Teaching Black Children to Read,* Joan C. Baratz and Roger W. Shuy (eds.). Washington, D. C.: Center for Applied Linguistics, 1969, 92–114.

8. Baratz, Joan C. and Roger W. Shuy (eds.), *Teaching Black Children to Read.* Washington D. C.: Center for Applied Linguistics, 1969.

9. Bauer, Evelyn, "Teaching English to North American Indians in BIA Schools," *The Linguistic Reporter* (August 1968), 1–2.

10. Bell, Paul W. "A Beginning Reading Program for the Linguistically Handicapped," in *Vistas in Reading,* II, Part 1, J. Allen Figurel (ed.), Proceedings, International Reading Association, 1967, 361–366.

11. Bereiter, Carl and Siegfried Engelmann, "An Academically Oriented Preschool for Disadvantaged Children; Results From the Initial Experimental Group," *Psychology and Early Childhood Education,* Daniel Brinson and Jane Hill (eds.). Toronto: Ontario Institute for Studies in Education, 1968, 17–36.

12. Bereiter, Carl and Siegfried Engelmann, *Teaching Disadvantaged Children in the Preschool.* Englewood Cliffs, N. J.: Prentice-Hall, Inc., 1966.

13. Brazziel, William F. and Mary Terrell, "An Experiment in the Development of Readiness in a Culturally Disadvantaged Group of First Grade Children," *The Journal of Negro Education* (Winter 1962), 4–7.

14. Brooks, Charlotte K. "Some Approaches to Teaching Standard English as a Second Language," *Elementary English* (November 1964), 728–733.

15. Burton, Dwight L. and Nancy Larrick, "Literature for Children and Youth," in *Development In and Through Reading,* NSSE Yearbook LX, Part I, 1961, 189–208.

16. Cheyney, Arnold B. *Teaching Culturally Disadvantaged in the Elementary School.* Columbus, Ohio: Charles E. Merrill Publishing Company, 1967.

17. Chisholm, Johnnie Bishop, *What Makes a Good Head Start?* Wolfe City, Texas: Henington Publishing Company, 1968.

18. Cohen, S. Alan, "Some Conclusions About Teaching Reading To Disadvantaged Children," *The Reading Teacher* (February 1967), 433–435.

19. Cohen, S. Alan, *Teach Them All to Read.* New York: Random House, 1969.

20. Crittenden, Brian S. "A Critique of the Bereiter-Engelmann Preschool Program," *School Review* (February 1970), 145–167.

21. Datta, Lois-ellin, *A Report on Evaluation Studies of Project Head Start.* Washington, D. C.: Department of Health, Education, and Welfare, 1969.

22. Davis, A. L. "Dialect Research and the Needs of the Schools," *Elementary English* (May 1968), 558–560, 608.

23. Davis, Allison, "Teaching Language and Reading to Disadvantaged Negro Children," *Elementary English* (November 1965), 791–797.

24. Deutsch, Martin, "Facilitating Development in the Preschool Child: Social and Psychological Perspectives," *The Merrill Palmer Quarterly,* (Spring 1964), 249–263.

25. Ecroyd, Donald H. "Negro Children and Language Arts," *The Reading Teacher,* (April 1968), 624–633.

26. Fantini, Mario D. and Gerald Weinstein, *The Disadvantaged.* New York: Harper and Row, Publishers, 1968.

27. Frost, Joe L. and Glenn R. Hawkes, (ed.), *The Disadvantaged Child.* New York: Houghton Mifflin Co., 1966.

28. Gladney, Mildred R. and Lloyd Leaverton, "A Model for Teaching Standard English to Non-Standard English Speakers," *Elementary English* (October 1968), 758–763.

29. Goldberg, Miriam L. "Adapting Teacher Style to Pupil Differences: Teachers for Disadvantaged Children," in *The Disadvantaged Child: Issues and Innovations,* Joe L. Frost and Glenn R. Hawkes (eds.). Boston: Houghton-Mifflin Company, 1966, 345–359.

30. Goodman, Kenneth, "Dialect Barriers to Reading Comprehension," *Elementary English* (December 1965), 853–860.

31. Goodman, Kenneth S. "Dialect Rejection and Reading: A Response," *Reading Research Quarterly* (Summer 1970), 600–603.

32. Goodman, Kenneth, Hans C. Olsen, Cynthia M. Colvin and Louis F. Vander Linde, *Choosing Materials to Teach Reading.* Detroit: Wayne State University Press, 1966.

33. Gray, Susan W. and Rupert Klaus, "An Experimental Preschool Program for Culturally Deprived Children," *Child Development,* 36, (1965), 887–898.

34. Hagerman, Barbara, and Terry Saario, "Non-Standard Dialect Interference in Reading" in *Claremont Reading Conference,* Malcolm P. Douglass, (ed.), Thirty-Third Yearbook, 1959, 158–167.

35. Harris, Albert J., Blanche L. Serwer and Lawrence Gold, "Comparing Reading Approaches With Disadvantaged Children-Extended into Second Grade," *The Reading Teacher* (May 1967), 698–703.

36. Haubrich, Vernon F. "The Culturally Disadvantaged and Teacher Education," *The Reading Teacher* (March 1965), 499–505.

37. Horn, Thomas D. (ed.), *Reading for the Disadvantaged: Problems of Linguistically Different Learners.* New York: Harcourt Brace Jovanovich, 1970.

38. Jensen, Arthur R. "The Culturally Disadvantaged: Psychological and Educational Aspects" *Social Psychology* (December 1967), 4–19.

39. John, Vera P. "Research Related to Language Development in Disadvantaged Children," *IRCD Bulletin* (November 1965).

40. Johnson, Kenneth R. "Pedagogical Problems of Using Second Language Techniques for Teaching Standard English to Speakers of Non-Standard Negro Dialect," *The Florida FL Reporter,* Alfred C. Aarons, Barbara Y. Gordon, and William A. Stewart (eds.), (Spring/Summer 1969), 78–80, 154.

41. Jongsma, Eugene A. "Preschool Education and the Culturally Disadvantaged," *Viewpoints* (May 1970), 95–116.

42. Keener, Beverly M. "Individualized Reading and the Disadvantaged," *The Reading Teacher* (February 1967), 410–412.

43. Kohlberg, L. "Montessori With the Culturally Disadvantaged," in *Early Education: Current Theory Research and Action,* Robert Hess and Roberta Meyer Bear (eds.) Chicago: Aldine Publishing Co., 1966.

44. Labov, William, "Language Characteristics of Specific Groups: Blacks," in *Reading for the Disadvantaged: Problems of Linguistically Different Learners,* Thomas D. Horn (ed.). New York: Harcourt Brace Jovanovich 1970, 155–156.

45. ———, "The Logic of Non-Standard English," *The Florida FL Reporter,* Alfred C. Aarons, Barbara Gordon, and William A. Stewart (eds.) (Spring/Summer 1969), 169.

46. Leaverton, Lloyd, et al. *Psycholinguistics Oral Language Program — A Bi-Dialectal Approach* (Experimental Ed.), Part I. Chicago: Board of Education, City of Chicago, 1968.

47. Leaverton, Lloyd, Olga Davis and Mildred Gladney, *The Psychollinguistics Reading Series—A Bi-Dialectal Approach* (Teachers' Manual). Chicago: Board of Education, City of Chicago, 1969.

48. Loban, Walter, "Teaching Children Who Speak Social Class Dialects," *Elementary English* (May 1968), 592–599, 618.

49. Loretan, Joseph O. and Shelley Umans, *Teaching the Disadvantaged.* New York: Columbia University, Teachers College Press, 1966.

50. McDavid, Raven I. Jr. "Dialectology and the Teaching of Reading," *The Reading Teacher* (December 1964), 206–213.

51. Martin, Clyde and Alberta M. Castaneda, "Nursery School and Kindergarten," in *Reading for the Disadvantaged: Problems of Linguistically Different Learners,* Thomas D. Horn (ed.). New York: Harcourt Brace Jovanovich, 1970.

52. Mills, Queenie B. "The Preschool-Disadvantaged Child," in *Vistas in Reading.* Proceedings, International Reading Association, 11, Part I, 1967, 345–349.

53. Montessori, Maria, *The Montessori Method.* New York: Schocken Books, 1964.

54. Moore, Walter, "Teaching Reading to Children from Culturally Disadvantaged and Non-English Speaking Homes," in *The Teaching of Reading,* John J. DeBoer and Martha Dallmann (eds.). New York: Holt, Rinehart, and Winston, Inc., 1970, 529–531.

55. Orem, R. C. (ed.) *Montessori for the Disadvantaged.* New York: G. P. Putnam's Sons, 1967.

56. Prendergast, Raymond, "Pre-Reading Skills Developed in Montessori and Conventional Nursery Schools," *The Elementary School Journal* (December 1969), 136–141.

57. Reissman, Frank, *The Culturally Deprived Child.* New York. Harper and Brothers. 1962.

58. Roberts, Hermese E. "Don't Teach Them to Read," *Elementary English* (May 1970), 638–640.

59. Robinson, Helen M. and Rose Mukerji, "Language, Concepts and the Disadvantaged," *Educational Leadership* (November 1965), 133–142.

60. Rystrom, Richard, "Dialect Training and Reading: A Further Look," *Reading Research Quarterly* (Summer 1970), 581–599.

61. Saville, Muriel R. "Language and the Disadvantaged," in *Reading for the Disadvantaged: Problems of Linguistically Different Learners,* Thomas D. Horn (ed.). New York: Harcourt Brace Jovanovich, 1970, 115–130.

62. Sherk, John K., Jr. "Dialect — The Invisible Barrier to Progress in the Language Arts," *The Allyn and Bacon Reading Bulletin,* #131, 1–4.

63. Shuy, Roger W. "Some Considerations for Developing Beginning Reading Materials for Ghetto Children," in *Language and Reading: An Interdisciplinary Approach,* Doris V. Gunderson (ed.). Washington, D. C.: Center for Applied Linguistics, 1970, 88–97.

64. Skinner, Vincent P. "Why Many Appalachian Children Are Problem Readers — We Create the Problems," *Journal of Reading* (November 1967), 130–131.

65. Spencer, Doris U. "Individualized Versus A Basal Reader Program in Rural Communities — Grades One and Two, " *The Reading Teacher* (October 1967), 17.

66. Stauffer, Russell G. *The Language-Experience Approach to the Teaching of Reading.* New York: Harper and Row Publishers, 1970.

67. Stemmler, Anne O. "An Experimental Approach to the Teaching of Oral Language and Reading," *Harvard Educational Review,* (Winter 1966), 42–59.

68. ———, "What Have We Learned About Teaching Reading to Spanish-Speaking Children?" *Highlights* of the Pre-Convention Institutes on Reading for the Disadvantaged, Millard H. Black (ed.). Newark, Delaware: International Reading Association, 1966, 11–24.

69. Stevens, George L. "Implications of Montessori for the War on Poverty," in *Montessori For the Disadvantaged,* R. C. Orem (ed.). New York: G. P. Putnam's Sons, 1967, 32–48.

70. Stewart, William, "Negro Dialect In the Teaching of Reading," in *Teaching Black Children to Read,* Joan C. Baratz and Roger W. Shuy (eds.). Washington, D. C.: Center for Applied Linguistics, 1969, 182-201.

71. Taba, Hilda, and Deborah Elkins, *Teaching Strategies for the Culturally Disadvantaged.* Chicago: Rand McNally and Company, 1966.

72. Tatham, Susan Masland, "Reading Comprehension of Materials Written With Select Oral Language Patterns: A Study at Grades Two and Four," *Reading Research Quarterly* (Spring 1970), 405–426.

73. White, William F. *Tactics for Teaching the Disadvantaged.* New York: McGraw-Hill Book Company, 1971.

74. Wolfram, Walter, "Sociolinguistic Alternatives in Teaching Reading to Non-Standard Speakers," *Reading Research Quarterly* (Fall 1970), 9–33.

75. Wood, Mildred H. "An Analysis of Beginning Reading Programs for the Disadvantaged," *Viewpoints* (May 1970), 149–188.

76. Worley, Stinson E., and William E. Story, "Socioeconomic Status and Language Facility of Beginning First Graders," *The Reading Teacher* (February 1967), 400–403.

77. Williams, Frederick (ed.), *Language and Poverty: Perspectives on a Theme*. Chicago: Markham Publishing Company, 1970.

78. Yonemura, Margaret, *Developing Language Programs for Young Disadvantaged Children*. New York: Columbia University, Teachers College Press, 1969.

79. York, L. Jean, and Dorothy Ebert, "Implications for Teachers, Primary Level: Grades 1–3," in *Reading for the Disadvantaged: Problems of Linguistically Different Learners*, Thomas D. Horn (ed.). New York: Harcourt Brace Jovanovich, 1970.

III

Beginning Reading: The Instructional Program

Although Chapter 4 deals with the concept of readiness and Chapters 5 and 6 with beginning instruction, the activities involved under both these labels are viewed as a continuum rather than as separate learning stages. In the past decade *beginning reading instruction* and *materials* have received unprecedented attention. A number of proposals for beginning instruction are described and analyzed. Some facets of code-cracking are discussed in each of the Chapters 4 to 9. However, repetition is avoided through the selective use of different illustrative teaching procedures. The same is true of certain linguistic insights, an example of which is the role of intonation in reading.

The discussion of individualized reading appears to fit equally well in this section and in the one that follows. Included here, it will hopefully convey the impression that individualizing instruction should begin early without implying that it diminishes in importance beyond beginning reading.

4

Assessing and Developing Readiness for Reading

Reading readiness is a concept that had to be invented after a society had committed itself to certain educational practices and expectations. Some of the conditions that gave rise to an emphasis on reading readiness will be noted but not discussed in detail. The first factor is the legal requirement that all children begin formal education on the basis of chronological age. While this practice has some virtue from the standpoint of administration, it has little relationship to learning the complicated process of reading. Many children are absorbed into a school environment that resembles an assembly line. Each child is expected to move a specified distance along an instructional continuum within a specified time. However, some children are simply not ready to move at this predetermined rate.

A second factor is the *value* that the society has placed on *learning to read**. Our society decrees that every child must learn to read and that he must make a certain amount of progress in the first calendar year of formal instruction.

A third factor is traceable to materials and methodology. These may differ a bit from district to district, but within a given class-

---

*Note that the high value is placed on "learning the process" rather than on reading itself.

room the materials and methodology are rather fixed. Usually, practices found within this classroom seem to indicate a philosophy that children are interchangeable units. Each child is expected to profit equally with all others from whatever goes on in that classroom.

In summary, the above practices and expectations negate what we purport to know about individual differences. When our overt behaviors refute a principle which we allege to hold with conviction, then lip service to that principle must be intensified. Thus, given the conditions that children start school on the basis of chronological age, that reading *is* the curriculum, that all children must learn how to read because they are in school, and that they must learn with the materials and methodology adopted locally, something is almost certain to go wrong.

The thing that went wrong is that a goodly number of children failed to learn to read under these conditions. In one sense failure in reading is analogous to the human body running a temperature. This serves as a warning that all is not well. The temperature does not tell you what is wrong, just that something is wrong. Good doctors vary their prescriptions to include aspirin, laxatives, antibiotics, and surgery. Hopefully, they do not prescribe on the basis of the temperature alone. They must also know "Where does it hurt?" and "Is there a swelling?"

Since there is an *a priori* consensus that significant changes in education are difficult, if not impossible, we do not deal with causes but only with the symptom of the temperature. We have opted for aspirin under the trade name Reading Readiness. Since the premises underlying the concept of readiness are humane, we tend to stress these rather than to question the outcomes they achieve.

**The Concept
of Readiness**

Readiness is a factor at all reading levels, but here we will focus on readiness for beginning reading instruction. All children have been getting ready for reading throughout their pre-school careers — some much more so than others — but entrance into first grade is not necessarily based on readiness for what will transpire there.

For several decades the term reading readiness has been used as if it had some universally accepted meaning. Recently, certain ambiguities in this concept have been discussed. MacGinitie points out that the question, "Is the child ready to read?" is poorly phrased on at least two counts. First it ignores that learning to read is a long term process not a fixed point on a continuum. "Reading is a process that takes some time for any person at any age. Part way through the process, the child becomes ready to profit from experience he would have found meaningless at the beginning." (36) Secondly, he raises the question as to how readiness scores can predict reading achievement when actual methodology and instruction have not been specified.

In general, the readiness period is viewed as an attempt to synthesize new experiences with the previous experiences that children have had. These previous experiences, or the lack of them, are extremely important, since they determine to a large degree the kind and the amount of experience that is still needed and which the school must provide prior to formal instruction in reading. How accurately the teacher discerns what is still needed, and how successful she is in filling these needs, may well be the most important factor in determining each child's later success or failure in reading.

A good readiness program would include activities for individual pupils which lead to their later maximum success in reading. It is not aimed at removing individual differences among pupils, but at seeing that each child has experiences which will remove blocks to learning. It can be thought of as a filling in and smoothing out process.

Thus, it would be difficult to defend a readiness program that involved all children doing the same things for equal periods of time. Such a program would ignore the known facts about individual differences and would negate any instructional cues that might be disclosed by readiness tests. On the other hand, it must be kept in mind that there are many activities which can involve all children.

A good readiness program achieves a high degree of flexibility. In practice, however, some first grade teachers follow a schedule of a given number of weeks of readiness activities followed by instruction in reading. At this point, responses to instruction tend to separate children into groups in which they might be labeled unready, partially ready, and ready.

When a readiness program is determined primarily by a calendar, the unready are likely to suffer at about the same intensity levels as if readiness had been totally ignored. In dealing with the unready, teachers face very difficult decisions. Both the school and the community operate from the premise that since children are in school they must be ready for what the school has planned — in grade one this is the learning of reading. Ironically, teachers frequently rationalize some of their practices on the grounds that "parents insist that their children start reading" or that "the school administration expects it." This is another example of teacher knowledge being ahead of practice. If teachers are professionally qualified, it is essential that they work toward achieving conditions in which it will not be necessary for them to sacrifice their profesisonal integrity and their pupils' psychological well-being because of pressures from the community.

Hopefully, the preceding discussion will not lead the reader to infer that the readiness period is a waiting period. It is educational malpractice to force children to come to school and then require them to wait for the unfolding of some maturational milestone. Flexibility does not imply laissez faire; it includes structure and a deliberately planned program. At least in theory, it weighs both the school's goals for the child and the child's capabilities and needs in relation to these goals.

Readiness and Reading:
Not a Dichotomy

A misconception that might arise is that there are a number of readiness activities that are distinct from other activities that are labeled "beginning reading instruction." The literature on the teaching of reading has developed in such a way that differences seem to be as real as they are apparent. One's belief in the concept of readiness need not be weakened by the perception that readiness activities blend almost imperceptibly, into beginning reading instruction.

For example, a good first grade teacher may honestly believe that she doesn't use a readiness program or teach readiness activities. The odds are, however, that she will also go on record that she "moves along with reading at a pace the children can follow." If she were observed by individuals who strongly believe in "readiness activities" they might well agree that her readiness program is the best in the district.

For a concrete example, assume you see a film clip of a group being taught the visual pattern M and the association of this letter symbol with the initial sound heard in the words *Mike* and *Mary*. Could you say with assurance that you are observing a readiness activity or reading instruction? Some teachers use this technique the first day of school and again (or a variation of it) in December and February. Teachers in higher grades should also use it with any child who has not mastered this letter-sound relationship.

Some instructional materials have designated certain tasks as "pre-reading" activities, and this term is widely accepted as a synonym for readiness activities. Providing practice in discriminating rhyming elements in words is one excellent and widely used pre-reading activity. However, work with rhyming elements will be used again and again throughout the period in which letter-sound relationships are taught and not just at the pre-reading level.

Assessing Readiness for Reading

Since there are noticeable differences between children who enter first grade, it is rightly assumed that some of these differences have considerable effect on their learning to read. Hundreds of studies have attempted to pinpoint "which differences" have the most impact on learning to read. Some of the factors studied include chronological age, mental age, knowledge of letter names, language facility, knowledge of word meanings, and the ability to make visual discriminations (between letters, words, geometric figures, etc.), follow directions, make auditory discrimination of speech sounds within words, and draw the human figure. Subtests found on most readiness tests purport to measure a number of these variables.

Teacher estimates of readiness

A number of studies, Karlin (30), Annesley, et al. (1), Koppman and La Pray (32), and Henig (24) report that teacher estimates of pupil success in reading, made without knowledge of readiness scores, correlate with reading achievement at approximately the same level as do the actual test scores. It is interesting to note that an early study (1934) by Lee and Clark (33) reported that only about half of the teachers in that study were as effective in predicting pupil achievement as was a readiness test. This might suggest that, over the years, teachers have become more sensitive to readiness factors. Regardless of teachers' ability to judge readiness, there is little evidence that schools rely on teacher judgment to the exclusion of readiness tests. Results from a national survey (Austin et al.) (2) indicated that approximately 80 percent of responding schools reported using readiness tests for evaluation.

Reading readiness tests

These tests are standardized instruments designed to assess the child's ability to profit from formal instruction in reading. They fulfill their purpose insofar as they predict success in learning to read. That is, the score made on the test itself must be indicative of what can be expected in achievement in reading during the first year or two of formal reading instruction. Readiness tests are, as a rule, administered as group tests, though some may contain one or more subtests which must be given individually. Representative test items include:

1. *Associating pictured objects with the spoken word for that object.* The child has before him a series of four or five pictures in a line across the page. The pictures might be of a frog, a boat, a shoe, and a turkey. He is asked to "underline (or circle) the shoe."

2. *Visual discrimination.* Four or five similar objects are shown. One is already circled or checked. One other picture in the row is exactly like this one. The child is to mark the identical picture. Variations of this test include the recognition of one or more digits or letters which are identical to the stimulus at the beginning of the line.

3. *Sentence comprehension.* The child must grasp the meaning of an entire sentence. Before him are pictures of a calendar, clock, lawnmower, and thermometer. "Mark the one which tells us the time."

4. *Drawing a human figure.* In a space provided in the test booklet, the child is asked to draw a man or a woman.

5. *Ability to count and to write numbers.* A series of identical objects are shown, and the child is told to mark the second, fourth, or fifth object from the left.

    To test his ability to recognize digits, he is told to underline or put an "X" on a certain digit in a series.

6. *Word recognition.* A common object (doll, house, barn, cow, man, etc.) is pictured. Three or four words, including the symbol for the picture, are shown, and the child is to mark the word represented by the picture.

7. *Copying a model.* A series of geometric figures and capital letters serve as models. The child is to duplicate the stimulus.

8. *Auditory discrimination.* On a group test this might consist of a series of pictures placed horizontally across the page. At the left of each series is a stimulus picture. The child

marks each object in the series whose name begins with the same initial sound as the name of the stimulus. If the first picture is that of a dog, for example, it might be followed by illustrations of a doll, a cow, a door, and a ball. Another test situation would be marking each picture whose name rhymes with the name of the stimulus picture.

Readiness tests vary as to the types of skills tested. Some of the older tests lack provision for measuring auditory discrimination, but most of the more recently published ones include such a subtest. In general, norms are based on total scores which determine pupil placement in categories such as superior, above average, average, or poor. Since the chief objective of readiness tests is prediction of success in learning to read, it is hoped that the test will separate the ready from the non-ready and that, when first grade pupils are thus identified, the school will adjust the curriculum accordingly. This brings us to the question of just how accurately reading readiness tests predict success in beginning reading.

Predictive value of readiness tests

During the past forty years, hundreds of studies involving the use of readiness tests have been reported. Any attempt to distill and interpret this large amount of data is complicated by a number of factors. Few studies are actually comparable, since different studies used different population samples, measured the impact of different variables, controlled some variables and ignored others, and used different tests, statistical treatments, and limits of significance.

In addition, test items on readiness tests may purport to measure a particular skill which is generally viewed as an absolute necessity for learning to read. (Examples might be visual and auditory discrimination skills.) However, even though test items focus on a particular skill, they may call for responses that do not parallel the actual tasks children perform in reading. Insignificant correlations have been reported between two subtests (from different tests) which were designed to measure the same readiness factor.

Dykstra (16) studied the relationship between auditory discrimination and reading achievement. His pre-test battery consisted of seven subtests from several different readiness tests. Two subtests measured auditory discrimination of speech sounds. One of these subtests, "Making Auditory Discriminations" (Harrison-Stroud Readiness Test), required children to draw a line from a stimulus picture to another picture whose naming word began with the same initial sound as the stimulus picture. This subtest made the highest contribution to prediction of reading achievement at the end of grade one.

Another subtest, "Auditory Discrimination of Beginning Sounds" (Murphy-Durrell Readiness Test), required pupils to place an X on a given picture if the name of that picture began with the same sound as a stimulus word pronounced by the examiner. This subtest failed to contribute significantly to any predictive multiple regression equation. Dykstra commented, "Furthermore the correlation between these two tests was only .30, a very insignificant relationship in light of the similarity of the task the two tests were designed to measure." (17)

MacGinitie (36) has identified two popular approaches used to establish the relationship between particular readiness skills and reading achievement. One is to measure children with a readiness test prior to reading instruction. The scores on a reading test administered at the end of grade one are correlated with the scores on the readiness measure. The predictive values of the various readiness subtests can then be charted. The second approach is to identify *good* and *poor* readers after a period of instruction and then test both groups on certain readiness variables believed to be related to reading. If poor readers have low scores and good readers have high scores on subtest X, causal relationships are frequently inferred. As noted earlier, MacGinitie suggests that generalizing from any particular study must be limited because the *method of teaching* has traditionally been ignored in both of these approaches.

Despite these and other methodological problems, the research data shows a rather remarkable internal consistency. If summary statements relative to the predictive value of readiness tests had been made at the close of each of the past four decades, they would be very much alike. On the whole, readiness scores alone lack precision in predicting reading achievement for individual pupils. In general, though, the experimental data indicate a positive relationship between scores on readiness tests and success in beginning reading. Referring to relationships found between readiness test scores and reading achievement, Dykstra writes, ". . . . predictive validity correlation coefficients are in general quite consistent. Most of the relationships can be found in the range .40 to .60 with a few extremes on either end." (17)

Subtest vs *battery*

Most reading readiness tests consist of six or seven subtests, and scores from the entire battery are usually used for predicting reading achievement. In recent years, due to the availability of computers and more sophisticated statistical techniques, more attention has been paid to the relative predictive value of each subtest in a total battery. Data from a number of studies present evidence that scores from a single subtest will often predict reading achievement approximately as accurately as does the entire test. Linehan (34), Barrett (5), and Dykstra (17) report studies in which children's knowledge of letter names was the best predictor of later success in reading. This finding was supported by an analysis of data from the Cooperative First Grade (10) and Second Grade (18) Studies.

Thus, experimental data suggest that readiness tests, intelligence tests, and teacher evaluations appear to be about equally effective in predicting success in beginning reading. This does not imply that readiness tests have little value to teachers, but it does suggest that educators should not project into these tests a degree of predictive infallibility which they do not possess. It appears that some readiness tests "overrate" children in regard to reading readiness. It is possible that some of the tasks on such tests are more closely related to the child's previous experiences than to what he will actually encounter in beginning reading.

It must be kept in mind that readiness tests measure only selected factors which are believed to be related to reading. There are many other factors which affect learning to read, such as the instruction the child receives, his attitude toward his teacher and toward reading, his reaction to varying degrees of success and failure, his home stability, and the like. This points up the need for intelligent use of readiness test results. The purpose of administering such tests is not to get a score for each child or to rank or compare children in the group, but rather to secure data for planning experiences which will promote successful learning.

In fact, unless the teacher is alert, actual scores may divert attention from child behavior which merits close scrutiny. This tendency is particularly marked when the administration of tests has become an end in itself. When this occurs, the inevitable result is that many trees become obscured by the forest. If teachers would analyze readiness test results, and if they could adjust their teaching to each child's needs, numerous reading problems might be averted.

Factors Associated with Readiness for Reading

Numerous factors have been studied in relation to their impact on learning to read. Since reading is a very complicated process, it is very difficult either to establish precise relationships or to completely rule out certain factors as being of no importance. The following discussion will be limited to only a few factors whose importance in learning to read has been widely accepted.

Mental age (the intelligence factor)

During the 1930s and 1940s, the importance of mental age appeared to be settled once and for all. A most interesting phenomenon of this period was the almost universal acceptance that children should have attained a mental age (M.A.) of 6-5 (years and months) before they were instructed in reading. This concept was based on the report and conclusions of one study published in 1931 by Morphett and Washburne (40).

They reported data for 141 first grade children who were given an intelligence test at the beginning of the school year and tested on reading achievement in February. The subjects were then divided into nine groups on the basis of mental age. The lowest range was 4-5 to 4-11, the highest 8-6 to 9-0 (these figures represent years and months of mental age). Of approximately 100 children who had attained an M.A. of 6-6 or higher, 78 percent made satisfactory progress in general reading and 87 percent made satisfactory progress in sight words. Of a group of twenty children whose M.A. ranged from 6-0 to 6-5, 52 percent made satisfactory progress in reading and 41 percent in sight words. Children below this range in M.A. showed little success in reading achievement.

In a follow-up study, Washburne (56) reported on a group of twenty-five pupils who were delayed in beginning reading instruction until the middle of second grade. Their reading achievement was compared with a number of control pupils who began reading at the usual time in first grade. By the end of the third grade, the experimental group had caught up with the controls; by the end of the fourth grade they had surpassed them; and at the end of seventh grade they were approximately one year ahead of the controls in reading. Unfortunately, the original experimental group of twenty-five had been reduced to approximately half that number by the end of the experiment and drawing conclusions on such a small sample is precarious. In addition there were, according to the author, important variables which could not be controlled.

During the 1950s and 1960s the criterion of 6–6 years of mental age for beginning reading instruction was the most prominent finding in reading research. This criterion persisted despite the fact that the study suggesting it was never replicated. Another interesting phenomenon is that during the same decade Gates published a study (next paragraph) containing data which was contradictory to that of Morphett and Washburne. Recently, Durkin* has suggested that the unquestioning attitude toward the 6–6 years mental age concept was perhaps due to the fact it was in harmony with popular beliefs at the time.

Gates (21) unequivocally challenged the contention that research data have established a "critical point" on the M.A. continuum below which reading cannot be mastered. He stated, "The fact remains ... that it has by no means been proved as yet that a mental age of six and a half years is a proper minimum to prescribe for learning to read by all school methods or organizations or *all* types of teaching skills and procedures." In a study of four different first grade classes, Gates reports the correlation between M.A. and reading achievement as .62, .55, .44, and .34. He postulated that much of the discrepancy between these figures was actually accounted for by the instructional procedures found in the classrooms and that good instruction results in a higher correlation between pupil M.A. and success in reading.

MacGinitie (36) supports Gate's position in his statement, ". . . it is hazardous to interpret the findings of readiness studies when the teaching method and materials are not specified, particularly when the sample is small." An analysis of the data from the First Grade Studies led Bond and Dykstra (10) to conclude that teaching is probably the most important variable in determining beginning reading achievement.

The objective in discussing mental age was not to minimize its importance in learning to read, but rather to place it in its proper perspective. The data available attest to the importance of M.A., but at the same time do not establish a particular point on the mental-age continuum as the point below which children will not achieve success in reading. To posit that 6–6 mental age is such a point implies that all children with this M.A. are alike and ignores the fact that teachers, teaching methods, and programs are not everywhere comparable.

Other investigations attest to the importance of factors such as pre-reading activities, methodology, and readiness programs in de-

---

*Dolores Durkin, "What Does Research Say about the Time to Begin Reading Instruction?" *Journal of Educational Research*, 64 (October 1970), 51–56.

termining how well children learn to read. One such study, carried on in first grade, reports that some children with an M.A. of 5-6 who had had no specific readiness program did not achieve up to grade norms in reading, while a group with M.A.'s of 5-0 who had had an extensive twelve-week readiness program did achieve up to national norms. Furthermore, a number of children who did poorly on readiness tests, and for whom prognosis in reading achievement was poor, achieved up to grade norm following specific readiness instruction.*

Pre-School experience and informational background

Pre-school experience and informational background have been studied to determine their relationship to reading readiness. In one study, scores made by first grade children on a readiness test correlated .49 with later achievement in reading. However, when only the scores of those children who had attended kindergarten were treated separately, the correlation between the two measures was .68. (33) After studying a group of children who had kindergarten experience and a group which had no such experience, Pratt (45) questioned the validity of using the same reading readiness tests and applying the same assumptions to both groups.

In a study designed to show the relationship between children's informational background and progress in reading, first grade children were tested on vocabulary, picture completion, and previous experience. On the basis of data secured, children were divided into "rich background" and "meager background" groups. Reading readiness tests were administered to all children at the beginning of first grade. Reading achievement tests were administered to first graders in January and again in December of their second year. The rich background group was superior on both readiness tests and later reading achievement although there was no significant difference between the groups in mental age. (28)

Both the school and society have recently focused attention on the preschool experiences of children who are economically deprived or whose cultural background and language patterns differ significantly from that of middle class or "mainstream" children. The reason for the concern stems from the fact that many children who come from culturally different backgrounds exhibit difficulty in adjusting to a curriculum that was developed without regard for their previous experience.

---

*Edmiston, R. W., and Bessie Peyton, "Improving First Grade Achievement by Readiness Instruction," *School and Society*, LXXI (April 1950).

In theory, our educational philosophy is that the school will adjust to the child's needs and "meet him where he is" with regard to what to teach. However, in actual practice, the schools frequently expect the child to "adjust" to a curriculum that is quite foreign to his present needs and past experiences. As children fail to learn under these circumstances, the school consciously or unconsciously places the blame on the learner. Instead of making necessary adjustments in methodology and content many schools gradually abdicate their role as educational institutions and function as "holding actions" for meeting the legal age requirements for keeping a child in school. The problem of culturally different children is discussed in detail in Chapter 3.

Auditory Discrimination

Some studies indicate that impaired readers lack skill in the discrimination of speech sounds. Robinson (47) points out that this skill is linked to success in reading on two counts: its relation to language and speech, and its role in phonic analysis. Durrell and Murphy (15) state, "Although there are many factors which combine to determine the child's success in learning to read, it is apparent that his ability to notice the separate sounds in spoken words is a highly important one." The authors indicate that most children who are referred for clinical help in reading because they have not achieved beyond first grade level are unable to discriminate between speech sounds in words. Tests usually reveal that the problem of these children is not a hearing loss but an inability to discriminate between minute differences in speech sounds.

Hildreth (26) asserts that the rapid noting of auditory clues results in more efficient reading. Betts (6) stresses a substantial relationship between a child's inability to name the letters and impaired reading. He adds that this does not imply that rote memorization of the alphabet is desirable. Walter B. Barbe and others identified the types of reading difficulties found among eighty remedial readers receiving help at a reading clinic. More than forty different problems were noted and tabulated. The weakness showing the highest incidence was sound of letters not known (found in 95 percent of cases at the primary and 62 percent at the intermediate age levels).

Other studies suggest the importance of the ability to synthesize or fuse phonetic elements of words (42). Hester, (25) reporting data

gathered on approximately 200 children admitted to a reading laboratory, states that blending of consonant sounds was particularly difficult for these children. Another study of over one hundred remedial readers (retarded two years or more on the basis of M.A.) indicated that these impaired readers were below average on auditory memory span as measured by specific subtests on the Stanford Binet. (48)

A series of studies conducted at Boston University which tested over 1500 first grade children led Durrell to conclude that "most reading difficulties can be prevented by an instructional program which provides early instruction in letter names and sounds, followed by applied phonics and accompanied by suitable practice in meaningful sight vocabulary and aids to attentive silent reading."*

---

*Donald D. Durrell, Ed., "Success In First Grade Reading," Boston University, *Journal of Education*, (February 1958).

Rudisell (49) reports data from a study which compared achievement of children who participated in a planned program emphasizing letter-sound relationships, with the achievement of a matched group which did not receive this instruction. At the end of eight months the experimental group had mean reading achievement and spelling scores which were superior to the mean scores of the control group at the end of sixteen months.

Modality strengths

Recent discussion has focused on the desirability of determining whether a child learns better through exposure to visual or auditory oriented instruction. (59) One theory being that instruction should be geared to the child's strength, Wepman (57) reported that the ability to discriminate speech sounds is influenced by maturational factors and that frequently this skill is not achieved until the child reaches eight years of age. He reported a positive relationship between poor auditory discrimination and poor reading achievement. Wepman suggested that in cases where there are marked differences in visual and auditory discrimination, beginning reading instruction should emphasize the modality in which the learner has developed the most efficiency.

Bateman* separated first graders into two groups, "auditory" and "visual," on the basis of their scores on selected subtests of The Illinois Test of Linguistic Ability. The group that scored highest on the auditory factor were taught by a method that emphasized phonics. The group selected for visual instruction were taught with materials which stressed learning sight words and included a minimum amount of phonics instruction. The auditory group scored significantly higher on reading achievement at the end of grade one than did the visual group.

In evaluating this data, one must keep in mind that in a large number of studies, the subjects were not selected on the criterion noted above. Instructional programs which included systematic phonics resulted in reading achievement that was significantly higher than that reported for programs which included little or no systematic phonics instruction. In regard to modality based instruc-

---

*Barbara Bateman, "The Efficacy of an Auditory and a Visual Method of First Grade Reading Instruction with Auditory and Visual Learners." *Perception and Reading*, Proceedings, International Reading Association, 12, Part 4, 1968, 105–12.

tion, there are several unsettled issues: First, how much of a discrepancy in visual-auditory perception must be present for the difference to be considered significant. Second, in the case of children who are not learning disability cases, would teaching to the weaker modality be as advantageous as teaching to the stronger one? Finally, can children become independent readers without developing *both* visual and auditory discrimination skills.

The normal child's linguistic base

The six-year-old child who has had normal development in understanding and using speech will have acquired one type of proficiency in auditory discrimination. He can distinguish between the pronunciations of words which sound very much alike such as *bath–path, drink–drank, feed–feet*. Although the differences in each pair of examples is caused by interchanging one phoneme (front-middle-last), the child hears each of the words globally.

The fact that a child can make these whole word distinctions is not evidence that he will have equal success in noting the speech-sound representations of letters in printed words. Neither is it assured that he will be able to simultaneously associate sounds with visual letter forms and blend a series of sounds to solve a word he uses orally but which he does not recognize in print.

For instance, assume a child recognizes the printed word *bath* and a number of words which begin with *p* and *l*. He should be able to solve the printed words *path* and *lath*. Some children have trouble making this type of transfer or substitution of speech sounds. After learning the above words, they may fail to note the *ath* combination in *path, bath, lath* is the same sound represented by the *ath* in *athletic*. Fortunately, most children learn these letter sound relationships step by step. If they fail to acquire this skill, they *inevitably* experience difficulty in becoming independent readers.

In the early stages of reading it is possible for a child to learn some "sight words" without noting letter-sound relationships. When he recognizes a word configuration as a whole (cat), he is not forced to translate letter-to-sound and to blend the sounds to arrive at the pronunciation *cat*. However, as more and more word symbols are met, the ability to sound and blend becomes an absolute necessity. For example the following words differ from *cat* in only one letter: *cat, cut, cab, bat, fat, hat, can, cap, car, mat, pat, sat*. These minimal visual differences become harder to detect with the absence of phonics clues.

Pronunciation problems and dialects

Another problem in developing auditory discrimination for speech sounds is faulty pronunciation. An illustration is provided by a third grade boy who read the word *wish* as *woush*. When asked, "What did you call this word?" he responded, "woush." The teacher said, "You mean *wish*, don't you?" He replied, "Sure, that's right, *woush*." The child who repeatedly says *tauk* for *talk*, *with* for *width*, *mus* for *must*, and *excep* for *accept* is laying the foundations for trouble in later work in phonetic analysis as well as in spelling. After a child has said *artic* or *Febuary* fifty to a hundred times, he does not hear *arc tic* or *Feb ru ary*, even if enunciated clearly by another person. A related issue and one that poses considerable difficulty is the linguistic habit of systematically dropping or changing phonemes in oral language usage. This characteristic is frequently found in the speech of several culturally different groups; it is not caused by faulty perception of speech, but rather *is* the speech pattern of these groups. This problem is discussed in more detail in Chapter 3.

Procedures for developing auditory discrimination

The major objective of auditory discrimination activities is to help the child become conscious of speech sounds within words. Specifically, he should become able to recognize the same sound at the beginnings or ends of words, rhyming elements, blended sounds, and the like. The readiness and beginning reading program should provide sufficient experience and drill to assure that every child develops a good foundation in auditory discrimination of speech sounds. Some children will need much more instruction in this area than will others. A few suggestions follow.

Rhyming elements in words

Prior to each exercise, review the concept of rhyming words and explain the activity.

1. *Number rhymes:* Review the number-words from one to ten. Then say, "I will say two words that rhyme. You give me a *number word* that rhymes with these two words:

    1. *Late* and *gate* rhyme with _____. (eight)
    2. *Alive* and *dive* rhyme with _____. (five)
    3. *Sun* and *fun* rhyme with _____. (one)

    4. *Hen* and *pen* rhyme with _____. (ten)
    5. *Do* and *shoe* rhyme with _____. (two)
    6. *Fine* and *mine* rhyme with _____. (nine)
    7. *Store* and *floor* rhyme with _____. (four)
    8. *Free* and *bee* rhyme with _____. (three)
    9. *Sticks* and *mix* rhyme with _____. (six)
   10. *Heaven* and *eleven* rhyme with _____. (seven)

2. *Color-name rhymes:* "Name a color that rhymes with _____."

    1. *Say and day* _____ (gray)
    2. *Said* and *Fred* _____ (red)
    3. *Flew* and *chew* _____ (blue)
    4. *Mean* and *seen* _____ (green)
    5. *Mellow* and *Jello* _____ (yellow)
    6. *Down* and *frown* _____ (brown)
    7. *Fan* and *man* _____ (tan)
    8. *Tack* and *shack* _____ (black)
    9. *Wink* and *drink* _____ (pink)
   10. *Night* and *sight* _____ (white)

3. *Animal-name rhymes:* "Name an animal that rhymes with _____."

    now (cow); *cantelope* (antelope); *trunk* (skunk); *box* (fox); *sat* (cat/rat); *deep* (sheep); *coat* (goat); *fog* (dog/frog); *hair* (bear)

4. *Intonation* and rhyming *elements* may be stressed in jingles and rhyming lines. These usually involve longer language units which also provide experiences for developing *auditory memory*. The example that follows uses number words and calls for children to discriminate the word that is stressed and to complete the statement with a number-word that rhymes with that word.

    a. I saw a number on the *door.*
       The number that I saw was _____.
    b. The snakes I counted in the *den*
       were more than six—I counted _____.
    c. Words like *bee* and *tree* and *see*
       rhyme with good old number _____.

    d. To keep this rhyming game *alive*
        we have to say the number _____.*

Drill on initial sounds in words

1. Explain to the children that you will say some words that begin with the same sound. (At this stage the children do not need to identify the *letter* that represents this initial sound.) Children are then to think of, and say, any word that begins with the same sound as the stimulus words.

*l*ook, *l*ine, *l*ake
*b*ird, *b*at, *b*oat
*m*oney, *m*onkey, *m*an
etc.

2. *Use of children's names.* "Listen to the sound that begins Mike's name—*M*ike. Can you think of any other children's first names which begin with this sound?" (*M*ary, *M*ark, *M*arcia.) The beginning sound should be emphasized but not distorted. The names of different children in the class may be used as stimulus words. Several names beginning with the same letter-sound may be written in a column on the board to provide the child with the visual pattern (letter form) that represents the initial sound.

Sue	Cathy	John	Pat	Herman
Sam	Carl	James	Paul	Helen
Sally	Carol	Jerry	Peggy	Harry

3. *Use of pictures:* Secure a large number of pictures from workbooks, magazines, or catalogues. Select those pictures whose naming words illustrate the sound that is to be taught.

    a. Place several pictures along the chalktray: *b*ird, *t*elevision, *h*ouse. Have volunteers tell which picture name begins with the same sound as stimulus words pronounced orally: *b*oy, *h*at, *t*able.

    b. Select 4 or 5 pictures, all of whose naming words except one begin with the same sound: *b*ird, *b*at, *b*ug, *h*and. A

---

*Arthur W. Heilman and Ann Holmes, *Smuggling Language into the Teaching of Reading.* Columbus, Ohio: Charles E. Merrill Publishing Company, 1972.

volunteer pronounces all of the picture names that begin with the same sound.

   After letter sound relationships have been taught children identify the letter that represents the initial sound: "*b*ird, *b*at and *b*ug all begin with *b*; *h*and begins with *h*."

c. Place in random order on the chalkboard pictures which have been selected so that several of their naming words begin with the same sound: *h*oe, *f*an, *f*ence, (*t*ub), *h*en, (*t*ire), *f*oot, (*t*eeth) *h*orn. Children arrange the pictures into groups according to the initial sound heard in the picture names.

Final sounds in words

The same procedures used for working with initial sounds can be used for teaching discrimination of final sounds in words.

1. Children match or group pictures whose naming words end with the same sound: ne*t*-ba*t*; ma*n*-fa*n*.
2. Pronounce three words, two of which end with the same sound. Pupils repeat the words that end with the same sound: *door*, house, *car*.
3. After letter-sound relationships have been taught, children name or write the letter which represents the final sound heard in picture names or stimulus words spoken orally.

Developing listening skills

In developing listening skills, one deals with a much broader area than auditory discrimination of speech sounds. Listening is involved in every facet of the curriculum and the school is programmed in such a way that children's listening skills must be effective if learning is to take place. Listening is required for following directions, developing and expanding concepts, maintaining discipline, planning curricular activities, and the like. Listening is closely related to many reading behaviors such as utilizing intonation patterns in reading, developing auditory memory, and processing language presented orally in stories or discussion.

   Children differ noticeably in listening ability. Some children come to school with poor listening habits, and others develop inadequate habits early in their school careers. This naturally has an impact on classroom activities and specifically results in impaired learning.

For example, the child who does not use the intonation patterns of English speech in his reading will never enjoy reading in English because his habits will interfere with reading for meaning.

If we judge educators' interest in, and respect for, listening by their statements about its importance, we might conclude that there is a high degree of respect for listening as a means of learning. However, until very recently the research on listening has been meager, despite the fact that during the past decade there has been more research and more writing on listening than in the previous half century. Much of this work is at the college level and has little relationship to children beginning school.

Listening involves more than being physically present and immobile while the teacher is speaking. It is just as important to provide experience-listening if we want learning to take place as it is to provide experience-*reading*. It is inevitable that there will be a great number of learning activities in the school which depend on listening. These include listening to recordings of stories, poetry, and songs; listening to music and acting out what the music suggests; listening to the teacher read stories; participating in speaking-listener situations; and many other experiences which need little explanation. A few exercises which can be used in pre-reading as well as at higher levels are briefly described below.

Identifying sounds

1. Assemble a number of objects which can be used for making distinctive sounds. Examples might include using an egg-beater, bouncing a ball, ringing a small bell, hammering a nail, pouring water from a narrow-neck bottle, ringing an alarm clock, sandpapering wood, pouring water from a pitcher to a glass, using a stapler, etc. Conduct the exercise so that children cannot see the objects being used. After each presentation call on a volunteer to identify the sound.
2. Same idea as above except use a commercial recording or prepare a pre-recorded tape and present it on the tape recorder. Use of the tape recorder permits using a wider range of sounds (birds singing, a train pounding by, a telephone ringing, a bus stopping or starting, cafeteria sounds, playground noises, etc.)
3. Drawing letter forms on chalkboard. For this activity children must be familiar with the letter forms used. They close their eyes or rest their heads on their desks. Using bold

strokes, draw a capital letter on the chalkboard. Children listen to the strokes and volunteer to identify the letter without looking at the chalkboard.

The difficulty level of the task can be varied. The teacher may say, "I am going to make either a capital O or a capital E"; or "I am going to draw either a capital A or a capital M." Later steps can involve giving no clues.

Critical listening

The following activities involve the child in listening to and interpreting language units ranging from single sentences through paragraphs and stories. The learner is called upon to attend, process, retain, and respond to language stimuli.

Critical listening from which to draw conclusions. Here the teacher reads short descriptive passages, and the children are asked to identify or draw a picture of what is described. This technique can be tied in with motor coordination and imagination.

1. I grow outdoors.
   I grow tall.
   In summer I am full
   of leaves. Birds sit
   on my branches and sing.
   What am I?
   Draw a picture of me.

2. People live in me.
   I have windows and doors.
   I come in many different
   sizes and colors.
   Draw a picture of me.

The descriptions the teacher reads can vary in length and complexity, depending on the maturity or age level of the group. These exercises can help teachers discover many things about their pupils such as:

1. Which children can listen effectively and which cannot.
2. Which children are self-sufficient and able to work on their own initiative.
3. Which children are dependent and receive clues from others.
4. Information relative to the degree of maturity of each child.

5. Unusual responses which may suggest other problems needing attention.

Story periods. Practically all children can be held spellbound by a good story well told. When the teacher tells or reads stories, she plants the idea in the children's minds that good listening is the key to enjoyment of the story. Equally important is the fact that she can stress a purpose for listening, whether for enjoyment, for information, for answers to specific questions, or for practice in social living.

Following directions can be used either as a class exercise, with small groups within a class, or with individual pupils. Several short commands are stated and the child, or the group, is to execute them in the order given. The performance will reveal ability to attend to oral directions and the ability to hold these in memory.

Finishing the story provides practice in developing language skills in listening, use of imagination, practice in using language, and expecting logic and meaning from reading. The teacher, while reading a story, interrupts it at a point of high interest and asks the children, "What happens next?"

"Once upon a time Jack went to visit his grandfather and grandmother. They lived on a farm. He went with his father and mother in their car. When they drove up to grandfather's house a big dog rushed out to the car and barked and barked. The boy and his parents had never seen this dog before. Father said '_____.'" (Child finishes story.)

"Jane and Henry were tired of running and playing. They sat down on the porch to rest and talk. Jane said, 'Henry, let's ask mother to make us some lemonade.'

"'Good,' said Henry, 'cold lemonade; I'm so thirsty I could drink three glasses.' They started into the house and Henry said: 'Jane, do you think your mother would make enough lemonade so we could have a lemonade stand and sell lemonade in paper cups?'

"Jane said, '_____.'"

Completing the sentence is a variation of the above in which the child supplies a word which has been omitted. "A big dog came up to the car and _____ at them." "Jim was tired of running. He sat down to _____." This exercise gives practice in listening and in getting meanings from context.

What word disagrees with the picture? While looking at a picture, pupils listen to the teacher as she says a series of four words, one of which could not be logically associated with the picture. Children are then asked to identify the word which does not belong. This can be a challenging game, because children must observe closely, listen carefully, and remember the word while other stimuli are presented.

Retelling a story.   The teacher reads a story or passage to one group who then tell the story to children who have not heard it. This experience motivates children to be good listeners since they must pay attention and comprehend if they are to retell the story successfully.

Emphasizing expression.   The teacher reads a sentence or short passage word by word, without inflection, then reads it with good expression. Pupils are lead to see that how a passage is read affects its interpretation.

Silly sayings.   Read the following or similar sentences one at a time. After each sentence call on a volunteer to explain what is wrong with the sentence and how it might be changed to make sense.

1. Mother cooked the corn in an old shoe.
2. The boys played baseball in the sand box.
3. John turned on the radio to watch a program.
4. The elephant drank water through his ear.
5. Mary read the book from back to front.
6. The man went in the jewelry store and ordered breakfast.

Listen and do.   Prepare a series of commands or tasks. Explain that you will describe a task and will then call on a volunteer to carry it out. Children must listen carefully since they do not know ahead of time who will be called upon.

1. Repeat this sentence: "George Washington was our first President."
2. Come to the front of the room and roar like a lion.
3. Stand up, turn around completely, sit down.
4. Move like an elephant (rabbit, snake, turtle, etc.).
5. Go to the blackboard, make two marks, then erase one of them.

Whisper a sentence.   Whisper a sentence to a child who in turn whispers it to another child, continuing until four or five children have participated. The last child says the sentence aloud. Then determine what changes were made in the message. A number of groups or teams may participate at the same time using the same message.

Visual Factors

Here the teacher must be concerned with two developmental factors: the child's vision as it relates to reading and the task of developing skill in visual discrimination. Steps in acquiring visual discrimination include the visual readiness program, learning to recognize letters and words, mastering a left-to-right sequence, and the like.

Vision

The bulk of all visual work in reading is at close range. The stimulus is about fourteen inches from the eyes. The retinas of both eyes reflect the image seen, in this case word symbols. For proper vision, the tiny images on both retinas must be perfectly synchronized or "fused." If fusion does not take place, the image will be blurred or, in extreme cases, two distinct images will appear. When the stimulus is near the eyes, as in reading a book, the eyes must converge slightly. This convergence is accomplished by muscles in each eye. Any muscular imbalance between the eyes can result in the lack of fusion described above.

Other muscles operate to put pressure on the lens of the eye, which is capable of changing its shape (degree of convexity). This adjustment is essential in order to compensate for differences in the reflected light rays striking the two eyes. The muscular action determining the degree of convexity of the lens is called *accommodation.**

Ruling out the more serious visual defects which prevent the child from seeing printed word symbols, it is difficult, on the basis of published research, to come to a conclusion regarding the precise relationship between visual problems and reading deficiency. However, many educators have warned that the school may be expecting too much physiologically of some children as they begin school and attempt to cope with the tasks the school has prescribed. John Dewey, in about 1898, cautioned that children six years of age were physiologically immature "for more than incidental attention to visual and written language forms." A number of authorities have

---

*For further discussion and illustrations of the structure of the eye, see: William Kottmeyer, *Teachers Guide for Remedial Reading* (Manchester, Mo.: Webster Publishing 1959), pp. 49–64.

suggested deferring the teaching of reading past the age at which it is currently begun. In discussing the relationship between poor vision and reading problems among children between six and eight, one might conclude from research that the problem stems from a lack of maturation, or slow development, of good binocular vision, rather than from actual visual defects. This point of view finds support among investigators in the area of child development who are not primarily concerned with reading behavior.

More recently, Eames (19) has conducted research which he interprets as refuting the "claims that children's eyes are too immature for them to start reading safely at the usual ages of school entrance. Children five years of age were found to have *more* accommodative power than at any subsequent age." Poor visual acuity (near vision) was not found to be a significant factor which would interfere with the child's reading of the usual textbook material.

One of the most common visual problems found among children beginning school is farsightedness (hyperopia). A child with this problem may see quite adequately and pass a far vision test such as the Snellen or be able to read an experience chart at the front of the room, and still be poorly equipped visually to deal with material in a book twelve to fourteen inches from his eyes. Any test of vision which purports to have a relationship to actual reading must include a test of near vision. The farsighted child may be able to compensate by straining eye muscles for short periods of time to correct some refractional problem, but he cannot do this for any great duration without causing strain and fatigue. If the teacher can detect the visually immature child, she may be able to protect him from too much close work.

Teachers are not optometrists

Since it is so obvious that adequate vision is important in reading, it is often suggested that teachers of reading should thoroughly understand the anatomy of the eye and the nature of problems such as myopia, hyperopia, astigmatism, fusion, and strabismus, as well as be proficient in administering tests such as the Snellen, Eames, and Keystone telebinocular.* It might be well for teachers to resist such responsibilities, or at least to question seriously whether they

---

The Snellen Chart, American Optical Co., Southbridge, Mass.; *The Eames Eye Test* (Tarrytown-On-Hudson, N. Y.: World Book Co.); *Keystone Visual Survey Test Telebinocular* (Meadville, Pa.: Keystone View Co.).

should take the time to become proficient in the use of eye charts, audiometers, or the telebinocular. If these devices are available in the school system, a trained person should use them. Elementary school teachers have more than enough to do in today's classrooms without getting involved in these procedures. Furthermore, if the teacher is not expert in the use of these instruments, she may create the illusion that her pupils have been adequately examined, an illusion which could be a serious matter for the child whose diagnosis is faulty. The less the classroom teacher gets involved in this type of diagnosis, the better. The less she gets involved in these matters, the more time she will have for the teaching of reading. The issue here is not whether such a diagnosis should be made, but rather who should make it. The teacher, however, should be alert in detecting vision problems and children with problems should be referred to a vision specialist.

Visual discrimination

By the time he comes to school, a child has had thousands of experiences in seeing and noting likenesses and differences. He has developed the ability to make fairly high-order visual discriminations, in many cases based on relatively small clues. At the age of three years he was able to identify and claim his tricycle from a group of three-wheelers, even though he was not able to tell us the exact criteria he used in this identification. All we do know is that it was a visual discrimination. Later, two coins much the same size but bearing different symbols will not confuse him. The pictured head of a man or woman no larger than a postage stamp will contain enough visual clues for correct identification. Common trademarks are correctly identified on the basis of size, color, and configuration. A pack of playing cards can be sorted correctly as to suit on the basis of visual perception.

The child's need to make fine visual discriminations is self-evident since the symbols which must be read are visual stimuli. Even a cursory examination of words is sufficient to establish that many of them look very much alike. A child who cannot differentiate between the various words in a passage cannot possibly get meaning from that passage. The widely accepted definition that "reading is getting meaning from printed symbols" does, to some degree, slight the sensory skills which are absolutely essential before reading can become "getting the meaning."

There are a number of studies which have attempted to establish the relationship between visual discrimination and achievement in reading. Goins (22) reports a study of first grade children designed to determine (1) the relationship between visual perception and reading ability and (2) whether training in rapid recognition of digits and geometric and abstract figures would aid children in beginning reading achievement. A visual perception test consisting of fourteen subtests was designed. It included no verbal or reading content such as letters or words, but did include numerous items of matching pictures and geometrical figures, completion of geometric designs which had a part missing, finding a reversed picture in a series otherwise identical, and a test of closure in which incomplete pictures were the stimulus and the child identified what was represented by the incomplete drawing.

The total scores of first grade pupils on the visual discrimination test showed a correlation of .49 with reading achievement at the end of grade one. Certain of the visual discrimination subtests showed considerable value in predicting first grade reading achievement. Further, certain of the subtests indicated that among first grade children, poor and good readers appear to be "different types of perceivers." This was particularly true of the ability to achieve "closure" and to keep in mind a particular configuration. The hypothesis was advanced that children who are widely different in these skills possibly should be taught reading by different methods in grade one.

It was found that training with the tachistoscope (flashing digits and figures on a screen for extremely brief exposures) was helpful with good readers in improving *their visual perception of such forms* but that this type of training resulted in no appreciable improvement in reading achievement. (22) Barrett (4) found that visual discrimination factors, namely, the ability to name letters and numbers was the best single predictor of reading achievement at the end of grade one. However, he cautions that the predictive precision of these factors does not warrant their being used exclusively to predict first grade achievement.

Barrett (5) summarized the research which focused on the relationship between visual discrimination measures administered prior to reading instruction and reading achievement at the end of grade one. He reports that studies show that "matching" letters and matching whole words have about the same predictive value. However, children's ability to name letters has a higher predictive value than the ability to match letter or word forms. Shea* tested beginning first graders on visual discrimination-memory of word forms. At mid-year, the subjects were tested on word recognition of those words which had been presented thus far in their basal program. The author reported relatively high relationships between scores on these two measures with the highest predictive value occurring among pupils who scored in the lowest quartile on the mid-year test.

Maturation cannot be hastened, but visual discrimination can be sharpened through experience and practice. The school must provide as much of this experience as is needed, and different children will need different amounts. Fortunately, there are many ready-made exercises which the teacher can use. Reading readiness books provide practice in developing the ability to make finer and finer discriminations. Both reading readiness tests and workbooks can aid the teacher in evaluating the child's progress, provided they are used with diagnosis in mind.

For the child who needs more practice than is provided in these activities, a number of teacher-made exercises can be developed. Such exercises take time to build; therefore, they should be duplicated in quantities and used from year to year. They never become outdated with one class use. One thorough preparation will provide for many pupils who need this particular type of experience.

A few examples of visual discrimination exercises follow. Each example could be developed by the teacher into a full page of work.

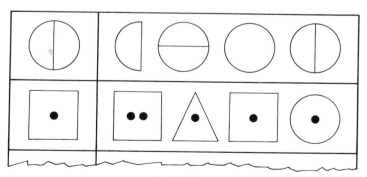

FIGURE 1

Underline the Figure That Is Exactly Like the Sample at the Left.

*Shea, Carol Ann, "Visual Discrimination of Words and Reading Readiness," *The Reading Teacher* (January 1968), 361–67.

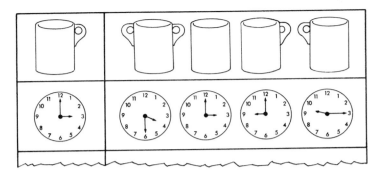

FIGURE 2

Underline the Object That Is Exactly Like the One at the Left.

Teaching letter recognition

Reference has been made to studies which report that the ability to recognize letter forms is the best single predictor of reading achievement at the end of grade one. Further, the ability to discriminate between letter forms is essential for instruction in phonics. If a child cannot discriminate visually between *b* and *p* or *l* and *t*, he will be confused when instructed to associate a particular sound with these letter forms. A few illustrative approaches for teaching and reviewing letter recognition are provided.

After a few letter-forms have been taught at the chalkboard or with flashcards, children may be provided with two or more letter-cards. One letter such as a   e   b is printed on both sides of a card. The group is then invited to "hold up the letter e," then *a*, *b*, etc. As the children's responses are observed, the teacher notes diagnostic clues which become the basis for smaller group or individual practice.

M	N W M Z U
WHO	HOW WON WHO WAH

FIGURE 3

Underline the Letter or Word That Is Exactly Like the One at the Left.

E - - - - - e
  m
  a
	M h
	     f
	     m
		R s
		     r
		     n

H   n
     h
     m
	A a	G g
		     h
		     f

FIGURE 4

Match Capital and Lower Case Letters. Connect Capital and Lower Case Letter Forms With a Line.

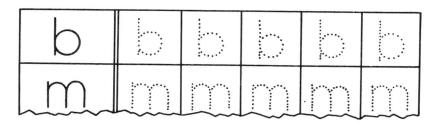

FIGURE 5

Practice Tracing Letter Forms.

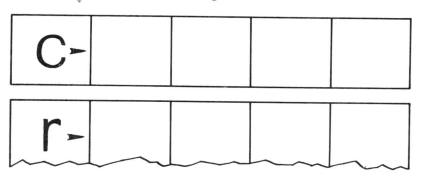

FIGURE 6

Write Letter Forms Using a Visual Model.

shall	Sally	shot	hall	shut
from	frog	flap	fry	free

FIGURE 7

Underline the Beginning of Each Word That Is Exactly Like the Sample.

hat	hit	hot	cat	has
hill	beil	mill	fill	call
ball	fall	pill	call	halt

FIGURE 8

Underline the Ending of Words Which Are Exactly Like the Sample.

a	a small black ant ate it all
l	a small lady led the lads

FIGURE 9

Underline Each Letter in the Sentence Which Is Like the Sample at the Left.

Recognizing words

The objective of the various experiences in the visual readiness program is to prepare the child for making very fine visual discriminations between words which look very much alike. It is as easy for a person who reads to see the difference between *cat* and *dog* as it is for the six-year-old to see the difference between *a* cat and *a* dog. Yet the child beginning to read must very rapidly develop the ability to distinguish between hundreds of written word symbols.

Prior to the use of pre-primers and long after their introduction, most teachers will provide classroom activities aimed at helping children to learn to recognize words. Teachers will employ different methods, but most prefer to teach words related to the child's actual experience. Discussion of the experience method and the use of experience charts is found in Chapter 6, "Beginning Reading." Examples of readiness experiences commonly used to help children in word recognition are briefly described here.

1. *Child's name.* Probably the easiest word to teach a child is his own name. He sees his name on his readiness book and on his pictures and drawings which the teacher displays. In addition, there will be many occasions when the teacher will write pupils' names on the board for birthdays, committees, special assignments, and the like. The child will notice similarities between his own name and other pupils' names and will learn a few words in this manner.

2. *Color names.* To teach color names, large circles cut from solid-color construction paper can be placed on the blackboard or a table. Names of colors are printed on white cards. The pupil selects a card, says the word, and places the color name on the proper colored circle.

3. *Matching words with pictures.* All children in the readiness group are capable of identifying a great number of objects and pictures of objects. Familiar pictures are found and word names are printed on separate cards: *car, swing, duck, cow, house.* Each child selects a word and places it beneath the proper picture.

4. *Objects in classroom.* A word card is made for familiar objects in the classroom such as door, table, window, book, chair. A child selects a word card, shows it to the group, and touches the object.

5. *Following directions.* Words previously studied can be used in "direction sentences" printed on heavy paper or oaktag. A child

selects a sentence, reads it aloud, and does what it suggests: *walk to the door; clap your hands; ask John to stand.*

In any exercise that uses single words as stimuli, the teacher can ask that the word be used in a sentence. As she writes on the board, she pronounces each word and then the whole sentence. Emphasis can be placed on visual clues found in words, on the sentence as a meaning unit, and on left-to-right progression in reading.

Left-to-right sequence

It is important during the readiness period and beginning reading stages that children learn that the eyes move from left to right across the page while reading. There is apparently only one reason why teachers would neglect this skill: they might think that all children have mastered it. It is easy to project this ability onto children because, to adults who have learned to read, the technique appears to be one of the most simple of the procedures which make up reading. It is also true that the majority of children learn the proper sequence without trouble. A child may identify words without realizing that the conventional way to interpret words and sentences is left to right. However, embarking on the next steps in learning to read without having mastered this response can develop other serious and harmful reading habits including reversals, omissions, losing place, and pointing with the finger. This skill should never be taken for granted by the teacher, and "overlearning" it would certainly be justified.

There are a number of ways in which left-to-right sequence can be emphasized. Readiness workbooks contain training exercises calling for a line to be drawn from left to right over a series of dots. Sometimes the point of such an exercise is not grasped if the child fails to relate it to reading. A large square can be drawn on the blackboard with short horizontal lines representing words. The teacher states, "Let's play that this is a page from a book. The heavy little lines are words. Where should I start reading?" Children can draw a line through the "words" moving from left to right. In using experience charts the teacher can demonstrate left-to-right reading with hand or pointer.

Rearranging pictures

This exercise consists of two or more picture cards which tell a story when arranged properly from left to right. The cards are laid out in improper arrangement, and after a child corrects the sequence, he relates the story the cards tell. Telling the story forces him to progress from left to right, note details, see relationships, and organize the material in a logical manner. Figure 10 illustrates two teacher-made series. A pupil's story for each example is given here:

Story A. "The tallest candle should be in the first picture — then it burns down a little and the third picture shows it real small."

Story B. "Mother is baking pies. In the first picture she puts one on the table, then two on the table. In the third picture there are three pies."

A. "The candle is burning."

B. "Mother is baking pies."

FIGURE 10

Language

Reading is a language process. When we read we translate graphic symbols into the language they represent. What we read is not speech written down, but it comes as close to this as the graphic system permits. It is probably impossible to overemphasize the relationships that exist between a child's language facility and learning to read. On the other hand, many instructional programs can and do sleight this relationship. The worst possible outcome of such instruction is that many children will fail to grasp the fact that reading must recreate the melody of language. Such failure will be detrimental to learning to read.

The discussion of language as it relates to reading is discussed in more detail in Chapters 13 and 3, *Developing and Expanding Concepts* and *The Culturally Different Child*. Here the discussion will involve a brief overview of (1) language as a catalyst in social, emotional and mental development; and (2) language and readiness including a few illustrative experiences that might be incorporated into readiness activities.

Language and socialization

The school is very much involved in guiding the social growth of its pupils. In the case of normal children, socialization is almost exclusively built around communication. Up to the time children reach school age, spoken language is the chief means of communication. There is no better tool than language facility for gauging the social needs or social maturity of children. Among the first experiences provided in the modern school's curriculum are those which have to do with social growth. The logic of this is apparent. Many children have had little or no experience in a group as large as that in which they will find themselves upon beginning school. There will be many learning situations which will call for group coherence. Each member of the group will have to follow certain social patterns in order not to disrupt the learning situation for the others in the group.

Gradually, step by step, the teacher moves in the direction of establishing social control within the class so that learning can take place. Whether the teacher structures this control on an authoritarian basis or has the group control evolve out of the group itself, the medium for establishing control will be language. Many group activities in the classroom, if they are to end successfully, will call for cooperation and sharing among pupils. Language is the most important basis for cooperation. Cooperation and sharing help the child grow and develop from a very self-centered organism into a social being. If the process breaks down and the individual, for any reason, does not learn the social rules, or does not within certain limits follow them, his behavior sets him apart from the group. When his peer group reacts to this behavior, he and the group are out of adjustment.

These maladjustments among children beginning school are almost inevitable because some children have further to go in order to live up to the group standards, some learn slowly, and some have learned to use anti-social responses when attempting to satisfy their needs. A teacher who does not perceive the symptoms of maladjustment fairly early may soon have cases of non-affiliation in her class. These can develop rapidly into isolates, or children rejected by the group. The teacher may be the best teacher of reading in the district, but if she lets the security of some children become seriously threatened in the school situation, the odds are that she will not teach them reading. In their unskilled efforts to strike back at threats they do not understand, these pupils may disrupt the learning for others in the group.

Language and emotional adjustment

Clinicians state that language is the most sensitive indicator of maladjustment and psychological needs. The classroom, the playground, in fact the total environment, is one never-ending projective technique if one but heeds the language of children. Both as adults and as teachers, we sometimes learn very little about children from children. This happens when we consciously or unconsciously feel that what children say is not important. The truth of the matter is that their language mirrors their needs, feelings, aspirations, and fears; and if one's job is to help children grow, sensitivity to these is essential.

A child's need for ego satisfaction seems to increase by a geometric ratio in the face of frustration. That is, a little denial of love, attention, and acceptance, or a little threat to self worth and integrity, is reacted to by an increased drive for these goals. If rebuffed, the child seems to redouble his efforts to maintain his prestige and self worth. It is apparent that when children are trying to fulfill ego needs, they invariably use behavior which by adult logic seems ill-conceived and not likely to achieve the child's goal. The child who wants and needs friendship and is rebuffed may resort to the use of aggressive, hostile, or abusive language, perhaps feeling that he can force acceptance or that his language will reduce the stature of those persons to whom it is addressed. Another child, after each failure, may withdraw more and more and make very few language overtures to others in his peer group. This non-use of language is itself a clue which should have diagnostic value for the teacher. Here is a child who has elected to withdraw from the arena, but the fight to salvage his ego will go on within himself. This child, at the moment, poses no problem to the teacher or society, but his response is potentially more dangerous than overt aggression.

Language and mental growth

Psychologists agree that the most valuable insights into the child's mental growth are gained from a study of the development of language facility. A brief though acceptable definition of intelligence is that it is "the ability to do abstract thinking." Stated another way, it is the ability to manipulate in a meaningful manner symbolic materials of which language is our best example. Intelligence itself cannot be measured but is inferred from behavior which can be measured. We measure certain behavior which by agreement is said to be representative of intelligence. The one kind of behavior most universally measured on intelligence tests is language behavior. Our society puts a high value on the ability to use and understand language. The degree of the child's mastery of communication skills determines to a large extent his readiness to do school tasks and to profit from instruction. Although he cannot read, spell, or write when he starts school, he has had years of experience with language. His language proficiency is used as an index of his mental growth, just as it provides data for appraisal of social and emotional growth and adjustment.

Furthermore, when we wish to assess what the student has learned at any grade level, we rely on language usage. Language reveals the number and breadth of concepts acquired. All concepts exist within the framework of some symbolic process and all are arrived at, and refined through, thought processes which in turn depend on the manipulation of language symbols. In other words, a change in language behavior is often the sole criterion of learning.

A society such as we have today could not have evolved without language. It is equally obvious that education would not have developed along the lines it has without language. Language provides a bridge which permits ideas, information, and data to pass between parent and child, teacher and pupil, and child and peer. As an individual masters new forms of language usage, he is developing "mind tools" which he can use from that time forward in the pursuit of knowledge. Reading is our best example of such a tool.

Language development and reading

The role of the school in preparing children for reading begins the first day of school and continues for varying lengths of time for different children. Whatever the school does in the reading readiness period will be done in order to guide each child into being a "good risk" as a beginning reader. The school attempts to structure the situation so that each child will acquire the right combination of abilities, skills, and attitudes. The study of how children acquire language is both interesting and rewarding. The understanding of this process is a prerequisite to planning a curriculum for children or putting it into practice.

Reading readiness is not confined specifically to experiences found on readiness tests. As a child grows and matures in all phases of human growth—intellectual, social, emotional, and physiological—he is growing into reading. Children can "grow" without a professionally planned curriculum. However, the school's function is to provide guidance and direction, to structure learning situations so that certain experiences are likely to result. A program aimed at preparing children for beginning reading is limited only by the facilities and resources of the school and the understanding and creativity of the teacher. A great majority of pre-reading activities can be encompassed under the heading *language.*

The child first develops oral language, acquiring the ability to make sounds in isolation and then in combination. As sounds are combined into words, they become associated with meanings. The range of meaningful language one uses is referred to as *speaking vocabulary.* The child beginning school has a speaking vocabulary of several thousand words. He can say, and has concepts for, a great variety of speech sounds, such as *horse, train, jet, farm, elephant, river.* In addition, he will have some concept for the relationship of *up* to *down, over* to *under, high* to *low, hot* to *cold, dry* to *wet, large* to *small, dark* to *light.* Speech sounds, coupled with the mysteries of meaning, fascinate the child. Some first graders will tend to "talk over their heads," to use speech sounds for which they have not learned meanings. Every child at this age has been exposed to more language than he has absorbed.

It is inevitable that the child will harbor many misconceptions, and come to school with varying degrees of insight into certain concepts. He will probably be vague about *good* and *bad, right* and *wrong, justice, government, God, Heaven,* and *death.* Many decades later, even if he has earned the title of Philosopher, he may still be attempting to develop, extend, and clarify some of these concepts.

Language cuts across every goal and function of the school. Everything that is taught in the school must pass through a communication process before it is learned by a pupil. Excellent books have been written about objectives, the impact of the school's curriculum on our culture, and the factors in our culture which in turn shape the school curriculum. The merits of various curricular philosophies such as the "traditional," "progressive," "integrated," and "core" are often debated. In these debates the point is sometimes overlooked that the real function of the school is to provide children with guidance in developing concepts. Our schools at all levels rely heavily on reading as the means of building and extending these concepts in all subject areas.

No matter how the curriculum is organized, the school can do no more than guide and direct the development of concepts. Therefore, the debate must center on *what* concepts, *when* to teach them, and *how* best to teach them. The effectiveness of any curriculum cannot be judged by the statements in the curriculum guide, but rather by the learning which takes place in the classroom.

Individuals learn and use language skills in social, cultural, emotional settings. The teacher is expected, and to some degree is trained, to become cognizant of, and concerned with, all facets of human growth and development — physical, social, emotional, and intellectual. The one reason why the school *must* be concerned is that these factors influence learning.

Over and above what the child's language usage can tell the teacher about all aspects of his development is the relationship of previous language experiences to the specific learning task called *reading*. Skillful, effective teaching of beginning reading is based on the teacher's understanding:

1. That reading is related to all language functions found in the curriculum.
2. That learning to read is related to, and built upon, past language experiences.
3. That learning to read should be a natural outgrowth of these past language experiences.
4. That learning to read is a developmental process that involves years of guided study.
5. That different methods of teaching reading may be justified, but the one criterion a method should meet is that it builds logically and systematically.

It is important for teachers who are preparing children for reading to be aware of the experiences and growth which have taken place during the pre-school years. The range of previous experiences among first grade children is tremendous. Some children will have had many pleasant experiences with books and with parents who read to them frequently. They will be able to identify the duck, the owl, the moose, the pony, the baby bear, or the tug boat and tell what each is doing in a picture, having learned to find meaning in pictures. Some children will be able to recite almost word for word certain of their favorite stories. Others will have a surprisingly large stock of concepts derived from viewing television, from travel, or from contact with adults. On the other hand, some children will have been read to rarely if at all. A limiting home environment will undoubtedly be reflected in a child's language usage and stock of concepts.

The curriculum of the first grade must be related to the child's previous development since what is done in the classroom must of necessity be built on previous experience. Even before the child begins to read, the numerous activities included in the curriculum are related to reading. This relationship is easy to see in such activities as hikes, excursions, field trips, bulletin boards, stories read by teachers, and the like. But other activities, such as drawing, painting, rhythm, sharing periods, planning periods, play, and problem-solving, are also related. All are bound together with language and communication; all involve developing and extending concepts. Each of these in turn is fixed by word symbols. Reading is an extension of the communicative process which involves learning the printed equivalent for the known spoken symbols.

There are certain differences between the language experiences which children have before coming to school and those they encounter early in the school situation. The first new adjustment will be using speech in groups larger than those in which the child has thus far participated. More speech responses will have to be inhibited, since the child will have to share talking time with so many others. His pre-school language was probably more ego-involved than will be acceptable in school. Here the speaker must consider his listeners or lose them. The pre-schooler can flit from topic to topic; his response need not dovetail with what has just been said by another. However, in the group discussion in the classroom, there is usually a central topic, and the children must gradually learn to follow a discussion and to build logically on what has been said previously. (29)

Learning to read is probably one of the most important accomplishments that the child will achieve during his formal schooling. This is not to imply that learning to read will be his most difficult or dramatic academic achievement, for if he gets off to a good start the whole process may be so uneventful that he will not recall how this particular learning took place. On the other hand, if he fails in reading, the frustrations and defeats which can beset him in the future are so numerous and varied that they have never been tabulated in one source. Thus, the experiences which the school arranges for children prior to launching into the formal teaching of reading are extremely important.

Programs of instruction designed to develop children's language should differ considerably from classroom to classroom. Activities which are suitable for some children will be unnecessary for others. If one were to recommend that a particular program be adopted for all children, this would negate what is known about individual differences. The following discussion suggests a limited number of activities which are illustrative of approaches which might have merit in certain situations.

Language experiences

There are many types of experiences which the school arranges so that skill in language and communication will be developed as rapidly as possible. Some of these tasks may at first seem unrelated to teaching reading. However, they involve skills used in reading, such as perception in noting details and making comparisons, extending the span of attention, learning to see relationships between events, and drawing inferences. What follows is a representative but not exhaustive list of such experiences:

1. Coloring, cutting, pasting
2. Working a jigsaw puzzle
3. An excursion to observe animals:
   a. at a farm
   b. at a zoo
4. Listening to musical records. "Do what the music tells you."
5. Listening to the teacher read a story
6. Celebrating birthdays
7. Bringing pets to the classroom — parakeet, puppy, duck, rabbit
8. Gathering leaves
9. Discussing the seasons
10. Growing a sweet potato in a glass of water
11. Using a medicine dropper. How can it pick up water?
12. Imitating sounds of animals — rooster, horse, dog, cat, frog

13. Learning what objects float — wide-mouthed gallon jar and numerous objects
14. Discussing the eating habits of different animals — cow, chicken, fish, frog
15. Taking an excursion to observe different occupations — to a bakery, a dairy, a farm
16. Planning a party (experience chart)
17. Flying a kite. Why does it fly?
18. Using a balance (scale)
19. Observing animals that can swim — fish, frog, duck
20. Using an electric fan with a home-made weather vane
21. Going on a nature hike. Turn over a fair-sized rock — Why is it damp underneath? Why do we find worms here?
22. Pouring water from quart jar into funnel. Why does the funnel run over?
23. Watching plants grow (outside garden or inside window box)
24. Planning an excursion and making an experience chart
25. Using clay, fingerpaints, colored paper, pictures, objects to express ideas

All of these experiences involve the senses. It should be remembered that as the child matures, sensory impressions are automatically translated into language equivalents and are the basis for all learning. When the child feels the turtle's shell, he translates the sensation into language symbols. A duck is how a duck looks, how it swims, how it quacks, how it waddles, and how it eats. A concept of the wind grows out of sensory perceptions of paper blowing across a yard, sand or grit against one's face, a hat blown off, and trees and bushes bending. This process, like reading, is developmental in nature and illustrates how concepts evolve and develop.

"Show and Tell"

A technique used frequently to help children develop language facility and extend concepts is "show and tell," or sharing periods. The child brings something to school or makes something in school which he thinks may be of interest to the group. Since he is familiar with the object, even the shy child can tell something about it. Attention is focused on the object rather than on the child and his speaking. This has psychological value for those children who fear speaking to the group. It is a situation that can be kept concrete.

"I brought a box full of my rocks. I want to show you some of the ones I like. I collect these when we go on trips. This one is quartz. This one has iron in it. It's heavy. You can see the iron in it. These rocks are very smooth. They came from Lake Michigan. The waves rub the rocks with sand. They get smooth and round."

Precise descriptions with full explanations of processes and smooth transitions may be lacking, but communication has taken place, self-confidence has been strengthened, status has been enhanced. The speaker is asked some questions, and he answers with considerable poise. The teacher compliments him on his fine talk. He senses that when he has something interesting to tell, others will listen. "Show and tell" can be a very ego-satisfying experience for children.

Not all children will be successful. Some will have a difficult time even stating what they are showing the group. The teacher is the only hope of salvaging something from such a situation. A question at the right moment may possibly evoke a response. The tone of voice in which the question is asked will condition the group's reaction to the speaker. A child who cannot speak successfully to the entire class may be able to speak to a smaller group, but this can come about only if the teacher perceives the child's problem and structures the situation so that he participates.

"Show and tell" experiences can contribute much to the child's social and language development, but there are some pitfalls which must be avoided if this practice is to contribute its maximum to children's growth. Some teachers use the "show and tell" period as a means of obtaining a little time for their daily administrative chores. They call on youngsters and try to give the impression that they are avidly interested, but they actually are filling out attendance reports, checking lunch money, tabulating returns from a P.T.A. questionnaire which the children brought from home, setting up schedules for parents' conferences, and so forth.

Another factor which can detract from the effectiveness of this practice is the unequal distribution of experiences. Unless the teacher keeps some record, certain children will monopolize the "show and tell" periods while others will rarely have an opportunity to contribute. This may result in a neglect of those who need the experience most. The shy, unsure child is not likely to volunteer, although he may have come to class with some object in his pocket about which he had hoped to talk.

An illustration of this tendency is provided by an experienced teacher who checked back on the past week's activity in the sharing period and found that she had inadvertently been calling on the most persistent volunteers and more or less ignoring some of the other children. Figure 11 sets down her data for the most-called-on five children and the least-called-on in the "show and tell" period. Even if we assume some inaccuracy due to faulty memory, the data are suggestive of how easy it is to let some children develop habits of non-participation.

Pupil	1	2	3	4	5		26	27	28	29	30
Mon.	P		P	P							
Tues.	P	P		P	P			P			
Wed.	P	P	P				P				
Thurs.	P	P		P	P				P		
Fri.	P	P	P		P						

FIGURE 11

A Teacher's Retrospective Record of the Five Students Who Participated Most and the Five Who Participated Least in One Week's "Show and Tell" Activities. The Symbol P Indicates Participation.

Conversation groups

Dividing the class into conversation groups is another method of helping children acquire facility in using language. The advantage in this device is that more children can participate in a given period of time and the teacher can spend more time with the group that most needs her guidance. However, the children must have developed the ability to cooperate with and respect others in order for this method to be effective.

Other means of practicing language usage that are more or less self-explanatory include:

Telling a story (not about self)
"My pet . . . ."
"We took a trip to . . . ." (Either a group experience or an individual child's experience)
"I have a riddle"
"My three wishes are . . . ."
"Who am I describing?" (A child in class or a well-known person)

Discussing trips and excursions

Discussion of class trips or excursions to a farm, the zoo, a dairy, or the airport will result in some learning for all of the children who participate. Children differ in the amount they learn and in the degree of thoroughness with which they form certain concepts because of differences in previous experience and sensory perceptions. They cannot all have the same experiences when they are visiting the same farm, zoo, market, or TV station. Therefore, visiting these interesting places is not the only important phase of the total experience. Equally important is the planning which tells the child what to look for and the discussion which follows the excursion. This discussion can extend partial concepts or clear up hazy concepts. Here again, the teacher can structure these sharing experiences so that all children become involved. The shy child or the one who will have only a limited contribution can often be called on early in the discussion. This precaution assures that their ideas will not have been advanced before they have an opportunity to speak.

Contact with books, stories, and pictures

A child may come to school with an interest in learning to read, and this interest may grow or it may be inhibited by school experience. Most children particularly enjoy a well-told story in school.

After hearing the story, a picture of some dramatic incident in the story can be used to focus discussion and comment or to enhance understanding. One important way to arouse interest in reading is to instill the feeling that the reading itself is a key to the resulting pleasure.

It is very important that the child have access to numerous books. The actual handling of books, turning pages, studying pictures, and the like, are an important part of readiness for reading. Most basal reader series contain good art work, are colorful, emphasize the story approach, and hold the student's interest until he moves on to the next higher level. However, in the case of a poor reader, the continued, uninterrupted diet of one or two books can color attitudes toward reading. The teacher and the school must assume responsibility for having available numerous good supplementary books at various reading levels.

Using pictures

The use of pictures is an excellent method of drawing children to books. A picture illustrating a familiar story may give the child a sense of security. On the other hand, a picture illustrating a story new to the child may be so exciting that he will want to hear the story. If the teacher has made it clear that she will, on occasion, read stories selected by pupils, the child will have an added incentive to seek and find a "good story." If the class enjoys "his story," he will experience keen satisfaction that will be associated with the reading process; at the same time, he will reinforce the knowledge that he can get "meaning" from pictures. After selecting a picture illustrating an unknown story, the child can be invited to tell what he thinks the story will be. Using this technique, the teacher can get some measure of the child's creative ability and his language facility. The use of pictures can help develop various other needed skills such as visual discrimination, attention to detail, and extension of concepts.

Summary

Learning to read is an extension of language skills which the child has already developed. Yet reading calls for several skills which are very much different from those previously learned. Specific examples include visual discrimination of letters and word forms, auditory discrimination of speech sounds within words, association of printed letters with the sounds they represent, and the blending of a number of letter sounds to arrive at the pronunciation of words in one's oral vocabulary, but which are not known as sight words. Failure to make adequate progress in these skills will inevitably slow or disrupt the entire developmental process of reading. Despite the importance of these factors, preparing for reading involves many other skills and capacities. Growing into reading is part of the child's total growth pattern. Certainly social-emotional factors are the key to success or failure in beginning reading for some children. These factors are not measured on reading readiness tests, and possibly this may be one reason why the predictive value of these tests is not higher.

The readiness period should not be thought of as ending with a calendar date or dealing with a limited number of specific skills measured by readiness tests. The length of the readiness period should vary for different children, since no pre-determined school schedule could possibly fit all children's development. The readiness program does not attempt to remove individual differences among pupils. It does give the school the opportunity to work with children who have deficiencies in skills which are believed to be important to progress in reading. No part of the readiness period should be thought of as a waiting period. Preparing for reading implies activity on the part of the child and a deliberate structuring of experiences on the part of the school.

Concern for a child's readiness to read is highly justifiable. Expecting a child to read before he is ready violates an important principle of teaching reading. The chief aim of the readiness period is to assure that children get off to a good start in learning to read. Experiencing failure in the early stages of learning to read can lead to attitudes which have far-reaching influence on later development.

YOUR POINT OF VIEW?

What is the basis for your agreement or disagreement with each of the following propositions?

1. American schools' emphasis on reading readiness is more apparent than real. The concept of readiness is verbally embraced, but a large number of pupils are subjected to reading instruction before they are ready.

2. The school provides readiness activities in order to assure that all pupils have a common experience background on which to build future instruction.

3. Reading readiness tests could also be defined as intelligence tests.

4. The extent to which pictures are used in beginning reading materials is unsound since some children form the habit of depending on the picture clues rather than mastering sight words.

5. Language usage is the best single indicator of a child's mental ability.

6. Readiness scores of pupils from culturally/economically depressed backgrounds can be expected to be low. The readiness experiences which the school traditionally provides are inappropriate for this group of children.

7. Teaching children to listen is, in general, neglected in the American elementary school.

BIBLIOGRAPHY

1. Annesley, Fred, Fred Odhner, Ellen Madoff, and Norman Chansky, "Identifying the First Grade Underachiever," *Journal of Educational Research* (July–August 1970), 459–462.

2. Austin, Mary C., et al., *The Torch Lighters: Tomorrow's Teachers of Reading.* Cambridge: Harvard University Press, 1961.

3. Bagford, Jack, "Reading Readiness Scores and Success In Reading," *Reading Teacher* (January 1968), 324–328.

4. Barrett, Thomas C. "Visual Discrimination Tasks as Predictors of First Grade Reading Achievement," *Reading Teacher* (January 1965), 276–83.

5. _____, The Relationship Between Measures of Pre-Reading Visual Discrimination and First Grade Reading Achievement: A Review of the Literature, *Reading Research Quarterly* (Fall 1965), 51–75.

6. Betts, Emmett Albert, "Reading: Perceptual Learning," *Education* (April–May 1969), 291–297.

7. Bing, Lois B. "Vision and Reading," *Reading Teacher* (March 1961), 241–44.

8. Blakely, W. Paul, and Erma M. Shadle, "A Study of Two Readiness-for-Reading Programs in Kindergarten," *Elementary English* (November 1961), 502–6.

9. Bougere, Marguerite Bondy, Selected Factors in Oral Language Related to First-Grade Reading Achievement, *Reading Research Quarterly* (Fall 1969), 31–58.

10. Bond, Guy L. and Robert Dykstra, "The Cooperative Research Program in First-Grade Reading Instruction," *Reading Research Quarterly* (Summer 1967), 5–142.

11. Bremer, Neville, "Do Readiness Tests Predict Success in Reading?" *Elementary School Journal* (January 1959), 222–24.

12. Dechant, Emerald V. *Improving the Teaching of Reading* (2nd ed.), Englewood Cliffs, N. J.: Prentice-Hall, Inc., 1970, Chapters 6 and 7.

13. Duggins, Lydia A. *Developing Children's Perceptual Skills in Reading*. Wilton, Conn.: Mediax, Inc., 1968.

14. Duker, Sam, "Listening and Reading," *Elementary School Journal* (March 1965), 321–30.

15. Durrell, Donald D. and Helen A. Murphy, "The Auditory Discrimination Factor in Reading Readiness and Reading Disability," *Education* (May 1953), 556–60.

16. Dykstra, Robert, "Auditory Discrimination Abilities and Beginning Reading Achievement," *Reading Research Quarterly* (Spring 1966), 5–34.

17. _____, "The use of Reading Readiness Tests for Prediction and Diagnosis: A Critique," in *The Evaluation of Children's Reading Achievement*, T. C. Barrett (ed.). Newark, Del.: International Reading Association, 1967, 35–51.

18. _____, "Summary of Second-grade Phase of the Cooperative Research Program in Primary Reading Instruction," *Reading Research Quarterly* (Fall 1968), 49–70.

19. Eames, Thomas H. "Physical Factors in Reading," *Reading Teacher* (May 1962), 427–32.

20. Espenschade, Anna S. and Helen M. Eckert, *Motor Development*. Columbus, Ohio: Charles E. Merrill Publishing Co., 1967.

21. Gates, A. I. "The Necessary Mental Age for Beginning Reading," *Elementary School Journal* (March 1937), 497–508.

22. Goins, Jean Turner, *Visual Perceptual Abilities and Early Reading Progress*. Chicago: University of Chicago Press, Supplementary Educational Monographs no. 78, 1958.

23. Henderson, Edmund H. and Barbara H. Long, "Correlations of Reading Readiness Among Children of Varying Backgrounds," *The Reading Teacher* (October 1968), 40–44.

24. Henig, Max S. "Predictive Value of a Reading Readiness Test and of Teacher Forecasts," *Elementary School Journal* (September 1949), 41–46.

25. Hester, Kathleen B. "A Study of Phonetic Difficulties in Reading," *Elementary School Journal* (November 1942), 171–73.

26. Hildreth, Gertrude H. "The Role of Pronouncing and Sounding in Learning to Read," *Elementary School Journal* (November 1954), 141–47.

27. Hillerich, Robert L. "Kindergartners Are Ready! Are We?" *Elementary English* (May 1965), 569–74.

28. Hilliard, G. H. and Eleanor Troxell, "Informational Background as a Factor in the Reading Readiness Program," *Elementary School Journal* (December 1937), 255–63.

29. Johnson, Lois V. "Group Discussion and the Development of Oral Language," *Elementary English*, XXXIII (1956), 496–99.

30. Karlin, Robert, "The Prediction of Reading Success and Reading Readiness Tests," *Elementary English* (May 1957), 320–22.

31. King, Ethel M. and Siegmar Muehl, "Different Sensory Cues as Aids in Beginning Reading," *Reading Teacher* (December 1966), 163–68.

32. Koppman, Patricia S. and Margaret H. LaPray, "Teacher Ratings and Pupil Reading Readiness Scores," *Reading Teacher* (April 1969), 603–608.

33. Lee, J. M., W. W. Clark, and D. M. Lee, "Measuring Reading Readiness," *Elementary School Journal* (May 1934), 656–66.

34. Linehan, Eleanor B. "Early Instruction In Letter Names and Sound As Related to Success in Beginning Reading," *Journal of Education* (February 1968), 44–88.

35. Lundsteen, Sara W. "Critical Listening: An Experiment," *Elementary School Journal* (March 1966), 311–16.

36. McGinitie, Walter H. "Evaluating Readiness for Learning To Read: A Critical Review and Evaluation of Research," *Reading Research Quarterly* (Spring 1969), 396–410.

37. McKee, Paul, *Reading: A Program of Instruction for The Elementary School.* Boston: Houghton Mifflin Company, 1966, Chapters 1 and 3.

38. Miller, Wilma H. "Some Aspects of Visual Perception and Reading," *Education* (November–December 1969), 115–117.

39. Mitchell, Blythe C. "The Metropolitan Readiness Tests as Predictors of First Grade Achievement," *Educational and Psychological Measurement* (Winter 1962), 765–72.

40. Morphett, Mabel V. and Carleton Washburne, "When Should Children Begin to Read?" *Elementary School Journal* (March 1931), 496–503.

41. Mortenson, W. Paul, "Selected Pre-reading Tasks, Socio-economic Status and Sex," *The Reading Teacher* (October 1968), 45–49.

42. Mulder, Robert L. and James Curtin, "Vocal Phonic Ability and Silent Reading Achievement: A First Report," *Elementary School Journal* (November 1955), 121–23.

43. Newman, Robert E. "The Kindergarten Reading Controversy," *Elementary English* (March 1966), 235–40.

44. Olson, Arthur, "School Achievement, Reading Ability, and Specific Visual Perception Skills in the Third Grade," *Reading Teacher*, 19 (1966), 490–492.

45. Pratt, Willis E. "A Study of the Differences in the Prediction of Reading Success of Kindergarten and Non-Kindergarten Children," *Journal of Educational Research* (March 1949), 525–33.

46. *Reading Teacher* (October 1968). Entire issue devoted to reading readiness.

47. Robinson, Helen M. "Factors which Affect Success in Reading," *Elementary School Journal* (January 1955), 263–69.

48. Rose, Florence C. "The Occurrence of Short Auditory Memory Span among School Children Referred for Diagnosis of Reading Difficulties," *Journal of Educational Research* (February 1958), 459–64.

49. Rudisill, Mabel, "Sight, Sound, and Meaning in Learning to Read," *Elementary English* (October 1964), 622–30.

50. Scott, Ralph, "Perceptual Readiness as a Predictor of Success In Reading," *The Reading Teacher* (October 1968), 36–39.

51. Sister M. Edith, C.S.F.N. "Developing Listening Skills," *Catholic School Journal* (February 1964), 72.

52. Spache, George D. and Evelyn B. Spache, *Reading In the Elementary School* (Second Ed.). Boston: Allyn and Bacon, Inc., 1969.

53. Stanchfield, Jo M. "Development of Pre-Reading Skills in an Experimental Kindergarten Program," *The Reading Teacher* (May 1971), 699–707.

54. Tinker, Miles A. and Constance B. McCullough, *Teaching Elementary Reading* (Third Ed.). New York: Appleton-Century Crofts, 1968.

55. Vernon, M. D. "Ten More Important Sources of Information on Visual Perception In Relation To Reading," *Reading Teacher* (November 1966), 134–135.

56. Washburne, Carleton, "Individualized Plan of Instruction in Winnetka," *Adjusting Reading Programs to Individuals*, Wm. S. Gray, (ed.). Chicago: University of Chicago Press, 1941, 90–95.

57. Wepman, Joseph M. "Auditory Discrimination, Speech, and Reading," *Elementary School Journal* (March 1960), 325–33.

58. Witkin, Belle Ruth, "Auditory Perception-Implications For Language Development," *Journal of Research and Development In Education* (Fall 1969), 53–71.

59. Wolpert, Edward M. "Modality and Reading: A Perspective," *The Reading Teacher* (April 1971), 640–43.

5

Beginning Reading

PART I

In order to understand the problems and pressures facing the school in regard to beginning reading instruction, one has to understand the educational milieu in which this instruction takes place. Recent trends in American education have been influenced by several factors which include: sweeping changes in the curriculum of most subject fields, a tendency to force subject-content downward in the grades, and widespread criticism of reading instruction, particularly beginning instruction. These and other changes are forcing the school to reexamine how children are being taught to read.

The designers of various "new curriculums" in content areas have, in general, been experts in a given subject area such as mathematics, the sciences, or social studies. Curricular materials in these areas have usually been developed with primary concern for content and sequence — *what* to include and *where* to teach it. There has been less than adequate consideration of the learner and his readiness for the prescribed experiences. Since there is a consensus that the content of the new curriculums is "good," the question is not raised as to "good for whom."

The grade placement of materials in the subject areas is based on an a priori assumption that the would-be learners will have mastered a certain level of reading ability which is commensurate with the demands of the materials. It would be relatively simple to design textbooks and related materials if this assumption held, but it does not hold. The question we face today is whether we can have a "good" program in science, mathematics, and the social sciences if we base our judgment only on the content of these courses and do not consider the learners' ability to "mine" these materials.

The point has been raised that the upgrading of subject curriculums has resulted in the inclusion of many reading activities which are beyond the capabilities of many students found in the various grades. Our quest for excellence has resulted in a curriculum which is better suited to the more capable students. The student with average or less than average ability is pressured more than taught. Yet, the school continues to embrace the philosophy that every child should be taught at his level; and our schools continue to enroll all youth.

Objectives of
Beginning Reading Instruction

Regardless of the materials one elects to use in beginning reading, the goals of this level of instruction would be much the same. Instruction will focus on a number of specific skills which are related to the larger long-term goal of producing facile and critical readers. It is understandable that the teaching of a process as complicated as beginning reading will include many objectives, some of which have been dealt with in previous discussions: to structure experiences so that the child feels accepted and develops desirable attitudes toward reading and toward self; to provide for group participation, development of verbal facility, listening ability, and auditory and visual discrimination; to teach left-to-right sequence; and to encourage contact with books, stories, and pictures. Despite the fact that these activities are very appropriate in the reading readiness program, it is apparent that the teacher must not neglect any of these goals when instruction in reading becomes more formal.

The main objective in beginning instruction is to arouse and sustain the child's interest in reading. When this is achieved he becomes ego-involved in reading. Achieving the following objectives is crucial if the child's ego is to be kept harnessed to the reading task. Experiences must be provided so that beginning readers:

1. Expand their sight-recognition vocabulary.
2. Master letter-sound relationships.

3. Understand that printed words are made up of letters. These letters represent speech sounds that must be blended to arrive at the pronunciation of printed words that are not recognized.
4. Develop the necessary visual and auditory discrimination skills that are needed for these code-cracking activities.
5. Grasp the fact that reading is a meaning making process; that meaning is conveyed in sentence units; and one arrives at meaning by supplying the intonation patterns that recreate the melody of spoken language.
6. Practice oral language usage and understand that reading is working with language.
7. Develop and expand concepts noting that ideas are expressed through language.
8. Learn that some words have many different meanings and that the various meanings are "signaled" by context clues.
9. Develop critical thinking through experiences which sharpen both critical listening ability and analysis of printed messages.
10. Gradually acquire independent work habits.
11. Progress smoothly in the mastery of the mechanics of reading such as heeding punctuation, reducing the number of regressions, and combining words into phrases.

These and other goals can be achieved when the results of individual on-going diagnosis are used as a blueprint for instruction. Obviously, some provision will have to be made for individual and small group instruction to assure that teaching becomes flexible and meaningful.

Defining Reading

It is difficult to understand why, with all the available written material on *reading* and all the efforts expended in teaching it, that there is no universally accepted definition of reading. Everyone who reads is sure he knows what reading is. It is only when he attempts to put his understanding into a definition that the ambiguity becomes apparent. The question of "what is reading" is of little consequence to the man in the street, bookstore proprietor, editor of the local paper, or the community's most successful professional writer. However, one's concept of what reading is would seem to be of considerable importance to the person whose primary task is to teach reading. With this as justification, the following - discussion is included in this book on teaching reading. A brief restatement of a few premises is necessary.

1. Language is oral, and to use language one must string together a number of speech sounds in a limited number of "patterns." The structure of a given language dictates what patterns are acceptable.
2. A graphic representation of English has been developed so that anything spoken in English can be "written" using 26 letter characters.
3. In any alphabetic language, of which English is one example, the graphic letter symbols stand for the same speech sound in thousands of different words. In English this correspondence between letter seen and sound represented is rather imperfect for certain letters and letter combinations.

Ab se bo sem fleebat is a series of speech sounds frequently heard in English, but to speak the above with *any* of several intonation patterns would not meet the requirement of language usage. One important criterion of language is missing. There has been no agreement as to the meaning of those speech sounds in the order found here.

1. Anyone who speaks English can "say" the sounds represented in the opening line of this paragraph.
2. Anyone who can read English can _____ that material.

What word belongs in the blank space? After considerable deliberation, the word you decide upon can well provide insight into *your* definition of reading.

If *ab se bo sem fleebat* happened to be the graphic representation of an utterance found in the English language, one could not "read" it unless he knew or could discover what spoken words were represented by the graphic symbols. The potential reader might:

1. Know each printed word symbol as a sight word.
2. Recognize some words at sight and analyze letter sounds in others until he "hits" upon the pronunciation of each of the printed word symbols.

3. Assign intonation patterns which at least approximate those which would be acceptable in oral English usage.

Would he also, in order to qualify as a reader, have to ascribe particular meanings to each word symbol as well as to the "total word combination?"

A third grader had just been asked to interpret this sentence, " 'I will sample your wares,' said the traveler." Following the child's response, the teacher said in a kindly voice, "John, I believe you read that wrong — the traveler was going to *buy* something from the peddler, not *sell* him something." The point of this illustration is that the teacher had not heard John read the sentence in question, yet she said, "I believe you *read* it wrong."

A further insight might be gained by reference to another sentence in English. "As face answereth face in water so the heart of man speaketh to man." Many primary-level readers could read aloud (i.e., pronounce) each word in this passage, but many of these same children could not arrive at an understanding of its meaning. (In essence, no further context is needed.) A school curriculum committee examining a science or social science text which contained many concepts at the difficulty level of this example would agree that, "This book is too difficult for third graders to read." Few, if any, critics of this position would counter with "most third graders can recognize the words in this book. I recommend it be adopted."

The following are English sentences. Anyone who reads English will have no trouble with word recognition or intonation:

1. "No square has four sides."
2. "Thomas Jefferson was a friend of tyranny."

These sentences, like all reading situations, demand reader interaction. The person reading "No square has four sides" might react in any of a number of ways: "This is a misprint — it should say, *all* squares have four sides. No, maybe that's not the kind of square it means; Michael Philbutt is a square and he doesn't have four sides. No, that's not what it means. Now a square is a plane figure, but it has a front and back, or does it have a back side? That's either five or six sides. What is the author talking about? Well, no matter what he means, I don't see how he can say that no square has four sides. Maybe this is one of those trick statements. I better read another paragraph or two. If that doesn't help, I'll ask someone."

In sentence 2, a reader with no background knowledge about Jefferson might reason, "Well, it's good to be apprised of this man's character. I'll be suspicious of everything he says or writes, particularly about government and people's rights." With any degree of historical background, however, one immediately says, "How ridiculous! Who is writing this stuff; where was this book published? I better read a little more, this might be a misprint. Didn't Jefferson say, 'I have sworn eternal hostility to every form of tyranny over the mind of man?' This statement is weird."

While the above discussion has not provided a specific definition of reading, it has attempted to put the two essentials, decoding and arriving at meaning, in proper perspective. Recognizing, or distinguishing between, printed word symbols is an absolutely necessary prerequisite for reading. But the mere pronunciation of words is not reading until this act of recognition evokes meaning(s) which the written words-in-combination carry in oral language usage.

There are simpler concepts as to what the reading process involves. A number of these concepts, however, fail to take into consideration the interdependent relationship between word recognition and word meaning. Teachers of reading, as well as of other school subjects, must understand the complex nature of reading. Accepting a definition which is too simple can easily result in overemphasis on one facet of the learning process.

Learning a Symbol System

In order that we may partially recapture the challenge of learning a symbolic process like reading, let us look at a number of familiar symbols and a number which are new. On the left of the list below are pairs of short word-symbols which are very much alike. For an adult it is extremely simple to distinguish between them. On the right are the same word symbols built from a different alphabet which at this point is unknown to the reader. The new word symbols

thin	than
play	plan
some	same

are no more alike than the words on the left, but it is much more difficult to distinguish between them.

The unknown symbols on the right are actually easier to learn than the ones on the left for these reasons:

1. All letters are composed of three or fewer straight lines.
2. The lines are always horizontal or vertical (no slanting lines like *A, X, K, M;* no curved lines like *S, C, U;* no combinations of straight and curved lines like *D, B, P,* etc.).
3. The first thirteen letters of this alphabet are composed of long horizontal lines and short vertical lines and the last

Symbol	Letter	Symbol	Letter
──	A			N
═	B	‖	O
≡	C	‖‖	P
L	D	┐	Q
L	E	┤	R
⊥	F	╡	S
⌐	G	⌐	T
⌐	H	╛	U
┌	I	Γ	V
┌	J	F	W
⊤	K	┣	X
┐	L	L	Y
┐	M	┗	Z

FIGURE 12

Passage A

(symbols)

Passage B

(symbols)

thirteen letters are composed of long vertical and shorter horizontal lines.

This new alphabet, with its equivalent in English, is found in Figure 12 on page 169.

Two short reading passages using this new symbol system are presented below Figure 12. The purpose is not to present a situation precisely analogous to beginning reading, since the reader will have to study the new alphabet in Figure 12 prior to reading. Attempting to read the passages will illustrate the difficulty of mastering a symbolic task in which the symbols are unknown. In this respect, the task is similar to beginning reading.

There are eleven different letter symbols and twelve word symbols in Passage A. Among the twelve words there are only six different words. Thus the vocabulary was carefully controlled. All of these words are found in the first few pages of pre-primers and have been used thousands of times by the reader. These factors might suggest that this reading exercise will be quite easy. Passage B should be extremely easy to read since, in this sixteen-word passage, only four new letters and four new words are introduced. Seventy-five percent of the words are repeated from the first lesson.

If you had a little trouble reading these simple passages (translations below*), the experiment was worth the effort. The objective was to demonstrate that any symbolic process is potentially difficult and that when the symbols appear very much alike, it becomes doubly so. Before the child is confronted with a task as exacting as reading passages A or B (above), he will have had many hours of practice aimed at helping him make finer and finer visual discriminations. He will also have had many experiences with the printed form of words in readiness books, in experience charts, and on bulletin boards.

Structuring the Climate for Learning

There are many things that can go wrong in beginning reading instruction. Learning to read is a highly complex task and the pres-

---

*Passage A:	look oh look	Passage B:	baby likes to play
	see baby play		look at baby play
	look at baby		oh oh see baby
	play baby play		play with me baby

sures that have become attached to "learning-to-read" often interfere with mastery of this symbol system. A little failure can create and nourish interferences to learning; thus it is essential to maintain a classroom climate that arouses and sustains the child's interest in reading.

Fortunately, there are potentially powerful motivators available to every classroom. No child has an innate drive not to learn to read. Most children come to school eager to explore the mysteries of print. Every child has ego needs which for a period of time can be fulfilled in part by success in learning to read. Another exceptionally powerful asset is the fact that reading is a language process and that children love to use and manipulate language. Unfortunately the magic and power of language is frequently not utilized to its fullest in reading instruction. If reading is divorced from language, then learning to read becomes mechanistic. Interest wanes, and even if learning occurs, it tends to lose some of its self-sustaining ingredients.

Building on what the child knows

In teaching reading, as well as in other learning situations, the wise teacher builds on what the child has learned previously. The typical child comes to school with a remarkably well-developed ability to use and understand his language. Here we use the linguistic definition of language — language is oral — thus referring exclusively to speech. In teaching reading, the child must be taught that the printed marks he sees as visual stimuli represent speech patterns he already knows.

If the child has learned the language of instruction used in the school, he is better equipped for the tasks the school has planned than if his language differs significantly from this norm.*

Reading is, in essence, a process of converting graphic symbols into their oral counterparts. One must decode the graphic representations, and in so doing he arrives at the known, or familiar, which is his speech. Teaching this fundamental relationship has always been one of the tasks of the first grade teacher. When a child reads in a monotone or emphasizes each word as a separate utterance (word-by-word reading), teachers characteristically say, "John, let's read that again. This time read it with *expression*. Read it like you would say it. How did Billy feel when it appeared he could not make the trip to Grandfather's farm? How do you think Billy said, 'Oh, no! This can't be. We just have to go.' "

---

*Cultural and dialect differences are discussed in Chapter 3.

In addition to having developed the use of language, the child will have had many experiences which in different ways can be translated into language usage. However, children have had vastly different experiences, and how to tie these to learning to read will tax the teacher's ingenuity. The readiness activities discussed in Chapter 4 can help to provide a smooth transition from previous experience to reading experience.

Since beginning reading is the logical extension of a readiness program, there is no break between the two, no point where one ends and the other begins. In a well-organized first grade, the transition is so gradual that the children hardly perceive it. The use of pre-primers and experience charts and stories is seen simply as an extension of work done yesterday and last week. The period of beginning reading should provide intelligent, systematic guidance in activities which make learning to read a meaningful and natural growth process.

Classroom
Management

The need for classroom organization stems from pupil differences within the classroom. As they relate to learning, the most significant of these differences are: previous learnings, present instructional needs, the rate at which learning can take place, and attitudes toward self as a learner. Taken together, these factors provide the basis for the fact that whatever instructional approach a teacher may use, it will not be equally appropriate for all pupils in her class.

Good teachers attempt to organize the total learning environment so as to permit differentation of instruction. This is the most difficult task facing educators. It was noted in Chapter 2 that any history of education that dealt with instructional practices would be primarily a catalogue of attempts to deal with individual differences of pupils being taught in a group situation. The search for a solution to this problem still continues. The chapter on *Individualizing Instruction* deals, in part, with this topic.

Administrative procedures for dealing with individual differences

Classroom organization involves many factors, such as providing for pupils an adequate supply of materials at various difficulty levels; selecting concepts and skills to be taught; devising a sequence for teaching these; evaluating the teaching-learning situation to determine what has been accomplished; assigning blocks of time for particular teachings; providing for class, group, and individual instruction. These considerations deal primarily with differentiation of instruction, but there remains the problem of how the teacher manages the actual teacher-pupil interaction necessary for learning. Two approaches to this problem are briefly discussed.

In-class grouping

Grouping pupils on the basis of previous learnings and present instructional needs is a practice of long standing in our schools.*

In recent years, grouping based on pupil ability has received considerable criticism. Indefensible practices such as Round-Robin Reading and infrequent shifting of pupils within groups were far too commonplace in our schools. The central issue is whether such practices could be identified and rectified without proscribing all grouping procedures.

It is realistic to assume that grouping per se is neither inherently good nor bad. Practices carried out under any plan of grouping may enhance pupil growth or become a meaningless and even harmful educational ritual. Grouping pupils on the basis of instructional needs can provide the framework within which an alert teacher can develop meaningful differentiated instruction. Grouping can narrow the range of differences and reading problems with which a teacher has to cope during a given instructional period. As a result, she can focus on particular short-term goals for specific pupils.

There are always practical considerations which limit the degree and type of grouping. Many authorities in the past suggested that the class be divided into three groups. Five or six groups might well overtax the teacher, dividing her time with pupils in blocks too small to be effective. Two groups would undoubtedly leave her with too heterogeneous a collection of pupils in both groups.

Grouping practices should be extremely flexible. Good teachers are always more conscious of the goals of grouping than they are of the mechanics of the practice. They do not think of equal num-

---

*For an historical account of the development and rationale of grouping practices found in schools since 1900, see: Kathleen B. Hester, *Teaching Every Child to Read*, 2nd ed. (New York: Harper & Row, Publishers, 1964), Chap. 18.

Further discussion of grouping practice may be found in *The Reading Teacher*, II (1957). This entire issue is devoted to the theme "Classroom Organization: Differing Viewpoints."

bers of pupils in each group or of groups being rigid and final or that every pupil can be accommodated equally well within a three-group structure. They know from experience that one or more pupils may not fit logically into any of three groups. This point is best illustrated by the extreme cases found in every classroom — the very poor reader and the very accelerated reader.

Different classrooms at a given grade level will differ to such a degree that it is impracticable to outline any particular plan of grouping with the expectation that it will be equally appropriate for all. Factors other than the abilities of the pupils also influence grouping practices. These include class size; space for activities; and the availability of supplementary books, film strips, recordings, and the like. The teacher's method is also a factor. Relying heavily on basal readers may call for a structure different from the widespread use of the unit or project approach.

The psychological impact of grouping

Grouping is sometimes discussed as being potentially threatening to pupils. There are various points of view as to how the grouping within a classroom is to take place so as not to introduce comparisons between children. Suggestions include calling the groups group one, group two, and group three; giving the groups some irrelevant titles such as bluebirds, redbirds, robins — the teacher knowing which is the superior group; referring to the groups by the names of children in the group. The latter has the merit of being a straightforward approach. No one is being humiliated on the basis of reading ability, and it does not appear that the teacher thinks every pupil should have a certain ability in reading. Psychologically, it is inadvisable for a teacher to attempt to hide differences among beginning readers. It is impossible to fool the children about their reading, and when the poorer readers see through the bluebirds versus the blackbirds, they too start attaching a stigma to poor reading ability. This of course is what the teacher has done, but she did not do it openly.

A wise teacher has had different groups of children doing different things at the same time throughout the year, and no significance was attached to this by either the teacher or the pupils. This teacher probably did not start all children reading from the pre-primer on the same day. She observed children closely and identified those who were ready. When she started this group on a pre-primer, other groups worked on reading also. Some children worked in a readiness workbook, some worked on teacher-prepared readiness materials, and some did preparation for making an experience chart. The teacher, in a natural way, had planted the idea that groups of pupils would be reading from different books and would be working on different pages of workbooks. The teacher who is successful in doing this helps her pupils in many ways.

1. She helps children build a foundation for independent work habits.
2. Competition and feelings of failure are reduced, since children are not arrayed against each other on the same reading tasks.

3. Tension and bad attitudes toward reading are held to a minimum.
4. Each child is permitted to progress at his own rate, and intergroup rivalry is minimized.
5. The teacher is prevented from embracing, consciously or unconsciously, a grouping system that is too rigid.
6. The teacher is granted flexibility in reducing the size of a group she works with by having some children work independently while she works intensively with others.

The ungraded primary

The concept of the ungraded primary represents another approach to dealing with the problem of pupil differences. The ungraded primary usually embraces the first three years of formal schooling; the children are designated as being in the primary school or at the primary level. They are not promoted or non-promoted at the end of years one and two. A recent study indicates that neither promotion or non-promotion is in itself a very satisfactory solution to low achievement in reading. It is suggested that more flexible curriculums, methods, and materials are needed "in a type of school organization which encourages continuous pupil progress." (36)

While instruction in the conventional grade-level system is geared to the mean, experience tells us that pupils do not cluster closely around an achievement mean. Differences in achievement are marked, and they increase with instruction. The ungraded primary starts from the premise that each child should progress at his own rate, and the instructional program centers on each child's need at the moment. This is accomplished by breaking the primary years into a number of units of accomplishment or levels of competency. As each child develops competency at one level, he is moved on into work at the next level. The number of levels and the skills to be mastered at each level are worked out co-operatively by teachers in the program.

Austin (3) describes an ungraded primary school that was eminently successful from the standpoint of both teachers and parents. No official reference is made to grade level; all primary grades, which cover the first three years of school, are simply designated primary rooms. Parents are always kept informed of their children's progress. Teachers are encouraged to work with the same group of children for more than one year, and new teachers are initiated into the program with a workshop held before the opening of school.

No single learning curve fits first graders' achievement, and pupil variability in achievement increases in succeeding grades. There is evidence that if the children are allowed three years of instruction to achieve the third-grade level, there will be fewer failures than there would be if all of the children had had to meet arbitrary standards at the end of grades one and two. Maturity and growth cannot be forced, and growth is characterized by both spurts and plateaus. The ungraded primary encourages continuous pupil progress without specifying precise amounts of growth which are to take place in a given year. Such a plan has particular merit for the child who starts slowly but later shows rapid progress. (16, 17)

Some of the educational advantages believed to be inherent in the ungraded primary plan are summarized below.

1. It is easier to provide for the child's reading growth *early* in his reading career if one is not thinking of "grade level norms" the first year.
2. There is likely to be less failure and frustration in the reading situation if there is less emphasis on comparison and promotion.
3. A teacher often stays with the same group of students two years or longer. This gives her an opportunity to know pupils better. She is less likely to push a student beyond his ability during the first year, since she expects to work with him the next year.
4. Students always work at the level on which they need instruction; i.e., they are not likely to miss some facet of instruction because they were absent several weeks.
5. The slower learner will not repeat the first or second grade, but he may take four years to move up from the primary level.
6. The ungraded plan is flexible in allowing pupils to cover some phases of learning quite rapidly when they are capable of doing so and in giving them more time when it is needed.
7. Bright pupils would not "skip a grade" and possibly be deficient in some skill taught there. They would simply go through the entire primary curriculum at a faster rate.

No method of grouping will automatically solve all instructional problems, and the ungraded primary plan is certainly not a panacea. If a shift to the ungraded plan is not accompanied by an understanding of the goals to be achieved, none of the potential benefits are likely to be realized. If teachers or parents continue to think in terms of a grade-level system, the plan is doomed from the start. On the other hand, if the philosophy of the plan is believed sound and the chief reason for adopting it is to help children grow in reading, problems which do arise will not be insurmountable.

Developing independent work habits

Learning to read is part of the total development of children. The period devoted to bringing reading instruction is not too early to help children develop self-responsibility and a degree of independence in their work habits. While many teachers would agree with this premise, it is possible we have underestimated the relationship between these factors and success or failure in reading.

In any discussion of reading readiness one invariably meets the term *immaturity*. An immature child has not attained a specific

level of behavior associated with his chronological age. Lack of responsibility or self-dependence is universally cited as evidence of immaturity. The child of six who has avoided or who has been prevented from developing independence and self-reliance is not likely to become self-reliant and independent in school unless he receives some specific guidance. The point is that immaturity, in the psychological sense, has been learned. The child's behavior may have developed out of the parents' need to keep the child dependent. It should be kept in mind that one of the easiest things to learn in early life is a pattern of abdicating responsibility. The child who learns this pattern has become accustomed to social controls from without. He will naturally find it difficult to develop self-discipline or controls from within. In this connection, Staiger (31) suggests that some children fail to learn to read because they have never had to do anything and therefore feel that they do not have to learn to read. Delays, procrastination, and lack of self-responsibility can only increase the difficulty of learning to read. In other situations where this behavior was learned, the parents can eventually make a response which resolves the problem. They can hang up the clothes, pick up the toys, write an excuse for the child when he is tardy, and take him to school in the car if he misses the bus. But learning to read is a task which no parent can perform for the child.

The aim of instruction in beginning reading is to make the child an independent reader. It is here that the child will develop habits of reading and study which will help or hinder him throughout his academic career. Independent work habits and self-responsibility are essential for children in today's schools because of group instruction in which children have to work out their own problems. Grouping practices create a problem since the teacher must divide her time among several different groups, thus leaving the child on his own during a good part of the time devoted to reading instruction.

Training for responsibility begins early and involves guidance from adults. This guidance must take into consideration that children learn self-responsibility only by practicing it. There is no single blueprint of teacher-behaviors that would be effective for each child in a class, and while expectations for individual children will differ, every child needs consistency from the adult authority.

The child who develops independence and self-discipline in his work habits early in the process of learning to read is not likely to become a severely retarded reader. The child who loses, or never gains, confidence in himself, the child who cannot work alone, complete tasks, and in general assume some responsibility for learning, is not well-prepared to weather a learning crisis. There are a number of ways in which a teacher can help pupils get off to a proper start in developing good work habits.

Give responsibility to all children and not just those who are already confident and at ease. Collecting workbooks or readers, stacking them neatly, cleaning up after art work, arranging chairs after group work, and stopping or beginning a task when requested to do so help develop self-discipline. It should be remembered that children learn best through experience.

Do not give a child tasks that he does not understand or cannot do. He will lose interest, procrastinate, daydream, and soon conclude that this is what one does in school.

Set short-term goals which can be readily achieved. The teacher should never tell her students that she will look at their work when it is finished and then fail to do so. The child wants a reward, and the teacher's approval of the completed task is interpreted as a reward. The child will then have many experiences of success which he associates with the reading situation.

It is stated above that children should learn to begin and stop activities when requested to do so. If a child is engrossed in a task, such as coloring, printing, or working a page in a readiness book, permitting him to complete it might be better than interrupting and insisting that he join a group to do something else. When grouping is flexible and a good learning climate exists, he will be able to join the group in a few minutes without disrupting the activity. Furthermore, children have a relatively short attention span and become tired even of tasks they enjoy.

If a child works slowly on an activity that the teacher feels should be completed, she can give a moment's help and then praise the child for completing the task, thus instilling the idea that this is the standard of performance which she expects from him. Children's reading behavior should be observed very closely so that no child experiences too much failure and frustration with reading. Children should be praised when they try, even if their accomplishment falls short of arbitrary standards.

Instructional Materials and Philosophy of Instruction

How reading should be taught has for many decades been the most widely debated topic in American education. Always the major concern and emphasis has been on beginning reading instruction. In recent years this debate has been intensified.

It is interesting to note that for years our schools used basal reader materials almost exclusively.* All such materials provided an instructional program covering the entire elementary school period. In contrast, the past fifteen years have seen many materials and methodologies introduced which focus only on beginning reading.

The materials available for beginning reading instruction reflect different philosophies which in large measure determine initial instructional strategies. The major differences in materials can be traced to the way the following pedogogical issues are treated.

1. The way initial reading-vocabulary is controlled.
2. The amount of phonics (letter-sound relationships) taught.
3. The emphasis on *meaning* in beginning instruction.
4. The degree to which various facets of the total language-arts program are integrated, specifically the emphasis on children's writing.
5. The temporary use of respellings or alphabet modifications.
6. "Content" of materials. (This of course is determined by prior decisions made in regard to items 1, 2, 3 above.)

Newer Methods and Materials

In this section we will discuss a number of materials which have the following common characteristics.

1. Each in its own way emphasizes "cracking the code" and achieving a *fast start* in beginning reading.
2. Each has its own specific set of instructional materials which are an integral part of the methodology.
3. Each focuses on beginning reading instruction offering little in instructional strategy beyond this stage.

English writing is based upon 26 letter symbols and follows the alphabetic principle of graphic signs representing speech sounds. While approximately half of the letters are quite consistent with the sound they represent, other letters and letter combinations rep-

---

*Basal materials and the language experience approach are discussed in the following chapter; Individualized Reading is discussed in Chapter 11.

resent several sounds. There is little room to doubt that the degree of inconsistency of letter-sound relationships adds to the difficulty of learning to read English. There have been numerous attempts to devise modifications of the English printing so as to mitigate this inconsistency.*

All attempts thus far to resolve inconsistent letter-sound relationships have centered on two approaches (or a combination of the two): (1) The use of additional printed signs to represent particular sounds; (2) respelling of English words so that the orthography parallels speech sounds hard. The first of these might be illustrated by Fry's (13) *Diacritical Marking System:* a bar over vowels representing long vowel sounds; a slant line through silent letters; underlining of digraphs; a dot over vowels indicating the *schwa* sound; and a bar under letters representing irregular sounds for that letter. A sample sentence follows:

"Oncé upon à time Littlé Red Hen livéd in a barn with her fivé chiçks." This system preserves the traditional spelling of words but adds clues to pronunciation.

Learn English the New Way by Frank C. Laubach utilizes a slant line following any vowel which has its long sound, and in addition respells many words: *smile*—smi/l; *quite*—qui/t; *snake*—sna/k; *told*—to/ld; *woman*—wuumun; *Asia*—A/zhaa; *cease*—seass; *deceive*—de/seev; *pronounced*—pro/nounsst.**

i/t/a (Initial Teaching Alphabet)

Sir James Pitman of England devised a new orthography which consists of a 44 character alphabet. This alphabet dropped the letters Q and X and added 18 new characters to the traditional English alphabet. Materials printed in this initial teaching alphabet (i/t/a) were used experimentally in certain English schools beginning in 1960. Since that time a number of American schools have used beginning reading materials printed in this augmented alphabet.

The purpose behind the development of this orthographic system was to permit a one-letter character to represent only one English

---

*See: Edward Fry, "New Alphabet Approaches," *First Grade Reading Programs*, Newark: International Reading Association Perspectives in Reading, No. 5 (1965), 72–85.
**Frank C. Laubach, *Learn English The New Way*, New Readers Press, Syracuse, New York, 1962.

sound or phoneme. Allowing for some irregularities in phoneme-grapheme relationships, the augmented alphabet does approximate a one-to-one relationship between letters seen and speech sounds heard. Use of the augmented alphabet was proposed only for teaching beginning reading. In general, this was envisioned to be the first year of formal instruction for the average child, and possibly less for the accelerated learner.

Issues

1. *Transfer to traditional English writing.* The questions most frequently raised regarding this approach to beginning reading focus on the issue of "what will the reader do when he transfers from the one-to-one relationship of letter-sound found in i/t/a materials and meets the frequently inconsistent graphic representations (i.e., spellings) of traditional English writing?" In some quarters this problem was somewhat summarily dismissed with the response that "there appears to be no problem of transfer." This opinion was often tied to "early reports from experimentation carried out in England" which conceivably lost something in translation.

Discussion by John A. Downing of the early English experiments reveals caution on this point. He writes:

> If teachers *opinions* are supported by the results of the objective tests conducted last month [March 1963], we may feel encouraged in our *hopes* that all children will pass through the transfer stage with success, but *we must urge the greatest caution in drawing final conclusion or taking action on the basis of this preliminary trial* . . . the full effects of the transfer cannot be judged until the majority of these children have been put on to books in conventional print for their everyday reading. *Even then the final assessment cannot be made until some years have elapsed* and we can determine the extent to which (i/t/a) pupils, at various ability levels, are able to maintain the advantage made possible through their early (i/t/a) experience. [Emphasis added.] (8)

Some evidence as to the ease with which pupils transfer from i/t/a to regular print is supplied by several studies of American pupils. Mazurkiewicz, (25) reporting on a population of 451 i/t/a taught pupils (1963-64 school year), indicates that only 26 percent made the transition. In a second study covering the academic year

1964–65 and involving 417 i/t/a taught pupils, "almost half the i/t/a population had not made transition to the T.O. [traditional orthography] standard in instruction." Hayes and Nemeth (21) report a lower figure, 26 percent having not made the transfer.

2. *Amount of Phonics Instruction Involved in i/t/a.* There are numerous studies which indicate that emphasis on phonics instruction in grade one has a salutory effect on reading achievement, as measured by first grade achievement tests, when such programs are compared with others which include significantly less phonics. The i/t/a program does include intensive systematic teaching of letter-sound analysis. The child's first learnings center on the sound associated with each graphic symbol. This stress is logical because the underlying principle of the system is uniformity of letter-sound relationships.

This discussion is not concerned with judging the value of such early phonics emphasis. The issue is that the intensive phonics emphasis found in i/t/a is an important factor which is ignored if reading achievement is attributed exclusively to the variable of the i/t/a orthography.

3. *Emphasis on Children's Writing in i/t/a Programs.* In i/t/a instructional programs there is considerable stress on children's writing, using the i/t/a symbols. This is also a feature of the language-experience approach and other integrated language arts programs. Although available data are inconclusive, it is generally hypothesized that such integration of reading and writing enhances the learning of the reading process. If this hypothesis proves tenable, the heavy emphasis on children's writing is a second variable which clouds the efficacy of the initial teaching alphabet.

A second and more immediate question is, if the child is to transfer from the initial teaching medium to traditional orthography within the first year of instruction, why should he learn and reinforce the augmented alphabet in his own writing? The question does not relate to the value of children's writing in grade one, but upon the medium in which that writing will be done. It is true that many letters are exactly the same in both systems, and in these particular cases transfer should be 100 percent. On the other hand, there is no question that using i/t/a symbols in writing is more difficult than writing using traditional orthography, because one meets such letter characters as   æ , ɛ , œ , ꜰ , ꞎ , ŋ , ω , ω , and the like.

4. *Respelling of Irregularly Spelled English Words.* In the promotional materials for i/t/a, it is claimed that there is a high degree of compatibility between spellings in i/t/a and traditional orthography. The question is asked, "Are the traditional alphabet and spelling of English important causes of failure in beginning reading?" The answer is that problems in learning to read English do not stem from the traditional alphabet but from the spellings of words. A fact that is often overlooked is that in addition to the changed alphabet in i/t/a, a great number of words are changed to phonetic spellings. The following examples come from one small first grade book of less than primer difficulty.*

was—woz	watched—wotcht	walked—waukt
excited—eksieted	enough—enuf	thought—thaut
called—cauld	once—wunz	next—nekst
large—larj	find—fiend	boxes—boksez
busy—bizy	some—sum	George—Jorj
come—cum	one—wun	six—siks

i/t/a actually attempts to follow the traditional "rules" found in most phonic approaches, particularly with regard to the "two vowel" and "final e" rules. When words do not follow the rules, they are spelled phonetically:

one—wun	said—sed
some—sum	board—bord
once—wunz	couple—cupl
more—mor	head—hed
have—hav	laugh—laf

In such instances, i/t/a ceases to be a method for "cracking the code" (which is English writing) and becomes a substitute code. The respellings are logical; but the issue is that children will soon be exposed to the irrational spellings, and they will have to learn these word symbols as sight words whether or not they begin reading with i/t/a or regular orthography. Since all words met in i/t/a writing can be sounded out by heeding the individual letters, the learner will inevitably develop a set to utilize this approach. This habit will not serve him well when he meets hundreds of irregularly spelled words following the transition.

---

*"A Seesied Holidae for Jaen and Toeby," Ann Thwaite (Cunstabl and Company, Limited, Lundon). [*sic*]

5. *Results of i/t/a Instruction.* Data from various studies have failed to indicate any significant superiority in reading achievement at the end of grade one which accrues from the use of i/t/a. Hahn (19) compared the reading achievement of three groups of children taught respectively by i/t/a, basal programs, and a language arts approach. His conclusion was that no one approach was consistently superior to the others although significant differences favoring each approach were found on some particular reading subtests. Fry (14) found no significant differences in silent or oral reading achievement of first-grade children taught by i/t/a, the Fry Diacritical Marking System or the Sheldon Basal Readers (Allyn-Bacon).

Tanyzer and Alpert (33) compared the efficacy of i/t/a, the Lippincott basal program, and the Scott Foresman basal program. Reading achievement of pupils taught by both the Lippincott materials and i/t/a were significantly superior to that of pupils taught by the Scott Foresman basals on each of the subtests of the Stanford Achievement Test. The group taught by the Lippincott materials was significantly superior to the group taught with i/t/a on vocabulary and spelling. No significant differences were found between these groups on Word Reading, Paragraph Meaning and Word Study Skills.

Mazurkiewicz (25) found no significant differences in reading achievement between children taught by i/t/a and traditional orthography as measured by the subtests Word Reading, Paragraph Meaning, Vocabulary, and Word-Study Skills, on the Stanford Achievement Test. Pupils taught in traditional orthography were significantly superior in spelling.

Hayes and Nemeth (21) compared four instructional approaches: i/t/a, Lippincott basal series, Scott Foresman basals, plus the use of *Phonics and Word Power* * and Scott Foresman basals alone. It should be noted that the first three include a considerable amount of phonics while the Scott Foresman basals introduce a relatively small amount of letter-analysis in grade one materials. On the word reading subtest, no significant differences were found between i/t/a and Lippincott approaches but both were superior to the Scott Foresman basal program alone. There was no significant difference between i/t/a and Scott Foresman materials supplemented by the Phonics and Word Power Program. On paragraph meaning, no significant differences were found between i/t/a and any of the other approaches. On Word Study Skills, no significant differences were found between i/t/a, Lippincott, and Scott Foresman supplemented by *Phonics and Word Power*, while each of these was significantly superior to Scott Foresman basals alone.

One important finding which emerges from a number of these studies is that when programs which utilize extensive phonics instruction are compared, no significant differences in reading achievement appear at the end of grade one. However, phonics-emphasis programs appear to result in higher reading achievement (as measured by existing standardized tests) than do programs which include significantly less letter-sound analysis.

This tends to support the contention that studies which have purported to be dealing with the efficacy of i/t/a orthography as compared with traditional orthography have failed to control an important variable — the amount of phonics instruction in the programs being compared. The contribution of the augmented alphabet in learning to read can be evaluated only if the stress on phonics instruction is equated in comparative studies.

---

*American Education Publications, Columbus, Ohio, 1964.

Words in color

This is a system for teaching beginning reading, developed by Caleb Gattengo. (15) Initial instruction involves the use of visual stimuli which provide two visual clues: (1) the traditional letter configurations, and (2) color. In this approach, 39 colors are used, each of which represents a speech sound in English. Any letter or combination of letters which represent a given speech sound will be presented as a visual stimulus in the particular color assigned to that speech sound. For instance, the long vowel sound of Ā is represented by the following combinations:

a — able	*eigh* — weight
ey — they	*aigh* — straight
ay — play	*ei* — their
ai — mail	*ea* — great

Each group of italicized letters above would be one color (green). The sound of ă, regardless of letters which represent it, is shown in white; the sound of ē is represented by vermillion, etc.

The actual teaching of this color code is done through the use of a number of large wall charts. Twenty-one charts contain words, and eight phonic-code charts contain letters and letter combinations which represent given sounds. The only other learning experiences which utilize color are those in which the teacher may write on the chalk board using different colored chalk. *ALL other printed material which the child uses is printed in black on white.* Thus the wall charts are nothing more than "keys" to which the child may turn to see the color of particular letters. The following are some pertinent facts about *Words in Color*.

1. This approach places considerable emphasis on phonics instruction. Children learn "sounds" of letters rather than letter names. Instruction starts with short vowel sounds and then moves into consonant sounds. These are taught systematically and with a good deal of repetition.

2. At the time of this writing, there has been no research which suggests that the addition of color to *letter forms* has any positive effects on learning either letter configuration or sounds associated with letters.

3. The use of thirty-nine colors can make the learning process quite confusing. In the absence of letter configuration clues, many adults have difficulty in determining whether certain

color samples are actually the "same" or "different." It is likely that some six-year-olds also have trouble in discriminating between colors which are very much alike. One series of color shades includes: dark green, olive green, cadmium green, yellow green no. 15, yellow green no. 47, light green, deep green, emerald green no. 45, emerald green no. 26, leaf green, yellow ochre, and brown ochre.

4. It is difficult to justify the emphasis on colored letters considering the fact that the child never reads any material printed in colors. His contact with words in color is limited to classroom charts composed of individual words, but no sustained reading matter.

5. Children who learn to *rely* on *color cues* could not read outside of class since the charts they depend on are large, bulky and expensive. It is highly improbable that these "aids" would ever become household fixtures.

Programmed reading

Programmed reading materials fall into two categories: (1) those the purpose of which is to teach facts and understanding in any one of the numerous subject areas; (2) those whose chief aim is to teach the child *how* to read, i.e., dealing with various skills which make up the reading process. This discussion will deal only with the latter in the form of workbook-type programmed materials.

There are a number of such materials available. One example which may be considered fairly representative is *Programmed Reading* (Webster Division, McGraw-Hill Book Company). The materials in this program, which are designed for grade one, consist of seven conventional-sized workbooks. The pupil writes a letter or word or circles a response in each frame. There is considerable emphasis on "phonics," or associating printed letters with speech sounds. Initial teaching involves short vowel sounds and consonant sounds in words which enjoy "regular spellings." This term implies that the sound represented by individual letters is the most common or characteristic sound of those particular letters (cat, rat, fat, mat, etc.)

Before beginning to work with the programmed materials, the child must have mastered a sizable number of phonic skills including the following:

1. The names of the letters of the alphabet (capital and small).
2. How to print all the capital and small letters.

3. That letters stand for sounds.
4. What sounds to associate with the letters *a, f, m, n, p, t, th,* and *i,* which are used as the points of departure for the programmed readers.
5. That letters are read from left to right.
6. That groups of letters form words.
7. The words *yes* and *no* by sight, how to discriminate the words *ant, man,* and *mat* from each other, and how to read the sentences, *I am an ant, I am a man, I am a mat, I am a pin, I am a pan, I am tan, I am thin, I am fat.*

These skills are taught in a stage called *programmed pre-reading* which, by the nature of what is taught, represents a rather heavy saturation of phonic analysis early in beginning reading.

One strength of programmed reading is that it makes possible individualized instruction. While every child would be using the same material, each may progress through it at his own rate. A second virtue is that even though programmed materials deal primarily with mechanical aspects of the reading process, many of these skills have to be practiced until they become automatic responses on the part of the learner. Thus, a well-planned program can relieve a teacher from a certain amount of repetitive drill and leave her more time for other important aspects of instruction. This assumes, of course, that programmed materials represent only one part of the instructional program.

The "linguistic" regular spelling approach

In the April and May issues (1942) of *The Elementary English Review* Leonard Bloomfield outlined an approach for beginning reading instruction. In essence, Bloomfield suggested a very rigid vocabulary control in which children's first attempts at reading would be limited to "words with regular spellings." Regular spellings are those words in which each grapheme (written letter) represents the one sound most frequently associated with that letter. Thus the words *cat* and *hum* enjoy regular spellings while *cent* and *come* are irregular (*c* in *cent* represents *s*; *o* in *come* represents the short sound of *u*).

Opposition to phonics instruction

The regular spelling approach is similar to i/t/a, *Words in Color,* and *Programmed Reading* in that it deals with beginning reading instruction and calls for use of special materials. However, it differs from these methodologies in one important way. They emphasize phonics instruction (or the systematic teaching of letter-sound relationships) and Bloomfield was unequivocally opposed to this method. Present day proponents of Bloomfield's method have remained loyal to this dictum.

In order to understand certain important methodological considerations in Bloomfield's proposal, one must be aware of his position as outlined in *Let's Read*. (5) His opposition to phonics instruction is based on two erroneous premises. The first of these is the misconception voiced by Bloomfield that the purpose of phonics instruction is to teach the child how to *pronounce* words by teaching him speech sounds. Bloomfield writes:

> The inventors of these (phonic) methods confuse writing with speech. They plan the work as though the child were being taught to speak.... If a child has not learned to utter the speech sounds of our language, the only sensible course is to postpone reading until he has learned to speak. As a matter of fact, nearly all six-year-old children have long ago learned to speak their native language; they have no need whatever of the drill which is given by phonic methods. (5: p. 27)

The second misconception about phonics which one finds in the writing of Bloomfield and others is found in their belief as to how phonics is taught. Bloomfield states:

> The second error of the phonic methods is that of isolating the speech sounds. The authors of these methods tell us to show the child a letter, for instance *t*, and to make him react by uttering the *t*-sound; that is the English speech sound which occurs at the beginning of a word like *two* or *ten*. This sound to be uttered either all by itself or else with an obscure vowel sound after it. (5: p. 28)

This description of phonics instruction was valid for an earlier era, but this practice had largely disappeared by the time Bloomfield inveighed against it. It is true that one cannot separately pronounce letter sounds, which taken together constitute the pronunciation of English words, and children are not asked to do so. They are taught that a particular letter represents the same speech sound in many different words, and they are invited to think or subvocalize this sound when the letter occurs in a word they are attempting to solve.

The program

The materials and methodology described here is outlined by Bloomfield and Barnhart in *Let's Read: A Linguistic Approach* (5). The program consists of 245 separate lessons which present five thousand words. The first 97 lessons deal with words with regular spellings. The remaining 148 lessons present words with irregular spellings. Prior to instruction in reading, the child must have developed certain pre-reading skills which include the ability to identify (name) the letters of the English alphabet. Capital letters are learned first, then lower case forms. Letters are taught in alphabetical order stressing left-to-right progression.

Teaching "regular spelling" words

Each of the lessons 1–36 introduces a different series of words which contain identical final phonograms (*at, an, op, ag, ip, ed, un, ot,* etc.). Thus, the words in a given lesson differ from each other only in the initial letter (sound) *c*at, *b*at, *m*at, *h*at. The teaching of CVC (consonant, vowel, consonant) words is followed by lessons dealing with other patterns such as CVCC (*lamp*); CCVC (*snap*); CCVCC (*stamp*); CVVC (*deep*), etc.

Lesson one presents the words *can, Dan, fan, man, Nan, pan, ran, tan, an, ban, van.* Bloomfield describes the method of teaching as follows:

> The word *can* is printed on the blackboard or a card. The child knows the names of the letters, and is now asked to read off those names in their order:
>
> see   aye   en
>
> The parent or teacher says, "Now we have spelled the word. Now we are going to *read* it. The word is *can*. Read it: *can*." (5:41)

Other words are taught in the same manner. It is suggested that no more than two or three words be presented per lesson since this learning calls for "a severe intellectual effort."

Bloomfield is quite precise as to *what* the child is to learn from the presentation of two words such as *can* and *fan*. "The aim is now to make the child distinguish between the two words — that is, to get him to read each of the words correctly when it is shown by itself, and, when the two words are shown together, to say the right one when the parent or the teacher points to it, and to point to the right one when the parent or the teacher pronounces it." (5: p-41)

In this teaching method children are asked to learn every word as a sight word, or to arrive at its pronunciation by saying the letter names. "All he (the child) needs to do is read off the names of successive letters, from left to right" (5:36). Bloomfield's example *"see aye en* — read it *can"* is all the evidence one needs in order to understand why the alphabet method (the spelling of words to arrive at their pronunciation) was discarded years ago. Letter *names* do not coincide with the sounds that letters represent in words.

Teaching irregular words

It should be pointed out that words with regular spellings constitute less than forty percent of the five thousand words listed in the *Let's Read* program*. Bloomfield's suggestion for teaching words with irregular spellings is somewhat astounding: "When it comes to teaching irregular and special words each word will demand a separate effort and separate practice" (5:206). Elsewhere in criticizing the sight word method, Bloomfield correctly points out the difficulty (or impossibility) of teaching many thousands of words in this manner. The child who has been taught phonics will find that he can apply something of what he has learned to a majority of irregular words. Since letter-sound relationships are not taught with the regular spelling words, the proponents of this approach cannot talk in terms of *transfer*. Thus they must fall back on the vague and impractical suggestion that each new word demands a separate effort and separate practice.

This is not to say that there is no virtue in presenting "family words," "word patterns," or words with minimal grapheme-phoneme differences in teaching reading. Gray** wrote favorably on this practice under the trade name "mental substitution of initial consonant sounds." Research by Wylie and Durrell† supports the fact that first grade children find it easier to identify words when they work

---

*This statement is based on Bloomfield's designation of words. It should be pointed out that he used much stricter criteria for regular spellings than is necessary if one's goal is teaching reading.

**William S. Gray, *On Their Own In Reading.* Chicago: Scott, Foresman and Company, 1960.

†Richard E. Wylie and Donald O. Durrell "Teaching Vowels Through Phonograms," *Elementary English* (October 1970), 787–791.

with rhyming phonograms (i.e., identical final letter-combinations). However, these individuals also advocate the systematic teaching of letter-sound relationships which turns out to be the missing ingredient in Bloomfield's approach.

Meaning and reading

The methodological decision to teach regular spelling words (and include all words that fit a given "pattern") definitely limits story content or material that will be meaningful to children. Both Bloomfield and others, who have developed materials based on regular spellings, reject the thesis that beginning reading instruction should be concerned with meaning. The rejection of meaning is not so much a well-founded pedagogical principle as it is an expediency when one is limited to using only those words which qualify as regular spellings. Normal English sentences are difficult to build when one decides to use only words which follow regular spelling patterns. For example, in Bloomfield's material, after 66 words have been taught (roughly equivalent to three pre-primers in a representative basal series), one finds only the most contrived sentences and absolutely no story line:

Pat had ham.	Sam ran.
Nat had jam.	Can Sam tag Pam?
Sam had a cap.	Can Pam tag Sam?
Dan had a hat.	Dan had a ram. (5:65)

After 200 words have been learned, the child reads these sentences:

Let Dan bat.	Let us in, Sis!
Did Al get wet?	Sis, let us in!
Van had a pet cat.	Let Sid pet a pup.
Get up Tad!	Jim let Pam tag him. (5:87)

Computer assisted instruction (CAI)

While computer programed instruction is quite different from the materials and methodology just discussed, it does meet the criteria of being a newer approach. Thus far (in reading) it has been used for initial instruction, and has focused mainly on teaching the code-cracking skills.

A decade ago both proponents and critics of computerized instruction agreed that "within a few years" computers were destined to play a major role in classroom instruction. There were an unprecedented number of mergers of big business (technology) and educational publishers.* Apparently it was believed that simply bringing these two elements under one management would lead to very rapid development of computer-instructional programs.

While no miracles have been wrought, it has been demonstrated that given time and enough resources, instructional programs for teaching mathematics, beginning reading, science, spelling, and even methods courses for teachers could be developed. At the moment most program development has been experimental in nature, involving only a few hundred or at most a few thousand students. Most programs, after being used in this limited fashion, were stored, shelved and forgotten. The major stumbling block in the path of widespread use of computer assisted instruction has not been program development but the problem of delivery to where the students are.

There is little reason to believe that computerized instruction will not increase in our schools. As far as reading instruction is concerned, it appears that computer technology is ideally suited for teaching a number of the essential skills associated with beginning instruction. Included would be letter recognition, association of letter forms with the sounds they represent, recognition of words which undergo structural changes (plurals, affixes compounds), and teaching irregularly-spelled sight words. The computer also has potential for bridging the instructional gap between dialect speakers and the standard English of the school.

Computer capabilities for teaching reading

Teachers of reading should understand the capabilities of computer assisted instruction as these relate to reading. The purpose here is not to explain the hardware, program writing, circuitry, and the like. When the program has been written, the system is in operation, and a child is sitting at the terminal, this instructional system has the following capabilities. The terminal at which the child works can consist of any or all of the following:

1. The child views a television set (cathode ray tube) on which can be shown:

---

*Examples include Raytheon — D. C. Heath; RCA — Random House; Xerox Corp. — American Educational Publications; Bell and Howell — Charles E. Merrill; Litton Industries — American Book Co.; IBM — Science Research Associates; General Learning Corporation — a union of Time-Life, General Electric, and Silver Burdett Publishers.

    a. Anything that may appear in a workbook, or any material ordinarily presented via chalkboard or overhead projector.

    b. The child can "register" responses directly on the tube by use of a light pen which leaves no marks but electronically registers the response made.

    c. A typewriter keyboard may also be part of the circuit in which case the learner types responses.

2. The auditory (voice) component can provide explanations, give directions, or present supplementary data.

3. The computer has the capacity to function much like an animated cartoon. A stick man can appear and take away a letter that is not sounded — (k)nee, (w)rap — or these letters can drop down the screen and disappear while the audio explains that the letter is not sounded but that it will always appear when these words are met in print.

4. If all goes well electronically, the learner can within a second's time receive a response to his response. This instant feedback can be visual, auditory, or both.

5. Every response a learner makes can be recorded and stored.

6. A child can be absent for a period of time. Upon his return, the "system" can pick him up at exactly the spot he was prior to his absence. If he has forgotten a crucial principle, the program can ascertain this by his error pattern and he can be "branched" back through a review or to easy material that fits his present need.

The possibilities above represent those capabilities already achieved in programming. Rapid changes and improvements can be expected.

Limitations of computer assisted instruction

Computer instruction involves a highly complex electronic system. It does break down, and when it does the party is over until an expert gets the lint out of the carburetor. If the system is crowded (maximum use), the instant feedback can be delayed a few seconds. During such intervals the student may wander mentally or physically; if the learner is "gone" the teaching can't go on.

Research reports have avoided mention of learners being "turned off" by computer instruction. It is highly unlikely that everyone has the same threshold of tolerance for this type of instruction. There is a hint of a problem in reports of how learners deliberately make "errors" in order to see how the computer will handle them. While the system is adept at recognizing and recording errors, it is vulnerable in analysis of what *caused* the error. In some cases this is of minor importance, in others it can be a crucial issue in the learning process.

One of the virtues of CAI is that it *can* maximize individual instruction. Through meticulous programming it can provide child *x* and child *y* with exactly what they need in instruction. When designing a program to be used by many thousands of students, the cost of developing, storing, and delivering an ideal program for each child becomes prohibitive (just as it is without computers). In essence, while the potential is there, it is highly unlikely that it can be used to its maximum.

YOUR POINT OF VIEW?

Would you defend or attack the following premises? Why?

1. "In-class grouping" has not helped teachers in dealing effectively with individual differences.

2. The ungraded primary is, in essence, an attempt to break away from grade-level standards of achievement.

3. One's definition of reading would in the final analysis have little impact on practices followed in teaching the reading process.

4. Programmed reading materials permit different pupils to be working on different skills and to work at different rates. This statement applies with equal validity to any workbook or series of workbooks.

5. Despite grouping practices and educators' expressed concern for individual differences among pupils, the grade-level system inevitably results in "teaching to the mean of the group."

6. Children cannot learn letter-sound relationships if they cannot discriminate visually between the various printed letter-forms.

7. When a child can consistently name the letters of the alphabet, this demonstrates that he can distinguish visually every letter form from every other letter form.

Respond to the following problems:

1. *Premise*: "There are certain reading skills which can be taught as effectively by a computer as by the classroom teacher." Discuss and identify these skills.

2. *Premise:* "If a given instructional technique is effective with a given child and does not inhibit his later growth in reading, the use of this technique is justifiable." State whether or not you accept this premise and support your decision.

BIBLIOGRAPHY

1. Atkinson, Richard C. and Duncan N. Hansen, "Computer-Assisted Instruction in Initial Reading: The Stanford Project," *Reading Research Quarterly*, (Fall 1966), 5–25.

2. Aukerman, Robert C. *Approaches to Beginning Reading*. New York: John Wiley and Sons, Inc., 1971.

3. Austin Kent C. "The Ungraded Primary School," *Childhood Education* (February 1957), 260–63.

4. Bliesmer, Emery P. "Problems of Research Design In Classroom Studies," *Journal of Reading Behavior* (Winter 1970), 3–17.

5. Bloomfield, Leonard, and Clarence L. Barnhart, *Let's Read, A Linguistic Approach*. Detroit: Wayne State University Press, 1961.

6. Bond, Guy L. and Eva Bond Wagner, *Teaching the Child to Read* (4th ed.). New York: The Macmillan Company, 1966, Chapters 3, 5, and 6.

7. Bond, Guy L. "First-Grade Reading Studies: An Overview," *Elementary English* (May 1966), 464–70.

8. Downing, John A. *Experiments with Pitman's Initial Teaching Alphabet In British Schools*. New York: Initial Teaching Alphabet Publications, Inc., 1963, 25.

9. Downing, J .and W. Lathram, "A Follow-Up of Children in the First i.t.a. Experiment," *British Journal of Educational Psychology* (November 1969), 303–305.

10. Feldhusen, Hazel J., Pose Lamb, and John Feldhusen, "Prediction of Reading Achievement Under Programmed and Traditional Instruction, *Reading Teacher* (February 1970), 446–454.

11. Fitzgibbon, Norrine H. and John H. Grate, "CAI: Where Do We Go From Here?" *Elementary English* (November 1970), 917–21.

12. Fleming, James T. "Oral Language and Beginning Reading: Another Look," *The Reading Teacher* (October 1968), 24–29.

13. Fry, Edward, "A Diacritical Marking System to Aid Beginning Reading Instruction," *Elementary English* (May 1964), 526–29.

14. Fry, Edward Bernard, *First Grade Reading Instruction Using a Diacritical Marking System, The Initial Teaching Alphabet and a Basal Reading System*. USOE Cooperative Research Project No. 2745, 1965.

15. Gattengo, Caleb, *Words In Color*. Chicago: Learning Materials, Inc., 1962.

16. Goodlad, John I. "Ungrading the Elementary Grades," *NEA Journal* (March 1955), 170–71.

17. _____, and Robert H. Anderson, *The Nongraded Elementary School*. New York: Harcourt, Brace & World, 1959.

18. Green, Donald Ross, Richard L. Henderson, and Herbert C. Richards, "Learning to Recognize Words and Letters on a CAI Terminal," *Reading and Realism*, Proceedings, International Reading Association, 13, Part I, 658–664.

19. Hahn, Harry T. *A Study of The Relative Effectiveness of Three Methods of Teaching Reading in Grade One*. USOE, Cooperative Research Project No. 2687, 1965.

20. Harris, Albert J. and Blanche L. Serwer, "The Craft Project: Instructional Time in Reading Research," *Reading Research Quarterly* (Fall 1966), 27–56.

21. Hayes, Robert B., and Joseph S. Nemeth, *An Attempt To Secure Additional Evidence Concerning Factors Affecting Learning to Read*. USOE, Cooperative Research Project No. 2697, 1965, 34.

22. Kerfoot, James F. (ed.), *First Grade Reading Programs*. Perspectives in Reading no. 5. Newark, Del.: International Reading Association, Inc., 1965.

23. King, Ethel M. and Siegmar Muehl, "Different Sensory Cues as Aids in Beginning Reading," *Reading Teacher* (December 1965), 163–68.

24. Marsh, R. W. "Some Cautionary Notes on the Results of the London i.t.a. Experiment," *Reading Research Quarterly* (Fall 1966), 119–126.

25. Mazurkiewicz, Albert J. "Lehigh-Bethlehem — I/T/A Study Interim Report Six," *Journal of the Reading Specialist* (September 1964), 3.

26. _____, First Grade Reading Using Modified Co-Basal Versus The Initial Teaching Alphabet. USOE, Cooperative Research Project No. 2676, 1965.

27. Ohanian, Vera, "Control Populations In I/T/A Experiments," *Elementary English* (April 1966), 373–80.

28. Serwer, Blanche and Lawrence M. Stolurow, "Computer-Assisted Learning in Language Arts," *Elementary English* (May 1970), 641–50.

29. Shuy, Roger W. "Some Considerations for Developing Beginning Reading Materials for Ghetto Children," *Journal of Reading Behavior* (Spring 1969), 33–43.

30. Southgate, Vera, "Approaching i.t.a. Results with Caution," *Reading Research Quarterly* (Spring 1966), 35–56.

31. Staiger, Ralph C. "Self Responsibility and Reading," *Education* (May 1957), 561–5.

32. Stone, Clarence R. "Questionable Trends in Beginning Reading," *Elementary School Journal* (January 1966), 214–22.

33. Tanyzer, Harold J., and Harvey Alpert, *Effectiveness of Three Different Basal Reading Systems on First Grade Reading Achievement.* USOE, Cooperative Research Project No. 2720, 1965.

34. Veatch, Jeannette, *Reading In The Elementary School.* New York: The Ronald Press Company, 1966, Chapter 9.

35. Wilson, Richard C. "Criteria for Effective Grouping," in *Forging Ahead In Reading*, J. Allen Figurel (ed.), Proceedings, International Reading Association, 275–77.

36. Worth, Walter H. and Harlan Shores, "Does Nonpromotion Improve Achievement in the Language Arts?" *Elementary English* (January 1960), 49–52.

6

Beginning Reading

PART II

Chapter 5 included a definition of reading, the goals of beginning instruction, suggestions for developing a proper climate for learning, and an overview of selected newer materials available for beginning instruction. This chapter continues the discussion of methodology, specifically basal materials, the language experience approach, and the major facets of a balanced instructional program for beginning reading.

The process of learning to read is not dependent upon moving through a particular body of content. It consists of mastering a derived language process which is a long-term developmental endeavor. The child can learn needed reading skills through the use of any of a number of printed passages. These materials may be children's books, stories dictated by the child himself, basal texts, experience charts, myths, biographies, riddles, children's newspapers, programmed work books, or subject matter content in any area. The one criterion that any material would have to meet is that of appropriateness to the reader's present level of development.

The major question in reading instruction is not what printed material to teach from, but rather to determine what skills to teach and when and how to teach them. However, when an individual addresses himself to these questions, he usually develops a set of materials which reflect previous decisions about what to teach and where on the educational continuum to teach particular skills. Materials also reflect *how* to teach particular facets of reading.

Language-Experience Materials

Regardless of what other materials may have been adopted by schools or used by teachers, most teachers of beginning reading include teacher-written charts and stories in their reading programs. Pupil experiences used as the content for writing charts and stories is a practice of long standing. Throughout the years, modifications and extensions have resulted in renewed emphasis on this procedure. For a comprehensive history of the language experience approach, the reader might consult Smith (31) and Hildreth (11). In addition to these sources, two early publications devoted to descriptions of experience-based materials are Gans' (8) *Guiding Children's Reading Through Experience* and Lamoreaux and Lee's (15) *Learning to Read Through Experience*.

The latter work (1943) describes the rationale, as well as concrete procedures, for using teacher-written experience charts. These materials, written by teachers, were envisioned as the basic instructional program. A revision (1963) by Lee and Allen (17) deals not only with experience charts for use with the class as a whole, but stresses the advantages of teachers' writing individual stories for individual students.

The experience chart

The experience chart is a means of capturing the interest of children by tying their personal experiences to reading activities. The chart, which tells about a shared activity, is a story produced cooperatively by the teacher and the class. This is a natural extension of earlier and less difficult experiences wherein the teacher wrote single words, short sentences, days of the week, names of months, the seasons, children's birthdays, and holidays, on the chalkboard. The experience chart provides practice in a number of developmental skills which are closely related to reading. For example:

1. Oral language usage in group-planning prior to a trip and in recounting the experience, for chart building, after a trip
2. The give-and-take of ideas as the experience is discussed

3. Sharpening sensory acuity, particularly visual and auditory, while on excursions
4. Expanding concepts and vocabulary
5. Reinforcing the habit of reading from left to right
6. Experience in learning words as wholes, thus building sight vocabulary
7. Reading the sentence as a unit
8. Reading about one's own experiences, emphasizing that reading is getting meaning from printed words

All of the points cited above are appropriate both to readiness and to beginning reading, and the experience chart should not be thought of as belonging exclusively to one stage of development. The experience chart has merit in proportion to the degree to which certain logical practices are followed. For instance, vocabulary must be simple, and sentences short; a minimum of sentences must be used, and each sentence must contribute to the story. There should be deliberate repetition of common sight words.

Preparing a group experience story

The teacher and children plan for a visit to the zoo, a nearby farm, or the library. Let us assume that the teacher has been able to make all of the necessary arrangements for a trip to the community library. She has arranged for the use of the school bus and has spoken to the librarian, who has volunteered to read the class a story and set up a display of children's books. When she has the attention of the entire class, the teacher might say, "I talked to Mrs. Winters, the librarian, the other day and she invited all of you to come to the library and look at the new books — maybe some of you would want to take a book home with you. I wonder if it would be fun if we took a trip to the library?"

CHILDREN: "Let's go!"
"I'd like that."
TEACHER: "If we go, we'll have to make plans first. What are some things we should decide?"
BILLY: "Can we go today?"
TEACHER: "Billy asks when can we go? We can't go today; we have to make our plans first."
CHILD: "Let's go tomorrow."
TEACHER: "How many would like to go tomorrow?"
(General agreement)

TEACHER: "How shall we get to the library?"
MIKE: "Let's walk."
MARY: "Can we go in a car?"
TEACHER: "Mike suggests we walk, but it's quite a long way from here; Mary suggested we go in a car, but it would take a lot of cars for all of us. Maybe we could go in the school bus."

(Excitement heightens in the class.)

The class and the teacher talk about what they should do and what they should not do at the library. Following each discussion, the teacher writes the decision on the board; from this activity an experience chart emerges. The chart itself may not be the most important outcome of this educational endeavor. The children have experienced how the group process works; co-operative planning and individual contributions have resulted in identifying and structuring a goal. The children are now ego-involved in a trip to the library. Their experience chart follows:

Plans for Our Trip

We will go to the library.
We will go tomorrow.
We will go in the school bus.
This will be fun.
We can look at books.
We will sit in our chairs.
We will hear a story.

The children enjoyed the trip to the library. Mrs. Winters, the librarian, had three tables of children's books available; she showed where the children's books were kept on the shelves and on a book rack. She talked about how to treat books — not to fold pages or tear the paper cover. The children were permitted to look at the books and the pictures. Finally, Mrs. Winters read them the story *Stone Soup.** The children clapped their hands when Mrs. Winters finished the story. They thanked her and then returned to their classroom on the school bus.

That same day they discussed their trip and the things they saw and did and heard. The natural outcome was to "write a story"

---

*Marcia Brown (New York: Charles Scribner's Sons, 1947).

about their experience. The teacher asked questions and occasionally substituted words to keep the vocabulary reasonable. The following discussion developed the title for the story.

TEACHER: "What shall we call our story?"

BOB: "What we did at the library."

TEACHER: "That's a good suggestion; does anyone else have a name for our story?"

MARY: "I think it should be called 'We have a nice time at the library.' "

TEACHER: "Fine — anyone else?"

RUTH: "Things we did on our trip to the library."

TEACHER: "Those are all fine — we did have a very nice visit, we did learn many things and we did enjoy the story Mrs. Winters read us. Would it be all right to call our story 'Our Trip to the Library'?"

Since the children agreed to the title, she printed it on the chalkboard, saying each word as she wrote it and then reading the entire line, being careful to move her hand slowly from left to right as she read. Next, she inquired what incidents should be related in the story and accepted the various suggestions while attempting to keep the vocabulary as simple as possible. Each line of the story was developed in much the same way as the title was. The teacher was careful to see that all of the students participated. The following chart is the result:

Our Trip to the Library

We rode in the school bus.
The bus took us to the library.
We looked at many books.
We sat at tables.
We looked at books and pictures.
Mrs. Winters read us a story.
The story was *Stone Soup.*
We thanked Mrs. Winters.
Our trip was fun.

The teacher read each line as soon as she printed it on the board, again being careful to move her hand under the line from left to right as she read. The teacher and children then read the complete story. Next, a child was asked to point out the line that told how they had traveled to the library, the line that told the name of the story they had heard, the line that told where the children sat in the library, and so forth. In each case the child pointed out the desired line and attempted to read it.

The same chart may be used in other ways. Each line in the chart may be duplicated on a strip of heavy paper: *We thanked Mrs. Winters.* A child is handed a sentence and is asked to find this line on the chart. Individual words may also be printed on oaktag or cardboard and held up by the teacher while a child points out that particular word on the chart: *books, us, bus.* Word cards may be prepared for each word in a particular line. These are handed to a child in mixed order, and he is to arrange them in proper order to correspond with the line on the chart. These tasks can be either seatwork or boardwork. The experience chart can be used with the class as a whole and also with various reading groups. After its main use with a unit, it may be referred to incidentally when certain words used on the chart come up in other contexts and in other activities.

Individual experience stories

Children enjoy talking about their experiences, particularly about incidents which involve them, their families, their pets, and the like. One of the best ways to take advantage of such motivation is to write individual experience stories. These language productions are usually brief, ranging from one to several sentences which deal with one incident. In the early stages of reading, the stories are usually dictated by the pupils and written by the teacher.

Some of the major principles which provide the rationale for language experience stories have been outlined by Lee and Allen (17) and include:

1. What a child thinks about, he can talk about.
2. What one talks about can be expressed in writing.
3. Anything the child or teacher writes can be read.
4. One can read what he writes and what other people write.
5. What a child has to say is as important to him as what other people have written for him to read.

Since these brief stories relate the child's own experiences, they involve his ego with the reading situation. The stories are always meaningful and are written in complete sentences which closely parallel the child's own language usage. In some cases, the teacher can write brief stories based on her observation of children and events which occur in class. An excellent description of how one teacher introduced the writing of experience stories is provided by Lindberg:

> "I have something to share with you, too," the teacher says to the first graders. "I like to write books for boys and girls. Here are the ones I wrote last night. Let me read them to you."
>
> She holds up a gay booklet, "This one is called *Susan's Red Shoes*." Susan looks up. Can it be! She does have new red shoes. The other children look at Susan. They are very aware of her bright new sandals because she talked of nothing else yesterday.
>
> The teacher opens the cover and reads the first page, "Susan has new red shoes." She turns to the next page. "Her father bought them for her at Smith's Shoe Store. They cost $3.98." Now the children know for certain that it is their Susan, and Susan is beaming.
>
> The teacher continues to read. "See me stand on one foot," says Susan. "Now see me stand on the other. Now watch me jump."
>
> "I have written the story," says the teacher to Susan, "but there are no pictures in the book. Perhaps you can make some."
>
> The other children lean forward. What is in the other books?
>
> "Read some more. Read one about me," are the cries from the first graders. So they are read. *Terry's Tooth, Jane's Trip to the Farm, Harry and His Big Brother, Roy's Birthday Cake, Cowboy Joe, Here Comes Josephine* are the titles.
>
> "But there wasn't one about me!" is the refrain when all of the books have been read.
>
> "See that pile of books on my desk? There isn't anything written in them. Why don't you tell me what to write — then you will have a book, too."
>
> During their work period, several children dictate stories. These will be read to the others the next morning. (19)

Experience stories need not be limited to accounts of personal experiences. Observations of the world outside the classroom can also serve as story topics: a seed growing into a plant, astronauts exploring the moon, squirrels gathering nuts in the fall, a hurricane in the news for several days striking a community, an oilspill threatening wildlife. As children talk, describe, and interpret such events, their own language is written down. As they practice reading, they also expand their concepts and enlarge their world; the magic of language is thus transferred to reading.

The amount of magic that gets into the method depends on the teacher. The experience approach can be open-ended, flexible, and highly motivating. It can also become highly structured or overly dominated by the teacher. Obviously the most difficult task is to somehow make the transition between the child's highly developed language usage and his developing ability to cope with the graphic representation of that language. Sessions devoted to skills development must somehow be included in the instructional program. Good teachers are learning that *language* can be smuggled into the teaching of skills.

The experience approach as method

Experience charts and stories can be used in any method of teaching reading. When a program limits instructional materials to this one type, the resulting instruction might be referred to as the *experience method*. Any procedure may have both merits and limitations, and this seems particularly true of the experience approach to teaching reading. The major strengths of experience stories and charts have been discussed previously; some potential weaknesses which may result from *overreliance* on teacher-written materials are:

1. It is difficult to control vocabulary. Too many words may be introduced at one time.
2. Basic sight words may not be repeated often enough to insure mastery.
3. When used exclusively as a *method*, it puts too much of a burden on the teacher, demands much time and a high level of training.
4. It is difficult to adapt this type of instruction to the needs and abilities of *all* children.
5. It encourages memorization rather than mastery of sight words.

The strengths and weaknesses of the experience method are relative and not inherent in the method itself. Under certain conditions, all of the advantages of the method might be lost through overemphasis, misuse, or lack of understanding. In other situations the effects of certain of the cited disadvantages could be held to a minimum through a teacher's skill, experience, and clear understanding of objectives. In the writer's opinion, the experience approach is most vulnerable when advocated as a complete method in itself.

Most teachers prefer to use the experience chart as a supplement to basals and other materials. This permits certain of the weaknesses to be minimized. The basic readers provide drill on sight vocabulary and control over the introduction of new words. The use of experience charts adds flexibility and interest to the program.

The Basal Reader Approach to Teaching Reading

For decades, basal reader series have served as one of the chief instructional materials used in the elementary grades for teaching reading. These materials are widely used today despite the fact that in recent years basals have been widely criticized. Critics have alleged that:

1. The materials are dull, insipid, and too repetitive.
2. The language used is somewhat removed from the child's own language usage.
3. Story material often lacks literary merit.
4. Too little emphasis is placed on teaching letter-sound relationships in grade one.
5. Content deals almost exclusively with characters and incidents drawn from middle class strata; and conversely minority groups were practically ignored. (25)

Throughout the 1950's and early 1960's all basal series tended to be very much alike. Significant innovations were held to a minimum, and the above criticisms, as they related to many materials, were justified. (16) On the other hand, there were a number of indefensible teaching practices found in the schools which were not suggested or condoned by any basal program. However, certain critics of basals contended that these practices were inevitable outcomes of using basals. For instance, when using basals, teachers will:

1. Have a group of children read "round-robin" every story they read. Each child will be asked to focus his attention on the same line at a given time.
2. Without exception resort to "three groups" within a classroom, and these groups will remain static throughout the year.
3. Make no provision for individual differences beyond this "three-group" pattern.

4. Hold the more facile reader to the basal material only, forcing him to move through this material at a pace far below his capacity.
5. Prohibit children from selecting and reading other books in which they may be interested.

Unfortunately, the above practices could be found in certain classrooms. Removing basals from these classrooms, however, would not get at the basic problem which essentially is poor teaching. The following is a description of the materials usually found in any basal reading series. These materials are arranged to parallel the grade-level system. They range in difficulty from a work-type readiness book (containing pictures, geometrical forms, and letter-matching exercises) to rather massive anthologies at seventh- and eighth-grade levels.

Readiness books

At the readiness level one might find picture books in which a picture or series of pictures suggests a child-centered story. From the pictures the teacher and the pupils develop a story. The more skillful the teacher is in providing background and involving the pupils in participation and interpretation, the more successful the use of these materials will be. Other readiness books may call for children to identify and mark similar objects, letters, or words, to facilitate the development of visual perception. To strengthen auditory discrimination, the child will identify two pictures in a group whose naming words rhyme. Identifying other pairs of pictures which start with the same sound gives practice in the discrimination of initial sounds.

Pre-primers

The readiness books are followed by a series of three or four pre-primers in which the characters are the same ones the children met and talked about in the readiness books. The pre-primers introduce pupils to printed words *along with pictures*. The first few pages may have single words which are "naming words" to go with the picture. Gradually more words and sentences per page are used.

Many basal materials are characterized by a rather rigid vocabulary control in the pre-primer and primer stages. This control does not involve *which* words are introduced, but rather the *rate* at which they are introduced. Thus the introduction of twenty to twenty-five different words would be representative of most first pre-primers (pp¹). Usually there are three or four pre-primers in a given series, and each of these will introduce approximately this same number of new words while systematically repeating those words previously introduced.

Since stories in the first pre-primer are limited to two dozen different words, the story, of necessity, lacks literary merit. Adult critics have described this material as "dull, insipid, contrived, and offensive to the eye and ear." It is much easier to level such criticisms against materials than it is to solve the problem of how to present vibrant prose to six year olds who cannot as yet read anything in print. In defense of criticism, the truth is that for several decades basal materials did remain quite static. During this period, the frequent "revisions" of these materials were quite meaningless.

Until the mid 1960's, the primary difference between competing basals was to be found in the names of the characters who pulled the little red wagons and called to the housebroken doggies. However, at the present time there are basal materials available which represent a wider philosophical continuum. Some basals stress meaning and an early emphasis on sight vocabulary, others emphasize code cracking, and some attempt to achieve a balance between these two polar positions. Most basals now include materials deliberately chosen to meet the psychological needs and interests of boys — a belated effort to close the reading achievement gap between boys and girls. Story characters and life situations involving minority groups are now the rule rather than the exception. The literary quality of materials for use beyond the beginning stage has been upgraded. While basals have changed more in the past decade than during the previous thirty years, some critics hold that the changes are more apparent than real.

Primers

The primer is the first hard-back book in the series. It carefully builds on what has gone before, using the same characters the children are familiar with and reviewing the words already met, while it introduces 100 to 150 new words.

First readers

Some series contain a single first reader; others have two (1¹ level and 1² level). Different series vary as to vocabulary load introduced, but a range between 315 and 400 words for first grade is representative.

Graded readers

Each subsequent grade level introduces one or more basal reading books. Many series provide two books at each of the grade levels, second through fourth, and one book at grades five and beyond. These are usually designated by grade number plus a subscript which indicates first or second half of the year (2^1–2^2, 3^1–3^2, 4–5–6–7–8).

Workbooks

Separate workbooks which parallel each level (pre-primers, primers, first readers 2^1–2^2, etc.) are available. The workbooks present material arranged as teaching exercises. These are usually designed so that one concept or skill is dealt with on each page. The exercises reinforce the teaching of skills which are being dealt with in the readers. In some cases, workbook pages are tied to specific stories in the reader. In others, skill-building exercises are independent of story content and could be used whether or not a particular basal reader were available.

Supplementary materials

It is becoming more common at all grade levels for basic reader series to include some supplementary books to be used in conjunction with the regular graded series. There has always been an abundant supply of these supplementary materials available at the intermediate level. Recently, good supplementary books have appeared at the early primary level where they are sorely needed. Some of these are easy to read, introducing very few words other than those already met in the regular basal texts. Others are designed for the more advanced readers and are more difficult and more challenging than the regular graded series.

Other supplementary materials include large poster-size wall charts or spiral-book charts which exactly duplicate a pre-primer. The large picture and large print have obvious advantages for classroom use. There has been considerable emphasis on film strips designed for use with basic readers series. The reading gains reported as resulting from the systematic use of film strips and other visual aids are encouraging. (20, 21)

Teacher manuals

Teacher manuals or guide books, containing suggestions for effective use of materials, accompany each reading level. That is, a separate manual is available for the pre-primer, primer, and first reader stages as well as for each subsequent level (2^1–2^2–3^1–3^2, etc.). These manuals are discussed in more detail in the following section.

Using a
Basal Reader Series

The purpose here is to deal with the framework of basal programs as designed for the first year of instruction. The major advantages of using a good series include:

1. Modern reader series are characterized by excellent use of pictures and art work.
2. A number of the first books used deal with the same characters, giving children a feeling of familiarity with the material and adding to their confidence in reading.
3. The books are graded to provide systematic instruction from the pre-readiness level through the upper elementary grades.
4. These graded materials permit teachers a great deal of flexibility in dealing with individual differences and in working with children grouped according to attained reading skill.
5. Excellent teacher guides are provided for each book or level. These provide suggestions for a step-by-step teaching program.
6. If used properly, the basic reader series deals with all phases of the reading program, guarding against overemphasis on some aspects and neglect of others.
7. Practice of new skills is introduced in a logical sequence.
8. A great deal of review is provided in deliberate, well-thought-out procedures.
9. The vocabulary is rigidly controlled to prevent frustration in beginning reading.
10. Use of prepared materials saves teachers considerable time.

A well-balanced program

Providing a well-balanced program is a virtue of basal series, particularly in the beginning reading stage. They provide for silent and oral reading, and by means of grouping and through individual work, the teacher can vary the emphasis for different pupils. The preparation of pupils for tasks is thoroughly outlined in the teacher's manual. During the readiness period, the children have used a pre-reading book which included a number of pictures. Through these pictures the children were introduced to the characters that they will meet again in the pre-primer, primer, and first reader. The teacher acquaints the children with the names of these characters and prints their names on the chalkboard, thus preparing them for the first words they will encounter in the pre-primer. The pictures are specific in that they represent *particular* persons, but they are general in that the characters in them are doing things that most children understand. Out of these picture situations, discussion can grow and provide an intoduction to formal reading in basal materials.

The first few pages of the pre-primer may be only pictures, but very soon words are introduced. These will probably be the names of the boy and girl who have been met previously in pictures — Jane, Sally, Ted, or Jack. The teacher will probably use the chalkboard and flash cards for both teaching and reviewing words. During seatwork, the children will draw a line from the word (*Sally, father, Ted,* etc.) to a picture the word represents. They might be asked to underline one of three sentences which describe a picture:

> Sally rides in the wagon.
> Sally plays with Spot.
> Sally plays with Father.

Such exercises help children learn words in the first pre-primer. Soon, more than one familiar word will appear on each page but rarely more than one *new* word.

The repetition of words in beginning reading can dull the child's appetite for reading. The teacher must guide the pupils into both imaginative and reminiscent "building of ideas and stories." The book may contain the words "Look, Mother" under the picture. These words, with the help of the picture, can serve as the basis for a great number of interesting and logical questions and conjectures. Perhaps from the following, one might easily visualize the picture that accompanies "Look, Mother."

> "Who is in the picture?"
> "Yes, what is Tom doing?"
> "Does Spot like to wear Tom's hat?"
> "What is Tom's mother doing?"
> "Is she watching Tom?"
> "Would he like for her to see Spot?"
> "Does Spot look funny?"
> "What does Tom say to his mother—who will read what he says?"

Many other points could have been discussed—pets in general, kindness to pets (Tom was not hurting Spot, but playing). Why wasn't mother watching? (Sometimes mothers are busy.) Why was she picking flowers? (Innumerable good responses.) What season of the year was this? As the child learns more words, he has less need for pictures which suggest the context or hold attention. As the pupils move through the basal series and master sight words, they need less story analysis by the teacher.

Comprehension and meaning are emphasized as children select the best titles for paragraphs or short stories or as they recall sequences of events. Concepts of time, number, size, and direction are developed through seatwork which calls for children to follow directions, to perceive relationships, to grasp main ideas, and to anticipate events. Auditory discrimination exercises are provided in the form of rhyming exercises and an emphasis on the initial sounds of words. Motor coordination of small muscles is developed in exercises such as tracing, coloring outlined forms, drawing connecting lines between matching words, and copying words from a model.

Teacher's guides

One of the greatest advantages in using a good series is the availability of excellent teacher guides. These guides are carefully worked out by the authors with the total reading program in mind. Sound laws of learning are followed, specific techniques are suggested, lesson plans are given in great detail, and the reasons for using certain approaches are explained. The beginning teacher would be remiss in not following the teacher guides and in not becoming very familiar with the rationale and concrete suggestions they contain. Experienced teachers might find the detail of these manuals a bit tedious, but they know that they can take what is offered and adapt it in light of their own experience.

The thorough and extensive treatment typical of teacher guides is exemplified in the manual for the readiness book, *Getting Ready To Read.** This teacher guide contains over one hundred pages of suggestions and directions for use with a pre-reading program. In the Robinson, et al., series, a teacher's guide consisting of over 250 pages is available for use with two pre-primers.** Considering that these pre-primers contain 75 different words, it is obvious that the guide is thorough and goes beyond the mechanical aspects of in-

---

*Paul McKee and M. Lucile Harrison (4th ed.; Boston: Houghton Mifflin Company, 1966).

**Helen M. Robinson, et al., "The New Basic Readers" Guidebook, Second and Third Pre-Primers (Chicago: Scott, Foresman and Company, 1965).

struction at this level. Separate manuals for the primer and first reader each contain approximately 250 pages of material addressed to the teacher.

With this type of meticulous concern for every facet of the reading program, the various guides can be excused for sometimes stressing the inevitable as if it were a deliberately planned virtue of the basic readers. It is common practice to find teacher's guides making much of the fact that pre-primers, primers, and first readers "do not require children to deal with concepts beyond their experience level." Considering the small number of words found in these materials, it would be a challenge, using only this vocabulary, to confront the child with concepts beyond his experience level. He uses twenty to thirty times the number of words and understands many more.

The foregoing discussion has touched on the alleged major weakness of the basic reader series. The concern for controlling the introduction of new words puts a limit on the variety of reading material which can be accommodated within the desired framework. The teacher must motivate children to identify themselves with the characters and the situations depicted, even though these may be somewhat alien to children of certain socio-economic groups. Without identification, the vicarious experiences gained from reading about a set of middle-class siblings, their parents, and their dog, may not seem half as fascinating as television. If one reads the guides carefully, it will be obvious that a major portion of their content is devoted to suggesting ways and means of bringing in background and of extending the concepts and the meanings actually found in the reading materials. This is important because the child's interest must not be permitted to lag.

Use of workbooks

As pointed out previously, workbooks constitute one of the important supplementary features of basal reader series. The educational value of using workbooks has been debated for years. It is true that seatwork in the form of workbook exercises can deteriorate into nothing more than "busy work" if teachers permit this to occur. However, this is only a potential danger not an inevitable outcome. A child may "learn" to daydream or doodle in workbook sessions. But with the right type of guidance, he can develop self-reliance and independence in work habits.

Workbooks properly used can have considerable educational value. Since a wide variety of skills are dealt with, it is likely that some exercises can be found that provide needed and meaningful practice in mastering essential skills. Workbooks can serve as diagnostic instruments since they will identify those children who do not understand a particular step in the reading process. A study of errors made by children will suggest to the alert teacher where further instruction is needed.

For some children, workbook exercises have value in that they are brief—usually one page. This factor is especially appealing to the child with a short attention span. A given workbook or developmental series deals with a wide variety of tasks. This provides work on new skills as well as review of skills partially mastered. Workbooks, like all other instructional media, are neither inherently good or bad. The way they are used can result in either of these outcomes.

Economy of time

Economy of teachers' time is a major factor in the widespread use of basal series. This is closely related to the previous point of a balanced reading program. No teacher would ever have the time to match the meticulous planning that is reflected in the total program of a good basal series. When a teacher has materials available for teaching and drill on every facet of reading, she will have more time to prepare supplementary exercises as needed. It will still be necessary to prepare these for certain pupils, since the basal program cannot possibly meet all individual needs. However, it is easier to prepare supplementary lessons for a few than it is to build the entire program for all pupils.

Providing for individual differences

Since a basal series includes many levels of difficulty, the teacher who understands her pupils and who is not compulsive in her teaching will be able to use these materials to advantage. Proficient readers may complete grade level materials much more rapidly than do the other children. These readers should then be encouraged to read supplementary trade books. The poorest reader should not be expected to read the same book month after month or year after year. Other basal materials (at the child's reading level) should be available. Impaired readers will have more success with "graded" materials than they will with books which reflect a minimum of vocabulary control.

From the standpoint of the busy teacher, one of the major contributions of any good basal series is the seatwork which is provided in workbooks. A separate workbook is available at every level — readiness, pre-primer, primer, and first reader. Many exercises are tied to particular stories in the reading text; others are independent of actual stories but closely parallel or supplement the new tasks. This varied nature of the workbooks in the basal series allows for flexibility in assignments, which is an aid to the teacher searching for ways to accommodate individual differences. Figure 13 attempts to illustrate the different levels one is likely to find among children in a given first grade and the correlative materials available in a basal reader series.

1. Readiness work, auditory discrimination, beginning sound in words, rhymes, etc., visual discriminations, has not learned enough sight words to read pre-primer

2. Making progress in PP$^{2-3}$

3. Successful reading of primer

4. Successful first readers

5. Can read in 2^1 readers

6. Can read in 2^2 readers

7. Third readers or above

FIGURE 13

A Graphic Representation of the Reading Levels Which Could Be Expected for a Given Class Near the End of Grade One.

Review

Adequate review is systematically provided in basal series. Children do not learn sight words, the sound of letters, initial blends, inflectional endings, and the like, as a result of one or two experiences. The introduction of new words is carefully controlled, and once a word or concept is introduced, it will be repeated many times. Tests, designed to show pupils' mastery of all skills previously introduced, are provided in workbooks. These workbooks, when used properly, can serve as diagnostic tools to indicate where more teaching or review is needed.

The previous discussion is not meant to imply that basal reader series *are* the reading program. A teacher may rely quite heavily on these materials and still teach reading through the use of bulletin boards, labeling objects, drawings and pictures, experience charts, and reading stories and poetry. These reading experiences are not incidental but are deliberately planned.

Trade Books

In addition to materials designed specifically for teaching children how to read, there are a number of "trade" or story books published every year. These materials are often referred to as "library books," but in any sound reading program such books will be present in

abundance in every classroom. Until recently the number of such books which children with first grade reading ability might read were quite limited. Today, hundreds of titles are available. Representative series include: *Beginner Books, Easy to Read Books, Early I Can Read Books, I Can Read Books*. Both the number of books and publishers producing such books are constantly being augmented.

Trade, or story, books for beginning readers follow the principle of controlled vocabulary. The easier books contain as few as 75 different words. At a somewhat higher difficulty level, children may participate vicariously in a space flight while reading a book containing no more than 300 different words. This vocabulary, abetted by excellent illustrations, manages to deal with some fairly high-level concepts. Thus, in addition to story-type materials, there are also many books available in such areas as science, travel, biography, and exploration.

The extensive use of self-selected trade books as an integral part of the reading program is one of the basic trends of the individualized teaching movement. This approach is discussed in more detail in Chapter 11.

**Three Major
Instructional Tasks**

Insofar as mastering the reading process is concerned, there are three instructional tasks which represent the major thrust of beginning reading instruction. Their importance diminishes little, if any, throughout the entire process of learning to read. These instructional tasks are: Helping the child

1. Develop and expand a sight vocabulary.
2. Learn to associate visual symbols with speech sounds.
3. See that reading is always a meaning-making process, and that printed word symbols represent speech.

Some instructional materials tend to treat the first two of these facets of instruction as independent skills which should be taught in sequence, either 1. first or 2. first, over an extended period of time. Children can learn much of what is taught in such an instructional approach, but in doing so they run the risk of developing attitudes and habits which "color" their concept of the reading process. When beginning reading instruction overemphasizes letter analysis, learning sight words, or reliance on context, children tend to become overdependent on the particular skill emphasized.

It is easy to inculcate pupils with a "set" which may neglect one or more of these important clues. This is uneconomical and may result in habits which handicap the reader in his later development. For instance, a child may develop a set to sound out every word he meets. This means he will be sounding out the same word the tenth, twentieth, or even the fiftieth time it is met in reading situations. He has learned that reading is "sounding out words," and this becomes his goal in all reading situations.

On the other hand, overemphasis on learning sight words in the absence of letter-sounding techniques overburdens the child with the task of making minute visual discriminations, where minimal sounding techniques would have made his task much easier. Sight words, plus context, plus the use of the minimal sounding clues necessary to solve unknown printed words, is more efficient than overreliance on one technique alone.

The premise underlying this discussion is that the major instructional tasks identified above are inseparable parts of one total instructional process. Each of these skills — expanding sight vocabulary, learning letter-sound relationships, and using context — are essential at each point on the learning continuum. They interact and complement each other in every reading situation. Thus, the major task of reading instruction is to arrive at the proper blending of those three instructional components.

What makes reading instruction complicated is that there is no blueprint which spells out precisely where and how much instructional time and effort should be devoted to each of these skills. And second, there is no blueprint which tells us what particular instructional techniques will have the most efficacy with particular learners. Understanding individual differences among learners become the key to these questions.

Synchronizing the Teaching of the Essential Skills

There is little basis for questioning the fact that children can learn to recognize "words as wholes." However, if this is seen as the exclusive approach to teaching beginning reading, the time quickly comes when distinguishing words becomes extremely confusing. The learning process is slowed or even halted. The child needs to apply the knowledge that a given letter in different words represents the same speech sound. For example, he must learn that an unknown printed word which begins with *M* must start with the same sound as any other *known* word which begins with *M*.

No matter how much letter-sound analysis a child learns, it is essential that he also continuously increase the number of words that he can recognize instantly. Letter analysis and contextual setting has helped him arrive at the speech equivalent of a number of printed word symbols. Repetition of a given response to particular printed word patterns has reinforced that response to the point where further clues are not needed. On the same page which contains dozens of known sight words, there will be found words which the reader is still solving through the help of letter analysis. When these words have been met and solved many times, they too become sight words; but analysis is still used with other less frequently met words.

This process is never-ending for the person who continues to read and who reads widely. No individual has ever mastered all of the approximately 600,000 words in the English language, but his sight vocabulary grows as he reads. The average reader in a third grade class will have mastered hundreds of frequently met words as "sight words." If he has not done so, he does not meet the criterion of being an average third grade reader.

Context clues can be useful aids in solving unknown words if the reader demands meaning from what he reads. Context plus a minimal amount of letter analysis focused on the beginning of the words is much superior to context alone. This combination of clues is also much superior to intensive analysis on a word-by-word basis which ignores the contextual setting of the unknown word.

In the following illustrations a blank line is used to represent an unknown word.

"The boy waved goodbye as the train left the _____." Even when the sentence has a blank line substituted for the word, most readers have no problem in supplying the correct word. One would have to strain in order to miscall the unknown word if he heeded the first letter supplied below:

"The boy waved goodbye as the train left the s_____."

Other reading situations will present more difficult problems. For example:

"The girl waved goodbye to her _____."

Here quite a number of possible word choices would make meaning: friend, mother, sister, teacher, brother, parents, family, playmate, aunt, cousin, uncle, etc. Select *any* word that makes meaning and insert only its first letter in the blank space. Note how many of the words that were possibilities are now eliminated when the reader heeds the sound associated with that initial letter.

The efficacy of combining skills is often more dramatically illustrated in larger contexts. In the first version of a story provided below, it is possible to get the sense of the story even if one is not sure of the identity of a number of the missing words. The second version provides only the initial letter of each missing word.

> John and his Cousin_____started on their fishing trip. John said, "I have my trusty _____ pole, a _____ full of lunch, and a can of _____." After walking a long time, John said, "Not far from here there is a _____ across the stream. We can sit on the _____ and fish." When they started fishing, John said, "I'm not going to _____ from this _____ until I catch a _____ _____." Finally _____ said, "I am tired of sitting on the _____. I am going to take a walk along the _____." _____ had walked only a short way when he lost his _____ and fell into the stream. The water was not very deep and he waded out. "Hey," said John, "you're lucky. You won't have to take a _____ when we get home."

The version below inserts the initial letter in each unknown word, which in all cases happens to be the letter *b*.

> John and his Cousin B _ _ started out on their fishing trip. John said, "I have my trusty b _ _ _ _ pole, a b _ _ full of lunch, and a can of b _ _ _." After walking a long time, John said, "Not far from here there is a b _ _ _ _ _ across the stream. We can sit on the b _ _ _ _ _ and fish." When they started fishing, John said, "I'm not going to b _ _ _ _ from this b _ _ _ _ _ until I catch a b _ _ b _ _ _." Finally B _ _ said, "I am tired of sitting on the b _ _ _ _ _. I am going to take a walk along the b _ _ _." B _ _ had walked only a short way when he lost his b _ _ _ _ _ _ and fell into the stream. The water was not very deep and he waded out. "Hey," said John, "you're lucky. You won't have to take a b _ _ _ when we get home."*

---

*Words in the order of their omission are: Bob, bamboo, bag, bait, bridge, bridge, budge, bridge, big bass, Bob, bridge, bank, Bob, balance, bath.

Mistakes in reading can be made even in situations where one has the ability to recognize all the words in a passage.

> Mary had a little lamp
> Its base was white as snow.

The child who knows the verse about Mary and her lamb may well be trapped into miscalling *lamb* for *lamp* and *face* for *base*, but as he reads further his mistake should become obvious.

> Mary had a little lamp
> Its base was white as snow,
> She turned it on when she came in
> And off, when out she'd go.

Since the reader has been taught to read for meaning, the mistakes on the first two lines do not permit a good fit with the concluding two lines. The reader would likely reason somewhat as follows: "Slow down — look again; that doesn't make sense; this is not about a lamb in school."

Advocating the simultaneous teaching of sight words, letter analysis, and context clues does not mean that occasional instructional periods cannot be devoted primarily to one or another of these teachings. What it does mean is that the teacher need not feel compelled to teach 50–70 sight words before teaching any letter-sound analysis. Or conversely, she will not devote the first 8–10 weeks of instruction to letter-sound analysis to the total exclusion of building sight vocabulary. Furthermore, she will not withhold insights about the role of context clues for fear a child may become a "word guesser." To do this is to negate the one important learning which the child brings to reading — language is meaning bearing.

Developing and Expanding Sight Vocabulary

The normal child's experience with reading will result in his acquiring a constantly enlarging stock of sight words. He will have established automatic stimulus-response patterns for dozens of frequently used words such as: *that, with, will, be, come, are, and, some, was, it, an, the, in, which, to, than, no, what, stop, you, they, now, us, said, when, him, go, little, can,* and the like. A number of these structure words and other frequently used words must be "overlearned" to the point where recognizing them is automatic.

There is a difference between overlearning certain frequently used words and learning to overrely on one approach to beginning reading, whether that approach be whole words, letter analysis, or context. The normal pattern of learning dictates that the child develop a sight vocabulary or learn some words "as wholes." The purpose of the following discussion is to illustrate briefly a limited number of approaches which may help to facilitate learning.

Learning to read children's names

1. Probably the first printed word a child learns is his name. Many first grade teachers tape each child's first name on the front of his desk.

Mary	Mike	Sarah	Sandy

Children learn the names of other children, and many learn very quickly to recognize a number of names in printed form. The practice of learning names in printed form provides the basis for teaching letter-sound analysis, discussed later.

2. Use of blackboard announcements involving pupils' names.

Hand out books	*Water the plants*
John	Jean
Helen	Billy

Labeling objects in the room

The teacher prints a naming word on separate oak tag cards.

door	book	plant	blackboard	table

Each card is held up and a volunteer is selected to say the word and place the card on the object it names.

Association of printed word with a picture it names

1. Secure a number of pictures which depict objects or animals within the children's range of experience. Paste the picture on cardboard and print the naming word beneath it.

cat

cow

horse

house

2. To add the kinesthetic sensory mode to the words, duplicate a page of outline drawings and leave space for the children to write (copy) the names from models displayed on the chalk tray. In the first experience the printed words may be outlined with dots. The child then marks over the dots writing the words.

3. A later exercise may be one which omits the dotted outlines and the child copies from the printed models on the chalk tray, chalkboard, or bulletin board.

Reading teacher-printed sentences

1. Today is Tuesday.
    Today we have our music lesson.
    Miss Rogers comes to our room at 10:00 o'clock.

The teacher reads each sentence, then asks the class to read with her. Following this, she may ask different pupils to go to the board and underline particular words such as *have, our, today, room.*

2. Assembling scrambled sentences.

Individual words, from sentences used previously on the chalkboard, are printed on separate cards. These are presented in scrambled order, and volunteers are chosen to arrange the words in proper order to be followed by a card bearing the proper punctuation mark.

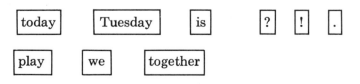

This is one of the many ways to provide repetition with particular frequently used words.

Joint teacher-pupil planning and reading of experience charts

Teacher prints on large easel or blackboard:

1. Daily happenings in classroom or school
2. Trips or visits
3. Special events charts (Valentines Day, Halloween, Thanksgiving Day, National Elections, Lincoln's or Washington's birthday, etc.)

Sentence completion exercises

The child selects the correct word from a pair of "look alike" words which completes the meaning of a sentence.

1. Child circles the correct word.
   a. Let's play _____. ball, tall
   b. In winter it is _____. hold, cold
2. At the next level of difficulty, the child may *write* the correct word in the blank space

Use of "classifying games" to teach common words

animals	clothing	food
dog	hat	milk
cat	shoes	cookies
cow	dress	pie

1. Place the underlined classification words on the board. The teacher points to and reads each word. Pupils repeat each word after the teacher pronounces it. Each of the other words to be used in the exercise is printed on oak tag or cardboard. The teacher holds up one word at a time and selects a volunteer to *pronounce* the word and to tell under which heading it belongs.

2. Variations include duplicated seatwork pages with headings such as *Toys, Plants, Months, Days.* A number of appropriate words are placed in a box at the bottom of the page and pupils copy the words under the correct heading.

Sight words are learned in myriad ways; from television, road signs, bulletin boards, labels on cartons, and the like. Obviously the most important source of learning is from meaningful reading situations as provided by charts, individual teacher-written stories, pre-primers, and easy to read trade books.

Thus far, the rationale for reading sight words has stressed only that to be a facile reader one must acquire an ever-increasing stock of "instant recognition words." The degree to which printed words are mastered as sight words is one of the most meaningful ways of differentiating between poor and accomplished readers at all grade levels. A skill of such significance to the total reading process should be taught effectively. A number of justifications for learning words as wholes are briefly summarized below:

1. If a child knows a number of words as sight words (instant recognition), he can be taught to see and to hear similarities between these known words and the new words he meets. Having a sight vocabulary is an invaluable tool in helping him "unlock" other words.
2. When words are recognized instantly, analysis is not necessary. The reader can put known words together in phrases, thus achieving intonation patterns that facilitate reading for meaning.
3. There are numerous high-frequency words which should be learned as units simply because they are met over and over in any reading situation. In addition, many of these words have irregular spellings which militates against "sounding them out."

Word Identification Skills

As noted earlier, simultaneously with developing a sight vocabulary, children must also acquire skills which will permit them to unlock or identify words which they do not instantly recognize as sight words. Since various English words are very much alike in their visual patterns, the child must learn that letters and letter combinations represent speech sounds. If English writing followed the alphabetic principle 100 percent, we could say that particular letters always represent the same sound in all words. However, this is true only of some letters, all of which are consonants.

Instruction which emphasizes associating letter forms with speech sounds has been labeled phonics instruction. The application of phonic analysis is undoubtedly the chief means used by readers to identify unknown words. It is only one of several approaches, most of which are identified in the following discussion.

Word analysis is an inclusive term which covers all methods of solving the pronunciation of printed word forms. These skills are not concerned with teaching the child how to pronounce words since he has already mastered this in learning oral language. Word analysis deals with helping the child discover what known oral language unit is *represented* by an unknown printed word symbol. The skills under discussion fall in the following categories:

1. Noting the unique appearance of words or distinctive parts of words
2. Utilizing structural analysis
   a. Prefixes and suffixes
   b. Inflectional endings *s, ed, ing,* etc.
   c. Compound words
3. Profiting from context clues
4. Applying phonic analysis
5. Using picture clues
6. Using various methods in combination

Unique letter configurations

In the early stages of reading, some children undoubtedly learn to distinguish between words on the basis of configuration or particular distinct visual features found in words. For example, the words *like* and *different* suggest the configurational patterns ⌐•⌐ and ⌐•___ . A child may develop the habit of paying special heed to the length of words, to position of tall and short letters, the dotted *i* or double letters such as *ee, tt, oo,* or *ff*.

This discussion does not advocate that such clues be pointed out or taught, but rather that children may stumble on such clues on their own. If written English consisted of word-writing (ideographic writing in which graphic symbols are not related to speech sounds), rather than being based on the alphabetic principle, this type of clue would be of paramount importance. However, the task of learning to read would be much more difficult and time-consuming.

As a matter of fact, *all* printed English words *can* be distinguished by the unique visual clues provided by letter arrangements. The only exception would be several dozen homographs, lĭve, līve; rĕcord, recŏrd; etc., whose identification depends entirely on context. But to rely solely on these minute visual clues will preclude the reader's ever becoming an independent facile reader. The task of distinguishing between twenty or thirty thousand word symbols on the basis of such minimal visual clues would be practically impossible. This approach would break down for practically all would-be readers during the primary stage of reading instruction.

The child may learn to recognize the word *look* because he notes "it has two eyes (oo) in the middle." Soon he meets a great number of other words which contain this letter combination (foot, took, wood, floor, pool, soon, food, room, good, book, stood, door, moon, boot, tooth, etc.). The double *o* ceases to be a unique identifying characteristic, and the letters which precede and follow become more important as aids in word identification.

Teaching analysis

Formal instruction in associating printed letters with speech sounds heard in words has been preceded by years of experience with related learnings. The child can discriminate rather minute differences in spoken words (*Ted, bed, fed, led, red*) (sat, sad, Sam, sack). He hears and learns these words globally rather than perceiving that each consists of three sounds (phonemes). Nevertheless, the six year old does distinguish thousands of words on the basis of minimal phoneme differences.

He understands that *cat, rat, sat* and *call, tall, ball* rhyme. He notes that the words *cat, bet, cot* do not have this quality even though they have a common concluding sound. Children cannot "explain" what is being pointed out here, but they have mastered the auditory discriminations involved.

The reading readiness program has extended the child's knowledge of language sounds by providing much practice in this area. A fairly large percent of children entering grade one have learned to make visual discriminations between some letter forms and all other letter forms. That is, they can name the letters *B, O, M, S, L, T*, etc., whenever they see these symbols. Most readiness programs now include formal instruction in letter recognition. The next step after learning to discriminate letter forms is to associate speech sounds with known letter forms. To achieve independence in reading, a child must master these leter-sound associations and be able to apply them in reading situations when he meets unknown printed words.

Phonics instruction in the schools today starts in the readiness period and extends through all stages of reading instruction. The teacher works with the children to make sure that they hear the similar beginnings or similar endings of these words. The next step is instruction on seeing that letter combinations correspond to the similar sounds in the beginnings or endings of words.

If the child recognizes *mine* and *many*, he is then led to perceive that *milk* and *mud* begin with the same symbol and thus the same sound. While he is learning sight words, he is also learning the sounds that initial letters contribute to words. If he knows the words *tell* and *sell*, he may be able to work out the word *bell*, since he also knows the words *be, by, boat,* and *boy.* Gray* calls this process "initial consonant substitution" and points out that this process can work only in relation to other *known* words. In addition to the clues just mentioned, if the child knows all of the words in the sentence except the one new word *bell,* the context in which the new word is found will also aid him in arriving at the correct choice.

The question is sometimes heard, "When should phonics instruction be introduced?" The question seems to imply that this instruction is not seen as an on-going integral part of the total reading program, but rather as a block of skills which might be plugged in at one or another point on the learning continuum. A further implication suggested by certain instructional materials is that when one decides to plug in phonics, this is done with a degree of emphasis which neglects related teachings. Evidence that balance can be achieved is provided by one teacher who describes her first phonics lesson as follows:

> I usually have a phonics lesson the first day of school. Prior to the opening of school, I print on oak tag the first name of every child assigned to my room. As the children enter, each is given his name tag. I introduce the children on a first name basis, "Class, this is Mary. Does anyone else have a name that begins the same way as Mary?" If I get a correct response, I build on it. If not, I say, "Now I want to introduce Mike, I think Mike's name begins like Mary's. Listen, children, as I say these two names; *Mike, Mary.* I hear the same sound at the beginning of both names." I then have these two children stand at the front of the room and hold their name cards so everyone can see them. I point out that if the children look closely they will *see* that each name begins with the same letter and that this letter is called M. I then print both names on the board; we pronounce the names and look carefully at the initial letter. We then move to other names such as *Bobby, Billy;* or *Henry, Harry, Helen.*

Observing in this teacher's classroom, one is impressed with the variety of approaches she uses to teach reading. All of these include some emphasis on word analysis. Every day she writes the day of the week, the month, and date, both in numbers and spelled out in words. These writings often contain words which begin with the same sounds: *Today is Tuesday, September sixth, November ninth.* In response to her questions, the children note that *Today* and *Tuesday* begin with a *T* that represents the same sound in both.

---

*William S. Gray, *On Their Own in Reading* (Rev. ed.). (Chicago: Scott, Foresman & Company, 1960).

They add other words which begin with the sound heard in *Today* and *Tuesday*, and the teacher writes these in a column on the chalkboard. They see the letter and say the words *t*omorrow, *t*ime, *t*ake, *t*ooth.

The teacher introduces the children to a game which involves participation, language usage, listening, observation of the environment, and word analysis. "I'm thinking of something in the room — its name begins like *dog* — what is it?" The children look around and respond *door, desk, David, dominos;* as well as *duck* and *dolphins,* which are seen in pictures on the bulletin board.

Every day the teacher lets three or four children come to the front of the room and dictate a "sentence story." If the child's story is a "run-on account" and becomes lengthy, the teacher and child abstract it to a sentence. This is placed on the board and read by the teacher. Then the child who dictated the story reads it to the class and chooses a pupil to underline a particular word in the sentence. This work on sight vocabulary is usually followed by some work on letter sounds. "Which two words begin with the same sound?" "There are two words that rhyme; what are they?" "Who can give a word that rhymes with *hand?*"

Techniques for teaching phonic skills are practically unlimited. A few examples follow:

1. Match two or more pictures of objects whose names begin with the same sound. The teacher secures pictures and pastes each one on cardboard. One picture from each letter series is placed on the chalk tray. As the children select a picture from the remaining pile, it is placed beside the picture whose name begins with the same sound:

fish	lamp	cake	tent	bus	horn
fence	lake	comb	turtle	book	horse

2. The final sounds in words may be stressed by using a different set of pictures:

hat	lamp	frog	book	bell	bus
boat	cup	flag	desk	towel	grapes

Interdependence of visual and auditory discrimination

Although visual and auditory discrimination may be discussed separately and lessons may be devised which emphasize one or the other, the two skills invariably work together in the reading situation. The child who learns to rely exclusively on visual clues will experience extreme difficulty as he meets hundreds of new printed words which have only minimal differences in letter configuration (*thumb, thump*). On the other hand, one cannot profit from learning letter-sound relationships if he cannot visually distinguish letters.

Attempting to teach the characteristic sound of *b* and *d* in such words as *big-dig, day-bay, dump-bump, bread-dread* cannot help the child "sound out" words unless he can instantly recognize the *b* and *d* configurations. First graders have learned to make hundreds of minute auditory discriminations required for understanding oral language. They can build upon this previous learning only if they learn to:

1. Focus on sounds (phonemes) which are blended into whole words.
2. Associate these speech sounds with the proper graphic representations (letters).

Eye and ear training

Combination eye and ear training usually comes after children have learned to recognize letters and some words. A series of work sheets can be prepared using single letters, letter blends, or words. This type of exercise may be viewed as moving beyond readiness activities, since the child must be able to recognize printed words.

1. The teacher says one of the letter symbols in each box and the child circles what he hears (*N—P—B—D*).

| (N)   M   R | B   (P)   D | S   C   (B) | T   B   (D) |

2. The teacher pronounces one word in each series (*flap, cap, tap, went*) and the child underlines that word.

clap	cap	map	*went*
flap	clap	top	want
slap	cat	*tap*	won't

3. The child marks the word in each box which rhymes with the stimulus word the teacher pronounces (*am, land, jump, day*).

hand	lamp	Jane	said
any	*sand*	came	sail
ham	fan	*dump*	*say*

4. Duplicate a number of three-word series of rhyming words:

a.	look	book	took
b.	pick	sick	kick
c.	name	game	fame

The teacher identifies the line and pronounces one of the words: "line a: *book*; line b: *pick*; line c: *name*." The children circle that word. In addition to providing practice in auditory and visual discrimination, such sheets have diagnostic value for the teacher. At a glance, she can see which children are experiencing difficulty on particular letter-sound combinations.

5. The same type of exercise can be devised to teach and test consonant blends and digraphs as well as short and long vowel sounds.

*t*rip	*d*rip	*g*rip
cheat	*w*heat	*sh*eet
bat	bet	b*i*t
b*ee*t	b*oa*t	b*i*te

6. Substitute initial letters to make new words. There are many frequently used words which end with the same two or three letters. These common elements are referred to as phonograms and words containing them were once referred to as "word families." Substituting initial letters in such words often helps children see and hear the letter-sound relationships.

Make a new word by placing a letter in the blank space in front of each word.

__at	__all	__and
__at	__all	__and
__at	__all	__and

The exercise can be made easier by providing letters which can be used *(b, f, h, s)*.

Variations

1. "Add a '*b*' in front of each word and listen carefully as you pronounce the new word."

__and	__it	__old	__eat	__end

"Add an '*s*' in front of the same words and listen carefully as you pronounce the new word."

___and   ___it   ___old   ___eat   ___end

2. (Vowels) "Make a new word by adding the vowel 'e' to each word in column B. Pronounce the old word under A and the new word under B. What happens to the vowel sounds you hear?"

A	B		A	B
at	at___		pin	pin___
past	past___		dim	dim___
cut	cut___		plan	plan___
rid	rid___		tub	tub___

Structural analysis

Structural analysis refers to the recognition of new words by noting known roots and

1. Inflectional endings to root words (s, ed, ing).
2. Words combined to produce a different word (compound word).
3. Prefixes or suffixes added to root words (derivatives).

Some inflectional endings are taught in first grade along with a few compound words. Prefixes and suffixes are usually introduced at a later period.

Structural and phonic analysis go hand-in-hand. The structural changes caused by adding inflectional endings also result in added phonemes. In most cases prefixes and suffixes are separate syllables. Thus, they function as visual, auditory and meaning bearing units.

Teacher-made exercises can be developed that help the child see the structural changes which take place in words. Examples of simple inflectional endings and compound words are found below.

A. Teaching endings: *s, ed, ing*
   Notice how new words are formed when we add s, ed, *or* ing *to words.*

Word we know	Add *s*	Add *ed*	Add *ing*
walk	walks	walked	walking
ask	asks	asked	asking
call	calls	called	calling
look	looks	looked	looking
jump	jumps	jumped	jumping
show	shows	showed	showing
cover	covers	covered	covering

B. Teaching sight recognition of compound words
   *Notice how words under A and B are put together to make a
   new word. Say each word and notice the word under C very
   carefully.*

A	B	C
any	one	anyone
up	on	upon
some	thing	something
in	to	into
when	ever	whenever
him	self	himself
snow	man	snowman
her	self	herself

In the following sentence the word in parentheses is unknown to
the child. "The boy was (looking) for the kitten." If no attention
is paid to the word itself, the context would permit several logical
guesses, such as *reaching, looking, waiting, hoping*. However, the
child has had experience with the root word *look*. The recognition
of this familiar root word permits no other choice except the correct
one. Structural analysis helps the child eliminate all incorrect
responses which are plausible in this particular context.

In the next example the first word is unknown. It is also one of
the longest words the child has met in his reading. " '*Somebody*
must get the ball,' said Billy." The sentence does not stand in
isolation as it does here. In the story the children have been playing
ball. The ball has rolled under the fence into Mrs. Brown's yard
and the game has momentarily come to a halt. Something logical
must be done and Billy suggests something. Previously the children
had learned the word *some*, and, prior to today's reading lesson,
they had had a workbook exercise dealing with compound words,
such as *sidewalk, playground, anyone, into,* and *anything*. If the
child recognizes *some*, this much analysis plus the context should
assure him of getting the word correct.

Further discussion and illustrations of teaching phonic analysis
is found in Chapter 7 which outlines the total word analysis program for the primary grades.

Summary

The school's failure to teach all children to read up to arbitrary
grade-level standards resulted in widespread criticism of reading

instruction during the past decade. Much criticism was aimed at basal readers, the chief instructional vehicle in a vast majority of American schools.

During the past few years beginning reading instruction has received more attention than any other facet of the school curriculum. Practically all of the "newer approaches to reading" (discussed in Chapter 5) were, in essence, materials and methodology focusing primarily on the beginning reading period. Materials were designed to emphasize certain premises which promised to be the best approach to reading instruction. Representative examples are augmented English alphabet, diacritical markings, basals following various philosophies, trade books, concomitant stress on reading and writing, programmed reading workbooks, boxed materials, and reading kits stressing particular facets of reading ranging from phonics to appreciation of literature.

The proliferation of teaching materials undoubtedly held some promise for the teaching of reading since teachers and schools would have many different materials available. However, there developed a tendency to place unwarranted faith in "new" materials and approaches. This false hope was undoubtedly nourished by the producers of some of the new materials. Advertisements and brochures attributed qualities to these materials which had not yet been established in the classroom. "Breakthroughs in reading instruction" were announced with startling frequency, and the popular press joined in building shaky hypotheses into specious proofs for many of the newer materials.

After a decade or more of disillusioned search for a reading instruction panacea, the concensus is that none will be found. There is less of a tendency today to become a partisan for or against particular materials. Many observers feel that the more rigid the teaching, the more likely one is to find reliance on one set of materials; conversely, creative teachers are less bound by loyalties to specific materials and methodology.

The fact that so many of the new materials emphasized the early and systematic teaching of letter-sound relationships has made this the foremost issue in reading instruction. Data from recent studies have reaffirmed the position that instructional programs which include considerable emphasis on phonics result in higher achievement at the end of grade one than do programs which include significantly less phonics instruction. Nevertheless, there are still a number of unanswered questions relative to beginning reading instruction, if one views learning to read as a long-term developmental process.

The 1964-65 USOE cooperative first grade studies support the above statements relative to early letter-sound analysis. They failed to establish any one method of instruction as being superior to all other approaches. In general, there was more variability in achievement among pupils taught by teachers using a given method than there was between groups of pupils taught by different methods. This adds further proof to the bank of data which attests to the fact that the teacher is the most important variable in any learning situation.

Topics for later discussion

Since learning to read is a long-term developmental process, there are numerous facets of instruction which could justifiably be treated at each instructional level. To avoid repetition, certain topics which cut across grade levels have been omitted at the beginning reading level. Examples include oral reading, use of standarized and informal tests, recreational reading, and comprehension skills which are discussed in later chapters.

YOUR POINT OF VIEW?

Would you defend or attack the following premises? Why?

1. "Context clues" are of little importance in first grade when instruction centers around a basic reader series because of "controlled vocabulary." (Be sure to use a representative basic reader series to illustrate your point of view.)

2. Teaching both sight words and letter-sound analysis as parallel or concommitant learnings will inevitably lead to confusion.

3. A justifiable criterion for judging good teaching in beginning reading is the extent to which a teacher uses different methods in her classroom. (Basic readers, experience method, individualized reading, etc.)

4. Normal developmental growth in reading reduces the efficacy of writing individual stories for pupils who are beyond the stage of beginning reading.

5. Deliberately teaching children to note and use context clues for solving unknown words is self-defeating since the possibility for "wrong guesses" is always present.

6. Many "trade books" for children deliberately limit the use of different words (i.e., follow the practice of "controlled vocabulary"). This is inevitably bad, as it curtails story content.

7. Any given experience-chart story will not be equally motivating for all pupils in a class.

8. There is little evidence that the reading material found in basal readers is inappropriate for children who come from depressed socio-economic backgrounds.

9. Since children use thousands of words in oral language, stories which they dictate will depart from the practice of controlled vocabulary and repetition.

BIBLIOGRAPHY

1. Aaron, I. E. "Using Basal Materials Effectively," *Improvement of Reading Through Classroom Practice*. Proceedings, International Reading Association, 9 (1964), 73–4.

2. Anderson, Verna Dieckman, *Reading and Young Children*. New York: The Macmillan Company, 1968, Chapters 6 and 7.

3. Bush, Clifford L. and Mildred H. Huebner, *Strategies For Reading in the Elementary School*. New York: The Macmillan Company, 1970. Chapters 8 and 10.

4. Denny, Terry and Samuel Weintraub, "First-Graders' Responses to Three Questions about Reading," *Elementary School Journal* (May 1966), 441–49.

5. Eller, William, "Contributions of the First and Second Grade Studies," *Reading and Realism*, J. Allen Figural (Ed.), Proceedings, International Reading Association, 13, Part 1, 1969, 585–88.

6. Frazier, Alexander and Esther E. Schatz, "Teaching a Picture Book as Literature," *Elementary English* (January 1966), 45–49.

7. Frymier, Jack R. "The Effect of Class Size Upon Reading Achievement in First Grade," *Reading Teacher* (November 1964), 90–3.

8. Gans, Roma, *Guiding Children's Reading Through Experiences*. New York: Bureau of Publications, Teachers College, Columbia University, 1941.

9. Hanson, Irene W. "First Grade Children Work with Variant Word Endings," *Reading Teacher* (April 1966), 505–7.

10. Harris, Albert J. and Edward R. Sipay, *Effective Teaching of Reading*, New York: David McKay Co., 1971, Chapters 3 and 4.

11. Hildreth, Gertrude H. "Experience-Related Reading for School Beginners," *Elementary English* (March 1965), 280–97.

12. Kendrick, William M. and Clayton L. Bennett, "A Comparative Study of Two First-Grade Language Arts Programs, *Reading Research Quarterly*, (Fall 1966), 83–118.

13. King, Ethel M. and Siegmar Muehl, "Different Sensory Cues as Aids in Beginning Reading," *Reading Teacher* (December 1965), 163–68.

14. King, Ethel M. "Beginning Reading: When and How," *Reading Teacher* (March 1969), 550–53.

15. Lamoreaux, L. A. and Dorris M. Lee, *Learning to Read Through Experience.* New York: Appleton-Century-Crofts, 1943.

16. Landau, Elliott D., "After They Learn to Read — What?" *Elementary English* (December 1964), 877–78.

17. Lee, Dorris M. and R. V. Allen, *Learning To Read Through Experience* (2nd ed.). New York: Appleton-Century-Crofts, 1963.

18. Lewis, Juanita, "A Critical Look at Instruction In Word Recognition at the Elementary Level," in *Forging Ahead In Reading*, J. Allen Figurel, (Ed.), Proceedings, International Reading Association, 12, Part 1, 55–59.

19. Lindberg, Lucile, "This Is Reading," *Improving Reading Instruction.* Joint Proceedings of the Twenty-fifth Reading Conference and First Intensive Summer Workshop, Volume I, University Park, Pa., 1963, 15.

20. McCracken, Glenn, "The Newcastle Reading Experiment: A Terminal Report," *Elementary English* (January 1953), 13–21.

21. _____, "The Value of the Correlated Visual Image," *Reading Teacher* (October 1959), 29–33.

22. McKee, Paul and William K. Durr, *Reading/a Program of Instruction for The Elementary School.* Boston: Houghton Mifflin Company, 1966, Chapters 1–5.

23. Meltzer, Nancy S. and Robert Herse, "The Boundaries of Written Words as seen By First Graders," *Journal of Reading Behavior* (Summer 1969), 3–14.

24. Murphy, Helen A. "A Balanced First Grade Reading Program," *Challenge and Experiment In Reading.* International Reading Association Proceedings, 7, 1962, 33–6.

25. Niemeyer, John H. "The Bank Street Readers: Support for Movement Toward an Integrated Society," *Reading Teacher* (April 1965), 542–45.

26. Pikulski, John,"Effects of Reinforcement on Word Recognition," *Reading Teacher* (March 1970), 516–522.

27. Porter, Para, "Pictures In Reading," *The Reading Teacher* (December 1968), 238–41.

28. Rosner, Jerome, "Perceptual Skills — A Concern of the Classroom Teacher," *The Reading Teacher* (March 1971), 543–49.

29. Sister Marilyn, O.S.F., "Reading for Meaning," *Catholic School Journal* (September 1965), 56.

30. Smith, Dora V. "Children's Literature Today," *Elementary English* (October 1970), 777–80.

31. Smith, Nila Banton, *American Reading Instruction*. Newark, Del.: International Reading Association, 1965.

32. Stauffer, Russell G. *The Language-Experience Approach to The Teaching of Reading*. New York: Harper and Row Publishers, 1970.

33. Wallen, Carl J. *Word Attack Skills In Reading*, Columbus, Ohio: Charles E. Merrill Publishing Co., 1969.

7

Phonics Instruction

The purpose of phonics instruction is to help the child develop the ability to work out the pronunciation (or approximate pronunciation) of printed word-symbols which at the moment he does not know as sight words. Phonics instruction in early reading does not focus on teaching the child *how* to pronounce words, but rather that printed letter-combinations *represent* a word he already knows and uses in his oral language. (27) Later, he learns to use a dictionary to ascertain the pronunciation of words he does not know how to pronounce.

Learning word analysis skills, including phonics, is an absolute necessity for learning to read. No child will learn to read, at what might be designated as fluent third grade level, unless he has mastered a number of insights into cracking the code. The term *code cracking*, as it is used extensively today, is simply a synonym for phonics. Both terms imply noting the relationship between printed letters and the speech sounds they represent. The teaching of phonics is teaching letter-sound relationships. When a child *applies* phonics in his reading, he translates graphic signs into known speech sounds and blends these sounds into words.

It is true that readers often make mistakes in reading which do not destroy or appreciably distort the meaning of a passage. When a substitution does not violate the syntactical requirements of

English speech and writing, the reader may still recreate the melody of language and not drastically alter the intended meaning.* Yet, it cannot be denied that an unknown word or words in a sentence poses a potential threat to reading for meaning. The substitution of a single phoneme-grapheme may call for a complete re-reading of a sentence, or invite the reader to make other changes in the sentence in order to maintain known syntax requirements. An example is changing *man* to *men* in the sentence, "The *man* was looking at the bottle."

The child's ability to associate letters with sounds is second in importance to no other skill in helping him to become an independent reader. It is difficult to understand how, over the years, so much controversy and emotional involvement could become attached to the issue of phonics instruction; undoubtedly, the pressures on schools and teachers today which are traceable to this issue are unprecedented. In the recent past, the most vociferous critics of reading instruction started from a number of questionable premises; chief among these were:

1. There is a sight word method of teaching reading which makes little or no provision for teaching phonic analysis skills.
2. All words met at various instructional levels are taught exclusively as "sight words."
3. Phonics instruction is "good" and children cannot get too much of a good thing.
4. If we were to go back to the phonics emphasis of the 1890's, reading problems in our schools would disappear.

Brief Review of Past Practices

Some knowledge of the history of phonics teaching in American education is undoubtedly helpful in understanding some of the problems, attitudes, and misunderstandings observable in educa-

---

*Kenneth S. Goodman, "Analysis of Oral Reading Miscues: Applied Psycholinguistics" *Reading Research Quarterly* (Fall 1965) 9–30.

Yetta M. Goodman, "Using Children's Miscues for New Teaching Strategies," *Reading Teacher* (February 1970) 455–59.

tion today. The following discussion is a very brief summary of phonic practices advocated in the past.*

Beginning around 1890 and continuing for a period of thirty or forty years, the cornerstone of reading instruction in American schools was a synthetic phonics method. Prior to this era much time was spent on the rote learning of the ABC's. Emphasis now shifted from drill on "letter names" to drill on the "sounds of the various letters." Here we have a form of phonics drill unrelated to meaning and in some instances unrelated to words in English. Children drilled on isolated sounds as illustrated below:

da	*ha*	*la*	*ma*	*pa*	*ra*
be	*se*	*te*	*ne*	*le*	*re*
pi	*mi*	*ti*	*si*	*li*	*ri*

This drill was not in context with reading, since the drills preceded the child's learning of words. It is easy to see that this type of introduction placed little, if any, emphasis on reading as a process of discovering meaning.

Rebecca Pollard's "Synthetic method," introduced about 1890,** advocated reducing reading to a number of mechanical procedures, each of which focused on a unit smaller than a word. Reading became very mechanistic and, when mastered, often produced individuals who were adept at working their way through a given word. The result among both teachers and pupils was that reading became equated with "facility in calling words." A few of the recommended procedures of this method were:

1. Drills in articulation were to precede any attempt at reading. The child was to drill on the "sounds of letters." Then he would be able, it was reasoned, to attack whole words.

---

*The reader who wishes a more detailed account of past practices will find the following sources helpful:

Nila B. Smith, "Phonics Then and Now," *Education* LXXV (1955), 560–65.

W. S. Gray, *On Their Own in Reading*, (Chicago: Scott, Foresman & Co., 1948), Chap. 1.

E. A. Betts, "Phonics: Practical Consideration Based on Research," *Elementary English*, XXXIII (1956), 357–71.

Nila B. Smith, *American Reading Instruction*, Newark, Del.: International Reading Association, 1965.

**Rebecca S. Pollard, *Pollard's Synthetic Method* (Chicago: Western Publishing House, 1889).

2. Single consonants were "sounded." Each consonant was given a sound equivalent to a syllable. Thus *b, c, d, p, h,* and *t* were sounded *buh, cuh, duh, puh, huh,* and *tuh.*
3. Drill on word families was stressed. This was unrelated to meaning. Sometimes children memorized lists of words ending in such common family phonograms as *ill, am ick, ate, old, ack.*
4. Diacritical markings were introduced in first grade, and children drilled on "marking sentences." For example:

The gh̸ōst wăs ā cŏmmŏn sigh̸t near the ẁre̸k. He knew the īṣlănd was ĕmpty.

A number of widely used reading texts adopted the suggestions of Pollard and, in many cases, extended them. For instance, if the objective of a unit were to teach the phonogram or "family" *ick,* a story might be built primarily from words in that family, without regard to meaning or lack of it in the passage. The following example is illustrative and, it is hoped, exaggerated.

Nick, flick the tick from the chick with a stick. Prick the tick from the chick with a thick stick. Nick, do not kick the brick, kick the stick.

The discerning reader will see the close relationship between this practice and one of the linguistic approaches to beginning reading which has recently enjoyed widespread publicity (see Chapter 4).

It is not implied that teaching word families is an indefensible practice but rather that some practices seem to have more merit than others. Drill on a column of words entirely unrelated to meaningful reading might be a poor learning technique. On the other hand, when children have learned the words *make* and *take* as sight words, and they meet the new word *lake* in a reading exercise, it would not be poor instruction to point out that this word, and certain others whose meanings are known, contain the common letters *ake* which in every case represent the same speech sound (*cake, bake, wake, snake, rake, shake*).

There is little point in opposing the teaching of "family groups" on the basis that a relatively small number of English words contain these families. This is not a sound argument because so many small, often used words *are* formed from some thirty such families, and these words are among those most frequently occurring in beginning reading materials (specifically such families as *an, at, it, am, in, as, ate, ake, et, ick, eat, arm, en, ing, ot, est, un, all, ell,* and *ame*). There are enough common or service words which are *not* phonetic to be learned as sight words that any clue, such as word families, that a child can pick up early in learning to read can be useful.

Wylie and Durrell* report that "whole phonograms are more easily identified by first grade children than the separate vowels contained in the phonograms, suggesting that the recognition unit is the phonogram rather than the separate vowel." They report that approximately 1,500 primary grade words include ending phonograms which contain a stable vowel sound.

Little Words in Big Words

Since some of the regular spelling families are also words (*am, is, and, ate, an, all, old, it, at, eat*), the practice of "looking for small words in large words" was advocated. The justification for this practice was that the little words were familiar to the child, and he could pronounce them. If he found little words he knew in larger unknown words, he had a start toward mastering the unknown larger word.

The procedure of looking for small words in larger words fails for two reasons. First, there is little logic in having the child see the word *ill* in the monosyllabic words *will, Bill, fill, mill, kill,* and *pill,* unless it is the association of *ill* with *pill,* which leaves much to be desired. In teaching reading today, the clue will not be the word *ill* but the sound of *ill* in conjunction with the sounds of various initial letters: *w, b, f, m, g, k, p,* and *h.*

The second charge against "finding little words" appears to be so serious as to remove the practice from the list of justifiable procedures. Many of the little words which retain some degree of pronounceable autonomy in single-syllable words lose this characteristic in words of more than one syllable. In *pan, can, man, fan, tan, ran* or in *ham, jam, Sam,* noting the little words *an* and *am* would not destroy the pronunciation of the words. However, seeing or pronouncing the *am* in *am*ong, *am*end, *am*en, *am*use, *am*ass would prevent a correct phonic analysis. Likewise, seeing or saying the word *as* in *as*hore, *As*ia, *as*ide, *as*leep; *it* in *it*em; *at* in *at*omic and *at*hlete; or *all* in *all*ow or *all*ege would hinder attempts at word analysis.

---

*Richard E. Wylie and Donald D. Durrell "Teaching Vowels Through Phonograms," Elementary English (October 1970), 787–791.

The "total emphasis" on phonics brought the method into disrepute during the 1920's. Reform was not advocated, but rather the discarding of the teaching of phonics. It was commonly alleged that the abuses of phonics teaching were responsible for the reading problems found at that time. Thus, what was *pre*scribed at one moment was *pro*scribed the next. There was much confusion among teachers, and this confusion seems not to have abated perceptibly today.

Learning Word Analysis Skills: A System of Cues

There are several cue systems which children can use in deciphering the pronunciation of printed words which at the moment are not recognized as sight words. These include:

1. *The unique appearance of words*

With the exception of a limited number of homographs (*re cord–rec ord; tear–tear; wind–wĭnd*) all words in English writing have unique visual patterns. While many children use this "uniqueness" cue in the earliest stages of learning to read, its utility diminishes with each new experience with reading.

The word *look* may be recognized because of the *oo* pattern. Then the child meets the word *book*. These words are different but they cannot be differentiated on the basis of the original unique cue *oo*. As the child meets *took, hook, door, floor, flood*, this *visual* clue ceases to be unique.

2. *Structural analysis*

Using structural analysis, the child gains mastery of a great number of words whose visual patterns are changed as a result of adding:
   a. Inflectional endings (*s, ed, ing, ly*)
   b. Prefixes and suffixes (*ex, pre, un; tent, ment, ous,* etc.)
   c. Root to root to form compounds (*sidewalk, farmyard, playground, sailboat*)

3. *Phonic analysis* (letter-sound relationships)

4. *Context clues*

5. *Above methods in combination*

Obviously the use of some of these techniques is predicated on previous learnings. For instance, for a child to use structural analysis in unlocking words with inflectional endings, he must recognize the root word (*help*) as a familiar unit or be able to sound out the root word. Then he solves the ending (*ing*) and blends the two (*helping*). A bit later this type of analysis should be uncalled for since he perceives the word *helping* as one familiar unit.

A child can use context clues only when he has the ability to recognize or sound out most of the words in a sentence that contains perhaps one unknown word. It should be emphasized that phonics is only one of many skills needed for facile reading. For instance, when a child does not know the meaning of a word, arriving at its *exact* pronunciation through phonic analysis will not help him. In the following sentence there is an unknown symbol:

"The man was attacked by a marbohem."

Everyone reading this page can sound out *mar-bo-hem*, but no one knows what attacked the man since saying *marbohem* does not convey meaning to the reader. Words can be substituted for *marbo-*

hem, and some readers would still have trouble with the meaning even though they successfully analyze the speech sounds in the words. For example:

1. The man was attacked by a peccary.
2. The man was attacked by a freebooter.
3. The man was attacked by a iconoclast.
4. The man was attacked by a fusilier.
5. The man was attacked by a hypochondriac.

Analysis is only a tool for use in the reading process and should not be confused with the process. It is a valuable technique in reading, but is not in itself a method of teaching reading.

**Tasks Involved in
Phonics Instruction**

There are a series of instructional tasks which taken together constitute the phonics program. Different phonic teaching materials will include a number of techniques which are common to all approaches. They may differ as to the sequence in which skills are introduced, the emphasis on children learning rules, the number of different steps taught and how much phonics instruction is included in beginning reading. An outline of the major phonics tasks which must be taught would include:

1. Auditory discrimination of speech sounds in words.
2. Written letters are used to represent these speech sounds.
3. The sound represented by a letter or letters in a known word can be used to unlock the pronunciation of unknown words in which these particular letters occur.
4. Sounds of consonants.
   a. Initial position in words
   b. Final position in words
5. Consonants which are blended.
6. Special consonant digraphs (*th, ch, sh, wh*).
7. Vowel sounds.
   a. Short vowel sounds
   b. Long vowel sounds
   c. Double vowels
      (1) Digraphs
      (2) Diphthongs

   d. Vowels followed by *r*
   e. Effect of final *e*
   f. Final *y* sounded as long *i*
8. Silent consonants.
9. Syllabication.
10. Accent.

   It should not be inferred that each of the above steps is of equal importance in learning to read, or that each should receive the same amount of instructional time. The steps listed are simply the framework, since some steps include many specific tasks. For instance, under syllabication one would deal with such teachings as "prefixes and suffixes are usually syllables; there are as many syllables as sounded vowels; two consonants coming between vowels usually divide (*gar·den*); double consonants usually divide (*let·ter, sum· mer*); the letter combinations *cle, ble, gle, dle, kle,* and *tle* at the ends of words are single syllables." There is no agreement as to the number of such rules or principles that should be taught in the reading process. Even a summary of all the suggestions found in the literature of teaching reading would be beyond the scope of this book.
   The actual learning of phonics as it relates to reading usually begins quite early in the pre-school years. The child learns a sound like *mommy,* and can easily differentiate it from similar sounds. He may have a pet *kitty* and a playmate *Kathy* and will differentiate if asked "where is *Kathy?*" even though the kitty is also present. Phonics instruction begins when an adult talks with an infant, thus providing the child with a model.
   When a child associates sounds with objects and does not confuse sounds that are very similar such as *mommy, money, monkey,* and *maybe,* he is mastering auditory discrimination, which is a prerequisite for phonic analysis in the reading process. None of the later "steps" in learning phonics can take place in the absence of mastery of this basic language function. Beginning reading instruction in the school builds on the child's previous language experiences. In reading, the child will have to make visual discriminations between written word symbols and learn that the written symbols represent the speech sounds of words he speaks and understands.

Teaching consonant sounds

Why Begin with Consonant Sounds? A large majority of instructional materials used in beginning reading advocate that the teaching of letter sounds begin with consonants. This position is supported by the following factors:

1. A number of consonants (*b, f, d, h, j, k, p, m, l, r, t*, etc.) have only one sound. Once the child masters these letter-sound associations, this skill can be transferred in attacking other words in which these letters occur. On the other hand, vowels in written words are notoriously inconsistent as to the sound they represent.
2. Children must learn to read from left-to-right. Since most English words begin with consonants, the first letter or letters a child must sound out in an unknown word will be consonants.
3. If a reader uses context along with sounding, the initial sound in the word helps eliminate most alternative possibilities. To illustrate, each of the following blank lines represents an unknown word.
   a. _____
   b. n_____
   The blank space in (a) can represent any word in English, while in (b) *all* words which do not begin with the *n* sound are eliminated. Below, each sentence contains a different unknown word. It is likely that the one-sentence context and the initial consonant will permit you to solve the unknown word. Larger contexts would make the task easier.
   c. "Pull that n_____ out of the board," said Grandfather.
   d. "What's the n_____of that song?" asked Mary. "It's on the n_____ record I bought yesterday."
   e. "The big right hander struck out in the last of the n_____."

The rationale for introducing vowel sounds first rests on the following assumptions. These have been gleaned from writings favorable to this practice and represent all of the justification this writer has found to date.

1. All words contain one or more vowels.
2. Vowels provide more important clues to pronunciation of words.
3. Consonants are blended with vowels and thus should not be sounded in isolation.

At first glance the above statements appear to have validity, but upon analysis they are seen to be relatively weak arguments. One might reverse the first statement and say, "all words contain consonants," but this is not a reason for teaching either consonants or vowels first. In the following sentence all consonant clues are removed:

—e—— ——y —o —ou—— ——e—e —o——

It would be a most difficult task to decipher the preceding sentence. The following sentence shows consonants and omits vowels.

L—ts tr— t— s——nd th—s— w—rds.

Reading this sentence is a much simpler task. Many other samples could be cited and the result would be to cast doubt on the premise that vowels provide the most important clues to pronunciation.

In regard to the third point above, *neither* consonants nor vowels should be sounded in isolation (*cat* = kah-ah-tuh). Since no instructional materials, with the exception of the Carden Method,* advocate sounding letters in isolation, the statement has little relevancy as an argument for teaching vowels first. It should be kept in mind that one of the most important clues to the sounds of vowels is provided by consonants which follow vowels. A consonant-vowel-consonant pattern usually results in a short vowel sound — *cat, den, can.* The same is true if the vowel is followed by two consonants (*cattle, dentist, canvas*).

Simultaneous learning of sight words and analysis

Teaching a limited number of sight words in beginning reading has been justified on the basis of the following rationale. First, the child has already mastered oral language in which he utilizes global word sounds rather than letter sounds. He has learned language as a meaningful process. Recognizing whole words builds on the child's previous language experience. That is, the child is taught the sight symbol *man* before he is taught the sounds of symbols *m*, *a*, and *n*. The word *man* is much more meaningful than the three symbols of which it is formed because the child:

1. Understands the meaning of the sound *man* in many contexts.

---

*Mae Carden, *The Carden Method*, Glen Rock, New Jersey.

2. Can make this sound himself and associates it with its referent.
3. Can recognize a picture (sight symbol or representation) of a *man*.

Thus, it is easy to move from what is known to the new and unknown — the printed word *man* used in any context familiar to the child.

Second, any word instantly recognized will serve as a phonic model for analyzing identical letter-sound combinations found in other words. This is predicated on the child's ability to recognize printed letters and associate a particular sound with that letter.

This discussion is not intended to suggest that teaching sight words without recourse to sounding letters goes on for any lengthy, fixed period of time. Building a sight vocabulary and utilizing sounding techniques (which should lead to further expansion of one's sight vocabulary) are parts of the same process. The most difficult task in beginning reading instruction is to arrive at the proper emphasis of both skills.

Teaching initial consonant sounds

Starting from the premise that the child has learned to recognize a few words, which for illustrative purposes we will assume includes any of the words *be, back,* or *ball,* he is now ready to associate the sound of *b* in these words with the written symbol *b*.

The teacher prints a capital *B* on the chalkboard and says, "Today we will learn all about the letter *B*. Next to the big *B* I will print a little *b*. This big *B* is called a capital *B*. Now I am going to write some words which begin with little *b*." (She writes *be, back,* and *ball*.) "Who can give us another word that begins with the *b* sound? Yes, *bear, boat, big* — *Bobby* we write with a large (or capital) *B* because it is somebody's name."

```
B  b
   be
   back
   ball
   boat
   Bobby
```

When a number of examples have been given, the teacher asks, "What do we notice about the sound of each of these words?" "That's right, they all begin with the sound of *b* — *bear, ball, boat, bat, big, bomb*." As the words are called out by the children, they are added to the list on the board and the teacher asks, "What do we *see* that is the same in all of these words? That's right, they all begin with *b*." It should be noted that in no instance were the children asked to sound the letter *b* in isolation, although it may have been emphasized without distortion.

In addition to the group work just described, there will be workbook exercises giving each child an opportunity to do seatwork which parallels the concept taught. These exercises use both visual stimuli and sounds associated with pictures, letters, and words. A few typical examples are:

1. In the row of pictures below, the child is to mark those objects whose names begin with the same sound as the name of the object in the picture on the extreme left.

FIGURE 14

2. A picture of a familiar object is shown along with the word represented by the object in the picture. The example is a bell (Figure 15). Here the child can see and hear the *b* sound. He is then to mark all the other words in a supplied list which begin with the same sound.

FIGURE 15

3. Figure 16 shows a series of words in columns, some of which begin with the same sound and the same letter. The child is to draw a line from the word in column *A* to the word in column *B* which begins with the same sound.

FIGURE 16

A word of caution should be injected here to point out that many exercises found in workbooks which aim to provide auditory practice can result in nothing but visual discrimination exercises, unless the teacher is careful to see that each child actually *sounds* the word symbols which are given as stimuli. To illustrate, the following exercise is patterned after Figure 16 and can be correctly marked using only visual clues. Incorporating auditory practice would require associating sounds with each initial symbol.

FIGURE 17

4. A pictured object is shown, followed by four words, none of which stand for the picture, but one or more of which begin with the same sound as the name of the pictured object.

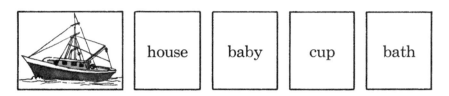

FIGURE 18

5. A series of boxes is shown, each containing three words. The teacher pronounces one of the words and the pupil underlines the word pronounced. (See Figure 19.) He need not know all of the words as sight words, provided he is familiar with the initial sound of each. In the following example, the teacher could pronounce *bank, tell, bill, may, bat*. There are many other types of exercises and many variations of those illustrated.

1	2	3	4	5
call	*tell*	hill	*may*	hat
bank	sell	fill	pay	show
play	fell	*bill*	say	*bat*

FIGURE 19

Substitution of initial sounds

The next important skill to be learned is to substitute known letter sounds in attacking unknown words. Assume the child knows the words *take* and *make* and meets the unknown word *rake*. He should be able to combine the *r* sound (which he knows in words like *run, rain,* or *ride*), with the sound of *ake* in *take*. By this process of "thinking the sounds," he should unlock the new word. (23) If the reader has mastered the steps in phonics previously introduced, this step also starts from that which is known, i.e., sight words and the sounds initial consonants contribute to words.

In beginning reading it is a common practice to teach a number of monosyllabic words which contain frequently used phonograms. Practically all workbooks use these "word families" as a means of teaching new words. Work on the substitution of initial consonants parallels the primers and first readers. Moving through the primer, the child meets such words as *back, came, day, fun, gate, hand, just, king, lake, met, not, pin, rest, sun, tall,* and *wet*. Each of these words contains a familiar and often occurring phonogram. Children should not receive drill on these word endings in isolation (*ack, ame, ay, ate, est, ust, ing, ake, ot, in, un, all, et*). Nevertheless, a number of important words can be solved independently when the child knows some sight words containing often used letter combinations and can substitute initial letter sounds.

Substitution of single consonant sounds at the ends of words

Some teachers prefer to teach consonant sounds at the ends of words at the same time that they deal with a particular initial consonant sound. Other teachers work through the initial sounds and then work on single consonant sounds at the ends of words. Regardless of which procedure is followed, the child is taught to notice visually and auditorily the final consonants in short words. He knows words such as *men, log, pen, bold, leg* and the sounds of letters, including *t*. He is now asked to substitute the *t* sound at the end of the words to get *met, lot, pet, bolt,* and *let.*

Initial blends

In dealing with many words that the child will meet early in the process of learning to read, sounding only the initial consonant will result in confusion. These words fall into two classes: simple consonant blends, and a smaller group of two-consonant combinations representing special speech sounds in English (*th, sh, ch, wh*).

The twenty-five two- and three-letter blends may be divided into three major groups on the basis of a common letter:

1. Those which begin with *s: sc, sk, sm, sn, sp, st, sw, str*
2. Those which conclude with *l: bl, cl, fl, gl, pl, sl, spl*
3. Those which conclude with *r: br, cr, dr, fr, gr, pr, tr, scr, spr, str*

The above arrangement is not intended to suggest a particular order in which blends should be taught. A logical sequence would probably be determined by the vocabulary found in the instructional materials actually used in beginning reading.

There is a great deal of variance among teachers as well as among basal readers as to (a) when blends are dealt with, (b) which are taught first, and (c) how rapidly the blends are covered. Most materials suggest teaching initial blends first and later stressing blends and special consonant sounds at the ends of words (chur*ch*, tra*sh*, che*st*, che*ck*, fla*sh*, fre*sh*, fro*st*, smoo*th*, whi*ch*, thi*ck*). While there are numerous approaches for teaching consonant blends, the objectives of all methods are to lead the child:

1. To see the printed letters involved.
2. To understand that in every instance the letter sounds combine into a blended sound.
3. To discriminate auditorily between the sound of individual letters and blends — *d*ug, *r*ug, *dr*ug; *s*old, *c*old, *sc*old.

Any procedure for teaching initial consonant sounds can be utilized for teaching each of the different consonant blends. A few techniques are illustrated below.

1. Secure a number of pictures of concrete objects whose names begin with a blend. Show the pictures one at a time and have the children write, or say orally, the blended letters. (They are not to simply name the picture.) Examples: *sk*ate, *tr*ain, *br*idge, *pl*ate, *gr*apes, *sl*ed, *fr*og, *cl*ock, *st*ar, *bl*anket, *sn*ake, *st*ore, *pl*ow, *cl*own, *sw*ing, *sch*ool.

2. Prepare and duplicate a series of sentences which contain a number of blends. Have pupils underline each blend.
   A. The *bl*ack *cr*ow *fl*ew away *fr*om the *tr*ee.
   B. *Pr*etty *br*ight *fl*owers *gr*ew near the *br*idge.
   C. What is the *pr*ice of the *gr*een *dr*ess in the *st*ore window?
   D. We will re*st* when we reach the coa*st* about du*sk*.

3. Add one of the letters *c, g, p, t* in front of each word to produce a consonant blend. Underline the letters which blend.

___reat	___roud	___rain	___rop
___reek	___rail	___rice	___ruly
___rint	___reen	___row	___rize
___rip	___rack	___ree	___rand

4. Step 1. Place on the chalkboard a list of words which begin with *p* and to which *s* can be added as a first letter to form the *sp* blend. Pronounce these words with the children.

Step 2: Write the *sp* blend word to the right of each word. Have the children note the visual pattern *sp* at the beginning of each word. Guide the children in pronouncing the two words in each pair in rapid succession and in noting the blended sound in the second word in each pair (*pin=spin; pot=spot*, etc.).

Step I	Step II
pot	spot
pin	spin
pill	spill
peak	speak
pool	spool
poke	spoke
park	spark

Most of the other initial blends can be handled in much the same manner. Illustrative word pairs with *tr*: race–trace; rain–train; rip–trip; rust–trust; rap–trap; rail–trail; ray–tray. etc. In teaching *sl*: lid–slid; lap–slap; lip–slip; led–sled; low–slow; lack–slack; lick–slick.

Teaching consonant digraphs

A digraph is a combination of two letters which when pronounced results in one speech sound. This sound is not a blend of the two letters. Some digraphs have more than one sound (*ch=k* in character; *sh* in chiffon; *ch* in church). Techniques used in teaching consonants and blends and the illustration of teaching *ch* which follows will apply to teaching other digraphs.

Teaching the sound of ch and sh

1. a. Place words beginning with *ch* on the board.
   b. Direct children's attention to these initial letters.
   c. Pronounce each word, inviting pupils to *listen* to the sound of *ch* in each word.
   d. In pronouncing, emphasize but do not distort the *ch* sound.
   e. Have pupils pronounce words.
   f. Ask class to provide other words which begin with the *ch* sound heard in *chair*, *child*, etc.

Ch
chair
child
chance

2. Contrast single initial consonant sounds and initial digraph sounds in words.

   Place words shown in Column *A* on the chalkboard and pronounce these words with the children.

   Next, write the words in Column *B*, inviting children to note the visual pattern *sh* at the beginning of each word. Have the children pronounce each pair of words (*hip*–*ship*) to contrast the initial sounds in each pair of words.

A	*B*
hip	ship
hop	shop
hot	shot
hark	shark
hare	share
harp	sharp

3. The procedure outlined above may be used with words that begin with *s* or *sh*.

   As the children contrast the initial sound in the words in each pair they note the visual pattern (*s–sh*) and hear the initial sound represented by these letters.

sell	shell
sort	short
sip	ship
save	shave
self	shelf
sock	shock

At a later time children will be taught that:

ch = k: *ch*orus, *ch*emistry, *ch*rome, *ch*aracter.
ch = sh: *ch*auffeur, *ch*amois, *ch*ef, *Ch*icago.
Other frequently met digraphs include *sh, wh, th, gh, ng, ph*.
The sounds of these letter combinations are:
sh = Sound heard in *sh*oe, *sh*op, *sh*ell, *sh*ort, wi*sh*, fi*sh*.
wh = *hw*: *wh*en — *hw*en; *wh*eel — *hw*eel; *wh*ich — *hw*ich.
wh followed by *o*, the *w* is silent: *wh*ole — *h*ole; *wh*ose — *h*ooz; *wh*om — *h*oom.
th = two sounds, voiced: *th*em, *th*ere, *th*ey, wi*th*.
   voiceless: *th*in, *th*ree, *th*row, wid*th*
gh = sound of *f* in: lau*gh*, tou*gh*, cou*gh*, etc.
   silent in: ni*gh*t, bou*gh*, ei*gh*t, thou*gh*t, etc.
ng = sounded as in: sa*ng*, wi*ng*, so*ng*, ru*ng*.
ph = usually sounded as *f*: *ph*one, ne*ph*ew, gra*ph*.

Limitations of Phonics Instruction

The efficacy of teaching and applying phonics analysis skills in the reading of English is limited by the spelling patterns (phoneme-grapheme relationships) found in English writing. Spoken English is of course "phonetic." The spoken words *love, would, said, rough, ocean, of, sure, they, two, was*, pose no problem to anyone wishing to transcribe the phonemes heard in these words.

However, such irregular grapheme-phoneme relationships in hundreds of high frequency words do result in severe difficulties for many individuals learning to read English. Although the irregularities of English spellings cannot be discussed here at length, a few of the problems are identified below:

1. The English language contains thousands of words "borrowed" from other languages. The spelling of these words are often confusing (yacht, beret, chassis, adieu, alias, naive, chaos, fjord, reign, chamois, bizarre, etc.).

2. Words with the same pronunciation will have different spelling patterns both of which meet the criteria of regular spellings:

   pain–pane; waist–waste; beat–beet; steel–steal; wail–whale; plain–plane; weak–week.

3. Some pairs of words have the same pronunciation, one following a regular spelling pattern, the other being irregular: ate–eight; sun–son; brake–break; wood–would; herd–heard; way–weigh.

4. The most troublesome grapheme-phoneme relationships involve vowel letters. The material below illustrates a few spelling patterns that represent long vowel sounds in English writing.

$\bar{a}$	(ay)	(a+e)	(ai)	(ea)	(ey)	(ei)
	pl*ay*	c*a*k*e*	m*ai*l	br*ea*k	gr*ey*	w*ei*gh
$\bar{e}$	(ee)	(ea)	(e)	(ie)	(ey)	(eo+e)
	b*ee*t	s*ea*t	m*e*	n*ie*ce	k*ey*	p*eo*pl*e*
$\bar{i}$	(i+e)	(i+gh)	(e+e)	(ai)	(ui+e)	(y)
	b*i*t*e*	h*i*gh	*e*y*e*	*ai*sle	g*ui*d*e*	m*y*
$\bar{o}$	(oa)	(o+ld)	(o+e)	(ow)	(oe)	(ou+e)
	s*oa*p	g*o*ld	b*o*n*e*	sl*ow*	h*oe*	c*ou*rs*e*
$\bar{u}(\ddot{u})$	(u+e)	(ue)	(ui)	(u)	(ui+e)	(ew)
	r*u*l*e*	gl*ue*	s*ui*t	R*u*th	j*ui*c*e*	fl*ew*

Spelling reform

The preceding illustrations represent only a few examples of irregular grapheme-phoneme relationships in English spelling. Over the years, there have been numerous proposals for reform of English spelling, but such reform, advocated as a humanitarian gesture toward children who have to learn to read English, has never been taken seriously. Reform of English spelling will come, and when it does it will be for economic reasons. Computers which have been programmed to read English have a tendency to become schizophrenic; and attempting to teach all children to read English is relatively expensive. As soon as a computer is programmed to divulge how much it costs to maintain this sacred cow, a national committee will be formed to plot its demise.

Phonic rules

In lieu of spelling reform, potential readers are offered a number of rules or generalizations designed to help them arrive at which sound is represented by a letter or letters in particular words. An example of a rule is that a vowel letter usually represents its short sound if it is the only vowel in a syllable or word and does not come at the end of the word or syllable. (Also stated "one vowel in medial position usually has its short sound".)

The above generalization is considered one of the better ones since it applies in most three letter words and in a number of four-

and five-letter words. Even so, there are many words which meet "the one vowel within the word" criterion but which violate the rule. When we meet *gold, sold, told, bold, cold, fold, hold,* etc., we amend the rule to "o followed by *ld* usually represents its long sound." Also, the vowel *i* followed by *nd* or *ld* usually has its long sound (*mind, find, blind, kind; mild, child, wild*). Any vowel followed by *r* is modified by this controller; *i* followed by *gh* represents the long sound. These examples are not cited to discourage the teaching of "rules," but rather to emphasize that over-reliance on generalizations can lead to confusion.

There are a number of studies which have explored the degree to which phonics rules can be depended upon. That is, what percent of words that meet the criterion specified in the rule actually follow the rule. Oaks (32) analyzed the vowel situations occurring in a number of basal series, primer through third grade. From among all the phonic generalizations that were advanced to cover these letter-sound relationships, she concluded that only eight principles applied often enough to merit their being taught. In this study, the eight generalizations were applicable in only about 50 percent of the cases that the rules were designed to cover.

In a more recent study, Clymer (13) tested the percent of cases in which various rules or phonic generalizations actually applied in words met in four basal series (grades 1–3), plus the words on the Gates Primary Reading Vocabulary (not found in the basals). Some twenty-six hundred words constituted the sample. Forty-five phonic generalizations were applied to these words to determine what percent of the words followed the rule and what percent were exceptions.

Clymer suggested that two criteria be met in order for a rule to be classified as useful. First, the situation covered by a rule must occur in a minimum of twenty words found in the twenty-six-hundred-word sample; second, the rule should apply in at least 75 percent of the cases it was designed to cover. Of the forty-five phonic generalizations studied, twenty-three covered vowel situations. Only five of this number met the criteria stated above. Ten vowel rules applied in less than 50 percent of the cases; seven rules applied more than 50 percent (but in fewer than three out of four instances); and one rule-situation occurred in only ten words in the entire sample.

Burrows and Lourie (10) report an intensive study of the frequency with which one widely taught vowel rule applied to the five thousand highest frequency words on the Rinsland List. The rule under discussion states, "when there are two adjacent vowels in a word, the first usually has its long sound and the second is silent." Children are often taught this rule as, "when two vowels go walking, the first does the talking." In the five-thousand-word sample a total of 1,728 words met the two-vowel criterion. However, only 628 (approximately 40 percent) followed the rule.

Emans (19) tested the frequency with which phonic generalizations applied to words found in materials written for pupils above the primary grades. In regard to the utility of phonic rules, intermediate level materials did not enjoy a significant advantage over beginning materials. Studies by Bailey (3) and Burmeister (8) reported data that was in general agreement with the findings cited above. However, different researchers have suggested different criteria for assessing the "utility" of phonic generalizations.

Teaching vowel sounds

Vowels are the worst offenders in any audit of grapheme-phoneme irregularities. Regardless of these irregularities, mastering letter-sound relationships is absolutely essential. The function of the teacher and school is to provide guidance, and most children gain proficiency in phonic analysis more quickly and more surely with guidance that leads to insights. To require rote memorization of a great number of rules will hinder some children in understanding the relationship between the rule and their reading. They may become so involved with learning the rules that they miss the application. On the other hand, having a generalization verbalized is often a help to learning.

Short vowel sounds

Techniques for teaching letter-sound relationships are unlimited. Each illustration presented will deal with only one vowel-letter sound since all of the other vowel sounds can be taught in the same manner simply by changing stimulus words. Practically any lesson can be presented via the chalkboard, overhead projector, or on duplicated pages for seatwork.

1. *Visual-auditory association* (illustration using short ĕ). (a) Select a few easy words which have been used previously and which contain the vowel pattern being taught. (b) Write these words in a column and pronounce each word with the children. (c) Have children note the vowel letter in the middle of the word and emphasize the sound it represents in *met, set, pet*, etc.

The material below might constitute three different presentations on different days. Column A contains one pattern CVA words, Column B mixed patterns, and Column C longer words.

A	B	C
met	leg	desk
set	men	bell
pet	bed	dress
bet	pep	sled
let	wet	best
jet	hen	help

2. *Discriminating rhyming elements* (illustration using short ă). Pronounce pairs of words selected so that the first word in each pair contains the short sound of ă. The second word either rhymes with the first or differs only in the vowel sound. As a pair of words is pronounced, children tell whether the words rhyme (both contain ă) or whether the vowel sounds differ.

Stimulus word-pairs	*Children's responses*
map–cap	Both have the short sound of ă.
rag–rug	Different vowel sounds.
dad–mad	etc.
pat–sat	etc.
hat–hit (tag–bag, fan–fun, dad–did, man–can, had–hid, pan–ran, bat–bet, bag–tag, etc.)	

3. *Review of all short vowel sounds.* Pronounce stimulus words, each of which contains a short vowel sound. Call on a volunteer to repeat the word, name a rhyming word, and identify the vowel sound heard in the two words.

Stimulus word	*Illustrative children's responses*
mop	mop–hop have the short o sound.
bug	bug–rug have the short u sound.
wig	wig–pig have the short i sound.
set	set–met have the short e sound.
had	had–bad have the short a sound.

4. *Contrasting short vowel sounds in words*

   a. Write a column of identical initial and final consonants leaving a blank space for adding a vowel letter (Step 1).
   b. Insert a vowel letter to complete the first word; call on a volunteer to name the word.
   c. Continue using a different vowel letter for each blank space.
   d. When the column is complete, have the children read the words in rapid succession to contrast the vowel sounds.

Example:

Step 1	Step 2 (Insert vowel)	Step 3 (Children name word)	Step 4
b__g	(i)	big	(Pronounce the
b__g	(e)	beg	series of words
b__g	(u)	bug	in rapid succession)
b__g	(a)	bag	

Other stimulus patterns: (bud bid bad bed; pan pun pin pen; pat pet pit pot; hut hit hot hat).

5. *Using sentence context.* Prepare simple sentences each of which contains a blank space. Each sentence is followed by two words which differ only as to vowel letter. One of these words fits in the sentence. If done orally via the chalkboard, a child *names* and *spells* the correct word which is then written in the blank space to complete the sentence. (If the exercise is seatwork, the child reads both words and then writes the correct word in the blank space.)

Example sentences:

1. The cat drank milk from the _____. (cap/cup)
2. Tom hit the ball with the _____. (bat/bit)
3. The _____ was in the pen. (peg/pig)
4. We have _____ fingers. (tin/ten)
5. John had a _____ of candy. (bag/bug)

Long vowel sounds

Generalizations covering vowel letter-sound relationships are quite numerous. Illustrative teaching procedures will be cited for two adjacent vowels (*ea, ai, ee, oa* patterns), effect of final *e*, long vowel sounds at the end of short words, and vowels followed by consonant controllers, and dipthongs.

Adjacent vowels (same syllable)

When two adjacent vowels represent a single sound they are referred to as vowel digraphs (*feet, boat, sail, mean*). One of the more widely quoted generalizations relates to vowel digraphs. "When two vowels come together they usually represent the long vowel sound of the first vowel," or, "the first vowel has its long sound and the second is not sounded." When this rule is applied to all two-vowel situations, there are about as many exceptions as instances where it applies. Clymer (13) found this rule to apply less than half the time in the sample he tested. However, he also reported that for specific vowel situations it holds much more frequently. For instance, words containing *ee* (98 percent), *oa* (97 percent), *ea* (66 percent), *ai* (64 percent).

Contrast single-double vowel patterns. Prepare lists of words selected so that the first has a single vowel (m*e*t), the second is identical except for an added vowel (m*ea*t).

Children read the first word under A and listen for the short vowel sound. Then they read the first word under B, note the two-vowel pattern and listen for the long vowel sound.

As a final step, read each pair in rapid succession to note the contrasting vowel sound (met–meat; led–lead, etc.).

A	B	A	B	A	B
e	*ea*	*a*	*ai*	*e*	*ee*
met	meat	man	main	fed	feed
led	lead	lad	laid	met	meet
men	mean	pal	pail	pep	peep
bed	bead	ran	rain	bet	beet
stem	steam	bat	bait	wed	weed
set	seat	plan	plain	step	steep

Words containing *o–oa*: *cot–coat*; *got–goat*; *rod–road*; *cost–coast*.

Different visual patterns represent the same sound. Prepare lists of homonyms in which one word in each pair contains either the *ai* or *a–e* pattern. Other pairs contain either the *ea* or *ee* pattern.

The following exercise may be used for group work at the chalkboard or duplicated for independent seat work.

Two words may sound alike
but not be spelled alike

Are these words		Spelled alike? (Yes/No)	Pronounced alike? (Yes/No)	Vowel Sound you hear
1	2			
sail	sale	_____	_____	_____
weak	week	_____	_____	_____
heel	heal	_____	_____	_____
made	maid	_____	_____	_____
pail	pale	_____	_____	_____
beet	beat	_____	_____	_____
plain	plane	_____	_____	_____
steel	steal	_____	_____	_____

Recognizing different vowel patterns as rhyming elements. Prepare a number of four-word series each of which includes two rhyming words with different spelling patterns.

Underline the two words that rhyme

boat	not	note	both
can't	cane	ran	rain
met	feet	seat	felt
sail	tall	walk	whale
sold	soap	rose	rope
paid	made	path	hand
while	well	wheel	meal
pain	plan	plane	pan

The effect of final e

1. Write a column of CVC words on the chalkboard, each of which contains the medial vowel *a*. (Step I) As these words are pronounced have the children tell which vowel sound they hear in the words (*ă*).

Explain that you will change each word by adding the letter *e* at the end of each word (print the words shown in Step II).

Step I	*Step II*
can	cane
hat	hate
mad	made
pal	pale
rat	rate
plan	plane

As these words are pronounced, have the children note the *a–e* pattern and tell the vowel sound heard in each of the words (*ā*).

Have the children explain what vowel sound they hear in words with two vowels when one is a final *e*. Their explanations may then be restated, "In many short words showing two vowels, a final *e* is not sounded while the first vowel has its long sound."

Word pairs for other final *e* series: bit–bite, pin–pine, hid–hide, kit–kite, rid–ride, slid–slide, not–note, hop–hope, rod–rode, rob–robe.

2. Prepare an exercise for either chalkboard presentatioin or independent seatwork. Supply a list of CVC words some of which can be changed to another word by adding a final *e*.

Children read the stimulus word and "think the long vowel sound" to determine if this will make a known word. The word is named (if an oral exercise) or they write the word on the space provided.

Directions: If the word can be changed into another word by adding a final *e*, write the new word on the line provided. If adding an *e* does not make a word, leave the line blank.

can	_____		hid	_____	
rat	_____		sob	_____	*
top	_____	*	mad	_____	
plan	_____		bit	_____	
kit	_____		not	_____	
hop	_____		tap	_____	
cat	_____	*	rob	_____	
cut	_____		big	_____	*

(*spaces left blank)

Long vowel sounds at the end of short words

There are two generalizations which cover single vowels at the end of words: "If a word has only one vowel which ends the word, the vowel sound usually is long;" and, "If a word has no other vowel and ends with *y*, the letter *y* serves as a vowel and is pronounced as long *i*. These generalizations apply in a limited number of high frequency words and can be taught at the chalkboard using columns of words.

be	by	try	go
me	my	sky	no
he	cry	fly	so
we	why	fry	ho
she	dry	shy	yo-yo

Vowels affected by particular consonants

The long and short vowel sounds are by far the most important vowel clues in helping children unlock the pronunciation of words. In addition, there are other vowel situations which should be explained, even though they may be of lesser importance in phonic analysis. When a vowel is followed by *r*, the sound of that vowel is affected by the *r*. Usually a blend results, which is neither the long nor the short sound of the vowel (*car, curl, fir, for, park*). When the vowel *a* is followed by *l* or *w*, the resultant sound is a blend (*awl, tall, awful, talcum, awning, ball*).

While a number of words contain a vowel followed by *r*, it is debatable whether this particular letter-sound combination causes beginning readers much trouble. That is, if children master the long and short vowel relationships they are not likely to experience serious trouble with vowels followed by *r*. Undoubtedly there are many successful readers who are unaware of the difference between the vowel sounds in the words *can* and *car*.

Diphthongs

Diphthongs are two adjacent vowels, each of which is sounded, as the *ou* in *house, oi* in *oil, oy* in *boy, ow* in *how* (but not the *ow* in *blow, grow, throw,* or *sow,* where the sound is long *o*). It is doubtful that teaching diphthongs is of major importance in the total phonics program. These sounds are met in a number of words that are learned as sight words, and certain of these words can serve as key words to help the pupil hear the sound (*house, oil, boy, how*).

1. To teach that the visual pattern *ow* has two sounds, place two columns of words on the board. In column B the *ow* represents long *o*; in Column A the *ow* is a diphthong.

	A	B
Have children note that words in a column rhyme, but that words under *A* do not rhyme with those under *B*.	now	low
	how	snow
	cow	grow
	plow	blow

2. Write some three-word series and have the children identify the two words that rhyme.

1. plow	cow	slow	4. grown	clown	brown
2. snow	now	grow	5. crow	cow	low
3. how	now	low	6. clown	own	down

3. Write several columns of words selected so that each word contains the same diphthong and represents the same sound. Have children read the words in unison, noting the visual pattern and sound represented.

oil	*out*	*saw*	*boy*
boil	*mouth*	*jaw*	*joy*
soil	*south*	*law*	*Roy*
toil	*shout*	*paw*	*toy*
spoil	*found*	*raw*	

Summary of rules related to vowel sounds

1. A single vowel followed by a consonant in a word or syllable usually has the short sound: *can* in *cancel.*
2. A single vowel which concludes a word or syllable usually has the long sound (*me, ti ger, lo co mo tive*).
3. In the vowel digraphs *oa, ea, ee, ai, ay,* the first vowel is usually long and the second is silent (*coat, reap, bead, wait, play*). The digraphs *oo, au,* and *ew* form a single sound which is not the long sound of the first vowel (*food, good, haul, few*).

4. In words containing two vowels, one of which is final *e*, the final *e* is usually silent and the preceding vowel is long.
5. Single vowels followed by *r* usually result in a blend sound (*fir, car, burn, fur*). The vowel *a* followed by *l* or *w* usually results in a blend sound (*awl, tall, claw, awful*).
6. The letter *y* at the end of words containing no other vowel has the long sound of *i* (*my, try, sky, shy*).
7. Diphthongs are two-vowel combinations in which both vowels contribute to the speech sound (h*ou*se, b*oy* c*ow*).

Applying structural analysis

In applying structural analysis skills to solve unknown words, the child is aided if he recognizes parts of words that he may already have studied. These familiar parts may be roots, inflectional endings, affixes, and the combining elements in compounds. He must also understand that a number of identical letter-units are added either to the front or end of many different words to form new words (*pre, un, re, dis; s, ed, ing, ment, tive, able, ness*, etc.). Exercises which illustrate these frequently-met structural changes are often helpful to the learner. A few teaching examples follow:

1. Adding *s, ed, ing* to words.
   "In the space provided, add *s, ed,* or *ing* to the stimulus word. Then pronounce each word."

	s	*ed*	*ing*
play			
look			
call			
flap			
want			
rain			
work			

2. Adding *er, est, ly* to words.
   In the space provided add *er, est, ly* to the stimulus word. Then pronounce each word.

	er	*est*	*ly*
warm			
great			
high			
soft			
kind			

3. "In each blank space add a prefix or suffix to make a word."
Use: *in, dis, re*; and *ment, able, ness*.

_____agree	disagree_____	_____agree_____
_____direct	indirect_____	_____direct_____
_____fill	refill_____	_____fill_____

4. Working with compounds (different levels of difficulty)

a. Each line below contains one compound word. Underline the compound word and write it on the blank space at the end of the line.

1.	children	dancing	hotdog	_____
2.	someone	beaches	crawling	_____
3.	alike	mousetrap	puzzle	_____
4.	downpour	happily	permitted	_____
5.	autumn	mistake	handbag	_____

b. Illustrating how the same word may be used in a number of compound words. Write three compound words for each group of words.

Example:

	air	plane	craft	port
		_____	_____	_____
1.	book	case	keeper	worm
		_____	_____	_____
2.	door	way	man	mat
		_____	_____	_____
3.	candle	light	maker	stick
		_____	_____	_____
4.	moon	glow	shot	light
		_____	_____	_____

c. Complete each sentence by writing a compound word in the blank space.

1. A player can hit a home run in the game of _____.
2. The teacher wrote on the _____ with a piece of chalk.
3. November 25 is _____ Day.
4. The front window in a car is called the _____.
5. The mailman puts mail in our _____.

Syllabication

A syllable is a vowel, or group of letters containing a vowel, which is pronounced as a unit. A child must be able to break unknown polysyllabic words into syllables if he is to approximate the pronounciation of these words. This ability grows out of knowing both the structural and the phonetic features of words. Children usually learn a number of one-syllable root words prior to meeting polysyllabic words. As they meet longer words, they learn that most prefixes and suffixes and come inflectional endings constitute syllables. During the child's early experience with high frequency affixes, he breaks the word into parts and then combines the parts into the whole: *re* read *ing, pre* heat *ed, bi* week *ly, dis* appear *ance*. After many experiences, he reduces his reliance on this type of analysis, and the blending of the parts into the whole becomes much smoother.

A knowledge of vowel behavior within words is the second major aid in breaking words into syllables. The sounds of vowels and letter combinations are not as consistent as prefixes and suffixes. Nevertheless, many phonetic generalizations are useful. Although the following examples are not words, the letter combinations can be broken into syllables: *comration, ragmotex, obsebong, fasnotel*. The likely syllabication is: *com·ra·tion, rag·mo·tex, ob·se·bong, fas·no·tel*. Most facile readers would pronounce these nonsense words in substantially the same way. These readers probably would not recite rules to themselves before attempting to pronounce the above words, but they would probably be subconsciously influenced by rules they had learned.

When generalizations applicable to syllabication are taught, children should be provided with a number of examples and then led to see for themselves what happens. Out of this experience, rules can develop. Starting with the question, "What usually happens when two consonants come between vowels?" the teacher can place on the board a number of words such as:

af ter	win dow	rab bit	let ter
gar den	can dy	din ner	sum mer
fas ter	pen cil	lit tle	cot ton

The generalization will then emerge that "when two consonants come between vowels, the syllable division comes between the consonants" or "one consonant goes with each vowel." It should be pointed out that this rule will not always hold, but that it is the best guess to make when trying to pronounce an unknown word.

In the case of double consonants (le*tt*er, su*mm*er), there are few exceptions to the rule.

To teach what happens when one consonant comes between two vowels, a list of known sight words may be placed on the board:

be gin	fe ver	to tal	de cide
o ver	di rect	ti ger	me ter
fa tal	mo ment	pu pil	ho tel

From these examples children will both see and hear that "the single consonant goes with the following syllable." They will also note that when "the syllable is a vowel or ends with a vowel, it usually has the long sound." These two generalizations should be taught together because they work together. In cases where the first of two vowels separated by a single consonant has its short sound, the single intervening consonant closes the first syllable (*cam el, mag a zine*).

A few generalizations about common word endings as they relate to syllabication might be taught. Children have had experience with prefixes and suffixes and may follow these rules even though they are not able to verbalize them.

1. Common endings which begin with a vowel such as *ing, est,* or *er* are usually sounded as syllables (look *ing,* long *er,* long *est*). This is not true of *ed* except when preceded by *t* or *d* (want*ed,* need*ed*).
2. Most one-syllable words remain intact as syllables when endings are added. In many instances this violates the "divide between consonants" rule stated earlier. This is not a problem to children if they have learned to see prefixes and suffixes as units. Examples might include spell *ing,* want *ed,* tell *ing* (not spel *ling,* wan *ted,* tel *ling*).
3. Certain letter combinations, when found at the ends of words, are rarely divided and thus stand as the final syllable.

un *cle*	fa *ble*	bu *gle*	sad *dle*
cir *cle*	tum *ble*	sin *gle*	can *dle*
bicy *cle*	mar *ble*	ea *gle*	nee *dle*
mus *cle*	dou *ble*	strug *gle*	bun *dle*
sam *ple*	gen *tle*	puz *zle*	an *kle*
tem *ple*	rat *tle*	daz *zle*	spar *kle*
sim *ple*	whis *tle*	muz *zle*	ran *kle*
pur *ple*	ti *tle*	fraz *zle*	twin *kle*

The generalizations are:

1. The letter combinations *cle, ble, gle, dle, zle, kle, ple, tle* at the end of words usually stand as the final syllable.
2. The final *e* is silent, and the sound contains the *l* blended.
3. This final syllable is not accented.

Accent

Certain words in sentences receive more stress than others, and this is also true of syllables in polysyllabic words. As he learns his native language, the child masters the stress and intonation patterns of sentences and longer words. To say that a child knows the pronunciation of a word implies that he knows its pattern of stress in normal speech. However, when one is attempting to sound out a word not known as a sight word, determining the syllable stress is important.

Teaching accent is usually one of the later steps in phonic analysis, primarily because the learner must be at a stage of development where he can use a dictionary and note primary and secondary accent marks. Memorization of a set of rules to apply in determining accent is probably not desirable since there are numerous exceptions to most such rules. However, structuring learning situations in which the child is invited to make observations and note certain "pronunciation clues" is undoubtedly defensible. To facilitate such learnings, one might provide brief lists of words and have the child or class mark the accent and then state an observation which applies to the group of words. Several illustrations follow.

1. *Two-syllable words*

dentist	den' tist	anvil	an' vil
barley	bar' ley	wisdom	wis' dom
wizard	wiz' ard	column	col' umn
journal	jour' nal	local	lo' cal
symbol	sym' bol	tailor	tai' lor

Observation: In two-syllable words, the first syllable is accented. Present following new data:

appoint	ap point'	parade	pa rade'
subdue	sub due'	complain	com plain'
receive	re ceive'	reveal	re veal'
proceed	pro ceed'	astound	a stound'

Modify observation: In two-syllable words, the first syllable is usually accented *unless* the second syllable contains two vowels, in which case it is usually accented.

2. *Compound words*

evergreen (ever′ green)
newscast (news′ cast)
shoehorn (shoe′ horn)
censorship (cen′ sor ship)
waterfall (wa′ ter fall)

underdog (un′ der dog)
makeshift (make′ shift)
passport (pass′ port)
drawbridge (draw′ bridge)

Observation: Compound words are usually accented on or within the first word.

3. *Three syllable words*

an′ ces tor
cap′ i tal
sat′ el lite
in dig′ nant
fi na′ le

sta′ di um
fan tas′ tik
pa′ tri ot
col′ o ny
bat tal′ ion

syl′ la ble
ho ri′ zon
in′ ci dent
chem′ is try
al′ ma nac

Observation: Three-syllable words are usually accented on the first or second syllable.

4. *Words containing primary and secondary accent*

con′ den sa′ tion
op′ po si′ tion
sep′ a ra′ tion
sen′ ti men′ tal

su′ per sti′ tions
ad′ van ta′ geous
in′ ter mis′ sion
mi′ cro scop′ ic

Observations: (a) Words of four or more syllables have a primary and secondary accent.

(b) The primary accent usually falls on the syllable preceding suffixes such as *tion, ous, al, ic, sion.*

5. *Shift in accent*

sep′ a rate → sep a ra′ tion
re spon′ si ble → re spon si bil′ i ty
sen′ ti ment → sen ti men′ tal → sen ti men tal′ i ty

Observation: Primary accent often shifts in derived forms of root words (adding suffixes).

Conclusion

In order to become an independent reader, a child must learn to associate printed symbols with the sounds these symbols represent. When a child successfully applies phonics skills, he blends a series of sounds so as to arrive at the pronunciation of a word he does not recognize on sight. Phonics is undoubtedly the most important of the word identification skills which also include word configuration, structural analysis, and context clues. The facile reader does not overrely on one skill, but tends to use various clues in combination. In teaching phonic skills, the following principles should be kept in mind.

Principles to follow in teaching phonics

One of the principles cited in chapter one recognizes the importance of phonics: "Early in the learning process the child must acquire ways of gaining independence in identifying words whose meanings are known to him but which are unknown to him as sight words."

As one begins teaching children letter-sound relationships, more concrete guidelines can be formulated and added to this general statement:

1. Before a child is taught that a given letter represents a particular sound in words, he must be able to discriminate visually that letter form from other letter forms.
2. Also, he must be able to discriminate auditorially the sound under consideration from other speech sounds in words. These considerations are valid even in methodological approaches which temporarily bypass the teaching of letter names but which invite learners to associate sounds with letter symbols directly.
3. There is an unlimited number of ways that letter-sound relationship can be taught. Any technique that proves successful for a child is a justifiable procedure for him providing:
   (a) What he is taught today does not inhibit his later growth, and (b) that the instructional approach is reasonably economical in time and effort expended.
4. Children should not be taught to overrely on phonic analysis techniques. Examples of overreliance include sounding out the same words hundreds of times (sight recognition must replace analysis); and attempting to sound out words which do not lend themselves to letter-sound analysis:

once, knight, freight, some, one, eight, love, know, head, move, none, have, laugh, etc.

5. Children differ as to how much instruction is needed while they are learning letter-sound relationships. Diagnosis that reveals what a child knows and does not know is essential for good instruction. In the final analysis, the *optimum* amount of phonics instruction for every child is the *minimum* that he needs to become an independent reader.

CONCLUSION AND YOUR POINT OF VIEW?

Space limitations prohibit a thorough discussion of all of the educational issues involved in phonics instruction. Therefore, as a conclusion to this chapter a number of questions will be posed, followed by brief answers which do not cite research findings. In some instances these questions and answers may serve as a stimulus for further discussion and library research.

1. In learning to read, how important are phonic (letter-sound analyses) skills? The child learning to read English writing *must* learn to associate printed letters with speech sounds. One cannot become an independent reader without this skill. It follows that if a cluster of skills are this important, they should be well taught.

2. What is the purpose of phonics instruction as it relates to learning to read? Applying phonic skills permits the reader to "work out" the pronunciation or the approximate pronunciation of printed words NOT known as sight words. The child is not learning "how to pronounce" the word in question, he is learning that a particular series of letters represents a particular word which is part of his speaking vocabulary.

3. Should children be taught to learn words-as-wholes (sight words)? All facile readers at *every* grade level recognize words as wholes and their stock of sight words is constantly enlarged month by month and year by year.

4. Is it possible to teach children to overrely on phonic analysis? It is possible to teach children to overrely on any word recognition technique (sight words, context, letter analysis). Learning to read involves the *simultaneous* application of all of these approaches; each is part of a unitary process called *reading.* When children overrely on phonics analysis, they have a "set" to sound out each

word (a habit which precludes getting meaning from larger language units). They sound out the same words many times, continuing to do so long after they should have learned the word as a unit. The child who sounds out every word in a story *is a seriously impaired reader.*

5. Does every child need the same amount of phonics instruction? Since the answer here obviously is no, the question is posed mainly to focus on phonic instructional materials which tend to ignore this issue. These types of materials suggest that lengthy periods of time be devoted to phonics each day. All children perform the same tasks and in so doing many are subjected to much more than the optimum amount of such instruction.

6. What is the optimum amount of phonics instruction? The optimum is the minimum amount of phonics which permits the child to become an independent reader. Ongoing diagnosis provides the teacher with information as to what skills are needed.

7. What is the relationship between memorizing "phonic rules" and applying them in reading situations? It is likely that some children profit from familiarity with certain phonic generalizations. On the other hand, it is known that some children can memorize "rules" and yet be unable to apply them in reading situations. It is debatable whether children should be asked to memorize rules which have very limited application to words they will meet in reading.

What is the basis for your agreement or disagreement with each of the following statements:

1. There is little justification for the deliberate teaching of letter names to first grade children.

2. The sequence in which phonic skills are taught is of little significance.

3. Since a child must learn letter-sound relationships before he can become an independent reader, this skill should be taught before "reading for meaning" is stressed.

4. Reform of English spelling would have little impact on children's learning to read English writing.

BIBLIOGRAPHY

1. Agnew, Donald C. *Effect of Varied Amounts of Phonic Training on Primary Reading.* Durham, N. C.: Duke University Press, 1939.

2. Bagford, Jack, *Phonics: Its Role in Teaching Reading.* Iowa City: Sernoll, Inc., 1967.

3. Bailey, Mildred Hart, "The Utility of Phonic Generalizations in Grades One Through Six," *Reading Teacher* (February 1967) 413–18.

4. Bear, David E. "Two Methods of Teaching Phonics: A Longitudinal Study," *Elementary School Journal* (February 1964), 273–79.

5. Bliesmer, Emery P. and Betty H. Yarborough, "A Comparison of Ten Different Beginning Reading Programs In First Grade," *Phi Delta Kappan* (June 1965), 500–504.

6. Botel, Morton, "Strategies for Teaching Sound-Letter Relationships," *Vistas In Reading,* International Reading Association Proceedings, 2, Part I, 1966, 156–59.

7. Brzeinski, Joseph E. "When Should Phonics Instruction Begin?" *Reading as an Intellectual Activity.* International Reading Association Proceedings 8, 1963, 228–32.

8. Burmeister, Lou E. "Vowel Pairs," *Reading Teacher* (February 1968), 445–52.

9. ———, "Final Vowel-Consonant-e," *The Reading Teacher* (February 1971), 439–42.

10. Burrows, Alvina Trent and Zyra Lourie, "Two Vowels Go Walking," *Reading Teacher* (November 1963), 79–82.

11. Chall, Jeanne, Florence G. Roswell, and Susan Halm Blumenthall, "Auditory Blending Ability: A Factor in Success in Beginning Reading," *Reading Teacher* (November 1963), 113–18.

12. Chall, Jeanne, *Learning To Read — The Great Debate.* New York: McGraw-Hill Book Company, 1967.

13. Clymer, Theodore, "The Utility of Phonic Generalizations in the Primary Grades," *Reading Teacher* (January 1963), 252–58.

14. Cordts, Anna D. "When Phonics is Functional," *Elementary English* (November 1963), 748–50.

15. ———, *Phonics for the Reading Teacher.* New York: Holt, Rinehart & Winston, Inc., 1965.

16. Curry, Robert L. and Toby W. Rigby, *Reading Independence Through Word Analysis.* Columbus, Ohio: Charles E. Merrill Publishing Company, 1969.

17. Dechant, Emerald V. *Improving the Teaching of Reading* (2nd Ed.). Englewood Cliffs, N. J.: Prentice-Hall, Inc., 1970. Chapters 10 and 11.

18. Durrell, Donald D. "Phonics Problems in Beginning Reading," in *Forging Ahead In Reading,* J. Allen Figurel (ed.), Proceedings, International Reading Association, 12, Part I, 1968, 19–25.

19. Emans, Robert, "The Usefulness of Phonic Generalizations Above the Primary Grades," *Reading Teacher* (February 1967) 419–25.

20. ————, "Phonics: A Look Ahead," *Elementary English* (May 1969), 575–582.

21. Fry, Edward, "A Frequency Approach to Phonics," *Elementary English* (November 1964), 759–65.

22. Goodman, Kenneth S. "A Linguistic Study of Cues and Miscues in Reading," *Elementary English* (October 1965), 639–43.

23. Gray, William, *On Their Own in Reading* (rev. ed.). Chicago: Scott, Foresman & Company, 1960.

24. Gurren, Louise and Ann Hughes, "Intensive Phonics vs. Gradual Phonics in Beginning Reading: A Review," *Journal of Educational Research* (April 1965), 339–46.

25. Haggard, J. Kendall, "Phonics in Directed Reading Activities," *Reading Teacher* (December 1955), 90.

26. Hanson, Irene W., "First Grade Children Work with Variant Word Endings," *Reading Teacher* (April 1966), 505–7.

27. Heilman, Arthur W. *Phonics In Proper Perspective* (Second Ed.). Columbus, Ohio: Charles E. Merrill Publishing Company, 1968.

28. Hull, Marion A. *Phonics for the Teacher of Reading.* Columbus, Ohio: Charles E. Merrill Publishing Co., 1969.

29. King, Ethel M. and Siegmar Muehl, "Different Sensory Cues as Aids in Beginning Reading," *Reading Teacher* (December 1965), 163–68.

30. Marchbanks, Gabrielle and Harry Levin, "Cues by Which Children Recognize Words," *Journal of Educational Psychology* (April 1965), 57–61.

31. Marlin, R. G. "Decoding and The Quest of Meaning," *Journal of Reading Behavior* (Fall 1969), 22–29.

32. Oaks, Ruth E. "A Study of the Vowel Situations in a Primary Vocabulary," *Education* (May 1952), 604–17.

33. Piekarz, Josephine A. "Common Sense About Phonics," *Reading Teacher* (November 1964), 114–17.

34. Potts, Marion and Savino, Carl, "The Relative Achievement of First Graders Under Three Different Reading Programs," *The Journal of Educational Research*, (July-August 1968), 447–450.

35. Ramsey, Z. Wallace, "Will Tomorrow's Teachers Know and Teach Phonics?" *Reading Teacher* (January 1962), 241–45.

36. Robinson, H. Alan, "A Study of the Techniques of Word Identification," *Reading Teacher* (January 1963), 238–42.

37. Rystrom, Richard, "Whole-word and Phonics Methods and Current Linguistic Findings," *Elementary English* (March 1965), 265–68.

38. _____, "Listening, Decoding, Comprehension and Reading," *The Reading Teacher* (December 1970), 261–266.

39. Sabaroff, Rose, "Breaking The Code: What Method? Introducing an Integrated Linguistic Approach to Beginning Reading," *Elementary School Journal* (November 1966), 95–103.

40. Scott, Louise Binder and J. J. Thompson, *Phonics.* Manchester, Mo.: Webster Publishing, 1962.

41. Smith, Carl Bernard, "The Double Vowel and Linguistic Research," *Reading Teacher* (April 1966), 512–14.

42. Soffietti, James P. "Why Children Fail to Read: A Linguistic Analysis," *Harvard Educational Review* (Spring 1955), 63–84.

43. Sparks, Paul E. and Leo C. Fay, "An Evaluation of Two Methods of Teaching Reading," *Elementary School Journal* (April 1957), 386–90.

44. Weintraub, Samuel, "A Critique of a Review of Phonics Studies," *Elementary School Journal* (October 1966), 34–41.

45. Wilson, Robert M. and MaryAnne Hall, *Programmed Word Attack for Teachers.* Columbus, Ohio: Charles E. Merrill Publishing Company, 1968.

46. Winkley, Carol K. "The Applicability of Accent Generalizations," *Academic Therapy Quarterly* (Fall 1966), 2–9.

47. _____, "Why Not an Intensive-Gradual Phonic Approach," *The Reading Teacher* (April 1970), 611–617.

8

Diagnosis of
Reading Ability

It has been pointed out that children entering school show great differences in readiness to learn, and the differences in reading skills and ability increase in each succeeding grade. Since some children in second grade read at the primer level, their teacher must function at least part of the time as a first grade teacher. In most third and fourth grade classrooms, there will be pupils who need instruction on skills *introduced* at earlier levels. Also, these same classrooms will contain children who are already fairly competent in the skills which are scheduled to be taught in these grades. For these children, more drill on mechanics which they have already mastered would be both wasteful and highly unmotivating. Figure 20 attempts to illustrate the overlap between grades and the range of reading abilities found at the primary level.

These facts, which apply to practically every classroom, emphasize the need for flexible or differentiated instruction. The one criterion that distinguishes excellent reading programs from others is the degree to which individual needs are ascertained and met. Teachers must be alert to differences among pupils in order to follow sound principles of teaching. Only through diagnosis will the teacher be able to assess needs and plan instruction for children whose needs vary considerably. Diagnosis should be thought of as continuous since children change rapidly. A diagnosis in September may be followed by a breakthrough on the part of the child

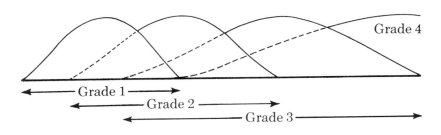

FIGURE 20

*Graphic Representation of Reading Abilities in the Primary
Grades. (Note that the Range of Abilities Increases at each
Succeeding Grade Level.)*

in some vital skill or by a child's failure to master some new step in
the reading process. In either case, the earlier diagnosis is obsolete.

Reading weaknesses and reading achievement can be assessed by
either standardized or informal teacher-made tests. Although tests
are designed for use at every grade level, no purpose would be served
in a reading textbook by a separate discussion of tests each time
a different instructional level is under consideration. The following
discussion of tests and testing applies to the various levels of the
elementary school with the exception that reading readiness tests
are dealt with in Chapter 4.

**Standardized
Tests**

These are commercially printed tests which fall into two classes:
those designed for group administration, and those designed to be
administered individually. In both, credits are given for acceptable
responses, and the child's score is determined by his correct responses, lack of errors, and rate of reading. Norms are usually
provided, and any child's score can be translated into a grade-level
equivalent. Usually subtests are scored separately, permitting the
plotting of a profile which will indicate the areas of pupil strengths
and weaknesses. Standardized tests are widely used in our schools,
and a larger number of them are becoming available each year.
Most of these have real merit, yet it is doubtful that reading instruction is improving as a direct result of these tests. This is para-

doxical. If tests have real merit, how could their widespread use not result in appreciable improvement in reading instruction?

The answer to this question is to be found in the way the tests are used. (27) As pointed out in Chapter 1, the only justifiable purpose for the use of reading tests is to secure data about a child's reading ability so that a reading program for him can be built from the data secured. In actual practice, some schools and some teachers gain comfort from the use of tests because they are convinced that testing programs per se have educational value. Testing becomes an end in itself rather than a basis for instruction. In some communities a metal filing cabinet "with a folder for each pupil" is interpreted as prima facie evidence of good teaching practices. This reaction suggests that the school has lost sight of the principle that diagnosis alone has no salutary effect on the pupil diagnosed.

Group tests

Tests designed for groups have some very obvious weaknesses. A second grade teacher testing a large number of children at one time cannot hope to find out much about any individual child's reading needs or weaknesses. Such a test will differentiate between poor and good readers, but a formal test may not be the most economical method of securing these data. A considerable amount of teacher time must be spent in learning the precise procedure for administering and scoring the test and in analyzing the results. The skilled teacher who uses equal time and effort in informal reading situations will certainly arrive at an equally reliable division of pupils. In addition, she will also have a better idea of what specific weaknesses certain children have developed. From the standpoint of instruction, this is more important than simply knowing which children are impaired readers.

Another drawback to the use of group tests is that pupils' scores can be influenced by such factors as the misunderstanding of directions, the guessing of answers, and confusion in marking responses. If these go undetected in the group-administered test, the analysis of test scores will result in a distorted picture of the child's reading ability. (25)

All achievement batteries designed to test pupils in the elementary school contain reading tests. Often these reading subtests are available in individual booklets which can be secured and administered independently of the rest of the battery. (The *California*, *SRA* and *Metropolitan* achievement batteries and the *Coordinated*

Scales of Attainment are examples.) Since there are so many different reading tests, it is to be expected that many of them will measure virtually the same aspects of reading. Nevertheless, there are major differences among tests as to what they measure, the level of difficulty for which they are designed, the care which went into their construction, and the ease with which they are administered. Each of these factors affects two important attributes of reading tests — the consistency with which they measure reading skills, and the degree to which they actually measure the skills that they allegedly measure.

No full-time elementary teacher would have the time or the need to become thoroughly conversant with all standardized reading tests. However, it might be well to know where one can go for information about tests when that information is needed. Probably the most authoritative source for such information is *The Mental Measurements Yearbook*, edited by Buros.* Information regarding tests can also be secured from publishers of tests and sample sets of tests can be purchased. In addition, many universities and colleges maintain testing bureaus which are equipped to advise teachers and administrators concerning tests and testing programs.

Individual tests

Individual tests can minimize some of the shortcomings attributed to group tests. Teachers can observe one child quite closely during the administration of the test. This permits much more precise knowledge of reading errors made and whether or not the child understands the test directions. Individual standardized tests range in content from a single paragraph of oral reading at each grade level to a number of subtests including silent reading, oral reading with comprehension questions, spelling, letter recognition, sounding of blends, word meanings, and rapid recognition of sight words in isolation. The most significant subtests are the oral reading passages at each grade level. These are usually relatively short reading passages upon which the grade norms are based and, as a result, tend to rate pupils higher than their actual reading level on sustained reading material. Table 3 presents data on the number of

---

*Oscar Krisen Buros, ed., *The Sixth Mental Measurements Yearbook* (Highland Park, N.J.: The Gryphon Press, 1965.) Also see Oscar Krisen Buros, *Reading Tests and Reviews.* Highland Park, N.J.: The Gryphon Press, 1968.

running words (total number of words in the reading passage at each grade level) found in several reading tests designed for use in the elementary grades.

TABLE 3

Number of Running Words Found on Representative Reading Tests, Grades 1–6

	Running Words Found on:		
Grade Level	*Durrell Analysis of Reading Difficulty**	*Gray Oral Reading Paragraphs Test†*	*Gilmore Oral Reading Tests**
1	21	49	26
2	51	49	50
3	55	49	51
4	72	62	67
5	78	62	107
6	97	62	107

*World Book Co., New York
†Public School Publishing Co., Bloomington, Indiana

Representative tests

A brief description of a limited number of both group and individual tests follows. These tests are selected because they illustrate different types of reading tests and because, in most cases, they are recent publications or recent revisions.

Group tests

1. *Gates-MacGinitie Reading Tests* (1965). Publisher: Teachers College Press, Columbia University. Six separate tests are available for testing grades one through nine.

	Grade	*Subtests*	*Forms*
Primary A	1	Vocabulary, Comprehension	1–2
Primary B	2	Vocabulary, Comprehension	1–2
Primary C	3	Vocabulary, Comprehension	1–2
Primary CS	2.5–3	Speed, Accuracy	1–2–3
Survey D*	4–5–6	Speed, Vocabulary, Comprehension	1–2–3
Survey E*	7–8–9	Speed, Vocabulary, Comprehension	1–2–3

*Available in both hand-scored and machine-scored editions.

2. *Nelson-Lohmann Reading Test* (Grades 4–8). Publisher: Educational Test Bureau, Educational Publishers, Inc. This is a paragraph test using multiple-choice questions to measure the pupil's grasp of central ideas; word meanings derived from context, and details; and the pupil's ability to integrate ideas. There are separate tests for each grade level 4–8. Two comparable forms are available.

These tests are also part of the battery: *Coordinated Scales of Attainment*.

3. *S.R.A. Achievement Series* (1964). Publisher: Science Research Associates, Inc. These materials consist of three separate batteries for use at grade levels 1–2; 2–4; 4–9. There are subtests for each area of the curriculum. The following data refer only to the reading subtests.

Grades 1–2.   The reading test contains 4 subtests: verbal-picture association, language perception, comprehension, and vocabulary. Forms C-D.

Grades 2–4.   The reading test consists of two subtests: vocabulary and comprehension. Forms C-D.

Grades 4–9.   Three separate batteries are published in a single booklet. Batteries are for grade levels as follows:

> 4.5 to 5.5
> 6.5 to 8.0
> 8   to 9

Subtests: Comprehension, Vocabulary. Forms C-D.

4. *California Achievement Test Batteries* (1957 edition with 1963 norms). Publisher: California Test Bureau.

A. Lower Primary, Grades 1–2
B. Upper Primary, Grades 3–4
C. Elementary, Grades 4–6
D. Junior High, Grades 7–9
E. Advanced, Grades 9–14

Reading skills measured: Reading vocabulary and reading comprehension are tested. Each is covered by several subtests which yield part scores. The reading tests, which are part of the achievement battery, are available as separate tests under the title *California Reading Test*.

Four forms: W, X, Y, Z

5. *Stanford Achievement Tests* (1964). Publisher: Harcourt, Brace Jovanovich, Inc. Five separate batteries cover grades 1–9. Each battery contains a number of subtests on reading.

Primary Battery I. Grades 1–2.5 (Word Reading, Paragraph Meaning, Vocabulary, Spelling, Word Study Skills).

Primary Battery II. Grades 2–3 (Word Meaning, Paragraph Meaning, Spelling, Word Study Skills, Language).

Intermediate Battery I. Grades 4–5 (same subtests as above).

Intermediate Battery II. Grades 5–6 (Word Meaning, Paragraph Meaning, Spelling, Language).

Advanced Battery. Grades 7–9 (Paragraph Meaning, Spelling, Language).

Each of the above batteries is available in forms: W, X, Y, Z.

6. *Iowa Tests of Basic Skills* (Grades 3–9). Publisher: Houghton Mifflin Company (3 alternate forms). This achievement battery yields eleven separate scores in the following major areas: vocabulary, reading comprehension, language skills, work-study skills, and arithmetic skills.

All of the subtests for each grade, three through nine, are included in one spiral booklet of ninety-six pages. These booklets are reusable since responses are made on separate answer sheets.

The reading comprehension test requires approximately one hour for administration at *each* grade level. It consists of a number of stories of graduated length and difficulty. Comprehension is tested by means of multiple choice items, the reader selecting the one best answer from among the four available. As noted above, the reading comprehension test is available only as part of the entire Basic Skills Battery.

7. *American School Achievement Tests* (Part I, Test of Reading). Publisher: The Bobbs-Merrill Co., Inc.

A. Primary Battery, Grades 2–3
B. Intermediate Battery, Grades 4–6
C. Advanced Battery, Grades 7–9

Reading skills measured (all levels): Sentence and word meaning, paragraph meaning, and total reading score.
Four forms: D, E, F, G

Individual Tests

1. *Durrell Analysis of Reading Difficulty* (Grades 1–6). Major subtests include a separate series of paragraphs for oral reading and recall, silent reading and recall, and listening comprehension. Other subtests measure visual recognition of letters and words, ability to give sounds of letters and blends, and spelling. Each individual test folder contains an extensive checklist of potential reading difficulties. This test has several limitations: only one form is available; grade level norms are based on rate but not on comprehension; and comprehension questions rely heavily on recall of detail, thus slighting other facets of comprehension.

2. *Gates-McKillop Reading Diagnostic Tests.* (Grades 2–6, a 1962 Revision of the *Gates Reading Diagnostic Tests*). Publisher: Teachers Press, Teachers College, Columbia University. This test consists of subtests measuring oral reading, rapid recognition of whole words, untimed sight-word recognition, auditory blending, spelling, recognizing word parts and oral vocabulary (meaning). The total test yields 28 scores, is somewhat complicated to administer, and is time-consuming.

3. *Gilmore Oral Reading Test* (Grades 1–8). Publisher: World Book Company. This test consists of ten paragraphs, arranged in order of difficulty, which form a continuous story. Each paragraph, representing a grade level, is followed by five comprehension questions. There are two forms of the test, both of which are included in the same spiral-bound booklet. The test yields separate scores on rate of reading, comprehension, and accuracy (pronunciation of vocabulary). The individual record blank permits a detailed record of reading errors.

4. *Gray Oral Reading Test* (1963). Publisher: The Bobbs-Merrill Co., Inc. This test consists of a series of 13 paragraphs of increasing difficulty. As the subject reads orally, the examiner marks on an identical passage the errors noted such as mispronunciation, words not attempted, omission, substitution, repetitions, and the like. Comprehension of each paragraph is checked by a series of four questions. Each paragraph is timed. Scoring involves recording the number of errors, type of errors, time elapsed in reading each paragraph, and a comprehension score. Total score can be converted into a grade-equivalent score. There are four alternate forms of the test: A, B, C, D.

Informal
Teacher-Made Tests

Teachers can devise informal tests for any classroom purpose. (4) The simplest screening test might consist of having a child read a paragraph or two from a book to determine whether he can successfully read that particular book. (22) More thorough informal tests will yield important data about children's reading, and these tests have certain advantages for classroom use. First, they are simple to construct since the teacher has available graded reading materials from the pre-primer level through the upper grades. Second, the child can be tested over longer passages of sustained reading than are characteristically found on standardized tests. Third, the use of teacher-made tests avoids the formality of the usual test situation. Informal testing is not likely to arouse the pupil tensions which sometimes accompany testing and which occasionally influence pupil performance. In this respect, the informal test more closely parallels the actual reading situations which the child encounters in the classroom. (23) Finally, the teacher-made test is inexpensive and demands no more teacher time for administration and analysis than do other tests. At the same time, it yields very specific data on each child's weaknesses and needs, as do the individual standardized tests. The following steps might serve as a guide in the construction of an informal test.

Devise a checklist of reading behaviors. This is usually one page upon which the teacher can rapidly record reading errors and observations of related behavior. Figure 21 is an example which could be duplicated and filled out for each child in the class. The checklist can be used with any graded reading materials.

Testing
Mechanical Skills

In the final analysis, the act of reading is a type of global behavior that is made possible by the simultaneous application of a great number of skills. (13) The terms *mechanical skills* and *comprehension skills*, as used in this chapter should not lead the reader to visualize a dichotomy. The simple fact is that critical reading or *comprehending* depends on the mastery of a myriad of related skills. It is true that when we give children assignments in reading we

FIGURE 21

Reading Behavior Record

Name_____ Age_____ Grade_____ Date_____

School_____ Teacher_____

Examiner_____

I. *Word Analysis*
   A.   Knows names of letters?   Yes   No
        Needs work with:_____
   B.   Attacks initial sound of words?   Yes   No
        Deficiencies noted:_____
   C.   Can substitute initial letter-sounds?   Yes   No
        Further drill needed: _____
   D.   Can sound out initial blends and digraphs?   Yes   No
        Deficiencies noted:_____
   E.   If root word is known, can solve words
        formed by adding prefixes and suffixes.   Yes   No

II. *Sight Words* (Check if applicable)
   _____Knows a word one time, misses it later.
   _____Guesses at unknown words.
       _____Errors frequently do not change intended meaning.
       _____Errors indicate not reading for meaning.
   _____Frequently adds words.
   _____Omits unknown words.
       _____Reads on.
       _____Fills in omitted word.
   _____Omits or skips words he knows or can solve.

III. *Reading Habits Noted*
   _____Reads word by word   _____Loses place frequently
   _____Phrasing inadequate   _____Does not utilize punctuation
   _____Poor intonation   _____Lacks persistence
   _____Dialect interference: Explain _____

IV. *Sustained Reading* (Basal, textbook, trade book)

Book	Grade Level	Approx. Number of Running Words	Number of Errors
1.			
2.			

FIGURE 21 (cont.)

IV. *Sustained Reading* (cont.)

Errors noted (example): Said *lied* for *lying; banged* for *bumped; stuck* for *start* (corrected)

Needed help with: *clown, stomach, curious, squeal.*

Read with some hesitation, not smoothly, etc.

	Excellent	Average	Below Average
V. Comprehension			
Recall of facts			
Recognizes main ideas			
Draws inferences			
Maintains sequence of events			
Understands humor			
Interprets figurative expressions			
VI. Oral Reading Skills			
Relates with audience			
Enunciation			
Adequate volume			
Reads with intonation			
Phrases for meaning			
VII. Behaviors Related to Reading			
Attitude toward reading			
Self confidence			
Background knowledge			
Language facility			
Originality of expression			
Range of vocabulary			
Stock of concepts			
Variety of sentence patterns			

VIII. Other Comments: _____

imply that the reader is to use the global skill labeled critical reading. However, actual instruction in reading almost always focuses on one or a limited number of skills.

The following pages provide illustrative materials which can be used or adapted for determining a child's present level of functioning in regard to a number of skills such as:

1. Letter recognition.
2. Associating printed letters with sounds they represent.
3. Auditory discrimination of speech sounds in words.
4. Structural analysis (involving root words to which affixes have been added).
5. Syllabication.
6. Sight recognition of high frequency words.

Letter recognition

To determine if a child recognizes capital and lower case letter forms, prepare a set of alphabet cards each of which shows a capital letter on one side and its lower case form on the other side.

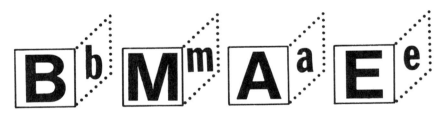

1. Present cards in mixed order and record errors made.

   Alternate approaches:
2. Present letter forms in mixed order on page or large cardboard. Child points to and names each letter.

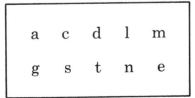

B	L	M	G	P
K	S	D	F	H

a	c	d	l	m
g	s	t	n	e

3. Matching capital and lower case forms: Duplicate a page of boxes similar to below. Child draws line to, or circles, matching lower case form.

	b		e		d		h
M	c	A	a	D	p	G	r
	m		h		b		g

Letter-sound relationships (Initial and final consonants, medial vowels)

Prepare a page of pictures. Below each picture is a line on which the child is to do *one* of the following tasks.

Write the letter that represents

a. the first sound heard in the picture naming word.
b. the last sound heard in the picture naming word.
c. the vowel sound heard in the picture naming word.

More difficult task: Child writes letter for initial, medial, and final sounds. (Picture naming words limited to three phonemes)

Initial consonants in sentence format

Each sentence emphasizes one initial letter-sound and can provide clues as to whether a child is experiencing trouble with any particular initial letter-sound.

1. Bobby brought back bunches of bananas.
2. Candy, the cat, can't come to class.
3. Dad didn't drop the dozen doughnuts on Dave's desk.
4. Father feels fine after falling four feet from the fir tree.
5. Go get a gun and a good guide if you hunt geese.
6. Henry hurt his hand with the heavy hammer.
7. Jean joined Joe in playing a joke on Jack.
8. Kate keeps the key in the kitchen.
9. The lucky lady located the lovely locket that she had lost at lunch.
10. My mother made Mike move the muddy mess.
11. Nick noticed a number of new nails in the workshop.
12. Polly put the pitcher in the pantry.
13. The rabbit ate the raw radishes, then ran rapidly down the ranch road.
14. Six surprised sailors saw Sam sneeze suddenly.
15. Ted tried to teach the tiny tot to talk.
16. On Wednesday, Wendy was washing the windows.
17. Yes, your younger brother yelled in the yard yesterday.
18. Zelda saw a zebra at the zoo.

Blends and digraphs

These words test the ability to sound most two-letter blends and digraphs in initial and final positions.

blank	church	slump	smart	skunk	speech
trump	brisk	plant	cloth	grand	champ
present	slant	which	drink	frost	chest
charm	fresh	crash	stand	crisp	swing

Auditory discrimination

1. The teacher pronounces the four words in each series. The child repeats the one word that differs from the first word in the phoneme being tested.

A. *Initial Consonants*

toy	pat	did	wind	dark	farm
tall	pet	kid	went	drink	warm
hall	cot	doll	bend	dash	find
tack	put	dull	well	bark	full
ball	hard	lack	kick	march	rode
pull	yard	lock	pick	much	load
back	hunt	lamp	kill	met	right
burn	hurt	damp	kind	net	race

B. *Endings of Words*
Child repeats the one word which does not rhyme.

pig	bake	ball	wet	bug	bag
dig	make	full	bet	hug	rug
big	bark	tall	pet	did	rag
bag	wake	wall	sat	mug	sag
pot	lick	leg	cut	fell	then
not	stuck	peg	hit	fill	hen
got	stick	lap	hut	sell	thin
God	kick	keg	but	bell	pen

C. *Initial Blends*
Child repeats the word which does not begin with the blend sound.

dress	sled	blue	step	tree	plan
drop	sack	blow	sack	truck	pain
draw	slip	bank	stop	train	place
down	slap	black	steep	turn	play

D. *Vowel Sounds*
Child repeats word having short vowel sound.

mate	fame	fight	joke	cute	team
mail	fan	mile	lock	dull	tell
mad	table	fine	note	true	see
take	flame	skim	snow	tube	feed

2. Testing child's ability to associate letter forms with sounds they represent using nonsense syllables which follow the CVC, CVVC, CVCV, and CVCC patterns. (Explain that the following are not words. Invite the child to pronounce each letter-pattern as if it were a word.)

baf	nem	gog	lut
kep	pab	med	bol
foz	ras	jum	pib
dut	hos	sug	taf
lig	tuv	vax	lod

(CVVC and CVCV)

beel	pean	taid	doat
heam	reet	gode	lume
kine	saim	feaf	daik
fote	mave	cabe	heef

(CVCC)

banf	polt	mulk	deng
hent	resk	saft	milt
dist	fland	hamp	goft
juld	tilp	lonk	zold

Structural analysis

The sight-word tests on page 304 contain only common root words. The words below test the child's ability to deal with inflectional endings, affixes, compounds and contractions.

A. *Easy root words plus endings* s, ed, ing

running	seated	playing	comes	played
asks	talking	lived	wanted	going
looked	wants	jumps	talks	sees
helps	coming	lives	walking	helping
wanting	likes	pleased	talked	looks
sits	helped	finding	runs	sitting
living	stops	plays	seeing	jumped

B. *Contractions, compound words, and derived forms usually learned at second grade level*

happily	belong	I'll	slowly	behind	hadn't
bakery	didn't	friendly	report	surely	himself
princess	outside	loudest	I'd	everybody	believe

quickly	afternoon	return	herself	you'll	politely
I've	it's	really	suddenly	everyone	shouted
isn't	warmer	everything	doesn't	couldn't	yourself
beside	anything	can't	between	into	wasn't

C. *Contractions, compound words, and derived forms usually learned at third grade level*

expect	explain	disappear	comfortable	rapidly
afternoon	ourselves	happiness	halfway	sawmill
you've	discover	invite	safety	invisible
family	they'll	include	upward	Thanksgiving
enjoy	unless	gentleman	peaceful	eyebrow
funniest	experiment	foolish	enchanted	firecrackers
finally	we've	contentment	bathroom	telescope

Syllabication

Words taken from spelling books at 3rd, 4th, and 5th grade level to test child's ability to break words into syllables. Pupil writes words in Column B. First word serves as sample.

Primer level		Intermediate level	
A	B	A	B
yesterday	yes ter day	beautiful	beau ti ful
grandfather	_____	geography	_____
birthday	_____	studying	_____
money	_____	history	_____
yellow	_____	interesting	_____
Easter	_____	difference	_____
stockings	_____	medium	_____
only	_____	electric	_____
afternoon	_____	average	_____
lessons	_____	citizen	_____

Word recognition

Children who are progressing satisfactorily in mastering the developmental skills of reading are constantly expanding their sight vocabulary. To test sight vocabulary one could use the Dolch Basic Sight Word Test* of 220 words. The material below consists of one hundred high frequency words taken from first grade basal materials. Any list of high frequency words, including the one

*Garrard Press, Champaign, Illinois.

below, will show considerable overlap with the Dolch List. (16) While reading words in isolation is not reading, tests can reveal whether or not the child has mastered a number of high frequency "service words." If these words are not recognized instantly, the child will find reading, even at the primary level, a most frustrating task.

we	horse	they	boat
with	a	jump	to
yes	an	big	walk
stop	look	come	want
like	was	go	on
help	find	think	house
very	little	and	my
all	best	could	can
this	old	boy	talk
some	try	may	girl
the	see	again	said
ball	mother	pretty	will
friend	any	which	father
went	over	then	small
did	wagon	live	blue
good	not	run	had
in	play	arm	she
me	what	up	your
hat	do	each	after
man	ran	his	clean
that	new	got	many
saw	wish	red	most
you	dog	there	around
here	under	please	open
sure	ride	name	every

High frequency words (Irregular spellings)

a	I	any	are	all	too	the
been	come	do	get	head	they	his
put	good	would	have	two	very	you
give	is	use	put	done	their	what
once	of	gone	there	who	sure	does
look	some	know	said	many	was	your
one	here	only	to	could	walk	were

Testing for reversals

Each of the following words is also a word when spelled backwords. In exercise *A*, children read the words in isolation. In exercise *B*, each sentence contains a number of reversable words.

A

was	pin	no	pal	rats
step	tub	spot	on	nip
saw	trap	net	tip	lap
tap	rat	part	pot	star
pan	ten	tops	nap	pit
cop	but	pat	tar	pets

B

1. Pam will pat the dog named Spot.
2. There was no top to put on the pot.
3. The words *star* and *tar* rhyme; but *pin* and *pan* do not.
4. Who was it that I saw pin the star on the net?
5. His pets Nip and Pal took a nap in the tub.

Measuring Comprehension

Any situation in which a child reads can provide clues to his reading strengths and instructional needs. Even the responses that children make on workbook pages can provide important diagnostic clues. Undoubtedly one of the best ways to evaluate reading is to listen to the child read a paragraph or two from a basal reader, social studies, or science text, or from a trade book.

Comprehension tasks for silent reading can also focus on important facets of critical reading. (20) Some illustrations of exercises that might be used for this purpose are included in the following pages. Examples are:

1. Tests of ability to use context clues.
   a. Sentence meaning
   b. Cloze procedures, paragraph length
   c. Sentences that do not "fit"
2. Drawing inferences

3. Following directions
   a. Sentence tasks
   b. Problem solving
4. Test of word meanings (malapropisms)
5. Determining *fact* or opinion

Obviously, any idea that is incorporated into informal testing will have to be adapted to fit the difficulty level of the pupils involved.

Comprehension in oral reading

Material for a test over sustained reading can consist of passages read from textbooks (basals, social studies, science, etc.) or tradebooks. An alternative is to assemble pages or copies of pages in order of difficulty in a teacher-made folder. Comprehension questions are carefully developed for each passage. Some teachers prefer to have extra copies of the passages so that they can mark each error and weakness observed. A checklist such as shown on pages 296-97 can be used to record inadequacies such as letter-sound relationships, sight vocabulary word meaning problems, punctuation, intonation and the like.

Use of context clues in sentences

In each of the following sentences two words are omitted. Read each sentence and fill in the words that complete the meaning of the sentence.

1. It is warmer in _____ than in _____.
2. The bird built a _____ in the _____.
3. A week has seven _____; a year has _____ months.
4. Apples, _____, and _____ are fruit.
5. When you _____ five and three the _____ is eight.
6. Leaves fall from the _____ in the _____.
7. Put a _____ on the letter and mail _____.
8. John runs very _____ but Bill runs even _____.
9. A decade is _____ years and a century is _____ years.
10. A baby cow is a _____ and a baby bear is a _____.

Use of Context Clues in Sustained Reading (Cloze Procedure) (29)

In the following passage, every sixth word is missing. The reader writes a word in each blank space and in doing so reveals an accurate picture of his comprehension of the passage. For further discussion of the cloze technique see Taylor (33) and Bormuth (5).

A helicopter is an aircraft _____ whirling wings. Pilots call it _____ whirlybird or a chopper. The _____ blades, called rotors, go round _____ round like a propeller on _____ back, but they really lift _____ copter just the way a _____ wing does.

The wonderful thing _____ rotors is that they can _____ the copter almost straight up _____ the ground and bring it _____ almost straight down. They can _____ it fly backward as well _____ forward. Or they can keep _____ hovering above one spot. This _____ that a helicopter needs no _____ runway for landing or taking _____. A space just a little _____ than its rotors is usually _____.*

Sentences that do not belong

In each of the following paragraphs there is one sentence that "does not fit." Underline that sentence and tell why it does not fit in the paragraph.

1. John visited grandfather's farm. He saw some ducks and cows. John never liked lions. He helped grandfather feed the chickens.

2. Mary loves sports. She plays tennis and basketball. This summer she earned ten dollars. Mary enjoys watching sports on television.

3. Mark Twain wrote the book *Tom Sawyer*. It is about a boy who lives on the Mississippi River. One of Tom's friends is called Huckleberry Finn. The Colorado River formed the Grand Canyon.

4. The beaver is intelligent and works very hard. He has sharp teeth and can cut down small trees. The beaver can build dams in streams. He can blow water out of his trunk. Beavers do not eat fish.

5. One of the problems troubling our country today is pollution of our air and water. Automobiles, factories, and care-

*Elting, Mary. *Aircraft at Work*. Irvington-on-Hudson, New York: Harvey House, Inc., 1964. Pg. 50 (Words in original 1. with, 2. a, 3. long, 4. and 5. its, 6. the, 7, fixed, 8. about, 9. take, 10. from, 11. back, 12. make, 13. as, 14. it, 15. means, 16. long, 17. off, 18. wider, 19. enough.

less individuals all contribute to the problem. Everywhere, people are pleased with the environment. It will take years and great sums of money to clean up the air and water.

Comprehension through drawing inferences

Read each numbered sentence and the statements a, b, c beneath it. Circle the statement you think is most logical.

Sample: The children went outside to build a snowman.
a. It was May.
b. It was August.
c. It was January.

1. As we were riding along, father slammed on the brakes.
a. It had started to rain.
b. We were out of gas.
c. A dog ran in front of the car.

2. The rooster crowed in the dim light.
a. He was hungry.
b. The sun was about to rise.
c. He was saying "Good night."

3. The class went to the zoo and saw:
a. A herd of cows.
b. Two elephants.
c. Donald Duck.

4. When the window broke the boy ran.
a. He had broken the window.
b. He was late for school.
c. The noise frightened him.

5. There were an elephant and a giraffe in the barn.
a. They had run away from the zoo.
b. The farmer was a big game hunter.
c. The farmer was taking care of the animals for a circus.

6. The woman ran into the store holding a newspaper over her head.
a. It was raining.
b. She was going to buy the paper.
c. She was telling everyone the news.

7. The ambulance roared down the street sounding its siren.
a. The ambulance was part of a parade.

b. Traffic was very light.
c. There has been an accident.
8. The family climbed into the car which was crowded with suitcases.
a. They were going to a suitcase sale.
b. It was vacation time.
c. Father was going to the bank.

Following written directions (sentence tasks)

1. Put the letter *l* in front of each word if it will form a new word.

__and   __end   __make   __ate   __old   __ice   __ink

2. Write the plural form of each of the following words.

house_____   bird_____   glass_____
brush_____   box_____   bench_____

3. Add the ending *ed* if this will make another word.

know____   light____   men____   park____   wish____
talk____   ring____   visit____   jerk____   shoot____

4. Underline all compound words.

somewhere swimming upon   waterproof overnight movement
wonderful newspaper important broadcast careless silverware

5. Rewrite the following words to make a sentence.
the station train of rolled out the

6. Circle each word to which we could add *s* to form another word.

fun   city   hurt   rub   came   run   seed   tell

7. Circle each word that can mean a person or persons.

going   he   Mary   pretty   they   someone   upon

8. Put the letter *s* in front of each word if this will form a new word.

__and   __car   __hot   __make   __lip   __kill
__pray   __ate   __mile   __nail   __ask   __win

9. Write the following words in alphabetical order.

elephant   elm   eel   envelope   easy

_____

10. Place the correct number in the blank space.
1   2   4   8   16   ____

Problem solving: following written directions

Each of the directions below asks you to study *Box A* and *Box B*. Then carry out the directions found in each of the numbered sentences.

1. If the sum of two odd numbers is always an even number, place a small X in the middle figure in line one, Box B.
2. If the sum of the third and fourth numbers in Box A is equal to the seventh number, circle A in Box A.
3. If this is an odd numbered sentence, circle the digit 6 in Box A.
4. If both lines 1 and 2 in Box B contain a square, put an X in the square on line 2.

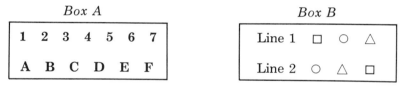

5. If the sum of the digits in Box A is greater than 28, underline D in Box A.
6. If there are the same number of digits in Box A as there are letters, place a dot (.) in the circle on Line 2 of Box B.
7. If there are more odd numbers than there are even numbers in Box A, circle the E in Box A.
8. If the sum of the first two digits in Box A equals the third digit, circle the sixth letter in Box A.
9. If there are three vowels in Box A, circle one of the triangles in Box B.

Word recognition and meaning

People often use one word when they mean to use a different one. In each of the following sentences there is one word that "does not fit." a. Underline this word. b. On the blank space following each sentence, write the word you think was intended.

1. She was selling magazine prescriptions.   _____
2. Lincoln was a grate president   _____

3. The picture for the baseball team
was hurt.   _____
4. The waiter said, "I hope your
stake is delicious."   _____
5. The word *big* is a cinnamon for *large*. _____
6. Desert land must be irritated
to grow crops.   _____
7. The doctor said, "This child has
an inflection."   _____
8. After a rain, the humility is
quite high.   _____
9. The cliffs had become withered
from the wind and rain.   _____
10. "Aisle be seeing you" he said.   _____

Conclusion

The reading ability of children in any given classroom will cover a wide range of achievement. Diagnosis is a prerequisite for differentiation of instruction which, in turn, is an essential for a sound reading program. One of the principles stressed in Chapter 1 is that diagnosis provides the blueprint for instruction.

Formal testing involving the use of standardized tests is one type of diagnosis. Unfortunately, in some schools the administration of these tests is dictated by the calendar rather than by sound instructional philosophy. If the chief aim of testing is to arrive at grade-level scores for individuals and mean scores for classes, diagnosis is reduced to an educational ritual. Test results must be carefully analyzed for clues to each child's strengths and weaknesses.

Meaningful diagnosis must be ongoing. It should be remembered that anytime a child reads, he provides clues to his instructional needs. Listening to a child's oral reading of a paragraph or two from any textbook will provide as much information per time unit invested as will any testing situation. The alert teacher will note whether the material is too difficult, what types of errors are made, and whether the child's sight vocabulary, word attack skills, and phrasing are adequate. The child's responses in this reading situation will suggest what other informal diagnostic approaches are now appropriate. Examples of brief testing materials have been provided throughout this chapter.

YOUR POINT OF VIEW?

Respond to the following problems:

1. During the first week of school you suspect that Johnny cannot read the social studies text that has been adopted for class use. You have five minutes to work with him and you wish to verify or refute the above hypothesis. How would you use this time?

2. Assume that the use of standardized reading tests in the elementary grades was prohibited for the next five years. Suggest logical hypotheses as to what would happen in reading instruction if this unlikely event occurred.

3. A careful study reveals that a certain percent of third grade pupils do not see reading as a source of enjoyment. Complete the following statement so that it would apply to at least 90 percent of these pupils:
   "These pupils _____."
   (examples: ". . . are poor readers," ". . . do not read with expression," ". . . have experienced failure.")

Defend or attack the following statements:

1. Informal teacher-made tests can yield as much data about an individual child's reading as can standardized tests.

2. In many schools the potential values which might be achieved from the use of standardized tests are lost because the school is more concerned with the ritual of administering tests than in "mining the test data."

3. The cloze procedure is a valid measure of reading comprehension.

BIBLIOGRAPHY

1. Anderson, Verna Dieckman, *Reading and Young Children*. New York: The Macmillan Company, 1968, Chapter 12.

2. Balow, Bruce and James Curtin, "Ability Grouping of Bright Pupils," *Elementary School Journal* (March 1966), 321–27.

3. Barrett, Thomas C. (ed.) *The Evaluation of Children's Reading Achievement* (Perspectives No. 8), Newark, Del.: International Reading Association, 1967.

4. Beldin, H. O. "Informal Reading Testing: Historical Review and Review of the Research," *Reading Difficulties: Diagnosis Correction and Remediation*, Newark, Del.: International Reading Association, 1970, 67–84.

5. Bormuth, John R. "Factor Validity of Cloze Tests as Measures of Reading Comprehension Ability," *Reading Research Quarterly* (Spring 1969), 358–365.

6. Botel, Morton, "Ascertaining Instructional Levels," in *Forging Ahead In Reading*, J. Allen Figurel (ed.) Proceedings, International Reading Association, 12, Part 1, 171–74.

7. Brillain, Mary M. "Informal Reading Procedures: Some Motivational Considerations," *Reading Teacher* (December 1970), 216–220.

8. Burnett, Richard W. "The Diagnostic Proficiency of Teachers of Reading," *Reading Teacher* (January 1963), 229–34.

9. Burns, Paul C. "Evaluation of Silent Reading," *Education* (March 1964), 411–14.

10. Cushenbery, Donald C. "Two Methods of Grouping for Reading Instruction," *Elementary School Journal* (February 1966), 267–72.

11. Dechant, Emerald V. *Improving the Teaching of Reading* (2nd Ed.), Englewood Cliffs, N. J.: Prentice-Hall, Inc., 1970, Chapter 14.

12. Della-Piana Gabriel, "Analysis of Oral Reading Errors: Standardization, Norms and Validity," *Reading Teacher* (January 1962), 254–57.

13. Farr, Roger, *Reading: What Can be Measured*. Newark, Del.: International Reading Association, 1969.

14. ――――, and Virginia L. Brown. "Evaluation and Decision Making," *The Reading Teacher* (January 1971), 341–46.

15. Harris, Albert J. *How To Increase Reading Ability* (Fifth Ed.). New York: David McKay Company, 1970, Chapters 7 and 8.

16. Johnson, Dale D. "The Dolch List Reexamined," *The Reading Teacher* (February 1971), 449–57.

17. Karlin, Robert and Hayden Jolly, "The Use of Alternate Forms of Standardized Reading Tests," *Reading Teacher* (December 1966), 187–91.

18. Karlin, Robert, *Teaching Elementary Reading*. New York: Harcourt Brace Jovanovich, Inc., 1971, Chapter 2.

19. Kastner, Marie A. "Instructing and Motivating Pupils in the Light of Test Results," *Catholic Educational Review* (February 1969), 106–10.

20. King, Martha L. "New Developments in the Evaluation of Critical Reading," *Forging Ahead In Reading*, J. Allen Figurel (ed.), Proceedings, International Reading Association, 12, Part 1, 179–85.

21. Ladd, Eleanor M. "More Than Test Scores," *The Reading Teacher* (January 1971), 305–311.

22. McCracken, Robert A. "Using Reading As a Basis for Grouping," *Education* (February 1964), 357–59.

23. _____, "The Informal Reading Inventory as a Means of Improving Instruction" in Thomas C. Barrett (ed.), *The Evaluation of Children's Reading Achievement.* Newark, Del.: International Reading Association, 1967, 79–96.

24. MacDonald, James B. and James D. Raths, "Should We Group by Creative Abilities?" *Elementary School Journal* (December 1964), 137–143.

25. Mitchell, Addie S. "Values and Limitations of Standardized Reading Tests," in *Forging Ahead In Reading*, J. Allen Figurel (ed.), Proceedings, International Reading Association, 12, Part 1, 163–67.

26. Prescott, George A. "Criterion-Referenced Test Interpretation In Reading," *The Reading Teacher* (January 1971), 347–54.

27. Putt, Robert C. and Darrel D. Ray, "Putting Test Results to Work," *Elementary School Journal* (May 1965), 439–44.

28. Ramsey, Wallace, "The Value and Limitations of Diagnostic Reading Tests for Evaluation in the Classroom." *The Evaluation of Children's Reading Achievement*, Thomas C. Barrett (ed.), Newark, Del.: International Reading Association, 1967, 65–77.

29. Ransom, Peggy E. "Determining Reading Levels of Elementary School Children by Cloze Testing," *Forging Ahead in Reading*, J. Allen Figural (ed.), Proeedings, International Reading Association, 12, Part 1, 477–82.

30. *Reading Teacher* (January 1971). Entire issue devoted to Testing.

31. Robinson, H. Alan and Earl Hanson, "Reliability of Measures of Reading Achievement," *The Reading Teacher* (January 1968), 307–13.

32. Sipay, Edward R. "A Comparison of Standardized Reading Scores and Functional Reading Levels," *Reading Teacher* (January 1964), 265–72.

33. Taylor, Wilson L. "Cloze-Procedure: A New Tool for Measuring Readability," *Journalism Quarterly* (Fall 1953), 415–433.

34. Trela, Thaddeus M. "What Do Diagnostic Reading Tests Diagnose?" *Elementary English* (April 1966), 370–72.

9

Linguistics and Reading

Various facets of linguistics are discussed throughout this book. For example, both the phonology and syntax of non-standard dialect speakers are treated in the chapter on *The Culturally Different*. The linguistic (regular spelling) approach to beginning reading is described in Chapter 5, and exercises for teaching intonation in reading are found in *Primary Instruction* and *Developing and Expanding Concepts*. The following material attempts to explore some of the areas which appear to be contiguous to linguistics and reading instruction.

Linguists are justifiably sensitive about non-linguists attempting to summarize or popularize linguistic discoveries. The purpose here is not to interpret the technical findings of this discipline but rather to examine the suggestions made by certain linguists relative to reading instruction. In order to understand what linguists have proposed, why they disagree about reading instruction, and why linguists as a group will never develop *The* Linguistic Method of Teaching Reading, we must have some understanding of the terms linguist and linguistics.

In attempting definitions of these terms one might keep in mind a linguist's advice, "We must define a linguist rather strictly because the term has become dangerously popular, emulating the more extensive term scientist."*

Linguists are trained individuals who make a scientific study of human language. Such study implies accurate observation and recording of data.

The linguist studies and identifies the building blocks of language called speech sounds or phonemes. He discerns how these are combined into words and word parts which have assigned meanings (morphemes). This is the groundwork for further study of language, namely the *patterns* in which words may occur and those patterns which cannot occur in a particular language. When these discoveries are made, one has the key to the structure or the grammar of a language.

The linguist discovers facts which are unique to each language and others that are common to various languages. The layman can verbalize some of these findings without grasping their full significance. For instance, the linguist states, *language is arbitrary*. This applies to all facets of language. The normal child growing up in an English-speaking environment learns to make many speech sounds which he will have to discard if he restricts his language usage to English. The sounds he will use are not a matter of individual choice. This matter has been arbitrarily established, along with the patterns or sequence in which sounds may be combined.

The order in which words may be combined into utterances has also been established. Language has a definite structure. The linguist notes that this structure permits a sentence like, "I runned all the way home," but that common usage dictates, "I ran all the way home," and English structure cannot accommodate, "I all the ran home way." While six-year-old children have mastered a tremendously large portion of English grammar, they project certain characteristics into word meanings which do not exist. When asked Piaget's question "Can the sun be called the moon?" they answer: "No, because the moon comes up at night," or "No, because the sun is brighter." This reaction that the meaning resides in the word is not confined to children.

Adults can also have hazy concepts about language. An example is the manner in which adults think the grammar of a language might best be taught to students who have already mastered it in practice. Fries (15) states that traditional grammar starts with

---

*Raven I. McDavid, Jr., "The Role of the Linguist in the Teaching of Reading," *Changing Concepts of Reading Instruction*. International Reading Association Proceedings, 6 (1961), 253–56.

the assigning of meaning to any given sentence and then moves to the labeling of words or groups of words and whole utterances. Thus, sentences become *declarative, interrogative,* or *imperative.* Within each sentence there is a subject and verb; to this may be added a direct object and an array of modifiers attached to each of those parts.

This approach, according to Fries, starts with an assumption that *grammatical meanings* are intuitive. A number of structural linguists reject this assumption. They posit that "grammatical meanings" are of considerable importance and that meanings are conveyed by signal or structure words which permit certain meanings and exclude others. A few examples of these structure words are *a* man, *the* man, *these* men, *that* man, *this* man, *some* men, *no* man. A further discussion of structure words will be found later in this chapter.

Linguistics is a broad term which can cover many orientations to language study. One linguist may be primarily interested in comparing different languages, another with the sound patterns of a language, another with the structural (grammatical word order) features of one or more languages, and another in the changes (phonological and structural) which occur in any living language. While linguists rarely deal with only one isolated facet of language, they do tend to become somewhat specialized.

The Application of Linguistic Findings to Reading Instruction

Linguists as scientists are in no way responsible for finding applications for their discoveries. Few have actively engaged in relating their discoveries to the school curriculum. As a result, linguistics has had little impact on the content of the curriculum, particularly at the elementary level. University faculties have devised courses of study for students whose educational goal is to become linguists or specialists in a particular language. Certain related fields, such as speech therapy, draw heavily on linguistics since therapists must distinguish speech sounds and understand the anatomical involvement in their production.

How children learn to read and how the reading process should be taught is not a part of linguistic science. However, there is little doubt that certain linguistic insights can be analyzed in such a way as to be extremely useful in reading instruction. Recently, some linguists have turned their attention to the reading process, and there were high hopes that a significant instructional breakthrough would be achieved fairly rapidly. This optimism was soon tempered by reality when it was discovered that a real communication barrier separated linguists and reading teachers.

Linguistic science has moved rapidly in the past fifty years because linguists were able to agree on the precise meaning of many crucial terms. Linguists were the first, and possibly the only, group who thus far agreed on the definition of language. Their definition is that "language is oral." To reading specialists, psychologists, and general semanticists, this definition may seem to be somewhat narrow, but the mark of a science is that its basic terms are unequivocal.

On the other hand, the field of reading provides many examples of terms which are used frequently but for which there is no universal agreement as to meaning. Examples include *reading, phonics method, individualized reading, critical reading, sightword method, reading disability, traditional method, remedial reading* and *phonics instruction.* All of these represent concepts, but none have a fixed meaning for all of the people who use them. Obviously, confusion results. The problem is accentuated when persons in different disciplines attempt to cooperate in the absence of an agreement on the meaning of the terms which both groups use. An illustration is provided in the use of the term *language* at a recent national reading conference.

A linguist, speaking to teachers of reading, remarked that he had little patience for the educators who made such absurd statements as, "English is not a phonetic language," or "English is not phonetically lawful." He stated that "English is perfectly phonetic — 100 percent phonetic." He was followed on the same platform by a teacher of reading who, probably not having heard his predecessor, stated: "One of the major problems of teaching children to read is the fact that English is not phonetic. The language contains a large number of phonetically irregular words."

Each of the speakers started from different premises based on different connotations for the words he used. Each was correct if one granted his original premise. The linguist worked from the linguistic definition of language that "language is oral — language is speech." Thus, all English language (speech) is 100 percent phonetically regular. Such words as *freight, light, come,* and all other words can be transcribed within the framework of English phonemes.

The teacher of reading used language to mean written English. The linguist, of course, would refer to this as "a graphic representation of language." The teacher of reading meant that many English spellings were irregular; that there was not a one-to-one relationship between printed letters seen and speech sounds heard when one is reading English. With this the linguist would agree, but he would convey this information by using the terms *phoneme-grapheme relationship.*

Communication between reading teachers and linguists depends on each making an effort to understand the other. In recent years terminology from the science of linguistics has been used frequently in material addressed to the reading teacher. These terms have fixed meanings, and there is little point in not adopting them for use in discussion of reading instruction.

Phoneme: The smallest unit of sound within a language. When the word *man* is pronounced, three phonemes are utilized: /m/ /ae/ /n/. The basic consonant and vowel sound are called *segmental phonemes.* In addition to these 31 to 33 basic sounds, the English language utilizes twelve intonational phonemes.

Intonation: In addition to the consonant and vowel phonemes just mentioned, English utilizes a number of intonational phonemes. Speech consists of a flow of words arranged in particular patterns which result in distinctive rhythms or melodies which are unique to English. The melody is created in part by several levels of pitch, several degrees of stress or emphasis on word components, and by pauses or stops in the flow of speech.

Individuals learn the intonation patterns of their native tongue without being aware of the significance of these signals, and certainly without any conscious labeling of the variations in pitch, stress, and pace. The pre-school child with normal hearing inevitably "picks up" the intonation patterns of the particular language he hears around him. Later, as an adult he may experience considerable difficulty in mastering the intonation patterns of a foreign language. He may have little difficulty in learning the pronunciation and meaning of *words* (vocabulary). The problem lies in stringing the words together, in acquiring the flow or the melody of the new language.

English writing, and the act of reading this writing, poses a somewhat similar problem. First, writing is an imperfect representation of speech. One cannot accurately depict intonation or melody of speech. (31,40) Many nuances are lost in setting down the graphic representation of speech. The reader's task now becomes that of putting the intonation back into the graphic signs. He has some very useful hints in the form of punctuation which suggests some pauses and stops. He is aided by other orthographic devices such as underlined or italicized words. But in the final analysis the reader is left to project or "think in" much of the meaning-making melody which is not depicted in print. The following discussion provides brief illustrations of the three major intonational components: juncture, stress, and pitch.

Junctures and terminals: Speech includes a number of pauses which serve as signals to the listener. In general four classes of junctures and terminals are identified in English speech, these are:

Open Juncture / – / which represents the most minute interruptions which occur between some syllables within words and between words. These breaks in speech enable one to follow such patterns as:

> "I *am a Tory* but not an *amatory* Tory."
> "He used a jar to keep the door ajar."
> *(amiss–a miss; a bet–abet; add dresses–addresses).*

Level juncture is a pause between parts of a total utterance in which the pause does not demand a rise or falling off of pitch. In the following illustrative sentence, examples A and B represent level terminal where everything preceding the phrase *was blind* is spoken without noticeable variation in pitch. Example C indicates a different reading.

> A. The man ⟶ speaking to me ⟶ was blind.↘
> B. The man speaking to me ⟶was blind.↘
> C. The man speaking to me ↘ was blind.↘

Rise and fall terminals are examples of speech signals which terminate all sentences, and which are frequently found separating major groupings of words within sentences. (Sentence C above.) The symbol / ↘ / represents a falling off or fading pitch accompanied by a pause which characteristically terminates declarative sentences. Many interrogative sentences end with a fading, higher pitch, indicated by the symbol / ↗ /. Both of these terminals contain a signal which goes beyond the mere pause in the flow of words.

> "The train arrives at six o'clock." ↘
> "What time does the train leave?"↗

Pitch, as this term is used in describing a particular characteristic of human speech, should be thought of as a continuum. However, this continuum does not consist of innumerable points, but rather a discrete number of segments or ranges. These ranges have been labeled low, normal, high, and extra high, and are frequently designated by the numbers 1–2–3–4. The absence of pitch variations in speech is called monotone, or in essence, one-level pitch.

Pitch interacts with stress and juncture and every statement in English has a "pitch contour" which can be plotted using one or another marking system such as /1–2 3 4 /;/ low normal high etc/.

Stress indicates the degree of emphasis placed on syllables or words in utterances. As in the case of pitch there are four levels or degrees of stress: heavy, medium, light, weak.* As noted earlier, the graphic representation of speech provides a rather incomplete record of intonation. Stress, pitch, and juncture are represented only partially by means of punctuation marks such as beginning a sentence with a capital letter and the use of the comma, semi-colon, period, exclamation mark, and question mark. In addition, one may indicate emphasis through underlining or italicizing a particular word.

> *He* was really a tall man.
> He was *really* a tall man.
> He was really a *tall* man.

Morpheme: The smallest meaningful units of language. Thus, *son* is a morpheme composed of three phonemes. If one adds an *s* to form a plural, *sons*, the final *s* in this situation is a morpheme. Here, the same grapheme (s) functions in the initial part of the word as a phoneme, and when it is used at the end of the word to change the meaning to "more than one son," it functions as a morpheme. When used to show possession, *his son's house*, it illustrates another morpheme.

There are two classes of morphemes determined by function. A *free morpheme is* one that functions independently in larger language units (cat, man, son). *Bound morphemes* must combine with another morpheme. This class includes affixes and inflectional endings. The prefix *un* in *unlock* is a bound morpheme while the same graphemes in *union* stand for two phonemes.

Alphabetic Principle: English is one of the many languages for which an alphabet has been devised for writing. We use 26 letters to represent graphically the sounds of English. Thus, English is an

---

*Levels of stress are also designated as primary ($/$), secondary ($\wedge$), tertiary ($\setminus$) and weak ($\cup$). See Henry Lee Smith, Jr., "The Teacher and The World of Language," College English, 20, (January, 1959), 172–78.

alphabetic language. English writing follows an alphabetical principle, i.e., certain graphic signs represent speech sounds. However, English spellings used in writing of words do not follow a one-to-one relationship of grapheme seen, phoneme heard. Exceptions are discussed in relation to phonics instruction (Chapter 7).

The irregular spellings of English words creates a problem for the person attempting to learn to write or read English. The fact that a large majority of English words follow regular grapheme-phoneme patterns leads some individuals to minimize the effect of irregular spellings on learning these two derived language processes. Establishing what percent of the 10,000 most frequently used words happen to be regular in grapheme-phoneme relationships and then generalizing from this data to the reading process ignores the *frequency of the use* of irregularly spelled words. This point becomes clearer as we examine structure words.

Structure words is a term used to cover some three-hundred or more frequently used words which have no concrete referent. Various other descriptive terms have been used to describe these words. These include "signal words," "glue words," "service words," and for reasons discussed below, they have also been referred to as "basic sight words." Each of the above has some validity. Structure words do signal the listener, or more important, the reader, that a particular syntactical pattern is coming.

Lefevre (29) refers to structure words as "empty" words used primarily to signal the coming use of noun or verb phrases, dependent clauses, and questions. In one analysis he indicates that approximately half of the words on the Dolch Basic Sight Word Test* are structure or "empty" words. A few examples of markers are:

> Noun markers: *my* house, *any* house, *this* house, *a* house, *some* houses, *the* house
>
> Verb markers: *am* coming, *are* coming, *is* coming, *was* coming
>
> Clause markers: *now, like, until, if, although, since, before, however*
>
> Question indicators: *when, where, who, which, why*

It is easy to see why structure words have been called "the glue words of the English language," or "service words." Both of these concepts are consistent with the way these words function in sen-

---

*The Dolch Basic Sight Word Test consists of 220 words and is available from Garrard Press, Champaign, Illinois.

tences. They both introduce and bind together utterances while not conveying meaning in and of themselves. Many structure words have irregular spellings which accounts for their being designated "sight words." Both their irregular spellings and their high frequency of usage make it mandatory that they be instantly recognized in print.

The frequency with which particular words are used will of course vary with the material under consideration. The previous sentence uses eight different structure words for a total of ten running words (the, with, which, used, will, of, course, with, the, under). Whether one is talking about reading material specifically designed for the primary grades or the professional writing of historians and linguists, these words will comprise from 25 to 50 percent of all running words, regardless of how many different words are encountered.

Structure words pose no problem for facile readers. But with seriously impaired readers, these are the words they have been unable to learn or recognize even after hundreds of experiences of seeing them in print and various types of drills designed to facilitate their becoming "sight words."

Syntax is a term used to describe the meaning patterns found within any language, in essence, the *grammar* of that language. Syntax includes the various word order patterns in which words can be strung together. The following word orders represent a correct sentence in English, an extreme regional expression, and a non-English pattern: "I go up the steps"; "I go the steps up"; "Up the go I steps."

Syntax includes the ways in which words may function in different patterns. The same word may function as a verb, noun, or adverb: *Light* the fire; She saw the *light;* He danced *lightly* across the ring and threw a *lightening* punch. English syntax rules out "He danced *lightening* across the ring and threw a *lighted* punch." A careful study of the syntax of a language will permit one to describe the basic sentence patterns which occur in that language, as well as the ways in which these patterns may be varied by means of expansion, substitution, and inversion.

Linguists have made a thorough and scientific analysis of the English language, and their writings should be consulted by individuals interested in linguistic findings. The purpose of the preceding discussion was to provide a few definitions which might be useful to non-linguists.

**Emphasis on
Phonology**

Leonard Bloomfield was probably the first linguist to concern himself with the application of linguistic findings to the teaching of reading. His proposals for beginning reading materials and methodology are outlined in chapter five and are listed here without discussion.

1. The materials for beginning reading should consist of words which have regular spellings. (These are words in which each letter symbol represents the sound most frequently associated with that letter.)
2. The first 36 lessons present three-letter words which follow the CVC pattern. Each lesson consists of words which end with the same phonogram *an, at, ad, ap, ag, am,* etc.
3. Bloomfield was opposed to phonics instruction and children are *not* taught letter sound relationships. They are asked to spell each word: "*See–aye–en* spells can."
4. Children see and spell the same words many times. Since they are not taught letter-sound relationships, they cannot *transfer* this skill to unknown words.
5. There is no methodology for teaching the thousands of irregularly spelled words beyond the admonition: "Teaching irregular words will demand a separate effort and separate practice." (8)

Bloomfield's approach aims at protecting the child from the irrational spelling patterns which have been allowed to occur and to continue in English writing. Of course the child cannot be protected long. The shock of reality can only be postponed. Bloomfield states, "Learning to read consists of learning the very abstract equation printed letter=speech sound to be spoken." This equation fits the words taught initially but does not hold for the irregular words which soon are to come.

**Structural Linguistics and
the Reading Process**

A language has a total structure within which will be found a number of sub-structures. The phonemic sub-structure determines which speech sounds are found in the language and the patterns in which these may be combined in words. However, the total structure cannot be grasped by focusing on the identifiable sounds in words or even by studying words as units. The larger or controlling structure is that which governs the possible word combinations found in utterances—the variations in which words may be strung together.

Structural linguistics is one of the broad fields of language research. It is an integral part of linguistic science which deals with how a given language actually functions when used by persons who learned it as their native tongue. Structural linguistics is often equated with the grammar of a language. This is not to be confused with a course of study usually found in English courses which has come to be labeled "traditional grammar." The structural linguist is concerned with *how* language is used, not with formulating theories as to how it *should* be used.

Individuals who would apply structural linguistics to reading instruction suggest that emphasis be placed on having the learner see the relationship between his use of spoken English and the decoding of written English. A statement frequently met is that "speech is primary and reading is secondary—or a derived process." This statement means more than that speech is learned before one learns how to read. Insofar as structural linguistics relates to reading instuction, this concept implies that speech is involved in the reading process. If the child does not grasp that in his reading he must reproduce the intonation patterns of English speech, he will not arrive at the meanings which are graphically represented.

Lefevre (29), in *Linguistics and the Teaching of Reading*, has attempted to build a communicative bridge between the structural linguist and the reading teacher. While stating his awareness of the complex nature of reading problems and the possibility of a number of causal factors, he states that, "The basic fault in poor reading (viewed as a crippled language process) is poor sentence sense, demonstrated orally in word-calling, or in reading various nonstructural fragments of language patterns as units." If a child reads word by word, he treats each separate word as an utterance and will utilize a fade-fall terminal/ \ /after each word.

The/boy/went/to/the/store/.

This habit will inevitably destroy the melody of spoken English and thus preclude reading for meaning.

Tyler (43) makes a number of references to the melody one must seek out when reading. "A writer wants his reader to hear the unspoken melody of his words"; primary-grade pupils have "an extensive lexicon of sentence melodies." Stress patterns are referred to as an "upward-downward melody." Lloyd (31) states, *"The ability to relate the melody of speech to the written page is the key to good reading.* Good readers do it; poor readers don't do it." Stevens (40) suggests that once pupils are able to recognize words in print, "they must be taught to see the sentence that they already hear. Only with help in perceiving this melody in its varied patterns will they ultimately become literate."

Although there is general agreement that children must learn to recreate the melody of language in their reading, there is little research data that bears on this issue. The results of two recent studies do suggest that intonation is closely related to reading comprehension and that intonation can be taught in beginning reading.

Means (35) studied the relationship between third grade children's use of intonation in oral reading and reading comprehension. He reported statistically significant relationships (.01) between appropriate use of each of three intonation variables (pitch, stress, and juncture) and comprehension scores on reading tests. Those children making the lowest number of "errors" on a measure of intonation, made significantly higher scores on measures of both oral and silent reading.

Ahlvers (1) demonstrated that first grade children can profit from instruction which focuses on teaching intonation patterns. She designed a program consisting of thirty lessons, each of approximately ten minutes duration. Children who received this instruction scored significantly higher on a test of intonation than did children in a control group who had no special training in intonation. However, no significant difference in reading achievement was found between the two groups on a reading test administered near the end of grade one. A hypothesis related to this finding was that possibly the content of first grade reading achievement tests may not reflect the contribution of intonation skills to the same degree as do tests designed for later grade levels.

The concept of melody of language does not concern itself with the selection of words but rather with the structural arrangements found in English. The child comes to school with an ear for this melody already developed. His use of oral language fits the pattern, and his understanding of oral English rests on this tremendous accomplishment. The seven-year-old speaks a melodic English comparable to that of his teacher. Both have learned the same structure.

In another sense the child has much to learn from his teachers and from experience which will enhance his use and understanding of the melody of language; this is in the choice of words which he can fit into the sentence structures permitted in the English language. This is illustrated by the title of a book of poems by Emily Dickinson, *Bolts of Melody.** This title is a most apt choice of words to describe the poet's art, the manipulation of language.

Evaluation of Linguistic Proposals

It would be difficult to find two more diametrically opposed approaches to beginning reading instruction than the "regular spellings" and the structural "melody of language" schools discussed above. Barnhart's statement that "a linguistic system separates the study of word form from word meaning" seems to imply that *all* linguistic approaches would, of necessity, start with materials in which the vocabulary consisted of regularly spelled words. Many linguists reject this thesis.

The regular-spelling approach

The science of linguistics has not established that beginning reading instructional materials should deal only with regular spellings or that pictures should be omitted from children's books. These are pedagogical decisions unrelated to linguistic science. These and other suggestions may prove to have merit, but their validity must be tested in the classroom like any other proposals. Their efficacy is not established a priori because they are labeled "linguistic approach." Raven McDavid (34) makes this point most succinctly by suggesting that the layman may have difficulty in distinguishing between when the linguist is speaking from his professional competence and when he is speaking as any other citizen. "When the linguist attempts to produce (basal) readers, he can expect them to be criticized on both linguistic and other grounds."

In discussing Bloomfield's and Fries' phonological approach to reading instruction, it might be pointed out that their linguistic scholarship was immensely broad; but the segment of linguistic

---

Bolts of Melody — New Poems of Emily Dickinson, Mabel Loomis Todd and Millicent Todd Bingham, eds., (New York: Harper & Row, Publishers, 1945).

knowledge they choose to utilize in their approach to reading instruction is extremely narrow. Bloomfield's ignoring of much of his own significant research (inflection patterns, signaling devices, sentence type, and word order), in the words of Lefevre (27) constitutes "an unsolved mystery of twentieth century linguistic scholarship."

It would appear that based on training and experience, any linguist might evolve any one of a number of approaches to reading instruction. This would indicate that suggestions about how reading should be taught are less influenced by linguistic training than by one's own concept of "what is reading." This leads to an important educational issue posed by certain newer materials. Should the materials and methodology used in beginning reading be evaluated from the standpoint of the concept of reading which they inculcate in beginning readers?

The Reader's "Set"
in Beginning Reading

The proponents of the phonological approach to beginning reading instruction are unequivocal in their rejection of the thesis that "beginning reading instruction should be a meaning-making process." In the words of Clarence Barnhart, co-author of *Let's Read* (8), "We find Bloomfield's system of teaching reading is a linguistic system. Essentially a linguistic system of teaching reading separates the problem of the study of word form from the study of word meaning." (p. 9) Bloomfield concurs; "Aside from their silliness, the stories in a child's first reader are of little use because the child is too busy with the mechanics of reading to get anything of the content. . . . This does not mean that we must forego the use of sentences and connected stories, but it does mean that these are not essential to the first steps. We need not fear to use disconnected words and even senseless syllables; and above all we must not, for the sake of a story, upset the child's scarcely formed habits by presenting him with irregularities of spelling for which he is not prepared." (p. 34)

Fries (15), in *Linguistics and Reading*, states: "Seeking an extraneous interest in a story as a story during the earliest steps of reading is more likely to hinder than to help the efforts put forth by the pupil himself." (p. 199) A non-linguist who supports the methodology under discussion writes, "Reading, thus, is the act of producing correct sounds from symbols. If the reader does not know the meaning of a word he can still 'read' it if he knows the alphabetical system. The reader of English can read 'gan' and 'foggle' and many other nonsense and real words because he knows the alphabetical system." (13)

That Fries (16) is bothered by the issue of meaning is evidenced in a later writing where he states: "As a matter of fact the primary *objective* of our materials built upon linguistic understanding *is the ability to read for meanings.*" The better part of a page is devoted to an explanation of the cumulative meanings the child must grasp in reading the material:

Nat is a cat.
Nat is fat.
Nat is a fat cat.

Recently there has been considerable emphasis on research related to beginning reading. The chief goal of much of this research has centered on identifying those materials and methodology whose use would result in higher achievement test scores at the end of grade one. In addition to their impact on initial achievement, materials and methodology will also influence pupils' perception of reading.

Concomitant with the interest in beginning reading, there has been a tendency to lose sight of the fact that learning to read is a long-term developmental process. The habits, attitudes (and "set" as to what is involved in reading), which a child acquires during this period can have a significant impact on all future reading behavior. If educators become overly concerned with pupils achieving a fast start in reading, it is possible that they might fail to note that achieving this initial rapid growth under certain methodological conditions might also produce side effects which lead to later problems for the reader.

It is not suggested here that lesser achievement in grade one is a virtue, but rather that it is possible to achieve an initial spurt at the expense of the long-term goal of producing facile, critical readers. There is no suggestion that "cracking-the-code" is not an essential part of the beginning reading process, but the issue centers on whether certain methodology and materials maintain a proper balance between this facet of instruction and teaching reading as a meaning-making process.

Intonation-melody-of-language emphasis

Structuralists emphasize that the sentence is the meaning-bearing unit and that reading instruction should focus not on words or phrases but on the sentence. This theory holds that the child should start with oral reading of sentences and that instruction should emphasize his noting and practicing intonation patterns he uses in his speech.

This position is somewhat reminiscent of a methodology used some years ago which was labeled the sentence or memory approach. Using material on the chalkboard or from a book, the teacher would read a sentence orally. Immediately following, the children would recite the sentence while hopefully noting the printed equivalent. This practice was not effective in teaching children how to read and it was soon replaced by various types of "skills" emphasis which moved from sounding out individual letters to drill on recognition of sight words.

The problem, of course, is that *reading* involves the simultaneous application of many skills. When one essential skill is neglected we produce unwanted reading behaviors. Thus, while proponents of a melody of language emphasis may be justified in criticizing reading instruction that overemphasizes skills, the fact remains that children without the necessary skills cannot project intonation into their reading.

In order to read a sentence with proper intonation, the child must recognize or instantly solve all or most of the words that make up the sentence. His ability to deal with all of the parts of a sentence enables him to combine the parts and arrive at the proper intonation. An unknown word interrupts the melody as does miscalling or substituting words. Thus it is a mistake to attempt to dichotomize mechanical skills and intonation.

Good instruction is predicated on achieving the right combination of emphasis on code cracking and meaning. *Every* approach to teaching reading should include provisions for helping children to use proper intonation in reading and to understand how intonation influences meaning. On the other hand, it would be quite difficult to devise a method of teaching reading that stressed this ability alone and slighted other essential mechanics of reading.

Conclusion

Linguistics is the scientific study of language. Without doubt, reading instruction can be strengthened as teachers acquire some of the important insights which linguists have discovered. On the other hand, linguists as scientists are in no way responsible for finding applications for their discoveries. Few have actively engaged in relating their discoveries to the school curriculum. As a result, linguistics has had little impact on the content of the curriculum, particularly at the elementary level.

Recently there has been an awakening of interest in the question of how linguistic findings might aid the school in developing more meaningful educational experiences. Some linguists have turned their attention to the teaching of the reading process. It has been difficult for these linguists to apply the same scientific rigor to reading instruction that they applied to the study of language.

Linguists have evolved theories relative to instructional materials and methodology, but these have not been tested longitudinally in the classroom. There is little research data upon which to base conclusions. Linguistic science has not been concerned with the issue of *how children learn to read*, and some linguists have started with an assumption of how they *should* learn this process. This factor, ignoring the learner, may inhibit the efficacy of some suggestions advanced by linguists.

There can be no official linguistic approach to reading instruction because the science of linguistics is not concerned with teaching children to read. However, any linguist is free to theorize and experiment in the area of reading instruction. Such experiences on the part of linguists may result in insights which eventually lead to significant changes in reading instruction.

There are certain important concepts which do relate to reading which may have been slighted in both past and current methodology. The following are illustrative:

1. Despite irregularities in English spelling, important phoneme-grapheme *patterns* do exist, and possibly these should be exploited to a larger degree in reading instruction.
2. Reading instruction can overemphasize dealing with words as units. Graphic symbols must be read to parallel normal sentence tunes. The reader must "put together meaning bearing patterns."
3. The printed page represents language which is oral. The child beginning to read knows the melody (i.e., grammar or syntax) of oral language. However, the printed pages do not contain all the language clues found in speech. The "graphic representation" of language does not indicate various levels of pitch and stress. Punctuation (which indicates junctures) is the only graphic intonational help that is provided; and it too is somewhat imperfect. Intona-

tion-juncture, stress, and pitch are part of the language, not optional additives.

4. The purpose and function of structure words need to be better understood for the mastery of the reading process. These approximately 300 words, sometimes referred to as "glue words" or "service words," have little or no meaning in and of themselves; but they provide significant clues as to the type of patterns they introduce (questions, noun markers, verb markers, parallel constructions).

5. Language has a definite structure and this structure plays an important role in conveying meaning. Structure is revealed in sentence patterns not by word units.

6. Linguists describe language as *it is used* not as they or others think it should be used. Thus, a given dialect is not incorrect, nor is standard English superior to other dialects.

7. While linguists have and will continue to provide accurate descriptions of the phonology and syntax of various non-standard dialects, the problem of how to teach reading to dialect speakers is still unresolved.

8. The science of linguistics should not be moved downward into the elementary school curriculum. However, linguistic findings can and should be *translated* into meaningful curricular changes in the school. Teachers of reading should place more emphasis on teaching children *about* language and how it functions. Reading is a language function.

YOUR POINT OF VIEW?

Defend or attack the following statements.

1. Evidence is lacking that if children learn to read using materials which present only "regular spellings" they will master the recognition of irregularly spelled words faster because of this initial experience.

2. No branch of linguistics deals with the phenomenon of how children learn to read.

3. The study of *language* is unquestionably neglected in our schools.

4. Based on training, psychologists, linguists, sociologists, and novelists should be approximately equally adept at preparing reading materials for six-year-olds.

5. All reading-instruction materials which follow the structure and patterns of English usage can be said to be "linguistically sound" or "linguistic methods."

6. Approximately the same percentage of sixth graders have mastered the "melody of language" in their reading as have first graders in their oral language usage.

BIBLIOGRAPHY

1. Ahlvers, Elizabeth R. *A Study of the Effect of Teaching Intonation Skills on Reading Comprehension in Grade One.* Unpublished Doctoral Dissertation, The Pennsylvania State University, 1970.

2. Allen, Robert, "An Approach to Better Reading Through Recognition of Grammatical Relationships," *Improvement of Reading through Classroom Practice.* Proceedings, International Reading Association, 9, 1964, 224–25.

3. _____, "Better Reading Through the Recognition of Grammatical Relationships," *Reading Teacher* (December 1964), 194–98.

4. Barney, LeRoy, "Linguistics Applied to the Elementary Classroom," *The Reading Teacher* (December 1970), 221–226.

5. Bateman, Barbara and Janis Wetherell, "A Critique of Bloomfield's Linguistic Approach to the Teaching of Reading," *Reading Teacher* (November 1964), 98–104.

6. Betts, Emmett A. "Structure in the Reading Program," *Elementary English* (March 1965), 238–42.

7. Bloomfield, Leonard, *Language.* New York: Holt, Rinehart & Winston, Inc., 1933.

8. _____, and Clarence L. Barnhart, *Let's Read — a Linguistic Approach.* Detroit: Wayne State University Press, 1961.

9. Burke, Carolyn L. and Kenneth S. Goodman, "When A Child Reads: A Psycholinguistic Analysis," *Elementary English* (January 1970), 121–129.

10. Carroll, John B. *Language and Thought.* Englewood Cliffs, N. J.: Prentice-Hall, Inc., 1964.

11. Clay, Marie M. "Reading Errors and Self-Correction Behavior," *British Journal of Educational Psychology* (February 1969), 47–56.

12. Creswell, Thomas J. and Virginia McDavid, "Linguistics and the Teaching of Reading," *Elementary English* (January 1963), 93–6.

13. Dawkins, John, "Reading Theory — An Important Distinction," *Elementary English* (October 1961), 389–92.

14. Edward, Sister Mary, P.B.V.M. "A Modified Linguistic Versus a Composite Basal Reading Program," *Reading Teacher* (April 1964), 511–15.

15. Fries, Charles C. *Linguistics and Reading.* New York: Holt, Rinehart & Winston, Inc., 1963.

16. _____, "Linguistics and Reading Problems at the Junior High School Level," *Reading and Inquiry.* Proceedings, International Reading Association, 10, 1965, 244–47.

17. Frost, Joe L. *Issues and Innovations in the Teaching of Reading.* Glenview, Ill. Scott, Foresman and Company, 1967, Part V.

18. Goodman, Kenneth S. (ed.), *The Psycholinguistic Nature of the Reading Process.* Detroit: Wayne State University Press, 1968.

19. _____, "Linguistics In a Relevant Curriculum," *Education,* (April–May 1969), 303–306.

20. _____, "Analysis of Oral Reading Miscues: Applied Psycholinguistics," *Reading Research Quarterly* (Fall 1969), 9–30.

21. Goodman, Yetta M. "Using Children's Reading Miscues for New Teaching Strategies," *Reading Teacher* (February 1970), 455–459.

22. Gunderson, Doris V. *Language and Reading An Interdisciplinary Approach.* Washington, D. C.: Center for Applied Linguistics, 1970.

23. Ives, Josephine Piekarz, "Linguistic Principles and Reading Practices in the Elementary School," *Reading and Realism,* J. Allen Figurel, (ed.), Proceedings, International Reading Association, 13, Part 1, 1969, 88–93.

24. Lamb, Pose, *Linguistics in Proper Perspective.* Columbus, Ohio: Charles E. Merrill Publishing Company, 1967.

25. Lefcourt, Ann, "Linguistics and Elementary School Textbooks," *Elementary English* (October 1963), 598–601.

26. Lefevre, Carl A. "The Sounds and Tunes We Read By," *New Dimensions in Reading.* University of Pittsburgh Conference Proceedings, 19, 1963, 61–68.

27. _____, "A Longer Look at Let's Read," *Elementary English* (March 1964), 199–206.

28. _____, "A Comprehensive Linguistic Approach to Reading," *Elementary English* (October 1965), 651–60.

29. _____, *Linguistics and The Teaching of Reading.* New York: McGraw-Hill Book Company, 1964.

30. *Linguistics In School Programs,* The Sixty-Ninth Yearbook of the National Society for the Study of Education, Part II, 1970.

31. Lloyd, Donald J. "Reading American English Sound Patterns." New York: Harper & Row, Publishers, 1962, Monograph No. 104.

32. McCullough, Constance M. "Linguistics, Psychology, and The Teaching of Reading," *Elementary English* (April 1967), 353–62.

33. McDavid, Raven J., Jr. "The Role of the Linguist In The Teaching of Reading," *Changing Concepts of Reading Instruction.* Proceedings, International Reading Association, 6, 1961, 253–56.

34. ————, "Remarks on B. Robert Tabachnick's Paper," in *Reading and the Language Arts,* H. Alan Robinson (ed.), Supplementary Educational Monographs No. 93. Chicago: University of Chicago Press, 1963, 112.

35. Means, Chalmers Edward, *A Study of the Relationship Between the Use of Intonation Patterns In Oral Reading and Comprehension In Reading.* Unpublished Doctoral Dissertation, The Pennsylvania State University, 1969.

36. Olsen, Hans C. "Linguistic Principles and the Selection of Materials" in *Reading and Realism,* J. Allen Figural (ed.), Proceedings, International Reading Association, 13, Part 1, 1969, 189–93.

37. Ryan, Ellen Bouchard and Melvyn I. Semmel, "Reading as a Constructive Language Process," *Reading Research Quarterly* (Fall 1969), 59–83.

38. Rystrom, Richard, "Whole-Word and Phonics Methods and Current Linguistic Findings," *Elementary English* (March 1965), 265–68.

39. Soffietti, James P. "Why Children Fail To Read: A Linguistic Analysis," *Harvard Educational Review* (Spring 1955), 63–84.

40. Stevens, Martin, "Intonation in the Teachings of Reading," *Elementary English* (March 1965), 231–37.

41. Strickland, Ruth G. "Implication of Research in Linguistics for Elementary Teaching," *Elementary English* (February 1963), 168–71.

42. Tilley, Winthrop, "Linguistics: Stern-Faced Science or Deadpan Frivolity?' *Elementary English* (February 1967), 158–61.

43. Tyler, Priscilla, "Sound, Pattern and Sense," *Changing Concepts of Reading Instruction.* Proceedings, International Reading Association, 6, 1961, 259–63.

44. Weber, Rose Marie, "The Study of Oral Reading Errors: A Survey of the Literature," *Reading Research Quarterly* (Fall 1968), 96–119.

10

Teaching Reading in
the Primary Grades

The term primary refers to the first three years of formal instruction, and this may be thought of as a somewhat fixed segment on the educational time line. These same years are more difficult to characterize on the curriculum continuum since they cut across both the "beginning" and "independent" reading stages. Although widely used, these two terms are vague because they have never been defined with reference to the time line or instructional practices. The logic for using the terms *beginning* and *independent* stages may stem from the fact that children who learn how to read do exhibit behaviors that these terms describe.

Having discussed beginning reading (Chapters 5 and 6), we are here concerned only with the later primary years. Since practically every reading skill is developmental, each must be extended at every level of instruction. The teacher will continue to stress the same fundamental skills introduced in beginning reading instruction; for example, instant recognition of words, phonic analysis and using context clues are stressed in beginning reading. However, the need for these skills becomes more acute in the primary and intermediate grades because new words are introduced with increased frequency at these levels. Learning the reading process involves both increased mastery of skills previously introduced and adding new skills to the repertory.

339

In the past, the concept of grade level has occasionally caused instruction to lose sight of the learner. Therefore, in this chapter few if any references will be made to specific grade levels. It is easy to accept the idea that the second grade teacher teaches second graders and that third grades are populated by third graders. Experience in the classroom indicates that this idea is not very useful for instructional purposes since the classification of second or third grader does not define pupil achievement but merely identifies the room which certain pupils are currently occupying.

Objectives of the Primary Period

The primary grades find the majority of pupils making rather rapid progress in reading. Significant changes which have an impact on reading are taking place among children. They develop abilities which are prerequisites for improving reading, and interests which enhance the value of reading ability. Pupils in the primary years acquire a large store of general information, a wider interest in events not directly involving their own lives, and an increasing ability to deal with the abstract. They are now mature enough to concentrate for relatively long periods, developing capabilities for both independent work and teamwork.

An almost unlimited number of objectives for primary reading instruction could be advanced. Many of those listed here cannot be thought of as belonging exclusively to the primary period. Some were important in beginning reading and others will continue to be important throughout the intermediate, junior high, and secondary school levels. These objectives are to help the child:

1. Develop a large sight vocabulary.
2. Expand his stock of concepts and word meanings.
3. Learn and apply phonic principles for sounding out unknown words.
4. Review and extend knowledge of language sounds associated with vowel and consonant combinations.
5. Use punctuation for smooth meaningful reading.
6. Develop the skill of reading several words together as thought units, either phrases or sentences.
7. Reduce the number of occurrences of reading errors such as hesitations, regression, repetition, substitutions, or omissions.

8. Develop the ability to recognize known root words in new word forms which include prefixes or inflectional endings.
9. Further develop the attitude that reading is always purposeful and that he must clarify his purpose in specific reading tasks.
10. Use the context as an aid in attacking unknown words.
11. Enjoy and appreciate the vicarious experiences which are open to him in reading.

In addition to a systematic effort to extend skills previously introduced, many new developmental tasks are undertaken. Particular emphasis is placed on phonic and structural analysis. A number of prefixes and suffixes are taught with an emphasis on both structural and meaning changes involved. Silent consonants (*k*nife, com*b*, island, li*gh*t) and other spelling irregularities will receive attention along with syllabication and simple alphabetizing.

Comprehension skills are developmental also and should be developed systematically in the primary grades. Context clues become more important as unknown sight words are met more frequently. It is essential to learn new connotations for many words, and literal meanings cannot be insisted on for figurative expressions. The reader must follow the sequence of ideas and see their relationship to each other. The ability to analyze the meaning of sentences must be extended to paragraphs and larger units so that the main ideas of these larger units of material can be grasped.

The pace at which reading skills are taught in the primary grades is increased and the progress expected of pupils in a given period of time, such as a semester or year, is practically doubled when compared with the goals of beginning reading. The program necessarily includes simultaneous emphasis on the development of the mechanics of reading and the development of those comprehension skills which make reading rewarding and satisfying.

Materials and Teaching Schedule

Use of basal materials

The relation of basal reader series to the total reading program is much the same in grades two and three as in beginning reading. Growth in reading is developmental, and basal reader materials are designed with this fact in mind. Most facets of instruction are provided for in a logical sequence and each receives proper emphasis.

The essence of primary-level instruction is continuity and a systematic building of skills. When a child's growth does not parallel the materials found at his grade level, it is the pupil's achievement and rate of growth, not the materials, that must determine the instructional program. The basal reader materials at this level not only stress the mechanical skills of reading but also emphasize comprehension, cultivating in the reader an attitude that demands comprehension from reading. While vocabulary is still controlled, the expansion of the reading vocabulary at this level permits practice in reading for information, organization of data, and interpretation and appreciation of literature. (5) These skills systematically taught in reading instruction should easily transfer to all reading situations involving subject area materials and textbooks. Instructional procedures for developing the mechanics of reading and comprehension skills are discussed later in this chapter.

When basal materials are used in grade one, their use will likely continue in the primary grades. Such programs are based on the concept of viewing the ongoing mastery of reading skills as a developmental process, and most essential facets of instruction are provided for in a defensible sequence. The basal materials stress not only the mechanical skills but they also emphasize comprehension, cultivating in the reader an attitude that demands comprehension from reading.

Vocabulary control is still practiced in these materials. This could be considered a virtue in the case of some children who are progressing slowly. On the other hand, children who can do so should be permitted and encouraged to move through basals at a faster pace. These pupils will then need to rely more heavily on self selection and wide reading of other materials.

In the transition from beginning reading to independent reading, changes take place in the materials which children read. Pictures will still be found in basal readers, but there will be fewer of them, and the decline of the importance of pictures in providing context clues will be quite obvious. Stories will be much longer, more interesting, and include more concepts. These will not be built around the "one family" theme. There will be fairy tales and tales of animals who think and talk and have feelings. There will be stories of children who live in different lands and do unusual things. The lives and contributions of great men and women will be studied. Materials at this level call for the reader to make interpretations. He must detect clues as to the mood of characters, see the relationship between events, and grasp the intended meaning of figurative or idiomatic expressions. (28) Humor may not always be overt, and inferences may have to be drawn in the absence of absolute statements. (12) The ability to read each word in a passage is not the only criterion of reading. The child must also be able to tell "if grandfather was serious or just playing a joke on the boys" or "if Jerry was frightened by what he overheard" or "how the storm affected the plans for a vacation."

Supplementary materials

While basal reader series can provide the foundation for systematic instruction at this level, these materials should not be thought of as *the* reading program. Certainly the continued use of experience charts is justifiable in grades two and three. Experience stories written by individual pupils, as well as charts produced by the class as a whole, can be used extensively at the primary level. Since the sight vocabulary of pupils has been enlarged, this particular problem in the use of experience charts is minimized in the upper primary grades.

Bulletin boards also have many potential uses since children can now engage in independent reading and find materials which bear on topics under discussion. Pictures and newspaper and magazine articles offer interesting sources of material. When children know that there is a certain space in the room reserved for the use of such materials, they are motivated to do outside reading to find appropriate display materials. The bulletin board can be particularly effective when the teacher is working with units.

Another type of supplementary material that represents considerable potential is the graded news magazines. Examples are *News Pilot, News Ranger,* and *News Trails* for grades one, two, and three respectively.* These are weekly magazines containing news-related articles, puzzles, cartoons, humor, and illustrated stories of children from many lands. *My Weekly Reader*** is a graded magazine with different editions for each grade from kindergarten through advanced levels. These weeklies have certain advantages over texts in that they deal with timely topics which permit children to read and discuss controversial issues. Enjoying this flexi-

---

*Scholastic Book Services, Englewood Cliffs, New Jersey and Pleasanton, California
**American Educational Publications, Columbus, Ohio 43216

bility, these childrens magazines might score higher than certain other instructional materials when measured on the criteria of relevancy and interest.

Trade books

During the past 20 years, a number of instructional materials for teaching reading have become available. While many of these have had little impact on instruction, one significant development was the publication of an almost unlimited assortment of "trade books" which could be read by children in the primary grades. (8, 11) Today there are beginning books on a wide variety of topics ranging through fairy tales, joke books, space travel, poetry, ecology, and sports. This development has permitted creative primary teachers to provide their classes with a literary mix that formerly was available only at much higher grade levels.

Impact on sex differences in reading, and minority groups

Other educational advantages may accrue from the almost unlimited number of trade books now available. Indications are that the learning environment for both boys and blacks is now a little more meaningful. There is no question but that recent publishing trends have made available a large number of trade books that have the potential for catching and holding the interest of boys.* Such materials are helping to make reading more enticing to boys.

Black children now have a much better chance of reading *in school* about black heroes and blacks who have made substantial contributions to American culture. Undoubtedly of equal importance is the fact that non-blacks now also have this opportunity. One can only speculate as to what human tragedies might have been avoided and what benefits might have accrued to our society if this particular "right-to-read" had been realized much earlier.

Teaching schedule

Teachers in the primary grades should have definite daily time periods scheduled for reading instruction. This should not suggest that reading be thought of as a subject analogous to mathematics, science, social studies, and the like, but that in addition to emphasizing reading in these areas, there must be time for teaching needed

---

*See Chapter 2 for discussion of "Sex Differences in Learning to Read."

skills. Having a definite time period for reading instruction need not result in lockstep activities. Teacher-pupil contact need not be the same for all pupils every day. For instance, a number of poor readers may be given extra practice in word-attack skills while those pupils fairly proficient in this skill read independently in a subject area text or for recreation. At other times, the teacher may participate in the discussion of a story with a group of advanced readers while other pupils do seatwork on skill oriented teacher-prepared lesson sheets.

There is no one specific amount of time per day which can be said to be ideal for systematic reading instruction. Factors such as class size, pupils' achievement, the teacher's skill, and classroom organization would have to be considered in arriving at a schedule. (19) In grade two, for example, an hour each morning and possibly a slightly shorter period in the afternoon would certainly be considered a minimum amount of time for scheduled instruction. Other short periods throughout the week should be devoted to particular reading problems as they arise in other instructional activities. Problems in word meaning, word attack, punctuation, and exploration of concepts all involve reading instruction and should be dealt with whether or not the curricular task is in the area of reading or language arts.

The Instructional Program

The instructional program in the primary grades must be based on the belief that reading growth is developmental in nature. Those children who learned the skills taught in beginning reading are now equipped to make more rapid growth in the reading process. Having mastered a number of letter-sound relationships, they can continue to build systematically on these insights. Children who can recognize several hundred words without recourse to analysis will continue to enlarge their sight vocabulary as a result of repeated experience with other as yet unknown words. If children developed the *set* to demand *meaning* from their reading, they will become more proficient at profiting from context clues and their meaning vocabularies will be expanded as a result of wider reading. The remainder of this chapter presents discussion and illustrations of teaching procedures that focus on a number of the goals of primary reading instruction.

Expanding sight word vocabulary

In other contexts throughout this book, the point is stressed that all mechanical skills and reading habits are closely related to comprehension of printed material. This relationship is reaffirmed here because in the following materials particular skills are of necessity discussed separately. In the actual reading process, no skill is applied in isolation. One does not read simply to profit from punctuation, phrase material properly, or apply analysis skills.

Developing sight vocabulary is one of the most important goals in the primary reading program. The pupil who fails to do so is in trouble as a reader. The child in the first grade will meet several hundred words on experience charts, on bulletin boards, and in basal readers. If he masters as sight words all the words he meets in the pre-primer, primer, and first reader of a given basal series, he will know between three and four hundred words, although this figure is too high to be used as an estimated average for all pupils beginning their second year of school. If at the end of the second grade, a child knew only the words met thus far in any one basal reader series, he would know between 800 and 1000 sight words. In the third year, he would again double his stock of sight words. Throughout the primary period, pupils read from a variety of sources, a practice which helps to expand sight vocabulary. (15)

A number of procedures and exercises for helping children extend sight vocabulary are found in basal reader workbooks. In many instances, teachers can devise additional seatwork lessons for pupils who need added experience. A few typical techniques follow:

1. Chalkboard work on new words which are introduced in the day's reading assignment. It is considered desirable to study these new words prior to having children read the story silently. The new words are pronounced as they are printed on the board (*stump, footprints, suddenly, ocean*). Similarities to other words previously learned are pointed out, i.e., the *st* in *stump*, the word *foot* in the compound word *footprints*, the root word *sudden* in *suddenly*. Learning *ocean* as a sight word is stressed because of the difficulty of sounding it.

2. Using experience charts and personal experience records, labeling objects in the room, and matching captions with pictures. A series of pictures can be displayed and appropriate titles consisting of words, phrases, or sentences can be prepared on oak tag or card-

board. Children then match the proper written caption with each picture:

"The box is empty"   "A jet plane"
"Evergreens"   "Children in a school bus"
"A brown cow"   "Two boys"
"The tree has no leaves"   "A boy and a dog"

3. Using picture-word cards to teach "naming words." A picture of an object is pasted on one side of the card and the word for the picture printed on the other side:

house, car, tractor, bridge, shirt, television, giraffe, piano, dress, swing, policeman, cowboy, hammer, etc.

4. Introducing exercises which call for pupils to select the proper word to fill in a space left blank in a sentence. These exercises stress both meaning and differentiation between similar appearing words.

The kittens were asleep on the _____.
                                        (stay/straw)
The bird built its nest in the _____.
                                   (tree/tray)
They made a _____ for the puppy.
            (bad/bed)
Mr. Brown sells _____ in his store.
                (hats/hates)

A more difficult task is illustrated below where two similar appearing words are to be placed in two blanks in a sentence.

It was their _____ to go by _____. (plane/plan)
The _____ is about a _____ from here. (mile/mill)
The dog took the _____ to the _____. (bone/barn)
The train whistle went _____ _____. (toot/toot, two/too)
We must _____ to write on the _____. (line/learn)

5. Using word-drill periods and work sheets for seatwork which stress seeing the difference between similar appearing words.

a. The easiest drill usually involves "family" words in which the initial letter or initial blend is the important visual cue:

*l*ake, *t*ake, *m*ake, *c*ake, *r*ake
*h*at, *c*at, *m*at, *f*at, *p*at, *r*at
*f*all, *c*all, *t*all, *b*all, *h*all, *w*all

b. A child is to supply a word containing the same ending as a pair of cue words.

make   take
They used a boat to cross the l_____.

told   mold

The teacher showed them how to f_____ the paper.

   c. Practice may be provided in discriminating between common service words which have marked similarities.

> *their, there; where, when, which; stay, stop;*
> *must, much; many, may; than, then, thin;*
> *horse, house; every, very; think, thank.*

   d. Practice may be given in rapid recognition of vowels in medial position. (To be read orally):

> pin, pen, pan, pun
> men, tan, fun, fin, son
> sack, sick, sock, suck
> duck, kick, back, lock, neck
> fell, fall, full, fill
> bat, fit, hut, got, let

   6. Combining phrases to form meaningful sentences. This exercise forces attention on both the configuration of words and their meanings. In a *finish the sentence* exercise, children draw a line from the phrase in Column *A* to the phrase in Column *B* which completes the meaning:

A	*B*
The car	is on his head.
Around the house	give us milk.
The horse	is a beautiful lawn.
A straw hat	moves down the road.
Cows	drink milk.
Cats	has a beautiful saddle.

   7. Identifying root words in inflected forms. The child writes the root in the space provided.

taken	_____	using	_____
carried	_____	goes	_____
earlier	_____	laziest	_____
parties	_____	angrily	_____
reaching	_____	wagged	_____

Developing word analysis skills

Word analysis includes all methods of arriving at the pronunciation of unknown words. Gaining independence in reading implies a mastery of those techniques which will permit a child to read a passage containing words which he does not recognize instantly as sight words. Instruction in the primary grades will continue to focus on most of the word analysis skills taught in beginning reading, specifically phonics, structural analysis, and context and methods in combination. These skills become increasingly important because they are prerequisites for independent reading.

Phonic analysis

Letter-sound relationship is one of the most important of the mechanical skills taught in the primary grades. The child must gain insight into a large number of these relationships and be able to apply them if he is to become an independent reader. In some instances, pupils in the primary grades are not systematically taught skills they need because these were included in the curriculum of previous grades. In an effort to mitigate against teachers associating particular phonics teachings with a particular grade level, an overview of the entire program is presented in Chapter 7, *Phonics Instruction.* Much of the material in Chapter 7 is germane to the primary grades; however, some teaching illustrations not included in that discussion will be presented here.

It should be kept in mind that children cannot profit from phonics instruction unless they are able (1) to discriminate visually between letter-forms; and (2) discriminate auditorially between speech sounds that printed letters represent. Any child who has not mastered these skills should be provided further instruction regardless of his grade level. (17)

Review of initial consonant sounds. Certain children will not have mastered this skill, others will need some review, while some pupils will need little if any further work. The following exercises for teaching mental substitution of initial consonants and blends illustrate the type of activities which may be used.

1. *Add a letter to the front of each word to make a different word. Write the new word on the line provided.*

it	(hit)	is	_____	and	_____
in	_____	ox	_____	ink	_____
at	_____	up	_____	am	_____
us	_____	ice	_____	ear	_____
an	_____	any	_____	all	_____

2. *Change the first letter to make a naming word for an* animal. *Write the animal name on the line provided.*

mat	(cat)	wig	_____	loose	_____
dish	_____	hole	_____	pen	_____

now	_____	box	_____	love	_____
boat	_____	house	_____	tub	_____
cup	_____	wear	_____	mitten	_____

3. *Change the first letter to make a child's name.*

back	_____	fancy	_____	due	_____
like	_____	hoe	_____	pail	_____
pane	_____	hose	_____	jam	_____
day	_____	sob	_____	hilly	_____
him	_____	drank	_____	loan	_____
late	_____	mill	_____	hat	_____

4. *Initial Blends: Form a new word by adding one of these blends to the front of each word.*

st	*sp*	*sk*

_____ate	_____ill	_____out
_____in	_____and	_____age
_____all	_____ring	_____ink
_____end	_____air	_____ice

5. *Take away the first letter and then add an initial blend to form a new word.*

lake	_____	nap	_____	tape	_____
dog	_____	late	_____	now	_____
mad	_____	sand	_____	sail	_____
door	_____	bee	_____	may	_____
bag	_____	rider	_____	mice	_____

6. *Initial digraphs: Take away the first letter and add wh, ch, sh, th to form a new word.*

lick	_____	mile	_____	rake	_____
sale	_____	but	_____	kite	_____
tower	_____	fin	_____	sick	_____
hen	_____	bank	_____	bird	_____
boot	_____	deer	_____	feel	_____

Irregular consonant sounds. The following material focuses on the two sounds of *g* and *c*, the unsounded letters in *kn* and *wr* words, and the digraph *ph*.

7. *On each blank space write g or j to show the sound that g represents.*

_____giant	_____giraffe	_____gold	_____general
_____got	_____gang	_____gem	_____Gipsy
_____gate	_____George	_____gas	_____gym

8. *On each blank space write* k *or* s *to show the sound that* c *represents.*

_____cake	_____cent	_____cuff	_____cycle
_____cider	_____coat	_____city	_____cut
_____color	_____catch	_____cold	_____certain
_____cypress	_____circle	_____cellar	_____course

9. *On the blank space write the letter which represents the* first *sound heard in each word.*

_____knee	_____wrap	_____phone	_____wrote
_____knob	_____write	_____photo	_____knight
_____know	_____wring	_____phonics	_____Phillip

Working with vowel sounds. Children will have had considerable experience in discriminating between vowel sounds and the letter combinations representing these sounds. Some children will need further review of concepts covered in Chapter 7. The following exercises represent only a few of the teaching formats that might be used with primary-level pupils.

1. *Auditory discrimination:* "Draw a card" is a game that can be played by pairs of children, a small group, several teams, or by the entire class. Paste each of a number of pictures on a separate card. (These may be limited to pictures whose naming words contain either a short or long vowel sound.) Shuffle the cards and place them face down on the playing area. Children take turns drawing a card. Each child names his picture and tells the vowel sound heard in the naming word:

> "I drew a *fox* — I hear short *o* in *fox*."
> "I drew a *tree* — I hear long *e* in *tree*."
> "I drew a *vase* — I hear long *a* in *vase*."
> Etc.

2. *Auditory-visual discrimination:* Prepare and duplicate a page containing a number of word pairs. The words in each pair are identical except for vowel letters and vowel sounds. Pronounce one word in each pair. The children are to underline the word pronounced. In the examples below, the word to be pronounced is in italics.

1. *bed*	2. plan	3. *coat*	4. *pal*	5. met
bead	*plane*	cot	pale	*meet*

6. pan	7. *rod*	8. fed	9. *cute*	10. *rid*
pain	road	*feed*	cut	ride

11. *us*	12. *slide*	13. *not*	14. cub	15. *win*
use	slid	note	*cube*	wine

3. *Mental substitution of vowel letter-sounds:* Duplicate a work sheet similar to the format shown below. The top of the sheet contains a box containing the vowel letters. A stimulus word is shown at the left followed by three blank spaces. Children are to write three words in which only the vowel letter is changed. Words must be sounded out since all vowel letters cannot be used in the series.

a	e	i	o	u

	(hat)	(hot)	(hut)
hit			
pup	____	____	____
beg	____	____	____
pop	____	____	____
bid	____	____	____
hum	____	____	____
pet	____	____	____
ham	____	____	____

4. *Homonyms* (Two Vowel Patterns): Explain the concept that some words are pronounced the same but have different meanings and spellings. All the words in the following exercise follow regular spelling patterns and contain one of the vowel patterns *ee, ea, ai, a+e*. The purpose of the exercise is to have the child associate these visual patterns with the long vowel sound they represent.

Directions: *On each blank space write a word that sounds like the first word. The new word will have a different meaning and spelling.*

week	(weak)	main	(mane)
beet	____	sail	____
steal	____	made	____
heal	____	mail	____
meat	____	pale	____
creek	____	waste	____
seem	____	plain	____
real	____	tail	____
peel	____	pane	____

5. *Decode the mystery word:* This is an exercise that provides practice in associating letter-sounds in initial, medial, and final positions. In its simplest form it consists of three pictures whose naming

words are made up of three letter-sounds. The pictures are arranged so that when the child uses the first letter-sound from the naming word of the first picture, the second from the second picture, and the final letter-sound from the third picture, he arrives at a CVC word.

First Letter   Middle Letter   Last Letter

b __ __   __ u __   __ __ g   bug

6. *Context and phonic clues:* Prepare a series of sentences each of which contains one or more short-vowel words in which the vowel letter has been omitted. Children read the sentence using context clues to identify the word. They then write the vowel letter that represents the sound heard in that word.

1. The c__t drank milk from the c__p.
2. We had f__n on the b__s.
3. Two m__n wore r__d c__ps.
4. Did the p__p s__t on the r__g?
5. Billy's d__d read the m__p.

7. *Long and short vowel words:* Each sentence shows two blank spaces and is followed by two words which, when placed in the proper blank spaces, will make "sentence sense." Children read the sentence and write the correct word in each blank space.

1. Our _____ won _____ games. (*ten/team*)
2. John and his _____ filled the _____. (*pail/pal*)
3. The children put their _____ on the _____. (*cot/coats*)
4. They used their scissors to _____ out _____ designs. (*cut/cute*)
5. The boys _____ down the _____. (*slide/slid*)

Structural analysis

The teaching of structural cues should receive considerable emphasis in the primary grades. In their reading, children will meet every type of structural change in word form found in English writing. Also, the frequency with which they meet inflected forms and affixes will increase drastically. Instruction should include a review and extension of children's experience with compounds, common word endings including plurals and contractions, affixes, and the like.

Compound words will not be difficult for the child who forms the habit of examining unknown words. The compound words he meets will be composed of shorter words that he has already learned. Basal reader series introduce a few compound words at first grade level and provide drill on recognition and analysis at each succeeding grade level.

1. Noticing the structure of compound words.

    a. *The two words in columns 1 and 2 can be placed together*

to form one word. Write the two words together under
3 and say the compound that is formed.

1	2	3
after	noon	afternoon
with	out	_____
every	one	_____
club	house	_____
air	plane	_____
door	way	_____
some	time	_____

  b. *Each word under 1 can be placed with a word under 2 to make a compound word. The first one is done for you.*

1	2	3
*after	way	afternoon
with	time	_____
every	plane	_____
club	one	_____
air	*noon	_____
door	out	_____
	house	_____

  c. *Building compound words from materials provided below. Combine one word from the box with a word from the list to form a compound word.*

type	tooth	snap	after
any	grand	bed	light

_____ache	_____one
_____noon	_____write
_____father	_____shot
_____house	_____room

  d. *Recognizing compound words in sentence context. Underline each compound word. Draw a line between the two words in each compound word* [mail/box].

   (1) Everyone went to the football game that afternoon.
   (2) John is upstairs writing in his scrapbook with his ballpoint pen.
   (3) We ran halfway to the clubhouse without stopping.
   (4) Frank received a flashlight, a raincoat, and a sailboat for his birthday.

(5) He read the newspaper headline, "Big fire at saw-mill."

(6) They saw the shipwreck from a hilltop near the lighthouse.

2. Forming plurals by adding *es*.

Many plurals are formed by simply adding s, *as in* boys, girls, trees, farms, cats. *In many words* es *is added to form plurals.*

fox	foxes	inch	inches
box	_____	dress	_____
dish	_____	lunch	_____
brush	_____	mix	_____
bus	_____	match	_____
class	_____	fish	_____

All of the above words end with *s, ss, sh, ch,* or *x*. Make a rule for adding *es* to form plurals.

3. Forming the plural of words ending in *y*.
   Change the y *to* i, *then add* es.

funny	funnies	body	bodies
fly	_____	army	_____
baby	_____	party	_____
puppy	_____	cherry	_____
lady	_____	family	_____

4. Recognizing contractions.

The two words in column A are often combined to form a different word found in column B. The apostrophe (') in these words indicates that a letter or letters have been omitted in forming the new word.

A		B
I am	=	I'm
I will	=	I'll
he will	=	he'll
he is	=	he's
has not	=	hasn't
I have	=	I've
have not	=	haven't

(In follow-up work sheets only column A is presented and the child writes the contraction.)

do not	_____
was not	_____
they have	_____
you will	_____
it is	_____
does not	_____

5. Doubling final consonants: The rule covering doubling of consonants is quite lengthy and involved. Most children, however, learn to do it without being conscious of a rule. In essence, the final consonant is doubled in a *one vowel word* when the last two letters are a vowel and consonant. If the one vowel word ends with two consonants, there is no doubling. An exercise such as the following might help children master this spelling and structural phenomena.

One vowel

One consonant   *Double the consonant before adding* ed, ing, er.

can	canned	canning	canner
plan	_____	_____	_____
skip	_____	_____	_____
pop	_____	_____	_____
drag	_____	_____	_____
stop	_____	_____	_____

Two consonants   *Just add the endings* ed, ing, er.

help	*helped*	*helping*	*helper*
click	_____	_____	_____
dish	_____	_____	_____
earn	_____	_____	_____
march	_____	_____	_____
climb	_____	_____	_____

6. Possessives: An apostrophe and the letter *s* (*'s*) indicate possession.

John has a bike.	This is John's bike.
Many girls have new hats.	These are the girls' new hats.
The cat eats from this dish.	This is the cat's dish.

Write the correct word in each blank space:

1. Two _____ were eating from the _____ bowl.
   (*cat's/cats*)
2. This is the _____ time to watch T.V.
   (*children/children's*)

7. Comparative forms:

Write the word that makes the sentence correct.

1. John is_____ than Bill, but Ted is the_____ runner on the team.
   (*fast/faster/fastest*)
2. November is _____ than July.
   (*cold/colder/coldest*)
3. If they took the _____ trail they should arrive in a _____ time.
   (*short/shorter/shortest*)
4. Our town has many _____ buildings, but not the _____ one in the state.
   (*tall/taller/tallest*)
5. We crossed the _____ bridge I ever saw.
   (*long/longer/longest*)

The structure or visual stimulus pattern of words is changed by a syllable added either at the beginning or at the end of that word. A child may know the symbol *load* as a sight word, but the first few times he sees *unload, reload, or unloading,* he may not see what is familiar. Instead, he may see the whole new configuration as unfamiliar. Thus, recognizing common prefixes will be an aid in learning new words where the root word is known. (27) Children use words which contain prefixes and suffixes in spoken language long before coming to school. These words are often learned as sight words before formal instruction deals with the meanings of these suffixes.

Instruction cannot deal exclusively with the structural changes resulting from the addition of prefixes or suffixes. Exercises should force attention both to the structural change and the modification of meaning. Workbooks of all basal series have lessons devoted to the study of prefixes, but the teacher does not have to wait for a particular time or page in a workbook. The curriculum of the modern school does not impose such rigidity. It is just as appropriate to show pupils that prefixes change the meanings of words in a science, arithmetic, hygiene, or geography class as it is to discuss this point during the period devoted to reading instruction.

8. *Make a sentence with each of the following words. What happens to the meaning of each word lettered* b? *What can you say about the prefix* un?

a. clean	a. load
b. *un*clean	b. *un*load
a. fair	a. kind
b. *un*fair	b. *un*kind

9. *Make a sentence with each of the following words. What happens to the meaning of each word lettered* b? *What can you say about the prefix* re?

a. fill	a. read	a. visit
b. *re*fill	b. *re*read	b. *re*visit

10. *Make a sentence with the following words. Each word lettered* b *has a prefix. Explain what each prefix does to the word meaning.*

a. view	a. ability	a. agree
b. *pre*view	b. *in*ability	b. *dis*agree

Suffixes are word endings which give root words different shades of meaning (*er, or, ist, an, al, ure, ty, ment, ism, age, is, en, el, ive, ish, ant, ful, ly, less,* etc.). Since there are a great number of suffixes and very few have an absolutely fixed meaning, an attempt to teach concrete meanings for the majority would probably produce more confusion than learning. If a child develops the habit of *seeing* the more common endings so that he is not prevented from recognizing known root words, the new word is not likely to cause trouble. Composing sentences using the different forms of a word is a better method of teaching than having the child attempt to tell the precise difference between words like joy*ful*, joy*fully*, joy*ous*; depend*ent*, depend*able*, depend*ency*.

The English language is rich in the number of prefabricated units that can be attached to any number of root words to form new words:

heat:	heated, preheated, reheat, preheating, heatedly
war:	postwar, warlike, warring, prewar, wartime
luck:	lucky, unluckiest, luckily, unlucky
place:	placing, displace, replaced, replaceable

Assume that the word *happy* is a known sight word. Identifying the word *unhappily* theoretically calls for these skills: recognizing the prefix *un* and the suffix *ly* as units, perceiving the root word *happy*, applying the rule that words ending in *y* change *y* to *i* before adding an ending, and understanding syllabication — i.e., prefixes and suffixes usually stand as syllables and two like consonants usually divide, thus giving the pronunciation *un hap pi ly*. It is doubtful, however, that any reader goes through all of these mental steps since the process would be most uneconomical. The reader also has the context to suggest the word, and after he has met a word on several occasions, he will probably have mastered it as a sight word and will not have to resort to analysis.

Context and methods in combination

At practically all points on the reading continuum, the one ability that sets the good readers apart from poor readers is the degree to which the context helps the reader get unknown words. When children do not profit from context clues, this weakness is easy to detect by observing their reading behavior — either they do not "try" words or they insert words which do not belong. On the other hand, when a passage is read correctly, it is difficult for an observer to determine to what degree dependence on context clues contributed to the successful reading.

The good reader keeps in mind what has been read and how the sentence he is reading builds on this meaning. If context is not enough, he glances through the word to detect a prefix, the root word, or an inflectional ending. When no prefix is found, the first syllable is isolated. This may unlock the word. If not, he will work further through the word. These operations are performed so rapidly by a good reader that there may be no perceptible pause between the different modes of attack. If the word is not solved by this attack, the reader may go on past the word for additional context clues. This step may call for rereading the sentence, but if it is successful, meaning will have been reached.

When each method of attacking unknown words is discussed and examined separately, one might conclude that in a given situation a reader uses only one method. The exclusive use of one method in this way makes for slow and inefficient reading, although some children approach reading in this manner. The more ability a reader has in profiting from structural, phonic, and context clues, the less likely it is that he can tell which one was the key in helping him solve a particular word. The smooth, facile reader is one who attacks an unknown word simultaneously on every front on which it is vulnerable to analysis. Early in the first grade the child learns to sound the initial letters of words. This skill, plus pictures and context clues, makes it possible to eliminate many of the words that might otherwise have been plausible choices.

The more difficult the level of the material, the less likely it is that the immediate context alone will be an adequate tool for analyzing unknown words, but often with the smallest additional clue the word is easily solved. Assume that the pupil meets a sentence containing an unknown word: "Jack was sure his _____ would let him go." This is the opening line of a story and the author has yet to unfold the plot or background. There are many words which might complete an idea when this is all we know. Is Jack being held a prisoner? The word could be *captors*. Is he thinking of "getting permission?" The word might be *mother, father, friends, teacher.* If the reader notes something about the unknown word, he may get a valuable clue. For instance, "Jack was sure his p_____ would let him go." *Mother, father, teacher, friends* are eliminated if the reader can use initial sounds. Several possibilities remain, such as *pal, playmates, principal, parents.* The word *play* is known as a sight word. It is not found in this unknown word, so playmates is not suggested. It is possible that word configuration (length of word) might help the reader decide between *pal* or *parents*. With enough skill at phonic analysis to work his way through the first syllable, the reader is almost assured of arriving at the correct response. If he should try PA rents or PAR ents, either pronunciation will be close enough to suggest the correct word.

"It's my _____," said Jimmy. Here a number of possibilities occur to the reader: my *idea, turn, guess, opinion* or any number of possessions. This sentence alone does not provide enough context but rarely does such a sentence stand alone. As we take into consideration the context supplied by several previous sentences, the unknown word falls into place.

> The boys searched everywhere but they did not find the little lost puppy. "I hope Blackie doesn't get hit by a car," said Billy. Jimmy was very sad. He had been thinking all afternoon about not closing the gate when he had gone to mail the letter. The puppy must have gotten out when he left the gate open. "It's my _____," said Jimmy. Then he told about the gate.

Comprehension skills

In one sense the topic heading *Comprehension Skills* is misleading, for all reading skills are related to comprehension. For example, learning to use punctuation might appear to be totally within the framework of mechanics, yet nothing can more quickly distort meaning than the inability to profit from the clues that punctuation provides. Word-by-word reading has implications other than just in the skills area. In addition to slowing the reading rate, this habit tends to force attention on words rather than on larger units. Discussion of types of skills and specific skills within types is justified solely on the ground that this permits the reader to work with concepts that can be handled more easily. In the final analysis, reading must be thought of as a unitary process that is more than the simple sum of its parts. When a child is asked to read a sentence or a larger unit, he must employ every skill that the situation requires regardless of how or what these skills have been labeled.

Expansion of meanings

Children's development of concepts cannot be left to chance. The school deliberately seeks to provide an environment which will lead to the development and expansion of concepts in every area of the curriculum. The following procedures can be used in helping children develop meanings. They are not limited to a particular grade level. While many of these techniques are used in the formal reading program, they are appropriate for teaching terms and concepts in all subject areas.

Using pictures. The use of pictures is an excellent method of expanding concepts and clearing up misconceptions. The role of pictures in beginning reading has been discussed previously in relation to helping pupils master sight words by suggesting context. Here we deal with the utility of pictures in developing and expanding concepts. A picture of an eroded hillside is much more effective in fixing the concept of *erosion* than is a word definition of the term. Early basal readers rely heavily on pictures, but it is actually in the context areas that pictures have greatest value. Pictures are more likely to fix accurate concepts of *colonial architecture,* the *iron-plated Monitor,* an *anteater,* a *Chinese junk, terrace farming* or the *human circulatory system* than is language alone.

The same picture can be used at different levels for teaching words and meanings. For example, let us imagine a picture which would be available to almost any teacher — a downtown scene in a small city. We see a bus, a boy on a bicycle, various store fronts and offices, a policeman directing traffic, a fire hydrant, the city hall across from a parking lot.* Without going into more detail, we might build a hierarchy of concepts.

"*Where is the policeman?*"
> "In the *street*."

"Yes, he is really standing in the middle of where two streets cross — what is that called?"
> "That's an *intersection*."

(The class level will determine whether the teacher should explain the term intersection.)

"*How many kinds of travel or transportation do we see?*"
> "Some people are *walking*."
> "A boy on a *bicycle*."
> "There's a *bus*. It's a city bus."
> "There are lots of *cars*."
> "I see an *airplane* above the city."

"*What kinds of transportation are not seen in the picture?*"
> "*Trains*."
> "Don't see any *boats*."
> "There are no big *trucks* — big trailers."

(Teacher points to the symbol which identifies the telephone company office.)

"*What is in this building?*"
> "That must be the telephone office."
> "What's this sign across the street?"
> "City Water Company, it says."

"*What do we call these types of businesses?*"
> (no response)

"Did you ever hear the term *utilities* or *public utilities?*
(The teacher prints the word on the board.)
"What other *utilities* do you think this city has — what others besides telephone company and water company?"
> "Electricity."

"That's right — what other name might it have?"
> "Light Company"
> "Power Company"

"Do you think of any other *utility* companies? Would there be a gas company?"

Other meanings the teacher can lead into are:
> "Four stories high"

---

*This is a description of the poster picture "The City" found in *Readiness Pictures* (New York: The Macmillan Company).

"This canvas over the sidewalk is an *awning* or a *canopy*."
"This is a parcel post truck. Its purpose is to serve the people. How is it like the power company? How is it different?"

The picture we have attempted to visualize is a simple one which could be used at various grade levels. Through its use the teacher can stress:

1. Noticing details
2. Symbols standing for things (the telephone symbol on a window)
3. Many different *names* standing for the same things
   a. Power company, public service company, utility company, etc.
   b. Canopy, awning
4. The same word having different meanings according to usage (i.e., *meter*: parking meter, gas meter, electric meter; meters in cars: speedometers, gas meter, and mileage meter)

The value of pictures lies in their wealth of detail and the fact that they stay in focus or can be referred to after a discussion has led away to other things.

Developing different meanings for the same word

The child's early language development is characterized by mastery of the concrete first and then a gradual moving up the ladder of abstraction. He may know such words as *air, blue, mine, broadcast, fence,* and he may know several meanings for each word; yet he will not be familiar with all the meanings of these words. The child will probably have mastered a number of meanings for the word *air*.

1. My daddy put *air* in the tires.
2. We hang clothes outside to *air* them.
3. We breathe *air*.

The same child may be confused by the following:

1. If asked to "*air* his views."
2. To hear that "his older brother gave his girlfriend the *air*."
3. That Mrs. Jones is disliked in the neighborhood because "she puts on *airs*."

The child may understand what is meant by *blue* in the sentence, "The boy had a *blue* boat." He may not be familiar with "The boy felt *blue* when his aunt left." He may understand "Grandfather rode the *horse*," but not have a concept of "The coach warned the boys not to *horse* around" or the expression "That's a *horse* of a different color" or "The mayor accused the council of beating a dead *horse*."

He may know one or two meanings of mine but some of the usages or concepts involving the word *mine* will undoubtedly be beyond him.

1. "The book is *mine*."
2. "Joe's father worked in the coal *mine*."
3. "That corner store is a gold *mine*."
4. "The tank was damaged by a land *mine*."
5. "Don't under*mine* the confidence of the people."
6. "Our break is over, let's get back to the salt *mine*."
7. "He was stationed aboard a *mine* sweeper."

The above examples point up how difficult it is to measure "size of vocabulary," for each child has several different kinds of vocabularies. The word *mine* would be in a child's meaning, speaking, and reading vocabularies if he could read sentence (a) above, even though that was the only usage which was familiar to him. And in some instances, if the child could "read" — that is, correctly say all the words in the sentence (d) — it would be concluded that *mine* was in his *reading vocabulary* whether or not he could explain the sentence. Inability to explain the usage would indicate only that the child did not understand this particular concept.

Adults' meaning vocabularies are larger than their speaking, writing, or reading vocabularies. The sounds "klee-shay" may conjure up meaning for an individual when he hears the word used in context, yet the written symbol cliché may be meaningless if he sounds "clish." The word *cache* may be mispronounced in reading but still produce meaning in the sentence "The bandits, under cover of darkness, returned to the mountain cache for their stolen loot." Meaning may escape the individual when the T.V. badman says, "Let's go, boys, we have to beat the posse to the kash."

Learning meanings is a fascinating and highly motivating experience for children. The teacher can point out that most words carry several different meanings according to how they are used. She might illustrate with simple words like *can*, *stick*, *run*, or *set*. As the teacher asks for different usages, she will write the children's responses on the board, at the same time attempting to fix the various meanings by using other known words.

"I *can* spell my name." — *can* means *able*

"I bought a *can* of beans." — *can* means a *container*

"Put the garbage in the *garbage can.*" — another type of *container*

"My mother said, 'Tomorrow I will *can* the peaches.' " — *can* means to *preserve food.*

The last example may not be given by any child in an early elementary grade in an urban school, but this usage may be known to almost every child in the same grade in a rural locality. Some other usages of the word *can* may not be appropriate for an early grade level, but would be at a higher grade level.

"Can it, Mack." — an order to stop talking

"If you leave now, the boss will can you." — dismiss from job

"Why don't you trade in that old tin can and get an automobile?" — a battered old car

After several group exercises which stress that the objective is to supply different meanings of a word, not simply different sentences, the teacher can suggest a written game. Each child works independently, selecting his own words for illustrating different usages. In order not to handicap the poorer spellers, the teacher may offer to spell any words the children want to use in their sentences. "Just hold up your hand and I'll come to your desk and write out the word you want to use." This exercise has considerable diagnostic value in that it yields data on spelling ability, language facility, legibility of handwriting, ability to follow directions, and ability to work independently.

Some specific findings reported by one teacher include:

1. Despite what appeared to be a thorough explanation of the objective, a number of pupils missed the point of the exercise and wrote different sentences using the same meaning of the word selected.

2. Several pupils misspelled words which they could spell correctly when the teacher pronounced or dictated these words. (The pupils slurred or omitted syllables when they said these words silently.)

3. The papers revealed many words misspelled *which the pupils thought they spelled correctly.* This data served as a basis for spelling review.

4. The handwriting was inferior to that which the child would do on a writing test.
5. This exercise disclosed great differences among pupils in their ability to use expressive language as well as exposing paucity of concepts among some pupils.
6. Misconceptions were found on many pages. These could be corrected individually with the pupil.

Synonyms

The pupils are reminded that words which have the same meaning are called *synonyms*. "Give me another word that means the same as *big, work, fast*" will as a rule elicit responses from everyone in the group. Exercises that permit group participation can be followed by individual work involving a series of three-by-five cards each containing the directions "Go to the board and write the word _____. Under it write as many synonyms as you can." Another series of cards may include a number of words some of which are synonyms for the stimulus word. The pupil selects the synonyms and writes them under the stimulus word. This latter task is the easier of the two and permits pupils of differing ability to participate. The following exercises illustrate this type of activity.

1. Write the word *timid* on the board. Under it write as many synonyms as you can think of.

2. Write the word *rapid* on the board. Under it write any word from the following group which is similar in meaning:

quick	speedy
shave	light
fast	fleet
grasp	throw
inquire	reduce
hastily	swift

3. On the board write the word *release* and under it write any word in the following group which is nearly the *opposite* in meaning:

grasp	trap
relief	free
hold	captive
clutch	repeat
dismiss	catch
receive	keep
mistake	

4. Another exercise might call for the child to underline two words in a series which are similar in meaning:

almost	together	certainly	*nearly*
thrilling	spinning	exciting	frightening
nonsense	terrible	scolding	awful
matches	money	penny	postcard

Work sheets of varying difficulty can be used with pupils of different ability levels in a class. Similar exercises are applicable to expanding word meanings by teaching words of *opposite meanings*. The objective should always be to work out lesson plans that will assure that the pupils:

See the words
Hear them pronounced
Experience their use in sentences

Sentence comprehension exercises can be used in which the child reads to determine whether two sentences carry the same meaning:

> *Read the two sentences below marked a. Do they have the same meaning? If so, write* S *in the box to indicate they have the* Same *meaning. Write* D *if the sentences have a* Different *meaning. Do the same for sentences b, c, d, etc.*

a. Bill took his dog for a ride.　▢
a. Bill took his dog in the house.

b. The park is not far from where Mary lives.　▢
b. Mary's house is near the park.

c. Tom has a cat and a pony at the farm.　▢
c. Tom has a pet goat at the farm.

Homonyms

Homonyms are words which sound exactly alike and are spelled differently. They are potential sources of trouble to young readers since both sight recognition and meanings may be confusing. Many common homonyms look very much like (*their, their; see, sea; hear, here; beat, beet; dear, deer; course, coarse*). The reader in the primary grades gets meaning from hearing the following sounds in these combinations, but he may not recognize all of the written symbols.

1. *Their* coats are over *there.*
2. The *plane* landed safely on the *plain.*
3. *Would* you please carry in some *wood?*
4. He felt *weak* for a *week* after he was sick.
5. *"Oh,"* he said, "how much do I *owe* you?"
6. The boy *ate eight* pieces of candy.
7. *See* the ship on the *sea.*
8. *No,* I do not *know* where it is.

One method of expanding both sight and usage vocabularies is to list homonyms in columns with the word the child is most likely to be familiar with on the left. An exercise calling for the use of each word in a sentence will provide a check on the mastery of meanings.

The words in columns A and B are pronounced the same.

A	B	A	B
do	dew	sail	sale
deer	deer	hair	hare
way	weigh	made	maid
hall	haul	one	won
pair	pare	poor	pour

For children who have trouble with these words, simple card games can be devised for two or more players in which one word of each pair is included in a draw pile and the other words shuffled and dealt to the players. When a card in the draw pile is turned up, whoever has the homonym for it in his hand pronounces the word on the stack and gives its meaning, then gives the meaning for the word in his hand. If he does each without help, he "takes" both cards. There are many variations which can be used with such cards.

Following is a list of easier homonyms which the child usually meets in the primary grades.

beat	beet	red	read
know	no	ring	wring
do	dew	would	wood
dear	deer	whole	hole
to two	too	sail	sale
knew	new	hall	haul
mail	male	pair	pare
road	rode	tail	tale
wait	weight	steal	steel

there	their	birth	berth
sun	son	ate	eight
oh	owe	some	sum
waist	waste	pain	pane
rap	wrap	so	sew
bee	be	by	buy
one	won	not	knot
see	sea	hear	here
hair	hare	our	hour
week	weak	maid	made
fair	fare	piece	peace

Figurative language and idiomatic expressions

Figurative language and idiomatic expressions are quite widely used both in basal readers and in subject texts. (18) These expressions pose virtually no problem for some readers, but can be stumbling blocks for other children in getting the meaning. This occurs because some readers have developed the habit of expecting the words they read to have literal meanings. It has also been noted that some children can both use and understand such expressions in oral communication but are still confused or misled when they attempt to read them. (20)

Some examples of expressions that will be met in the primary or elementary grades follow. The mere fact that a child can read these correctly is not assurance that he interprets them correctly.

The old sailor *spun a yarn* for the boys.
Soon *night fell.*
Don't *throw your money away* at the circus.
Before long they were driving through *rolling hills.*
The *rich earth* spread for miles along the river.
He returned *heavy-hearted.*
The waves *pitched the boat* up and down.
Give me a *lift.*
They *picked themselves up.*
He *made his mark* as a successful coach early in his career.
The captain *barked* his orders.
A *finger* of light moved around the airport.

Workbooks have a limited number of exercises which attempt to give practice in interpretation of figurative language. The teacher must be alert when these exercises are used, however, for a pupil may check the correct response without clearly understanding the intended meaning. When a child makes an error in interpretation and his response is marked wrong by the teacher, all he has to do is erase his X and place it in the remaining choice, thus "correcting his error." Learning may not have taken place even though the exercise is corrected.

Although teachers understand that some pupils will need extra practice in developing skills, they often do not find the time to construct teacher-made work sheets. If exercises are duplicated, one preparation can be used with successive classes, and if several teachers at various grade levels co-operate, they will find work sheets designed for use at one grade level are appropriate for particular children in other grades. Pooling their effort will save time, add variety, and enhance the teaching in that school. The examples of exercises below were designed by teachers in grades three through five in one elementary school. These were then made available to all teachers.

1. What is the meaning of the words that are underlined? Write "same" before the sentence which explains the underlined words.

    a. Father said: "I was walking through the park and Mr. Brown gave me a lift."
    _____picked father up in his arms.
    _____lifted father off the ground.
    _____gave father a ride home.

2. Finish the sentence with the one group of words (phrases) that makes the best meaning.

    a. The stones in the showcase were _____.
    as big as watermelons.
    as high as a mountain.
    as shiny as diamonds.

3. Can you tell in your own words what each of the following expressions means? If any puzzle you, ask the teacher for help.

    a. A wolf in sheep's clothing.
    b. Keep the wolf from the door.
    c. Flew into a rage.
    d. The ship was watertight.

Analyzing and dramatizing stories

Some stories need to be analyzed and discussed. The discussion should not be conducted from the standpoint of "who remembers something from the story" but by skillfully leading the children to see how the author is able to picture each character and show the type of person he is, how he conveys the characters' attitudes toward each other and toward themselves, how the reader is led to see the difference between unkindness and thoughtlessness, to see how people feel after making mistakes, what they do about them, and why it is not always possible to do exactly what one wants. Analysis of stories is not a testing period or a time for the recitation of facts. Analysis should lay the foundation for the type of insight Emily Dickinson developed before she could write, "There is no frigate like a book to bear us lands away."

Dramatizing stories or incidents from stories helps children develop understanding, imagination, and appreciation. To dramatize a story or scene, children must read the material critically and understand the author's purpose and the feelings he wishes to convey. In the dramatization these would find expression through tone of voice, emphasis, gesture, facial expression, and the like. In selecting material to be acted out, children will have to make correct judgments on the dramatic potential of various stories or situations. A story about a man lost on a mountain might be extremely interesting reading, but it is not well-suited to a third grade dramatic production. One drawback is that only one character is involved.

Intonation as an aid to comprehension

Since intonation is discussed in detail in Chapter 9, we will focus here on techniques for helping children to develop acceptable intonation patterns in reading. Much has been written about the necessity for children who are learning to read to recreate the melody of spoken language.* This melody is determined by the reader's use of pitch, stress, and juncture (terminating the flow of speech). Teachers of reading have always posited a relationship between reading with "expression" and getting meaning. This concept is on the same continuum as Lloyd's statement *"The ability to relate the melody of speech to the written page is the key to good reading. Good readers do it; poor readers don't do it."***

Profiting from punctuation. In oral language, intonation is provided by the speaker. In decoding printed material, arriving at the proper intonation is primarily the responsibility of the reader. However, punctuation is a set of conventions by which the writer provides important cues to help the reader arrive at a proper interpretation. If these cues are not heeded by the reader, meaning is distorted or destroyed. The lack of ability to use punctuation in making reading a smooth and meaningful process appears with surprising frequency among impaired readers. Experience in working with poor readers indicates that this habit is not exceptionally difficult to eradicate. The ignoring of punctuation is one of the easiest defects to detect on any oral reading analysis, a fact which suggests that the importance of learning to use punctuation is underrated in reading instruction. The following techniques can help children understand the importance of punctuation.

1. One of the most effective methods of dramatizing the utility of punctuation is through the use of a tape recorder. The reader records a passage. On the playback, he follows the printed passage

---

*See statements by LeFevre, Lloyd, Tyler, et al in Chapter 9.
**Donald J. Lloyd, *Reading American English Sound Patterns*. Row, Peterson and Company, Monograph 104, 1962, p. 2.

as he listens to his recorded version. Errors are easily detected and insight comes a little easier when the child acts as his own critic.

2. *Punctuating sentences:* Duplicate a series of sentences which are ambiguous or whose meaning can be altered by use of punctuation. After several illustrations on the chalkboard, children can work independently.

Examples:

Father called Bill a touchdown.
"Father," called Bill, "a touchdown!"

A. That little girl said her mother is hungry.
   (Punctuate B so that the little girl is hungry.)
B. That little girl said her mother is hungry.

A. The policeman said his brother should get the reward.
   (Punctuate B so that the "brother" is talking. Who should get the reward now?)
B. The policeman said his brother should get the reward.

A. The newspaper said the mayor is a bit confused.
   (Punctuate B so that the mayor is critical of the newspaper.)
B. The newspaper said the mayor is a bit confused.

A. The doctor said his friend is ill.
   (Punctuate B to show the doctor is ill.)
B. The doctor said his friend is ill.

A. The dog said John is barking again.
   (Punctuate B so that John stops barking.)
B. The dog said John is barking again.

3. Another procedure is to deliberately displace punctuation in a passage and thus illustrate how the meaning becomes lost. The same passage can be reproduced several times with varying degrees of distortion. The pupil sees how difficult it is to get meaning from a passage so treated. In the following three paragraphs, the first version completely obscures the meaning, the second version is frustrating but not impossible, and the third is reproduced correctly.

How Punctuation Helps the Reader

Billy listened, carefully as the teacher. Explained how punctuation helps. The reader commas periods exclamation marks and question marks? All help a reader get meaning. From the printed page. Billy wondered what would happen. If the printer got the punctuation marks mixed. Up it was hard for him to imagine. What this would do to a story.

Billy listened carefully as the teacher explained. How punctuation helps the reader. Commas periods, exclamation marks and question marks all help. A reader get meaning from the printed page. Billy wondered. What would happen if the printer got the punctuation marks mixed up. It was hard for him to imagine what this would do. To a story.

Billy listened carefully as the teacher explained how punctuation helps the reader. Commas, periods, exclamation marks, and question marks all help a reader get meaning from the printed page. Billy wondered what would happen if the printer got the punctuation marks mixed up. It was hard for him to imagine what this would do to a story.

Choral reading

Choral reading offers many potential virtues, one of which is helping children develop good intonation in oral reading. Obviously, it is hoped that as they hear and use good models of intonation this skill will transfer to silent reading and enhance their ability to read for meaning.

Choral reading should not be thought of as an activity reserved for expert readers. It can and should be used at various instructional levels and for a variety of goals. The reading ability of the participants simply determines the materials which might be used successfully. For example, a teacher discovered quite by accident that choral reading had extremely high motivational value for her third grade class. She was showing a text-film of a story that the class had not read before. Each frame consisted of an attractive picture in color and two or three lines of text. She normally would call on individual children to read this material but would occasionally say, "Let's all read." The response was so enthusiastic that she printed on chart paper poems such as "The Wind," "Watching Clouds," "Railroad Reverie," "The Owl and the Pussy Cat," "Hold Hands," or any number of limericks. Later she prepared duplicated sheets which contained several pieces of material appropriate for choral reading. She observed that choral reading was always the motivational peak of the day's activity.

In addition to the fact that it is an enjoyable activity, other values of choral reading are often cited:

1. It is a good technique for getting all children to participate.
2. Can be a means of motivating children to want to read. The shy child or the poor reader is not likely to experience failure or frustration in this type of group reading experience.

3. Provides an opportunity to teach good pronunciation and reading with expression.
4. Permits the use of different materials for emphasizing different objectives such as phonic analysis, profiting from punctuation, and proper phrasing.
5. Can be a creative experience since children can suggest different ways a poem or passage can be interpreted.
6. Helps develop an appreciation for fine literature or poetry.

Oral reading

Instruction in oral reading must be considered in light of the purposes for which it is used, the materials used, and how it is incorporated into the total reading program.

Opinions as to the relative value of teaching oral reading have changed considerably during the present century. At one time oral reading was widely practiced without much attention to the justification of the classroom procedures that were followed. Oral reading was equated with the school's reading program. The term *oral reading* may call to mind children in a circle reading round robin from the same book with each child in the group reading silently along with, behind, or ahead of the child performing orally. The poorer reader took his turn along with the rest and sighed, mumbled, and coughed his embarrassed way through the allotted paragraph.

The evils that result from a particular educational practice may be remembered long after the practice has either been discontinued or substantially modified. In some cases oral reading was overemphasized and children spent most of their time reading aloud. As a result, they read slowly, putting all the emphasis on the mechanics of reading and little emphasis on meaning. Gray (16) tells of a boy reading a long passage orally. He read with expression and good interpretation. The teacher asked him a question about the content of what he had just read. His reply was that he could not answer because he "wasn't listening."

Another abuse was that oral reading was often advanced as an end in itself rather than a means to several desirable ends. Oral reading was practiced in artificial situations with little thought given to creating a true audience situation. As these abuses were pointed out in the literature on teaching reading, a reaction against oral reading took place. The disadvantages and potential weaknesses were stressed to the point where many teachers may have thought that the issue was oral reading versus silent reading, rather than the *intelligent use* of oral reading. At the moment, the most popular position is the middle ground which embraces the position that a proper balance should be maintained between silent and oral reading. It is difficult to argue with the logic of this latter position; nevertheless, it is almost impossible to find what constitutes a proper balance. What is adequate and desirable for one teacher with a particular class may be an improper diet in another situation.

Teachers of beginning reading will use oral reading for a number of purposes, and its values can be found in many natural classroom situations. The most common situation is one in which a child reads aloud in order to convey information or pleasure to an audience of his classmates. Regardless of the situation, oral reading can be justified only when the purposes are logical, the goals educationally sound, and the preparation adequate to the occasion. There is much written in teacher's manuals about the preparation of students for reading tasks, but there are no reading tasks which make more justified demands for adequate preparation than does oral reading.

Reading in an audience situation can be an ego-building experience for the reader. Personal and social growth as well as self-confidence can be achieved. But the child must be able to read satisfactorily in order to elicit approval from others, and he should not be expected to read to a group unless adequately prepared. Furthermore, having one child read aloud from a book while others follow the same passage in their book minimizes the audience situation. Oral reading should, insofar as possible, make use of materials other than basal series used for instructional purposes with the class.

Oral reading can be an excellent means of teaching reading skills such as good phrasing, use of punctuation, reading with expression, and fluent reading without hesitations or repetitions. Oral reading is a logical extension of the language usage characteristic of children as they enter school. Practice in oral reading can help the child associate printed words with their speech equivalents.

It is often stated that oral reading provides an excellent opportunity for the diagnosis of reading skills and the discovery of pupils' reading weaknesses. This diagnostic function is a pupil-teacher situation centered around a teacher purpose and probably would not involve the child's reading to a group. It could be argued that this is not a true oral-reading situation since pupil purpose, informing an audience, is not paramount. However, reading to the teacher is a highly motivating situation for most children, providing the teacher is encouraging rather than critical.

It cannot be denied that oral reading provides many clues to the actual weakness in a child's reading. A child's response after reading silently may indicate that he is a poor reader, or that he is performing below a certain grade level. Such a diagnosis may not disclose *why* the child reads poorly. If the teacher can *hear* and *observe* the child's reading, she can discover important clues to his competence in sight vocabulary, attacking unknown words, use of context, use of punctuation, and whether he views reading as getting meaning. The teacher will not rely on only one sample of oral reading as an adequate diagnosis, but each instance of oral reading will be seen as a part of an ongoing diagnosis.

It is generally agreed that oral reading is a more difficult task than silent reading. Kovas (21) emphasizes this, pointing out that in oral reading the reader must know all the words and must get the author's point and mood so that he can convey it to the listeners. To do this he must use proper phrasing, paying heed to punctuation, while at the same time reading loud enough to reach all his listeners. Children will inevitably face situations which call for reading aloud. Since almost all purposeful oral reading takes place in a social setting, these instances will be important to the reader whose performance will place him in the position of being judged by others.

In summary, the following considerations should be observed when using oral reading:

1. The reader must have a purpose for the oral reading. He must have interesting data which he wishes to share with others.

2. The reader must be prepared. He must have mastered the mechanical skills required and have arrived at an acceptable interpretation of the author's intent.

3. Children are not always well-trained to *listen*. When children cannot listen critically, the primary justification for oral reading is missing.

4. Instruction during the oral reading itself will usually destroy the value of oral reading.

5. Too much oral reading can diminish its effectiveness. The stress should be on good oral reading, not on an endurance contest for either readers or listeners.

6. Oral reading must not become so artificial or mechanical for the reader that he forgets that he is reading for meaning.

7. The teacher should be ready to provide a good model of oral reading when such a model is needed by the group or an individual child.

8. It should be remembered that the larger the group involved, the more the problems.
9. Oral reading may be a considerable threat to some pupils. These cases should be handled with sympathetic understanding.

Summary

Reading instruction in the primary grades is a challenge to teachers because successful readers must utilize a great number of skills concommitantly. Any child who is deficient in one or more essential skills will be error-prone in his reading. Errors made while reading tend to produce other errors, the cumulative effect of which is to impair the child's self-confidence and influence his attitude toward reading. Undetected weaknesses result in a child reinforcing whatever bad habits he has at the moment.

Thus, in order to provide pupils with the instruction they need, it is essential to achieve a thorough diagnosis of each child's reading achievement. Diagnosis as the basis for a program is quite essential at this instructional level because children are going through a stage of rapid development and are entering into independent reading. Furthermore, the curricular materials are designed based on the assumption that pupils have achieved a certain level of competence in reading.

In the primary grades children meet a number of concepts in reading which are strange or unknown to them. They encounter an increasing number of words not in their sight vocabulary, a fact which calls for a higher level of word recognition skill. The accelerated pace at which new tasks are introduced makes it essential that sound principles of teaching reading be followed. Growth in reading must be treated as developmental. Practically all skills previously taught must now be reinforced and extended. Mechanical and comprehension skills must be developed simultaneously and at a rate of growth which is considerably beyond that found in beginning reading. To prevent both gaps in learning and overemphasis of particular skills, instruction must be systematic and planned.

The primary grades are a period in which children's experience with reading will mold their later attitudes and reading habits. Great damage can be done to some children by expecting them to read materials which at the moment they are incapable of handling. Other children may form mal-attitudes if they are forced to perform mechanical activities when they are capable of wide and extensive reading for pleasure and profit. Thus, a successful program in the primary grades, probably as much as at any instructional level, depends on the right combination of instruction in all facets of reading.

YOUR POINT OF VIEW?

Would you defend or attack the following premises? Why?

1. Oral reading has little educational value in the primary grades.

2. One of the strengths of American schools is their success in arousing and maintaining pupil interest in recreational reading.

3. Recently, reading instruction has tended to focus more on materials and methodology than on "the child as a learner."

4. A child made normal progress in beginning reading, but is now experiencing considerable difficulty in reading in grade two. The most tenable hypothesis as to his problem is that he has failed to master letter-sound relationships.

5. When a child in the primary grades is not making expected progress in reading, more instruction time should be devoted to reading even if this involves less time for other established areas of the curriculum.

Respond to the following problems:

1. Select the one variable below that you think is the most important factor in producing low achievement in the primary grades. Defend your choice.
   a. The child's inability to work effectively in a group situation.
   b. Negative self-concept and expectation of non-success.
   c. Disparity between school tasks and home-neighborhood experiences.

2. Assume it is established that third grade social studies textbooks are more difficult to read than are third grade basal readers. What factors might account for this?

BIBLIOGRAPHY

1. Austin, Mary C. and Coleman, Morrison, *The First R: The Harvard Report on Reading In Elementary Schools.* New York: The MacMillan Company, 1963, 19–20.

2. Balow, Bruce and James Curtin, "Ability Grouping of Bright Pupils," *Elementary School Journal* (March 1966), 321–27.

3. Balow, Irving H. "A Longitudinal Evaluation of Reading Achievement in Small Classes," *Elementary English* (February 1969), 184–187.

4. Brekke, Gerald W. "Actual and Recommended Allotments of Time for Reading," *Reading Teacher* (January 1963), 234–37.

5. Buelke, Eleanor, "The Drama of Teaching Reading Through Creative Writing," *Reading Teacher* (January 1966), 267–72.

6. Byers, Loretta, "Pupils' Interests and the Content of Primary Reading Texts," *Reading Teacher* (January 1964), 227–33.

7. Cohen, Dorothy H. "Word Meaning and the Literary Experience in Early Childhood," *Elementary English* (November 1969), 914–925.

8. Cox, Donald R. "Criteria for Evaluation of Reading Materials," *The Reading Teacher* (November 1970), 140–145.

9. Cushenbery, Donald C. "Two Methods of Grouping for Reading Instruction," *Elementary School Journal* (February 1966), 267–72.

10. Dykstra, Robert, "Summary of the second-grade phase of the Cooperative Research Program in Primary Reading Instruction," *Reading Research Quarterly* (Fall 1968), 49–70.

11. Ekwall, Eldon E. and Ida Bell Henry, "How To Find Books Children Can Read," *The Reading Teacher* (December 1968), 230–32.

12. Endres, Raymond J. "Humor, Poetry, and Children," *Reading Teacher* (January 1966), 247–52.

13. Frame, Norman, "The Availability of Reading Materials for Teachers and Pupils at the Primary Level," *Elementary English* (March 1964), 224–30.

14. Froese, Victor, "Word Recognition Tests: Are They Useful Beyond Grade Three," *The Reading Teacher* (February 1971), 432–38.

15. Gates, Arthur I. "The Word Recognition Ability and the Reading Vocabulary of Second- and Third-Grade Children," *Reading Teacher* (May 1962), 443–48.

16. Gray, Lillian, *Teaching Children To Read* (3rd ed.). New York: The Ronald Press, 1963, 276.

17. Gray, William S. *On Their Own in Reading* (rev. ed.). Chicago: Scott, Foresman & Company, 1960.

18. Grosbeck, Hulda, *The Comprehension of Figurative Language by Elementary Pupils: A Study of Transfer.* Unpublished Doctoral Thesis, Oklahoma University, 1961.

19. Harris, Albert J. "Key Factors In A Successful Reading Program," *Elementary English* (January 1969), 69–76.

20. Holmes, Elizabeth Ann, *Children's Knowledge of Figurative Language*. Unpublished Masters Thesis, Oklahoma University, 1959.

21. Kovas, Helen, "The Place of Oral Reading," *Elementary English* (November 1957), 462–66.

22. Lloyd, Bruce A. "Helping The Disabled Reader at the Elementary Level," in *Reading and Realism*, J. Allen Figural (ed.), Proceedings, International Reading Association, 13, Part 1, 1969, 171–76.

23. McCracken, Robert A. "Using Reading As a Basis for Grouping," *Education* (February 1964), 357–59.

24. MacDonald, James B. and James D. Raths, "Should We Group by Creative Abilities?" *Elementary School Journal* (December 1964), 137–143.

25. Manning, John C. "Eclectic Reading Instruction for Primary Grade Success," in *Reading and Realism*, J. Allen Figural (ed.), Proceedings, International Reading Association, 13, Part 1, 1969, 332–37.

26. Martin, John E. "Guidelines for Planning Special Reading Facilities," *The Reading Teacher* (December 1970), 203–208.

27. Otterman, Lois M. "The Value of Teaching Prefixes and Word Roots," *Journal of Educational Research* (April 1955), 611–16.

28. Painter, Helen W. "Critical Reading In The Primary Grades," *Reading Teacher* (October 1965), 35–39.

29. Personke, Carl R. "The Listening Post in Beginning Reading," *Reading Teacher* (November 1968), 130–135.

30. Raven, Ronald J. and Richard T. Salzer, "Piaget and Reading Instruction," *The Reading Teacher* (April 1971), 630–39.

31. *Reading Teacher* (March 1970). Entire issue devoted to primary reading.

32. Robinett, Ralph F. "An Interdisciplinary Approach To Oral Language and Conceptual Development: A Progress Report," *Elementary English* (April 1971), 203–08.

33. Stauffer, Russell G. "Certain Convictions About Reading Instruction," *Elementary English* (January 1969), 85–89.

34. Vite, Irene W. "Grouping Practices in Reading," *Elementary English* (February 1961), 91–103.

11

Individualizing
Reading Instruction

A history of American education dealing primarily with classroom practices would be in essence a history of the attempts to deal with pupil differences. The first publicly supported schools in America were one-room rural schools which housed pupils of all ages and achievement levels. Out of necessity and logic, teachers in the one-room schools divided the total class into smaller groups of students; groupings being based roughly on reading ability, chronological age, or both. While the teacher taught one group, the remaining pupils worked at their desks in preparation for recitation.

As urbanization gained momentum, school enrollments grew larger. This necessitated establishing several classrooms within a school, each of which was presided over by one teacher. When multiple classroom-teacher units existed under one roof, pupils could be assigned to different classrooms on the basis of any one of a number of criteria.

Pupils entered school on the basis of chronological age, and it was easy to discern differences between pupils of widely divergent ages. This perception gave rise to questions such as, "When there are a number of classrooms in a building, why should each room contain pupils ranging from six to thirteen or fourteen years of age? Why not group pupils in such a way as to reduce the wide age and achievement differences?"

Thus, the graded system replaced the totally heterogeneous class-room. The theory on which the graded system rested was that pupils would move upward through the grades on the same basis as they entered school — chronological age — and further, that pupils exposed to the same instruction for a school year would be similar in achievement at the end of that period. Therefore, all children would be equally ready to move to the next higher level of instruction.

With such an organizational pattern in the school, it was logical that learning tasks were arranged on an ascending scale of difficulty. The formal curriculum evolved into a "sequence of tasks" which were placed at particular levels or grades. Once there was a general agreement as to sequence and grade placement of tasks, graded instructional materials were developed so that over the years instruction became more and more dependent on such materials.

It was soon discovered that differences among pupils of a given chronological age were so great that a fixed curriculum was not effective for all pupils. As a solution to this problem, non-promotion was tried. Students who had not mastered necessary skills to do satisfactory work in the next grade were held back a year. It has been estimated that during one period of our history between 20 and 25 percent of all students reaching the sixth grade had been retained in a grade at least once. Non-promoted pupils simply went through the same educational experience with the same teacher. This solution to the problem had little salutary effect upon the non-promoted child. It gradually became apparent that non-promotion was indefensible for it emphasized failure and made it visible to all. In this sense it was a form of punishment which could, and often did, effect the child's chance of returning to a normal growth pattern.

It was then reasoned that practically all children should continue through the graded system with their age-group peers. This practice, called "social promotion," caused further confusion by moving a child to a higher grade in which mastery of prescribed learning tasks was dependent upon skills which he had not previously acquired. Inevitably this also doomed the child to failure.

Over the years a number of approaches have been inaugurated in an attempt to deal with pupil differences. In the past fifty years, instructional and administrative innovations have been numerous. These include the Dalton and Winnetka plans; activity-related programs; the experience approach utilizing experience-derived materials; homogeneous and ability grouping; non-graded schools; the

Joplin plan; the language experience approach; and programmed instructional materials.

Reports of the success of new approaches held out hope for reform. Once the initial enthusiasm began to wane, however, teaching tended to fall back on the old established order. Perhaps this occurs because *any* plan of individualizing instruction takes more skill and energy than simply treating a classroom of pupils as interchangeable parts. As Smith (29) noted, "It seems, however, that the seeds of these passing innovations lie dormant for a time and then spring up again in revised and better forms."

Each attempted reform started from sound premises and embraced commendable goals. No matter what plan was attempted, however, the school tended to gradually return to the graded system with its graded curricular materials. Treating a classroom of students as though all were alike in their instructional needs or present achievement inevitably results in poor teaching, simply because the premise is false.

Although the problem has remained unsolved, one favorable omen is the large number of reforms currently being proposed. Nevertheless there is danger that these proposals may be viewed as competing alternatives which must be either adopted in toto or rejected. Since schools, communities, and teachers differ radically, it is likely that no one plan would be equally good in all situations. Perhaps an *eclectic* approach (choosing practices and procedures from various approaches) would be best. (2) The following discussion centers on the individualized reading movement which, to many observers, has over the years broadened its appeal by curbing early tendencies toward proscription of materials and practices.

The Individualized
Reading Movement

During the 1950s, frustration with the *status quo* in reading instruction reached a new high, and the climate for change seemed particularly good. A new emphasis on gearing reading instruction to individual pupil's needs and interests evolved through a movement which came to be called *individualized reading*.

Proponents of this reform movement had enthusiasm and fervor, both of which were essential if change were to be achieved. Two educational practices in particular, the use of basal readers and grouping by ability, came under fire.

There is little question that certain indefensible practices were to be found in the use of basals and grouping. Some teachers over-relied on basal texts to the exclusion of other materials. When this occurred, reading and learning to read could easily be reduced to deadly routines. Some pupils who had the ability to move through basals fairly rapidly were kept with the group with the result that their reading was severely rationed. These students were asked to complete tasks, such as workbook exercises, which added nothing to their growth in reading because they could already do these things.

Children at the other end of the achievement continuum were kept reading the same primer and first reader for two or more years even though their progress was not improved by this repetition. Overreliance on basals (or any other material) implies less than optimum use of other instructional techniques and materials.

The other area of concern, that of dividing a class into three groups, took on the characteristics of a mechanical ritual unrelated to caring for individual differences and meeting individual needs. In some classrooms, children did read "round-robin," but poorer readers were not only embarrassed, but provided unacceptable models of oral reading for the remainder of the group. It was probably impossible to enjoy a story read under such adverse conditions. These practices were not inherent in the use of basals or grouping, but rather had grown as a result of teachers and school systems failing to be creative in teaching. In an effort to bring about reform, some proponents of change made sweeping indictments against basal materials and grouping practices. It is generally agreed that it would have been more logical to focus on the actual *abuses* of basals and achievement grouping which were found in classrooms rather than to attempt to proscribe them altogether. (32) Although extreme positions have been adandoned by most advocates of individualized reading, a few examples are cited here for historical perspective:

> "Individualized reading requires the complete abandonment of the basal reader and the basal reader system."

> "One source of bias in many critics (of individualized reading), it should be recognized in advance, is the intellectual and emotional involvement in authorship of basal series."

> ". . . it is everywhere reported that children who have disliked reading change their minds. It is reported that maladjusted

children change their attitudes and fit in with the group in other activities. Everywhere it is reported that the children do quantities of reading, not only the good readers but all of them."

"Seldom are two children ready to be taught reading from the same materials at the same time."

"First, we must admit that our group reading system is a rather dismal failure when it comes to teaching sounding."

No sound educational purpose can be served by making criticism the central issue for discussion, and such generalizations raised more questions than they settled. They caused some teachers to overlook the positive contributions offered by individualized reading. The potential dangers posed by such views have been mitigated as a result of moderation in the more recent criticism made by the very people who originally were most prescriptive.

Individual Reading Defined

Like so many terms associated with reading instruction, there is no universally accepted definition of individualized reading. The term includes both instructional practices and classroom organization. If one thinks of a *method* as embracing a set of materials which provide for the systematic teaching of necessary reading skills over a relatively long period of time, individualized reading does not qualify as a method.

As Jacobs (11) states, "In the first place, 'individualized reading' is not a single method, with predetermined steps in procedure to be followed." Brogan and Fox (3) concur, adding, ". . . the term refers to the variety of practices through which resourceful, sensitive teachers, working with and taking their clues from individual children, are helping each of them appropriately to move ahead in reading."

In one sense, individualized reading focuses on the child-as-reader more than the teacher-as-teacher. Reading is seen as an act of personal involvement which is synchronized with the child's growth and development. The emphasis on child growth is commendable, but many teachers who favor this approach find the literature vague as to how one achieves reading goals. One frequently finds statements such as, "individualized reading is a state of mind"; "a new attitude"; "a philosophy or a way of thinking about reading instruction."

It would be difficult, if not impossible, to provide a blueprint for instruction which rested on such commendable but vague attributes. As a result, as Larrick (14) points out, much of what has been written about individualized reading has tended to deal with organizational mechanics, "how many minutes per child, how to keep records, how to sign up for the books, how to manage the class." These problems, she believes, teachers can work out for themselves once they view reading as a personal involvement of pupils and once teaching ceases to be dominated by the demand to cover a stipulated content.

Individualized reading rejects the lockstep instruction which tended to become standardized within the framework of the graded system and traditional graded materials. However, with freedom from routine there comes the responsibility of replacing the routine with creative teaching. The success or failure of an individualized program rests almost exclusively with the teacher. She is free to develop a program, utilize a wide array of materials, diagnose pupils' needs, and teach skills utilizing any number of approaches. Thus, freedom for teacher innovation is one of the strengths of individualized reading, but it is also one of the reasons why it is difficult both to define and evaluate.

Over the years a number of practices have become associated with individualized reading. (26) These include self-selection of materials by pupils, self-pacing in reading, individual pupil conferences with the teacher, and emphasis on record-keeping by teacher, pupil, or both. One other notable characteristic is the absolute need for a wide variety of reading material in each classroom. This becomes mandatory if each pupil is to select books in which he is interested and which he can read.

Principles and Practices of Self-Selection

Self-pacing of reading and self-selection of reading materials are basic to the philosophy of individualized reading. Olson's (21, 22) writing is frequently cited as the basis for the emphasis on seeking, self-selection, and self-pacing. While these concepts are not new to education, the individualized reading movement has given them a new emphasis focused on reading instruction.

The principle underlying the advocacy of self-selection is psychologically sound. Since there are tremendous individual differences among pupils in a given classroom, there is little justification for assuming that different pupils' needs and interests will be met equally well by one basal series or a single text.

The efficacy of the practice of self-selection of reading materials is influenced by several factors. First, the child must have some interests he wishes to explore further. This ties the ego to the reading situation. Second, there must be materials available which fit his interests and which he can read independently.

The theory is that when these conditions are met, the child will seek out the materials which fit his needs, interests, and present reading level. If he selects wisely, he grows. Much depends on pupil success, and some proponents of seeking, self-selection, and self-pacing appear to have assumed that success is assured by this formula.

Carried to extremes, this idea of individualized reading can minimize the role of the teacher in guiding pupils to materials to the degree that self-selection almost becomes a fetish. There is some danger in attempting to close debate by re-asserting that "pupils, when permitted to do so, will select materials they can read." This may be true in a number of cases, but it is not an inevitable law of child behavior. As Spache (30) points out, many pupils have no felt need for reading, do not seek reading, have not ascribed any personally relevant values to reading, and are not "sufficiently insightful into their personal or social needs either to recognize their needs or to find solutions through the medium of reading."

Self-selection on the part of pupils is to a degree limited a priori by the fact that the teacher or some authority has previously chosen the one or two hundred books found in the classroom from among thousands which are available. This infringement on the principle of self-selection is not decried simply because we accept the gathering of materials as part of the teacher's role. Individualized reading and self-selection do not preclude the teacher from recommending books or guiding pupils toward certain materials, but this type of guidance does call for a high level of teacher competency. She must know the child's interest, his reading ability, and the difficulty level of materials if her suggestions are to help her pupils grow.

The factor of economy in the teacher-learning situation must also be considered. If after a period of "seeking" a child has not made a selection and settled down to reading, his behavior may indicate that he is not yet ready for self-selection. There is no evidence that a teacher praising a book or offering suggestions to pupils will result in undesirable psychological side effects. On the contrary, there is evidence that pupils respect teacher judgments and tend to be favorably disposed toward materials recommended by understanding teachers. With many pupils, self-selection can safely be tempered with guidance.

Teacher-Pupil Conference

The teacher-pupil conference is one of the major identifying features of individualized reading and is potentially one of its great strengths. This potential is realized only when the teacher is skillful in achieving desirable goals. The conference is a brief session in which the teacher gives her whole attention to one pupil so that he may express himself on a story which he has selected and read prior to the conference. The primary goal of the conference is to assure the child he has an appreciative audience.

The chief value of the conference is that it ties ego-satisfaction to the reading process. For a student to share his feelings about a book with his teacher is an excellent ego-building experience. If

the conference is to yield maximum pupil growth, however, the teacher must be more than a listener. If she is only a passive listener, the pupil will tend to standardize his role in the conference. The type of responses he makes the first time will tend to set the pattern for subsequent conferences. In addition to being an appreciative audience, the teacher must also assume some responsibility for helping the child develop a higher level of values and self-understanding, goals often best achieved through judicious questioning.

The structure and prevalent practices of most of today's schools are not conducive to close personal relations between teacher and pupils. Large classes, too many classes per day, and administrative and instructional busy work often stand as barriers between teacher and pupil. We extol creativity and yet teach to the "golden mean." We establish professional philosophy which stresses the importance of teaching to children's needs and interests, yet it is possible for a student to complete his formal education without ever having had ten minutes of a teacher's undivided attention.

The teacher-pupil conference is worthy of further consideration because it also has possible therapeutic value. The conference serves as a catalyst which helps to produce teacher-pupil rapport, a factor which is highly underrated in its influence on learning. For some pupils, the teacher's positive response to their reading is a stronger motivation than the actual act of reading itself. The skillful sympathetic teacher can provide this extrinsic reward while slowly moving the child toward accepting reading as its own reward. (33)

The conference provides the means by which the teacher can learn important facts about a child's psychological needs and the means he has adopted for fulfilling these needs. With this knowledge, the alert teacher is in a position to become a party to sound bibliotherapeutic practices. Discussing his reading with a respectful adult will help a child gain insights into his own problems and afford him examples of how others have met such difficulties. (24)

Preparing for the conference

The brief discussion which follows is not intended as a prescription for the only way to approach the teacher-pupil conference; rather, it is intended as a guide for forming one's own approach. Veatch has listed the factors which teachers may wish to consider in setting up conferences. (33)

1. As a general rule, the pupils inform the teacher when they feel ready to participate in a conference.

2. The teacher should be familiar with the book or story which a child plans to discuss.
3. Pupils are informed when and in what order they will be scheduled for the conference.
4. Provision must be made for all other pupils in the class to be engaged in some other meaningful activity. One suggestion is to have them selecting and reading books independently.
5. The teacher must be prepared to stimulate pupils through the use of questions. These should be questions that stimulate thought instead of asking only for factual information.
6. The class and teacher will have worked out some system for pupils to receive help pronouncing unknown words during their independent reading.

For helping students pronounce unknown words, a large number of possibilities exist. Some teachers permit the child to come to her and point out the troublesome word, and she whispers its pronunciation. If pupils do not abuse this privilege, it need not disrupt the teacher-pupil conference in progress. Other teachers feel that such interruptions detract from the intimate nature of the conference, and they appoint "helpers." These are the more proficient readers in the class who can usually help the other pupils.

Sperber (31) suggests that a seating arrangement be worked out so that the class falls into three groups, each containing one or more good readers. These better readers serve as resources for helping other pupils in the group with words they may not know as sight words.

On occasion an entire class may be involved in a writing assignment while the teacher is engaged in conferences. In one first grade classroom the children were observed while writing a letter to a classmate in the hospital. The teacher printed a dozen words on the board, explaining that these might be words the pupils would be using and that they could look at the board for help on spelling. The words were: *dear, Susan, hope, soon, well, sorry, you, love, sick, missed, get, school, from.* This selection of words anticipated a large percentage of the "spelling interruptions" which might have ordinarily occurred.

Another approach is to encourage pupils to "spell the words the way you think they are spelled." Such free writing exercises can have a diagnostic value for the teaching of spelling and the analysis of phonic skills.

Frequency and length of conferences

The related problems of length and frequency of conferences have received considerable attention. These matters are still the basis for questions from teachers. Although the individual conference is one of the key features of the movement which broke up the rigid stereotyped practices prevelant in reading instruction, there still has been a tendency for the thinking and writing about the conference to become somewhat fixed and formalized.

One of the problems has been that the length and frequency schedule will necessarily vary with the size of the class. A schedule which is logical for a classroom of 24 pupils will become unworkable with a class of 35 pupils. Furthermore, the length and frequency of the conference will also vary with different grade levels and different ability levels within the grade. A still further complicating factor is the difference found among readers themselves. The child who has read a story consisting of only several hundred words will probably not take as much sharing time with his teacher as the pupil who read *Charlotte's Web*.

Format of conference

Since the conference is a technique for dealing with individual differences, it should not acquire a "standardized format." There is always the possibility that teachers may develop the habit of treating the conference as a set ritual, tending to make the same remarks, ask the same questions, and follow the same procedures with each pupil time after time.

The conference is in one sense a teaching tool that varies with individual pupil needs; and a set formula is not desirable. In no sense is it necessary to think of all conferences as embracing the same procedures or lasting for the same duration. Some conferences might be exclusively a sharing time; others might be devoted to helping the child become oriented to the self-selection process. During a given week, a teacher may schedule nothing but 2–3 minute diagnostic conferences, planning on a minimum of two per pupil. Many teachers would be amazed at how much they can learn about a pupil's reading from such a practice.

In the case of a facile reader who needs little encouragement to read, a brief exchange between the teacher and pupil would suffice on some occasions. A word of praise, a question about whether there are still a number of books in the classroom that he wishes to read, and an offer of help when he needs it could be considered adequate, providing his previous conference was a full-fledged "sharing period."

Since the sharing-type conference is primarily an ego-building experience, it is obvious that some children will need more attention than others. Some pupils continually avoid a conference because reading is a threat rather than a pleasure. Unlike the good reader who fulfills his ego-needs through the success and enjoyment derived from reading, these pupils need constant encouragement.

Expansion of the role of the conference

Up to this point, the discussion about the teacher-pupil conference has been restricted to the goal outlined above — providing a time for the child to share a favorite reading passage with a very appreciative audience, his teacher. Questions have been raised, however, as to when and how other facets of instruction are to be included. Specific examples include the diagnosis of the pupil's reading and the teaching of needed skills.

In much of the more recent writing on individualized reading, both of these vitally important aspects of reading instruction have been included as activities of the teacher-pupil conference. It is obvious that the inclusion of diagnosis and teaching of skills change the nature of the conference, and the original purpose of the conference would of necessity be diluted. However, it should be kept in mind that this expansion of the role of the conference is not mandatory simply because it is suggested in the descriptive literature. Teachers who evolve other solutions for including diagnosis and skill teaching can still preserve the original intent of the teacher-pupil conference.

Meaningful class activities during the teacher-pupil conference

Individualized reading calls for a high degree of planning by the teacher, much of which will likely include pupil participation in outlining independent activities. Such activities are unlimited. The following brief listing is only illustrative. The tasks are not identified by grade level since many may be adapted to various levels. The listing includes class, group, and individual activities, covering skill development, recreational reading, reading in curricular areas, and creative activities.

1. Children select books or other reading materials. This will likely include browsing and sampling. Selection is followed by independent reading of materials.

2. Conducting library research for an individual or group report. Such activity may relate to a unit in some other subject.

3. Creative writing experiences might include writing original stories; poems; letters to a classmate in the hospital or one who has moved away; invitations to parents to visit school; a riddle composition to be read to the class during a period set aside for such activities.

4. Preparing art work such as:
   a. Drawing or pasting pictures in a picture dictionary.
   b. Drawing a picture to accompany a pupil-dictated, teacher-written story.
   c. Preparing posters or book covers to illustrate the high point in a book or story which the pupil has read.

5. Using workbook pages or teacher-prepared seatwork guides for the development of particular skills such as:
   a. A dictionary exercise which follows an introduction of a skill such as alphabetizing by initial letter, or by two or more letters, use of guide words, pronunciation guides, or syllabication.
   b. Word analysis skills (associating sounds with graphic symbols, noting compound words, abbreviations, and the like).
   c. Study skills involving effective use of parts of a book such as the index, table of contents, glossary, appendix, library card catalogue, reference materials.

6. Using an appropriate film strip with the entire class, a smaller group, or a pair of pupils. In each case, one pupil is appointed to move the frames.

7. Teaching and testing word meanings.
   a. Workbook pages or teacher-prepared seatwork may be provided.
   b. Children may work on "vocabulary building" cards or notebooks in which they write one or more common meanings for new or unknown words met in their reading.
   c. The teacher may place a list of words on the board. Pupils write as many sentences as possible, using a different connotation for the word in each sentence. Example: *Light* — light in weight; light as to color; light the fire; light on his feet; her eyes lighted up; light-hearted; etc.

8. Making a tape recording of a story. A group of 4–6 pupils may each read the part of one character. Practice reading

and the actual recording may be done in the rear of the classroom or in any available space in the building.

9. Testing or diagnostic activities may be arranged. The entire class or any size group may take a standardized test (or reading subtest); tests which accompany basal series; *My Weekly Reader* tests; or informal, teacher-made tests. These will be scored and studied for the diagnostic information they yield.

10. Preparing interest corners, bulletin boards; devising choral reading activities for later presentation to the class.

These represent only a few of the reading-related activities which can be used. Teachers are limited only by their experience, creative ability, and the degree to which the pupils in their class have learned to function in independent activities.

Record keeping

Record-keeping receives considerable attention in the description of individualized reading programs. This term is not at all synonymous with diagnosis, although some aspects of diagnosis include record-keeping. For the most part, record-keeping has dealt with such items as listing the title of the book read; author; type of book (biography, fiction, myth, science, etc.); number of pages in the book; some notation as to difficulty level of the book; and the date the pupil began and finished the book.

When records consisting primarily of factors such as these are kept, they have limited diagnostic value. The teacher may note that a particular child reads nothing but fairy tales or stories about horses, or that a pupil consistently chooses easy books. Such information must be supplemented by observations which focus on the process of reading. Most records contain a column for teacher's comments such as the following: "needs help on phonic analysis"; "needs to read more smoothly"; "word attack poor"; "weak on developing sequence of a story." Such observations, however, are only the first step in the diagnostic process. Each is an invitation to a further diagnosis to ascertain why these reading behaviors are present.

The type of records under discussion can be prepared by the teacher, the individual pupil, or both. Many pupils enjoy keeping a log of books read. There is ego-building potential in seeing one's list of books grow. A note of caution is necessary, however; sometimes the pupils' listing of books can become the primary motive for reading. Thus, that which started out as an extrinsic motivator becomes intrinsic, and the child reads just to be reading and misses its primary purpose.

Also, if too much emphasis is placed on the number of books read, the competition of compiling a list may be detrimental to slower readers. They cannot keep pace with the more facile readers in the group. Lists of books read will be compared and low output can become a psychological factor which turns some children away from reading.

Neither of these potential weaknesses should be thought of as an inevitable outcome of pupil record-keeping. However, since one of the positive strengths of self-selection and individualized reading is that competition and comparison between pupils is avoided, the teacher must be alert to see that this potential strength is not lost.

Jacobs (11) differentiates between record-keeping and evaluation procedures noting that "appraisal is integral with teaching." Many teachers supplement the child's reading records with checklists or cumulative accounts of observed reading behaviors. Checklists of difficulties can take many forms, but usually they make provision for teacher's responses to a large number of skills and reading habits ranging from knowledge of sight words and sounding ability to use of study skills and reading interests. Figures 22 and 23, found on the following pages, are illustrative.

Problems Related to
Individualized Reading

Within the framework of individualized reading, some concepts are new and the procedures for achieving reading objectives are varied. This has given rise to a number of questions by teachers who are interested in this approach. It has been mentioned previously that despite the considerable amount of information available, there is no blueprint which outlines individualized reading as a total program.

In fact, divergent opinions and a multitude of procedures can be, and are, accommodated within the structure of individualized reading. The fact that the basic principles are so flexible has given rise to a number of questions such as: "What practices are included in individualized reading? How does one initiate an individualized program? What materials are needed? How does one take care of

FIGURE 22

Pupil Checklist (Skills)

NAME:_____

AGE:_____ GRADE:_____ DATE:_____

   I. *Basic Sight Vocabulary*   Test Used:_____
      No. of Words Tested_____No. of Words Missed_____
      Words Not Known_____

  II. *Difficulties Noted*
       __ Reads Word by Word   __ Easily Distracted
       __ Omits Words*   __ Guesses Words
       __ Poor Phrasing   __ Word Analysis Poor**
       __ Does Not Profit from   __ Errors Not Corrected
            Punctuation***
       __ "Service Words" Missed****   __ Little Help From
       __ (Other)   Context Clues
          *Examples:
        **Examples:
       ***Examples:
      ****Examples:

 III. *Study Skills and Effective Use of Textbooks*
      Understands and Effectively Uses:

	Yes	No	Comments
A. Index	_____	_____	
B. Table of Contents	_____	_____	
C. Glossary	_____	_____	
D. Appendix	_____	_____	
E. Card Catalogue	_____	_____	
F. (Other)	_____	_____	

the remainder of the class during individual conferences? How and when is diagnosis of pupils' needs included? What are the provisions for teaching needed skills?" These problems will be briefly explored with the understanding that the material presented is not a prescription to follow but merely a synthesis of the information available.

FIGURE 23

Comprehension Check List

NAME:_____

AGE:_____ GRADE:_____ DATE:_____

Book Title and Author:_____

Date Started:_____ Finished:_____ No. Pages:_____ Level:_____

Recall of Material Read
1. Level of Language Usage:
2. Following Sequence of Story:
3. Recall of Details: (unaided)_____
   with Questions:_____
4. Knowledge of Word Meanings (special connotations, figurative language, etc.)
   Examples Tested:_____
   _____
   _____
   _____

5. Examples of Pupil Responses:
   A. Describing Particular Character:
   B. Main Point of Story:
   C. Part Liked Best:
   D. Ability to Draw Inferences:
   E. Evaluation of Book (Does he recommend it highly — why or why not?):_____
   _____
   _____

   F. Ideas Expressed by Pupil:
6. Pupil Interest in Reading (teacher judgment):
7. Does pupil need guidance in selection of material?

Practices Included in Individualized Reading

As mentioned earlier, individualized reading does not have a universally accepted definition, and as a result questions have arisen as to what practices are included and excluded. Fortunately, there is less of this type of questioning now than a decade ago. At that time the majority of descriptive articles focused on a limited number of practices such as self-selection, self-pacing, teacher-pupil conferences, record-keeping, and the like. While these practices have obvious merits, many teachers declined to accept them as a total reading program.

The fact that some articulate proponents of various approaches opposed the use of basals, grouping, and other practices probably added to the confusion. Such suggestions tended to divide teachers into two camps, pro- and anti-individualized reading. The tendency to proscribe classroom practices has subsided in favor of a much broader and more inclusive base. There has never been any sound educational basis for questioning the need for individualized instruction. There are obvious reasons why there should always be room for a wide array of different practices for achieving this goal.

The either/or phraseology of "individualized *vs* grouping" never has represented a true dichotomy since neither represents a methodological approach. It was gradually recognized that individualized practices and grouping practices complemented each other and that they did not necessarily represent mutually exclusive teaching philosophies. (10) Indefensible practices can flourish under any label, and such practices should be eliminated without regard to philosophical or methodological loyalties. This tendency to move toward "middle ground" is based on the recognition that poor teaching is not inherent in any philosophy, set of materials, or administrative arrangements, but rather in the manner in which they are utilized. By the same token, no combination of philosophy and materials by themselves can make a school or classroom immune to poor teaching.

The tremendous differences found among teachers strongly suggest that they cannot achieve equally successful results using a given set of procedures. This, plus the fact that teachers work under vastly different circumstances and attempt to cope with vastly different pupil needs, militates against any a priori exclusion of teaching techniques and materials.

Thus, teachers A and B in schools I and II, which house pupils of quite different cultural and socio-economic backgrounds, may have developed excellent but quite different individualized reading programs. One would not ask the question, "Well, which program, A or B, is individualized?" or "Which comes closest to being individualized?" Such questions could arise only if there existed an agreed definition of individualized reading and a standardized list of accepted procedures.

If teachers A and B exchanged classrooms, it is likely that their respective programs might be less effective than the programs in their previous classroom environments. Individualized reading practices will vary because differences among teachers precludes all teachers being equally successful with a given technique or procedure. A teacher who has strong reservations about pupils keeping records of books read might at the moment be incapable of making this practice work effectively in her class. Another may use basals extensively with a group of pupils slow in developing sight vocabulary and use trade books extensively with another group.

Needed Materials

A reading program embracing self-selection and self-pacing and designed to meet individual pupil interests cannot function in a learning environment which does not include a wide array of reading materials. This should not be thought of as a special problem related only to the individualized reading. There is no justification for any classroom or school not meeting this criterion regardless of methodological approach or program. Therefore, the need for materials is not a unique feature of individualized reading but rather a factor which has been justifiably emphasized in this approach.

While there is little point in attempting to settle upon a fixed number of books which would be considered adequate, a minimum figure frequently mentioned is approximately one-hundred different trade-book titles per classroom. Assuming that the same hundred books should suffice throughout the year, a hundred books in a third grade would be totally inadequate.

Factors which must be considered include: grade level; range of interests and abilities of pupils; class size; whether books can be rotated with other classrooms; whether the school supports a central library; and whether the same materials are used extensively in other subject areas such as social studies and science in the preparation of units.

Materials should not be tightly equated with trade books alone, although these would likely be the major source. Classrooms should contain magazines, newspapers, various reading kits, *My Weekly Reader, Readers Digest* (Skill-Builder Materials), and most other reading materials children might choose to work with. Reading material would of necessity cover many areas such as biography, science, sports, exploration, hobbies, fairytales, medicine, space, poetry, humor, adventure, myths, and travel.

**Starting
a Program**

All elementary teachers are likely to be doing some things which
fit logically under the heading "individualization." Any of the
formal aspects of individualized reading such as self-selection or
individual conferences can be started with one pupil, a small group,
or the entire class. Obviously, the latter approach would present
the most problems; therefore, perhaps one should start with one of
the other alternatives.

The first prerequisite is, of course, the availability of materials;
and to this must be added the prerequisite that the child be able
to read some of these materials. A reading vocabulary of twenty
words is needed to handle a pre-primer, and with a few more words,
a reader could make the transition to similar materials in different
basal series. A sight vocabulary of fifty words and some ability
at sounding out words would permit a reader to start his first
trade book.

Within this ability range, a portion of the child's reading material
might well be individual stories dictated by the pupil and printed
by the teacher. This practice may be identified with the language-
experience approach, but its practice is not precluded in individualized reading. Commercial picture dictionaries and teacher-pupil-
prepared dictionaries would also be appropriate at this level.

Starting an individualized program by involving a small group
of the more proficient readers in the class is another logical way
to begin. This approach will present fewer organizational problems
than involvement of the entire class. The teacher begins by calling
together the students she has selected and explaining that she
would like them to select their own books to read at their desks
during the reading period.

Prior to this group conference, the teacher has gathered a number
of books and placed them on the reading table. She has been careful
to see that a number of "new books" are included and has deliberately included books which she thinks will appeal to the five or six
students in the group. There would be nothing wrong with calling
the children's attention to certain books.

She concludes the group conference with, "When you have
selected the book you wish to read, go to your desk and read it
silently; you may keep the book at your desk until you finish it.
For the rest of this week I am appointing Bill as a special helper.
If you come to a word you cannot sound out, you may ask Bill;
if he does not know the word, you should print it on one of these

cards along with the number of the page on which it is found. Sometime during the morning I will come to your desks and help you read the sentences which have the hard words."

These directions and explanations have taken only a minute or two. The teacher now turns her attention to the remainder of the class, explains a seatwork assignment to a portion of the class, and conducts a planned session on word-analysis techniques with a selected group of students. She will observe how the pupils function in the newly organized individualized group. Do they find a book in a reasonable length of time? Is it at a level they can handle? How does the "helper" manage — do the other pupils bother him for help so often that it interferes with his own reading? This information may call for adjustments and further clarification.

Within a day or two the teacher will again briefly assemble the pupils in the individualized group and explain that she would like to have each student tell her something about the book he is reading and for him to read to her a part of the book he particularly likes. In order to do this, she will schedule an individual conference with each pupil. Pupils are to tell her when they are ready for their conference, and she will schedule the time.

Providing for Diagnosis

Individualized reading is an organizational-instructional approach which by its very nature calls for considerable diagnosis if children are to progress smoothly in reading growth. Achievement of individualization may soon be thwarted for some pupils in the absence of on-going diagnosis. It is doubtful that such potentially excellent procedures as self-selection and self-pacing were ever envisioned to operate independently of diagnosis and teacher guidance.

In the absence of teaching built on diagnosis, pupils tend to reinforce whatever poor reading habits they have at present. The same mistakes will be made time after time, and it may be weeks before "self-correction" is worked out. One example is the case of a child who consistently miscalled a word throughout the entire length of a story. "In one class a child read a story about an old man and a 'termite' for four days. On the fifth day during his conference he discovered the word was 'turnip.' No wonder he had missed comprehension and the humor." (23)

There are no diagnostic techniques which are associated exclusively with individualized reading, nor are there any which need be thought to be foreign to it. The individual teacher-pupil conference may in some instances be a major source of diagnostic information, but the conference cannot be the only time and place where diagnosis takes place. Diagnosis must be on-going, and every reading activity in the classroom should be viewed as serving some diagnostic purpose. (8)

All seatwork, whether teacher-prepared or conventional workbook exercises, has diagnostic value. A student's spelling performance, both on formal weekly tests and in his creative writing, will give clues to his ability to associate letter sounds with letters and letter combinations. Brief informal tests may be developed for testing any facet of reading from recognition of words to understanding figurative language.

**Teaching
Reading Skills**

The early individualized movement was in part a reaction against reading instruction which often stressed individual skills at the expense of the "total reading process." In some classrooms, all pupils received the same instruction, worked on the same skill-building exercises, and read the same materials. When these practices were prevalent, there was room for suspicion that instruction was predetermined rather than based on pupil needs and abilities. Such uniform practices inevitably resulted in some children becoming bored with reading instruction, and thus there existed a need for reform.

Unfortunately, the attack on uniform skills instruction for everyone tended to spread to the teaching of skills per se. Actually, skills-teaching was not explicitly rejected, but this facet of individualized reading instruction was neglected. In recent years the importance of skills-teaching has been accepted by practically all proponents of individualized reading. But the vagueness as to how and when the teaching is incorporated into the program still lingers. Questions relative to teaching skills elicited two frequently repeated responses: 1. "Teach some skills in the teacher-pupil conference"; and 2. "Teach other skills as they are needed by the pupils."

The first answer suggests what is, on the whole, an uneconomical procedure, unless the child participating in the conference is the only one in the class who can profit from the instruction that is given. Any reading skill that can justifiably be taught to the entire class should be taught to the whole group. Those students who learn with the first presentation should be doing something else when subsequent presentations are made to pupils who did not learn. Assume that eventually only one child in the class has need for further instruction; provision is now made for him to receive it individually. This may be done by the teacher; a classmate may function for a few minutes as a "helper"; the materials may be on a filmstrip and the learner may operate the projector himself; or the child may work on a teacher-prepared worksheet or with a commercially prepared programmed lesson. Where reading instruction is integrated school-wide, the child may join five or six pupils from other classes, regardless of grade level, who have the same instructional need. This latter solution may fit under any one of a number of administrative titles such as "remedial reading," "modified Joplin plan," "ungraded primary," etc. The actual instruction may be provided by a full-time remedial teacher, a one-day-a-week teacher, a teacher aide, or a student teacher working under supervision.

The basic validity of the second response, "teach skills when they are needed," cannot be faulted, but it can be argued that it is both vague and difficult to implement when each child in the class is reading a different book. Concern for providing differentiation of skills-instruction need not start from the premise that no two pupils, or larger groups in a class, cannot profit from the same instruction or drill. This extreme position is simply the antithesis of the practice which implies that all children in a class *could* profit from the same amount of time spent with the same book. Reliance on diagnosis, not slogans, is the only safe way to resolve what is appropriate instruction.

There are dozens of abilities and habits which may be listed under the heading *basic skills*. The three major areas with which the elementary teacher must be constantly concerned are *word recognition, ability to sound out or pronounce unknown words, and the knowledge of word meanings*. This is true regardless of the materials used, organization pattern followed, or one's philosophy of teaching.

Conclusion

In the absence of eternal vigilance and the search for creative responses to existing problems, reading instruction tends to lose vitality and become stereotyped. In American schools the tendency toward standardized teaching practices has been accentuated by two factors: the grade level system and the overreliance on graded instructional materials. Individualized reading represents a new emphasis on evolving classroom practices which fit individual pupil needs.

Seeking to find means of individualizing instruction is evidence of the awareness of pupil differences. Such awareness is absolutely essential to a sound reading program. However, what one does in actual practice as a result of this perception may or may not be sound.

In the early stages of the movement, lines were somewhat closely drawn as to what practices were included and which were proscribed. As Miel stated, "With any way of teaching which is hailed as promising there is always the danger that formalism will set in and that essential features of the proposal will be distorted in well-meant attempts to popularize the idea and secure wide-scale trial of it."*

An effective individualized reading program of necessity must rest on a rather broad base. It may include, but cannot be limited to, children selecting books, reading these at their own rate, and occasionally reporting to the teacher on their reading. Individualized reading does not exclude practices which may be thought of as integral parts of other instructional approaches.

Any instructional program must include the teaching of all facets of reading. A few examples are study skills, word-recognition techniques, library research techniques, integration of reading instruction with other subject-matter, expansion of meaning vocabulary and concepts, and appreciation of poetry and literature. These are essential skills, and they should be taught. This position is not rejected by those who advocate individualized reading. But the details of how and when such essentials are to be taught have not been carefully delineated.

It also must be remembered that both the virtues and defects ascribed to individualized reading are potential and not inherent in the approach. The achieving of potentials and the avoidance of pitfalls is exclusively a function of individual teachers in specific classroom situations. This is not unique to individualized reading. Precisely the same conditions hold for *any* method or instructional framework.

---

*Alice Miel, ed., *Individualizing Reading Practices*, Bureau of Publications, Teachers College, Columbia University, VI (1958).

Many authorities feel that individualized reading instruction calls for relatively high teacher competence. It is likely that this hypothesis is well-grounded. One reason for this would be that with the exception of self-selection, self-pacing, and the teacher-pupil conference, few concrete procedures have been spelled out in the system. Individualized reading lacks the structure that is found in the teacher's manuals of basal series.

Assuming this rationale is fairly accurate, it would appear we are faced with a paradox. The greatest potential weakness of individualized reading is that it lacks a blueprint for instruction, but blue-print-type structure leads to stereotyped unimaginative teaching, which was the chief factor in the rise of the individualized movement.

The implication is clear. Teachers who fit this analysis failed to recognize indefensible practices as poor instruction. Further, there is a suggestion that these teachers lack the training and insights necessary to function under the high degree of freedom and the resultant responsibility which is an integral feature of individualized reading. The conclusion seems warranted that training in reading instruction has not reached the degree of competency that our society should expect at this point in the twentieth century.

YOUR POINT OF VIEW?

Respond to the following problems:

1. A certain school has been using the Individualized Reading Approach for a number of years. A study of children's reading performance led to the conclusion that "children seem to be reinforcing a number of poor reading habits." What sound principles of instruction would you hypothesize are being neglected in this program?

2. Assume a teacher knew a great deal about a particular pupil (reading level, interests, instructional needs, etc.). Would pupil-self-selection of reading material be inherently superior to this teacher's suggestions relative to appropriate reading materials?

3. Assume you wish to set up an ideal individualized reading program. Which of the following materials would you feel free to use?

Trade books	Basal readers
Experience charts	Individual teacher-written
My Weekly Reader	stories
Programmed reading materials	Workbooks

Assume you are a first grade teacher and that you are free to use only three of the above types of material. Which three would you choose?

Assume you are a sixth grade teacher, would your choices remain the same?

Defend or attack the following statements.

1. Any practice which leads to children reading appropriate material would fit under the label individualized reading instruction.

2. Most of the individualized reading programs which have been described have more efficacy for better readers in a class than for poorer readers in the group.

3. It is impossible to establish and maintain an individualized reading program in the absence of individual teacher-pupil conferences.

BIBLIOGRAPHY

1. Ashley, L. F. "Children's Reading Interests and Individualized Reading," *Elementary English* (December 1970), 1088–1096.

2. Blakely, W. Paul and Beverly McKay, "Individualized Reading as Part of an Eclectic Reading Program," *Elementary English* (March 1966), 214–20.

3. Brogan, Peggy and Loren K. Fox, *Helping Children Read*. New York: Holt, Rinehart & Winston, Inc., 1961, 5.

4. Burton, William H. and Joseph Ilika, "Some Arguments About Reading," *Education* (March 1964), 387–92.

5. Bush, Clifford and Mildred H. Huebner, *Strategies for Reading in the Elementary School*. New York: The Macmillan Company, 1970.

6. Duker, Sam, "Masters Studies of Individualized Reading II," *Elementary English* (May 1970), 655–60.

7. Eisenhardt, Catheryn T. "Individualization of Instruction," *Elementary English* (March 1971), 341–45.

8. Evans, Robert, "Teacher Evaluations of Reading Skills and Individualized Reading," *Elementary English* (March 1965), 258–60.

9. Fay, Leo, "Basic Reading Skills," *Education* (September 1961), 10–12.

10. Hunt, Lyman C., Jr. "A Grouping Plan Capitalizing on the Individualized Reading Approach," in *Forging Ahead In Reading*,

J. Allen Figurel (ed.), Proceedings, International Reading Association, 12, Part 1, 290–95.

11. Jacobs, Leland B. "Individualized Reading Is Not a Thing," in *Individualizing Reading Practices*, Alice Miel (ed.), Bureau of Publications, Teachers College, Columbia University, 1958.

12. Johnson, Rodney H. "Individualized and Basal Primary Reading Programs," *Elementary English* (December 1965), 902–04.

13. Karlin, Robert, "Some Reactions to Individualized Reading," *Reading Teacher* (December 1957), 95–98.

14. Larrick, Nancy, "Individualizing The Teaching of Reading," in *Reading, Learning and The Curriculum*. Proceedings of the Twelfth Annual Reading Conference, Lehigh University, Bethlehem, Pa., 1963, 35–38.

15. Metzler, Helen, "Providing for Individual Differences In Reading," *Improvement of Reading Through Classroom Practice*. Proceedings, International Reading Association, 9, 1964, 95–96.

16. Miller, Janet S. "Individualized Instruction," *Elementary School Journal* (April 1966), 393–96.

17. Miller, Wilma H. "Organizing a First Grade Classroom for Individualized Reading Instruction," *The Reading Teacher* (May 1971), 748–52.

18. Morrison, Coleman, "Individualized Reading: Some Unanswered Questions," *Improvement of Reading Through Classroom Practice*, International Reading Association Proceedings, 9, 1964, 93–94.

19. Morrison, Virginia, "Teacher-Pupil Interaction in Three Types of Elementary Situations," *The Reading Teacher* (December 1968), 271–275.

20. Odom, Sterling C. "Individualizing a Reading Program," *The Reading Teacher* (February 1971), 403–10.

21. Olson, Willard C. *Child Development*. Boston: D. C. Heath and Company, 1949.

22. ———, "Seeking Self-Selection and Pacing in the Use of Books by Children," in *Individualizing Your Reading Program*, Jeannette Veatch. New York: G. P. Putnam's Sons, 1959.

23. Putnam, Lillian R. "Controversial Aspects of Individualized Reading," *Improvement of Reading Through Classroom Practice*. International Reading Association Proceedings, 9, 1964, 99–100.

24. Reeves, Harriet Ramsey, "Individual Conferences-Diagnostic Tools," *The Reading Teacher* (February 1971), 411–15.

25. Sartain, Harry W. "What Are the Advantages and Disadvantages of Individualized Instruction?" in *Current Issues In Reading*,

Nila Banton Smith (ed.), Proceedings, International Reading Association, 13, Part 2, 1969, 328–43.

26. Sipay, Edward R. "Individualized Reading: Theory and Practice," *Children Can Learn To Read — But How?* Rhode Island College Reading Conference Proceedings, Providence, 1964, 82–93.

27. Sister Aloysius Clare Maher, "Individualizing The Teaching of Reading Through Tape Recordings," *Changing Concepts of Reading Instruction,* Proceedings, International Reading Association, 6, 1961, 179–81.

28. Smith, Nila Banton, *Reading Instruction for Today's Children.* Englewood Cliffs, N. J.: Prentice-Hall, Inc., 1963, Chapter 7.

29. ———, *American Reading Instruction.* Newark, Del.: International Reading Association, 1965, 378.

30. Spache, George D. and Evelyn B. Spache, *Reading In the Elementary School.* (Second ed.). Boston: Allyn and Bacon, Inc., 1969, Chapters 4 and 11.

31. Sperber, Robert, "An Individualized Reading Program In a Third Grade," *Individualizing Reading Practices.* Bureau of Publications, Teachers College, Columbia University, 1958, 44–54.

32. Sucher, Floyd, "Use of Basal Readers In Individualizing Reading Instruction," in *Reading and Realism,* J. Allen Figurel (ed.), Proceedings, International Reading Association, 13, Part 1, 1969, 136–43.

33. Veatch, Jeannette, "Self-Selection and the Individual Conference in Reading Instruction," *Improving Reading Instruction.* Joint Proceedings of Reading Conference and Summer Workshop, Vol. 1, The Pennsylvania State University, 1963, 19–25.

34. ———, "What Research Says About Individualized Reading," *Children Can Learn to Read — But How?* Rhode Island Reading Conference Proceedings, Providence, 1964, 94–101.

35. ———, *Reading in the Elementary School.* New York: The Ronald Press Company, 1966.

IV

Beyond Beginning Reading

The next four chapters deal with the instructional program for the intermediate and middle-school grades. Chapter 12 presents an overview of objectives and problems encountered at this level. Chapter 13 *Developing and Expanding Concepts* covers the elementary years with emphasis on the upper grades. Chapters 14 and 15 focus on teaching study skills and developing critical reading.

413

12

The Intermediate Grades — Problems and Challenges

The intermediate grades constitute one of the crucial instructional periods in the child's education. The curriculum for this period has developed out of a series of adult concepts and theories as to what children *should* be learning. Theory, however, often does not take into account all aspects of the learning situation. As a result some goals and classroom practices of the school fit children as we wish them to be, rather than as they actually are.

The intermediate grades coincide with a period in child development during which learning should be a natural, pleasurable experience. Unfortunately this highly desirable outcome is not achieved by the large majority of pupils in these grades. It is true that children will have acquired enough reading ability and related language tools to permit them to read on many topics and to develop background in some areas of interest. It is reasonable to expect them to be able to move at a more accelerated pace than they did in the primary grades.

However, the school and the culture which supports it seem somewhat impatient with learners at this stage of their development. This is exemplified by two facts. First, the curricular materials are often beyond the present reading ability of many pupils. Second, there is a diminished emphasis upon teaching the language tools which are needed for "mining" all subjects, and an air of urgency about having pupils accumulate facts in various subject areas.

The school has become a party to the utilitarian delusion that you can move children along the road to becoming scientists and mathematicians before they have acquired mastery of the language tools which are essential in these and all other academic areas. It is paradoxical that *reading instruction* in the intermediate grades suffers because of our inordinate respect for knowledge. It will be alleged that reading skills are also respected, yet no provision is made for assuring that pupils will have developed reading ability commensurate with the demands of the various content curriculums. (27)

Goals of Intermediate-Level Instruction

In addition to working with the skills introduced in the primary grades, the intermediate-level teacher must provide guidance in a large number of even more complicated reading tasks. The application of skills previously taught also becomes more complex. For instance, visual discrimination taught in beginning reading involves perception of structural differences between whole word symbols. In grade four, the child must perceive minute differences within words in order to use a dictionary. Also, getting meaning from context was relatively simple in beginning reading since the connotation of an unknown sight word was undoubtedly in the child's meaning vocabulary. In addition, the unknown sight word was probably the only new word on the page. In the intermediate grades a paragraph in a social science text may contain a number of new and difficult concepts as well as several unknown sight words.

The following objectives, while perhaps not including every facet of instruction, do provide a fairly representative picture of the breadth of the reading program in the intermediate grades.

1. Individual evaluation should take place to determine the capacity of students and the present level of achievement in all facets of reading including:

    a. sight word vocabulary
    b. word-attack skills
    c. level of silent reading
    d. meaning vocabulary and concepts
    e. ability to profit from listening situations including oral directions
    f. oral reading skills
    g. facility in finding information, use of reference materials
    h. work habits and attitudes
    i. rate at which curricular materials can be read

2. Following diagnosis, the teacher should devise a flexible reading program to take care of individual differences and needs revealed in the initial diagnosis.

3. Reading instruction must be deliberate and systematic. Inestimable damage to children can result from the philosophy that "children learn to read in the primary grades and read to learn at the intermediate level." They must do both at each level.

4. In addition to specific reading instruction per se, instruction must also be incorporated with the teaching of all subject matter. Children must be *taught to read* science, mathematics, health, and social science materials. It is not intended that reading instruction be seen or treated as dichotomous, but rather that items 3 and 4 be complementary parts of a total program.

5. The child should be helped to expand his stock of concepts. This is essential in all content areas.

6. Practice should be provided in various types of functional reading — in newspapers, magazines, and books — to supplement basic texts in subject areas.

7. Guidance should be supplied in reading for recreation, pleasure, and personal growth.

8. The child's reading interest should be widened to build a sound foundation for life-long personal reading activities.

9. Appreciation should be developed for good literature, poetry and drama.

10. A wide selection of materials should be made available in all fields — science, literature, biography, current events, social studies, and the like.

11. A program should be devised for guiding the growth of intellectually gifted children.

12. Children should be helped to increase the rate at which they can comprehend printed word symbols in combination. This

skill becomes increasingly important at this instructional level since the curriculum materials in the various content areas make ever-widening demands on readers.

13. Steps should be taken to improve critical reading skills such as:
    a. Coping with figurative or picturesque language
    b. Drawing inferences
    c. Classifying ideas and selecting those that are germane to the reader's purpose
    d. Evaluating ideas and arriving at the author's purpose or intent
    e. Detecting bias and differentiating between fact and opinion
14. The following reading-study skills should be developed and extended:
    a. Using books effectively — making maximum use of the index, table of contents, and appendix
    b. Acquiring facility in the use of a dictionary
    c. Using reference books effectively
    d. Understanding graphs, maps, charts, and tables
    e. Using library resources, card catalogue, and periodical indexes
    f. Note-taking and outlining materials for a given purpose
15. Diagnosis should be continuous and ongoing throughout each instructional year. An initial diagnosis serves only for initial procedures.

Instructional Problems at the Intermediate Level

The intermediate grades present a formidable challenge to the teacher of reading. The pitfalls are as numerous and as serious as those found at any instructional level. Academic failures and loss of interest in school occur because of certain instructional practices which actually inhibit rather than enhance pupil growth. The following major barriers to good instruction are discussed in this chapter.

1. Diminished emphasis on systematic teaching of reading skills.
2. Failure to deal with variability among pupils in regard to mastery of reading skills.

3. Inadequate integration of reading instruction with the teaching of content subjects.

A transition period

Teachers agree that ideally the process of learning to read progresses smoothly without perceptible breaks through a series of grade levels. There are certain factors in the total school framework, however, which cause many teachers to feel that an abrupt transition occurs between third and fourth grades. The end of the third grade and the beginning of the fourth is often designated as the period of "independent reading." There is evidence in classroom behaviors that some teachers do succumb to the philosophy that the intermediate grades should be characterized by a shift in emphasis from "learning to read" to "reading to learn" in the various subject-matter areas. The use of a number of non-integrated textbooks in various content areas tends to substantiate the idea that this is a transitional period.

These factors form the basis for the generalization that reading skills are taught in the primary grades and applied in the intermediate and later grades. A further generalization is that since reading skills are taught in the primary grades, children who have been through these grades have mastered the skills. It is true that once pupils reach the intermediate level they are expected to do more reading, grade by grade, while less time is devoted to the actual process of learning to read. A study of the relationship between reading ability and a language-factor intelligence test at all grade levels indicated, however, that the correlation between these measures was lowest at grade four. The authors posited a "fourth grade hump in reading" which may be accounted for by the increased difficulty of concepts, style of writing, and specialized vocabulary found in reading materials at this level. A second hypothesis was that this finding might reflect a decline in the systematic teaching of reading at the fourth grade level. (22)

Every instructional level in the school presents its own unique challenges to teachers. Undoubtedly it is not intentional that the intermediate grades constitute a break in the continuity of instruction in the elementary school. Nevertheless, the emphasis on separate textbooks in the various subject areas is one of the chief sources of instructional problems. These books call for a fairly high level of independent reading ability and special facility in a number of reading-study skills such as the ability to use the dictionary, reference materials, graphs, charts, and tables.

These curricular materials confront the reader with an ever-increasing number of unknown and relatively difficult concepts. (17) In addition, much more complex sentence structure and a variety of organizational patterns are found which frustrate many pupils. It is necessary to know many new and more difficult connotations for words met previously and to understand a large number of idiomatic and figurative expressions. The amount of reading which is required is suddenly increased, and pupils must develop the ability to read and comprehend at a more rapid rate. They must also develop flexibility in their reading to be able to adjust rate to both difficulty level and purpose. Instructional procedures for coping with these and other problems are discussed in the remainder of this chapter.

Learning to Read is a Long-Term Developmental Process

The structure of American education is embedded in, and influenced by, the grade level system. The development of curricular materials for use in all grades is to some extent patterned on growth gradients in all subject areas. An underlying premise of the graded system is that students finishing a given grade have mastered the language skills and concepts that will prepare them for the developmental tasks of the next grade.

The theory is sound, but in actual practice a large number of students in the intermediate grades have not mastered reading skills *commensurate with the tasks they will be asked to perform in these grades.* Another group of students may be fairly close to the expected growth level, but as months and years go by, they fail to *advance* in reading ability at a pace equal to the reading demands placed upon them.

The recognition of a problem is the first step in arriving at a solution. Unfortunately, the problem under consideration is so large and so complex that little progress has been made in alleviating it. Since there are no easy solutions, educators at various levels (elementary, junior high, secondary, and teacher training institutions) all live in the hope that some group other than themselves will tackle the problem and evolve a solution.

The statement of *how* we might solve the reading problem in our schools makes the task seem deceivingly simple: The solution would be: "we must systematically teach reading more effectively and more extensively than is our present practice." Achieving this goal, up to the present at least, has escaped us. No teacher or educational administrator at any educational level argues against the importance of reading ability; however, many have not as yet become personally involved in helping to devise programs and guidance in the development of reading skills in all areas of the curriculum. (25)

Undoubtedly, one of the causes of the problem is the failure of the teacher to understand the nature of the reading process. The purpose here is to discuss the developmental nature of reading. In recent years the statement, "Reading is a developmental process," has been repeated so often that it now sounds almost like a cliché. This concept deserves more respect and attention than it has received. "Reading ability is a developmental process" means that the very complicated process of learning to read is not mastered at any particular time such as age ten or twelve. Nor can it be assumed that the ultimate ability to read critically is achieved at any particular point on the educational continuum.

Thus, an adequate reader at grade three may be considerably less efficient at grade four and be in serious trouble by grade six. The statement implies recognition that the nature of human learning and the nature of the reading task precludes the possibility of mastering the reading process by a given chronological age or a designated number of years of formal schooling. The developmental aspect of various reading skills is discussed in the following section.

Illustrations of developmental skills

Reading is an integrated total response which is made up of a very large number of separate skills, abilities, memory patterns, and the like. Any of the dozens of reading skills could serve as an example of how growth must take place at higher levels of efficiency. Without attempting to determine how many separate skills go into reading, we can isolate a few and illustrate how each is developmental in nature.

Acquisition of sight vocabulary

The development of a sight-word vocabulary is probably one of the more obvious examples of what is implied by the term "developmental process." Instant recognition of words is a basic skill which is a prerequisite for reading at any level. Although it is true that mere recognition of words is not reading, it must be remembered that the absence of this ability precludes reading. For example, the individual who has no sight-recognition vocabulary is not a reader. One who fails to recognize as few as 5 percent of the words in a passage is handicapped; one who is stopped on 10 percent is a seriously impaired reader. For these people, frustration is inevitable.

Along with expanding his sight vocabulary, the child will of course be using phonics and related word-attack skills. The point of the discussion is that the normal reader is constantly learning to instantly recognize new words. He may resort to letter-sound analysis the first few times he meets a new word. However, as he meets the same word time after time he should rely less and less on analysis. When a reader fails to add words to his sight vocabulary, he is not maintaining a "normal learning pattern." The following lines of words represent visual patterns of increasing difficulty which must be mastered as children move upward through the grades:

> an and hand sand band land baker barber barker
> banker barter medal metal meddle mental medical
> elegant element elephant elegance eloquence general
> generous generally genesis generalize national natural
> nationally naturally nationality

As an increasing number of new words are met, certain irregular spellings occur more frequently (combinations: *que, ph, igh, wr, mb, ch = k or s, psy, kn,* etc.). Many words containing these patterns are learned as sight words. Children will also meet many sight words which have come to English from other languages: *debris, corps, reign, cache, rouge, yacht, sphinx, chassis, suave, chaos.*

Word-attack skills

Applying word-attack skills is developmental in nature, at least up to the point where they are utilized automatically. Experience indicates that lack of ability in phonic analysis is a major stumbling block for many pupils in the middle and upper grades. Word attack skills must be both reviewed and extended at this level. The child who has experienced little difficulty with simple compound words such as *sidewalk, anyhow, somewhere* and *barnyard* may need drill and guidance in dealing with words like *floodgate, homespun, praiseworthy, foreshadow* and *supernatural.*

Children who have applied letter-sound relationships in solving shorter words often experience difficulty with multisyllabic words. Some children develop the habit of "giving up" on lengthy words because they lack skill in breaking these words into syllables. They need guided practice in order to gain the confidence needed to solve words such as *overproduction, reenforcement, unworthiness, misrepresentation,* and the like.

Children also need to develop an ear for accent within longer words. This is most logically taught along with dictionary usage. Exercises can be developed which stress accent-shift in longer words (examples: confírm – confirmátion; úniverse – univérsal; éligible – eligibílity).

Other developmental skills

The developmental nature of many other reading skills is self-evident. Examples would include locating information, use of library resources, improving rate of reading, expanding meaning vocabulary, and critical reading. A final illustration consists of six sentences each taken from a basal reader at successive grade levels. This material reflects the need for growth on the part of the reader in regard to sight words, sentence patterns, profiting from punctuation, using proper intonation, drawing inferences, as well as other skills.

Grade 1	"I will run and bring some water."
Grade 2	"I know where the field mouse lives down by the brook."
Grade 3	"The next night, when his father got home, Bob said, "I read that book about the other Bob."
Grade 4	"Sir," said the duck, who was trying to recover his dignity while hopping around on one foot — not an easy thing to do, "Sir, I am minding my own business and I suggest that you do the same."
Grade 5	The missile range was known as Station One, and when the men talked over the radio from there they would say, "This is Station One," or just, "This is One."
Grade 6	"We can be sure that the Trojans, on hearing this, will not risk bringing her wrath down upon themselves by destroying our offering."*

Need for systematic reading instruction

In order to assure that children continue to develop skills that are commensurate with the reading tasks they are asked to perform in

*David H. Russell et al., *The Ginn Readers* (Boston: Ginn and Company, 1961).

the intermediate grades, systematic instruction must be continued. Hopefully, some reading instruction will be incorporated with the teaching of all subject matter courses; however, such teaching is not likely to meet the needs of those children who are weak in a number of reading skills.

Systematic instruction does not imply that all pupils will be receiving the same instruction. This would be justifiable only if all pupils in a given class were at the same developmental level. Since this is never the case, instruction must be differentiated if it is to be relevant. While meaningful differentiation of instruction is difficult to achieve it is not impossible.

Coping with variability among pupils

Individual differences in reading ability tend to increase with reading instruction. A given group of pupils will show greater individual differences at the end of four years of schooling than they did at the end of the first year. Good teaching aims at moving every child along at his maximum rate. The gifted child will move further in a given period of time than will the average child. Thus, the better the teaching, the greater will be the differences between children's achievement. Although different facets of the reading program receive varying degrees of emphasis at different grade levels, in the intermediate grades the emphasis almost has to be on what the individual child needs regardless of what is found in the curriculum guide.

Basal materials continue to be used extensively at the intermediate level in many schools. Recent editions of these materials contain a much wider variety of content than did former editions. Nevertheless, the intelligent use of basals becomes more difficult at this level, primarily because of the wide range of pupils' needs and achievement levels. Faced with this diversity of reading ability, teachers cannot rely on a single grade-level text. Obviously, such material will be appropriate only for those children who are progressing at approximately the rate that matches the pace built into the material.

Importance of diagnosis

Diagnosis is essential to a successful reading program at the intermediate level. Principles of teaching reading do not vary with grade level or with the materials being used. The variability of pupils in the intermediate grades makes a number of principles, discussed previously, particularly appropriate to this period: 1. no child should be expected to deal with materials he cannot read; 2. instruction must be at the learner's present level; 3. a thorough diagnosis will single out the pupils needing special instruction and indicate the skills in which the student is deficient; 4. once weaknesses are discovered, instruction must be fitted to individual needs. (2)

An illustration of the importance of following sound principles of instruction is provided by the pupil who has failed to master phonic-analysis skills. Experienced teachers know how unlikely it is that he will simply outgrow his inadequacy. The fact that the child has come this far without developing insights and techniques for overcoming his problem is in itself evidence that he is not likely to do so in the absence of skillful guidance and teaching. If a child has not developed the ability to hear the differences between the first syllables of words such as *dim*ple, *dem*onstrate, *dum*found, *dom*inoes, *dam*sel; or *mar*ble, *mor*tal, *mur*mur, *mer*cy, *mir*acle, it is useless to attempt to teach him a number of rules regarding short vowels, long vowels, or vowels followed by varying numbers of consonants. The child must be taught to make auditory discriminations, and the fact that this is ordinarily taught in first grade does not alter the fact that in this case it will have to be done now. Until the inability to discriminate between speech sounds is overcome, the student can make little real progress in gaining independence in sounding. The principle of going back to where the child is applies to every learning step in phonic analysis, such as learning initial consonant sounds, learning substitution of initial sounds, recognizing blends, distinguishing between long and short vowel sounds, and understanding syllabication.

Standardized tests and teacher-made informal reading tests appropriate for all of the elementary grades have been discussed in detail in Chapter 8. The reader may wish to refer to this discussion found on pages 288-311. A commendable practice in the intermediate grades is the use of teacher-prepared comprehension questions over the various subject materials covered. Such tests can serve two purposes. They are diagnostic from the teacher's standpoint, and they can provide excellent guidance for the reader. To devise tests which serve both these purposes is difficult and time-consuming. As a result, many attempts at preparing such tests tend to isolate facts and details. In this connection, it should be remembered that the pupil at the intermediate level needs practice in evaluating ideas, seeing relationships, and drawing inferences.

Grouping of pupils for instructional purposes is essential in the intermediate grades. The great variety of reading materials available make possible a number of grouping practices which can be used effectively. Highly structured groups become less practical in the intermediate grades, yet all the virtues of grouping can be achieved if a variety of tasks at varying levels of difficulty are devised.

While the teacher works with a group of pupils who need review on word-attack skills, more advanced readers can be reading independently from supplementary sources. This reading can be influential in extending reading horizons and developing new reading interests. During some reading periods the teacher can work with the advanced group stressing appreciation or critical analysis of a poem or story while the skills group works independently on teacher-made or workbook skill-building exercises. At other times the teacher may not work with any particular group but will give individual help. There will be some situations where instruction can involve the entire class: for example, when giving instruction in the use of the dictionary, in group planning of a unit, in word meaning sessions, when reading to the group, or when giving instruction in how to find materials. These instances of class-wide instruction would undoubtedly be followed by grouping techniques based on pupils' present achievement and individual needs.

While a majority of the pupils in a social science class may profitably use the assigned textbook, there are numerous other materials available at all levels of difficulty. Some of these lend themselves to use by the entire class; other materials and tasks will be more appropriate for either accelerated or impaired readers.

1. A film may be shown to the entire class.
2. Pictures which illustrate a particular concept appropriate to the topic can be gathered and placed on the bulletin board. Perhaps this project can be carried out by some of the less competent readers.
3. A special vocabulary lesson can be worked out using new terms children are likely to meet in their reading.
4. Each child can also make his own "new word list" which grows out of his reading on the topic.
5. Newspaper and magazine articles may be read by some pupils in the class.
6. Models, charts, or other illustrations which clarify some facet of the project may be prepared and displayed. With some guidance from the teacher, this task may be made quite appealing to poorer readers.
7. Better readers may report to the class on material found in reference or other books.

The Intellectually
Capable

The problem of arousing and maintaining interest in reading is not confined to the below average reader. The excellent student also faces certain educational hazards in our schools. Since we teach great masses of children in large groups by textbook methods, it is almost inescapable that the more facile readers will not always be stimulated by our standardized methods and materials. The intermediate grades can become a very critical period for gifted students as far as maintaining interest in reading is concerned. The challenge of the intellectually able student is present at all grade levels but becomes more pronounced at the intermediate level because the child's abilities and interests are often beyond the standard curricular materials. When bright pupils are expected to "adjust" to this condition, they often become satisfied simply to get by or, worse, to become uncritical readers. They may plod through required reading which demands no mental exercise on their part.

It is true that there are marked differences in reading achievement and needs among pupils who are classed as intellectually capable. Some of this group will need instruction in the fundamental skills of reading. Their ability to deal with concepts may be far in advance of their reading level. A larger group of the extremely capable will be advanced both in the mechanical skills and in the ability to deal with concepts. For these pupils, graded materials at their grade placement level will be mastered without as much repetition and guidance as is characteristically given to the class. The problem will not be alleviated by having these children do more work at this level, i.e., simply reading other textbooks. This solution will not extend the talented, who will acquire little additional information by spending time with other texts.

While stating that every child should be educated to his maximum ability to profit from instruction, our schools have been relatively unsuccessful in achieving this goal with the intellectually capable. Regardless of high ideals, our mass educational structure has in many cases led us to gear instruction to the "golden" mean. This is not to be construed as an expression of disaffection for universal free education, but rather as a recognition of the need to effect a solution for one of its obvious shortcomings. If pupils are helped to develop study skills which lead to independence in reading and are provided easy access to interesting supplementary reading materials, the school has at least fulfilled its obvious obligations. However, there are many other instructional responsibilities which should be fulfilled for all children but which are particularly acute in the case of the intellectually capable.

The following procedures have been particularly successful in motivating the more able students.

1. If the school has a central library, pupils should be allowed to visit it whenever the need arises and not be restricted to specified library periods.

2. Pupils should be given systematic instruction in the use of library resources such as encyclopedias, *Readers Guide to Periodical Literature*, bulletins, newspapers, and current magazines.

3. Time should be provided for independent reading, and the reading done at such times should always be purposeful. The gifted child, or any child, should never be kept occupied with busy work.

4. As a child develops interest in a particular topic or field, he should be kept supplied with challenging materials which will extend his growth. He should be praised for all serious effort and accomplishment.

5. Children should be encouraged to make plans and carry them out independently after the initial planning with the teacher.

6. The teacher can afford to use more analysis of stories or literature with the more capable pupils. This might take place on an individual or small-group basis.

7. Those pupils capable of such work should be encouraged to participate in special creative activities such as:
   a. writing biographies of famous persons from material they have gathered from many sources.
   b. describing historical events based on wide reading about these happenings.
   c. writing plays or dialogue involving historical personages.
   d. making "resource maps" in social studies.
   e. giving oral reports based on outside reading which will be a contribution to the knowledge of the group. (29)

8. Children should be encouraged to gather resource materials on a topic on which the class is working. These would include pictures, current magazines, bulletins, books which deal with any facet of the topic, and films. Such materials could be used in developing an "interest corner."

9. Pupils should be given access to professional recordings of plays, poems, or prose. Such materials, as well as films and books, may be borrowed from libraries, curriculum centers, or the local state department of education depository.
10. Children should be encouraged to do research on topics which help them see the social forces which shape their society. This type of activity will make "learning for responsible leadership" more than an empty phrase.

The Impaired Reader

As noted earlier, the intermediate grades are characterized by an increased emphasis on various content areas. Those children with inadequate reading skills cannot function successfully in this educational environment. They are placed in the untenable position of being expected to read materials which they are incapable of reading. For these children, the systematic teaching of reading is an absolute necessity, yet their need is often ignored in the rush to "cover" textbooks in structured content areas.

It is an educational paradox that, as the number of impaired readers in our schools increased, the school tended to rely more and more on reading. Textbooks became more widely used, and the basic curricular materials became more rigid and inflexible. As a result of this trend, children who cannot read adequately now constitute the schools' greatest problem. This problem has been accentuated recently as the plight of the "culturally different" child is acknowledged by the society and the school. The real meaning behind the "Right To Read" slogan is a reaffirmation of the principle that children must be taught *how* to read if the school expects them *to* read.

There is also a tacit recognition of the fact that the time is past when mere tinkering with the educational system will be accepted as a satisfactory response. Children cannot be held indefinitely as hostages. Thus, the school is faced with an identity crisis. It must decide whether it is to be an educational or custodial institution.

Since the problem of inadequate readers in our schools is so serious, two chapters in this book are devoted to dealing with such readers in the *classroom setting*. In that discussion, the points are made that we cannot write off our failures by hypothesizing that upwards of 25 percent of our children have succumbed to mysterious maladies such as dyslexia. Nor do we need to devise another set of principles for teaching reading, or wait for newer instructional approaches. At the moment a child's right to read is determined in large part by the teachers he draws and by the learning environment the school provides.

Integrating Reading Instruction with Subject Matter

In previous discussion it was recommended that reading instruction be a definite part of the curriculum of the intermediate grades. However, it was not implied that instruction be limited to a scheduled period and ignored when content subjects are taught. The idea that various facets of reading must be taught concurrently with subject matter is constantly verbalized by teachers and educators. Even in schools which are departmentalized with one teacher responsible for social science, another for science, and so forth, a respect for the integration of reading and the content subjects emerges in the slogan "every teacher a teacher of reading." The nature of the reading materials and the great difference between pupils' instructional needs make it logical and even mandatory that some reading instruction be related to the social sciences, science, literature, arithmetic, and other subject areas. (6)

It is unfortunate when the school views the curriculum as a series of separate tasks only one of which involves reading instruction. It is occasionally suggested that the duty of the school is to teach children to read as quickly as possible so that they can cope with other areas of the curriculum. In one sense, no one can disagree with this position, but in this setting, reading can easily become thought of as an assortment of mechanical skills which the reader applies to subject matter. Here we have more than a hint of compartmentalization, and this attitude is easily transferred to pupils who think they "read" reading one hour, "do" arithmetic another, and "study" social science, health, or science at other times.

Working with reading skills in different content areas

There are two points of view, which are probably not mutually exclusive, that relate to the issue of teaching reading skills while teaching subject matter. The first is that the various subject areas (social studies, science, arithmetic, health and the like) require radically different types of reading and, therefore, call for different types of reading instruction. (2) The point is sometimes made that certain skills are more identifiable with certain subjects than with others. "It seems reasonable to expect that the reading skills required for science material will differ from those required for materials of history, mathematics, or other content areas, each of which requires its peculiar combination of abilities." (31)

This point is carried further by some educators who list the various skills which they feel are most closely associated with each content area. The following skills are examples, each of which has been identified with reading in science, mathematics, social studies, or English:

adjust rate to purpose
attitude of the reader
drawing conclusions
word attack skills
getting main ideas
locating information
specialized vocabulary

read for main ideas
noting and weighing details
using contextual clues
organizing ideas
discriminating between
    relevant and irrelevant
    information

Most teachers of reading would find it difficult to associate each of the skills listed above with just one of the content areas.

This leads us to the second point of view which holds that while there are a great number of reading skills which go toward making up the total skill of reading, it is doubtful that these skills divide along content or subject-matter lines. Granted there are a few specifics which are more likely to be needed in one area than in another, but these do not constitute the essence of reading. A few specific skills would include map reading in history, graphs and tables in geography, abbreviations of elements in science, understanding scale drawings or blueprints in shop work. The basic premise of this point of view is that reading ability is a total process involving the total person and that a reader functions in *any* reading situation under a given set of attitudes, interests, and skills.

It should be noted that there are not several sets of principles and practices in reading which divide along subject area lines. Whether the teacher is attempting to develop adequate concepts for *congruent, parallel, equivalent,* or *isosceles* in arithmetic or *plateau, pole, delta,* or *isthmus* in geography, the problem is working with word meanings. Drawing inferences should not be thought of as belonging exclusively to one area of the curriculum. A pupil may in the course of a day be asked to draw inferences as to what

happens when a decimal point is inserted between digits in two-digit numbers; what effect mountains, located between the sea and the plains, have on rainfall on the plains; and what happens to the circumference of a balloon placed in the freezer compartment of a refrigerator.

A factor which may lead to the hypothesis that certain essential skills of reading are more appropriate to one content area than another is that many pupils can read successfully from basal readers and yet do poorly in subject areas. The reasons for this have been discussed previously. The basal readers present a controlled vocabulary; teachers are alerted to new words and difficult concepts found in each lesson, and systematic instruction is provided to help the pupil over these potential difficulties. Since all reading skills are developmental, the real issue may well be the difficulty level of the material in subject-area textbooks. These materials call for a more extensive development of essential reading skills rather than a different configuration of skills for each content area. When one carefully analyzes the content of history, science, arithmetic, and geography books, he finds it difficult to isolate particular reading skills which are more characteristically needed in one area than in another.

What will inevitably be found is that the vocabulary and concepts met in each field are roadblocks for some pupils. Background or lack of background, interests, attitudes, ability to note details, grasp main ideas, use context clues and word attack skills, and the reader's purpose, are factors which operate in all reading situations. Reading which children are expected to do in many content areas is farther removed from their actual experiences than is the material in basal reader series. Textbooks which may be excellent from the standpoint of accuracy and breadth of content may be relatively poor from the standpoint of the reader's present vocabulary and concepts.

Textbooks and heavy concept load

Because of the rigid control of vocabulary in beginning reading materials, teachers frequently have the problem of arousing and maintaining interest in these materials. By the time the intermediate level is reached, the teacher's problem has traveled full circle. Difficult words and concepts are introduced in the content textbooks in such profusion that many pupils are frustrated and often lost.

Meaningful reading at the intermediate level depends on the acquisition and continual extension of concepts. Here, pupils are confronted with more difficulties per reading unit than they met in their primary reading. One of the major reading problems is coping with the gap which tends to develop between the child's store of meanings and the demands made by the curricular materials he is expected to read.

Hildreth (15) writes, "The middle-grade pupil can now expect to meet new words he has never seen before in the proportion of about 1 in 10, even in material prepared for his age group and a still larger proportion of strange words in difficult texts." The problem of meaningful reading is complicated by the fact that in the intermediate grades, as well as at higher levels, there are found a great number of idiomatic expressions, abstract terms, figurative terms, and new connotations for words met earlier. In the primary grades, even though the occurrence of these is less frequent, teachers are alerted to them through the teaching manuals accompanying the basal reader series used. Also, deliberate instruction is provided in the workbooks which supplement the reader series. With the shift to separate textbooks in the content areas, there tends to be less emphasis on helping pupils with meaning difficulties precisely at the point where help is most needed. Examples of difficult concepts from fourth and fifth grade geography, science, and arithmetic books are cited below. Teachers found that many pupils did not understand these concepts even after the material had been assigned and covered in class.

Many years and great sums of money will be needed to *harness the river.*

It (blood) is carried through other *branching tubes* called veins.

When you are frightened, your *pupils get bigger.*

Check by doing each example again.

You bite and chew your food with the *crowns of your teeth.*

Ornithologists have examined the crops of many birds to find out what kind of food they eat.

Most of the *infections* and *contagious* diseases are caused by bacteria.

Birds help to keep the *balance of nature.*

We can use a *ruler* to subtract fractions.

Cloud formations make what is called a *mackerel sky.*

The *red corpuscles are racing through the capillaries.*

To solve problems like this, turn your *multiplication table of eights into a division table.*

The native city is *backward* and ugly.

The Mediterranean became a *melting pot* for surrounding civilization.

The people who lived in *fixed settlements* made far greater progress than the Nomads.

Now, as in ancient times, the Mediterranean is a great *connecting* highway.

There is plenty of *home-grown wool.*

Business and industry were *paralyzed.*

Science has *unlocked the greatest force in nature.*

China was not entirely *sealed off* from her neighbors.

A *belt of irrigated land* stretches almost all the way along the coast.

In time, *the front of Europe shifted* from the Mediterranean Coast to the Atlantic Coast.

As the *globe* shows, Europe and Asia really form one *land mass.*

The *shrinking world* and new inventions have made this possible.

If some day the river is controlled it will be a great *life-saver*
instead of a *life-destroyer.*
Gradually the continent was opened up. Another "jewel" had
been added to the British crown.
The top of the world will have a new meaning in the future.
Almost every farmer grows some *cash crop* besides food for his
family.
Britain was busy for many years in getting *stepping stones*
along the sea-ways.*

The unit approach

A widely used method for integrating reading along with all language skills in the teaching of any subject is the unit approach.
The unit has been discussed in educational sources under many
different labels. Descriptive titles for this concept include *resource
units, teaching units, activity units, core units,* and *survey units.*
The unit method is a classroom procedure which attempts to
organize and integrate a number of learning activities around a
particular theme. A unit may be devised for any subject area and
can cover a time span of a few days during which pupils attempt
to find the answer to a particular question or, as is usually the
case, may extend over a period of weeks and culminate in some
class project. The culmination might be a play, a school program,
or a science fair consisting of many individual and committee
projects, all related to the central theme. While the unit approach
is not new, it is consistent with the aims of modern curriculum
planning. Unit study can help avoid the tendency toward fragmen-
tation of the curriculum into isolated, seemingly unrelated parts.
    Units lend themselves to two types of major emphasis. The first
type emphasizes pupil experiences built around a specific topic,
such as *How We Get Our Food.* Experiences related to this topic
might include visits to various types of farms, to a cannery, a cold
storage plant, a meat packing plant, a dairy, or a bakery. Pupils
may plant and care for a garden or a window box. The second major
emphasis is on wide reading. It is likely that emphasis on the
experience approach will come at the early elementary level, shifting to reading in the subject areas in the intermediate grades.
These two methods are extremely compatible, and the proper combination of the two approaches undoubtedly makes for a better
total learning situation.

---

*Unpublished data compiled by teachers in actual classroom situations.

The use of the unit approach that emphasizes wide reading is reserved for the intermediate grades because wide reading calls for mastery of the fundamentals of beginning reading. Also, a wide variety of interesting supplementary materials on a variety of topics are available. Finally, by the time they have reached the intermediate grades, pupils have had opportunities to learn to work both independently and co-operatively in small groups.

Advantages of the unit approach

The potential advantages of the unit approach are quite numerous. The actual benefits resulting from its use will vary with such factors as the teacher's skill, the reading ability and work habits of the pupils, and the amount of supplementary reading material available. Some of the more frequently mentioned advantages of the unit approach are summarized below.

1. The unit serves as the framework within which learning experiences are shaped into larger, more meaningful wholes.

The unit permits more than the superficial study of a topic and encourages wide and varied reading.

2. Units can be used in any area of the curriculum.

3. The pupils learn that reading is the key to getting information on all subjects and not just an operation performed in the basal reader and accompanying workbooks.

4. The unit approach can and should include a great variety of experiences related to reading, such as excursions, field trips, and small group participation in working on various facets of the problem.

5. Units structure the learning situation to make reading more varied, more meaningful, and more interesting.

6. Units permit pupils of widely different reading abilities to work on different facets of the same project. Reading materials at many levels of difficulty can be used, and children need not be directly compared as readers.

7. The unit approach gives the teacher flexibility and freedom to work with a child or a group of children engaged in some reading activity at their own level. The retarded and the accelerated reader can be working independently and successfully on something that is challenging.

8. Units aid independent reading and help to foster independence in research reading.

Examples of units

A unit on weather designed for a fourth grade class may be used as an illustration. The teacher had aroused the interest of the class through an assignment of watching weather reports on television, finding interesting pictures of weather stations, and a class discussion of stories dealing with weather. Out of this grew the class decision to have a study unit on weather. Pupils worked cooperatively in identifying objectives, finding questions to be answered, and working on individual projects which fell within the limits of the unit. These are listed below:

1. Objectives of unit on weather:
   a. To learn ways in which weather helps or harms man.
   b. To learn what causes various types of weather and changes of seasons.
   c. To learn the causes and effects of rainfall, temperature, fog.

    d. To become familiar with the instruments used in measuring or predicting weather changes.
2. Questions to be answered:
    a. How is a thermometer constructed and how does it work?
    b. What is fog?
    c. What causes hail?
    d. What is lightning? Why is it followed by thunder?
    e. Why do we have seasons such as winter and summer?
    f. Why are some parts of the earth always hot and others always cold?
    g. Why is there very little rainfall in one part of a country and a great deal in another part?
    h. Why is it important for man to be able to predict weather?
    i. What is a barometer? How does it work?
    j. What is humidity?
3. Representative activities or projects, both individual and group:
    a. Keeping a daily record of temperatures. Securing temperatures registered in cities in different parts of the country.
    b. Preparing charts and graphs which illustrate some aspect of weather.
      (1) Average rainfall for different states and countries.
      (2) The relationship between rainfall and the type of crops raised in a particular area.
      (3) The effect of rainfall on density of population.
      (4) Maps showing occurrence of tornadoes, hurricanes, or floods during past decade.
    c. Explaining and demonstrating a thermometer and barometer.
    d. Doing research on the work of the U.S. Weather Bureau in predicting weather — how it is done and why.
    e. Studying the effects of weather on human dress, shelter, or diet.
    f. Measuring rainfall during a rain.
    g. Securing pictures which illustrate any facet of weather or the effect of weather, such as floods, erosion, storms on land and sea, barren deserts, and permanent snows.
4. Culminating activity:
    It was decided that at the end of the unit the class would have a Weather Fair. All individual and group projects

would be displayed, including posters, graphs and charts, picture series, pupil-made instruments for measuring weather, and all written projects. Parents were invited to visit the class on a particular afternoon, and other classes in the school saw the display at certain times that day. Children explained their projects and received a great deal of ego-satisfaction from this culminating activity.

Units integrate work in all areas

This well-planned unit provided a variety of purposeful learning experiences; the teacher had structured activities so that all facets of the curriculum received attention.

Spelling. Many words were learned incidentally as children printed them on their posters or charts. New words were assigned and studied as part of the unit (*weather, thermometer, mercury, rainfall, temperature, erosion, bureau*).

Health. One popular topic, *How Weather Affects Our Health,* almost became a unit within a unit. The entire class participated, and each pupil was asked to write a brief account of anything he had found in his reading that answered the question. The teacher had a few references for those children who needed help in finding material. What was ostensibly a health lesson also became a lesson in communication skills as the children worked on their written assignments. Practice in oral language usage also received attention as children discussed or reported their findings to the class.

Arithmetic. A lack of understanding of the problems to be solved is more of a stumbling block in arithmetic in the intermediate grades than is lack of computational skills. Failure to read problems critically will result in hazy concepts. In unit work the arithmetic problems which are met emerge from the immediate experience of the learner. Problems such as finding the average rainfall, average temperature, or total foodstuffs raised, are related to larger goals and become meaningful in the goal-directed activity. The need for accurate measurement becomes apparent in building a barometer or measuring a rainfall.

Science. Basically the unit was a science unit. One topic that received emphasis at this particular grade level was how science predicts and tracks weather and the scientific instruments used in the process. In studying the thermometer and barometer, many scientific principles and questions evolved, such as the principle of expansion, the principles of gravity and pressure, and the questions of whether mercury is a metal, why it is used in these instruments, what the function of heat is in causing a thermometer to work.

Social Science. The discussion above on health led into social science topics. A discussion of diet in relation to health led to questions and discussion on how weather affects diet or the production of foodstuffs. A discussion of the economic value of climate would logically follow. The relationship of climate to certain natural resources was discussed, i.e., to forestry, deposits of coal, and petroleum. The relationships between rainfall, temperature, winds, forests, and the types of crops were discussed. Methods of cultivation and crop rotation were studied in relation to erosion of the land.

Reading. Reading was the process which provided the raw material for all of the curricular activities mentioned above. The unit stressed, in the pupils' minds, that they were getting information for science, health, and geography. This reading was purposeful. Neither the reading nor the teaching of it were the compulsive "let's get this workbook page finished" approach. The teacher kept in mind all the principles of teaching reading. She had to be particularly careful not to expect all children to read the same materials and to provide a variety of supplementary materials at many grade levels.

Use of the unit method in no way restricts the teacher in developing the reading skills of her pupils. In fact, once the preliminary planning of a unit is done, the creative teacher will find that she has as much time and opportunity to help individual pupils or small groups as she had when working with a conventional grouping arrangement. Most unit work introduces a fairly heavy vocabulary load. It follows that some time must be spent on sight word recognition problems. As the teacher has different children read for her and as pupils ask for help with unknown words, she can prepare several word lists of new words to be studied during the course of the unit. One such list might be taken from the more difficult sources and be used exclusively with the advanced reading group. Lists of easier words can be used in sight word exercises with average and poor readers. Many new and unknown words can be used for teaching phonic analysis and for stressing the importance of context clues in solving meaning difficulties.

In developing a unit, the teacher may find that her first important task is to secure materials at various levels. The references available will vary from school to school. Basal readers at all levels could serve for such a unit as well as selected reading from subject-matter texts. *My Weekly Reader* files would provide material on many topics, and a child is often pleased to bring to school his own books on some special topic. The following is a partial list of materials the teacher was able to assemble and make available.

Primary level (from basal readers)

The Thermometer	The Storm
Winter Is Coming	Adventures in Science
Rain-Sleet-Snow	The Wonderworld of Science
Changing Weather	The Thunderstorm
How Spring Came	What Time of Year

Intermediate level (basal materials)

Dogs and Weather (Poem)
Inside a Thunderhead
Weather Control
The Snowstorm (Poem)
Ways of the Weather

Trade Books

"Our Friend the Sun," Polgreen (Holt, Rinehart & Winston, Inc., 1963)

"The Sun and Its Planets," Hawkins (Holt, Rinehart & Winston, Inc., 1964)

"Air Is All Around You," Branley (Crowell, Collier & Macmillan, Inc., 1962)

"Weather and Weather Forecasting," Forsdyke (Grosset & Dunlap, 1970)

"How Weather Affects Us," Provis (Benefic Press, 1963)

"Weather Experiments," Feravolo (Garrard Publishing Co., 1963)

"Our American Weather," Kimble (McGraw-Hill, 1955)

"Poems for Weather Watching," Riswall (Holt, Rinehart & Winston, Inc., 1963)

"Tornadoes of the United States," Snowden (University of Oklahoma Press, 1964)

"Atlantic Hurricanes," Dunn and Miller (Louisiana State University Press, 1964)

Pamphlets and Magazines

Life Magazine
National Geographic Magazine
U. S. Weather Bureau, *Collection of Weather Publications*
Weatherwise (American Meterological Society, Boston, Mass.)

Summary

The intermediate-level teacher is faced with the formidable task of arriving at a meaningful differentiation of instruction which is geared to pupil differences. American education is continually searching for formulas and formats which will achieve this goal. All classroom and administrative innovations are attempts to focus on this problem. The difficulty lies in the fact that differentiation of instruction must rest on meaningful ongoing diagnosis of pupils' present abilities and instructional needs. Such diagnosis will reveal that no single textbook or other source will be equally good for all pupils in a grade.

A criticism of the secondary school, which is believed to have validity, is that it has abdicated this responsibility for teaching students "how to read subject matter." The same pressures which operate in the high school are presently being encountered in the elementary grades as content is "moved downward." There is little virtue in a strong academic curriculum unless the learner's reading ability is synchronized with the curriculum materials he is asked to read.

Learning to read is a long-term developmental process. The curricular tasks found in the intermediate grades call for wide and extensive reading. To meet these demands successfully, pupils will need guidance in reading *curricular materials*. This means that skill in reading geography, science, and mathematics must be developed in the actual study of these subjects as well as in a period devoted to "reading." In the intermediate grades there is danger of a too literal acceptance of the old dictum that "a pupil learns to read by reading" or "nothing improves one's reading like more and more reading." This is true for readers who have mastered the necessary reading skills, but there is a fallacy in these statements when applied to any child who is deficient in reading skills. The more reading a pupil with poor reading habits does, the more he reinforces his poor habits. Reading with instruction and guidance aimed at improvement is the key. Learning in all content areas, from this point on in the grades, depends primarily on reading skill. The facts taught in science, geography, history, and mathematics are important, but the school's basic task is to teach each child the reading skills which will enable him to read independently in any of these content areas. Since many children still need instruction in reading skills, any reduction of emphasis on this facet of reading is a serious omission.

YOUR POINT OF VIEW?

What is the basis for your agreement or disagreement with each of the following statements?

1. Variability among pupils in the intermediate grades could be reduced by improved teaching in earlier grades.

2. Using basal reader series as the basic instructional approach has less efficacy with accelerated readers than with those pupils who, on the basis of reading achievement, rank in the lower half of their grade.

3. There is little evidence in either the curriculum materials or instructional objectives to indicate that there is an educationally significant transition between the primary and intermediate grades.

4. The unit approach relies too much on incidental learning and slights systematic instruction in reading.

5. Good teaching in the intermediate grades will increase the individual differences in reading ability of children found in these classrooms.

6. In recent years the curriculum reforms in content areas have been geared to the intellectually capable child without adequate concern for the average learner.

Respond to the following problems:

1. Illustrate the concept that reading is a long term developmental process by tracing the developmental nature of learning in one of the following areas: *meaning vocabulary; use of library resources; appreciation of poetry or literature.*

2. *Premise:* The "grade level" score achieved on reading tests is more representative of the child's ability to deal with basal reading materials than it is of his ability to deal with textbooks in the content areas. Can you provide evidence that supports this assumption?

BIBLIOGRAPHY

1. Bond, Guy L. and Eva Bond Wagner, *Teaching The Child to Read* (4th ed.). New York: The Macmillan Company, 1966, Chapters 13 and 14.

2. Bracken, Dorothy Kendall, "Appraising Competence In Reading In Content Areas," in *Evaluation of Reading*, Helen M. Robinson, (ed.), Supplementary Educational Monographs No. 88. Chicago: University of Chicago Press, 1958, 56–60.

3. _____, "The Theme Approach for Reading Literature Critically," *Reading and Realism*, J. Allen Figurel (ed.), Proceedings, International Reading Association, 13, Part 1, 1969, 223–27.

4. Burns, Paul C. "Corrective Aspects of Elementary School Language Arts," *Elementary English* (December 1969), 1008–15.

5. _____, "Vocabulary Growth Through the Use of Context In Elementary Grades," *Forging Ahead In Reading*, J. Allen Figurel (ed.), Proceedings, International Reading Association, 12, Part 1, 79–85.

6. Cooper, J. Louis, "The Reading Program Spans the Total Curriculum," *Forging Ahead In Reading*, J. Allen Figurel (ed.), Proceedings, International Reading Association, 12, Part 1, 200–05.

7. Davis, J. E. "The Ability of Intermediate Grade Pupils to Distinguish Between Fact and Opinion," *The Reading Teacher* (February 1969), 419–22.

8. DeBoer, John J. and Dallmann, Martha, *The Teaching of Reading* (3rd Ed.). New York: Holt, Rinehart and Winston, Inc., 1970, Chapter 11.

9. Dolan, Sister Mary Edward, "Effects of a Modified Linguistic Word Recognition Program on Fourth-Grade Reading Achievement," *Reading Research Quarterly* (Summer 1966), 37–66.

10. Dulin, Kenneth L. "Using Context Clues in Word Recognition and Comprehension," *The Reading Teacher* (February 1970), 440–45.

11. Gans, Roma, *Common Sense in Teaching Reading*. Indianapolis: The Bobbs-Merrill Co., Inc., 1963, Chapters 8, 9, and 11.

12. Groff, Patrick, "How Do Children Read Biography About Adults?" *The Reading Teacher* (April 1971), 609–15.

13. Guszak, Frank J. "Questioning Strategies of Elementary Teachers In Relation To Comprehension," in *Reading and Realism*, J. Allen Figurel (ed.). Proceedings, International Reading Association, 13, Part 1, 1969, 110–116.

14. Harris, Albert J., *How To Increase Reading Ability* (5th Ed.). New York: David McKay Company, Inc., 1970, Chapter 4.

15. Hildreth, Gertrude, *Teaching Reading*. New York: Holt, Rinehart, & Winston, Inc., 1958.

16. Jacobs, Leland B. "Books for the Gifted," *Reading Teacher* (May 1963), 429–34.

17. Kennedy, Larry D. "Textbook Usage in the Intermediate-Upper Grades," *The Reading Teacher* (May 1971), 723–29.

18. Kline, Donald F. "Developing Resource Units," *Education* (December 1963), 221–25.

19. Klosterman, Sister Rita, "The Effectiveness of a Diagnostically Structured Reading Program," *The Reading Teacher* (November 1970), 159–62.

20. McAulay, J. D. "Integrating the Social Studies," *Education* (December 1959), 239–42.

21. McKee, Paul, *Reading: A Program of Instruction for the Elementary School*. Boston: Houghton Mifflin Company, 1966, Part Three.

22. Manolakes, George, and William D. Sheldon, "The Relation Between Reading-test Scores and Language-factors Intelligence Quotients," *Elementary School Journal* (February 1955), 346–50.

23. Millsap, Lucille, "The Ubiquitous Book Report," *The Reading Teacher* (November 1970), 99–105.

24. Morrison, Virginia B. "Teacher-Pupil Interaction in Three Types of Elementary Classroom Reading Situations," *The Reading Teacher* (December 1968), 271–75.

25. Rauch, Sidney J. "Reading In the Total School Curriculum," in *Forging Ahead In Reading*, J. Allen Figurel (ed.), Proceedings, International Reading Association, 12, Part 1, 212–17.

26. Robinson, H. Alan "Reading Skills Employed in Solving Social Studies Problems," *Reading Teacher* (January 1965), 263–70.

27. Roswell, Florence G. "When Children's Textbooks Are Too Difficult," *Elementary School Journal* (December 1959), 146–57.

28. Sauer, Lois E. "Fourth Grade Children's Knowledge of Grammatical Structure," *Elementary English* (October 1970), 807–13.

29. Schulte, Emerita Schroer, "Independent Reading Interests of Children in Grades Four, Five and Six," *Reading and Realism*, J. Allen Figurel (ed.), Proceedings, International Reading Association, 13, Part 1, 1969, 728–32.

30. Sheldon, William D. and Donald R. Lashinger, "A Summary of Research Studies Relating To Language Arts in Elementary Education: 1968," *Elementary English* (November 1969), 866–885.

31. Shores, J. Harlan, and J. L. Saupe, "Reading For Problem-Solving In Science," *Journal of Educational Psychology* (March 1953), 149–58.

32. Zirbes, Laura, "The Developmental Approach in Reading," *Reading Teacher* (March 1963), 347–52.

13

Developing and Expanding Concepts

An attempt to explain the purpose or function of the school usually results in a rather lengthy discussion of all of the hopes and fears of the larger society that supports the schools. On the other hand, a brief and concise statement can be advanced: *The purpose of the school is to develop and expand concepts and to help children develop the tools which will permit them to continue this process on their own.* After this much is agreed upon, interested parties may still debate *which* concepts and *how* to teach them (i.e., science, health, understanding self and others, literature, art, the role of government, ecology, etc.).

Language and Concepts

Regardless of which concepts the school elects to teach, the medium through which teaching and learning takes place is language. Although language is a system of agreements as to what words mean, it is not static. Within limits, the meanings of words have been established by previous generations over a period of many centuries. Nevertheless, each individual who uses language, whether receptively or as a form of expression, participates in a potentially creative act. This is analogous to the twentieth century artist using a chisel upon a block of marble. He did not invent the chisel, the hammer, or the art form of sculpture, yet what he does can be creative because the media is open-ended.

Language is both the raw material and the working capital of the learning process. (30) Practically all of the subject matter taught in the school is presented to the potential learner by means of language. The learner in turn must "break the code" of written language and assimilate word meanings and concepts. In essence, the educational process consists of transmitting meaning from the knower (author, teacher, etc.) to the learner.

When children enter school, they are able to understand and use several thousand words in their speech. From the standpoint of intellectual growth, the single most important educational achievement from kindergarten through college post-graduate work is the progressive mastery of word meanings and the acquisition of concepts which are fixed by words. The acquisition of concepts is based primarily upon experiences with language. (24) The process of mastering language is much the same for individuals within a given language or culture; yet the rate of acquisition and extent of mastery vary tremendously.

The teacher's problem is not necessarily to discover *new* ways to teach the meanings of words. What is needed is a more thorough and systematic application of the techniques already known. As teachers, we probably *do* need a bit more creativity in modifying practices which have been available for years in textbooks on reading, language arts, workbooks, and the like. We do need a little more enthusiasm for teaching language, developing concepts, and inculcating students with an understanding of and a respect for the power of language. (15)

Reading and
Language

The teaching of reading has a unique relationship to and with language. One often reads in the professional literature that reading is a "tool," and of course a fairly solid rationale can be built for this position. It might be better to go back one step and establish the fact that language is the *tool* involved and that reading is the manipulation or special use of the tool. The *ability* to read does not a priori expand the mind any more than the ability to swim or to run makes one physically fit. If reading results in interaction between the reader and the printed stimuli, growth on the part of the reader is assured; concepts are developed and expanded as a result of language experiences.

It is probably true that the process of "learning to read" can take place under circumstances that minimize the language component. The child who is learning to read may fail to see that he is really involved with a language process. This is true because we have developed ways to teach reading which pretty thoroughly divorces the act of reading from language involvement. Merely "learning to read" can provide its own motivation for only a limited time. Once the rudiments are mastered there is no self-sustaining mechanisms unless the power and beauty of language is experienced while reading. (17) Thus, the mastery of myriad reading skills must be accompanied by a sense of involvement with language.

Language is the only magic to be found in the schools. Everything else in the curriculum is "The Way It's Spozed to Be." A book can be a frigate to bear us lands away only when the reader transforms the book into a frigate. The captain of such a ship knows that both sail and rudder are synonyms for language. This is not a plea for the child's hasty entrance into great literature, but rather that he will have a chance to work with jokes, rhymes, riddles, proverbs, and both brief and lengthy language samples. Man is the only talking animal, and his language has a tremendous potential fascination for him. We must find ways to smuggle language into reading.

The following section illustrates how the teaching of reading can also involve teaching the reader something *about* his language, specifically that:

1. Intonation and punctuation influence meaning.
2. Words may have many different meanings.
3. Plurals are formed using several different patterns or visual formats.
4. Words may have different spellings and meanings and yet be pronounced the same.
5. Words may be spelled exactly alike and yet be pronounced differently and have different meanings.
6. New words are constantly being added to our language.

The role of intonation in reading situations

Learning to apply intonation while reading is a developmental process. This skill is not mastered once and for all time at any given grade level. As the difficulty level of material increases, the influence of intonation on understanding what is read increases. The importance of profiting from punctuation was stressed in the material on primary instruction. Here, a few teaching exercises which focus on the importance of stress pitch and terminals are cited. These illustrations may be used or adopted for helping children arrive at the melody of language while reading.

Word stress and meaning

Write the same sentence several times and have children read the sentence stressing a different word each time. Explain that they are to stress the word(s) that are underlined.

1. *I* said no. I *said*, no. I said *no*!
   Read this sentence as a question: I said no?

2. a. *This* is your lunch.
   b. This *is* your lunch.
   c. This is *your* lunch!
   d. This is your lunch?

3. a. *John* said, "Who lost a quarter?"
   b. John *said*, "Who lost a quarter?"
   c. John said, "*Who* lost a quarter?"
   d. John said, "Who *lost* a quarter?"

4. Alternate approach: A volunteer reads one of the numbered sentences. The group or another volunteer gives the number of the sentence based on the intonation pattern heard.
   a. *That* plane will never fly again.
   b. That *plane* will never fly again.
   c. That plane *will never* fly again.
   d. That plane will never *fly* again.

5. *Provide a clue* as to how the sentence is to be read (see column A), and have volunteers read statement B with the appropriate intonation.

A	B

(Clerk informing a customer)⟶ This hat costs ten dollars.
(Customer shocked
  at high price)⟶ This hat costs ten dollars.
(Customer surprised
  at low price)⟶ This hat costs ten dollars.
(Speaker happy
  with a gift)⟶ This is my birthday present.

(Speaker thinks the gift was meant
for his baby sister)——➤ This is my birthday present.
(Speaker is terribly
disappointed)——➤ This is my birthday present.

6. Showing emotions through use of intonation patterns.
Provide a number of mood-descriptive words followed by
several sentences. A volunteer reads a sentence using intonation that conveys one of the moods. Individuals or the
class identifies the emotion the speaker depicted.

---

sadness   disbelief   anger   surprise   disappointment   fear   etc.

---

 a. Which one of you wrote this?
 b. Put that thing down, John.
 c. Who is responsible for this mess?
 d. I don't believe he said it.
 e. Of course he didn't say it; how could he?
 f. Guess who won first prize?

7. Use intonation to express the opposite meaning.
 a. Oh that's just lovely.
 b. Man, I'm really going to like school this year.
 c. Did you see that brilliant play?
 d. That's the number one team in the country.
 e. Oh no it can't be raining again.

8. Devise *who, what, when, where* and *how* sentences. Have
different children read each sentence so as to stress —
    who (said or did something)
    what (was said or done)
    where (it happened)
    when (it happened)
    etc.

 a. The announcer said it rained very hard yesterday in
    Chicago.
 b. The players practiced very hard the week after they lost
    the game.
 c. John said the bridge was washed away by the flood.
 d. Two men boarded the plane at 3:00 P.M. through Gate
    10.
 e. A policeman put a ticket on the brown car parked in the
    driveway.

9. Noting the role of punctuation in arriving at intonation and meaning. Prepare material in which punctuation marks have been omitted. Provide clues that will determine what punctuation to use.

		Use punctuation to show that:
a.	Mike said Mary is always hungry.	(Mary is talking)
b.	Mike said Mary is always hungry.	(Mike is talking)
c.	That little boy said the teacher is smart.	(The boy is smart)
d.	The doctor said his friend is ill.	(The doctor is sick)
e.	The doctor said his friend is ill.	(The doctor is speaking)

The following material is written without punctuation marks or capital letters. Put in punctuation marks so that it is easy to get the meaning.

a. What do you like to eat some boys and girls like hamburgers milk and ice cream.

b. The farmer tried to hurry his horse was tired both sat down later the farmer got up to go on his horse wouldn't move.

c. Father said jack come and play we will play ball watch mother.

Note: exercises similar to the above may be presented via the chalkboard, overhead projector, or duplicated for seat work.

Different meanings for same word

Native speakers of English are frequently unaware that so many words we use have five, ten, twenty, or more different meanings. This does not imply that we do not use or understand many connotations for a given word. The point is we rarely think about the extent to which this feature of our language operates. (7) Thus, working with "different meanings" is an excellent way for children to learn about language while developing and expanding concepts.

The fact that many words have a large number of connotations adds to the problem of developing a precise order of difficulty of words, or the order in which words should be introduced and taught. Thus, the word *rhinoceros*, while very concrete in meaning, might be considered more difficult than the word *heavy* — but only if one is discussing a particular and limited connotation for *heavy*.

A child may acquire *a* meaning for *heavy* (opposed to light in weight) before he acquires a concept for, or the ability to, pronounce the term *rhinoceros*. But once he has had the experience of seeing a rhinoceros, or even a picture of one, he will have established a workable concept. He can learn many more details about this animal such as its average weight, height, habitat, feeding habits, agressiveness, and economic value.

The word heavy has dozens of connotations which range from fairly concrete to highly abstract.

> They had a *heavy* load on the wagon.
> The voters registered a *heavy* vote.
> The guide led them through a *heavy* fog.
> Meet the new light *heavy*weight champion.
> Time hung *heavy* on his hands.
> Their eyes became *heavy* with sleep.
> He carried a *heavy* load through life.
> The sad news made him *heavy*-hearted.
> The actor complained, "I am always cast as the *heavy*."

Multiple meanings for words was briefly alluded to in the discussion of primary reading. However, children at the intermediate and higher levels have been exposed to much more language usage. For these students the possibilities for learning about language and developing concepts are greatly extended. The following are a few illustrative teaching techniques.

After selecting a word such as *head* used below, explain that volunteers are to use this word in a sentence. They must *listen carefully* as the game proceeds, trying not to use a meaning that has already been given previously.

1. John scratched his head.
2. Mother bought a head of lettuce.
3. The candidate called his opponent a cabbage head.
4. That ranch supports 100 head of cattle.
5. You must be "out of your head" to talk like that.
6. The captain will head the ship into the storm.
7. Two heads are better than one.
8. The sheriff said "We'll head them off at the pass."
9. The coach said, "Don't lose your head — play it cool."

10. They couldn't make heads or tails of the code.
11. John was selected to head up the committee.
12. He gave an opinion off the top of his head.
13. May I speak to the head waiter please.
14. This course is over my head.

One fifth grade class decided to start each of their sentences the same way using *Joe* as the subject and using different meanings for the word *broke*.

Joe broke the dish.
Joe said, "I'm broke."
Joe watched as dawn broke.
Joe broke a rule.
Joe broke the bank (at Monte Carlo)
Joe broke the record.
Joe finally broke the silence.
Joe broke his $20 bill.
Joe broke in his catchers mitt.
Joe broke the news.

Joe broke into the big leagues.
Joe threw a curve that broke outside.
Joe watched as the crowd broke up.
Joe, playing fullback, broke into the open.
Joe broke up when he heard the story.
Joe said to the team,"let's go for broke!"

The number of connotations for a given word may be enlarged if the various inflected forms and different tenses of a word are used. The class added the following: Joe finally got a *break*; . . . sounds like a *broken* record; . . . jammed on the *brake*; . . . played for the *breaks*; . . . struck out on a *breaking* pitch; . . . was *broken* up by the news; . . . saw the waves *breaking* over the hull; . . . said, "the new cars have more *braking* power," etc.

The *Different Meanings* game provides an excellent medium for the development of written exercises. Children may work on these individually, as pupil pairs, or in teams of various sizes. Two teams may select the same word from a list and see which team can develop the most meanings for that word. Children's work can then be used for developing teaching exercises which consist of a duplicated page showing an extensive number of sentences, each of which illustrates a different connotation for the chosen word. Children then select a lesson sheet and study the meanings of any word in which they may be interested. Examples which might be used are unlimited: fence, light, handle, read, match, pack, state, pike, dead, free, grace, set, etc.

In developing different connotations for words, children often note that many of their usages are expressions: two *heads* are better than one; this is over my head; let's go for broke; her eyes lighted up; a person can be light headed; light hearted; light fingered; "I can read you like a book"; don't read something into that statement; etc. This is another characteristic of their language that is both enjoyable and profitable to study.

Figurative expressions

The English language is rich with expressions which we call figures of speech. Figurative language is colorful, flexible, picturesque, and vivid. One of the problems is that even though children may "read" such expressions flawlessly, they still may not understand the meaning intended. (32) Metaphor, similes, hyperbole, euphemisms, and irony should be explained to children although it may not be necessary to have them memorize dictionary definitions.

A study by Holmes (13) indicated that children in the intermediate grades have difficulty with the meanings of many figurative expressions found in reading and social studies textbooks. The problem involved more than not knowing meanings. When a child did not arrive at the intended meaning he tended to fall back on a concrete meaning for the words, which resulted in misconceptions.

Groesbeck (11) reported that significant transfer of learning occurred when children were given spaced systematic instruction in understanding figurative expressions and were later tested on materials which were not part of the instructional program. Considering the large number of idiomatic expressions found in textbooks, it appears that working with this facet of language is of considerable value to readers. The following are a few techniques which might be adapted to various instructional levels.

1. Match expressions with concrete meanings.
    Identify each definition on the right with the letter of the expressions that it explains.

Expressions	Definitions
a. Business will soon *pick up.*	___pay attention
b. March came in *like a lamb.*	___does not understand
c. *Jack stood up* for his friend	___will improve, become better
d. *"Mark my words,"* said father.	___very pleasant weather
e. I don't *dig the jive.*	___defended

2. *After each expression, write in your own words what it means.*
   a. *bury the hatchet.* _____
   b. *out of step with the times.* _____
   c. *lost in thought.* _____
   d. *chip off the old block.* _____
   e. *flew off the handle.* _____

3. *In each sentence below, a figurative expression is underlined. Rewrite each sentence so that it carries the same meaning but do not use the underlined phrase.*

   Sample: Old Mr. Brown was a man who often *flew off the handle.*

   Old Mr. Brown frequently got mad and lost his temper.

   a. The broadcast warned against dealing with *fly-by-night* business concerns.
   _____

   b. The bandit had a *price on his head.*
   _____

   c. "That fellow *rubs my fur the wrong way*", said big Bill.
   _____

   d. Wearing a suit and tie to the picnic, Wylie *stuck out like a sore thumb.*
   _____

   e. Old Mr. Jones was a *jack-of-all-trades.*
   _____

4. Prepare a study sheet that will help children in understanding and interpreting figurative expressions. The following is one example:

Just an Expression

   Some groups of words have special meanings. If someone writes "It was raining cats and dogs," he means it was raining very hard. He does not want the reader to take his words *literally*. (Is the meaning of the last word clear?) Basketball players are not "tall as mountains" or "as fast as greased lightening". However, this is a much more colorful and vivid way of saying one is very tall or that he moves quite rapidly.
   Expressions such as "stong as an ox," "patient as Job," "flew off the handle" are called figures of speech. They help us to draw vivid word images. With them we can make picturesque (*pik sure esk*) comparisons. With fig-

ures of speech, we can exaggerate or convey meaning by stating the opposite of what is meant. A few of the more common types of figurative language are:

a. Hyperbole (hy. per′ bow. lēē) : To exaggerate — an obvious overstatement.

"so hungry I could eat a bear"

b. Simile (sĭm′ ĭ. lē) : Is an actual comparison between things that are basically different. Usually these comparisons include the words *like* or *as*.

"Hearing this, he turned as *white as a sheet*."

"He drifted about town *like a ship without a rudder*."

"He was so tired he *slept like a kitten*."

c. Irony (ī′ rō. nĭ) : Humorous light sarcasm.

If you hand in a rough copy of a theme which contains misspellings, marked out passages, improper punctuation and no evidence of organization, your teacher may say,

"This a *fine* piece of work," but your grade on the theme should provide a clue as to what she meant.

d. Metaphor (met ă for) : An implied comparison between two different things. (27)

"The *ship plowed the ocean*."

"Tom remained *rooted to the spot*."

"The king had a *heart of stone*."

5. Illustrate over use of expressions: Prepare a passage or story in which the child is to underline each example of a figurative expression (underlining is provided in the sample below).

Directions: The following story contains too many figurative expressions! Many of the examples are used so often that we say they are *threadbare, shopworn, worked-to-death* expressions or *cliches* (*klee shays*). Figurative language is to the writer as seasoning is to the cook. Overuse may spoil the flavor. Underline each example of a figure of speech in the passage. (To illustrate, expressions have been underlined.)

Our hero Horatius Algerman left home <u>at a tender age</u> <u>to seek his fortune</u> in the <u>cold and heartless city</u>. He was a person of <u>sterling qualities</u> and had a <u>burning desire</u> to <u>prove his worth.</u> (Also his mettle.) One day he found himself <u>lost in the heart of the (heartless) city.</u> So with a lump in his throat he decided to follow his nose, meanwhile keeping one eye out for Indians. Remaining true to his upbringing he kept his other eye on the ball, his nose to the grindstone, shoulder to the wheel, and feet on the ground. However, he never let the grass grow under his feet. This was particularly difficult in the heart of the city as the grass sprang up fast as lightning and spread like wildfire.

Soon our hero was as hungry as a bear — so hungry in fact that he could eat a horse. Having no horse of his own, he declined to eat another's horse as this was a horse of a different color to Horatius.

The next day good fortune smiled on our hero. He was elected mayor of the cold heartless city. He vowed he would be a good servant of the people. He decided to learn the mayor business from the ground up. Since he always kept a straight face he soon earned the nickname "old oval jaw." That year March came in like a lion but Horatius kept a clear head, frequently put his foot down, weathered many storms, stormed every obstacle in his path, pushed his way to the top, rarely lost his head, and when he did he would find his tongue at the right moment. He also learned to hold his tongue at the right moment (some people thought he was odd).

Nevertheless, our Hero never wasted a minute and always made up for lost time, was up with the sun and never slept on the job, burned the candle at both ends, and became a Jack of all trades. We hear little more of our hero except for two conflicting stories. One has it that he threw his heart into his work and ended up a clinker. The other version — equally heart rending — is that one dark night, black as pitch, he was swallowed up by the city.

Children may "translate" or rewrite selected sentences, paragraphs or the entire passage, substituting other words for the underlined expressions.

6. Reserve space on the bulletin board where members of the class may put up examples of figurative language that they meet in their reading. A committee may then select the best of these and duplicate them for distribution to all members of the class.

Forming plurals

A good way to point up some interesting facts about written language is to have children study how plurals are formed in English writing. Such a study also impinges on reading since plurals change the visual pattern, meaning, and pronunciation of words. Examples of ways in which plurals are formed are listed below, followed by several generalizations which apply to large groups of words.

One	*More than one*
1. bird	birds
2. fox	foxes
3. fly	flies
4. shelf	shelves
5. potato	potatoes
6. man	men
7. deer	deer

It is possible to learn visual recognition and spelling patterns of plurals through repeated experiences with these patterns. Undoubtedly some children learn faster when they work with rules or generalizations which cover a number of singular-to-plural transformations. Such rules may be useful in working with some of the examples cited above:

1. Most plurals are formed by adding the letter *s*.
2. If words end with *s*, *ss*, *ch*, *sh*, or *x*, we usually add *es* to form plurals.
3. If final *y* is preceded by a consonant change, change *y* to *i* and add *es*.

Rules have also been formulated for other changes in spelling:

4. Words ending in *f* or *fe*: Sometimes we change these letters to *v* and then add *es* (shelf, shel*ves*).
5. Words concluding with a consonant and final *o*: Sometimes we add *es* to form plurals (hero, hero*es*).
6. and 7. The examples above show "irregular plurals." It would be very difficult to write a rule without including all "instances" as examples. Some teachers prefer to include items 4 and 5 as "irregulars" rather than teach relatively complicated rules to cover a very limited number of words.

Some children will be helped in learning language and reading skills through the use of exercises which focus on the changes that occur as singular forms are changed to plurals. The following are illustrative: Have children compile a list of words which are governed by any rule 2–7 above.

1. *Words ending with s – ss*	*Add es to make "more than one"*	*Words ending with ch*	*Add es to make "more than one"*
bus	buses	watch	watches
gas	gases	lunch	lunches
glass	glasses	inch	inches
dress	dresses	witch	witches
kiss	kisses	match	matches
guess	guesses	peach	peaches
address	addresses	church	churches

2. If final *y* is preceded by a consonant, change *y* to *i* and add *es*

fly	flies	army	armies
sky	skies	cherry	cherries
spy	spies	puppy	puppies
city	cities	lady	ladies
baby	babies	story	stories

3. If final *y* is preceded by a vowel, add *s*.

key	keys	boy	boys
toy	toys	day	days
turkey	turkeys	tray	trays
toe	toes	valley	valleys
way	ways	ray	rays

4. On words that end with *f*, change *f* to *v* and add *es*.

calf	calves	elf	elves
wolf	wolves	shelf	shelves
loaf	loaves	self	selves
half	halves	thief	thieves
leaf	leaves	sheaf	sheaves

5. Words which are spelled the same in both singular and plural form:

They saw a deer.	They saw many deer.
one moose.	several moose.
this sheep.	those sheep.
his hair.	their hair.
a bamboo shoot.	bamboo shoots.

6. man – men   woman – women
    tooth – teeth   louse – lice
    goose – geese   child – children
    mouse – mice   foot – feet

7. Children write the plural form for each singular stimulus word.

loaf_____   church_____   deer_____
goose_____   sheep_____   bus_____
woman_____   lion_____   match_____
fox_____   key_____   brush_____
dish_____   mouse_____   porch_____

Jack has one *sheep*   Jill has two_____.
John had a *tooth* pulled.   Jim had several_____
                               pulled.
Fred bought a *loaf* of bread. Ted bought three_____
                               of bread.
Mary has a paint *brush*.   Sue has a set of
                               paint_____.

Homonyms

Children can learn interesting facts about their language, expand concepts, and develop reading skills through the study of words with identical spellings which have different pronunciations and meanings, and words with different spellings and meanings which have the same pronunciations. Exercises dealing with homonyms should help the child learn both the visual patterns and meanings of these pairs of words. Exercises such as the following can be useful.

1. Word-meaning study: Provide definitions of words which may present meaning difficulties or whose meanings may be confused.

   raise: to elevate, cause to rise
   raze: to demolish, overthrow, completely remove

   principle: a fundamental or basic truth, law, or point
   principal: the chief officer, as head of a school

   reign: to exercise authority, to govern, "the king's reign was
          10 years"
   rein: a bridle to guide or control a horse

stationary: fixed in place, not moving
stationery: paper, and other items for writing

coarse: common, rough, inferior quality, unrefined
course: a course of study; a path such as a racecourse, golf course, etc.

2. Provide one word from a homonym-pair and have the child write the other word (homonym). The words children will need to write may be provided in mixed order (see box), or the child may work without such clues (see b. below).

a.

weigh	wave	wrap	waist	wring
would	weak	wait	write	won

one	_____	way	_____
right	_____	ring	_____
waive	_____	rap	_____
wood	_____	week	_____
waste	_____	weight	_____

b.

reel	_____	pail	_____	ate	_____
peak	_____	made	_____	night	_____
sent	_____	here	_____	due	_____
blew	_____	plain	_____	steak	_____

c. Devise sentences which "sound right" but which contain the wrong word from a pair of homonyms. The child underlines this word and then writes the word that belongs in the sentences.

(1) We eight our lunch together.   _____
(2) The old flower mill is closed down.   _____
(3) I do not believe in whiches or goblins.   _____
(4) The injured dear was easy pray for the wolves.   _____
(5) Please weight for me after school.   _____

Make the sentence correct by writing the two words in front of each sentence in the proper blank spaces.

bare   1. The_____was standing in a_____spot
bear   in the woods.

not   2. He did_____know how to tie the_____.
knot

their   3. Over_____on the hill stands_____
there   new home.

herd   4. The cowboys_____the thundering_____
heard   coming closer.

Homographs represent another interesting group of English word pairs. These are words which have identical spellings but which are different in pronunciation and meaning. The differences in pronunciation may be either in accent (*pro'duce, pro duce'*) or in both accent and syllabication (*re bel', reb'el*). Pronunciation and meaning clues are not found in the words themselves but rather in the "sentence context" in which they are found. Thus the same spelling may represent a noun, verb, adjective, etc., and the pronunciation is determined by the word's *function* in a sentence. Most common homographs are learned by ear, that is the word must "sound right" in the sentence context. Exercises employing various sentence formats may be used in helping children master and understand these words.

1. *In each sentence there is one italicized word. Write this word on the line following the sentence, showing how the word is broken into syllables and which syllable is accented.*

   Sample: The dentist said, "I will *extract*
   the tooth."   *ex tract'*

   a. "I *object*," said the lawyer.   _____
   b. The judge did not *convict* the man.   _____
   c. She opened the bottle of vanilla *extract*.   _____
   d. The store sells groceries, meats and *produce*. _____
   e. A rope will *contract* when it is wet.   _____

2. *Rewrite each italicized word on the space provided. Break the word into syllables and show which syllable is accented.*

   Sample: That *record* was quite difficult to *record*.

   rec' ord   re cord'

   a. One does not *desert* a friend in the middle of the *desert*.

   _____   _____

   b. The teacher will *record* all grades in her *record* book.

   _____   _____

   c. What caused the *rebels* to *rebel*?

   _____   _____

   d. Did the sanitation workers *refuse* to collect the *refuse*?

   _____   _____

   e. The coach was *present* to *present* the awards.

   _____   _____

3. *Use the accent and syllabication clues that are shown, and write a sentence using the stimulus word.*

   pro' duce   _____
   ob ject'   _____
   con' tract   _____
   per mit'   _____
   con tent'   _____

4. *Write sentences using one syllable homographs such as the following list. Mark the vowel sound heard (either –or˘) to indicate the pronunciation of the word.*

   wĭnd – wīnd   līve – lĭve   bāss – bˇass
   lēad – lĕad   rēad – rĕad

5. Present a word that has two meanings and pronunciations followed by a definition of one of its meanings. The student writes the proper word indicating syllabication and accent.

   Sample: desert: "to leave or abandon"   de' sert
   rebel: "one who fights against authority"   _____
   invalid: "not well, sick or disabled"   _____
   conduct: "to lead, carry or transmit"   _____
   moderate: "not extreme"   _____
   content: "satisfied, happy"   _____

Confusion of meanings

Some words which look very much alike are often confused in meaning. Wide reading, which insures meeting such words in many different contexts, is probably the most desirable method of expanding meanings. However, teacher-made exercises can also be useful and highly motivational. As a rule, children enjoy working with word meanings, particularly if the difficulty of the exercise material is geared to their needs. Below is an example of a teaching-testing exercise.

Working With Words Whose Meaning is Often Confused

   1. Some words which look very much alike are often confused as to *meaning*. Study the following words and then, in the sentences below, fill in the blanks with the proper word.

   alter: to change or modify   council: a governing group
   altar: place used in worship   counsel: to advise

medal:	a decoration awarded for service
meddle:	to interfere
cite:	to quote, or use as illustration
sight:	to see, act of seeing
site:	location

affect:	to influence
effect:	a result produced by a cause
carton:	a box or container
cartoon:	a drawing, a caricature

meddle – medal:
1. It might be a good idea to give a _____ to people who never _____ in others affairs.

alter – altar:
2. In over 500 years, no attempt had been made to _____ the _____.

carton – cartoon:
3. You will find a humorous _____ on every_____of breakfast food.

sight – site:
4. He hoped to catch _____ of the _____where the new club was to be built.

2. The meanings of the pairs of words which follow are not given above. Place the proper word in the blanks in each sentence. Use a dictionary if you are doubtful about the meaning of any word.

miner –minor:
1. Most states have laws which prohibit a _____ from working as a _____.

course – coarse:
2. The fairways of the golf _____ were covered with _____ grass.

dairy – diary:
3. During the day Bill worked in a _____, but each night he would write in his _____.

descend – decent:
4. We should try to find a _____ trail if we hope to _____ the mountain before dark.

precede – proceed:
cannon – canyon:
5. When an army is to p_____ through a c_____ surrounded by the enemy, it is the usual custom to have a barrage by c_____ p_____ _____ the march.

Words of recent origin

English is a living language and living things grow and change. The changes that take place in a language are determined by its users and not as a result of previously adopted rules. It is likely that more new words were added to English in the past thirty years than in any previous century. Children should be invited to think about this phenomenon and discuss possible causes for it. An excellent way to develop insight is to prepare a list of recently coined words and then place them in categories.

The following are some newly coined words that were suggested by one class. Children had worked in small teams relying both on their knowledge and on any and all materials available in the classroom and library.

Astronaut, transistor, groovy, soul, uptight, laser beam, flowchart, radar, talking typewriter, heat shield, computer, thermofax, keypunch, dune buggy, teflon, megaton, formica, rap, right on, panasonic, Medicare, orlon, dragstrip, smog, seat belt, skybus, astrodome, heart transplant, yippie, lunacart, cassette, antibiotics, aerospace, polyester, telestar, snowmobile, maxi-mini-midi, and dozens of other words.

As a next step they decided to group words into categories and some of the first that came to mind were *slang, medicine, transportation* and *space exploration*. In the process they found that headings such as "science" or "technology" were too broad since these terms cut across every other heading. There was quite a list of trade names for products: Thermofax, Formica, polyester, teflon, etc. Words such as *lunacart, Medicare,* and *telestar* were analyzed and provided insights into the logic of coining new words. The study of slang terms proved interesting, particularly when an older *Dictionary of Slang* was studied. It became obvious that this is one of the most prolific areas for new words, but also that the mortality rate is very high.

Working on a unit devoted to *New Words in English* leads to an understanding of how language works and how it develops. An increased respect for the power, precision, and flexibility of language is usually an outcome. Motivation is high during such study, particularly among students who have become satiated on "reading skills instruction." A great number of reading and writing experiences can grow out of the study of newly coined words.

Word analogies

Working with analogies is an excellent way to develop skill in seeing relationship, associating or contrasting word meanings, and applying analytical processes. Exercises involving analogies can be developed for working with practically any concepts with which the school deals and can be adapted to any difficulty level. The materials which follow illustrate working with a limited number of areas such as synonyms, irregular plurals, homonyms, sports, irregular verbs, mathematics, science, and social studies. Two different formats are shown. Each illustration can easily be expanded into larger units or full page exercises.

Explain that word analogies involve a relationship or similarity between words. The following might be used to illustrate some of these relationships.

Part to whole:	(finger – hand; toe – foot)
Sequence:	(six – seven; f – g)
Origin:	(paper – tree; wheat – bread)
Class:	(orange – fruit; carrot – vegetable)
Function:	(shoe – foot; glove – hand)
Opposites:	(weak – strong; cold – hot)
Synonyms:	(hate – despise; expand – enlarge)

1. *Complete the following analogies by underlining the one word on the right that completes the sense of the statement.*

Synonyms

1. Expand is to enlarge as
   contract is to: shrink   sign   annual
2. Awkward is to clumsy as
   funny is to: joke   luminous   childlike
3. Miniature is to small as
   average is to: ordinary   rare   peculiar
4. Huge is to massive as
   often is to: hasten   forever   frequently
5. Perfect is to flawless as
   exact is to: legal   peruse   accurate

Sports

a. Glove is to baseball as
   stick is to   tennis   wrestling   hockey
b. Football is to gridiron as
   baseball is to   diamond   summer   stadium
c. Five is to basketball as
   eleven is to   baseball   football   volleyball
d. Baseball is to sport as
   tennis is to   ball   net   sport
e. Swimming is to pool as
   hockey is to   ice   teams   soccer

Math

a. Foot is to yard as
   one is to   twelve   three   six
b. One is to four as five is to   ten   fifteen   twenty
c. Ten is to 100 as one is to   ten   twenty   1/10
d. Radius is to diameter as
   three is to   6   1½   9
e. Minute is to hour as
   second is to   first   hour   minute

Science

a. Magnet is to nail as
   light is to: dark   moth   electrons
b. Soft is to hard as
   bituminous is to   deposit   anthracite   coal
c. Stem is to flower as
   trunk is to   elephant   traveler   tree
d. Canal is to water as
   vein is to   leaves   blood   mining
e. Bark is to tree as
   scales are to   markets   music   fish

   f. Caterpillar is to butterfly
      as tadpole is to   frog   fishing   pond

Process

   a. Cream is to butter as
      apple is to   tree   bushel   jelly
   b. Leather is to shoe as
      flour is to   doughnut   wheat   mill
   c. Wood is to paper as
      sand is to   break   glass   clear
   d. Milk is to cow as
      wool is to   clothing   farmer   sheep
   e. Grass is to cow as
      mouse is to   trap   cat   rat

2. Complete the following analogies by writing the one word in the English language that will complete the sense of the statement.

Homonyms

   a. Piece is to peace as pain is to _____.
   b. Steel is to steal as sun is to _____.
   c. Deer is to dear as eight is to _____.
   d. Tale is to tail as reign is to _____.
   e. Blue is to blew as weight is to _____.

Irregular verbs

   a. Sing is to sang as bring is to _____.
   b. Write is to writen as speak is to _____.
   c. Give is to gave as dive is to _____.
   d. Fly is to flew as cry is to _____.
   e. See is to saw as flee is to _____.

Irregular plurals

   a. Nickel is to nickels as penny is to _____.
   b. Dog is to dogs as fox is to _____.
   c. Cow is to cows as deer is to _____.
   e. Pan is to pans as tooth is to _____.
   f. Book is to books as child is to _____.

Developing Concepts in the Content Areas

This section will deal briefly with several problems which are related to concept development in the school. The problems boil down to school practices which have become widespread: once a practice becomes well established, its presence then becomes justification for its continued existence. In an earlier discussion the point was made that the intermediate grades represent a somewhat abrupt transition. The emphasis shifts from learning-to-read to mastery of content areas. Both textbooks and teachers tend to take reading skills for granted as they push forward rapidly on all curricular fronts.

Determining "fact or opinion"

In reading materials in the various content areas, children are frequently faced with the task of deciding whether a statement is fact or opinion. Young readers (and older ones also) develop habits which are not always helpful in this type of problem solving. One such habit is the tendency to accept "what is written" as being factual. Second, when one strongly agrees with a statement, it is frequently accepted as a fact. Third, if a position is developed logically or if something is repeated often enough, it may be accepted as factual. Thus, the statement "finding a four leaf clover *always* brings good luck" may be doubted; while the statement "finding a four leaf clover *can* bring one good luck," may seem a bit more logical.

Probably the best way to help children develop skill in differentiating fact from opinion would be immediate discussion of statements as they are met in textual material. This is difficult to do because it would call for a particular and limited *set* in regard to the material. There are other goals which through practice have earned higher priorities. Another possibility is to collect statements of fact and opinion from various sources and devote a period to their discussion. Obviously all items could pertain to one subject area such as social science, health, geography, or literature. On the other hand, exercises might deal with general statements or cut across various content areas. The following example illustrates the latter approach.

Read each statement carefully. If the sentence states a fact *write* F *on the line in front of the sentence. If the sentence states an opinion, write* O.

    __ 1. The Mississippi River is the longest river in the U.S.
    __ 2. If you go swimming immediately after eating you will get cramps.
    __ 3. Americans are the happiest people in the world.
    __ 4. A pound of feathers weighs the same as a pound of rocks.
    __ 5. The best things in life are free.

___ 6. Alaska is the largest of the fifty states.
___ 7. Today will be yesterday tomorrow.
___ 8. Baseball is the most popular sport in the U.S.
___ 9. February is always the shortest month of the year.
___10. Democracy is the best form of government for man.

___ 1. Man will never be able to settle on the moon.
___ 2. A century is equal to ten decades.
___ 3. Wild animals will not attack if you do not run.
___ 4. One should practice what he preaches.
___ 5. English contains a large number of words borrowed from other languages.
___ 6. Pollution is the most serious problem in the world today.
___ 7. Opposite sides of a square must be parallel.
___ 8. There is no life on Venus.
___ 9. A fool and his money are soon parted.
___10. If today is Monday, tomorrow will be Tuesday.

Misconceptions

During the intermediate grades many children will encounter a number of words and concepts which will puzzle them. Many such instances will occur in subject-matter texts as well as in basal readers. Whereas the child comes to school with the "meanings" which are adequate for dealing with beginning reading, he is by no means familiar with the various connotations of the words with which he must cope in the primary and intermediate grades. A lack of concepts and insufficient knowledge of various connotations of words is not the only problem with which the teacher must deal in expanding meaning. A related problem is that of misconceptions harbored by pupils. The school cannot be held responsible for misconceptions which children have picked up elsewhere. It may be impossible in overcrowded classrooms to prevent misconceptions from arising or going undetected. Nevertheless, the extent to which this problem exists should motivate teachers to seek ways of modifying instructional techniques, for the confusion of meanings is a barrier to reading and learning.

One of the axioms of teaching reading is that "new" words in a lesson should be mastered both as sight words and as meaning-bearing units before the child is expected to read that lesson. Often little attention is given to mastering shades of meaning, and too much is taken for granted when the child is able to "call the word." As a result, many teachers would be shocked at the misconceptions still harbored by some children in their classes. The following responses on vocabulary tests illustrate some rather striking misconceptions, even though it is not difficult to imagine how some of these arose. The responses are given verbatim.

regard-	a. like you were guarding something
	b. to think of someone as a cousin
	c. to re-do your work
priceless-	a. something that doesn't cost anything
	b. you want to buy something and you think it's not worth it
brunette-	a. a kind of permanent
	b. a girl that dances
	c. a prune
shrewd-	a. when you're not polite
	b. being kind of cruel
	c. guess it means rude
lecture-	a. 'lected for president

When asked to give the meaning of "conquer," one boy volunteered, "It means like to *konk her* on the head." Another, when meeting the written word *mosquitoes* for the first time, concluded it was the name of a fairy — "most quiet toes." A pre-school child hearing an older sibling make a reference to a dinosaur immediately responded, "I like to go to the *dime store*." An eight-year-old listening around Christmas time to a choir on television asked, "What does the *si door im* mean?" His parents were at a loss until he repeated the line, "Oh come let us si door im."

Some of these examples illustrate what takes place when a child is confronted with concepts beyond his present grasp. He usually changes them to a more concrete meaning which is known to him. Although illustrating how the child deals with unknown words which he *hears*, these examples can also provide us with insight into what happens when a child *reads* unknown words.

Working with malapropisms

In speaking and writing, children often reveal misconceptions by their choice of words. They might be interested in the fact that there are approximately 600,000 words in English. Since no one can learn the meanings of all of these words, it is to be expected that sometimes we will use one word when we mean to use another. Perhaps the children can be introduced to Mrs. Malaprop, a character in a play* who continuously used words which had meanings different from what she intended. Once she hired a guide and said to him, "You lead the way and we will *preceed* you." When she meant to say that the guide would *escort* the party she said, "This gentleman will *exhort* us."

The author chose the name Mrs. Malaprop to emphasize this language characteristic. When someone makes a humorous mistake like the above examples, it is called a malapropism: The prefix *mal* = "bad"; the word apropos = "fitting, suitable, to the point." An exercise such as the following provides children with the opportunity to work on detecting and correcting inappropriate use of words.

Directions: Read each sentence and find a word that "does not fit." Underline this word. Then in the blank space following the sentence, write the word that you think was intended.

1. He looked very extinguished in his new suit. _____
2. The cook prepared bacon and eggs on the girdle. _____
3. Don't play near the fire hydrogen. _____
4. The old prospector saw a marriage on the dessert. _____
5. The police arrested a restless driver. _____
6. A man was walking his dog on a lease. _____
7. She has an analogy to pollen. _____
8. I enjoyed my conservation with the pilot. _____
9. There were many futile farms along the river. _____
10. Is the whale the largest manual? _____

Pronunciation and meaning problems

Problems can be dealt with in the context in which they are met, but there is nothing educationally unsound in reviewing or teaching a series of such words by means of either the chalkboard or a lesson sheet. One value of the latter procedure is that a given exercise can be used with only those pupils who reveal a need for it, several times if needed. A list of words that are difficult to pronounce might include: *aisle, fatigue, coyote, exit, plague, sieve, cache, posse, gauge,*

The Rivals by Richard Sheridan (1775).

corps, beau, feign, nephew, antique, bouquet, isthmus, agile, chaos,
ache, plateau, quay, bivouac, czar, recipe, stature, reign, viaduct,
suede. A number of exercises can be devised to teach the pronunciation and meaning of such words. A few are listed below:

1. In the first column the difficult words are listed and adjoining
columns contain the dictionary pronunciation and meaning:

cache	cāsh	a hole in the ground, or a hiding place
feign	fān	to imagine; invent, hence, to form and relate as if true
quay	kē	a stretch of paved bank or a solid artificial landing place made beside navigable water, for convenience in loading and unloading vessels
bivouac	bĭv oo ăk	an encampment for a very short sojourn, under improvised shelter or none.

2. Use the difficult word and a synonym in the same sentence:
"As they reached the *plateau* the guide said, 'It will be easier
walking on this *flat level* ground'."

"Climbing mountains is hard work," said the guide. "We will
rest when you feel *fatigued* so tell me when you get *tired.*"

3. Prepare a card for each word; one side of the card contains the
difficult word and its pronunciation; the other side has a sentence
using the word.

c h a o s (kā ŏs)	When a tornado strikes a community, *chaos* results. Houses are blown down, fires break out, fallen trees block the streets, telephone poles and wires are down, and the fire department cannot get through the streets.

4. Prepare a short paragraph in which the difficult word is used in
several contexts.

From the aerial photographs it was difficult for him to *gauge*
whether the railroad was narrow or regular *gauge.* He recalled
that the day the picture was made the fuel *gauge* registered
very nearly empty. He remembered attempting to *gauge* the
effect of a tail wind on his chances of returning safely.

**Teaching subject matter versus
teaching how to read subject matter**

Perceptive critics of our high schools have noted the tendency in these schools to ignore the reading ability of students while using teaching strategies which are posited upon ability to read. Lately, and to a disturbing degree, this practice has filtered down into the junior high and intermediate grades.

There is little doubt that students can learn a considerable amount in science, social studies, history, government, etc., without reliance on reading. However, the important point is that instruction in the schools is still structured in such a way that reading ability is a prime prerequisite. In other words, our schools are still "reading schools." As long as this condition prevails, it should be recognized, and instruction in the content fields should be built on this reality.

Recognition of this fact would preclude teachers absolving themselves of responsibility for integrating reading instruction with subject-matter instruction. Arguments such as "there is not enough time to do both" or that "students should know how to read by the time they get to this class" would be revealed as begging the question. We might then stop dichotomizing means and ends in education and see that these components are inseparable. Teachers should feel strongly that their subject matter is important. This is reason enough to assume some responsibility for helping students develop and apply efficient reading and study habits in the process of learning that subject matter.

Teachers should determine if the achievement of their goals is being thwarted by the practices they follow in teaching. Answering the following questions may help point out where theory and practice are incompatible.

Do I as a teacher:

1. Sincerely believe that material I teach is important?
2. Assume that my students must read in order to become proficient in the subject I teach?
3. Assign reading as part of the teaching-learning process?
4. Actually know the reading ability of each of the students I teach?
5. Note evidence that some students do not possess the reading ability necessary to read critically the materials I assign?
6. Think that when students are assigned material that they cannot successfully read (even though the material itself is excellent) they will profit from this experience?

7. Understand that assigning students material they cannot read and not providing guidance in reading is an unjustifiable educational ritual?
8. Believe that each of the above factors is closely related to effective teaching?

Are the Content Areas Fact Oriented and Anti-Now?

This chapter opened with a statement that the purpose of the school is to develop and expand concepts. There is no question but that our schools are busy doing this. It was further stated that there is always debate as to "which concepts" the school should focus on and how to teach them. At this particular time, many people have opinions about these issues. Critics charge that the curriculum stresses facts, but not how these relate to each other, that whatever learning takes place does so in an atmosphere of joylessness, that there is little relevance between school activities and the child's life and needs.

Ever since Sputnik there has been a tendency in the United States to blame the schools for every weakness, shortcoming, or failure that occurs in any sector of our society. In addition, when the society is frustrated beyond its usual threshold for pain by a declining stock market, an unpopular war, or out-groups reaching for power, it is much safer to attack the schools than the real problems. Nevertheless, it is hard to escape the feeling that many students would add eloquent testimony reflecting the schools' lack of relevance (if somewhere they had developed the tools of eloquence).

Most of us remember the recent but not too funny jokes about our capability to land men on the moon and our inability to motivate sixth graders to read about the world in which we live. This phenomena is difficult to rationalize since the world is full of mystery, suspense, puzzles, and patterns; it is crowded with adventure. There are amazing discoveries being made almost daily in the areas of space, medicine, communication, and human relations. Many of these are as fascinating as Columbus' famous discovery, and certainly as interesting as anything found in textbooks. The great advantage for teachers is that these discoveries are *now*. This advantage is nullified if the "world of now" cannot be smuggled into the classroom.

The school must break with its past; we must not overrely on textbooks, workbooks, mechanical gadgets, and a fragmented curriculum. The now world undoubtedly threatens many of us teachers more than it does children, but perhaps we can enter it as partners. Children are ready.

Those schools that are not quite ready are doing one little thing wrong (which in this case is analogous to permitting dust in the carburetor, the result being that the great school machine won't go!): These schools will not trust the children they teach to test for themselves whether great benefits, advantages, and opportunities accrue to those who learn to read. Such schools are not marketplaces for ideas; they are company stores which extort exorbitant prices for the few staples they stock.

These schools put too much faith in the curriculum they have worked out, and they are usually dominated by the materials they have selected for teaching that curriculum. In one sense the materials decide *what* concepts will be dealt with, *when* they will be explored, *where* each will fit in the sequence, and *how* each will be handled. The only decision the children make is how long they will attend to this ritual.

Children who do poorly in learning to read are very sad indeed. We try to convince them that they are missing something great. We even convince ourselves of this. This is an important part of the folklore of our educational system. If the child could only read, the school would make his life so full, so pleasant, so rewarding, so growth provoking. This is a fallacy that helps sustain teachers and schools.

Turning to those children who do master the reading process, are their school experiences as exhilarating as we have promised? Are these children taking mind-expanding journeys during the reading period? Does social studies really grab their minds? Does the ability to read help children "do their thing," or is there an establishment that calls the shots? If the ability to read pays such high dividends, how does one account for the fact that so many students who *can* read are not avid readers? Does the school really make a serious attempt to help the child collect all of the rewards that he has been told will accrue from *learning to read*?

We're beginning to suspect that the school does not use reading ability of students very creatively, and that those students who do crack the code find themselves in somewhat of a learning-reading straitjacket. The reward for cracking the code is a long term sentence to do innumerable, less than meaningful assignments such as reading chapters and answering factual questions. Within the framework of the school, learning to read does not inevitably bring freedom to read.* It may not provide escape from the humdrum. It

*See Carl R. Rogers, *Freedom to Learn*. (Columbus, Ohio: Charles E. Merrill Publishing Co., 1969.)

does not a priori usher one into the "wonderful world of books." Before one can enjoy all of the blessings that alledgedly reside in reading, one must participate in and become immersed in certain types of experiences. Unfortunately, some schools are the natural enemy of such experiences.

The previous discussion does not support the idea that children should determine the curriculum. However, they should be encouraged to contribute to some decisions along the way. For instance a two-page textbook stimulus on conservation could lead to a relatively unlimited unit on a number of current issues relative to ecology. Here students could select *their* topics which might range from "The Death of Lake Erie" to "How poisoning wolves in Alaska upset the balance of nature."

A study of several metropolitan newspapers (21) as part of a unit on "Mass Communication" could lead to the discussion of phenomena such as the following:

1. Newspapers from widely separated areas will carry identical, word-for-word, news stories. How does this come about?
2. The same "news" story in different newspapers may be found under vastly different headlines. That is, the different headlines may imply almost opposite conclusions based on the same "facts." Why?
3. Editorials on the same topic (legislation, foreign policy, education) may present diametrically opposed conclusions. How might this be accounted for?
4. The same editorial may appear in papers that have no connections with one another. Is this a coincidence? Who prepared the editorial? How did it get in dozens of different newspapers the same day or during the same week?
5. How are opinion polls conducted? What is their purpose? Are the results reliable? Are there any potential dangers in the widespread use of such polls?

With the world in revolution it is a somewhat old hat to study our own one great revolution exclusively in terms of the Boston Tea Party, Paul Revere and "one if by land and two if by sea," or Washington crossing the Delaware and surprising the Hessians on Christmas Day. We need not turn our back on these concepts, but we can make room for others which have relevance for today and which help us to understand the millions of people who are attempting their revolution now. Thomas Paine had a dream for *our* revolution which went beyond taxation without representation. He wrote:

> Oh ye that love mankind
> ye that dare oppose
> not only tyranny
> but the tyrant,
> Stand forth!
> ... receive the fugitive
> and prepare *in time*
> an asylum
> for mankind

Fact laden pages and chapters often fail to convey the crucial historical significance of a particular event or era.

Summary

The folklore of education attempts to convince the child that once he has learned to read he will have achieved a most precious freedom. The process of "learning to read" is seen as somewhat analogous to paying his dues and going through the initiation ritual. Once this is completed, he is to enjoy all the blessings and privileges of club membership. Henceforth, life in school will be pleasant, rewarding, and growth provoking.

Children soon perceive that this is folly. Reading *in the school* is often not an exhilarating experience. They have to read textbooks in reading, social studies, science, etc. Frequently these tasks fall short of the excitement anticipated. Reading is used for fulfilling assignments. They can read without feeling, without involvement. Although reading is a language process, both instruction in reading and the use of reading can fail to capitalize on the power and magic of language. When this occurs teachers are reduced to asking "how do you motivate children to want to read?"

The motivational challenge in "decoding words" deteriorates rapidly unless this activity is accompanied by decoding language. Reading instruction should deal with teaching children how their language functions. They need to know how intonation influences meaning, that some words have many different meanings, that English abounds with figurative expressions which have special meanings. Children need to have some understanding of the sentence-pattern and word-order options that English can accommodate. But above all, children need experiences. Above all, children need experiences which lead them to perceive the power, beauty flexibility and precision that their language affords. Thus they need more than textbooks and experience charts. They must interact with the language of feeling as well as that of facts.

YOUR POINT OF VIEW?

Respond to the following problems:

1. What would you have to add to the following statement to make it consistent with your definition of *the purpose of the school?*

   "The purpose and function of the school is to help the child develop and expand concepts, and to help him develop the language tools which will permit him to do this independently."

2. *Premise:* "Misconceptions are more likely to arise in the content areas than in the materials used for reading instruction." Based on a study of curriculum materials, provide data that would support this assumption.

Would you defend or attack the following premises? Supply a rationale for each of your choices.

1. Reading instruction in American schools tends to neglect helping the child to see reading as a language process.

2. A valid criticism of subject matter textbooks is that they present an unrealistically large number of concepts which are beyond the grasp of pupils in the grades for which the texts were designed.

3. Many children master the mechanics of reading, but fail to understand the role of intonation as it functions in reading for meaning.

4. Materials used for instruction in reading should include a sizable portion of content that "teaches the child about his language and how language operates."

5. At each successive grade level, a smaller percentage of children are avid readers, i.e., fewer children love to read as a free-choice activity.

BIBLIOGRAPHY

1. Butts, David P. "Content and Teachers In Oral Language Acquisition — Means or Ends?" *Elementary English* (March 1971), 290–97.

2. Carlton, Lessie and Robert H. Moore, *Reading, Self-Directive Dramatization and Self-Concept.* Columbus, Ohio: Charles E. Merrill Publishing Co., 1968.

3. Carroll, John B. "Words, Meanings and Concepts," *Harvard Educational Review* (Spring 1964), 178–202.

4. Cohen, Dorothy H. "Effect of a Special Program in Literature on Vocabulary and Reading Achievement," in *Reading and Realism,* J. Allen Figurel (ed.), Proceedings, International Reading Association, 13, Part 1, 1969, 754–57.

5. Crosby, Muriel, "Concept Building: Human Relations," *Education,* (September 1963), 36–39.

6. Early, Margaret (ed.), *Language Face to Face.* Syracuse University: The Reading and Language Arts Center, 1971.

7. Emans, Robert, "Use of Context Clues," in *Reading and Realism,* J. Allen Figurel (ed.), Proceedings, International Reading Association, 13, Part 1, 1969, 76–82.

8. Gast, David K. "The Dawning of the Age of Aquarius for Multi-Ethnic Children's Literature," *Elementary English* (May 1970), 661–65.

9. Golub, Lester S. "Teaching Literature as Language," *Elementary English,* (November 1970), 669–77.

10. Greenlaw, M. Jean, "Science Fiction: Impossible! Improbable! or Prophetic?" *Elementary English* (April 1971), 196–202.

11. Groesbeck, Hulda, The Comprehension of Figurative Language by Elementary Pupils: A Study of Transfer. Unpublished Doctoral Thesis, Oklahoma University, 1961.

12. Hildreth, Gertrude, *Teaching Reading.* New York: Holt, Rinehart, & Winston, Inc., 1958.

13. Holmes, Elizabeth Ann, Children's Knowledge of Figurative Language. Unpublished Masters Thesis, Oklahoma University, 1959.

14. Jenkins, William A. "Goals of Language Instruction, 1970," *Elementary English* (April 1971), 179–87.

15. Juliea, Sister M. "The Magic of Words," *Catholic School Journal* (March 1964), 57–8.

16. Leavitt, Hart Day and David A. Sohn, *Stop, Look, and Write,* New York: Bantam Books, Inc., 1964.

17. Loban, Walter, "The Limitless Possibilities for Increasing Knowledge About Language," *Elementary English* (May 1970), 624–30.

18. O'Leary, Helen F. "Vocabulary Presentation and Enrichment," *Elementary English* (October 1964), 613–15.

19. Robertson, Jean E. "Pupil Understanding of Connectives In Reading" in *Forging Ahead In Reading,* J. Allen Figural (ed.), Proceedings, International Reading Association, 12, Part 1, 581–88.

20. Root, Sheldon L., Jr. "Literary Understandings in the Reading Program of the Primary Grades," *Reading and Inquiry*. Proceedings, International Reading Association, 10, 1965, 70–72.

21. Sailer, Carl, "Building Reading Skills Via Reading the Newspapers," in *Reading and Realism*, J. Allen Figurel (ed.), Proceedings, International Reading Association, 13, Part 1, 127–32.

22. Schnepf, Virginia and Odessa Meyer, *Improving Your Reading Program*. New York: The Macmillan Company, 1971, 124–44.

23. Shapiro, Phyllis P. and Bernard J. Shapiro, "Two Methods of Teaching Poetry Writing In The Fourth Grade," *Elementary English* (April 1971), 225–28.

24. Sheldon, William D. and Donald R. Lashinger, "A Summary of Research Studies Relating to Language Arts In Elementary Education: 1968," *Elementary English* (November 1969), 866–85.

25. Smith, E. Brooks, Kenneth S. Goodman, and Robert Meredith, *Language and Thinking In the Elementary School*. New York: Holt, Rinehart and Winston, Inc., 1970.

26. Stauffer, Russell G. "Concept Development and Reading," *Reading Teacher* (November 1965), 100–5.

27. Stewig, John Warren, "Metaphor and Children's Writing," *Elementary English* (February 1966), 121–23.

28. Sutton, Rachel S. "Words Versus Concepts," *Education* (May 1963), 537–40.

29. Thompson, Ruby L. "Word Power: How to Use What They Like to Give Them What They Need," *Journal of Reading* (October 1971), 13–15.

30. Tiedt, Iris M. and Sidney W. Tiedt, "A Linguistic Library for Students," *Elementary English* (January 1968), 38–40.

31. Torrance, E. Paul, *Rewarding Creative Behavior*. Englewood Cliffs, N.J.: Prentice Hall, Inc., 1965.

32. Yandell, Maurine Dunn and Miles V. Zintz, "Some Difficulties Which Indian Children Encounter with Idioms in Reading," *Reading Teacher* (March 1961), 256–59.

14

Teaching
Reading-Study Skills

Formal education has many goals, one of which is to help the child become increasingly independent within the framework of the school setting. To achieve such independence the learner must master a number of related language tools or skills. One important cluster of skills has been designated reading-study skills or work-type reading skills. In our reading dominated schools, these skills are of primary importance. Yet, in actual classroom practice, they are not always treated with this same importance. Obviously, the need for these skills becomes more pronounced as students move upward through the grades. A review of the literature on reading reveals general agreement about the major areas of reading-study skills; these include:

1. Locating Information
2. Evaluating Material
3. Organizing and Summarizing Data
4. Retaining Essentials of What is Read
5. Flexibility, or Adjusting Rate to Purpose

Any one of these major topics would probably include numerous specific skills; for instance, locating information would cover:

    1. Effective use of books
       a. Table of Contents
       b. Index
          (1) knowledge of alphabetical order
          (2) use of key words
          (3) cross-listings
          (4) following subtopics
          (5) significance of abbreviations and signals commonly used, e.g., "see also . . .," or commas and hyphens in page listings
    2. Use of Special References
       a. Encyclopedia
       b. Atlas
       c. Dictionary
          (1) extended knowledge of alphabetical order
          (2) selection of proper connotation of word
          (3) recognition of inflected and derived forms of words
          (4) use of diacritical marks
       d. Use of Library Aids
          (1) card catalogue
          (2) *Reader's Guide*
          (3) bound periodicals

The study skills are an excellent illustration of what is meant by the term developmental. It can be seen that any given skill is not taught exclusively, or once for all time, at a given grade level. Each skill can be thought of as being a continuum which represents both increasing difficulty of learning tasks and increasing potential usefulness to the learner. For instance, skill in using a table of contents is first taught systematically in grade one when the teacher calls attention to the list of stories found in a pre-primer. With this experience, no child will have mastered this skill to a degree required for effective use of the table of contents in a sixth grade geography book. However, since the use of a table of contents, index, or appendix is not seen as part of the content of either geography, health, or arithmetic, these and other related study skills may be neglected in all courses of study. (14, 31)

Brewer (3) states that if students are to be able to work effectively in content areas, ". . . the school must accept greater responsibility for initial teaching and provide guided practice in using the reading study skills. It is essential that these be interpreted as fundamental, and treated as such in order to progress in all curriculum subjects." While it is true that some children will learn study skills incidentally, the importance of these skills suggests that they should not be left to incidental learning.

Locating
Information

As children become independent readers and attempt to find answers through wide and varied reading, they must understand and use all the hints and helps available in order to determine rapidly and accurately whether a particular book contains information in which they are interested. In other words, knowing how to use the book is a prerequisite for intelligent use of supplementary reading in the subject areas and in any unit work. In the intermediate grades, the increased need for study skills stems from the nature of the materials used, the need for wide reading, and the fact that supervision is not always readily available. While reading ability is a prerequisite for the development of study skills, this ability in itself does not assure that a pupil has mastered the study skills. When a pupil fails to develop adequate study skills, the educational process may become dull and unpleasant, and guidance and specific instruction must be provided to help children develop these skills. (1)

During the past few years, we have witnessed a tremendous expansion of the availability of books, professional journals, and other printed matter in practically every area of man's experience. This advance in knowledge in the past two decades, even when compared with previous centuries, has been so dramatic that the period since 1945 has been labeled the era of the "knowledge explosion." Competency in any given field has taken on a new meaning and educational methods, of necessity, will have to change radically to adapt to this new challenge.

The contents of any subject area cannot be encompassed within a single textbook or even a series of texts. The time lag between research, publication, and the adoption of textbooks causes even the most recent texts to be somewhat inadequate. Good teachers have always attempted to provide supplementary reading materials, but achieving this goal has not been easy. Today, providing a wide array of supplementary materials is not only desirable, it is an absolute necessity. Thus, study skills have rather abruptly increased in value to the learner while the school's respect for these skills and its ability to teach them effectively has lagged. The following discussion deals with facets of instruction that relate to locating information.

Effective Use of Books

In teaching any of the study skills, the teacher at each grade level starts from, and builds on, what the student presently knows. To do this, the present ability level of each student must be determined. A good place to begin is with the textbook adopted for a given course. Teachers have learned from experience that many students are not particularly adept at "mining" a book, but meaningful learning situations can lead to the development of this facility. (9)

It is easy to develop exercises that foster such growth. Some teachers do not particularly like the exercise approach, but we should keep in mind that any learning situation is, in essence, an exercise. The issue is how exercise materials and specific teachings are used in relation to the goals to be achieved. Some very important learnings deal with the mechanics of learning — *how* to use a card catalogue, *where* to look in an encyclopedia, *when* an appendix or glossary might be useful, *what* is likely to be found in an appendix or glossary, and the like.

Workbook exercises are often provided to help pupils understand the function of an index, table of contents, or appendix. It is common to find pupils who can work out correct solutions to workbook problems consisting of sample lines from an index but who still do not know how to get help from a real index. One of the best ways to teach children how to use a book effectively is to design a learning situation around a textbook which they will be using throughout the year. A social science, health, or other text would provide ample opportunities for teaching the functions of the table of contents, charts, indexes, or appendixes. The use of the text the child is using will give him something concrete to return to when he is in doubt. Skills learned in using one text should transfer to books in other areas.

Student deficiences in using a table of contents, index, glossary, and appendix are frequently not detected by teachers and often provisions may not be made for teaching these skills. Too often it is assumed these basic skills have been taught or are being taught elsewhere. For example, as an outcome of an in-service program, one group of teachers agreed to build a one-page testing-teaching exercise consisting of fifteen to twenty questions which would measure students' skill in using parts of a book. The exercise was to be specifically applicable to the textbook students were using in one of their courses. Although the books had been in use for nearly three months, few students were able to complete the exercise without error. Teachers discovered glaring deficiencies and tremendous individual differences in students' ability to use these reader aids. In one class, the time students took to do the "book mining" exercise was noted. The range was from six to twenty-two minutes (a range of 400 percent), with some students unable to complete the task. An exercise similar to that under discussion is shown on page 490.

Such an exercise might be used initially with an entire class. For the proficient student, it will be a justifiable review, and for others it will serve as a diagnostic instrument. The observant teacher will note which students have difficulty and what their problems are. Teaching small groups and individual students the skills they need should be an outgrowth of the teacher's findings. General concepts will also be taught in the process. This particular experience was constructed for use with a sixth grade social studies text.*

The exercise teaches a number of facts about the book. Question one takes the reader to the table of contents and requires that he be able to associate his home state with part of a larger geographical region of the United States. Question two calls attention to a sixteen-page atlas; and question three focuses on a second highly specialized table of contents which deals exclusively with maps.

Questions 4–8 deal with ways in which the index may be helpful. The reader must locate pictures through the use of key words and be prepared to look under different headings. (Grand Coulee Dam is found under Grand Coulee *Project*.) Topics may be listed as subheads under a more general heading. Thus, Dutch, English, Spanish and other explorations are all listed under *Exploration*. Questions 9–11 deal with information about pronunciation and meanings of more difficult words, and call attention to the fact that these aids are divided between the index and glossary.

Profiting from reader-aids

Students sometimes fail to realize that a number of reader-aids are included in most reference books and textbooks. Unfamiliarity with,

---

*Norman Carls, Philip Baron and Frank E. Sorenson, *Knowing Our Neighbors In The United States* (New York: Holt, Rinehart & Winston, Inc., 1966).

Page:

How to Use a Book

1. The region in which we live is discussed under the heading
   _____.

2. The last 16 pages in the book are called an Atlas. Looking at these pages can you define "atlas"? _____
   _____

3. On what page can you find a listing of all maps, graphs and diagrams found in the book? _____

4. Does the book contain a picture of Wonder Lake? _____ How did you go about answering this question? _____
   _____

5. Is there a picture of the Grand Coulee Dam in the text?
   _____

6. Under what heading must you look to find it? _____
   _____

7. In the index there is a main heading *Exploration*. What six subheadings are found under it? _____
   _____

8. The book contains a double page map called Main Air Routes in the U.S. There is no heading "Main Air Routes" in the index. How can you find this map? _____
   _____
   _____

9. There are two sections of the book which provide the pronunciation of difficult words, these are _____ and_____.

10. The pronunciation of the following words is provided in the _____. In the blank spaces show the pronunciation and page number where found:
    SHOSHONE _____ Page_____
    COMANCHE _____ Page_____
    FORT DUQUESNE _____ Page_____

11. A particular page contains the *definition* of difficult words used throughout the book. That page is called the _____
    _____ and is page number _____.

or disinclination to use, these aids will inhibit students from "mining" books with maximum efficiency. Although the student has a need for this skill, he does not always recognize this need since he is not aware of the value of these aids or how they might improve his learning.

It will be noted that, for one purpose, the table of contents might be skimmed. With other goals in mind, it must be read critically. A comparison of different books would disclose that a table of contents may consist exclusively of chapter titles. This is similar to an outline composed of nothing but major topics. In some books, chapter titles are followed by a number of topics in the order in which they are discussed. Students may note that this, in essence, is a modified index containing only major headings in *chronological* order. The index, on the other hand, is in *alphabetical* order, dealing with smaller topics, and cutting across chapters.

The major learnings are: (1) that parts of the book are deliberately designed as aids for the reader; (2) these are valuable aids and are used with profit by the efficient reader; (3) each of the different parts of a book has a definite purpose. The efficient reader must make instant decisions as to where to go for specific types of help; he learns what type of information is contained in each section, where the various aids are located, and how each may be used effectively. Once learned, this knowledge can be transferred and applied to any book. The following is an abbreviated treatment of what the reader might expect to gain from the helps found in most books:

As "Aids" for the Reader	Information the Reader Might Expect to Find
Title Page	Main title and subtitle. (The latter may set forth the limitations and narrow the topic.) Name of author, date published.
Table of Contents	Chapter titles followed by major topics discussed in each chapter. Is book divided into major parts (I, II, III)? What are these? Length of chapters give hint as to thoroughness of treatment.
Preface	To whom or to what group does the author address the book? What is his

	stated purpose? What new features does he stress? What unique features does he believe are found in the book?
Illustrations	Title, item and page where found.
Index	Major topics in alphabetical order; minor topics under each heading; key phrases, cross references, photographs, drawings, charts, tables.
Glossary	Difficult or specialized terms presented in alphabetical order, with a definition.
Appendix	Organized body of facts related to subject under consideration. For example, in a geography book the appendix may give the areas of states or nations, populations, state and national capitals, extent of manufacturing, exports, imports, mineral deposits, etc.

**Use of
Library**

Effective use of library resources may well be one of the most underrated and undertaught skills in the entire school program. The library is *basic* to the school's reading program (11). It is a place where children read and receive guidance in both the use of books and in research techniques. Children at all grade levels need the experience of frequent contacts with a good school library.

Some teachers use the library effectively themselves but do not assume responsibility for teaching students to do so. On the other hand, there are a number of teachers who would score low on any evaluation of their personal use of library facilities. To illustrate, one school librarian and principal were convinced that a substantial number of the teaching staff were somewhat derelict in their personal use of the library. Further, student use of the library for these teachers' courses seemed to be less than optimum. A one-hour library unit was incorporated into the total in-service program. Each teacher was relieved of his regularly scheduled duties for a one-hour period, and this time was spent in conference with the librarian.

The librarian assumed responsibility for discussing and pointing out resources which related directly to the various subjects taught by each teacher. Pamphlets, bound volumes, pertinent books, government documents, current magazines, and the like were located, and suggestions were made as to how the librarian might help the faculty member and the students in his classes.

Records disclosed that the attitude of a number of the teaching staff changed markedly after this experience. Some teachers visited the library more frequently, spent more time in the library, and checked out more materials. In addition, the students in these teachers' courses began to use the library much more effectively.

It is generally conceded that it is difficult to teach library usage in a classroom setting removed from the library materials themselves. However, certain facts related to the library can be discussed prior to a visit to the library.

Several teachers in one school built a model card catalogue drawer using a three-by-five index-card box and constructing approximately 100 author cards ranging from *A* through *G*. This model was used in the various classrooms and was particularly useful in working with individual students who were not yet competent in the use of the card catalogue.

Another useful teaching device consisted of a library checklist devised by teachers and the librarian. The list consisted of eight or ten specific tasks which the student was to perform in the library such as:

1. Find the book *King of the Wind* by Marguerite Henry.
2. a. Who is the author of the book *A Child's History of Art?* _____.
    b. What is the call number of this book? _____.
    c. Fill out a library card for this book_____.
3. Where are the bound volumes of *My Weekly Reader* located? _____.

These items provide guided practice in the use of title and author cards, location of books and journals on the shelves, and the proper filling out of library cards. Other tasks cover specific learnings related to the library.

To use this technique effectively, small groups or individual students go to the library at specific times. The librarian may give a brief explanation of how to use certain facilities in the library. Then each child may be handed a checklist of tasks. The problems may vary according to grade level and individual student needs. In some cases a student monitor may work one hour a week in the library helping other students with the checklist and other problems.

There are numerous ways in which teachers and the librarian may work together in teaching study skills. One account of such a cooperative endeavor describes a joint teaching venture in which one teacher and the librarian conducted a weekly library usage period. Topics included search techniques, organizing a paper, constructing a bibliography, outlining, and notetaking. (17)

At some stage of the program the *Dewey decimal system* might be explained. A duplicated sheet containing information may be studied in class or in a library visit. The amount of details included would be determined by teacher objectives and student readiness. Material such as the following might be included.

All books are divided into ten major groups and each group is numbered as follows:

000 - 099 general works, bibliographies, encyclopedias, periodicals
100 - 199 philosophy, psychology
200 - 299 religion
300 - 399 education, government, law, sociology
400 - 499 language
500 - 599 physical science, mathematics
600 - 699 medicine, engineering, agriculture
700 - 799 fine arts (painting, architecture, music)
800 - 899 literature
900 - 999 history, travel, biography

Reference materials

Using reference materials is an important study skill which, as a general rule, is not thoroughly taught in our schools. Many students reach high school or even college with only a hazy idea of how to make a systematic search of available materials. The child, both in and out of school, is constantly faced with the problem of locating material and deciding whether it is relevant to his purpose. (20) Although a few children in the upper primary level are ready for limited use of reference materials, it is in the intermediate grades that teachers have a major responsibility to teach these skills.

The encyclopedia

The use of encyclopedias and other reference books should be deliberately taught. If such materials are located in the room, different children or groups can be taught their use at various times. Instruction here will parallel points already covered above, i.e., topics are arranged in alphabetical order, books are numbered in series, the alphabetical range covered is indicated on the cover, and cross listings and key words will have to be used. The teacher can make a set of card exercises, each card containing a question: "What book and what page tell about coal?" "About the Suez Canal?" "About Iron Deposits?"

Teaching any given unit in any content area can provide the framework for teaching efficient use of the encyclopedia to those students who need this instruction. Assume a health class is developing the topic *The Advance of Medicine*. Students might be asked to list all of the possible headings under which they might list data which relates to *The Advance of Medicine*. The responses might range from one suggestion to "look under medicine" to a half page of suggestions which might include medicine, surgery, disease, medical research, drugs, germ theory, space medicine, and public health. Other headings might include particular diseases such as cancer, tuberculosis, yellow fever, diabetes, poliomyelitis; or the names of individuals who made significant medical discoveries such as Walter Reed, Jonas Salk, Louis Pasteur.

Interpreting and Evaluating Material

Locating information is an important part of the learning process, but this step is only a prelude to the ultimate goal of assimilation of material. The ability to locate information will have little impact on personal or academic growth if the student is unable to read the material he has located.

Teaching students how to read critically is undoubtedly the most difficult task attempted in our schools. In fact, if the matter is pressed beyond the usual textbook definitions, asking a group of teachers to *define* critical reading is more likely to result in chaos than in unanimity. Practically all of their definitions are abstractions, simply because critical reading involves so many variables.

Interpreting and evaluating material is probably as close a synonym for *critical reading* as can be found. Illustrations of the analytical abilities involved include:

1. Knowing what the author has said
2. Grasping the validity of statements and knowing when and how to check validity with other sources
3. Differentiating between facts and opinion
4. Noting when inferences are being drawn and drawing them when they are not stated
5. Detecting author bias as well as inaccuracies which might not be traceable to bias
6. Understanding one's own biases as these relate to what is being read
7. Taking into consideration an author's use of allusions, satire, humor, irony, and the like
8. Developing some criteria for judging an author's competency in the area in which he writes

Undoubtedly this list could be extended. Each of the above abilities is developmental in nature and should be taught at all grade levels. The reading tasks found in the intermediate grades are characterized by an increasing difficulty that requires a high degree of competency if the reader is to grow increasingly perceptive. This point holds even as we move into the high school and beyond. How many adults are immune to propaganda, know both sides of controversial issues, and do not let their emotions color interpretations while reading? Parke (22) suggests that students read for much the same reasons as do adults; namely, to keep informed, secure answers to questions, solve problems, follow directions, and share with others. It is likely that students do more reading that calls for interpretation and evaluation than do adults simply because this is the nature of being a student.

The test of critical reading often applied in our schools is the students' demonstration of the ability to restate or write what an author has said. The inability to discern what the author is saying may well be evidence of inability to read the material critically, but paraphrasing, by itself, is not evidence of critical reading either. Restating the gist of a passage but failing to detect author bias will result in a transfer of author bias to the reader's own thought. Knowing what the author is saying without seeing that some statements are contrary to fact will inhibit critical reading, as will reciting strongly expressed opinions as if these were statements of verifiable facts.

Interpreting and evaluating calls for the application of a number of the mechanical reading skills and higher level abilities listed above. Students need both guidance and systematic practice in developing work habits and study techniques, (30) a number of which are dealt with in the following discussion.

Retention of Material Read

The organization of our schools and the curricular materials used make learning very dependent upon reading. Once the mechanical process of recognizing printed words is fairly well established, the most frequently cited weakness of students at *all* educational levels relates to inefficient retention of what is read. Remembering what is read is synonymous with "learning from reading." Of most reading that students are expected to do, this is the primary goal.

When we subject students to an examination of materials read, we are in essence sampling the knowledge they have gleaned and retained. We often find that reading is relatively ineffective when judged by what students retain. Approximately the same degree of efficiency (or inefficiency) in retention is found when the material is presented orally via lecture. Some loss in the communicative process is inevitable. Since the role of the teacher is to guide and direct learning activities, we should seek to examine every approach or technique that will further that purpose.

Retention of material read is influenced by many factors, one of which is the reader's "set," a psychological term referring to perception. This is often discussed under the general heading of the "reader's purpose." It is probably true that, as teachers, we sometimes fail in helping students develop a meaningful purpose for reading. Sometimes more stress is placed on the ritual of covering material than on assimilation. This misemphasis is seen, for example, when a teacher gives a reading assignment just as a class period ends; or when there is no further elaboration than "your assignment for our next meeting is Chapter 8—read Chapter 8 for Friday."

Many students will follow these instructions with no appreciable learning taking place. It is also unlikely they will make contributions if the material is discussed in class. When the reader's only purpose is to fulfill an assignment, he will read Chapter 8, or any other chapter, without conscious interaction with the material. If, as he finishes the reading, his teacher were suddenly to appear and ask, "What have you just read?" the answer would be, "I don't know, I was just trying to finish the assignment."

Use of questioning to inculcate a learning set

Studies indicate that questions that are considered prior to the actual reading have a salutory effect on both learning and retention. (8) Questions provide a purpose for reading and alert the reader to important issues to be covered. In this sense, questions provide a preview of what will be met in the reading situation. This techinque is one of the highly justifiable procedures of most "study programs." (4)

The use of questions should not be limited to preparing students for assignment. A greater value for questions results from helping the student formulate concepts. Yet, as Smith (29) points out, questions per se have no inherent value. In any teaching situation, questions can be used most unimaginatively. The efficacy of questioning lies in the interaction which may take place between teacher and student as together they explore the *meaning* of what is being taught and learned. "The artful teacher initiates and sustains the kind of thoughtful discourse that helps students ruminate and organize ideas."

Using the Dictionary

The use of the dictionary is another important study skill associated with reading instruction at the intermediate level. The three major goals in dictionary instruction are learning to: (1) find a particular word, (2) determine its pronunciation, and (3) select the correct meaning of the word in the context in which it is used. Teaching dictionary skills is often neglected by teachers even when they acknowledge the value of these skills. This neglect might stem from a teacher's feeling of inadequacy about certain relatively difficult facets of dictionary use such as mastering diacritical markings or pronunciation keys. On the other hand, teaching may fall short of maximum efficiency when dictionary skills are taught as something extra rather than as an intrinsic part of the regular reading instruction. The use of the dictionary should always be seen by both teacher and pupil as a means of getting meaning, not as a form of rote drill or a penalty for making certain errors. (16)

Certain prerequisites are essential for successful use of the dictionary. A few of these skills or undertstandings are:

1. The knowledge of alphabetical order
2. The understanding that a word can have many different meanings
3. The knowledge of root words and the various inflected and derived forms of root words
4. The understanding that letters and combinations of letters have different sound values in different situations and that some letters are silent
5. The knowledge that *y* on the end of some words is changed to *i* before adding *es* for plurals

Facility in the use of the dictionary paves the way for a number of potential breakthroughs in the struggle for independence in reading because it:

1. Unlocks the sound or pronunciation of words
2. Discloses new meanings of words which may be known in

          only one or a limited number of connotations

  3. Confirms the spelling of a word when one can only approximate its correct spelling
  4. Expands vocabulary through mastery of inflected and derived forms of known root words

These skills are developmental in nature and must be refined and extended as the child moves upward through the grades. The alphabetizing ability which is adequate for successful fourth grade work will be inadequate for junior high or high school. The brunt of teaching dictionary skills falls on the intermediate grades simply because most of those skills are introduced during these years of instruction. The success the child feels and the utility he sees in dictionary usage can be most important factors in how he reacts to the dictionary as a tool for helping him in all facets of communication. He must be shown that dictionary skills are permanently needed; failure to master these skills can color his attitudes and learning development for many years to come.

A number of developmental tasks are associated with dictionary usage and there is general agreement among educators on what these tasks are and the order in which they should be presented.

Developmental tasks in dictionary mastery

  1. Recognize and differentiate between letters
  2. Associate letter names with letter symbols
  3. Learn the letters of the alphabet in order
  4. Arrange a number of words by alphabetical order of their initial letter
  5. Extend above skill to second and third letters of words, eventually working through all letters of a word if necessary
  6. Develop facility in rapid, effective use of dictionary, i.e., where does H, P, V come in the dictionary; open dictionary as near as possible to word being studied
  7. Develop the ability to use accent marks in arriving at the pronuonciation of words
  8. Learn to interpret phonetic spelling used in dictionary
  9. Use pronunciation key given somewhere on each double page of most dictionaries
 10. Work out different pronunciations and meanings of words which are spelled alike

11. Determine which is the preferred pronunciation when several are given
12. Select the meaning which fits the context
13. Profit from guide words found at the top of each page to tell at a glance if the page contains the word being sought
14. Use intelligently special sections of a dictionary; geographical terms and names, biographical data, foreign words and phrases

Although particular skills are characteristically taught at a given grade level, what the individual child has learned or not learned should determine what is taught. Fortunately, dictionaries are available at all levels of difficulty from simple picture dictionaries to massive unabridged editions. The needs of the child and the goals of the teacher should determine how these differences in dictionaries will be utilized in the classroom. A child who is expected to use a dictionary which calls for skills far beyond what he has mastered will profit little from the experience. Any classroom practice which puts the child in such a position has little if any educational justification.

Rate of Reading

The rate at which one can assimilate meaning from printed symbols becomes a reading problem when students are expected to understand curricular materials for which their reading skills, habits, and abilities are inadequate. (26) The intermediate grades are probably the first level at which a concern for rate of reading is justified since at this point emphasis begins to be placed on the various content areas. In recent years there has been considerable emphasis on the need for improving rate of reading. The impetus for this concern with rate undoubtedly came first at the college level, where, for the past several decades, considerable attention has been given to this problem. College reading improvement programs grew out of the conviction that many college students have the capacity to meet the demands of the college curriculum but that their reading habits make them poor academic risks. It is undoubtedly true that many teachers, ranging from high school to the intermediate levels, are convinced that this is also the case with many of their students.

Over the years the term *rate of reading* has been widely but not always wisely used. It has been a popular practice to speak of the rate of reading of the average high school senior, college freshman, or adult. The impression was often left that the figure quoted, such as 325 or 375 words per minute, had some real significance. The implication was that once an individual's rate for reading a given passage was established, this figure could be cited as though it were a constant for any reading situation. The emphasis on rate led some individuals to confuse the entire reading process with the number of words one could allegedly cover in a specified period of time. In an effort to lessen this tendency, it became popular to talk about "rate of comprehension," a term which emphasized that reading is getting meaning. But this term was also subject to semantic confusion since several factors are always at work in determining rate of comprehension. (28) There are a number of variables which influence the rate at which different reading materials can be assimilated:

1. The reader's knowledge of the general subject matter
2. The vocabulary load, difficulty level of words and concepts
3. The reader's degree of motivation
4. The reader's purpose for reading the material
5. The physiological state of the reader, whether fatigued, etc.
6. The length of the reading period
7. Mechanical factors such as size of print and length of line
8. The readability of the material as determined by such factors as style of writing, sentence structure, and sentence length
9. The reader's mastery of the mechanical skills of reading, such as number of words known as sight words, ability to sound unknown words, ability to profit from punctuation, and freedom from the habit of inserting, omitting, or repeating words or phrases
10. The number of figures, illustrations, cross-references, and footnotes the material contains

Consideration of these factors reveals that no one sample of reading behavior can provide a valid basis for establishing a person's rate of comprehension. Any figure arrived at would be valid only for the particular material read under the precise conditions which prevailed while it was being read. Regardless of the fact that the term *rate of reading* is vague and may lead to confusion, there is little question that the rate at which pupils read curricular materials is an instructional problem which tends to become more acute as they move through the grades.

Varying rate according to material and purpose for reading

A facile reader must develop several different rates for reading different types of printed matter. (5) This fact merits careful attention in the intermediate grades because here the pupil must read a great variety of materials in various content areas. The child should learn to adjust his reading behavior to the material and to the objectives he has for reading it. A magazine article may be read with good comprehension at several hundred words per minute while the same reader may have to spend several minutes in reading a mathematical problem stated in forty words. Or assume that a pupil, having read a particular passage, is attempting to recall the five largest cities of the United States. He has tentatively settled for New York, Chicago, and San Francisco, but the other two city names do not come to mind. As he rereads, it would be a slow and possibly wasteful effort to read carefully every word and sentence of the entire section which contains the desired information. If the pupil had mastered the technique of scanning material, he could quickly find the one or two sentences that contain the desired data; these could then be read carefully.

Developing flexibility

The term flexibility, as applied to reading, refers to the ability to read different materials at different rates. An analogy might be made between reading and walking. Just as most individuals have settled into a particular characteristic gait in walking, they have also developed a favorite reading pace. However, all individuals can walk faster when circumstance demands it. Examples would include the threat of rain, being late for an appointment, or the likelihood of missing a bus. In the absence of such motivators, the individual settles back into his characteristic gait.

It should be obvious to anyone who reads widely that there is little justification for reading all material at the same rate. Such a habit will be wasteful in many situations. The flexible reader is one who has developed the ability to "adjust to the terrain." He has developed the ability to discern where more rapid reading is appropriate, and he has developed the ability to read more rapidly in such situations.

Initial training in learning to read concentrates heavily on word recognition. It is obvious that the individual who fails continually to increase his sight vocabulary can hardly be expected to learn to read more rapidly or more efficiently. The need for growth in rate of reading is an excellent example of the developmental nature of reading. Unfortunately, formal instruction in reading makes little provision for helping students develop this skill.

Improving rate through improving reading skills

The problem of improving rate can be oversimplified unless we keep in mind that rate is influenced by the reader's skills, habits, and attitudes toward the material being read. It would be unrealistic to attempt to improve a slow rate of reading without dealing with those factors which are its basis. When slow reading is simply a habitual response stemming from a lack of basic reading skills, it can be dealt with by practice in those skills. Lack of skills, or the development of habits such as guessing, substituting or omitting words, adding words to salvage meaning, or ignoring punctuation, inevitably contribute to slow reading. Inadequate word-attack skills may prevent a child from arriving at correct pronunciation or cause him to arrive at the pronunciation very slowly. Word-by-word reading is usually related to these problems.

Reading in phrases is a skill which relates to rate of reading on two scores. Word-by-word reading is time-consuming and also tends to interfere with comprehension. A child who has been taught to read for meaning will have to repeat sentences and parts of sentences when he loses the thought because he has been so slow in piecing the various work units into a meaningful whole. When word-by-word reading is habitual—that is, when it has been reinforced by many thousands of reading experiences—it is sometimes advisable to give the reader practice in reading easy phrases. Gradually, more difficult reading material can be used. The teacher can make up drill exercises which use phrases in isolation, exercises which show logical phrases underlined, or short passages where the student underlines logical phrases. These three procedures are illustrated in Figure 24 below. Figure 25, on the following page, presents a sustained reading passage arranged in phrases.

FIGURE 24

1. The following phrases or short sentences are designed to give practice in reading a number of words as one thought unit. Some pupils read one word at a time — that is, they pause after each word: up, the, mountain. Since this is a logical thought unit it should be read: up the mountain. Read the phrases from left to right across the page.

In the car   down the hill   at the farm   from the house
had to leave soon   in the big house   he will be   has gone away
the white horse   eat some cake   ran to the house   the show
can see it   the pretty dress   will look good   we can see
much too much   the tiny boat   on the paper   to the fair

2. *In the following paragraph logical thought units have been separated. Be sure to read each phrase as a whole. There are many different ways we could read the same passage. The following is only one example.*

Billy saw the car   coming down the road.   He said to himself,
I hope I can get a ride   to town.   He began to wonder
if he should   accept a ride   if he didn't know   the driver.
The car pulled up   and slowed down.   He saw a man
and two boys   about his age.   The boys shouted,   "Hi, Billy."
He recognized the twins.

3. *Underline phrases which could be read as one unit. Remember that there may be several different ways to arrange words in thought units. Underline the way you think is best.*

The twins, Roger and Sandy, had moved to town several weeks ago. "Hop in the car," said Sandy. "Have you met my dad?" asked Roger. Billy shook hands with Mr. Farrell. As they neared town, Mr. Farrel said, "Can you come and play with the boys at our house or must you go straight home?"

FIGURE 25

The passage below tells something about the reading process. The material has been arranged in short phrases to provide practice in phrase reading. The ability to read in phrases is learned through practice. After reading this material several times, you should be reading it both faster and more smoothly. Try to apply this skill when you read other materials which have not been phrased.
(Read down the columns, reading each line as a unit.)

This exercise	"as one unit."	As you read
is arranged	That is —	other materials
in columns	do not read	which have not
of phrases	each/word/	been phrased,
to help you	as/a/unit/.	let your eyes
in developing	With practice,	and your mind
the habit of	you will find	cooperate
reading phrases.	you can read	in selecting
Try to read	several words	several words
each line	as units.	which are

"logical thoughts."
This will help you
to read
more rapidly,
more smoothly,
and with good
comprehension.
Your eyes
and your mind
are capable
of dealing
with several
smaller words
or with a
very large one.
For instance —
  Mississippi
  Rhode Island

cheerfulness
peppermint
in olden days
cold and rainy.
The examples
cited above
are relatively
long units.
They were easy
for you to read
because they are
familiar.
You have seen
each of them
many times
and you know
their meanings.
These phrases

were not related
to each other.
Other phrases
on this page
are related.
This is a bit
more difficult
to read smoothly.
First because
the thought units
vary in length.
Secondly,
some readers
might select
different
phrasing patterns
than shown here.

Conclusion

Study skills, which include locating information, organizing and evaluating material, effective use of library resources, and adjusting reading rate to purpose and material, are a most important cluster of reading skills. Their importance to the learner is not always paralleled by the effectiveness with which they are taught. One of the reasons for this is that these particular skills cut across all subject areas, while responsibility for teaching them is left vague.

Ideally, helping children develop efficient study skills should be an integral part of the *teaching* in all content areas. Ironically, in many classrooms the "content" itself takes precedence over the process of developing effective skills in locating, evaluating, and organizing this material.

When study skills are neglected, teaching often becomes ritualistic. All pupils read the same material and are given no guidance or even opportunity to explore the world of books. An example is provided by an observation of a study hall in which row after row of students were listlessly attempting to answer questions found at the end of a particular chapter in their history text. These children had read exclusively from this textbook, and were now required to respond to stimuli such as:

1. List three rulers of Persia.
2. Name three great conquerors.

3. Who is noted for asking questions? (Socrates — and the textbook authors had learned little from him.)

The time wasted in such busy work is a serious indictment of teaching and a sure way to stiffle interest in learning. To hold a child to reading only from a text which gives a larger treatment to the Roman Baths than to Roman Law (because the former can be illustrated with a half page of bad art), is totally indefensible. Here there can be no growth, no development of interest. What results is a reaction against Rome, Greece, and history in general.

Some important study skills do appear to deal primarily with mechanics. Examples include dictionary usage; profiting from reader aids such as a glossary, index, and appendix; use of the card catalogue and other library aids. However, these need not be taught mechanically. They are best learned as part of larger educational activities such as unit work which will call for ascertaining definitions and pronunciation of unusual terms, deciding upon the specific connotation of a word; and finding related materials in a wide variety of sources. These and other opportunities for learning are on-going — they occur daily. Thus, one need not resort to lengthy drill on dictionary or reference material skills. The study skills are developmental in nature and are best taught and learned as part of a total growth process.

YOUR POINT OF VIEW?

Respond to the following problems:

1. Group A consists of 100 sixth graders who consistently read material in a social studies text at 260 words per minute. Group B consists of 100 sixth graders who consistently read this material at 150 words per minute. Develop a hypothetical description which compares and contrasts the "skills and reading behaviors" of the pupils in these two groups.

2. Based on the study of a typical basal reader series, develop a definitive statement as to how thoroughly these materials deal with the teaching of the reading-study skills.

What are your reactions to the following statements?

1. While study skills are important, pupils who progress through the grades will master these skills through incidental learning.

2. Rate of reading or rate of comprehension is determined by such factors as intellectual level, background experience, and concepts held. Therefore, working directly on "speeding reading" will be ineffective unless these factors are dealt with.

3. As a general rule the questions found in intermediate and junior high school level textbooks deal with isolated facts and do not help the child to organize information and see relationships. (Why not destroy the opposing point of view by citing questions from two or three geography, health, history, or science texts?)

4. One of the strengths of American schools is their thoroughness and effectiveness in helping pupils develop study skills.

5. In regard to dictionary usage, there are few if any new skills introduced beyond fifth or sixth grade. Thus, learning dictionary skills is not developmental beyond this level.

6. A reader whose rate of reading does not vary appreciably as he reads different types of materials is probably an inefficient reader in some of these situations.

BIBLIOGRAPHY

1. Artley, A. Sterl, "Effective Study—Its Nature and Nurture" in *Forging Ahead In Reading*, J. Allen Figurel, (ed.), Proceedings, International Reading Association, 12, Part 1, 10–19.

2. Braam, Leonard, "Developing and Measuring Flexibility in Reading," *Reading Teacher* (January 1963), 247–51.

3. Brewer, A. Madison, "The Reading Study Skills," *Improving Reading Instruction*. Joint Proceedings of the Twenty-fifth Reading Conference and First Intensive Summer Workshop, Vol. I. The Pennsylvania State University, University Park, Pa., 1964, 25–30.

4. Carner, Richard L. "Levels of Questioning," *Education* (May 1963), 546–50.

5. Carrillo, Lawrence W. and William D. Sheldon, "The Flexibility of Reading Rate," *Journal of Educational Psychology*, XLIII, (1952), 299–305.

6. Cheyney, Arnold B. "A City-wide Effort Improves Study Skills," *Clearing House* (February 1962), 330–32.

7. Coleman, Mary Elizabeth, "How To Teach Dictionary-Index Skills," *Explorations In Reading*. Eleventh Annual Reading Conference Proceedings, Lehigh University, Vol. 2, Bethlehem, Pa., 1962, 51–56.

8. Daniels, Hazel, "Questioning—A Most Important Tool In The Teaching of Reading," *Education For Tomorrow-Reading.* Joint Proceedings of the Twenty-sixth Reading Conference and the Second Intensive Summer Workshop, Vol. II, The Pennsylvania State University, University Park, Pa., 1965, 61–65.

9. Dawson, Mildred A. "Learning To Use Books Effectively," *Education* (September 1962), 20–22.

10. DeBoer, John J. and Martha Dallmann, *The Teaching of Reading* (3rd Ed.). New York: Holt, Rinehart and Winston, Inc., 1970, Chapter 8.

11. Dechant, Emerald V. *Improving the Teaching of Reading* (2nd Ed.). Englewood Cliffs, N. J.: Prentice-Hall, Inc., 1970, Chapter 13.

12. Harris, Albert J. and Edward R. Sipay, *Effective Teaching of Reading.* New York: David McKay Co., 1971. Chapters 11 and 12.

13. Heilman, Arthur, "Teaching The Study-Reading Skills at The Elementary Level," *Reading, Learning and The Curriculum.* Proceedings of the Twelfth Annual Reading Conference, Lehigh University, Vol. 3, Bethlehem, Pa., 1963, 41–46.

14. Huus, Helen, "Antidote for Apathy—Acquiring Reading Skills for Social Studies," *Challenge and Experiment In Reading.* Proceedings, International Reading Association, 7, 1962, 81-88.

15. Jenkins, William A. "Reading Skills In Teaching Literature In The Elementary School," *Elementary English* (November 1964), 778–82.

16. Lake, Mary Louise, "Improve the Dictionary's Image," *Elementary English* (March 1971), 363–65.

17. Lauck, Mary Ruth, "Every Teacher a Reading Teacher," *Reading, Learning and The Curriculum.* Proceedings Twelfth Annual Reading Conference, Vol 3, Lehigh University, Bethlehem, Pa., 1963, 18–21.

18. Mahoney, Sally, "Basic Study Skills and Tools," *Elementary English* (December 1965), 905–15.

19. Massey, Will J. "Critical Reading In The Content Areas," *Reading as an Intellectual Activity.* Proceedings, International Reading Association, 8, 1963, 104–07.

20. McKee, Paul, *Reading—A Program of Instruction for The Elementary School.* Boston: Houghton Mifflin Company, 1966, Chapters 9 and 11.

21. McKim, Margaret G. and Helen Caskey, *Guiding Growth in Reading* (2nd ed.). New York: The Macmillan Company, 1963, Chapter 12.

22. Parke, Margaret B. "Reading For Specific Purposes," *Elementary English* (March 1964), 242–45.

23. Patterson, Charles W. "Pilot Project in Reading and Study Habits," *Reading Teacher* (April 1964), 531–35.

24. Pauk, Walter, "Study Skills and Scholastic Achievement," *Reading Teacher* (December 1965), 180–82.

25. Robinson, H. Alan, "Reading Skills Employed In Solving Social Studies Problems," *Reading Teacher* (January 1965), 263–69.

26. Robinson, Helen M. and Helen K. Smith, "Rate Problems in the Reading Clinic," *Reading Teacher* (May 1962), 421–26.

27. Schubert, Delwyn G. and Theodore L. Torgerson, *Improving Reading In The Elementary School*. Dubuque, Iowa: William C. Brown Company, Publishers, 1963, Chapters 6–7.

28. Shores, J. Harlan, "Dimensions of Reading Speed and Comprehension," *Elementary English* (January 1968), 23–28.

29. Smith, Nila Banton, *Reading Instruction for Today's Children*. Englewood Cliffs, N.J.: Prentice-Hall, Inc., 1963, Chapters 10, 11, 23, and 24.

30. Snoddy, James E. and J. Harlan Shores, "Teaching The Research Study Skills" in *Reading and Realism*, J. Allen Figurel (ed.), Proceedings, International Reading Association, 13, Part 1, 1969, 681–88.

31. Whipple, Gertrude, "Essential Types of Reading In the Content Fields," *Improvement of Reading Through Classroom Practice*. Proceedings, International Reading Association, 9, 1964, 31–33.

15

Critical
Reading

One of the basic difficulties in attempting a definition of critical reading is the fact that this concept has no fixed boundaries. Kerfoot, (22) while granting the complexity of reading comprehension, notes a high degree of ambiguity in various discussions of the term. Critical reading can take place on many levels. A high school senior, a college sophomore, and a doctoral candidate in English, may all critically read *Macbeth*, though the performance of the high school student would be considered inadequate at the higher educational levels. Reading matter covers a wide range of difficulty and complexity. Very few people explore the more difficult end of the continuum, yet the goal of formal education is to guide and direct each student to "explore to the maximum of his ability."

At a given moment, a reader can comprehend at a level commensurate with his academic background, experience, and intellectual level. In the final analysis, the catalyst between writer and reader is the manner in which the latter uses his past experiences in the reading situation. Thus, it is fruitless to talk about getting *the* meaning of a passage, since most serious writing lends itself to a number of interpretations. As Triggs (34) points out, the meaning which is attributed to written symbols in any reading situation is not intrinsic within the passage but is actually supplied by the reader. This would account for the variety of interpretations that good readers have given to the Constitution of the United States, laws on negligence, the Bible, or passage from Shakespeare. It is evident that such readers have brought something of themselves to the reading materials. Although reading cannot be defined as "what the reader brings to the reading situation," it is apparent that there must be interaction between the reader and the printed symbols. At the moment, "reading is thinking" has become a popular phrase, but reading and thinking are not always synonymous. To modify this phrase to "critical reading is thinking while reading" will help to satisfy some readers and to frustrate others. Reading is not the simple sum of its parts, because in every case the reader must be considered in the process and each reader is unique. Reading always involves the simultaneous application of a great number of mechanical and comprehension skills, all of which are influenced by the reader's attitudes, knowledge, and past experience. Reading is a complicated process.

Critical reading is developmental in nature. It is an ongoing process. Some second graders may merit the designation *critical readers*, but no one would suggest that their interpretation of the Constitution is adequate for our society. Nevertheless, if children are to become adept at critical reading, they must be guided toward this goal from the beginning. Helping the child develop ability to read critically is a problem and a challenge for teachers at all grade levels. Reading for meaning is emphasized by the authors of practically all basal reader series, and the emphasis is particularly noticeable at the beginning reading level. Pre-primers and primers contain instructions on building meanings around the few lines of print found in these books. Pictures are widely used to aid the child in extending concepts encountered at this level. One study of the degree of emphasis on critical skills found in a number of basal reader series lists thirty-three skills being stressed in the first six grades. (38)

As the child progresses in reading ability, the materials he reads increase in difficulty. The teacher's task becomes that of keeping children's concepts abreast of the material they are reading. This is easier in the prepared basal reading materials than it is in the content areas where more words and concepts are likely to be new to the child. In the stories children read there are many opportunities to sharpen critical reading powers if the teacher is able to take advantage of them. Children must develop the ability to interpret stories, determine whether places and characters are real or imaginary, discern moods of character, relate the sequence of events, and give plausible explanations of why persons felt and spoke as they did. (18)

In the content fields, the analysis is much the same, but the events may deal with natural phenomena rather than with storybook characters. (1) "What factors make it necessary for country X to import considerable foodstuffs?" (2) "There are a number of substances called minerals; each has a different melting point. What does this statement mean? What is its significance to man? Give examples." If the information necessary to answer these questions is gleaned through reading, critical reading has taken place.

Critical reading is not simply getting answers. Some exercises may get at certain facts but help very little in developing critical reading. Other types of questions are characteristically asked about material similar to that alluded to in the previous paragraph: "What are the main imports of country X?" "List the minerals discussed in this chapter." "What is the melting point of lead?" "Who discovered a process for making steel?" and the like. Correctly answering these questions may not be evidence of critical reading.

Seatwork or questions accompanying reading assignments are often dull. They may call for merely repeating sentences or words which answer questions or for scanning an entire article to find a synonym. Examples:

1. A story is read and a task is assigned. Fifteen statements, in jumbled order, are to be numbered to coincide with the order in which they appeared in the story.
2. Write a word that is used in this story for the word *large*.
3. Write the word which means a place where ships unload.
4. Copy the sentence that tells the number of lakes in Minnesota.

The appetite for critical reading is often dulled by thoughtless, time-consuming tasks such as these. Yet these and similar questions are referred to as aids to measuring or developing comprehension. Unfortunately, this type of busy-work is often encountered about the same time that the child is ready to do independent reading.

Prerequisites to Critical Reading

A number of abilities must be dealt with in teaching for critical reading. When the student develops these abilities, his reading skill is enhanced; when they are neglected, the result is likely to be inept and uncritical reading. Jenkins (20) raises and answers a question relative to the identity of these skills, "What are vital reading skills that must be considered when teaching literature in the elementary school? I think the list is as comprehensive as our knowledge of reading." A few of the frequently listed abilities are.*

1. The ability to recognize the meanings of words
2. The ability to select the one appropriate meaning of a word which may have many meanings
3. The ability to deal with figurative language, not insisting on literal meanings when the author does not intend literal interpretation
4. The ability to determine the author's main ideas
5. The ability to paraphrase, or restate, what the author has written
6. The ability to see the relationship between one part and another and of all parts to the whole
7. The ability to adjust to the author's organizational pattern
8. The ability to determine the author's purpose, his intent in writing, his point of view, his biases, or whom the author is addressing and with what goal in mind
9. The ability to draw inferences which are not specifically stated in the data
10. The ability to recognize literary devices such as humor, satire, or irony, and to detect mood or tone

Barriers to critical reading

Having listed a number of skills that are considered prerequisites for critical reading, we could logically infer that the *lack* of these skills constitute barriers to critical reading. This inference would be correct; however, there are other important and more subtle barriers which are traceable to school practices. We do not imply that the school consciously elects to follow self-defeating practices, but rather that some outcomes of instruction should cause us to question certain inputs. (17) The following discussion suggests some factors that may inhibit the production of critical readers.

Does Learning-to-Read Defeat Reading?

Children come to school excited about reading. They have an interest in learning to read, actually a felt need to learn this mysterious

---

*For an excellent summary of factors related to comprehension, see Frederick Davis (8, 9).

process. However, a great majority who learn to read seem to lose interest; they show little inclination to continue to use this ability learned at so much expense of time and energy. This phenomena needs to be studied more closely than it has been. One related hypothesis is that something happens in the learning-to-read process that turns children away from reading. Perhaps the early teaching of basic and essential skills has become too ritualistic, too intensive, too divorced from the beauty and power of language.

Perhaps we can gain some insights into why children lose interest in reading if we study the answers that some fifth and sixth graders gave to the question *"What is Reading?"* Daniels, in compiling the children's responses noted that "many show signs of insight and creative thinking; others lack the real understanding of what the printed page is." (7) The examples cited here are illustrative of the latter:

Children's Answers To: "What Is Reading?"

"Reading is a subject that contains a group of words that you read such as math, social studies and English."

"Putting letters together to make a word."

"Reading is a subject that most people like. Reading is good for you if you don't read too long."

"Reading is a lot of words that are all mixed up together to make neat letters and meaningful words. It is something that you pronounce with your tongue, lips, and teeth."

"Reading is looking at a book or paper and sounding out the letters and by doing that you are making words. Making those words as you go along is what is called reading."

"Reading is a subject in which you have a Book which has stories which you read. You also have a workbook which has something about the story which you read in the textbook. Also in your workbook you learn the vowel sounds."

These definitions of reading suggest that one of the major issues in reading instruction is whether we should continue doing what we have been doing, or whether we should attempt some other approaches to harnessing the child's ego to the reading task.

Beyond
Beginning Reading

An educational system can honestly claim its chief goal is to produce critical readers without noticing that its practices are defeating this purpose. We can condition students so that about 90 percent of the time they will make one type of response based on reading. Sergeant Friday of the Los Angeles Police (and not Mark Hopkins on one end of the log) is the patron saint of education. From primary grades through college, students hear echos of the same invitation: "Just gimme the facts mam; just the facts please."

There is no question that facts are essential. However, they become less so when isolated from other facts. While an experienced critical reader is contemplating a particular fact, every circuit in his system is "open" for the retrieval of and feed-in of related facts (or even facts that *might* be related). Within the classroom we seem always to be working within the framework of a given chapter where the facts come in orderly little columns unrelated to larger contexts.

> Where is Bolivia?
> How many Bolivians are there?
> Who is their George Washington?
> What is the most important industry?
> Yes, how much tin is exported?
> Who is the chief purchaser?

Chances are, it is not deliberately intended to limit the unit on Bolivia to the establishment of certain facts about tin mining, the relative size of the country, or the altitude of the capital (over 12,000 feet!). Unfortunately, exposure to a number of facts does not lead to more subtle generalizations about the country, its people, their poverty in the midst of great natural resources, and who benefits most from their labor. Thus, students are not prepared for reality. They cannot think their way into the minds of Bolivians and anticipate the paragraphs that will follow when emerging nations get to the point of writing. "When in the course of human events. . . ." Fact gathering is only a small part of critical reading.

The teachers' experiences as barrier

Having noted above how some children view reading, we might wonder how prospective teachers have fared after years of exposure to reading. An experience with a college class of prospective teachers illustrates how educational experiences mold the reading behavior of young adults.

In a course devoted to the teaching of reading, the discussion one day focused on the issue of how a teacher gets across to children that reading enhances human growth in all important areas. How can you convince children that through reading one can become what he hopes to be; that all the great thoughts of poets, philosophers, and statesmen belong to one who reads?

It was generally agreed that teachers are the key to whether or not children will see reading as the door to many treasures or an attempted confidence job on the part of the establishment. Teachers, it was agreed, cannot convince children of the many virtues which reside in reading unless they themselves are experiencing this. Teachers of reading must be *reading* teachers!

This seemed to be an excellent time to illustrate how reading had affected the lives of these students soon to be teachers. An impromptu assignment was given which was phrased somewhat as follows: "Assume that everything that has been written will mysteriously disappear from print at the end of this hour. However, each of you can preserve any passage or quotation that has been of importance to you. Write those quotes or passages that you wish to have preserved for future generations."

The unlikely calamity just posed seemed to paralyze the students; or perhaps they were intent on not preserving anything that was not worthy of preservation. They looked straight ahead, then at each other, then at their notebooks, then at each others' notebooks. Very few wrote anything. Something obviously was wrong and so the assignment was modified: "If you can't provide an exact quotation, paraphrase the idea, write it in your own words, give the essence of it." Not much happened even then. Gradually some participants did write something, but many of the class could conjure nothing to write. After a few minutes the activity was terminated.

The group was asked if they would like to discuss what had just occurred — or maybe it wasn't significant. The concensus was that it should be explored. The idea was rejected that the element of surprise would account for their inability to write something of value. It was agreed that everyone could have summarized something from a textbook that they had read that week, the chapter on study skills, for instance, or its counterpart for Psychology 201, or History 312, etc. Somehow they felt that none of this needed to be preserved for posterity. They could also have written the titles of books or plays they had read in high school or college. Their problem had been to distill something specific from these experiences.

Someone suggested that their experience with this assignment was probably somehow related to the then-current, vague but recurrent demand for "Relevance in Education." Prior to this they had not realized they had this educational deficit, so they had never missed what their education had failed to provide.

Developing
Critical Reading

There is little question but that critical reading does not automatically accompany an individual's ability to crack the first code. The first code refers to the mastery of letter-sound relationships and sight words. This skill is an essential mechanical aid used in cracking the deeper code of language and meaning. Chase (4) suggests that there are two kinds of illiteracy that threaten civilization. One is non-reading or failure to crack the first code. The second he calls the "higher illiteracy," wherein people who can read are incapable of thinking and feeling while they read. The following discussion identifies some of the areas in which the school must provide guidance if children are to become critical readers.

Meaning vocabulary

A number of techniques for developing word meanings were presented in Chapter 13, *Developing and Expanding Concepts*. The following material extends that discussion while emphasizing how deficiencies in vocabulary short circuit the critical reading process. An example is provided by the fourth grade boy who was quite adept at arithmetical computation, including division. He came to a page in his workbook in which the directions read, "Write the quotients for the following problems." The boy did not attempt to solve a single problem on the page because the word *quotient* baffled him. The problems looked very much like the ones he had done previously, but surely this strange word instructed him to do something new and unknown. The teacher had assumed that everyone in the class knew the word, since it had been discussed at length. The concept had not been mastered, at least by this student.

The content areas, such as science, mathematics, health, and social studies, use hundreds of words which can inhibit learning if not fully understood. Examples are *ratio, proportion, respiration, longitude, exponent, photosynthesis, plateau, congruent, catalyst, inertia, delta,* and *contagious.*

Cole (6) tells of a student in a chemistry class who asked his instructor for help in understanding the law: "The volume of a gas is inversely proportional to its density." The instructor tried without success to explain the concept embodied in the law. Finally, he asked the boy to define volume, volume of a gas, density, and inversely proportional. The boy had only one concept for *volume* — a book; *gas* was what is used in a stove; *density* meant thickness;

he had no concept to go with *inversely proportional.* The boy had actually "memorized" the law, a fact which emphasizes the futility of such effort in the absence of understanding.

The child's need for learning new words and concepts never abates, but sometimes the great mass of material to be taught may interfere with the effective teaching of meanings. In earlier chapters a number of procedures have been suggested for helping children master unknown words. Some of these procedures have merit for use in the upper grades and should be used when appropriate. A technique used with success by some teachers is the *word meaning period.* Ten- to fifteen-minute periods are used in which pupils present and discuss words whose meanings they had not known when they met them in their reading. A number of variations can be introduced to keep the period interesting. A pupil reads the sentence containing the word he has just learned and tells its meaning in that context. Other pupils can volunteer to use the word in different contexts, supply synonyms, or give other words which have the same root.

Another variation is a teacher-planned period devoted to learning important word roots and to demonstrating the possibilities of word building through the addition of prefixes, suffixes, and other roots. For example, *dict* is a root meaning "to say." To *predict* is to say in advance, and implies that an event is pre *dict* able. This same root permits one to say that if one is to *dict*ate, his *dict*ion in *dict*ating should be clear and that his pronunciation should not contra*dict* the *dict*ionary. The study of word meanings can be a fascinating and rewarding experience.

On the other hand, an assignment to learn a number of roots listed in one column and the common words made from each of these roots in an adjacent column, may not be highly motivating because the drill is detached from meaningful learning. In science, geography, or social science, however, words and concepts are met which need clarification. This provides an excellent opportunity for the integration of teaching meanings with teaching subjects. Terms and concept, such as *photosynthesis, extracting minerals, geology, biology, plywood,* and *perspective,* can be used as a starting point for a study of word derivations.

The teacher might use the following exercise for teaching how some of our common words were built from words borrowed from other languages. *Auto* is a Greek word meaning *self; graph* is also Greek and means to *write;* when we put these two roots together we have our English word autograph. Do you see how the meaning of this word is related to the Greek word from which it is built?

ROOT		ROOT		
photo	(light)	*graph*	(to write):	photograph
				(to write with light)
tele	(far)	*graph*	(to write):	telegraph
phono	(sound)	*graph*	(to write):	phonograph
geo	(earth)	*graphy*	(to write):	geography
bio	(life)	*logy*	(to study):	biology
geo	(earth)	*logy*	(to study):	geology

Word meanings can be further explained by studying roots and prefixes, and roots and suffixes.

PREFIX		ROOT		
con	(with, together)	*tract*	(to draw):	contract
re	(back)	*tract*	(to draw):	retract
ex	(out of)	*tract*	(to draw):	extract
im	(into)	*port*	(to carry):	import
trans	(across)	*port*	(to carry):	transport
re	(back)	*port*	(to carry):	report

ROOT		SUFFIX		
port	(to carry)	*able*	(capable of):	portable
dict	(to say)	*tion*	(act of):	diction
grat	(thanks)	*full*	(full of):	grateful

When pupils evince interest in word building (roots, prefixes, suffixes), the teacher can make available teacher-constructed exercises similar to the examples above. Knowledge of roots and prefixes will help a child work out the meaning of many words that at first glance may appear strange and difficult.

Selecting the appropriate meaning

Teachers in one school tested the children in all grade levels, first through high school, on a few common words like *set, run, stick,* and *mine*. The word *set* elicited approximately ten different meanings from first graders. The number of different meanings associated with this word increased through the grades and reached twenty-eight correct usages in a third-year high school class. Yet the word *set* is considered a rather simple word.

The ability to select the appropriate meaning of a particular word which has many meanings is essential for critical reading. The word *base* has many meanings: third base, the base of a triangle, the base line of a graph, a naval base, base motives, and a number of others. *Dividend* does not have the same meaning in mathematics that it does when used as an increment from investments in stocks and bonds. The literal definition of *island* as "a body of land entirely surrounded by water" is not the meaning implied by John Donne when he states, "no man is an island entire unto himself — each is a piece of the continent, a part of the whole." Nevertheless, this conventional meaning would have to be known in order to understand the author's intended meaning. The child's learning of various connotations of words is complicated by the widespread use of figures of speech. Although these expressions may increase the difficulty of a passage, they also add to its beauty or forcefulness. Cyrano De Bergerac, sword in hand but mortally wounded, describes the approach of death, "I stand — *clothed with marble, gloved with lead.*" Overstatements or gross exaggeration emphasize particular qualities — "He's as patient as Job," "strong as Hercules," "tall as a mountain." Likenesses are suggested through implied functions — "The ship *plowed* the waves," "The arrow *parted* his hair." Sometimes, in fact, words are used in such a way as to mean just their opposite. Obviously, understanding material containing such expressions depends on the reader's realization of the intended meanings.

The following passage is filled with expressions which probably would pose no problem for adults but which might mystify a child who reads slowly or literally.

> Joe, *flying down the stairs, rested his eye* on the hawk. Grandfather *buried his nose in a book* and acted as if he were *completely in the dark.* Grandmother and Sue *put their heads together* and tried to figure out *which way the wind was blowing.* Joe *tipped his hand* by carrying the gun. On the *spur of the moment* Grandmother *hit the nail on the head. Cool as a cucumber,* she called to Joe, *"Freeze in your tracks* and put that gun back upstairs!" Joe's *spirits fell* as his grandmother's words *took the wind out of his sail.* He *flew off the handle* and told about the hawk. *"That's a horse of a different color,"* said Grandmother, satisfied that she had *dug up the facts.* "Let the boy alone," said Grandfather. "He will *keep the wolf from the door."* Outside, Joe thought, "I'd better *make hay while the sun shines,"* as he *drew a bead* on the hawk.

Although these expressions may not bother most children, more difficult figures of speech will constantly confront them. The children who are baffled by such expression need more experience with them. For these pupils, the teacher should devise exercises over and above those which are found in workbooks at their grade level. If the reader is *thinking while reading*, he will probably develop the flexibility necessary to deal with this type of language.

Need for Background Knowledge

All of the skills required for critical reading are developmental in nature. The readers' previous experiences or lack of such experiences, impinge on each new reading situation. (19) Thus, factors such as how extensively and how effectively various skills have been practiced will have a bearing on the present level of critical reading.

As Durrell (12) points out, "The efficiency of transferring ideas from one person to another is seldom high," and there is an unavoidable loss for the reader in this process. Eller (14) lists a number of obstacles to critical reading found in the school, in society, or in both. Some of them follow:

1. Pupils form the opinion that anything in print is true.
2. Children are conditioned to accept authority blindly.
3. Schools have relied on single texts in the various content areas, and the teacher stresses "what the book says." Thus, children do not learn to look for differences of opinion or for interpretations.
4. Schools avoid controversial topics and emphasize uniformity.

Each of these points is inevitably tied in with experience, and is thus affected by a person's background and knowledge. It is likely that the greatest barrier to critical reading is the reader's lack of background and experience. The teacher has to deal with this problem regardless of the level or the curriculum area in which she teaches. In reality, we are dealing with two questions. First, what does the reader bring to the reading situation in the way of experience and understanding? And second, what does he need in order to understand the particular reading he is attempting? The higher one goes through the grades, the more need there is for this type of preparation because the reading materials deal with concepts which are often beyond the present stock of concepts held by some students in the room.

A third grade class is reading a story about bees storing honey in a hollow tree. The facts that the bees "belonged to a farmer," worked for him in a hive he provided, and yet one day swarmed and left the hive, may call for a good deal of explanation by the teacher, or by bee experts in the class, before all aspects of this story are meaningful to every member of that third grade class.

A high school or college student reading *John Brown's Plea to the Court* can hardly be expected to arrive at a sound critical analysis of this passage unless some background facts are also known: who was John Brown?; when did he live?; what political-social issue was involved?; what experiences did John Brown have in Kansas prior to the Harper's Ferry episode?; was John Brown's attitude shared by a large number of people living at that time?; how would one describe John Brown's emotional maturity?; is the real issue here the question of whether the end justifies the means?

Almost all the prerequisites for, and obstacles to, critical reading are related to the two skills of discerning a writer's purpose and of drawing inferences. The presence or absence of bias, a lack of background, the habit of accepting that which is in print or that which is allegedly backed by authority, and the lack of experience in dealing with controversial topics, all help to determine whether critical reading can take place. College students too have trouble discerning an author's purpose. Students in a reading improvement course, after reading and discussing several serious paragraphs, were given the following passage by Mark Twain. Each student was to read the passage silently and to write a sentence or two answering these questions: "What is the author's purpose? How does he achieve it? What is the author's mood?"

It was a crisp and spicy morning in early October. The lilacs and laburnums, lit with the glory fires of autumn, hung burning and flashing in the upper air; a fairy bridge provided by kind Nature for the wingless wild things, that have their home in the tree-tops and would visit together; the larch and the pomegranate flung their purple and yellow flames in brilliant broad splashes along the slanting sweep of the woodland; the sensuous fragrance of innumerable deciduous flowers rose upon the swooning atmosphere; far in the empty sky a solitary oesophagus slept upon motionless wing; everywhere brooded stillness, serenity, and the peace of God.*

Hundreds of students, and a smaller number of teachers and adults, have responded in essence: "It is a beautiful fall day. He describes nature, the beautiful colors, and the peace and quiet one

*Mark Twain, "A Detective Story," from *The Man That Corrupted Hadleyburg* (New York: Harper & Row, Publishers), 304.

finds in nature." Despite the first line a number of readers move the day into spring. Occasionally a reader says, "I wondered about the oesophagus, but thought it might be a tropical bird." However, once adults are shown the ridiculous nature of the passage, they seriously doubt that others would be so easily taken in by it.

The ten abilities related to critical reading operate in all reading situations, not just in those that occur during the clock-hour devoted to formal instruction in reading. They operate whenever reading is used in the pursuit of knowledge, whether in history, geography, economics, health, mathematics, science, or literature. (37) The reader must know the meaning of the words used and the different shades of meaning words have in different contexts. He must separate main thoughts or ideas from qualifications; he must detect the author's purpose, bias, and intent. From the first grade through college, the teacher has a major responsibility to structure reading situations so that these factors and many others are kept in proper focus.

Reading provides the needed background for clearing up vague and hazy concepts. It is difficult to determine the number of such

concepts that children harbor. One teacher discovered that many students in her class had vague ideas as to the origin and meaning of the term *Freedom of the Press*. These came to light as a result of an assignment which called for students to write briefly on the meaning of this term. Several recurring ideas were that freedom of the press was strictly an American invention, that what one printed had to be true, and that freedom did not extend to criticism of the government. The following are a few representative examples of students' comments.

Freedom of the press originated in the United States which made it possible for a person or a newspaper to express opinion without being persecuted.

The right to express our own ideas on any subject with the exception of derogatory remarks about our country or government.

This (freedom of the press) originated in the early 1800's as an outgrowth of the press being inhibited. It was brought about by a trial.

Freedom of the press means all men have the right to express their inner feelings in written or oral language. But there is a law saying that one cannot yell "fire" when there is no fire.

The right to report current happenings as factual information which is relatively free from personal or group bias.

Resisting propaganda depends to a large degree on the reader's background or "data bank," or in his being wise to the techniques people use when they use language that doesn't fit the facts. The critical reader assumes responsibility for questioning what he reads. While he respects language, he knows that some people use it to control the behavior of others. The purpose here is not to explain all of various propaganda techniques that are used to obscure meaning or take the reader on a detour. The teaching examples which follow might help students detect these devices.

I. List a number of popular propaganda techniques. Discuss these with the class and then have each student or teams write examples.

   1. *Beg the issue* or *Throw up a smoke screen.* Here one does not discuss the real issue, but switches the dis-

cussion to other topics. For example: Candidate A has charged that B has violated the law by not filing a statement of his campaign expenses. B replies, "A has accused me of not filing a statement of expenses. Why should he care? Is he a policeman? Have I ever lied to the voters? Who voted against raising taxes last year? I'll tell you who did — I did! And I'll tell you something else; A voted for the tax bill. I support every worthwhile charity in this community, I was born here, I went to school here! Can A make this statement?"

2. Generalize from too few cases.
3. Ignore the *idea* and attack the person suggesting it.
4. Use a false analogy.
5. Appeal to authority.
6. Rely on guilt by association.
7. Use a faulty cause-and-effect relationship.
8. Misuse figures or statistics.

II. *Step 1.* Prepare a number of propositions that might be an issue in any community.

   Step 2. Follow each proposition with an imaginary statement that someone included in a "Letter to the Editor." Students analyze and point out "what the writer was up to."

Proposition: "Should the city council pass an ordinance which would require fluoridation of the city water supply in an effort to decrease tooth decay among children of the community?"

Letter to the Editor: "Of course some people favor fluoridation, they spend so much time in the Roaring Twenties Bar that they probably don't drink enough water to care how it tastes."

Letter No. 2: "The real issue is that fluorine is a poison. We shouldn't poison our fine water supply." (Beware of jumping to a conclusion: Fluorine *is* a poison. What is the missing detail?)

Proposition: "Should the voters approve a proposed school bond issue?"

Letter to the Editor: "As Lincoln said, "You can fool all of the people some of the time," and this is one of those times! Our schools are as good as any in the country. The people pushing this school bond proposal want to raise your taxes. I say vote this bond issue down."

Proposition: "Should we adopt a city ordinance, proposed as a safety measure, which would prohibit the sale of fireworks?"

Letter to the Editor: "The Fourth of July is one of our great holidays. This proposal is unpatriotic. It is a direct slap at free enterprise. There are a lot of American firms which make fireworks. The next thing you know somebody will try to outlaw automobiles because people get hurt in accidents."

Proposition: "Should the city construct a swimming pool in city park?"

Letter to the Editor: "The people in this town do not want a municipal pool. It is obvious that if the people favored this hairbrained idea we would have had a pool by now!"

Proposition: "Should we extend the runways at our municipal airport so that jet planes can land here?"

Letter to the Editor: "When we built the airport the planners said the present layout would be adequate for at least twenty years. That was just ten years ago. Those people are experts and we should listen to them."

Clues to use while reading the news

Teachers use newspapers and other mass media for both the teaching of critical analysis and mechanical skills which relate to such analysis. The potential values in the use of such materials are numerous. There are also barriers to significant learning, two of which are inadequate planning and the tendency to avoid discussion of issues which might prove to be controversial. Children should be permitted and encouraged to interpret and analyze advertisements, political cartoons, editorials, and syndicated columns.

"Clues to use while reading the news" can be developed by noting and discussing details such as the following:

1. *Compare the editorials* found in four or five metropolitan papers which deal with a particular current issue. Assume there are apparent differences of opinion; what might account for these differences? (1) Political orientation of editor or publisher; or (2) does a particular newspaper have a standing policy on certain issues (labor-management, foreign aid).

2. *The political cartoon:* Gather cartoons, from different papers and drawn by different artists, which deal with the same topic. Ask students to analyze and put into words what the cartoon is attempting to say. Student interpretation of any given stimulus will vary considerably. This will facilitate discussion and help students to see the importance of "the reader's background" which includes bias, emotional attachments, and the like. Such factors always function in any interpretation of a cartoon, editorial, feature article, or news story.

3. *Detecting propaganda techniques:* The teacher or a committee of students might prepare and duplicate an editorial which by design contains biased statements, factual errors, and various propaganda techniques. Each student has a copy of the material and independently edits or rewrites the editorial. Next, have class discussion of the original material and substitutions, deletions, and corrections made by members of the group. Differences between student reactions will in many cases be marked, particularly if the topic is chosen wisely. In the discussion, students will be exposed to points they missed and points of view different from their own.

4. *Study a current issue longitudinally:*
   a. Compare different newspaper and news magazine treatment of this problem.
   b. Attempt to account for differences in editorial points of view.
   c. Study several columnists' or news analysts' interpretations.
   d. Analyze the day-to-day statements of the decision-makers or those spokesmen attempting to mold public opinion. Based on the issue being studied, these might be legislative leaders, State Department officials, labor leaders, candidates for high office, the President, White House staff, etc.

Paraphrasing

The ability to paraphrase, or restate in one's own words, the author's main ideas is usually the criterion by which the pupil's critical reading ability or comprehension is judged. The inability to paraphrase often implies one of two things: either the pupil did not fathom what the author was trying to tell him, or he lacks the language facility to restate what he read. Paraphrasing is one of the most effective and, at the same time, one of the least used techniques available to teachers at all levels. Walpole (36) states, "Paraphrasing provides a simple classroom technique which not only commits the pupil to a specific task of interpretation, but also enables him to study other versions and see how people interpret the same passage in widely varying ways." Paraphrasing exercises provide an almost ideal example of a means of integrating all of the language arts. First, the student gets experience in interpretive reading. Second, by writing he gains experience in all facets of composition, such as sentence and paragraph construction, organization of material, and grammatical usage. This technique can be highly motivating to students if care is exercised in the selection of reading passages.

In order to paraphrase accurately or restate the essence of what an author has written, one must be able to grasp the meaning as he reads. Paraphrasing demands that one see the relationships between various parts of a passage and how these parts are related to the total effect sought by an author. As a rule, good readers have developed the ability to read in "thought units." Thus, their reading habits lead them naturally into logical and meaningful phrasing. They have learned to see the relationships between words and how the author builds a pattern of thought units into a larger whole. The point under discussion cuts across several factors which have been listed as related to critical reading: main ideas, paraphrasing, adjusting to author's organization, and seeing the relationship between a part and the whole.

The following illustrations have been used with high school groups. In each case, passage A was read by the student who was then asked to write a sentence or two restating what the author said. Immediately following this, each pupil was given passage B which was the same passage divided into meaningful thought units. All of the students stated that it was easier to get meaning from passage B. The point of the exercise was to help students see that in their reading for meaning they must do what was done for them in passage B, i.e., read in meaningful thought units. Such an exercise can be developed for use at practically any reading level.

Passage A

A man rises, sometimes, and stands not, because he doth not, or is not believed to fill his place; and sometimes he stands not, because he overfills his place: He may bring so much virtue, so much justice, so much integrity to the position, as to be a libel upon his predecessor, and cast infamy upon him, and a burden upon his successor.*

---

*Paraphrased from John Donne, *Complete Poetry and Prose of John Donne* (New York: The Modern Library, 1946), 338.

Passage B

A man rises, sometimes,
and stands not,
because he does not,
or is not believed to fill his place;
And sometimes he stands not,
because he overfills his place:
He may bring
so much virtue,
so much justice,
so much integrity to the position,
as to be a libel upon his predecessor,
and cast infamy upon him,
and burden upon his successor.

Passage A

Man, of whom David had said (as the lowest diminution that
he could put upon him), 'I am a worm and no man' — he might
have gone lower, and said, I am a man and no worm.*

Passage B

Man,
of whom David had said,
(as the lowest diminution that he could put upon him)
'I am a worm and no man' —
He might have gone lower,
and said,
I am a man and no worm.

Developing Appreciation
Through Critical Reading

Developing an appreciation for poetry and literature is not a function of chronological age, grade placement, or mere contact with
good literature. One does not develop taste in literature as a result
of one experience; taste evolves as a result of crossing numerous literary thresholds. Every teacher at every grade level should assume
some responsibility for introducing her pupils to the world of good
literature. (33)

The purpose of teaching is to provide experiences which facilitate
personal growth. The ability to appreciate good literature assures
us of a lifetime source of pleasure. In addition, the reading and

_____

*Ibid., 369.

understanding of literature will inevitably lead to insights about self and the world about us. Literature is also a form of potential therapy for the alienated and those in flight from involvement. There are few human problems, fears, or aspirations which are not treated in literature.

Basic to helping children develop appreciation for literature is the recognition that appreciation comes only from actual participation. Reading is, in essence, a dialogue between reader and writer. Appreciation is personal; it cannot be standardized. Thus, appreciation may not result from such tactics as:

1. Urging students to read good literature.
2. Providing a list of acceptable authors or established literary classics.
3. Prescribing an inflexible agenda of reading materials for groups of students.
4. Assigning the same reading to all students in a given class.
5. Assuming that all students in a given class or school year have the readiness, and the skills needed, to "mine" a traditional reading list.
6. Relying on evaluative methods which imply that all students should arrive at the same interpretation of a story, analysis of a particular character, or insight into an author's purpose.

Unfortunately the above procedures, in modified and sometimes disguised form, are often followed in actual teaching situations. These practices, of course, negate what we know about reading, readers, the learning process, and the development of taste in reading. There is a consensus that the schools' approach to teaching literature fails a great number of students who undertake the study of literature. (27)

Enjoying poetry

In most instances the reading of poetry calls for a different reader-set than does narrative prose. While it is true that the poem is susceptible to more than one interpretation, the language of a poem must take precedence in determining the reading cadence. The poet's chief concern is not with facts but with feelings. To enjoy poetry one must have or develop an ear for language. The reader, like the poet, must be receptive to the language as it comes to him. (30)

The poem is designed to be heard. While one may of course hear the words and the language rhythms as he reads silently, there is no better introduction to poetry than to hear it read orally. The teacher who is skilled in reading poetry should read to students. If a teacher prefers, she may turn for help to expert readers who have recorded a wide array of great literature and poetry. A number of modern poets such as Robert Frost, Langston Hughes, Mary McLeod Bethune, Carl Sandburg, e. e. Cummings, Arna Bontemps have recorded portions of their own works. Dozens of highly competent artists including Julie Harris, Richard Burton, Jose Ferrar, Basil Rathbone, Sir Cedric Hardwicke and others have recorded a number of great classics.*

The poet is by definition and practice a word and concept craftsman. He uses imagery, allusion, analogy, and symbolism; words are selected not for meaning alone but also for sound and rhythm. Emily Dickinson explains the process.

> "Shall I take thee?" the poet said
> To the propounded word
> Be stationed with the candidates
> Till I have further tried**

Thus, to paraphrase a poem is to destroy it. This does not imply that meaning is sacrificed in order to get other effects; nor does it preclude analysis or even group discussion for arriving at meaning.

The chief cause of the failure of the school to inculcate students with an appreciation for poetry lies in the language barrier. An inadequate language background stalls the communicative process between poet and reader.

> Who goes to dine must take his feast
> or find the banquet mean;
> The table is not laid without
> till it is laid within†

While the reader must come to poetry prepared, he need not, as part of a planned curriculum, be continually exposed to that for

---

*A wide variety of recordings may be secured from the *National Council of Teachers of English*. These are completely catalogued in *Resources for The Teaching of English*, NCTE, 508 South Sixth Street, Champaign, Ill.

**Mabel Loomis Todd and Millicent Todd Bingham, ed., *Bolts of Melody— New Poems of Emily Dickinson* (New York: Harper & Row, Publishers, 1945), p. 228.

†*Bolts of Melody—New Poems of Emily Dickinson*, op. cit., p. 229.

which he is not prepared. Good poetry is distributed over a wide range of difficulty. The school's responsibility is to match the student's present ability with reading tasks of commensurate difficulty.

One excellent way to build understanding and appreciation for poetry is through encouraging children to write their own poetry. Many teachers have discovered that children have tremendous talent for the use of language. One poetic form that is a favorite of many children is Haiku, or stanzas composed of exactly seventeen syllables divided into three lines of five, seven and five syllables respectively. The following are examples of fourth graders' writing. The third poem titled *Now* illustrates an interesting pattern of repetition of the title.

> See the small bird fly
> He is just a beginner
> Oops! He fell again.

> Trees now with no leaves
> Plants gone to their winter beds
> All waiting for spring.

Now

> Winter has come now
> The snowflakes are falling now
> Winter has gone now

> Winter has gone now
> And spring is in the air now
> The birds are back now

> Spring too has gone now
> And summer has filled the air
> Soon it will be gone

> Summer is gone now
> Now all the leaves are falling
> The trees are bare now

Children and teachers working together can devise their own poem forms. One class* wrote poems patterned on the Cinquain

---

*The author regrets not having the data which would permit giving proper credit to the individual students and teacher(s) whose work is cited here.

form of five lines, but did not follow the syllable requirements of this form. Their poems were based on the following stanza form.

1st line:	one word (usually a naming word)
2nd line:	two words which constitute a synonym for line one
3rd line:	three words describing action
4th line:	four words which build on line three
5th line:	a one-word summary

The following are illustrative examples written by fourth and fifth grade pupils.

Maps
Giant papers
On the wall
Colors red and blue
Useful

Earth
Small planet
Spinning fast around
Rotating on its axis
Neat

Deer
Little fawns
Jumping far, playing
Jumping over big stones
Happy

Leaves
Shapes, colors
Falling slowly down
Through brown tree branches
Lonely

Developing Interests through Purposeful Reading

We make much of the fact that the child's reading must be purposeful, yet much of our actual reading instruction must appear to the child to be related only to *learning* to read! Children need guidance in discovering the values inherent in meaningful reading. While a large number of values could be cited, the one we are concerned with at the moment is the pleasure and growth potential to be found in this activity. There is no denying that pleasurable and purposeful reading is dependent upon the development of mechanical and comprehension skills. (26) Yet millions of individuals attain satisfactory proficiency in these skills without ever finding a deep personal satisfaction in reading. Persons who love to read find this fact difficult to believe. However, studies of the reading interests and activities of a great number of high school and college graduates demonstrate its truth.

No doubt the school shares the responsibility for this outcome. Perhaps the degree of emphasis that is placed on *learning* to read leads pupils to see this accomplishment as an end in itself rather than the means of many desirable ends. Whatever the cause, too many children experience an uncritical, unimaginative growth in reading. Reading should never deteriorate into a ritual but should serve as a means of awakening the senses and stirring the imagination and the emotions. Whether the child is exploring one of the man-made wonders of the world or one of nature's wonders, such as the functioning of an ant colony or the metamorphosis of the monarch butterfly, reading can feed the senses with raw material for building concepts. Feelings and images aroused by reading can also stimulate emotions. A poet speaks to his love:

> "I never think of you
> but what some new virtue
> is born in me."

A leader in the American Revolution, having been chided for a long absence from America, writes a friend a few observations in 1789:

> A thousand years hence, perhaps in less . . . the ruins of that liberty which thousands fought for, or suffered to obtain, may just furnish materials for a village tale. . . .
> When we contemplate the fall of empires and the extinction of nations of the ancient world, we see but little to excite our regret. . . . But when America shall fall, the subject for contemplative sorrow will be infinitely greater than crumbling brass or marble can inspire. It will not then be said, here stood a temple of vast antiquity, here rose a Babel of invisible height, or there a palace of sumptuous extravagance, but here, oh painful thought! The noblest work of human wisdom, the grandest scene of human glory, the fair cause of freedom rose and fell. Read this and then ask if I forget America.*

It is true that children in the primary grades do not read Cyrano De Bergerac or the letters of Thomas Paine. But the point is that they may never read these authors or Mark Twain, Frederick Douglass, Ralph Ellison, Oliver Wendell Holmes, Dostoievsky, Whitman, James Baldwin, or Gwendolyn Brooks if they do not learn to read for pleasure and develop an appreciation for reading. The primary

---

The Complete Writings of Thomas Paine, Philip S. Foner, ed. (New York: The Citadel Press, 1945), II, 1274.

grades are not too early to awaken the senses and emotions through reading. (31)

Reading relevancy

If we looked carefully at much of the assigned reading in our schools, we might wonder along with the students *why* they were asked to read certain works critically. In order for reading ability to have value to an individual or a society, it must be used to read something of value. One does not master the mysteries of reading in order to be led by Madison Avenue, but rather to interact with the exceptional minds of poets, philosophers, statesmen, and great teachers. With reading ability properly used, one should be able to bridge the gap between generations and, more important for all nations, between races. We must interact with John Donne's statement that "all mankind is of one author," and that, "any man's death diminishes me because I am involved in mankind."

Unfortunately, reading can be reduced to non-involvement, and this is the antithesis of teaching. As teachers we must become involved because we are part of mankind, but even more so because we are teachers! If the United States of America is to become one nation, indivisible, with freedom and justice for all, then its teachers must *want* this type of nation. We must explore with our students the barriers to this goal, and how these barriers can be surmounted. We have never done this, and thus we do not know if we can do it.

Because of pressures from the community, or possibly because of the schools' own inclination, there is a tendency to avoid reading and discussing topics that are considered controversial. To the degree to which this is true, the school waives responsibility for educating students. The school becomes a mirror image of the society rather than the cutting edge in "the race between education and catastrophe." This is not a plea that the schools deliberately seek embroilment in current controversies but rather that children's involvement with real issues facing their society should not be proscribed.

We must remember that everything a democracy holds sacred is by nature controversial. This is true for values and ideals as well as humanitarianism and brotherhood. If the school does not encourage children to read in these areas, can it continue to claim it is involved in *education?*

It would seem that the time has arrived when the school should take a few more *risks* in the educational process. For children to become critical readers they must read materials that demand critical reading. As educators, we must come to believe with Jefferson that "error of opinion can be tolerated where reason is left free to combat it"; and with Milton who asked "who ever knew truth to be bested in a free and open encounter?"

Children should be encouraged to go with Frost to the meadow when he invites "you come too." They must also be encouraged to *feel* with Langston Hughes the institutionalized injustice involved, and the frustration of a people that are revealed in *Merry-Go-Round*. The poem opens with the words

> Colored child
> at carnival . . .

and pursues the dilemma of both the victims and the designers of racism when neither can figure out which is front and back (i.e., Jim Crow section) on the Merry-Go-Round. The child finally inquires "Where's the horse for a kid that's black?"*

One might ask if the school has been derelict if children lack the concepts for understanding the line, "Here on the Edge of Hell stands Harlem"*; or *What Happens to a Dream Deferred.* Since concepts are built on experience, we produce cultural and educational deprivation when children have no opportunity to interact with these and similar stimuli. The school must become a party to the child's *Right To Read*.

Working with smaller units

Recalling the fifth and sixth graders' responses to "What Is Reading?" (discussed earlier in this chapter), one senses that the children quoted saw reading as a series of mechanical tasks. Their reading experiences had not introduced them to the power and beauty of language. The prospective teachers who found it difficult to recall any writing "that should be preserved" thought that their reading experiences in school put very little emphasis on savoring the beauty of language.

It is quite possible that in our haste to get into subject matter we assign chapters, books, and plays with the admonition that these be read critically. Obviously, no one can read a book or a chapter critically unless he can read paragraphs and sentences that way. This is often forgotten in actual practice. The school seems to have little time for analyzing the meaning of a sentence because it is so

---

*Langston Hughes, *The Panther and The Lash*, New York: Alfred A. Knopf 1967, Pages 92, 4, and 14 respectively.

busy assigning larger units. Thus, much of our behavior is self defeating.

The only way to teach critical reading is to take the necessary time. Students must develop their own interpretations of a passage and test them in open discussion with peers and teacher. Any passage that merits critical reading is in essence as much of a projective technique as a multi-colored inkblot. Whether one interprets the inkblot or the sentence "as face answereth face in water, so the heart of man speaketh to man," the interpretation draws upon his unique experiences.

Analyzing and discussing small units of printed matter permits children to become involved with language. They have dialogues with the author, they are exposed to interpretations radically different from their own. They often note how imprecise their peers are in explaining a concept; then they see this in their own efforts. As a result, they begin to learn that language is raw material that must be shaped and molded, that using language is a *creative activity*.

One excellent technique for developing discussion and understanding of language is to write a nonfactual sentence on the chalkboard. Children are then invited to vote as to whether the author is right or wrong. (The same result is achieved by having children indicate whether they *agree* or *disagree* with the statement.) An example which can be used at several different grade levels is: "Good men are more miserable than other men." Most groups divide on the issue of agreement or disagreement with the statement. Individuals then state the reasons they feel as they do. Such discussion provides valuable insights into the critical reading process: "A good man shouldn't be miserable"; "He has no reason to be miserable"; "Good men are made miserable when they see suffering, injustice, poverty, war," etc.

Many college students and adults show some hostility toward the assignment, raising such questions as "the material is taken out of context." What does he mean by "miserable?" "What's the definition of a 'good man'?" etc. As these and other questions are discussed, insights into reading are developed. It is established that the author is dead; we cannot ask him what he meant by *miserable* and *good men*. Soon the readers see that in the final analysis these words (and all words one reads) take on the meaning that each reader gives them.

The following are a few examples of sayings, proverbs, and quotations that might be used as stimulus statements for discussion. When discussions begin to extend far beyond the time you think should be allotted to this activity, you can assume that children are learning much about critical reading.

It is the good reader that makes a good book.

Character is what you are when no one is watching.

Don't criticize a man until you have walked in his shoes for a day.

The longest journey begins with the first step.

All mankind is of one author.

You must have a good memory to be a successful liar.

As a man sows, so shall he also reap.

You can judge a man by his enemies as well as by his friends.

The riches that are in the heart cannot be stolen.

Error of opinion may be tolerated where reason is left free to combat it.

People are lonely because they build walls instead of bridges.

Man is the only animal who can talk himself into problems that otherwise would not have existed.

**What the School
Can Do**

There are a number of practices which, if followed, will have some impact on improving instruction. The following list of procedures can serve as a summary on critical reading.

1. Do not violate the principles of teaching reading which apply particularly to critical reading.
   a. Diagnosis is essential in order to discover weaknesses before the child has a reaction formation against reading.
   b. Instruction should be based on pupil's needs.
   c. Reading is getting meaning.
   d. Many approaches and techniques are needed.
   e. Do not ask the child to read over his head. Asking a child to read something he cannot read is unjustifiable and asking him to read it critically is expecting the impossible.
2. Pre-teach difficult, new, or unknown words as they are encountered in any reading — particularly in subject areas. Work on both pronunciation and meaning.
3. Get rid of the idea that reading and the teaching of reading take place during the "reading period" and that during other periods subjects are taught.

4. There should be a deliberate effort to study the organization of sentences, paragraphs, and larger units.
    a. Stress the function of pronunciation for students needing this type of drill.
    b. Explain and analyze difficult sentence structure, dependent clauses, complex sentences, and inverted order.

5. Teach and expect orderliness, organization, and logic in written work.

6. Use all audio-visual aids available. Concepts are built through sensory experiences. And experience with word symbols alone is an ineffective way to broaden concepts. The concept of land erosion might be taught with words, i.e., "erosion is the wearing away of land by rain or the action of water." However, a single good picture of badly eroded land might fix this concept and make it much more meaningful. A film showing the cutting of forests, plowing, and lack of cover grass, will broaden the concept even more.

7. Use purposeful study questions in advance of pupil reading. Questions given prior to reading can be most effective in structuring any reading situation. Eventually the student should get in the habit of asking the proper questions for himself, but this takes time and experience. In order to master this technique the child needs guidance and direction. This is an excellent method for giving the student a motive or goal in his reading. Too often this technique is neglected or not used as a means of implementing critical reading.

8. Wide reading on fewer topics, rather than superficial reading on many topics, will permit students more practice in organizing, analyzing, seeing relationships, comparing sources, and determining whether information belongs or is related to the topic under discussion.

9. Teach interpretation of graphs, charts, tables, figures, wherever they occur in any subject area.

10. Explain and teach analogies and how the reader must always make sure the analogy applies.

11. Provide practice in recognizing bias, distortion, and various propaganda techniques. Sixth grade children can be taught to detect some propaganda used in materials they read. This does not mean they can become immune but that they can detect certain propaganda devices after periods of instruction aimed at helping them identify these techniques.

12. Help children develop a questioning attitude so that they will differentiate between fact and opinion, see cause and effect relationships, and use clues in evaluating the merit of a work. These clues might include the origin or context of the article (reputation of the magazine or publisher); the writing or publication date (have

significant advances taken place since publication?); and the reputation of the author (is he objective; is he selling a point of view?).

Conclusion

Without question, the most important task of the school is helping children develop critical reading ability. All facets of the curriculum demand this skill of students. Good teaching in any of the various subject areas will contribute to the child's ability to read materials in that area. Poor teaching assumes that students have the prerequisite skills for critical reading and tends to focus on learning facts rather than on the *process of mining* content materials.

Critical reading is not a skill that is acquired once and for all time. It is a developmental process that might be thought of as a continuum. To become and remain a critical reader requires continuous growth. Each successive grade level makes higher demands on the reader. If pupil growth does not keep pace with the demands of the curricular materials, learning is inhibited. Furthermore, the gap between reading ability and the demands of the school tends to widen once it is permitted to develop.

College students' and adults' reactions to the Mark Twain passage cited previously are illustrative of behavior which would naturally occur in a society which has not been perturbed by the obstacles to critical reading and thinking which have gradually accumulated in its mass educational system. It is a rare day when millions of people are not taken in by some form of advertising which in the final analysis is as divorced from meaning as is the Twain passage. Also, on numerous occasions, people are faced with political arguments which are equally meaningless. Whether or not our schools will produce more critical readers is an issue which has great significance for a democracy's future. Probably the most devastating criticism of the schools, which bears on this point, is that "the schools reflect the culture around them."

YOUR POINT OF VIEW?

What are your reactions to the following statements?

1. There is no particular group of skills needed for appreciation and understanding of literature that are not essential for critical reading in other situations such as the content areas.

2. The term *critical reading* implies the mastery and application of a great number of developmental skills. Therefore, a typical reader in third or fourth grade would not qualify as a critical reader.

3. If we agree that we cannot talk in terms of *the meaning* of a passage, we must conclude that it is impossible either to evaluate or to teach critical reading.

4. Since critical reading depends on the application of numerous reading skills, early reading instruction should focus less on critical reading and more on skill development.

5. In most classroom situations, critical reading is equated with supplying responses which arbitrarily have been decided upon as being correct. Creative reading which might lead to divergent interpretations is not encouraged.

6. A person with no training or background in physics or genetics could not read critically a series of conflicting reports on the effect of "atomic fallout."

7. A high school student could not arrive at a sound critical analysis of the effect of tariffs on American industrialization by critically reading only high school textbooks on American history.

8. Honest judges with equal ability in critical reading of statutes will agree on the constitutionality of a particular law. (Assuming, of course, that they have read the constitution critically.)

9. America's free public education system is the world's foremost example of "socialized education."

BIBLIOGRAPHY

1. Arbuthnot, May Hill, "Developing Life Values Through Reading," *Elementary English* (January 1966), 10–16.

2. Calder, Clarence R., Jr. and Zalatimo, Suleiman D. "Improving Children's Ability to Follow Directions," *The Reading Teacher* (December 1970), 227–231.

3. Caskey, Helen J. "Guidelines for Teaching Comprehension," *The Reading Teacher* (April, 1970), 649–654.

4. Chase, Francis S., "In the Next Decade," Supplemental Educational Monographs, no. 91, *Controversial Issues in Reading and Promising Solutions*, Helen M. Robinson (ed.). Chicago: University of Chicago Press, 1961, 7–18.

5. Cohn, Marvin L. "Structured Comprehension," *The Reading Teacher* (February 1969), 440–44.

6. Cole, Louella, *The Improvement of Reading*. New York: Farrar and Rinehart, Inc., 1938.

7. Daniels, H. Perk, Children's Answers to "What is Reading?" New York: Vantage Press, Inc., 1969. Used by permission of the author.

8. Davis, Frederick B. "Fundamental Factors in Comprehension in Reading," *Psychometrika* (September 1944), 185–97.

9. _____, "Research In Comprehension In Reading," *Reading Research Quarterly* (Summer 1968), 499–545.

10. Dawson, Mildred A. (ed.), "Developing Comprehension Including Critical Reading," Newark, Del.: International Reading Association, 1968.

11. Dulin, Kenneth. "Using Context Clues in Word Recognition and Comprehension," *Reading Teacher* (February 1970), 440–445.

12. Durrell, Donald D. "Development of Comprehension and Interpretation," *Reading in the Elementary School*. Forty-eighth Yearbook, Part II, National Society for the Study of Education. Chicago: University of Chicago Press, 1949.

13. Eisenman, Sister M. Victoria, "The Situation In Literature," *Elementary English* (October 1965), 644–45.

14. Eller, William, "Fundamentals of Critical Reading," in *The Reading Teachers' Reader*, Oscar S. Causey (ed.). New York: The Ronald Press Company, 1958, 30–34.

15. Gainsburg, Joseph C., "Critical Reading is Creative Reading and Needs Creative Teaching," *Reading Teacher* (December 1961), 185–92.

16. Gray, Marian M. "Research and Elementary School Critical Reading Instruction," *The Reading Teacher* (February 1969), 453–59.

17. Henderson, Edmund H. "Do We Apply What We Know About Comprehension?" *Current Issues In Reading*, Nila Banton Smith (ed.), Proceedings, International Reading Association, 13, Part 2, 1969, 85–96.

18. Homze, Alma, "Interpersonal Relations in Children's Literature 1920-1960," *Elementary English* (January 1966), 26–28.

19. Howards, Melvin. "The Conditions for Critical Reading," *Fusing Reading Skills and Content*. Newark, Del.: International Reading Association, 1969, 171–174.

20. Jenkins, William A., "Reading Skills in Teaching Literature in the Elementary School," *Improvement of Reading Through Classroom Practice*. International Reading Association (June 1964), 324–25.

21. Jenkinson, Marion E. D. "Reading—Developing the Mind," *Changing Concepts of Reading Instruction*. Proceedings, International Reading Association, (June 1961), 170–73.

22. Kerfoot, James F. "Problems and Research Considerations in Reading Comprehension," *Reading Teacher* (January 1965), 250–57.

23. Langman, Muriel Potter, "Teaching Reading as Thinking," *Education* (September 1961), 19–25.

24. McKee, Paul, *Reading—A Program of Instruction for the Elementary School*. Boston: Houghton Mifflin Company, 1966, Chapter 10.

25. Robertson, Jean E. "Pupil Understanding of Connectives In Reading," *Reading Research Quarterly* (Spring 1968), 387–417.

26. Robinson, H. Alan and Ellen Lamar Thomas (eds.). *Fusing Reading Skills and Content*. Newark, Del.: International Reading Association, 1969.

27. Russell, David H. in Robert B. Ruddell (ed.), *The Dynamics of Reading*. Waltham, Mass.: Ginn and Co., 1970.

28. Schneyer, J. Wesley, "Use of the Cloze Procedure for Improving Reading Comprehension," *Reading Teacher* (December 1966), 174–79.

29. Shnayer, Sidney W. "Relationships Between Reading Interest and Reading Comprehension" in *Reading and Realism*, J. Allen Figurel (ed.), Proceedings, International Reading Association, 13, Part 1, 1969, 698–702.

30. Sister M. Baptist, R. S. M. "The Promise That is Poetry," *Catholic School Journal* (May 1965), 45.

31. Stauffer, Russell G. *Directing Reading Maturity As A Cognitive Process*. New York: Harper & Row, Publishers, 1969.

32. Taba, Hilda, "The Teaching of Thinking," *Elementary English* (May 1965), 534–42.

33. Tinker, Miles A. and Constance M. McCullough, *Teaching Elementary Reading* (Third Ed.). New York: Appleton-Century Crofts, 1968, Chapter 9.

34. Triggs, Frances O. "Promoting Growth in Critical Reading," *Reading Teacher* (February 1959), 158–64.

35. Usery, Mary Lou, "Critical Thinking Through Children's Literature," *Elementary English* (February 1966), 115–18.

36. Walpole, Hugh R. "Promoting Development in Interpreting What Is Read in the Middle and Upper Grades," Supplementary Educational Monographs, University of Chicago. Chicago: University of Chicago Press, No. 61, 162–67.

37. Wardeberg, Helen L. "Do We Apply What We Know About Comprehension?" in (Con-Challenger) *Current Issues In Reading*, Nila Banton Smith (ed.), Proceedings, International Reading Association, 13, Part 2, 1969, 85–96.

38. Williams, Gertrude, "Provisions for Critical Reading in Basic Readers," *Elementary English* (May 1959), 323–31.

39. Wolf, Willavene, Martha L. King, and Charlotte S. Huck, "Teaching Critical Reading to Elementary School Children," *Reading Research Quarterly* (Summer 1968) 435–498.

40. Zintz, Miles V. *The Reading Process, The Teacher and The Learner.* Dubuque, Iowa: Wm. C. Brown Company, Publisher, 1970, Chapter 10.

V

The Impaired Reader in the Classroom

Practically all classrooms contain children who are experiencing difficulty in mastering the reading process. This fact contributes greatly to the complexity of teaching reading. It also justifies the discussion of instructional problems which will confront most teachers of reading. The following chapters reflect a deliberate effort to focus primarily on the type of problems that classroom teachers will meet and which they can hope to successfully cope with in the classroom setting.

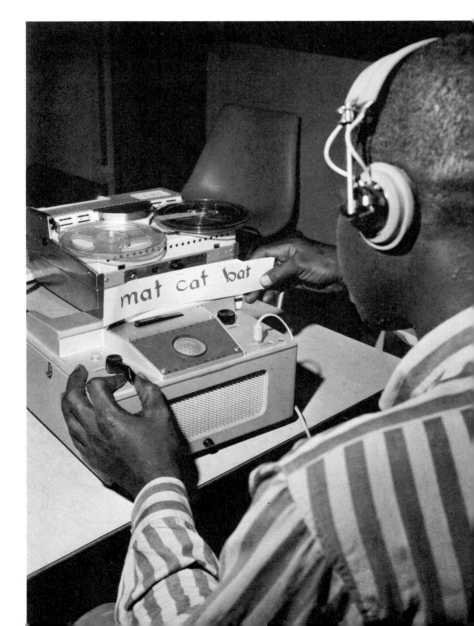

16

Remedial
Reading

Americans assign an extremely high value to literacy. For years it was taken for granted that the mere process of attending school would result in acquiring this prized asset, except in cases in which the individual was too dull or simply refused to learn. Individuals who were alleged to fit either of these categories usually dropped out of school, and there were numerous niches for them to fill in our society.

Gradually laws were passed which forbade dropping out of school prior to reaching a designated age, usually 16 to 18 years. "School" became much more of a threat to the twentieth-century severely impaired reader than hell was to his Puritan ancestors. But as soon as an individual fulfilled the requirements of the law, he could leave school and still find a niche in adult society.

Automation emerged as the most significant socio-economic factor since the industrial revolution and changed the picture drastically. The impaired reader could elect to stay in school until he reached the legal age minimum; get expelled from school for anti-social behavior; or drop out of high school (with the tacit approval of the authorities). Regardless of which option he elected, *there was no niche for him to fill in our complex society*. During the mid-sixties, as unemployment figures for the population as a whole dropped to unprecedented lows, the figures for the not-in-school age group 18 to 22 hit new highs with no encouraging signs of a better tomorrow.

The fervor of the fifties was expended on the "great talent search." The upgrading of the curriculum in mathematics, science, and languages was now focused on the more basic educational problem of how to equip students with the necessary reading skills demanded by the established curriculum.

The failure of large numbers of children to learn to read at a level commensurate with their intellectual ability may well be our number one educational problem. The serious nature of this problem has been known for years, but education at the local level could never muster the finances and trained personnel in such quantities as to be able to even slow down the growing number of impaired readers. As the severity of this problem was grasped by citizens and government alike, the needs of American youths in this area yielded its "local" status and became a matter of national interest. Education of youth and the goals and survival of society were reaffirmed as being inseparable.

The long years of neglect made the solution to this problem more difficult. When federal funds were made available in abundance, the first fact learned was that money alone could not produce a solution. Education is a process not a commodity. Education as a creative process had been stifled too long, and creative ideas could not be conjured up with the same rapidity with which congress voted appropriations. A number of practices which were supported by federal funds turned out to be rather unimaginative. One of these was the hastily assembled in-service program which paralleled course work and which failed to involve teachers in sharing activities and intensive study of research and other professional materials related to reading instruction. A second was the tendency of local schools to acquire a large supply of gadgets such as pacing devices and other mechanistic paraphernalia which had little relevancy to elementary reading instruction.

Remedial Reading
Defined

Unfortunately there is no universal agreement as to the meaning of the terms *remedial reading instruction* and *remedial readers*. In its broadest sense the term remedial reading covers special instruction for those individuals whose reading achievement is X amount lower than their expected achievement based on measured intellectual capacity for learning. There is also no universal agreement as to the value of X. Figures cited in some research suggest that this criterion might be a range of from six months to two years difference between achievement and capacity.

It should be noted that such a broad definition of remedial readers does not differentiate pupils on the basis of what might have caused their lack of growth in reading. Some specialists in the field would prefer that "remedial" be reserved for those cases in which there is evidence that the major cause is a neurological condition. Instruction involving other cases might then be labeled "corrective instruction."

There is general agreement that remedial reading instruction aims at removing the barriers to learning which inhibited learning in the past. It is not concerned with poor reading per se, but rather with bringing children's achievement closer to their actual ability. Remedial reading instruction is not concerned with providing special attention for all pupils who are reading below grade level or chronological age norms. To illustrate this point one might think of two third grade pupils of the same age who read at the same level as noted below:

| Child A | C. A. 8–4 | M. A. 9–2 | I. Q. 110 | Reads 1^2 |
| Child B | C. A. 8–4 | M. A. 7–0 | I. Q. 84 | Reads 1^2 |

Although both pupils are in the same grade and are reading at the same level, only pupil A should be thought of as a remedial reader. He has above-average intelligence, but he is learning at a rate far below his capacity. Child B, although in the third grade, is achieving as well as could be expected on the basis of his ability, and, according to the preceding definition, would not be a logical candidate for remedial reading. He is now learning about as rapidly and as thoroughly as can be expected. Should we decide to give him remedial instruction aimed at bringing him up to his grade level (or chronological age level), we would be implying that methodology or technique in instruction can actually compensate for a lack of ability in academic achievement. Since we do not believe this, it would be irrational to attempt to practice it. However, it is important to realize that when we take this position, we assume that our assessment of his ability is accurate. Pupil A, who is reading slowly in view of his ability, might profit from a change in technique and from individual instruction in certain mechanics of reading. These practices might help him to move forward at a rate commensurate with his ability. This in essence is the philosophy behind remedial instruction.

It has been pointed out previously that reading ability is held in very high esteem in our culture and that children are expected to achieve up to an arbitrary grade-level standard. The fact that at least a third of all pupils in a given grade fall below this standard is well-known to educators. Schools which are geared to mass education, a rigid grade-level structure, and promotion without regard to mastery of skills will continue to produce remedial readers.

Remedial reading, as it is usually understood, puts the onus of failure on the child who needs the remedy. Some authorities have suggested that the term should be *remedial teaching* to intimate that the teaching, not the pupil, is at fault. Neither position is always fair to either pupil or teacher when all factors in reading failures are considered.

It is easy for a teacher to blame the child who develops habits of laziness, inattention, disinterest, withdrawal, or aggression. It is just as easy for parents and critics of schools to blame schools and teaching methods or for teachers to blame parents and home environments. Fixing blame, unless the blame is clear-cut, is dangerous.

Common Misconceptions About Remedial Reading

Despite the widespead use of the term remedial reading, there is some degree of confusion regarding what it is, what practices it embodies, and who its practitioners are. Vague concepts often give rise to misconceptions. Some of these are discussed below.

The most widely held misconception is that remedial reading instruction is based on a set of principles which differ appreciably from those principles which are the basis for the school's regular developmental reading program. It is easy to see how such a misconception might develop. Virtually every college or university which prepares teachers in elementary education has one or more courses entitled "Remedial Reading," "Practices in Remedial Reading," or "Methods and Techniques in Remedial Reading." Many textbooks bear similar titles. Remedial reading clinics are found on almost every university campus. Schools hire "Remedial Reading Teachers." Workshops devoted to remedial reading are commonplace. With this much evidence it is easy to conclude that remedial reading is a subject matter different from the teaching of reading.

It is sometimes difficult to convince teachers that all of the principles and most of the practices which are characteristic of remedial reading are also applicable to developmental reading.

An illustration of this point is found in the behavior and attitudes of two groups of teachers enrolled in different sections of a course entitled "Remedial Techniques in Reading." In the first section the instructor stated that there were not two distinct approaches, one regular and the other remedial, to teaching reading. Some teachers seemed skeptical and were quite reluctant to accept this point of view. In the second class a different approach was tried. Each student was handed a sheet of paper and was asked to list all of the principles of teaching which she identified with remedial reading. The major points mentioned included:

1. Go back to the child's present reading level.
2. Do not expect the child to read material which forces him to experience failure, i.e., he must have developed readiness for the task.
3. Help the child build self-confidence—use abundant praise. Undue pressure in the learning situation may interfere with learning.
4. Use a variety of approaches.
5. Base instruction on a thorough diagnosis.
6. Build interest in reading—have a large stock of supplementary reading materials.

As each point was mentioned, the group noted that it applied equally well to any good classroom program. It was conceded that no principles had been listed which applied exclusively to remedial reading.

A second misconception centers around the practices and the procedures believed to be reserved for remedial reading instruction. Remedial reading is sometimes thought of as consisting of a bag of tricks which includes, among other items, a vast number of games and motivators. When experienced teachers attempt to list methods and procedures which might be identified as "remedial," it is obvious that these methods and procedures are equally justifiable for use during the months in which the pupil is becoming a remedial reader. It might be conceded that in remedial teaching there is more emphasis on devising unique ways of approaching a particular learning task. This emphasis is justified because the remedial reader usually needs more motivation for reading than does the successful reader. It should be pointed out that games and motivators are used to arouse the pupil's interests and to hold his attention in the hope

that this attention and energy can be directed toward reading. These "crutches" must be replaced with more effective and less time-consuming procedures as soon as the child can make the transition. Therefore, to make the use of motivators the identifying badge of remedial reading is misleading.

Experienced teachers often think of remedial reading as being composed of a number of highly specialized techniques which only the initiated can practice. For example, a group of teachers, as part of a course in remedial reading, were each to tutor a child whose reading achievement was considerably below his ability. There was a file available for each child which contained intelligence test results, notes from parent interviews, and a summary of the child's reading level and reading weaknesses. Later, several of these experienced teachers admitted that they "felt completely lost" during the first few sessions because they were not sure that they knew enough about remedial reading to work with the case. In a discussion, they admitted having had children in their regular classes with problems at least as serious as those found in the assigned case. They also indicated that they expected something special or extraordinary to be imparted to them in the area of remedial reading before they could work with an impaired reader. Once this notion had been dispelled, they taught successfully and with much creativity and insight.

A third misconception is that remedial reading is something that must be done outside of the regular classroom. It is true that in some school systems the remedial program develops as a sort of appendage to the regular structure, but remedial reading must of necessity be conducted in the classrooms of those schools which have no such special provision. Inevitably there are pupils in these classrooms who must be considered remedial readers. (6)

Differences Between Remedial and Regular Reading Instruction

The position has been taken that there may be little if any difference between the principles or the practices followed in remedial reading and the everyday instructional activities of a conscientious, reading classroom teacher. Nevertheless, when remedial programs supplement regular reading instruction, there are probably some real differences between the two. The chief cause of the differences has already been implied: in remedial reading we conscientiously adhere to the principles that we often only verbalize in the regular classroom instruction. Thus, when differences exist they probably stem from two sources:

1. *The attitudes and philosophy of administrators and teachers*
   a. In the remedial program, as a rule, there is no immediate conscious endeavor to get the child up to "grade level" or some other arbitrary standard. He will read materials which he can read with some degree of success regardless of his grade placement.
   b. The teaching-learning atmosphere will probably be more permissive. The child will not be labeled a failure, and he will be accepted as a person. Even though the objective is to read, pressure on the child to read will be lessened. As a result, he will be less threatened by the reading situation.
   c. In the remedial program more attention might be focused on the reasons for failure, thus revealing certain other factors which may have to be dealt with concurrently with the actual reading problem. Considerable emphasis will be placed on how to interest the child in reading; as a result, senseless drill is likely to be held to a minimum.

    d. There will be conferences with parents if it appears that the child is under pressure and tension at home.

    e. A great variety of reading materials will be available, and children will be permitted to choose what they wish to read. They will be encouraged to read books they *can* read, not necessarily books at their grade level. (12, 24)

    f. The teacher will know a great deal about the child, and she will know exactly his reading achievement as well as his instructional needs.

    g. There will be time for individual instruction as needed, and each child in the group will require such instruction.

    h. In the remedial program, there may be more emphasis on the use of "motivators." In the regular classroom only a few pupils need this type of instruction in order to learn.

    i. In remedial reading, the psychological needs of the child are considered to be very important. He is encouraged to set goals he can achieve and is praised for any accomplishment.

    j. In remedial reading, children never feel as if they are in reading competition with others. They may compete with their own previous performance, but they do not have to measure up to some arbitrary standard.

These attitudes and goals undoubtedly differentiate between remedial and regular instruction, yet the regular classroom teacher probably subscribes to all of them. They are universally advocated as sound classroom procedure. How, then, do these factors become more characteristic of remedial reading than of the regular classroom instruction? The answer is found in the second source of difference between regular and remedial instruction.

2. *The conditions under which teachers function*

These conditions have been briefly discussed in Chapter 1 under the heading, "Administrative Practices Affecting Instruction." Included were: too many pupils per teacher to permit individual instruction; universal promotion in a grade-level system; non-teaching activities of teachers; the schools' and the communities' disinclination to wait for readiness; school entrance based on C.A.; and others. Some first grade teachers have admitted to attempting to teach as many as forty children how to read. Fortunately, this would never happen in a remedial class. In the remedial class there is time for diagnosis, time for building a program to fit individual needs as disclosed by the diagnosis, and time to give individual attention where it is needed. Supplementary materials are available and competitive pressures are removed from the learning task. These steps are taken, because educators know that this is the way to get the job done, and they see to it that it is done this way. They also say that these are the principles and the practices to follow in the teaching of reading prior to the child's becoming a severely handicapped learner, but they somehow do not insist that conditions prevail which will permit these principles and practices to be followed.

It is a sad commentary on American education that sound principles of teaching a skill as important as reading can be followed only after many children suffer due to the inadequacy of the instruction. Teachers regret this terrible waste and the attendant risks of producing maladjustment and anti-social behavior. They have guilt feelings because teaching as a profession has not yet evolved the procedures which would prevent teaching under conditions that threaten the mental health of their pupils.

**Factors Related to
Success in Reading**

A survey of the literature on reading reveals a number of factors relating to success and failure in reading. (16, 18) Those which seem to be universally agreed upon are:

1. Physical handicaps
2. Intellectual capacity
3. Perceptual abilities
4. Emotional involvements
5. Environmental factors including both home and school

These topics are discussed in other chapters of this book. However, it should be noted that each of the topics covers an extensive range of causal factors, as illustrated below under the major headings of physical and educational factors.

1. Physical handicaps
   a. Impaired vision
   b. Hearing loss or a lack of facility in auditory discrimination
   c. Low vitality, lack of energy to apply to the learning task
   d. Inadequate attention span
   e. Absence from school due to illness at crucial instructional periods

      f. Specific language disability stemming from physiological impairment

  2. School-Environmental factors

      a. The child, having moved from school to school, has encountered different methods of teaching which may have produced confusion

      b. Lack of individual instruction when needed

      c. Failure of the school to detect reading weaknesses

      d. Universal promotion not related to the mastery of basic skills

      e. Inadequacy of the instruction stemming from poor teacher preparation

      f. Lack of an adequate supply of interesting reading materials at the pupil's reading level

In a majority of the reading problems it is unlikely that severe impairment can be traced to only one factor. If it is true that there are innumerable factors which affect learning to read, it is logical to surmise that these factors can work together in hundreds of different combinations. This makes diagnosis, particularly from the psychological standpoint, extremely difficult and complicated. Figure 26 attempts to illustrate the complexity of factors which may influence the development of good reading habits. While any one of these is sufficient to cause trouble in learning to read, it is unlikely that any one operates alone for any great length of time. Unresolved problems seem to hasten the growth of other problems.

When faced by a complex problem, most people prefer simple explanations and simple remedies. This is true of the complex problem of explaining how and why such a large number of school children with adequate intellectual endowment become seriously impaired readers. Earlier it was pointed out that at different times simple explanations and remedies for this problem enjoyed widespread acceptance. Inadequate intelligence, special disabilities, and the schools' lessened emphasis on the synthetic method of teaching phonics have at one time or another been advanced as the chief cause of reading problems. Certain of these theories have been downgraded as explanations of reading failures. Nevertheless, there is still the tendency to advance hypotheses which in the final analysis may be over-simplifications in that they neglect to take into consideration the interaction of various factors.

Another approach, thus far fruitless, is to start with a hypothesis which at the moment cannot be verified or refuted. Brain damage

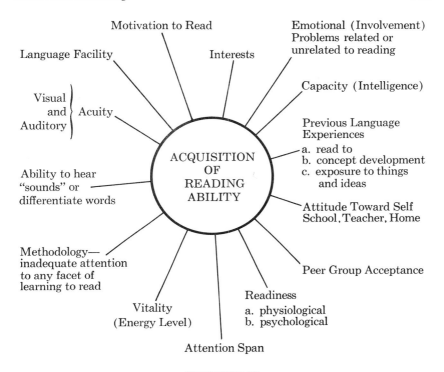

FIGURE 26

Some Factors Influencing the Acquisition of Reading Ability.

(and minimum brain damage) is a case in point. Since it would be most arbitrary to a priori rule this factor out, it is not long before some individuals suggest its presence in every impaired reader found in the schools.

The Dyslexia bandwagon

One of the major problems in discussing and/or working with impaired readers is that we have not actually isolated the problem with which we want to deal. Too much effort has gone into assigning labels which in the final analysis have little meaning. (22) The latest example is *dyslexia*. This term had been introduced decades previously, was found not to be particularly useful as a diagnostic entity, and was rarely used in reference to learning problems. Today, dyslexia is one of the most widely discussed terms in the literature on reading. Whatever meaning it once had has been blurred and diffused by its indiscriminate use in referring to every type and degree of reading malfunction. (4)

Dyslexia has been used as a synonym for word blindness, brain damage, neurological impairment, general language disability, learning disability, psycholinguistic malfunction, symbolic confusion, unilateral cerebral dominance, streptosymbolia, specific language disability, and variations on the above themes such as minimal brain damage, neurological dysfunction, and the like.

The sudden popularity of *dyslexia* provides an excellent example of the pendulum effect often found in education and in this case reading instruction in particular. Although educators during the early 1960s voiced concern about poor readers in the schools, there was still a degree of institutional optimism that the school could teach every child to read. This was the era in which educators and the community at large had great faith in the concept and practice of remedial reading instruction. Schools which had instituted remedial programs reported that these programs enjoyed some degree of success. The hope was that those children who were not making adequate progress would soon get the proper remedial treatment, and the idea that the school could not teach all children to read was simply not entertained.

The following incident is illustrative of this attitude. A group of teachers and administrators were discussing the problem of how to deal with stubborn cases of retarded reading when it had been established that intelligence was not the causative factor. Various proposals for remedial teaching were discussed. Suddenly the tenor of the meeting was changed when a speaker made the following statement:

"We all know that there are tremendous individual differences among pupils in every type of skill performance — music, athletics, composition, creativity, oral expression, computation, reasoning, and achievement in all subject matter courses. We accept individual differences in these areas, but not in reading. Although we find great differences in reading skill in every classroom, we insist that all children should be reading at an arbitrary level which we refer to as grade level. The inferior reader must 'be taught' to read at this arbitrary level whether or not we can teach him, whether or not he can learn, and whether or not he is interested. Do we really believe that we never meet a child, even though he is not below average in intelligence, who is just not going to learn to read?" This suggestion had a chilling effect on the discussion and it was promptly rejected.

It is not clear precisely what caused the change in so many attitudes about reading failures in American schools, but something shattered the uneasy confidence that the schools were equal to the task of solving the reading crisis. Criticism of reading instruction may have been a factor; or perhaps parents lost interest in the token value of "promotion" when they knew their children could not read at grade level. It also seems apparent that the change paralleled the publicity which accompanied the discovery of poverty and the ghettos in America and the student unrest which plagued the schools.

The educational establishment had up to this time reacted to impaired readers in the schools in much the same way as the larger society reacted to poverty and the ghettos. (Yes, there was poverty out there somewhere; and yes, minority groups by the millions lived under the most dire conditions, but we've solved our problems before....) Now as the pressures on the schools mounted and educators sensed that the schools were expected to (but could not) eradicate the *effects* of all the ills of society, dyslexia became an idea "whose time had come."

Considering the time and the problems faced, dyslexia happened to be the ideal hypothetical construct. Dyslexia is in the nervous system of the learner. It is sub-clinical in nature since its presence or absence cannot (at the moment) be scientifically established. By definition it does not stem from lack of intellectual capacity. Furthermore, it is not produced by inadequate instructional methodology. (15) The most harsh charge that can be sustained against methodology is that the instruction that was used was not equal to the task of overcoming the residual deficits that were already there. Here, an analogy might be drawn with medicine. The medical profession was not derelict with regard to the deaths of certain polio victims prior to 1954. However, the intervention programs used by doctors were not sufficient to prevent the casualties. Once the Salk vaccine was developed, tested, and approved by the medical profession, a new set of procedures and ground rules were in operation. At the time of this writing the combined efforts of medicine, education, and chemistry has not reached the Salk-point on the dyslexia intervention continuum.

At this point the analogy ceases. It is likely that no otherwise healthy person developed polio or died from it as a result of an erroneous diagnosis. A wrong diagnosis of dyslexia could well result in the death of a potential reader. The educational issue is not whether dyslexia exists. We can assume it does. The issue is its incidence in the school population. Until there is better evidence, we must resist the invitation issued by self appointed experts to join them in the belief that between 10 and 28 percent of the youth in our schools suffer from this malady.

Experience Determines
Point of View Toward Causes

Educators and clinicians who deal extensively with reading problems undoubtedly have vastly different experiences with readers.
There are significant differences in the role of each group and in the
work climate in which each group operates. The community expects
different types of behavior from educators and clinicians. Therefore,
it should not be considered unusual when divergent views emerge
as to the cause and cure of reading problems. It should be kept in
mind, however, that one's original premises as to the cause of reading problems will influence the procedures advocated for working
with impaired readers.

When blind men feel different parts of an elephant, each man
forms a disperate hypothesis on the nature and structure of elephants, even though all the men had a common experience labeled
"elephant feeling." This is demonstrated by the story of the five
blind men, each of whom felt only a part of the elephant, such as
the trunk, tail, leg, ear, and side. They variously described an elephant as being like a snake, a rope, a tree, a fan, and a wall. The
reasons for their varied conclusions are quite evident to the person
who entertains the total picture of an elephant. It is also quite obvious that, on the basis of their individual experiences, their deductions were quite plausible, despite the fact that not one of them
emerged with a good concept of an elephant.

All people who work with impaired or disabled readers do not
work from the same side of the elephant. Educators differ among
themselves regarding the origin and the cure of reading problems,
as do psychologists, clinicians, and therapists. This divergence of
opinion may have arisen from differences in training which lead to
dissimilarity in the relative emphasis placed on learning factors.

Most educators have reasoned that when a child has been exposed to reading instruction which has not "taken," it is obvious
that the instruction was not adequate for this particular child. (1)
The proper approach to such failure was to vary the method of
teaching and to introduce new techniques which might prove effective. Experiments were designed to test or establish this premise.
Groups of retarded readers were subjected to specific types of instruction for varying periods of time. Strangely enough, almost any
technique advocated and reported had a degree of efficacy with some
cases. The data for a group of retarded readers are given on reading
tests in the form of pre-test and end-test means, and the group gain
reported is often significant. In most cases, the test data show that
some individuals made no gain or even appeared to decline in read-

ing ability. The important conclusion of such studies, however, is that the group made a mean gain of so many months' reading when compared with a control group of retarded readers who were not exposed to these particular methods and techniques. The methods used to effect these changes gain widespread appeal among teachers having children who have failed in reading in their classes.

In our society the educator's duties include responsibility for methodology and for techniques of teaching. It is only natural that educators have tended to concentrate on experimentation in the area of method. Figure 27 attempts to illustrate the behavior most likely to result when one starts from the premise that methodology is the key to all reading problems.

If all children who failed to learn to read did learn to read as a result of varying techniques and methodology, the only necessary premise would be the one discussed above. Unfortunately, this is not the case. We know that some children have had several different teachers who used different approaches to teaching reading, but the children still failed to learn to read. Neither pressure, punishment, nor variation in procedures proved effective with these children. Quite often they developed behavioral problems and showed evidence of maladjustment. If the behavior problems were of the overt aggressive type, the child was probably referred to a child-guidance clinic, a reading laboratory, or psychiatric help if it were obtainable. Referrals undoubtedly included children with high intelligence who had not, over a period of years, profited from instruction.

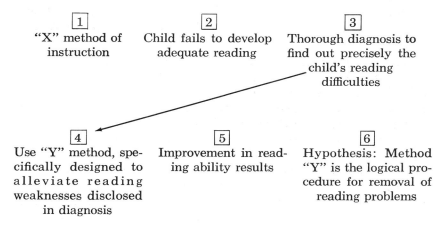

1	2	3
"X" method of instruction	Child fails to develop adequate reading	Thorough diagnosis to find out precisely the child's reading difficulties

4	5	6
Use "Y" method, specifically designed to alleviate reading weaknesses disclosed in diagnosis	Improvement in reading ability results	Hypothesis: Method "Y" is the logical procedure for removal of reading problems

FIGURE 27

Illustration of How the Attitude is Reinforced That Failure in Reading Can Be Remedied by Change in Method

The psychologist-clinician finds that most cases of referral for reading failures are not, at the time of referral, simple uncomplicated learning problems amenable to solution by methodology alone. The evidence already at hand makes it obvious that more work on the reading problems alone will probably not be any more effective than it has been in the classroom. The clinician may tend to see all reading problems in the light of his own experiences. His role, and the type of cases he is likely to see, may lead him to the premise that impaired reading ability and emotional problems are inseparable. Usually, prior to or along with any work on reading, some form of therapy is introduced. Regardless of the therapeutic approach, the goals of this therapy are likely to include:

1. Reduction of the tension connected with reading
2. Change of the child's attitude toward self (ego-rehabilitation, self-confidence, etc.)
3. Change of the child's attitudes toward authority (school and parents)
4. Building interest in reading

Figure 28 is an attempt to illustrate this concept.

The best informed opinion today seems to be that reading behavior is a part of total development. The reading process and the reader interact at all times. While one may be primarily interested in a child's reading behavior, this behavior is but one facet of the individual's total growth process. It is generally conceded that both conscious and unconscious motivations are involved in reading difficulties.

Reading difficulties stem from many causes; but, no matter what the cause, any child having difficulty with reading needs special help. Perhaps the child is socially immature or lacks experience. He may not have mastered a vocabulary sufficient to express his own ideas or to understand the ideas of others. Perhaps he comes from an underprivileged family and poverty has affected his health, leaving him undernourished or undersized. Perhaps his mind is undernourished, too, because his parents read very little to him or speak English imperfectly. He may lack security because his father keeps moving from job to job, thus interrupting his school work. It may be that his parents neglect him or favor a brighter child in the family. Or he may lack emotional maturity and cannot concentrate

(Methodology and techniques cannot always remove reading failures and concomitant behavior problems. Some reading problems have their roots outside the reading situation and a frontal attack on reading will not solve the problem.)

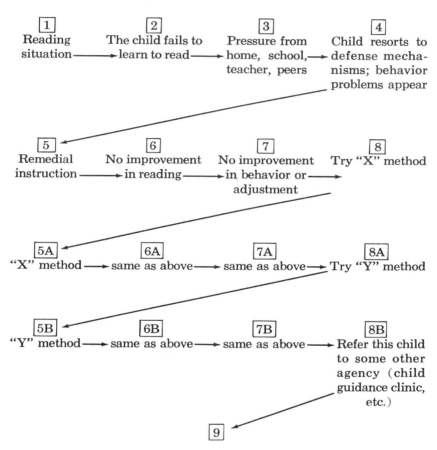

FIGURE 28

Hypothesis: Some emotional problem (possibly originally not related to reading) is still unresolved. The problem must be attacked and alleviated before the child can concentrate on the learning task.

on a difficult abstract skill such as reading because he is anxious, unhappy, hostile, or depressed. (21)

Characteristics of a
Sound Remedial Program

Previous discussion has suggested that techniques for remedial reading instruction do not differ radically from the instructional practices already found in the regular reading program. However, teaching a severely retarded reader may be complicated by his previous failure experiences and his reactions to them. For this reason the process of learning is more complex for remedial readers than for normal readers. (8)

The following discussion of practices in remedial reading focuses on those problems which it is believed can be handled in the school. The extreme cases of non-reading stem from genetic defect and call for diagnostic techniques and treatment which in most cases lie beyond the competence of the school to provide. In no case is it implied that there is a one best way to deal with slow-learning readers. There are a number of practices, however, which should be common to most programs because they can be accommodated within any framework designed for working with remedial readers. The topics discussed below are important because they relate to the teacher's daily contact with children and influence the degree of success her program will enjoy.

The first step — through diagnosis

In diagnosing the reading problems of children in a given class, a teacher must determine each child's full academic potential, as well as his present skills, weaknesses, and habits. (A diagnostic checklist dealing only with reading behavior is illustrated in Figure 21, Chapter 8.) When the etiology of a reading failure is not a simple one, a teacher needs a comprehensive set of data in order to work intelligently with the child. The diagnosis should extend not only to the reading but also to the reader, and should be concerned with all educational, emotional, and environmental factors. Knowing her pupils' psychological needs and observing their social behavior can help a teacher detect many signs of maladjustment which are, or may become, related to reading behavior. Figure 29 is a personal inventory containing items which focus the teacher's attention on social-emotional behavior and which may reveal the presence of unresolved problems.

If the school makes psychological assessments of pupils, a teacher should refer problem children as soon as possible after she detects behavior patterns which indicate poor adjustment. Even when

FIGURE 29

Personal Adjustment Inventory for Retarded Readers

NAME: _____

ADDRESS: _____

AGE: _____

GRADE: _____

Father: Living ( ) Deceased ( ) Occupation:_____

Mother: Living ( ) Deceased ( ) Occupation:_____

	Above Average			Average			Below Average		
Feeling of security	( )	( )	( )	( )	( )	( )	( )	( )	( )
Acceptance by peer group	( )	( )	( )	( )	( )	( )	( )	( )	( )
Attitude toward school	( )	( )	( )	( )	( )	( )	( )	( )	( )
Degree of self-confidence	( )	( )	( )	( )	( )	( )	( )	( )	( )
Reaction to frustration	( )	( )	( )	( )	( )	( )	( )	( )	( )
Language facility	( )	( )	( )	( )	( )	( )	( )	( )	( )
Ability to follow directions	( )	( )	( )	( )	( )	( )	( )	( )	( )
Independent work habits	( )	( )	( )	( )	( )	( )	( )	( )	( )
Concentration span	( )	( )	( )	( )	( )	( )	( )	( )	( )
Background and experiences which relate to reading	( )	( )	( )	( )	( )	( )	( )	( )	( )
Parents' attitude toward child's reading	( )	( )	( )	( )	( )	( )	( )	( )	( )
Parents' acceptance of child	( )	( )	( )	( )	( )	( )	( )	( )	( )
Estimate of home:									
(Socio-economic status)	( )	( )	( )	( )	( )	( )	( )	( )	( )
(Emotional climate)	( )	( )	( )	( )	( )	( )	( )	( )	( )

Observed behavior which is related to judgments on above items:

_____

_____

_____

_____

there are no clinical facilities available, a teacher aware of the fact that a particular child is under strain and tension may permit her relationships with this child to be more therapeutic than usual. The experienced teacher knows she must discover why non-learning or poor learning takes place. If the answer is simply poor teaching rather than emotional reactions that have become attached to the reading problem, remedial reading instruction is much different and much easier. Therefore, one of the obectives of remedial reading instruction is that the program must take into account both the individual's reading problems and why he has failed in his overall school efforts. In many cases it would be useless, if not unwise, to proceed without concern for the reasons why an individual has developed as he has.

The assessment of reading ability has been discussed in Chapter 8. The discussion of standardized and informal reading tests found there is equally applicable to remedial reading and will not be repeated here; however, one point should be reviewed. Although standardized tests may differ in merit, the best available test is almost useless without a careful evaluation of results in the light of the testee's individual characteristics. When emphasis is placed more on administering tests than on their instructional implications, it is easy to acquire the feeling that testing is an automatically desirable academic rite.

A group test, which yields a score that in turn is translated into grade-level or age norms, may not tell much about why a child reads poorly. Most standardized tests which are administered individually at the various grade levels are composed of relatively short reading passages. These tests tend to overestimate readers, placing their reading ability level somewhat higher than the level they can actually handle in sustained reading. Reading tests are designed to measure the same skills that a child is using in his daily reading activities. Therefore, it should be kept in mind that teachers have a number of procedures available in the classroom for discovering a child's strengths and needs in reading. These include:

> Standardized group and individual tests and informal teacher-made tests.
>
> Basal reader material. Having a child read orally for a few minutes will disclose whether he can read successfully the material he is attempting.
>
> Various word lists for sight-recognition tests.
>
> Worktype assignments such as workbook exercises for evaluating particular skills.
>
> Group participation situations in the classroom, which are the culmination of a reading assignment.
>
> Classroom achievements in spelling, writing, and unit work.
>
> Cumulative records which show the child's achievements and how he handled tasks over a period of time. These point up both the progress made and the skills yet to be mastered.

Diagnosis is continuous

The alert teacher guards against thinking of a standardized test or any testing situation as if it were terminal. No child reveals all there is to know about his reading in any one given sample of his reading behavior. When diagnosis is continuous, "patterns of errors" become more apparent. An isolated observation may in itself be valid, but it is the sum of many observations and their relationship to each other which gives a total picture of the remedial reader. Something is learned each time a child reads aloud to the teacher, each time he attempts seatwork or exercises. Group discussion may reveal clues like vocabulary weakness or misconceptions about words. Diagnosis must be seen as part of the whole remedial process, not just the prelude to remedial instruction.

Keeping a record of each remedial session is an important and closely related part of continuous diagnosis and the use of varied techniques. A record of what was done and the apparent success or usefulness of each procedure can serve as a guide to future preparations. Out of such a record will emerge a series of immediate goals.

Stress evidence of progress

The impaired reader has usually had a long history of failure and frustration associated with reading. These experiences have colored his attitude toward reading and toward himself as a reader. He expects to fail in reading. Since his level of aspiration is low, he needs experiences which will break the "I can try—and you can teach—but I'll fail" syndrome.

A thorough diagnosis will reveal certain mechanics of reading in which the child is weak. Using the results of such a diagnosis, it is a good policy to work on some phase of reading which will yield objective evidence of progress. Lack of confidence and aversion to reading must be overcome, and one of the best ways to do this is to dramatize progress. If the lack of a particular skill is an obstacle to further progress in reading, working on that specific skill is a highly justifiable procedure.

Help child gain insight

The attitudes toward self and reading which a child has formed while failing in reading are often inhibiting factors in remedial situations. Most remedial readers have been conditioned to suspect and dislike reading. If instruction is to be successful, the child must go through another conditioning process in which he finds reading pleasant and rewarding. Since his previous reading situations produced tension and threatened the child, a climate which he can tolerate must be developed.

Establishing rapport is primarily the responsibility of the teacher. In many cases the child conceals his real attitude toward reading, authority and books. A teacher may think she is working with a docile, cooperative child, but she may be working with one who has learned it is best to conceal resentment and hostility and to feign interest. Such a child is probably burning up energy which might well be channeled into the learning situation. His reading progress depends upon his perceiving and accepting the fact that he actually can succeed at reading, which in turn may depend on his gaining insight into the causes which have contributed to his poor reading. A remedial program should help the child gain such insights. This insight provides him with direction and motivation, and helps him obtain a degree of objectivity about himself and his capabilities.

Once he has gained insight, the child should be helped to set his own goals. Attainment of this objective can be the basis for a healthy teacher-pupil relationship. If the child is resentful of authority, his setting his own goals will have therapeutic value, especially if, with guidance, he can make these goals realistic.

Realistic goal-setting and insight into the causes of his reading problems should help the child overcome whatever poor work habits he may have developed. Many children have experienced difficulty in completing workbook assignments. They have learned to omit questions or problems which they do not understand because their asking for help calls attention to their inadequacy. They may develop the habits of guessing when in doubt, wasting time, or seeking ways of evading tasks which are distasteful. It may be a long road back to good work habits, but traveling this road is an important function of remedial instruction.

Need for a variety of materials

Supplying a variety of materials is a second special administrative and instructional problem. According to Whipple, (27) one of the first steps necessary to improve reading instruction in most schools is to secure a wide variety of supplementary reading material. She states, "Teachers have indicated that they need much more reading material in order to satisfy pupils' needs, especially supplementary material and less difficult reading material for retarded pupils." There are some obvious reasons why a great variety of materials is needed. Each child who fails to read in the elementary grades has failed while using the conventional classroom materials, composed of basal readers, workbook-type materials, and textbooks in the various curricular areas. Thus, in many instances, they develop an aversion for these materials.

Since these children are reading at a level below their grade placement, their experience level is often far in advance of their reading level. The content of basal reader materials which can be read successfully may be quite elementary. Poor readers of average or superior intellect have a special need for materials which are easy to read, from the standpoint of mechanics, and yet have a high interest potential. (24) As a general rule, a seriously impaired reader does not volunteer a multitude of topics that he is interested in exploring through reading. Anyone who has worked at length with such cases will recall those youngsters who maintained that they wanted to read only stories about horses, jets, fairy tales, cowboys, space travel, or some other specific topic. Such an interest is the most important lever available to the teacher, provided that she has such accessible materials at the child's reading level.

The more reading ability the child has, the easier it is to find supplementary material on any given subject. During recent years, more and more supplementary materials at the easier levels have been published. Teachers should be familiar with a number of books and series of books which are available and of particular interest to poor readers. In addition, teachers should be conversant with guides, reviews, and bibliographies which can be used as resources for finding new materials as they are published.

Developing and Maintaining Interest in Reading

Building rapport between teacher and pupil helps the child tolerate the reading situation, but success in reading provides the drive which will keep him at the task. Following a change in attitude toward reading, the next logical step is to help create within the child a desire to want to read. This can best be accomplished if the child's reading materials parallel his interests. Remedial readers, as a rule, do not respond helpfully to questions such as "What are you interested in?" or "What do you want to read today?" The answer is likely to be "nothing," said more or less politely. A number of techniques can be used either to discover or to arouse a remedial reader's interest:

1. Books with colorful jackets, or books opened to interesting pictures, may be left where they will be noticed. The teacher can observe the child's reactions to see which books he rejects and

which ones hold his attention. The teacher might discuss or read from one that captured the pupil's attention in order to whet his appetite for reading.

2. Thorough preparation of lesson plans is of great importance; the problems of motivation, interest, attitudes, work habits, and attention span are more acute with a remedial reader. Lesson plans should always include alternate tasks in case a particular task fails to motivate the remedial reader or hold his interest.

3. The child can be asked to participate in a sentence completion task wherein he supplies information:

    a. "When I grow up, if I am able to do the type of work I like to do best, I will be a_____."

    b. "The person I would like best to meet and talk with is _____."

    c. "If I could travel anywhere in the world, the place I would like most to visit is_____."

These and other items can be used to discover areas of the child's interest such as science, exploration, athletics, aviation, or medicine.

4. One teacher used this technique successfully: a child found her reading a book when he arrived for his session of individual instruction. The book was at his reading level, and was one she believed he would enjoy. The boy, noting that it was not an adult book, looked at the picture and read the text beneath it. "I can read that," he said. The teacher replied, "Good, someday you can read this book, but today we are going to review sight words, work on prefixes, read a story. . . ." The boy then interrupted with "I'd like to read that story." The fact that the teacher was reading and enjoying the book, plus the fact that the boy had demonstrated to himself he could read it, were factors in producing his reaction. The teacher was wise not to suggest immediately that the boy read the book. His own decision to do so made his reading "ego-involved," and he eventually asked to read other books in the series.

5. Another approach that proved successful in working with a child, who seemingly could not get interested in any reading matter, was leaving a tape recorder and microphone in a conspicuous place. The child walked in and immediately inquired, "What's that?" "Oh, that's a tape recorder — someone else was using it today." "Can I use it — can I record something?" "Sure, you can use it sometime." "How about today?" "Well, I don't know — if you can find something you want to read, I guess we can record it today."

The boy went at once to the shelf containing books at his reading level, looked at two books, put them back, and selected a third. It was a book about flying and airplanes which the teacher had unsuccessfully tried to get the child to choose and take home at a previous session. The novelty of recording interfered with reading for a few minutes, but then served as a highly motivational device for many succeeding sessions. Eventually the child was able to listen to the playback, correct his own errors, and point out the types of improvement he should work for.

This suggestion will not prove effective with every child. In one case, that of a boy of ten reading at the first grade level, the recorder was tried unsuccessfully. The slow, halty, error-ridden reading on the playback was too much for him. He volunteered that he did not want to use the recorder any more.

Administrative Considerations

Many schools and communities have inaugurated reading programs designed to help those children who have failed or who are not progressing at a rate commensurate with their ability. The administration and operation of programs differ, sometimes because of the belief that one administrative setup has certain inherent superiorities over all others, and in other cases because at the moment other approaches are not possible because of financial or other limiting factors. One of the most common or widely followed procedures is remedial reading carried on by the regular classroom teachers. (16, 29, 30) Most teachers group pupils on the basis of their reading ability. Whether or not this practice qualifies as remedial is determined by what goes on in the classroom. While grouping may be the first step toward providing remedial instruction, it is obvious that provision must be made for some individual instruction, or else the grouping will result in structure without substance. In a school which has no other method of dealing with impaired readers, the only remedial teaching which will be done will be provided by the regular classroom teachers. However, the fact that reading problems are not dealt with in a special setting is not prima facie evidence that they are being dealt with in the classroom.

A second approach is the use of a reading specialist or a remedial reading teacher. In some instances, such a teacher's duties consist exclusively of remedial work; she teaches no regular classes. In other situations, one or more teachers may divide their time between a regular assignment and remedial teaching. An interesting variation of this is the practice of the Dearborn schools, as reported by Jackson. (9) Elementary teachers spend five weeks in the Dearborn Reading Center working with cases and building materials. They then return to their regular classrooms with new insights in reading problems.

Another issue is whether to work with impaired readers as individuals or in small groups. Often the reading problems involved dictate the answer to this question. Group instruction probably should be used wherever it is feasible. This is done not only for the sake of economy, but also because grouping provides a social setting for the instruction. Small groups of five or six are sometimes superior to a group of two children. Two pupils often get involved in competing for the attention of the tutor. If one of the two is, or feels, inferior to the other in reading, the problem is accentuated by the direct comparison. Children will feel less singled out and possibly less threatened in a slightly larger group. Small group instruction in no way precludes individual work and individual help within the group. In any case, the size of the group should be adjusted to the instructional problems to be solved.

There are certain other administrative practices which do not fit the traditional framework of classroom instruction. One of these is the use of part of the summer as a make-up term. This practice, while not widespread, has in recent years found its way into a number of schools. In some instances, instruction is provided during the summer for children reading far below their ability level. This instruction might be for one or two hours per day, in small groups, one or more teachers from the school being hired for a specified number of weeks. In other cases such instruction is provided on a tuition basis. The latter practice can raise serious problems unless it is possible to enroll children who need instruction but who are unable to participate for financial reasons.

Summer programs are usually voluntary for the student, but some schools use the subtle pressure of tentative nonpromotion or of probationary promotion as a means of motivating the poor readers and the underachievers to participate in the program. Usually such pressures are not needed if an interesting program is developed and explained to children and parents.

Several such programs are described in recent publications. An article by Still (26) reports that a four-week summer remedial program, which enrolled 72 pupils ranging in age from 6 to 17 years, resulted in a mean gain of 10 months in reading achievement. Googins (7) describes a six-week summer program which featured materials entirely different from those used during the regular school year. This feature was instrumental in developing wider interests and more positive attitudes toward reading.

The scheduling of summer remedial reading programs has increased as a result of Title II and III funds available to local school districts. (28) A number of the initial projects funded by NDEA and ESEA may have erred in their emphasis on mechanical devices and gadgets. In some instances where this occurred, one of the objectives was to secure this relatively high-priced equipment for use in the school's regular reading program. Widespread use of such materials could result in deleterious side effects if schools substitute gadgetry for sound developmental instruction.

Providing for staff involvement

Regardless of what administrative procedure is followed, the resultant program can be successful. On the other hand, following any particular method will not in itself assure a successful program. Any administrative plan or organization is at best only the bare framework upon which a program can be built. The principles and practices which are followed determine the degree of success any remedial program will enjoy. Thus, the administrative details may vary without hindering a program as long as teachers follow sound practices. There are a number of general considerations which are very important in determining the success or failure of a special reading program. Some of these are listed below.

1. *In inaugurating a new program, the administrator should be certain to involve the teaching staff, since the teachers are ultimately responsible for making the program work.* A new program or a program change should evolve out of a cooperative effort of both administrators and teachers. Both have areas of responsibility, of training, and of competency, which will help them in foreseeing and solving the problems which are sure to arise.

2. *As new personnel come into the school, they must be thoroughly briefed on all phases of the program — its goals, how referrals are made, and each teacher's role and responsibility in the total effort.*

3. *All teachers should be totally familiar with both the goals and the limitations of the program.* It would be psychologically bad for teachers to expect more from the program than it is designed to deliver. For instance, remedial instruction outside of the classroom cannot be expected to relieve the regular classroom of pupil variability. Neither should such a program be permitted to become a dumping ground for all reading cases which merit some individual attention.

4. *The remedial instruction must not be an ego threat to the pupil.* It might be construed as a punishment if it is tacked on the end of the school day or if it takes the place of play, recess periods, or any other activity which the child values.

5. *The instruction should have regular curriculum status and should be integrated with all school goals in the teaching of reading.* If the remedial instruction is done outside of the classroom and is not integrated with the regular classroom instruction, the child may possibly be exposed to poor educational practices. In one situation he is expected and encouraged to read materials considerably below his grade level, while in the other situation he may be expected to cope with workbook exercises and textbooks at his grade level even though these materials are too difficult for him. Methods of approaching the same goal, such as phonic analysis or sight word study, may vary considerably or even be contradictory. One reading situation may be permissive, and the other may be rigidly structured.

6. *Releasing a teacher for remedial work at the expense of increasing the class size of other teachers may result in unconscious resentments against the program.* If teachers feel that they are forced to work under more difficult conditions, they may feel justified in attempting to shift any and all problem cases to the remedial reading teacher.

7. *If a special program is inaugurated, it is important to "take parents along."* An interview may help explain what the school is attempting to do — and that it is being done for the child's good.

8. *The basic criterion as to whether there is a program is whether the teacher or teachers have time to prepare lessons and materials.* If this important factor is missing, one can conclude that at the most there is only a "paper program."

9. *Where a special program or out-of-class teaching exists, there should be a clearly understood method of referral.* Most schools have a testing program, and test results coupled with teacher judgment are probably the most widely practiced referral procedure. Where reading, intelligence, and academic achievement scores are available, all should be used as criteria for referral.

Need for prevention

In addition to these administrative considerations, there are several special problems which are extremely important and which are both administrative and procedural in nature. The first of these is the recognition and referral of first-stage remedial cases, or emphasis on prevention rather than cure. The longer reading failures go uncorrected, the more complicated and severe they are likely to become. As a rule, reading problems become interwoven with social, emotional, and behavioral problems.

Ordinarily, children are not referred to a reading or child-guidance clinic until some time after the problem has developed. Also, it is undoubtedly true that many schools which attempt to provide some formal program of help for retarded readers fail to get the children and the special help together until poor habits and poor attitudes have had a chance to become solidified. Children who are experiencing difficulty in reading, often develop symptoms which are then advanced as the cause of the reading problem. Dawson (5) expresses the belief that, "many pupils learn to be poor readers, that bad habits and negative attitudes are learned, that many so-called remedial readers could have been effective and confident readers under a program of preventive teaching."

An analogy might be drawn between working with reading problems and the prevention and cure of tuberculosis. If the medical profession and our society had continued to attempt to cope with tuberculosis the way we still try to deal with reading problems, today we would undoubtedly be a nation of consumptives. Fortunately, medical practice and concern shifted from emphasis on "cure" to emphasis on prevention. Slum clearance, diet, sunlight, mobile X-ray units, health education, and stress on early detection — all practices evolving from sound principles — have, to a considerable extent, controlled this malady. Even if American education achieves a mushrooming of good reading sanatoriums aimed only at cure, we will never be able to cope with our reading problems because our educational system is geared to mass production. Unfortunately, it becomes very apparent that remedial reading is not thought of as concerned with prevention of reading problems but rather with their cure.

Perhaps one reason why teachers and schools do not get to reading cases earlier is the belief that these problems will disappear with passing time. Some problems perhaps do solve themselves. Others, when ignored, become stubborn, severe, complicated problems. When children with adequate ability fail to learn to read when exposed to the usual classroom procedures, they need help quickly. The school's failure to put emphasis on early detection and immediate help for children failing in reading is undoubtedly a factor in producing some reading difficulties which, once the process of cure is undertaken, are slow to improve.

Conclusion

Reading instruction has emerged as the number one problem of American education because seriously impaired readers cannot find a niche in our society. We have developed a highly complex society which, in turn, has created a greater need for communication skills. In recent years, as federal funds became available to local school districts for special projects, the number of proposals for remedial and other reading instructional programs exceeded all other areas of the curriculum combined.

Individuals who have followed a normal pattern in learning to read may find it difficult to accept the fact that large numbers of youth experience difficulty in mastering the reading process. Accepting the facts as they are still leaves the problem of rationalizing *why* this problem persists.

There will probably always be a number of children who fail to learn to read because of physiological and other clinical causes not yet fully understood. On the other hand, there are many children whose failure to learn could have been prevented by practices which are presently within the power of schools to apply and follow. If schools in a given community should embark on programs which aim at preventing failure in reading, there will be less need in those communities for remedial reading programs.

YOUR POINT OF VIEW?

Respond to the following problems:

1. You have been hired to assess the effectiveness of a remedial reading program. Identify the questions you want answered, and discuss the relative weight or importance you assign to each item.

2. Assume you are the director of a five-year state project, the aim of which is to reduce by 60 percent the number of children experiencing reading difficulties. You have adequate financial resources to do what you want to do. What would you propose doing?

3. Points a. and b. below are advanced as facts. If the reader accepts them as facts, the problem is to deal with the premise which follows.
   a. Classroom data indicates beyond doubt that individual differences of considerable magnitude in reading ability will occur among children of comparable capacity or ability.
   b. If capacity is held constant and equal amounts of expert instruction is given to all children in a class or group, those children who are lowest in reading achievement will make the smallest gain per unit of instructional time.

   Premise: "The degree of emphasis placed on remedial reading in the past fifteen years indicates a lack of willingness to accept the premise of individual differences in learning to read and applies special instruction where it will have the least impact on achievement."

Evaluate the following statements and provide a rationale for either accepting or rejecting each one:

1. Instructional practices associated with remedial reading do not differ markedly from practices which should be found in the regular classroom.

2. When a school system makes provisions for remedial reading instruction, it is likely that this instruction will follow sounder principles of teaching than does the regular instructional program.

3. Because of the nature of the teaching tasks in all elementary grades, teachers are inevitably remedial reading teachers if they teach all children in their respective classrooms.

4. The effectiveness of remedial instruction in reading is largely determined by the degree to which it meets the child's psychological needs.

BIBLIOGRAPHY

1. Bardon, Jack I. and Virginia D. C. Bennett, "When Teaching Does Not Take," *Elementary School Journal* (May 1966), 426–32.

2. Bliesmer, Emery P. "Evaluating Progress in Remedial Reading Programs," *Reading Teacher* (March 1962), 344–50.

3. Bond, Guy L. and Miles A. Tinker, *Reading Difficulties: Their Diagnosis and Correction* (Second Ed.). New York: Appleton-Century-Crofts, 1967.

4. Botel, Morton, "Dyslexia: Is There Such A Thing?" *Current Issues In Reading*, Proceedings, International Reading Association, 13, Part 2, 1969, 357–71.

5. Dawson, Mildred A. "Prevention Before Remediation," *Reading and Inquiry*. Proceedings, International Reading Association, 10, 1965, 171–73.

6. Frostig, Marianne, "Corrective Reading In the Classroom," *Reading Teacher* (April 1965), 573–80.

7. Googins, Duwane G. "Helping Retarded Readers within a Small School District," *Reading and Inquiry*. Proceedings, International Reading Association, 10, 1965, 178–79.

8. Harris, Albert J. *Casebook on Reading Disability*. New York: David McKay Co., 1970.

9. Jackson, Joseph, "A Reading Center Approach within the Classroom," *Journal of Educational Psychology*, XLVII (1956), 213–22.

10. Jellins, Miriam H. "Grouping for Remedial Reading on the Basis of Learner Needs" in *Forging Ahead In Reading*, J. Allen Figurel (ed.), Proceedings, International Reading Association, 12, Part 1, 282–87.

11. Johnson, Marjorie Seddon, "Reading Instruction in the Clinic," *Reading Teacher* (May 1962), 415–20.

12. Kasbohm, Mary Crowley, "Remedial Reading Materials," *Elementary English* (March 1966), 209–14.

13. Lovell, K. and A. Gorton, "Some Differences Between Backward and Normal Readers of Average Intelligence," *British Journal of Educational Psychology* (November 1968), 240–247.

14. Marksheffel, Ned D. "Therapy: An Interdisciplinary Approach," in *Reading and Inquiry*. Proceedings, International Reading Association, 10, 1965, 197–200.

15. Money, John (ed.), *Reading Disability Progress and Research Needs In Dyslexia*. Baltimore: The Johns Hopkins Press, 1962.

16. Otto, Wayne and Richard A. McMenemy, *Corrective and Remedial Teaching*. Boston: Houghton Mifflin Company, 1966.

17. Plessas, Gus P. "Reading Abilities of High and Low Auders," *Elementary School Journal* (January 1963), 223–26.

18. Pollack, M. F. W. and Josephine A. Piekarz, *Reading Problems and Problem Readers*. New York: David McKay Co., Inc., 1963.

19. Rasmussen, Glen R. and Hope W. Dunne, "A Longitudinal Evaluation of a Junior High School Corrective Reading Program," *Reading Teacher* (November 1962), 95–101.

20. *Reading Teacher* (January 1970). Entire issue devoted to Learning Disabilities.

21. Reich, Riva R. "More Than Remedial Reading." *Elementary English* (March 1962), 216–19.

22. Rosner, Stanley L. "Word Games In Reading Diagnosis," *The Reading Teacher* (January 1971), 331–35.

23. Rowe, Cecil Ann, "Techniques for Teaching Dyslexic Children: Using the Tape Recorder," *Academic Therapy Quarterly* (Spring 1968), 171.

24. Sister Mary Julitta, "A List of Books for Retarded Readers," *Elementary English* (February 1961), 79–87.

25. Spache, George D. (ed.), *Reading Disability and Perception*, Proceedings, International Reading Association, 12, Part 3, 1969.

26. Still, Jane S. "Evaluation of a Community Sponsored Summer Remedial Reading Program," *Elementary English* (May 1961), 342–43.

27. Whipple, Gertrude, "Desirable Materials, Facilities and Resources for Reading," *Reading In The Elementary School*. Forty-eighth Yearbook, N.S.S.E., Part II, 147–71.

28. Young, Virgil M. "Summer School for Poor Readers — A Title I Model Project," *The Reading Teacher* (March 1971), 526–31.

29. Zentgraf, Faith M. "Promoting Independent Reading by Retarded Readers," *Reading Teacher* (November 1963), 100–101.

30. Zintz, Miles V. *Corrective Reading* (Second Ed.). Dubuque, Iowa: William C. Brown Company, 1972.

17

Working with Reading Problems in the Classroom

The classroom teacher's role as defined by society is to teach all children who are assigned to her classroom. Because practically all teachers have impaired readers in their classrooms, they should be expected to ask the questions, "What should I do with these children now? What can I do to help them learn to read?" Such questions do not imply teachers do not know how to teach, but rather that they are enough professionally oriented to seek cures for their clients. Teachers are not hostile to theory, but they have every right to be impatient with theory that does not also spell out practices which will test the theory.

One of the major difficulties in discussing how to cope with the various reading difficulties found in the schools is the myriad of terms that have been used to describe these problems. If one reviews the literature on this topic, he must assume the burden of adjusting to and translating terms such as remedial, corrective, dyslexic; and etiologies such as primary, secondary, congenital, acquired, genetically based, and the like. One of the goals of this chapter is to not introduce new terms. Teachers are invited to think of children as readers within a framework that emphasizes how to approach teaching them to read.

**Types of Remedial
Reading Cases**

In the discussion which follows, an attempt is made to identify the
types of remedial reading cases on the basis of one important criterion which then becomes the key to how the remedial instruction
should be approached. More specifically, the classification is for the
purpose of suggesting whether a diagnosis indicates that the teacher
can hope for success in *working directly with the reading problem;*
whether the reading problem is tied to *emotional or other problems*
which need to be worked with simultaneously; or whether the solution of the problem requires *more than the usually prescribed educational procedures.* Identifying these types does not imply that all
cases which fall under a given type are alike, or that specific teaching techniques and methods should be associated with a particular
type of case. However, it is undoubtedly true that cases falling generally into one or another of these types are more alike than are
cases taken at random from the total population of remedial readers.

Type I

Type I indicates all remedial cases *in which the best treatment
would be immediate, straightforward, systematic instruction on the
skills the child should have mastered but which he has not yet
learned.*

Thus for children to qualify as Type I, they must have failed to
master certain *essential* skills and be judged capable of learning
these skills. The deficiencies which these children have at the
moment may fall anywhere on the continuum from mild to serious.
However, the important criterion is that there are no other complicating factors such as mashed egos, entrenched attitudes that
learning is impossible, or other serious unresolved emotional problems which will interfere with learning.

The root of the child's problem may have been non-readiness to
read, poor educational practices, or absence from school at critical
periods. However, it is not important to establish which of these
or countless other factors contributed to the problem, because knowing this will have little influence on what is done *now.* The important
thing is that the reading problem be diagnosed accurately. The
immediate and on-going diagnosis will serve as a blueprint for the
instructional program that will be followed. However, delay in working with a Type I child can be instrumental in producing a Type II
problem.

Type II

Type II includes the impaired reader (1) *whose reaction to his failure in reading is a significant factor,* or (2) *who has some other serious unresolved emotional problem which is a factor in his failure to learn.*

In working with these children, it is assumed that no matter how obvious the reading problem may be, it is probably unwise to attempt to resolve it through instructional techniques alone. We must deal with the child's reaction or attitude toward himself and toward reading. In other words, he is not emotionally ready to face the reality of his reading problem. As a rule, a program of therapy must be inaugurated either prior to or concommittantly with remedial reading instruction.

Part of the problem of a Type II may be "in his nervous system," so to speak, but it does not stem from any neurological dysfunction. He has an intact nervous system that will permit him to make the necessary visual-auditory discriminations, and to process these if he could bring his energies to bear on the complicated task of learning to read.

Type III

Type III *includes the more severe cases of impaired reading and non-reading. Many of these children have average or better intelligence but they have profited little from traditional classroom instruction. Future growth under regular instruction is likely to be quite limited.* It is widely hypothesized that these children suffer from some neural or brain dysfunction. Unfortunately, at the moment, there is a lack of diagnostic techniques which can *establish* the existence of neurological dysfunction. Therefore such a diagnosis is derived from "observable behaviors" of the subject.

Limitation in classifying remedial cases

In this attempt to identify types of remedial cases, the aim has been to provide a framework for leading teachers to a better understanding of reading problem cases. The aim has also been to suggest that different approaches are indicated in attempting to deal successfully with different types of readers, even though their reading problems may appear on the surface to be very similar. Teachers should guard against the several pitfalls in this process of classifying.

1. The boundaries between types should not be considered as rigid.

2. The correct diagnosis of a child as one problem type or another is not a permanent classification analogous to blood-type or fingerprints. As children have new experiences, their needs, attitudes toward self, others, and learning will change.
3. A teacher working with children may develop an unconscious bias which supports one particular hypothesis. This will, of course, interfere with accurate diagnosis, and an accurate diagnosis is the basis for all good remedial instruction.

Working with Reading-Problem-Cases

(Type I)

These cases have been defined as children who have the ability to learn but who, for some reason, have developed certain reading deficits. It is safe and desirable to work directly on their reading problems because these problems are as yet uncomplicated by other factors. A description of several cases and treatment follow.

Don was a second grader of average intelligence, seven years and eight months old. The family lived on a farm; Don attended a rural school and was doing poorly in reading. At a parent-teacher conference his teacher stated that he was not reading up to his ability and that she would not be able to give him the individual help he needed. His mother had neither the training nor the time to help Don, but she did make arrangements to have him receive individual instruction outside the school three evenings a week. Some of the more important conclusions abstracted from the diagnosis were that Don was weak in sight word recognition; often ignored or failed to profit from punctuation; substituted, added, and omitted words; and, as a consequence, read very slowly. He read well only at the primer level, although he could slowly work his way through material in a first reader. Don was not defensive about his poor reading. Neither his teacher nor the home had caused him to feel like a failure, and he did not feel that he was letting his parents down. He quite frankly admitted that he needed help in reading and was able to work effectively on reading problems from the very first individual meeting. In a few weeks Don could actually see that he was improving. He kept 48 consecutive appointments over a sixteen-week period. His teacher wisely used a variety of approaches and attacked several different problems in each hour session. Thus, fatigue and loss of interest were avoided. This, coupled with much praise, helped Don to build self-confidence in his ability as a reader.

Earlier it was stated that in working with uncomplicated cases (Type I), exact knowledge of how the problem developed is not of crucial importance. Occasionally, however, the attack-strategies that the child has learned to rely on become important in how one attempts to alleviate the problem. For example two fourth grade boys from the same classroom had been diagnosed as remedial cases, were reading at the same level, and having the same problem. Under stress situations, both boys had developed much the same reading behaviors, but their real problem and *instructional needs* were quite different.

Both boys had failed to make adequate progress in reading after a relatively successful beginning and were diagnosed as being handicapped by very poor phonic analysis skill. Their patterns of reading were very similar. The first boy attempted to sound words as a whole. He would not follow through on a word or divide unknown words by syllables. When he came to an unknown word, he would size it up as a unit and make a hurried guess. When he guessed wrong, he remained loyal to his response and, if necessary, would change, add, or omit words which followed, in order to salvage meaning from the passage. It was surprising to discover that he could correctly sound syllables if words were divided for him.

In the early stages of reading, he had been put under pressure by his parents not to hesitate or stall in pronouncing words, particularly words he had previously pronounced correctly. As a result, he learned the habit of "saying something" instead of relying on the slower method of analyzing the sound components. Many of his rapid responses were correct and the habit became reinforced. As the material he read became more difficult, his percentage of correct guesses declined, but the habit continued. Other poor reading habits were natural outgrowths of his attempts to *make* meaning from his reading.

The other fourth grader knew a considerable number of sight words, but, in contrast to the first boy, was completely incapable of sounding syllables or letters in combination, even in words he knew by sight. Also, recognizing meaning did not seem to be an objective of his reading. He miscalled, substituted, and omitted words, but not in an effort to salvage meaning. He did well in spelling on weekly tests, but, a short time after each test, he could not spell a fourth of the words he had previously spelled correctly. Spelling was a rote memory process.

The first boy overcame his word-attack problem in approximately twelve hourly sessions of instruction, much of it on syllabication. The second boy required a number of months to help him overcome his difficulty. He needed hours of drill on distinguishing speech sounds in words, including extensive work on such elementary phonic skills as initial consonants and consonant blends. Progress in mastering vowel sounds was slow, and it was necessary to give him constant praise for even the smallest accomplishments. At the time of diagnosis, both boys showed much the same reading behavior, with a crucial weakness in phonic analysis. However, the way in which each boy's problem had developed called for different approaches or solutions.

Both inadequate sight vocabulary and inability to sound out words are "generative" weaknesses. Each leads the reader into many other bad reading habits. When a child has a very limited sight vocabulary, he must "sound out" many words. These interruptions prevent smooth reading and cause the child to lose the meaning of what he is reading. In an attempt to compensate, he may develop the habit of "guessing" instead of resorting to phonic analysis. Figure 30 illustrates how a number of other poor reading habits are generated by low sight vocabulary.

(How low sight vocabulary becomes a contributing factor in other poor reading habits or mechanical weaknesses — which in turn are related to comprehension.)

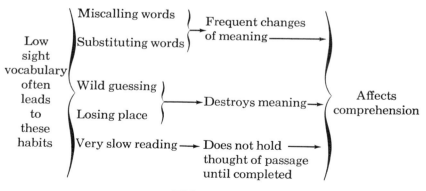

FIGURE 30

An interesting related phenomenon is that some expert readers develop the habit of omitting or at least slighting certain of the less essential words in a passage. Their reading is so meaning-oriented that they can sift out the chaff without really being conscious of doing so. Obviously, they must omit only those words that are expendable. The following is an illustration.

"Many writers have on occasion demonstrated that you can omit or strike out as many as one-fifth or one-sixth of the running words in a paragraph or on a page and still not distort or destroy the author's intended meaning."

In the following version 40 percent of the words are removed without any appreciable distortion of meaning:

"_____ writers have _____ demonstrated _____
you can omit _____ _____ _____ as many as one-
fifth or _____-sixth of the _____ words _____
_____ _____ _____ on a page and _____ not
distort _____ _____ the _____ intended meaning."

On the other hand, one or two substitutions may completely destroy the intended meaning. Assume the reader substitutes *hit* for *omit* and *runners* for *running* in the illustrative sentence above. We now have:

Many writers have on occasion demonstrated that you can hit or strike out as high as one-fifth or one-sixth of the runners . . .

With this much of an erroneous start, the reader will probably conclude he is reading about baseball. To salvage the meaning, he must change following words. Eventually he will have to begin again, thus introducing another reading fault—repetition. Moving his eyes back over words may cause him to make reversals (*was* for *saw*; *on* for *no*; *won* for *now*; *pot* for *top*.) He may change, omit, or transpose letters in his search for familiar words, leading to miscalling smaller words such as *sack, lacks; them, then; thin, than*. He may lose his place, skip lines, or reread passages, exhibiting the numerous habitual responses of the slow reader.

Case studies

The material that follows is a description of several children who had been referred to a reading laboratory for diagnosis and remedial instruction. The diagnosis of the first case is discussed in detail and several lesson plans are presented. The other cases are treated in less detail.

Study A: William

William was a nine-year-old boy with above average intelligence who had been referred because of very poor reading ability. For some time he had made no noticeable progress in reading and had been held in the third grade for a second year. The initial testing in reading included a standardized reading test, a recognition test of sight words in isolation, and an informal reading test using materials from basic readers. On the standardized test he failed the second grade level (a passage of 51 running words) because he was unable to recognize the words *began, rain, wanted,* and *know*, miscalled the words *by, little, took,* and *take*, added the word *it*, and omitted one word. The major weaknesses revealed by the diagnosis included:

1. Very slow and labored reading — many hesitations
2. Omitted words
3. Miscalled many easy words, with occasional self correction
4. Moved lips in silent reading
5. Poor or inadequate phrasing
6. Missed one fourth of the 220 words on the Dolch Sight Word Test*
7. Repetitions
8. Poor posture — pointed at words

Table 4 summarizes the child's reading behavior and illustrates a one-page form which might be utilized to record the results of diagnostic testing.

Results of any diagnosis, shown in a concrete manner, would alert a teacher to specific problems which need attention. Poor habits and the absence of needed skills become more obvious when precise errors are noted. As one studies this table, he sees that a small stock of sight words and lack of ability to sound words are major obstacles to reading progress. However, there is evidence that the boy did pay attention to initial consonants, but did not "follow through" the entire word. For example, he called chair

---

*Edward W. Dolch, *The Basic Sight Word Test* (Champaign, Ill.: Garrard Publishing Company, 1942).

TABLE 4

Diagnosis of Reading Problem Case Showing Tests Used and Types of Errors Found
(Boy, Age 9: I.Q. 110; Third Grade; Reading Level 1¹-1²)

Test Used	Grade Level	Sight Words Not Known	Words Miscalled	Repetitions	Words Omitted or Added	Rate
Durrell Analysis of Reading Difficulty	1st	Could not pronounce: *drink* (21 running words in passage)	*chair* ⟶ *couch*	2 repetitions in 21 running words	*is* (omitted)	21 running words 32 secs.
	2nd	Could not pronounce: *began, rain, wanted, know* (51 running words)	*big* ⟶ *little* *book* ⟶ *take*	3 repetitions	*it* — added; *away* — omitted	51 running words 80 secs. (scored middle first grade on rate)
Informal Reading Test	First Grade Reader	missed 6 words in 103 running words: *once, only, they, under, could*	*must* ⟶ *much* *cross* ⟶ *across* *then* ⟶ *when* *raised* ⟶ *rushed* *think* ⟶ *like* *point* ⟶ *plant*	5 repetitions	omitted: *far, any, my*	Very slow
Dolch Basic Sight Word Test	1st to 3rd	missed 1 out of 4 words — miscalled and then corrected a number of words	examples of words missed: *by, drink, any, kind, just, both, found, grow, first, away, cold, best, light, gave, hurt, red, try, only, there, woman, chose*			Very slow

593

couch; took, *take*; raised, *ru*shed; must, *mu*ch. He also appeared
to have considerable trouble with the initial blends *th*, *wh*, *ch*, and
others. His very slow rate suggested that he may not have developed instantaneous recognition of small service words, although,
after study, he may have named them correctly.

The remedial program for William.   One of the first entries made
by the tutor included the following:

> William's interest span is quite short, and motivating him for an
> hour is a problem. However, he is not a behavior problem and is
> very cooperative. He likes to talk and does talk quite fluently.
> His comprehension of what he reads is extremely good. This is
> surprising in view of his many poor reading habits and very slow
> reading. In addition to working on sight words and word anal-
> ysis, the boy's attitude toward reading must be changed. Work
> on these objectives can go on simultaneously.

Illustrative lessons used with William.   A few sample lessons taken
from the tutor's files are cited along with illustrations of actual
materials used.

> *Lesson 3*   We talked for a few minutes about things Bill has
> been doing at school. I told him he has an interesting way of
> expressing himself — I think he would have enjoyed talking
> for the full hour, but when I suggested we go to work he was
> quite co-operative and worked very well this period.
>   1. We worked with a film strip, *Vowel Sounds Help You**
> (10 minutes).
>   2. [We] worked on "hearing vowel sounds." I would drop
> the initial consonant from three-letter words and sound the
> remaining two letters. Bill was to:
>   a. tell which vowel was sounded.
>   b. say the letters which made the sound heard (i.e., um, et,
>   at, im, en, un, ug, ap, ip, etc.)
>   c. give a word which used this sound (i.e., hum, met, hat,
>   him, pen, sun, rug, cap, sip, etc.) (5 minutes).
>   3. We read from *Young Reader's Animal Stories* (12
> minutes).

---

*"Vowel Sounds Help You," "Your Eyes and Ears Are Good Helpers,"
"Test Yourself on Sounds," "The Vowel," "Backbone of a Syllable," are some
filmstrips on phonics available from The Society for Visual Education, Inc.,
Chicago, Illinois.

"Hearing Sounds in Words," "Letters Which Work Together," "Long Vowel
Sounds," and others are available from Popular Science Publishing Co., Audio
Visual Division, New York.

a. [We had] blackboard work on the words Bill missed during his reading (3–4 minutes).

During the reading I praised Bill for things he did well and tried to point out concretely how he was making progress in his reading. [I] also pointed out things we had to work on. He could supply some of these goals himself, which indicates he is gaining insight into reading problems.

4. [We] worked on syllabication (5 minutes). Stimulus words were presented in one column and the words were to be broken into syllables in an adjoining column (see the exercise below).

Divide each word into syllables. See sample on first line.

locomotive	lo-co-mo-tive	vacation	va-ca-tion
window		together	
yesterday		picture	
afternoon		valentine	
nothing		tomorrow	
pencil		halloween	
children		hundred	
another		grandmother	
stockings		arithmetic	

5. Billy read silently to get the answers to five questions given him prior to the reading. ([We] finished out the hour with discussion.)

Lesson 5

1. [We] worked (5 minutes) on attacking longer words — names of famous people, cities, states, and compound words:

Fold the paper on the dotted line. Pronounce the words in Column A. If you need help, see Column B where words are broken into syllables.

Column A		Column B
Steinmetz	.	Stein metz
blacksmith	.	black smith
George Washington		George Wash ing ton
Andrew Jackson	.	An drew Jack son
themselves	.	them selves
fisherman	.	fish er man
wonderful		won der ful
Benjamin Franklin	.	Ben ja min Frank lin
Canada	.	Can a da
President Cleveland	.	Pres i dent Cleve land
holiday	.	hol i day
fireplace	.	fire place
fairyland	.	fair y land

2. [We] used the tape recorder as Bill read from the book *Let's Look Around.* When we played the story back I noticed that Bill could fill in the words quite easily where he paused or was helped during the recording (20 minutes).

3. I read to Bill in the area of science. Afterward I asked him several questions over the material and he demonstrated good comprehension (10 minutes).

4. [We] worked on initial blends *br, fl, pl, tr, dr,* [and] used [a] separate card for each blend. [We] used cards containing easier words utilizing each initial blend (8 minutes) (see the following illustration).

Illustration of Cards Prepared to Facilitate Drill on Initial Consonant Blends

Card 1	Card 4	Card 8	Card 10	Card 3
brag	flag	plan	trip	drop
braid	flood	play	track	drink
brick	fled	plain	trap	dress
broke	flat	plant	train	drug
broom	flock	plug	tree	dream
bread	flash	plenty	trim	drive
brave	flame	plot	trust	draw
brain	flee	plum	tribe	drank
break	fleet	planned	trade	dry

5. Bill finished out the hour reading silently from a book he had selected.

Lesson 8

1. [We] played "word-pile" [with] 50 cards.*
2. Bill related a story which I took down verbatum.
3. Bill read silently from *Cowboy Sam and the Fair.*
   While Bill read, I typed the story he had just dictated.
4. [We had a] brief discussion of material read silently.
5. [We] worked on a special "sounding page," whose aim is to help Bill "go on through a word" when he is attempting to sound words. Longer phonetic words are in a column on the left. To the right are the same words with one syllable added

---

*A competitive game which permits drill on sight words. This game calls for two players, teacher and child, and an even number of cards. On one side each card bears a word which the child is in the process of learning. The back of the cards are blank. Cards are shuffled like dominoes in the middle of the table and each player draws 10 cards at a time. Players alternate in "leading" a card, which is then played on by opponent. However, the pupil *always* attempts to call or name both cards. If successful, he takes both cards for his pile. If he fails on either, both cards go to opponent. This game is extremely successful since the tutor can control the game by the way he plays his "difficult" and "easy" cards, and also by the words he includes in the game.

on each new line. The column on the right is covered with a card until a word on the left is missed, then the pupil looks at the word in its syllabic units. Of all the techniques for teaching sounding, this was the most successful with Bill (see the following illustration.

Pronounce the words in Column A. When you meet a word you cannot pronounce, go to Column B for help.

A	B	A	B
	No		Wash
November	Novem	Washington	Washing
	November		Washington
	in		sen
inventor	inven	senator	sena
	inventor		senator
	el		hol
elephant	ele	holiday	holi
	elephant		holiday
	lo		Wis
	loco	Wisconsin	Wiscon
locomotive	locomo		Wisconsin
	locomotive		im
	re	important	import
remember	remem		important
	remember		con
		continent	contin
			continent

6. Bill read [the] typed story he had dictated earlier. We then worked on the words he missed.

7. Bill selected the book *Riding the Pony Express* to take home.

From the sample lessons cited, note that a good balance was maintained between sustained reading and drill on mechanics. The reading program was designed to include a variety of interesting activities. ("William's interest span is quite short and motivating him for an hour is a problem.")

Study B: Martha

Martha was a ten-year-old girl in the fifth grade. She was a good student, had never repeated a grade, and was very personable and apparently well-liked by other children. She volunteered that she liked the subjects health, spelling, physical education, and music. She disliked science, reading, and social studies. Martha had developed a few bad reading habits which prevented her reading from being pleasurable. She had been referred to the reading laboratory, at least in part, because she did not like to read and, as a result, read very little. Without going into detail, the relevant findings disclosed by the diagnosis could be summarized as follows:

1. Martha ignored or failed to profit from punctuation.
2. She miscalled many words which she actually *could* get correctly.
3. She was not concerned by the fact that her frequent substitutions of words and ignoring of punctuation destroyed meaning.

In one brief reading session Martha made the following errors and did not correct any of them on her own initiative.

leading (called)	leaning	lessons	(called)	classes
pleasant "	present	grin	"	gleam
searching "	seeking	quickly	"	quietly
long "	large	echoed	"	shouted
called "	said	beamed	"	because
problem "	program	admiringly	"	approval
shaping "	shaking	Hale (proper name)		Hall

A majority of the errors indicate no effort at maintaining the sense of the passage. Context was simply ignored. Following the reading, Martha was asked to identify the words she missed, and she was able to do so in 80 percent of the cases.

Martha did admit to being interested in fairy tales and myths. Fortunately this was an area in which material at a reading level which held her interest was plentiful. It was pointed out from the very beginning that a change in two or three reading habits would make a noticeable improvement in her reading ("use punctuation"; "do not guess at or substitute words"; "be sure what you read makes sense").

Following are some of the procedures used in working with Martha.

1. If she ignored or missed punctuation, her teacher would read the same paragraph, asking Martha to listen. This served as a good model which Martha could hear as she followed the passage with her eyes.

2. A tape recorder was used for a few minutes each session. Martha was asked to criticize her own reading as she listened to the playback. She was able to point out errors, thus demonstrating that she understood the problem and that she was capable of a better performance.

3. It was agreed that when Martha miscalled a word and went on, her attention was to be called to the error. This emphasized reading for meaning, and gradually Martha was able to catch some of her errors without being prompted.

4. A limited amount of drill was provided each day on words that look alike, start alike, or sound alike. Martha was to pronounce each word, and, when asked, use it in a sentence. This type of drill emphasized that minute differences in words must be noticed, and that paying heed to the initial letter or blend is not enough to assure reading accuracy if the reader guesses from that point on (see the illustration which follows).

Below are columns of three words which look alike or sound alike. Pronounce each word carefully.

tired	tried	trial	farther	father	further
cease	crease	crash	crayon	canyon	canteen
mouth	month	moth	quiet	quite	guilt
flash	flush	flesh	with	which	width
board	broad	broth	except	accept	expect
adopt	adapt	adept	reflect	respect	relate
dairy	diary	daily	whether	weather	whither
seize	seige	size	thing	think	thank
desert	disturb	dessert	vary	very	every
easiest	earliest	earnest	advice	advise	adverse
brother	broth	bother	crash	cash	clash

5. As Martha paid more attention to the total word and made fewer errors and substitutions, her reading became more "meaning-centered." Reading became more interesting and challenging, and she was gradually guided into reading materials other than fairy tales and fables.

6. Thought questions were prepared on sustained reading materials, and these questions were given to Martha prior to having her read the passage.

7. Two-part plays and poems were occasionally used, the teacher reading one part, Martha the other. This type of

exercise helped stress accurate reading, attention to punctuation, and reading for meaning.

Martha may have had more reading ability than many remedial cases in that she knew many sight words and could sound out words. Nevertheless, she had reached the stage where she apparently could not resolve her reading problem by herself. In reality she had quite a serious reading problem, since her attitude toward reading made it a distasteful chore and a meaningless ritual. Fortunately, with guidance and individual help, she was able to overcome her poor reading habits. When her reading became meaningful, it also became pleasant and rewarding.

Study C: Jerry

Jerry was a nine-year-old fourth-grader and an only child. His father was successful in business and his mother was active in community and social affairs, but not to the point of neglecting her home. Following an interview with Jerry's mother, an experienced clinician characterized her as "not being rejecting, but somewhat cold and reserved." The mother made the following comments about Jerry's reading: "Jerry is concerned with his reading ability; in fact, he has been, even from the first grade. He seems nervous when he reads and he doesn't like to try reading situations. He lacks confidence and will not attack new words or words he doesn't know. He is very poor in spelling, too."

Jerry's behavior in reading is summarized in the following findings from the diagnostic tests:

1. Moves lips excessively in silent reading.
2. Reads slowly and seems threatened by this habit — tries to speed up and then miscalls words he knows; then he reads very choppy, missing punctuation, losing place, says, "just a minute" — rereads, etc.
3. Missed only 14 of 220 words on Dolch Sight Word Test and corrected all but four of these errors on second trial. Yet, in sustained reading situations, Jerry miscalls a number of these same words.
4. Repeats words and groups of words even when he knows all the words involved. This was a habit Jerry developed as a means of giving himself time to probe ahead into the remainder of the sentence; also this sometimes occurred when he was deliberately attempting to speed up his reading.

5. Phrasing is inadequate.
6. Occasionally ignores punctuation.
7. Not consistent in word attack or sounding.

Following are some conclusions which grew out of the testing and interview with the mother.

1. The parents had high aspirations for Jerry.
2. Jerry was very much aware that his father was successful, and he seemed to be attempting to measure up to his father.
3. Father and son got along fine, but the father apparently did not have enough time to spend with Jerry — at least not enough to meet Jerry's needs at the moment.
4. Jerry needed a tremendous amount of reassurance because he sensed he was not measuring up to his parent's academic standards and expectations.
5. Unconsciously, his parents had, and were, putting pressure on him to improve in his reading. Feeling that his relationship with his parents (love, respect, affection) was dependent on his performance in reading, he put pressure on himself to succeed.

Many of the procedures mentioned previously were used with Jerry. No opportunity was missed by the teacher to praise Jerry for his improvement in reading and his excellent attitude in the reading situation. His reading problems were played down. Speed of reading, which seemed to be very important to Jerry, was ignored during sustained reading. Eventually he stopped pushing for speed, and his mechanical errors declined in frequency. Speed was touched on indirectly in an exercise designed to help Jerry read in phrases or thought units. Jerry would read a series of phrases and the teacher would record the time and the number of errors. Then, later, in the hour or at the next session, Jerry would attempt to improve his scores. Before long he wanted to manipulate the stopwatch himself, mostly to prove beyond doubt that his improved scores were on the level. Columns of phrases are illustrated below.

near an old well	would swing very high
still on the ground	liked to count
mud on the fence	caught in the act
forgot to get up	then and there
saw the other neighbors	right in the middle
by the side	beat the drum

winked his eye	wanting to fly
gave him some	into the garden
plenty of cakes	funny little man
under the tree	book on the table
see the surprise	left them behind
when he looked	came over the hill
just what is	was very fine
eggs for breakfast	light as a feather
fishing near by	how much money
waved from the door	bother the robber
where the corn grew	a ride in the forest
must be something	tied in a knot

Jerry enjoyed role-playing. He pretended that he was a radio announcer when using the tape recorder. He became very ego-involved in this procedure, and the purely mechanical defects of his reading (repetitions, substituting smaller words, phrasing, and ignoring punctuation) were often present to a smaller degree than at other times. Since he played back these recorded sessions, it was easy to demonstrate improvement in his reading. He enjoyed working with jigsaw maps of the United States and of countries making up other continents. He would sound out the name of the state or country as he placed it and, when asked, would attempt to spell the names by syllables. Occasionally the teacher would print a state name on paper or the blackboard, and they would sound it together.

To conclude the discussion of Jerry, a few sentences from the first entry made by his tutor might be helpful: "Jerry is a very bright boy; he loves to talk, and he has had many experiences about which he talks quite intelligently. However, he talks most about his father, whom he reveres. In his reading Jerry shows signs of insecurity, reading with more volume than necessary, seems to go to pieces when attempting to read material that is difficult for him — will bite his nails during such a reading session."

When this was written, Jerry still qualified as a Type I problem. However, his lack of confidence and feeling of inadequacy were building up rapidly. With a few more months of failure, it is quite possible that his emotional involvements would have affected his learning to read.

A type II problem

Type II cases have developed severe reactions to a reading failure or they have some other unresolved emotional problem that interferes with learning. Here, the objective is to focus on whatever factors are preventing a child from profiting from regular instruction. It is hypothesized that if the treatment is successful, the learner will now be able to bring his energies to bear on learning. He will be able to tolerate and profit from systematic instruction that relates to his reading problems.

An illustrative case of Type II is that of Robert, a third grade child of above-average intelligence who had difficulty reading at primer level. At home, he had been drilled on reading by both parents, neither of whom had the patience that was needed to help Robert overcome his difficulty. His self-confidence had been destroyed and, as pressure in the reading situation mounted, his effectiveness as a reader decreased. He was an extremely frustrated child and was showing definite signs of withdrawal in the reading situation. His teacher was annoyed at some of the odd mistakes he made when reading or attempting to work independently in a workbook. The first step in helping Robert deal with his problem was a series of conferences with his parents. It was agreed that they would give up all their efforts to teach him reading themselves. This was not an easy decision for the parents to make since they naturally did not see the relationship between their behavior and his reading problem. In the next few months Robert showed very little measurable growth in reading ability. However, in this situation, Robert was accepted by his teacher in spite of his reading failure. As the pressures at home diminished, he was gradually able to concentrate his energy on reading, and he did begin to learn.

Emotional problems which were not originally related to reading can become contributing factors in severe disability cases. Here, the unresolved emotional problems are such strong barriers to learning that the child is at the moment uneducable (as far as learning to read is concerned). And yet, the lack of reading ability is only a symptom of some larger problem. Results cannot be expected from working with the symptoms alone. In most instances of this nature, it is necessary to inaugurate a program of therapy prior to attempting to work directly with the reading problem. A brief description of such a case follows:

Edward was a second-grader, seven and one-half years old, whose father was successful in business; both parents were well-educated. He had a younger sister four and one-half years old. Even though Edward was beginning the second grade, he was virtually a nonreader. His mother was quite concerned about his lack of academic success. Diagnosis showed that Edward was a very bright boy (a

Stanford-Binet I.Q. of 140) but on a reading test he knew practically no words. The examiner reported that he was very polite and cooperative and did everything that he was requested to do.

Edward's apparent willingness to work held out high hopes that through individual help he would learn to read. Here are brief descriptive passages abstracted from his tutor's daily reports (emphasis has been added).

> *Second meeting:* Edward stares hard at the words for a long time and *gives the appearance* of trying very hard.

> *Third meeting:* We took a trip to the museum and Edward dictated a story about what he saw and did. He enjoyed the trip very much. *He seemed panicky when I suggested he read our story about the trip.*

> *Fourth meeting:* An unsuccessful attempt was made to teach Edward words by the kinesthetic method. He writes the words mechanically and does not *remember* the pronunciation *immediately* after he has finished tracing a word.

> *Fifth meeting:* Edward appears to be testing the limits. Sometimes he is cooperative and appears to be trying his best; at others he appears to be trying to see what the tutor's reaction will be to things he says and does *which he probably considers bad and unacceptable*

> *Seventh meeting:* I definitely have the feeling that Edward is *trying not to learn to read* and at the same time leaves the impression that he is trying very hard.

At this point it became obvious that continued work on reading alone would not be advisable or profitable. This conclusion should have been arrived at sooner; however, too much emphasis was attached to high intelligence and seeming willingness to work cooperatively. From this time on, as each session was devoted more to therapy than to instruction, these facts emerged. Edward had strong feelings of hostility toward his younger sister and also toward his mother. He felt his sister was favored in the home, "[he] was punished more," "she could get by with more," "[he] was picked on," all symptoms of a feeling on his part of psychological rejection at home.

It was hypothesized that Edward was using non-reading as a means of getting revenge on his mother. He was asked who would be made most happy if he became a good reader. Without hesitation he replied, "My mother." Edward and the teacher discussed why a baby sister "could get by with more" than an older brother, how people sometimes got mad at their parents even though they loved them, and how almost everyone tried to "get even." Finally the teacher said to Edward, "I know you can learn to read whenever you want to, but you don't have to learn to read here if you don't want to; however, we would be happy if you did decide to learn to read." Edward could accept this because he had developed guilt feelings, but he had not been able, by himself, to find a way out. Being told "you will learn to read when you want to" and not being judged for his behavior gave him a chance to work out a solution. He seemed to make very little progress in reading in the tutoring sessions, but at school his behavior changed quite radically. He ceased being passive and retiring in the group, and his reading improved greatly. His need for non-reading was disappearing.

Emotional Needs
and Reading Failures

Most teachers are aware that children's school experiences are a most important factor in determining the kinds of persons they will be. Thus, the school may take partial credit when children learn at a level approximating their capacity or when they exhibit social and emotional behavior that society recognizes as acceptable and healthy. Yet few of us, as teachers, like to admit that the schools must also share the credit (or guilt) for pupil maladjustment. If reading disabilities are to be curbed, the school must seek out and attempt to mitigate its own contributions to pupil maladjustment.

Psychologists and psychiatrists as well as informed teachers know that maladjustments in the learning process (reading disabilities) do not stem from any one academic practice or malpractice as some popular writers seem to think. Methodology alone is not responsible for producing the host of impaired readers and non-readers that plague our schools, homes, and guidance clinics. While methodology may often be a contributory factor, the human organism is extremely flexible and it is a proven fact that children can and do learn to read under the most adverse methodological procedures, provided that they are physically and emotionally ready to read.

It is apparent from the literature on emotions and reading that there are two major hypotheses which might account for the interaction between emotions and reading disability.

1. Where emotional behavior and reading problems are found together, the emotional involvement stems from failure, frustration, tension, and pressure connected with the reading problem.

Reading failure ⟶ Emotional reactions

Here it is implied that the child's emotions become involved in reading through success or failure. While competition may not be new to the child, the type of competition he encounters in the reading situation *is* new to him. Never before has so much been expected from him by his parents and his teacher. Reading ability is very highly prized in our society, and pressures on the child from parents, teacher, and peers all seem to focus on this one front. He has not sensed this type of pressure in his drawing and coloring activities, in rhythm activities, in listening to stories the teacher has read, or in other activities found in the curriculum.

The child's frustrations mount as a result of failure and also as a result of his inability to please the figures of authority—parents and teachers. His attitudes toward himself are influenced by attitudes around him. Feelings of inferiority and personal inadequacy result. When one's ego is threatened, tension and emotional conflict are inevitable. Under these circumstances, the child resorts to some behavior which, irrational as it may appear to adults, seems to the child to be a means of escape from an untenable position.

It is amazing how varied the responses of different children are to frustration and ego-threatening situations. The same classroom stimulus will not produce like responses among different children. The teacher's remark, "now let's open our reading workbooks—we should be on page thirty-nine," may elicit responses varying from elation to nausea among the various pupils in the class. The individual child's past experiences both at home and school, and the impact these experiences have had on the child's attitudes toward himself, toward the teacher, and toward parents and peers, will all determine the response which this stimulus evokes. One child may give the appearance of functional deafness—he didn't hear the request; one may request to leave the room; another child may respond with the ultimate of conformity, and open his book to page 39, even though he has never worked successfully on any of the preceding pages or any preceding workbooks.

2. Unresolved emotional problems, which originally need not have been related to reading, may prevent the child from applying his energies to the learning task. The non-reading behavior is simply a symptom of the emotional problem.

Unresolved emotional problem———▶Reading problem

When reading problems and emotional involvements are found together, there may also be other factors contributing to the reading problem (i.e., physical factors, educational procedures used, learned responses to frustration).

Several principles of teaching reading discussed earlier are related to emotional problems and reading. In Chapter 1 it was pointed out that learning to read is a very complicated process and that language functions are among the most sensitive indicators of maladjustment. Unrelenting pressure brought to bear on a child to make him read will not always achieve desirable results. Further, it was suggested that sometime in the future it is likely that children with emotional problems severe enough to prevent learning will receive treatment before being expected to harness their energies to learning tasks.

The teacher's role in dealing with emotionally involved reading problems

What should the teacher do for children with reading problems who also show evidence that there is an emotional factor involved? Several factors make this question difficult to answer.

1. Some teachers, parents, school boards, and critics of education do not yet admit that in many cases non-learning and emotional problems are inextricably knit together. Nevertheless, the belief that the schools have a tremendous impact on ego-development or ego-starvation of pupils is gaining wider acceptance and teachers are coming to realize that they are necessarily involved in the process of dealing with social and emotional maladjustments. Yet there are many critics of American education who think that the school's concern with the social and emotional development of children is a tender-minded, do-gooder escape mechanism thrown up as a rearguard action by confused teachers engaged in a retreat from teaching.

It must be admitted that some teachers who verbally embrace the principle that the school should be concerned with the pupil's emotional health are hazy as to *why*. To some teachers the reason may appear to be more closely allied to public relations than to learning. These teachers may not be aware of the fact that the learning process is very sensitive to emotional and social disturbances and in the final analysis is affected by maladjustment in these areas. "Meeting the child's needs and interests" may have, through constant usage, been reduced to jargon, but it once was meaningful. "Educating the whole child" may share the same present-day reputation, but this too once had meaning. Both of these principles involved the recognition that all school experiences are related to learning. The school cannot meet the needs of children if it ignores psychological needs such as the need for success, self-realization, creativity, and an acceptable concept of self. Failure in school is the most important factor in thwarting the fulfillment of the child's needs.

2. The teacher's ego needs can contribute to the child's insecurity and pose threats to his adjustment and concept of self. The fact that some children fail to make progress commensurate with grade-level norms may become a threat to the teacher. This threat is often met with more pressure and sometimes with unconscious hostility.

3. Another important factor is the conviction on the part of teachers that they are not prepared to deal with emotional problems. This lack of preparation is undoubtedly the case with some teachers, some parents, some clinicians, and quite a few detention homes. Also, it is probably true that most of the maladjusted are not equipped to help themselves. There are some children who have emotional problems which teachers cannot hope to alleviate, just as there are some pupil maladjustments produced by the school which could have been prevented.

Teachers as therapists

In recent years, however, there has been an awareness on the part of many clinicians in child-guidance clinics as well as remedial clinics that the school — or, more correctly, the teacher — is in a therapeutic relationship to children because of the very nature of the school and the activities which are carried on there. This is not to imply that teachers should consider themselves trained therapists when they are not, but rather that, try as they may, they cannot escape the fact that much of the activity in the classroom is ego-involved and how they handle everyday situations has an impact on the mental health of pupils.

Woodruff, (32) in his book *The Psychology of Teaching* states, "Every teacher is of necessity a psychologist in *function*, with or *without training*." (Emphasis added.) He does not say that teachers are psychologists, but rather implies that their daily tasks in the classroom require them to deal with, understand, and influence human behavior (learning). This they do with or without training in understanding or influencing behavior. Actually, the average teacher does have some training for this part of her job, and the better the teacher the more she understands her limitations. But with or without limitations, she must find ways to help children grow, to help children face frustration, to help children accept reality, and to help children drain off tension so they can apply energy to learning tasks instead of burning it up in behavior not related to learning.

The issue is that, if teachers see themselves as exclusively concerned with methodological procedures or techniques, they are likely to find that some of their pupils do not seem to profit from any of the procedures or techniques used.

When classroom procedures fail, certain pupils may be referred to a reading or child-guidance clinic for help. If, as a result, they receive the right combination of attention to their psychological needs and attention to techniques aimed at the mechanics of reading, all may turn out well. In many cases there are no such facilities available, at least not until the child's behavior becomes so deviant that something *has to be done.* Can teachers themselves provide this right combination? Many teachers do practice a certain amount of therapy, and they rarely see it as something extraneous to the learning situation. It is simply part of the job of guiding the learning activities of children.

To illustrate, an elementary school arranged for a thorough diagnosis of a number of children with severe reading problems. One third grader, Mary, was a non-reader. She had intelligence adequate for learning and was attractive but shy and retiring. When asked about friends, she had only one friend, Miss Blank (her teacher). In answer to other questions, Whom do you like to play with? walk home with? visit? Miss Blank was the only human being mentioned. At noon, this child and teacher were observed in the cafeteria. All the children in the third grade sat around one long table, the teacher at one end. Mary sat next to her and was most possessive. She put her hand in the teacher's, looked at her most of the time, talked to her (not shy here). In fact, before the meal was over, she had managed to slip her chair up very close to the teacher and place her head on the teacher's lap. The teacher stroked her head and shoulder all the while talking to others around her and keeping in touch with all that was going on around the large table. As the group left, Mary and the teacher left hand-in-hand.

Later, Mary's problem was discussed. Her teacher brought up the matter of the child's complete dependence on her and stated that she had to be very careful that Mary's possessiveness did not arouse

antagonism among the other children. (There had been absolutely
no resentment shown in the cafeteria although this type of behavior
was a daily occurrence.) The teacher knew these facts: Mary lived
with grandparents; her parents were divorced, and the father worked
in another state. The child created fantasies of her father coming
to see her; he never came. Several months earlier the mother had
taken employment as a waitress in a large city several hundred
miles away and had not been home to visit her daughter during this
period. The grandparents fulfilled the child's physical needs, and
she was fairly well-dressed and clean. They completely failed to help
the child in her emotional problem, which stemmed from feelings
of rejection and attendant guilt feelings about her own contribution
to parental rejection.

While all of this history was known to everyone in the small community, including Mary's two previous teachers, none had sensed
the child's loneliness or great need for someone to tie to, until Miss
Blank. The important point is that Miss Blank did not feel that
she was doing something "nice" for Mary. She did not think of what
she was doing as therapy. Her problem, as she saw it, was to protect Mary by concealing from the other children the fact that Mary
was monopolizing the teacher. No change had yet occurred in
Mary's reading behavior, but gradually she was able to bring some
energy to bear on learning. Meeting the needs of children is therapy,
and the more flexible and creative the reading teacher is in discerning the child's real needs, the more likely it is that she will alleviate
present reading problems and forestall the appearance of others.

The use of bibliotherapy

Another type of therapy available to classroom teachers is found
in reading materials themselves. Reading provides vicarious experiences, and it is through experience that children work out their
problems. Whether these solutions are inadequate, unrealistic, or
desirable depends on the experiences and the person's reaction to
them. Russell and Shrodes* state: *"Bibliotherapy* may be defined
as a process of dynamic interaction between the personality of
the reader and literature — interaction which may be utilized for
personality assessment, adjustment and growth."

In order to see how literature affects individuals, we might start

---

*D.H. Russell and C. Shrodes, "Contributions of Research in Bibliotherapy
to the Language Arts Program," *School Review*, LVII (1950) 335–42.

with a discussion of the pre-school child. Children are enthralled by stories read to them. If you are a parent, you probably recall certain favorite stories which never seemed to lose their appeal for your child, regardless of how often the stories were heard. In fact, long after you felt that the child could not possibly be interested in hearing that story again, he would insist on hearing it. Maybe on some occasion you attempted to skip a page or two only to have him stop you and point out the omission. Perhaps you noticed that each time you went through a certain passage the child would ask the same question or make the same statement.

On the other hand, there would be certain stories which, after having heard once, the child never selected again. Some stories you might start to read only to have him select another one. It is doubtful that you attempted to determine the reasons for these choices. It was common sense to conclude that he liked some stories better than others. Also, at this age you could expect no help if you asked him why he liked this story. It would be hard to deny that something other than the literary tastes of two- or three-year-olds enters into these choices. The following is an excerpt from a case history, which, although a very small sample of behavior, is quite suggestive of a child's needs in relation to literature.

> A boy (age approximately 3 years), both parents living and together, social-economic status high. Child read to quite a good real, has many children's books. The mother relates the following: "He likes for me to read to him before he goes to bed and I do just about every night. His favorite story just now is the *Three Little Kittens*. He likes that to be the last story, but he will not go to bed until he has been assured several times that 'the naughty kittens are okay now.'"
> "Did they find their mittens?" he asks.
> "Yes, they found their mittens."
> "Kittens okay now?"
> "Yes, kittens are all right now."
> The mother states that the boy dislikes the poem "Dapple Grey." She thinks it is because the woman in the poem whipped the pony. The child has never been subjected to any corporal punishment with the exception of an occasional light slap on the hand accompanied by "no-no!"
> A tenable hypothesis is that the child identified with the three little kittens whose behavior displeased their mother. The kittens were in fact rejected for their behavior, but they were able to reinstate themselves in their mother's affection and they were fed pie, a most demonstrative form of affection

and reward. Having identified with the kittens, reassurance that all was well with them was necessary before the child felt entirely secure. Thus, the insistence on the happy ending. Even the wisest parent is sometimes unaware of the innumerable times each day a child of two or three years engages in behavior which results in reproof, scolding, and disapproval. The child, like the kittens, has much to learn about property and propriety, and while he cannot understand the terms which we have used to describe the situation, he does grasp the dynamics of the authority-child, affection-rejection situation.

The aim of the discussion above is to point up the fact that children use stories and literature as a means of finding parallels to their own problems and needs even before they can read themselves. The possibility of using bibliotherapy, of course, increases with age, understanding, and the acquisition of mental age and insight in dealing with concepts.

In an analysis of the bibliotherapeutic value of a series of books by Clara Ingalls Wilder, it is suggested that this author's writings help children with the solution to problems in such areas as gaining maturity, fears and misunderstandings, and physical, intellectual, and moral achievement, as well as dealing with the growing-up process which reflects the child's need for material and emotional security. Wenzel states: "There are many people who know a great deal about books and many others who are thoroughly familiar with children. It is only in the last few years, however, that attempts have been made to bring books and children together."* It is encouraging that an increasing number of teachers are becoming interested in the value of books and literature as a means of helping children help themselves in dealing with their personal problems.

There are many suggested helps in the literature for teachers desiring to use bibliotherapy in their classroom. Russell discusses procedures appropriate for use in guidance programs and lists books dealing with topics such as adoption and foster homes, belonging to the group, family relations, working with others, and the like.** Shrodes (27) stresses the value of using literature as a means of providing vicarious experiences, stating: "Bibliotherapy is made possible by the shock of recognition the reader experiences

---

*Evelyn Wenzel, "Little House" and "Books of Laura Ingalls Wilder," *Elementary English*, XXIX (1952), pp. 65–74.
**David H. Russell, "Adventuring in Literature with Children," *Association for Childhood Education*, Washington, D. C., Leaflet No. 5.

when he beholds himself, or those close to him, in a story or some other piece of literature."

Bibliotherapy, while particularly well-suited for children showing symptoms of maladjustment, should also be considered as a method of presenting challenging ideas, promoting growth in concepts, and developing insight into one's own behavior, for all children, whether maladjusted or not. Reading literature or viewing drama provides many psychological outlets. Any adult who can recall his own growing-up process can probably also recall some emotional experiences stemming from reading or seeing plays or movies. Reading lends itself to practically all of the mechanisms of adjustment: compensation for weaknesses and failures; identification with heroes, and, in the same process, the identification of qualities and behaviors which the society respects and rewards; a haven for withdrawal; a substitute for overt aggression.

One of the virtues of using reading as a form of therapy is that the reader remains in control of the degree to which he becomes involved in identifications. His discoveries of self will usually not be traumatic. He can gain insight into his own problems (and behaviors) at a pace which he can tolerate. Therapeutic values may be inherent in reading materials anywhere on the literary continuum from the *Three Little Kittens* to Dostoevsky's *Notes from the Underground*.

The teacher's task is to perceive the child's needs, bring the child and the right book together, draw out meanings from the book by questioning, and help the child develop confidence and self-assurance as insight permits him to see himself and his problems mirrored in what he reads.

Type III cases — a discussion

As noted earlier, Type III includes the most severe cases of impaired readers — those children who do not learn when exposed to instructional strategies that result in most children learning to read. By definition, the problems does not stem from lack of intelligence, previously existing emotional involvements, initial lack of interest in learning to read and other like causes. Type III would not include the child who achieves quite poorly for six months or a year and then "blossoms" into an average or better reader as a result of regular instruction. These children (it is posited) are handicapped by neurological deficits which are not ameliorated by the passing of time. These children do not "grow into reading."

Type III — a hypothetical construct

It should be kept in mind that, at the moment, the diagnosis of a Type III case — or a dyslexic — cannot be absolutely established on the basis of empirical tests. Certain behaviors are observed and these form the basis for the diagnosis.

There is general agreement as to the types of behavior that are useful in arriving at a diagnosis of neurologically-based reading deficiencies. However, many normal readers exhibit *some* of these behaviors. If an awkward boy is learning to read, his "general awkwardness" ceases to be significant as it relates to learning to read. In another case of a boy not learning to read, such behavior may be considered diagnostically significant. To forestall the inclusion of most children experiencing reading difficulties as Type III's, authorities suggest that a child should exhibit a syndrome of related behaviors. The following is a representative list of such behaviors.

The syndrome of behaviors associated with extreme reading disability obviously cuts across all of the essential skills that are needed in learning to read. Most symptoms can be included in one or more of the following developmental processes.

1. Visual discrimination
2. Auditory discrimination
3. Association of visual stimuli with sounds they represent
4. Motor deficiencies
5. Language processing

Each of these broad headings would include a number of specific behaviors such as:

Poor visual memory: The child has a low sight vocabulary. He may appear to have learned several words today but misses them tomorrow. He reverses letters and words, transposes letters within words, spells very poorly, even bizarrely. His reproduction of visual stimuli is inadequate. These problems do not disappear as a result of experience, but they tend to persist.

Auditory associations weak: The learner may experience extreme difficulty in associating speech sounds with letters and in blending several sounds. He may exhibit a number of speech irregularities (not to be confused with dialect differences). When success is achieved in the mastery of some letter-sound relationships, these must be constantly reinforced in order to be retained.

Motor Impairment: Handwriting and printing may be extremely immature and is often totally illegible. The subject exhibits confusion in left-right orientation, is unable to copy designs, lacks eye-hand coordination, is below age norms in activities such as throwing or catching a ball, maintaining balance, climbing, etc. Frequently, hyperactivity and impulsive behaviors will be noted.

Processing information: Here an important clue is the child's inability to handle sequence. He may have trouble naming the days of the week, months of the year, and the alphabet. In addition, he may have trouble remembering his birthdate, telephone number, and the like. Attention span and ability to concentrate may be quite limited, thus affecting his ability to organize activities and carry them through to a conclusion. Other areas in which the child is deficient or inconsistent are in discriminating similarities and differences, grasping relationships, and in temporal orientation.

Instructional programs

The instructional approaches designed for use with extreme cases of reading failure have a number of common elements such as stress on visual perceptual training, auditory discrimination activities and use of the kinesthetic component. Preliminary visual training may vary, but eventually it focuses on letter discrimination and word recognition. The auditory training involves teaching letter-sound relationships. In addition to the A-V emphasis, children also use the kinesthetic sense in finger tracing letter forms in the air or tracing letters and words on paper or outlined on sandpaper, etc. (V-A-K).

In summary, it can be said that these are phonic-emphasis programs. The systematic teaching of letter recognition, letter-sound relationships and tracing are not new concepts in the teaching of reading. Thus, the major differences between these remedial programs proposed for the seriously impaired reader and other school programs are to be found not so much in the content but rather in the philosophy and methodology. The major differences are:

1. The acceptance of a slower rate of progress on the part of children.
2. Drill on and repetition of particular teachings until they are mastered.
3. Use of kinesthetic mode along with the visual-auditory teachings.
4. The insistence on individual instruction (many feature one-to-one tutoring situations) and willingness to use volunteers or paraprofessionals to achieve this goal.

The kinesthetic method. This method is described in detail by Fernald (12) and involves utilizing the sense of touch in learning to differentiate between letters and words. It is also referred to as the *tracing method* or *visual-motor method* and employs the following steps.

1. A word is written or printed on a card.
2. The teacher says "This is the word *farm* — say it with me."
3. The child traces his finger over the word one or two times saying, "the letters f-a-r-m is *farm.*"
4. With the stimulus card out of sight, the child attempts to write the word from memory.
5. The child compares his efforts with the original and repeats the tracing and sounding until the word is mastered.

In addition to use with severely impaired readers, the kinesthetic method could be used with any child who consistently confuses certain words (these, those; were, where) or who reverses words (was, saw; no, on). It can also be used in learning difficult spellings. As a technique to aid in the teaching of reading this approach would probably not be used extensively except in extreme remedial cases. Since it is very time consuming, it would be uneconomical to use the method with children who could learn by faster methods.

The Gillingham-Stillman approach (15): This approach relies heavily on the teaching of letter discrimination (naming) and associating sounds with printed letter symbols. During the early stages of the program the child sees and repeats the names of individual letter forms. Then he receives drill on the sounds represented by letters and phonograms. These steps involve considerable visual-auditory practice. Next, considerable emphasis is placed on tracing letter forms and words while saying or blending the sounds represented by the letters. A later step involves writing letters and words from dictation which of course involves visual-auditory memory. The child is taught only cursive writing.

The program consists of many discrete steps and the child practices each step until he has mastered it. After he has learned the names and sounds associated with certain letters, the child traces and pronounces words built with these letters. As a number of words are learned, they are combined into sentences. The authors advocate a particular sequence for teaching these phonic skills and suggest no deviation from this sequence. Further, once the child is started in the program he is to attempt no work in reading outside the tutorial situation and is never to be exposed to regular classroom techniques or even be in the classroom while reading or writing is being taught there.

There are certain materials which are an integral part of the instructional program. These include separate sets of cards for letters, words, and syllabication, and prepared stories for later use. The authors point out that teachers attempting to use this approach must be thoroughly trained as to methodology and that the outlined steps and procedures must be followed in all cases. It is suggested that children with problems be identified in kindergarten and that they participate in the program for a minimum of two years — preferably four or five years.

David Sabatino has developed materials (as yet unpublished) to be used in teaching visual-perceptual skills in preschool and early primary level children. The material consists of some 800 discrimination tasks, beginning with the matching of geometric forms, then matching form and color, form and direction in which objects are facing or moving, letter forms, word pattern configurations, nonsense letter combinations, and actual word forms. The materials also provide practice in visual retention of letters and word forms. Experimental use of these materials have resulted in significant growth in visual perceptual skills.

Summary

Earlier chapters have emphasized the importance of a good start in reading while at the same time stressing that reading is a developmental process. Since reading is a developmental process, it is inevitable that barriers to successful reading will be found at all levels of instruction. This problem is accentuated by the fact that our schools operate on a grade level structure which permits pupils to move upward through the grades without having mastered the skills which are prerequisite for dealing with the planned curriculum. As a result, the reading abilities of some pupils and the curricular aims and the materials used to achieve them are not always synchronized.

There are an unlimited number of factors which can contribute to poor reading. Rarely, however, does one factor stand alone as the sole cause. The interaction of various factors makes it difficult to accurately evaluate causation of impairment in reading ability. This, in turn, makes it imperative that all available data be used in discovering causes, as well as any tentative prognosis as to what programs will lead to cure. Thorough and continuing diagnosis is essential in working with seriously impaired readers. The experience of failure in reading produces a complex teaching-learning situation. The longer the process of failure has operated, the more complex the problem is likely to be.

There is no dichotomy between remedial and regular classroom teaching, at least as far as principles and instructional practices are concerned. The most perceptible difference is that remedial programs are more likely to permit teachers to follow sound principles of teaching. Remedial reading has not been treated as a separate type of instruction, since it is believed that most regular classroom teachers will also be called upon to function as remedial teachers. This is true because they will most certainly have remedial readers in their classes. No particular administrative pattern for remedial programs has been singled out as superior. Factors in the local school system undoubtedly determine which of several approaches would be most productive. The mechanical details of operation are not the essence of a program; what each individual child does *is* the program.

Motivating the reader is the key to the success of any remedial program. After years of instruction, failure and drill, impaired readers are likely to resist all reading situations. It would be difficult to list all the factors which might conceivably be useful in motivating poor readers. Those factors, which have been discussed in some detail, include the necessity of having a variety of reading materials at the difficulty level the reader can handle; working on factors which will make the most difference in the child's reading, and which help to emphasize progress; helping the child to develop insight into his reading and allied problems; seeing that reading is always purposeful; helping the child regain self-confidence and accept the fact that he can learn to read. All of these are instrumental in reducing tension in the reading situation.

A good remedial program must consist of the proper blend of instruction and a degree of rapport between teacher and child which can lead to the child's acceptance of himself as a person and as a reader. If this is interpreted as therapy, then good teachers are therapists. Reading is a major part of an individual's total educational development.

YOUR POINT OF VIEW?

Respond to the following problems:

1. You are visiting school X to observe their reputedly excellent remedial reading program. The principal of the school was to be your guide, but just as you start on the tour he receives an emergency call and he says to you, "Just go down this long hall — you'll find the three remedial reading classes." Based *exclusively* on *instruction*, how would you know when you had found a remedial class?

2. Assume that you are assigned the task of materially reducing the number of remedial readers normally found in a given school system. Would your recommendations deal primarily with teaching methods, school practices other than methodology, or both? Would you also have to deal with parents' attitudes?

Defend or attack the following statements.

1. In most remedial reading situations methodology is less important in changing reading behavior than is the type of relationship established between teacher and child.

2. Due to automation and the knowledge explosion in recent years, reading ability is more important today than it was twenty-five or fifty years ago.

3. Emotional factors are no more important in the learning of reading than in any learning situation.

4. Many students who are academically in the top 15 percent of their class or age group are reading well below their potential.

5. Inadequate reading ability, or failure to learn to read well enough to meet the demands of the school curriculum, is a factor in producing anti-social behavior and delinquency.

BIBLIOGRAPHY

1. Abrams, Jules C. "Learning Disabilities — A Complex Phenomenon," *The Reading Teacher* (January 1970), 298–303.

2. Balow, Bruce, "The Long-Term Effect of Remedial Reading Instruction," *Reading Teacher* (April 1965), 581–86.

3. _____, "Perceptual-Motor Activities in the Treatment of Severe Reading Disability," *The Reading Teacher* (March 1971), 513–25.

4. Bliesmer, Emery P. "A Comparison of Results of Various Capacity Tests Used with Retarded Readers," *Elementary School Journal* (May 1956), 400–402.

5. Bloomer, Richard H. "Reading Patterns of the Rejected Child," *The Reading Teacher* (January 1969), 320–324.

6. Bryant, N. Dale, "Reading Disability: Part of a Syndrome of Neurological Dysfunctioning," *Challenge and Experiment In Reading.* Proceedings, International Reading Association, 7, 1962, 139–43.

7. _____, "Some Principles of Remedial Instruction for Dyslexia," *Reading Teacher* (April 1965), 567–72.

8. Cohn, Stella M. and Jack Cohn, *Teaching the Retarded Reader.* New York: The Odyssey Press, Inc., 1967.

9. Dechant, Emerald, *Diagnosis and Remediation of Reading Disability.* West Nyack, N.Y.: Parker Publishing Company, 1968.

10. Durr, William K. and Robert R. Schmatz, "Personality Differences Between High-Achieving and Low-Achieving Gifted Children," *Reading Teacher* (January 1964), 251–54.

11. Durr, William K. (ed.), *Reading Difficulties: Diagnosis, Correction and Remediation,* Newark, Del.: International Reading Association, 1970.

12. Fernald, Grace M., *Remedial Techniques in Basic School Subjects.* New York: McGraw-Hill Book Co., Inc., 1943.

13. Frierson, Edward C. and Walter B. Barbe, *Educating Children with Learning Disabilities.* New York: Appleton-Century-Crofts, 1967.

14. Gallant, Ruth, *Handbook In Corrective Reading: Basic Tasks,* Columbus, Ohio: Charles E. Merrill Publishing Co., 1970.

15. Gillingham, A. and B. Stillman, "Remedial Training for Children with Specific Disability in Reading, Spelling, and Penmanship." Cambridge, Mass.: Educators Publishing Service, 1960.

16. Graff, Virginia A. "Testing and Reporting Procedures for an Intensive Tutoring Program," *Reading Teacher* (January 1966), 288–91.

17. Heckelman, R. G. "A Neurological-Impress Method of Remedial-Reading Instruction," *Academic Therapy* (Summer 1969), 277–282.

18. Heckerl, John R. "Teaching Reading Skills: A Problem in Task Analysis," *Academic Therapy* (Fall 1969), 11–14.

19. Henderson, Edmund H., et al., "Self-Social Constructs of Achieving and Nonachieving Readers," *Reading Teacher* (November 1965), 114–18.

20. Hollingsworth, Paul M. "An Experiment with the Impress Method of Teaching Reading," *Reading Teacher* (November 1970), 112–114.

21. Lipton, Aaron, "Relating Remedial Strategies to Diagnostic Considerations," *The Reading Teacher* (January 1970), 353–59.

22. Mingoia, Edwin M. "A Program for Immature Readers," *Elementary English* (October 1964), 616–21.

23. Orton, Samuel T. *Reading, Writing and Speech Problems In Children.* New York: W. W. Norton & Company, Inc., 1937.

24. Sabatino, David A. "Auditory and Visual Perceptual Behavioral Function of Neurologically Impaired Children," *Perceptual and Motor Skills* 29 (1969), 35–40.

25. Senz, Edward H. "Neurologic Correlates In The Reading Progress," *Challenge and Experiment in Reading.* Proceedings, International Reading Association, 7, 1962, 217–18.

26. Shedd, Charles, "Dyslexia and Its Clinical Management," *Journal of Learning Disabilities* (March 1968), 171–185.

27. Shrodes, Caroline, "Bibliotherapy," *Reading Teacher*, IX (1955), 24–29.

28. Silver, Archie A. and Rosa A. Hagin, "Maturation of Perceptual Functions in Children with Specific Reading Disability," *Reading Teacher* (January 1966), 253–59.

29. Strom, Robert D. *Teaching in the Slum School.* Columbus, Ohio: Charles E. Merrill Publishing Company, 1965.

30. Stuart, Marion Fenwick, *Neurophysiological Insights Into Teaching.* Palo Alto, Calif.: Pacific Books, 1963.

31. Whipple, Clifford I. and Frank Kodman, Jr. "A Study of Discrimination and Perceptual Learning with Retarded Readers," *Journal of Educational Psychology* (January 1969), 1–5.

32. Woodruff, Asahel D. *The Psychology of Teaching* (3rd ed.). New York: Longmans, Green and Company, Inc. 1951, 8.

33. Zintz, Miles V., *Corrective Reading.* Dubuque, Iowa: William C. Brown Company, 1966.

Photo Credits

The author and the publisher wish to thank the following organizations for permission to use the photographs which illustrate this text. The Charles F. Kettering Foundation photos were taken in conjunction with the Dartmouth College Jersey City Project.

Index